THE ENCYCLOPEDIA OF FEATURE PLAYERS OF HOLLYWOOD

VOLUME THREE

RITA QUIGLEY • through • H.M. WYNANT

BY
TOM AND **JIM GOLDRUP**

BearManor Media
Albany, Georgia

The Encyclopedia of Feature Players of Hollywood, Volume 3
© 2012 Tom and Jim Goldrup. All rights reserved.

No part of this book may be reproduced in any form or by any means, electronic, mechanical, digital, photocopying or recording, except for the inclusion in a review, without permission in writing from the publisher.

Published in the USA by:
BearManor Media
PO Box 1129
Duncan, OK 73534-1129
www.BearManorMedia.com

ISBN-10: 1-59393-295-2
ISBN-13: 978-1-59393-295-4

Printed in the United States of America

Design and Layout by Allan T. Duffin.

TABLE OF CONTENTS

Acknowledgments   ix

Rita Quigley	3
Rex Reason	13
Marshall Reed	23
Walter Reed	27
Frank Richards	41
Keith Richards	49
Warner Richmond	57
Chuck Roberson	65
Robert Rockwell	73
Ric Roman	85
Henry Rowland	95
Herbert Rudley	101
Bing Russell	115
Gene Rutherford	125
James Seay	133
Robert Shayne	137
Marion Shilling	145
Richard Simmons	155

The Encyclopedia of Feature Players of Hollywood

Mickey Simpson	159
Jeremy Slate	169
Paul Sorensen	175
Arthur Space	183
Peggy Stewart	197
Harold J. Stone	207
Liam Sullivan	217
Lyle Talbot	231
Steve Terrell	245
Ruth Terry	253
Frank M. Thomas	261
Harry Townes	267
Virginia Vale	275
Russell Wade	283
Gregory Walcott	289
George Wallace	299
David Warner	311
Peggy Webber	321
Jacqueline White	333
Robert Wilke	339
Scott Wilson	349
Marie Windsor	363
Morgan Woodward	367

Table of Contents

Hank Worden	373
Than Wyenn	379
H.M. Wynant	391
About the Authors	401

ACKNOWLEDGMENTS

This book is dedicated to our parents, Eugene and Fernita (McKillop) Goldrup and to our very good friend, Walter Reed.

The stories included in these volumes are based on personal interviews that the authors had with the performers. Seven of these were through correspondence; eight were interviews with the actor by telephone; eight were with the next of kin to the deceased featured player, one we were given permission by the daughter to use information from the journal and scrapbooks of her deceased father; and the remaining one hundred and thirty-six were done in person with the performer.

We wish to offer acknowledgements to the following people who helped in making these books possible. First and foremost, we thank each of the performers that are included in this volume of works who kindly granted us personal interviews. Another hearty thank you goes to our editor, Annette Lloyd, and the typesetter, Allan Duffin, for their many hours devoted to helping make this book possible. In addition, our gratitude goes out to: Ed Begley Jr., Jim Bonisuthi, Beatrice Bratton, Jack Bray, Marion Carney, Eddie Firestone, Michael Fitzgerald, Bill Goldrup, Marilee Goldrup, Ray Goldrup, Sandy Grabman, Dorothy Harvey, Jamie, Nancy and Pat Haworth, Joe Haworth Jr., Edith Lane, Bob and Susan LaVarre, Jon Libby, Boyd and Donna Magers, Michelle McNair, John Nelson, Ray Nielsen, Ben Ohmart, Tony Paterson, Tony Phipps (of Screen Actors Guild), Frankie Prather, Mrs. Marshal Reed, Warner Richmond Jr., Ian Ritchie, Wayne Short, Reijo Sippola, Betty Strom, Susan Swann, and Frankie Thomas.

THE ENCYCLOPEDIA OF FEATURE PLAYERS OF HOLLYWOOD

RITA QUIGLEY

R ita Quigley, the daughter of Wayne Disque Quigley and Madeline McHaile, was born in Bell, Los Angeles County, California, on March 31, 1923, in back of one of the markets where her parents lived. "My father was in the grocery business," informed Rita. "Later we had an apartment over one of the markets, and then we had a home next door to our mother's sister. Daddy always felt that Hollywood was going to be so great, because people would laugh when they would see the films, and of course that was the time of Charlie Chaplin. Daddy thought that it would be a good place to head, so he opened markets in Hollywood." Recalling some fun times during her early childhood with her brother Quentin and sister Juanita, she mentioned, "We were always into mischief, we were always doing things. I had to be able to throw a football. We used to play out on the vacant lots. We made guns out of some old pieces of wood, would nailed clothespins to them, and made a rubber band out of an old inner-tube. We'd run through the vacant lot and shoot at each other. We had the theater close by, and would go there for ten cents to see the silent movies.

"When Daddy opened the Mandarin Market on Vine Street it was like a wonderful premier," Rita continued. "All the companies made miniatures. Oscar Meyer made miniature weenies, and Wonder Bread made loaves of tiny bread to put the Oscar Meyer weiners in. The mustard company was there with samples. It was just a grand affair. They had the Planters Peanut man on stilts, and I can still remember it. It was so great. Many of the stars were there, because it was the first drive-in market, and they used to literally come to his market in their cars and hand one of the box boys their grocery list. Daddy would fill it out or supervise the filling of the order and carry it out. He'd make change at the cars, so the stars never had to get out. He was doing very well and plans were afoot for them to go to Hawaii. He took home the money from one store and went and collected from another store that night. The next morning he had prepared a deposit. He went to the Bank of Hollywood and found that Beesmeyer had stolen all the money from the bank. He now had no operating money for his market, and they couldn't extend credit forever. So he closed the markets and was offered a position down in Brawley. We went down to Brawley, which is hell on earth. It was unbelievably hot. We went down in the summertime. Mother went to turn one of the water faucets on so I could get a drink and a cockroach shot out," she laughed. "So we sort of knew then what we were in for, and yet we had a lot of fun. Daddy worked for someone there and we went to school. It was a quiet time, but we still had fun doing things at home as a family. I think I was very fortunate to have enjoyed all this, because I carried it with me when I got married in order to do the same things with my family. When we came back to Hollywood and Daddy went to work for someone there, my sister and mother were walking down Hollywood Boulevard one day and Juanita was seen by an agent who took her to Universal to play Claudette Colbert's daughter in *Imitation of Life*. The hair-do that my sister had was exactly like Claudette Colbert's with the bangs. They said that Juanita was a natural to play her daughter. The studio changed her name to Baby Jane, and from then on she was in movies.

"MGM ultimately bought Juanita's contract from Universal," Rita went on to say, "and the casting director was a customer of my dad's. Daddy, by that time, had opened three or four markets in Culver City. I got into movies because the casting director had said to dad, 'Why don't you have Rita come on this interview for *Susan and God*; every kid in the country is coming on that interview.' I was sixteen. Mother was busy going to the studio with Juanita because the younger children had to be accompanied by an adult at all times on the studio lot, and daddy would have me come down and help him at the market. So I knew the casting director from helping him at the market, and helping dad. I used to take the deposits over to the bank in a paper bag, and nobody knew that I was carrying around thousands of dollars. I did go on the interview at MGM, and I guess I had a lot of hope." As good fortune would have it, it paid off for Rita.

"I had asked mom and dad if I could go to University High. It was in December 1939, I think, that I started at Uni High, and they had a wonderful Drama coach. I was reading for her one day and she said, 'Would you please stay after class? I'd like to ask you a question.' So I stayed after class, and she said, 'I have a young man who wants me to read with him. He's a former student, but I can't help him as much if I read with him because I'm concentrating on the way I'm reading. I think that you are a natural actress. If you would read with him, I could help both of you.' I said, 'I would love to do that.' She said, 'You wouldn't mind staying after school?' and I said, 'Not at all.' It turned out that the young man, whose name was Jerry Paacht, not only became a very famous attorney, but he also became one of our judges here in the state of California."

Before she got her part in *Susan and God*, Rita's father asked her what her future plans were. "Quentin was making plans to take Loyola by storm, and he was an excellent student; I was not. Juanita was doing very well in pictures and I guess daddy wondered what in the world was going to happen to this middle child, so he said, 'What would you like to do?' That's when I said I'd like to be an actress, and he said, 'Then do it. You do whatever you want to do and you'll do it better than anyone else.' When I did do *Susan and God*, I won a nationwide poll as the best supporting actress of the month."

Asked what inspired her to want to become an actress, Rita answered, "I was exposed to it by seeing so many of the movie people coming to my father's market, and then seeing Juanita working in pictures. I had visited the sets a lot and thought that it would be wonderful, that I would like to do that. Then when I went to Uni High, and talked with the teacher, she told me that she thought I was a great actress, and had me do political readings for her so she could see if I would be appropriate to read for her former student. The readings were mostly Ibsen plays, which were all of a political nature. That's what we rehearsed with, and he was very pleased with the way that I read with him. He knew how important it was for him to be a good attorney by being a good actor. That just made me feel all the more that if you never did anything in pictures, but could project whatever you wanted to project, you could be successful. And I do think that that was a great inspiration. And another thing that my teacher told me that I never forgot – and I was only there couple of weeks before I got the part in *Susan and God* – was always watch the way people walk. If I ever had to give a description of the way someone looked, my first thought would be how they walked. To this day the first thing I look for when I meet someone is how they walk, how they carry themselves. It was just that she impressed that on me to that degree. And then, of course, I was in the little red schoolhouse with Kathryn Grayson, Mickey Rooney, and Judy Garland. It was just a lot of fun. I did not sign a contract with MGM and that is to my regret, but of course I didn't really have anything to say about it. The studio would not negotiate with someone that didn't have an agent. I already had the part, and MCA, who happened to be Juanita's agent, was happy to have me. I was sixteen when I started *Susan and God*, and had my seventeenth birthday on the set."

Rather than signing a contract with MGM, the agency told Rita that their client, Mary Boland, was very unhappy with the young lady that was appearing with her in the play, *Meet the Wife*, because of a personality clash, and Mary had asked the agency to look for someone else. They recommended that Rita would be better off going on the summer circuit with Mary Boland in the play rather than going under contract with MGM. "That's a nebulous thing. How do you know that I wouldn't have been better off? If I stayed under contract to MGM, I now believe that they may have backed me for an Academy Award."

Reflecting on her work in *Susan and God*, Rita recalled, "When I was tested for it, George Cukor, who directed the picture, played the part of my father. He had told all the others who tested, 'Thank you, that was great,' but told me, 'You can do better than that. I know you can. Let's do it again.' I was so embarrassed in front of my peers that I could have died. We did it over and over again. Finally, I was on the break of tears, and we did it, and he said, 'Cut! Break for lunch,' and turned and walked away. I went in the dressing room and started to cry because he didn't say, 'We'll call you' or anything. My mother said, 'What's the matter? You just got it.' I said, 'No I didn't.' She said, 'Yes you did. That's how he works, and his crew knows. You got the part.' I didn't know until the next day. Fredric March was a great actor. And of course, Gloria DeHaven was a charming young woman in it, and she could sing, which is something I could never do, and Joan Crawford loved to hear her sing. Another thing which I remember is that Joan Crawford said to me one day at the beginning of a scene, 'Just because you're new in this business, don't think I'm going to throw anything your way. I'm going to fight to steal every scene I can from you.' I thought, 'Wow, this is one tough cookie.' But later she had her secretary come to the classroom and ask the teacher if I could be excused. So I was excused to go to Joan Crawford's dressing room, which was actually a little portable trailer-like home, and she said, 'Come in, Blossom.' She didn't call me Rita, she always called me Blossom, which was my name in the movie. She said, 'I just want to tell you something. I will do anything I can to help you because you are new in this business, but I also want to tell you that I'm the only one in this movie that will, so just be on your toes. Okay?' And I said, 'Well, thank you.' With that, she stood up and kissed me. I always loved her because I knew that she would help anyone, and I resented it terribly when her daughter wrote that book about her."

Rita mentioned that Joan Crawford was her most favorite actress she had worked with and that *Susan and God* was her favorite film. "It was a great part and a great story," she noted. "When my character wasn't on film, they were talking about me. It was a powerful part. It was difficult not to overact in it, because in those days everybody overacted. Something that George Cukor said to me was, 'Whatever you do, do not go to the drama coach on the lot here at MGM.' She came after me, and I said I had been informed not to take any lessons; that Mr. Cukor wanted me to get my direction strictly from him, and she said, 'Well, that's what I'm here for.' I told her that I would have to ask Mr. Cukor because he had asked me not to, and that caused a little friction. So he told her himself that he did not want anyone interfering, that I had a quality that he did not want them to destroy. *Susan and God* took a long time to make because George Cukor wanted everybody to know everyone very well before we ever turned the camera on. So we would sit around every afternoon and read the script. We read it from beginning to end, not once, but three times. Everybody was present to hear everybody else, so you were comfortable. You knew them, and you knew when they did better than other times and when they were at their prime. You got a gut feeling for everyone in the film. We rehearsed almost to the point where you wondered if it would still sound like it was fresh in your mind. That's one reason why you would think it would be very difficult to do a stage play, because you do it over and over and over again. But I think it's your audience in a stage performance that really keeps you alive, because you don't know what their reaction is going to be, and you feed from their reaction, and the audience is always different." Rita mentioned that George Cukor was her favorite director. "You can't even compare with him," she noted.

"George Cukor did something for all of the children," Rita continued. "They had a scene after I was glamorized, and it was supposed to be my birthday party. He wanted the party to be special so that all of the kids that were in that scene would have a great time, and we did. He went down to Santa Monica Pier and hired the man that made the saltwater taffy, and that man was on the set with all of his regalia, and making one kind of taffy after the other until we were all practically sick from eating it. But we had so much fun and a great time. I do remember that Joan Crawford had some gorgeous jewelry on in that scene and someone said, 'You don't want to get taffy on your rings.' And she said, 'These are just copies. These are fakes.' But they were copies of rings that Franchot Tone had given her, and she was madly in love with him.

"One of the funniest things happened when I used to have lunch in the commissary at MGM and my mother would accompany me. I would go in with no makeup. My makeup had to match Fredric March's because most of our scenes were together. So I had this pancake 29 on, no rouge, no nothing, no lipstick, and braces on my teeth. I would take the glasses off that I wore for the film, but the braces scratched the enamel so I had to be very careful with those. I'd go in and pass the big table where all the male stars, producers and directors sat, and they would throw dice to see who picked up the tab for the day. Clark Gable was always there and he'd always give me the biggest wink and smile, and then turn to somebody next to him and say, 'That kid's never going to make it.' And I used to hear him and think, 'Oh, you so and so, you.' But anyway, then when they made me up – Sydney Guilaroff did my hair, and Adrian did my own – I walked into the commissary and Clark Gable looked at me, sat back in his chair, and with two fingers gave the biggest wolf whistle you have ever heard," she laughed. "So I just smiled sweetly."

Reflecting on her tour with Mary Boland in *Meet the Wife*, Rita commented, "That was a wonderful trip. Quentin drove, and mother and Juanita went with me. We went across country and I memorized my lines as we drove. We started out in Maple Wood, New Jersey, and then toured. By the time we were starting to Toronto, Quentin received his call from the Army Air Force, so he had to turn around and drive back home. We went on, and flew home. But that was a wonderful performance. I guess it was in Quebec. I was standing in the wings waiting for my cue to go on, and my mother said, 'Oh, look at your shoe. You got something all over it.' There was a reporter there who was talking to me and writing up an interview for the French newspaper, so I handed mother my shoe and she gave me something else to put my foot in. I went on talking to this delightful young Frenchman with a beautiful accent, and all of a sudden I heard my cue and dashed on stage. I'm center stage, and I realize I have on one red shoe and one brown shoe. Now what am I going to do?" she laughed. "So at the first opportunity I exited stage left, ran around behind the curtain, got the shoe on that I should have had on, ran back, and came on stage. Everybody on stage stopped and looked at me like, 'Well, where have you been?' But the show went on and nobody seemed to notice except the young reporter who wrote a lengthy article. Fortunately it was all in French. The director knew, but he was a little mystified to think that Mary Boland did not get the coverage that I did. Everywhere I went, everything that I did in this business I can reflect on, it's all been joyous, and there's something funny that happened in all of it. I have nothing but the fondest memories of everyone that I worked with and everything that I did. I feel so sad to think that not everyone feels as I do, but there were instances of abuse, and mishandling of children's funds and things, and that was too bad. That was why they had to have the Jackie Coogan law, but I never experienced anything like that. Mickey Rooney – whom I dearly loved and was just a delightful person – had developed quite a name for himself. MGM wanted him to be known as the good boy, so I was considered a miss goody two-shoes, and they used to send Mickey and I out on dates, but they always had the chaperone from the publicity department with us and a limousine driven car. We had a lot of fun together."

Rita appeared with Cary Grant and Martha Scott in *The Howards of Virginia*. "Martha Scott and Cary Grant were absolutely so phenomenal that you wanted to just watch every breath they took when they were working. Martha Scott was a delightful person and very hard working. Being on film was a field new to her from stage, and she didn't want to overact. She had to underplay it because her tendency from being on the stage was to use much greater gestures. She was constantly aware of what she needed to do to compensate for film, and she would ask the director. And that was good, because you could learn from what was being said and use it if the opportunity ever came up for you to do so. Sir Cedric Hardwicke was never out of character. I'm sure it was because he was a very gentle person and had to play such a tough, mean, and totally heartless man in that picture." Asked how it was working with Cary Grant, Rita replied, "We used to double talk all the time, so you couldn't be serious around him. But that was just his way of doing things. He was a very charming man."

Reflecting on other films she had worked in, Rita stated:

"*Ride Kelly Ride* and *Jenny* were both done at Fox Studios. "Sol Wurtzel was the producer, and when you arrived at the studio at six o'clock in the morning he was there at the gate to say, 'Hi. Good to see you come to work so early. See you later on the set.' Not very many producers did that.

"I played a brat in *The Five Little Peppers in Trouble*. I was horrible in that one. My grandchildren saw it, and said, 'Oh, you were terrible.' And I said, 'What do you mean I <u>was</u>? You just better be careful. Now you know what I'm really like,' " she smiled.

"*Henry Aldrich, Editor* was just fun from beginning to end. That was a funny story and of course, Jimmy Lydon is delightful. A lot of good people and a lot of great acting.

"*The Human Comedy* was delightful. That was where I met David Holt. I know that it was L. B. Mayer's favorite movie. It was certainly a familiar story for anyone who had someone in the service: You knew there was always that time when you might get that terrible telegram. Frank Morgan and Mickey Rooney played that scene to perfection where Morgan dropped dead when the telegram came across the wire with the news that someone's favorite son had been killed, and Mickey Rooney had to take over from the teletype and deliver that message to the mother. It was a great scene. After that, I met William Sarayoan at Frank Thomas's home. I was also with Frank Thomas Jr. the night there was a notice on the radio that Carole Lombard had just died in a plane crash. So you made many friends, at least I did. I made many friends along the way, during the course of interesting historical happenings; things that you never forget when you see one another. You remember these things."

Rita married in 1944. "Neal Rauch, who was sometimes a writer for Luella Parsons, wrote a lengthy article about us years ago," she noted. "We had six children that died at birth. They were not in succession. We had three sons who were born prematurely. They were baptized and died within twenty-eight hours. And then we adopted a little boy whose parents reconciled and took him back. Then we lost another little boy, and then we adopted Judy. We lost another child and we adopted Martin, and then we had Paul and Theresa. We then lost the sixth child and then had Andy and Patrick. So there was a good many years when I wasn't doing very much of anything except being pregnant. My husband was not too thrilled with the idea of my being an actress. He didn't feel that people in the industry were all that good, but anybody that did anything wrong, their career was ruined. Mary Astor's career was almost ruined when her famous purple diary was discovered. In those days they were very particular about how the actors and actresses behaved and their private life was open to anyone. It was a tragedy for Mary Astor. But then she did a great movie, a beautiful movie with Claude Rains called *The Man Who Reclaimed His Head*.

"My husband's father was in the shoe business, so he inherited that when he came out of the service," Rita mentioned, speaking of her husband. "His uncle and my dad had kept his office opened for him, but of course shoes were rationed at the time so it made it very difficult. We were in the wholesale shoe business, and then after we had Judy we decided that he would open a shop of his own. So he bought leftovers from many of the big department stores. We were really one of the first stores that had what they called the closeouts. And it was very successful for many years. Then the man that held the master lease lost it, the building was sold, and we were in limbo for a while. That's when I started to work. I was well fitted to do bookkeeping and things like that. I had always helped my dad, and I helped my husband. So I faked a lot. I knew the acting was going to come in handy, so I told them I could do anything. I got along very well with people, and that was the most important thing. I could help them put on a successful event and a successful party, whether it was for business or for pleasure."

In 1947, Rita returned to the screen. "I guess it was because of my mental attitude. I needed a change; sometimes we do. I did *The Trap* and I did a Lassie. I don't even remember the name of the Lassie film, but it was just a vignette. I was on the set for just one day and we didn't even see the rest of the cast. I think what they did was simply send a camera crew to some little church out in Culver City, take a shot of us, and that was it. I did do an *Ironside* on TV. I think I did that about the time my husband's business was going sour for him. Things were not going well for him. I thought maybe I would get back in pictures, but I didn't have time – I had to go to work. I worked for a plastic surgeon, and then I went to work for a secretarial service for three years. Then I got the job at the Petroleum Club, which I had for about twenty years. When I worked there, I had learned a little bit about computers so that I could handle the payroll. They had a sophisticated regime, so they sent me to school to handle the payroll according to the way ADP wanted it. I did all the correspondence and was the hostess at all the parties. I helped with the arrangements for food and serving. At one point in time we had nine hundred and ninety-nine members and I think out of that there were three females, and I was the only female employee. They treated me like a queen. They couldn't have been nicer to me."

Talking about comedy, Rita mentioned, "Maybe one of the reasons one enjoys doing comedy is because you know someone's going to laugh. You're making people happy. This is what my dad felt would be so wonderful for people at the close of the Depression. There were people still bemoaning the fact that they didn't have money; they didn't have this or they lost that. He always felt, 'But if you laugh. If you laugh.' I think I preferred doing comedy, but I didn't get the opportunity of doing much of it. I was just happy to be acting. I really loved it. I have always felt that timing was so essential in comedy. People who play comedy never win awards – Look at Bob Hope, for example, probably one of the greatest actors of all time. His timing had to be impeccable. That to me seemed more of a challenge."

Asked what are some of the things she enjoys doing, Rita replied, "Oh, I enjoy everything. I think one of the greatest courses I ever took was etymology at UCLA, and to this day I'm fascinated with words, and the meaning and the root of the words. One of my favorite hobbies is reading the *Increase Your Power* from the *Reader's Digest*. I have some of my daughters-in-law interested in it too, so we play a game. We hear a word and we go look it up. You can find anything on the computer. I have four encyclopedias on my computer, so if I can't find something in one, I go to one of the others. And of course, children are my real love. My kids were everything. That was what I lived for." Does Rita miss acting at all? "Oh yes, terribly. But I couldn't have both.

"Did you know that two of my sons did commercials?" Rita asked. Andy did a marvelous Applejacks commercial, which was done in stop-action. Unfortunately, he had to eat applejacks and was out on a football field. First, a cloud would go in front of the sun and then an airplane would fly by, and he ate applejacks, and ate applejacks, and ate more. Finally they broke for lunch, but he didn't want anything to eat. We came back and finally somebody said, 'Don't swallow any more of those applejacks.' They put a container so he could spit it out instead of swallowing it after they did the take. To make a long story short, when they finally said, 'Cut! Print!' he turned around and looked at that container and threw up all of those applejacks, and they turned the camera back on. He was so embarrassed."

Looking back over her career, Rita summed up her feelings saying, "I enjoyed every minute of it, and I enjoyed everyone I had worked with. I loved Joan Crawford, and still do. She was a great lady. But they were all wonderful people. I was also thrilled to be able to read with the young attorney. That was a great honor, and to know that it helped him to become a great success as a superior court judge."

Rita passed away on August 25, 2008 at Arroyo Grande, California.

Film Credits: **1940**: Susan and God; Five Little Peppers in Trouble; The Howards of Virginia; Third Finger, Left Hand. **1941**: Jennie; Ride, Kelly, Ride; Blonde Inspection; Riot Squad. **1942**: Henry Aldrich, Editor; Keeper of the Flame. **1943**: The Human Comedy; Isle of Forgotten Sins; Women in Bondage; Whispering Footsteps. **1947**: The Trap. **1948**: Hills of Home.

REX REASON

Rex Reason was born November 30, 1928, in Berlin Germany. "My father was traveling with General Motors Acceptance Corporation," Rex began. "He and my mother were traveling around the world and it just happened that I was dropped off there in Berlin. We stayed there about two years so I don't have much of a memory of Europe." When the Reason's decided to come back to America in 1930, they chose to make their journey home on board the largest ship at that time, and on their way across the Atlantic were hit by the biggest hurricane of the year. "We were lucky," Rex stated, "there were a few ships that capsized in this storm. My dad was telling me how he belted me around him so I would be tight to him, and then stood in the doorway with his feet propped up alongside to try to maintain a balance. He was thrown down a couple of times with me, and finally he strapped himself to a heater in the room and we survived."

With his parents later being divorced, Rex was mostly raised in the country by his grandparents. The grandfather, who was the first Mayor of Glendale, California, had a large stable with many horses. "My brother, Rhodes, and I learned to ride when we were quite young," commented Rex, "the whole hillside that is Forest Lawn was the studio backdrops and they had all kinds of sets. I used to ride up there and enjoy myself like a cowboy; I loved riding bareback most of the time, and Rhodes and I rode up and down in the hills acting like cowboys and Indians. Anyway, it got in my blood at this time, the whole feeling of acting, of being somebody."

Rex went to live with his mother in Hollywood, and attended Hollywood High School through the eleventh year and transferred over to Hoover High for his senior year. During this last year, Rex was walking down the hall one day and was stopped by the dramatic coach, who said, "You are the one I want for my play." She had lost her leading man because he had pneumonia," Rex explained, "and I didn't do any theater up to this time. I had a mother who was interested in the theater when she was younger, but she never pushed me into the direction of the theater." Rex went home and told his mother about this, and she "was just so excited because it was like an answer to her prayers. She really wanted somebody to be in the theater because she was a part of us; she was just thrilled to death, and that's how it all started." Mrs. Reason worked with Rex, cueing his lines with him, helping him all she could to make her son's stage debut a success for him. One day Rex was in bed ill and she was cueing him; the grandmother would enter the room, view the scene, and say, "That's awful, let him alone." "Get out," came the reply. "I was really spoiled by my grandmother," Rex noted, "but my mother pushed me, pounded those lines into my head."

The name of the play was *Seventh Heaven*. The premise was that Chico, a fellow who worked in a sewer but felt like a king, was in love with a girl named Diane whom he would meet on the seventh floor of an apartment building, thus the title. There was a war and before Chico goes off to fight he takes the necklace off his neck and puts it over Diane's head, saying, "I take you as my wife." Then, pointing up toward Heaven, he says, "If there's any truth in the idea of You, make this a true marriage." "This kind of thing touched me and, as a result, I had a nice feeling toward the part and had a nice response from doing it," Rex reflected. It just so happened that a scout from Paramount Studio had seen the play and wanted Rex to come out and do a screen test. "No," was Rex's response, because "I didn't want to study, and I was kind of running around with my head off and enjoying life; I wasn't really a student."

Rex was now seventeen and getting close to graduating; all that stood between him and that great day were the final examinations just a couple of weeks away. "But," Rex noted, "I found that if I went into the Army I would get my diploma automatically once I had finished basic training." Rex thought that was wonderful; he wouldn't have to wait for the finals. At that time the length of military duty was only two years as opposed to the normal three or four years. "I hope you know what you are doing," voiced the school counselor. "Yes, I do," remarked Rex; so he went into the Army, finished basic training, received his diploma, and two years later was discharged.

"Then I had a decision to make," stated Rex, "I could have gone into Civil Engineering; even though I wasn't a very good student I was very good at mathematics. But I decided to go to Pasadena Playhouse." Rex thought he would just get on the stage and act, but a surprise was waiting in that they gave him thirteen different subjects that had to be taken for two years before getting on the main stage. Classes were held in costumes, history of literature in theater, radio, production, direction, etc. "I took about a year of it," Rex said, "and I thought, no, I want to get on stage. So, I went down to Hollywood and tried out for plays."

Rex Reason

Rex's first play was for the Ben Bard Players ("that's what I named my dogs, first dog was Ben, the other was Bard"). He auditioned, and "they took me for the lead for about a year and a half," mentioned Rex. The next step was an audition for a play that was bound for Broadway, and he was accepted. Before he left for New York, an agent, who had seen him in a little production, approached Rex. He asked, "Would you like to go out and audition for a picture that you'd be just right for?" Rex answered in the affirmative, and he was off to MGM for a screen test. They gave him what was known as an interrogation type test, where they sat him on a stool, started the camera rolling and asked him questions about himself. "Ricardo Montalban saw the test and came to my dressing room right after, and said, 'This is the best interrogation test I've seen.'" Then they had him do another test for the film part and two weeks later he had the lead in *Storm over Tibet*.

"Because of my stage background," Reason explained, "I was very disciplined. I memorized my lines; I was well prepared – unlike a lot of actors who just go into pictures: They don't have the discipline and worry the director with thirty-five takes. Believe it or not, I did every scene in *Storm over Tibet* in one take. We shot it in nine days," Rex concluded, "and I walked out with a contract with MGM."

The plot of the film concerned two pilots (played by Rex and Myron Healey) who were partners in their private flying business. They had the assignment of flying "over the hump" of the Himalayas and in their travels found the Mask of Sinja, which was a holy symbol to the Tibetans. Rex is tempted to steal it, but Healey argues that to do so would be akin to someone coming to America and stealing a crucifix from a church. They struggle, Rex is hurt, and so Healey flies the plane on the route Reason was originally supposed to and is killed in a crash. Sometime later in the USA, Rex begins to feel remorse, blaming himself for the accident and his guilt draws him back to the Himalayas. He's there yelling at the heavens, "Why did this happen?" and the shouting causes and avalanche that carries him away. He is found by Tibetan monks, who bring him to their shrine and nurse him back to health and there he sees the light.

Dore Schary, who had seen the rushes of the film and were considering releasing it, said, "There's a couple of scenes where Rex was pretty good," so put him under contract for six months and then, after no work, they let him go. "I went right over to Columbia," Rex noted, "because they're the ones that released the picture and they signed me up for the normal seven year contract." This was in 1952, and before he was again let go the following year he appeared in two additional films in support roles – *Salome* and *Mission over Korea*.

Rex next went to Universal, where he tried out for a part opposite Rock Hudson in *Taza, Son of Cochise*. They liked the test and signed him up to a seven year contract, but "I was out there for three years and then I was let go again." While he was at Universal, Rex starred or co-starred in eight motion pictures, including Westerns (*Raw Edge*, *Smoke Signal*, and *Taza*); science fiction/horror (*This Island Earth* and *Creature Walks Among Us*); and period pieces (*Kiss of Fire*, *Yankee Pasha* and *Lady Godiva*).

Universal Studios changed Rex's name to Bart Roberts for his two initial features at the studio. He learned of this when Rock Hudson greeted him with "Hi Bart." "What?" Rex asked. "Hi Bart, they changed your name," Rock smiled, and handed Rex a paper reading; "Rex Reason is now Bart Roberts." "I didn't like that," Rex informed us, "and when I got back to the studio I talked to the head-man, saying, "If my name was Bart Roberts, you'd probably want to change it to Rex Reason! Rex Reason is a darn good name." He talked them into it, but as the credits were set up already for *Taza* and *Yankee Pasha*, he was billed under Bart Roberts for these.

While under contract to Universal, Rex made the film he considered his most interesting. When asked if he had any favorites, he answered, "I wasn't really in there long enough to get a hold and really do something that I knew I was capable of; I never really got to that point." His most interesting film was *This Planet Earth*. He explained that "When we did it we obviously weren't up there on Metaluna, and the huge set in the background wasn't there; it was painted in with special effects brought later. But they were explaining this was over here and that over there; so we had to relate within our mind to the fact that we were on this monorail traveling through Metaluna with bombs exploding all over. But I loved the whole concept because it was futuristic, and all this was very interesting. So, *This Planet Earth* was my favorite." Another one Rex enjoyed was *Kiss of Fire* because he liked working with Jack Palance, and "it imposed a challenge because, even though I looked younger, I had to develop the attitude of a forty-five year old."

Of all the various types of films, Rex enjoyed period pieces the most. "I loved Westerns," Rex stated, "I loved the mountains, the horses; I enjoyed that very much. In fact, most of the period pieces I did, including *Kiss of Fire* and *Yankee Pasha*, I put on the make-up, the outfits, the goatee, and I felt comfortable like I've done this before, or in my past life I must have been a knight or something," he chuckled. "So I loved doing it, felt good doing it and it was always exciting when they said, 'Rex, you're going to have swordplay."

Rex told of an experience which happened while filming *Taza, Son of Cochise* on location. He was playing an Indian warrior named Naiche and had to find contact lenses to change his blue eyes to brown. "This was on a Friday afternoon and I had to be up at Moab, Utah on Monday morning," Rex said. Contact lenses were new at the time and were made of glass; it was hard to find a pair that would fit. They searched and finally found a colored pair that didn't fit properly, but he put them in his suitcase and took them up to Utah. As Naiche, "I wear a wig, I'm stripped to the waist and wearing heavy make-up, and its one hundred and twenty degrees up there in Moab," Rex commented. Late in the afternoon, just as the sun was starting to go down, they were shooting the last scene of the day "The scene," Rex explained, "was this covered wagon way out on the desert and we just killed everybody. I had gotten off my horse and was going to light the fire to the wagon; the other Indians were milling around on their horses, one was holding mine." Doug Sirk, the director, told Rex to stand off camera and that the grips would set the fire, starting the action. "It's as though you had already set it on fire and you're running from the wagon," Sirk directed. "When you're off camera you are going to jump on the horse, ride up here and rein him; if you get him to go back up on his hind legs that will be great, because the camera's going to look right at you as you're looking over the scene, then you turn and ride off with your men." They rehearsed it and everything went perfectly as planned. "Okay, let's do it," shouted Sirk. "Action!" Rex described what happened next: "The covered wagons went up in flames, it spooked the horses and they went all over the place. Here I am standing off camera, waiting for them to hit me on the shoulder and say 'Go, get on your horse.' So I switched the rifle over to my right hand, ran in and found my horse; grabbed a hold of the mane and swung over Indian style. I got on the horse and everything was fine. I was trying to hold the horse while the others were riding off. Now that's almost impossible, but I kept pulling it up to get him toward the camera where I could look down and then ride off. Well, he just kept going back, back, and went right over backward with me – ruined the whole shot -- and I hit my head and was out for a few seconds. I woke up and here was Doug Sirk standing over me, saying, 'No, no Rex, not like that.' Today, looking back, it's humorous, but at the time I didn't feel like it. I had a sore head for the rest of the picture and I lost my contact lenses, so whenever they got close, I squinted."

After being let go from the contract at Universal, Rex started to free-lance, making features at Warner Brothers, Allied Artists, and several at Twentieth Century Fox. At Warner's, Rex co-starred opposite Clark Gable in *Band of Angels*. He said of Gable: "I had the experience of meeting the man. There was quite an aura around him; strange, majestic and very powerful. He was very strong," Rex concluded, "and there was an unusual feeling about the man."

In 1957, Rex was signed to star as Adam MacLean, a crusading newspaperman in the old west, in the television series, *Man without a Gun*. "I did three and a half shows a week, six days a week; I was married then, had a couple of young children and the pressure was on me. I was doing my own stunts and it was a hard show."

After these months of pushing himself Rex collapsed and came down with brain fever. "They were planning for my funeral," remarked Rex. "After six days my fever was up to one hundred and nine degrees, and I still survived." Rex spent ten months of that year on his back, and had to learn to walk, write, pick up a glass – everything, all over again. "So it was a period of time that was paid by my residuals because the first thirty-nine episodes were run over and over again. I had one hundred percent residuals, so had a lot of money coming in." After Rex recovered he filmed another thirteen episodes a year later.

After *Man without a Gun* ended Rex was offered another series titled *The Borderline*, which was about a casino that straddled the Utah-Nevada border. "It sounded interesting," Rex noted. "This is what I wanted to do, but then Warner Brothers came up with a good opportunity called *The Roaring Twenties*." Rex signed with them to play Scott Norris, an investigative reporter in New York City during the Prohibition era. This series ran from 1960 through 1962. When he signed his contract to Warners a six month writers' strike began so the series was postponed until the strike was settled. "In the meantime I was just sitting around doing nothing so I asked if I could do the heavies in the existing series, which I did." Rex worked at Warners on such shows as *Sugarfoot*, *Bronco*, *77 Sunset Strip*, *Bourbon Street Beat* and *The Alaskans*, as well as on other shows such as *Wagon Train*, *Perry Mason*, and *Trackdown*. "It was a lot of fun," he reflected. "In fact, I think most of my fan mail was when I did all of those characters. Then finally we did *Roaring Twenties*, and that's when I decided to leave the business."

We asked Rex why he chose to give up his acting career, and he answered, "I started when I was very young; twenty-two when they gave me a lead. They kept telling me to think twenty-eight; as I got older, think older, and I kept getting older parts. At Universal, James Mason turned down a role and they put me in his role in *Kiss of Fire* because I had the heavy voice and stature; they thought I could handle it. Well, from twenty-two on I didn't really grow up," Rex continued. "I never went through the experiences of a normal twenty-two year old – going off skiing, having fun, and getting into trouble. I was just disciplined and worked hard, learned it at a young age. I worked, was always on time, and I just felt empty; I really felt empty inside. I thought, 'I've got to do something different.' My whole life, my whole being, my whole security was the motion picture business, and to leave it was quite a traumatic experience for me. It took about three years – it's like a withdrawal from drugs; the process is the same thing. You have to let go of something and you don't know where you're going; it's difficult and frightening. Finally one day, just before I left Warner Brothers because I bought out my contract in 1962, I said I was leaving. The agent said, 'You can't do that. You're a million dollar product!' 'Well, sorry, I got to do it.' He said, 'I'm going to blackball you. I'll see you never work again!' That was his reaction, but I couldn't help it," Rex concluded. "It was my life."

Rex was going through a divorce at the time and he and his wife went to court. "Mr. Reason," the judge stated, "you have your children; your wife wants one-third of your earnings for the rest of your years in the business." "Well," Rex replied, "I'm not going to be acting anymore. I'm now a student going to real estate school." "You can't…" the judge stopped himself before completing his thought, which was "You can't do that. You've got to go back to motion pictures; that's where the money is." But he had stopped because he knew he could not dictate to Rex about where he was going to work. "That was the transition right there," Rex told us, "because I made up my mind it was real estate."

Why did Rex decide on a career in real estate? There is an interesting answer to this question, and it starts with Rex being in the process of selling an old gas station corner that the family owned. He met with a real estate broker to discuss the sale, and about his decision to leave the picture business came up in the conversation. "You have a great mind for real estate," the broker told him. "You ought to get into it." "A couple of weeks later," Rex told us, "I was in a little house behind the family home, which I had built and designed as a one bedroom studio to study and be by myself. As I continued designing it, it grew to be a fifteen hundred square foot house, so this was where I was staying. I did a lot of reading; I read the bible and a lot of religious books that helped me through this transition." Two weeks after he had talked to the broker, Rex was sitting in his living room by the table when his mother came out from the big house and told him that Sedell, who was the broker, called and wanted him to work with him. "That was like an answer to prayer, and it hit me like a chill down my spine. I got the answer and somebody wanted to help me. I didn't know how to go out there into the world; being an actor you're kind of babied in the industry. You drive into the studio and you're in another world, but to be able to walk on your own, go out and get a job, that's all new to me."

So Rex was sponsored, went to school, passed the test, and became a salesman for Sedell. There is where he met Shirley, who was to become his wife. "Very interesting," Rex noted, "because I had my own religious experience within myself and she had one, unbeknownst to each other." Rex stated that he was still Hollywood in the sense that he still had an actor's ego – his appearance still meant a lot to him. So whenever Rex saw a pretty girl he would say 'Hi" and hope they'd look at him. But this girl, a redhead, came out of the broker's office and walked right by him, not even looking at the young man sitting at his desk. "That bothered me," Rex confessed. "I walked back to her booth and saw a letter on her desk; at the beginning of the letter it read, 'The Kingdom of God is within you,' and because I was reading the Bible I was really geared for the proposition. I asked if I could read that letter." Shirley thought, "The audacity of this son of a gun. This is personal." But something in her said, "Let him look at it." It's a letter from her father; this was the kind of relationship she's having with him all of her life. He was always feeding her with wonderful thoughts about life and a relationship with God. "I read it," Rex stated, "and said it's beautiful." He then invited Shirley to go to the Title Company meeting, which as a group they were supposed to go through and learn related services. "How would you like me to pick you up and take you to the meeting?" She replied, "No, I would like to borrow your lock-box key. I have a house I have to look at tonight and I don't have one." Rex loaned her his key and told her, "You can return it Sunday. I'm having an open house up in Burbank." She came, and that's when Rex really enjoyed her conversation, although she knew he was an actor and didn't believe all the things he told her, like that he wasn't married. Rex asked, "I'd like to take you to the next meeting," and she finally agreed. "We went to the backyard and looked over the fence at the sunset, and that's where we fell for one another," Rex confided.

Rex and Shirley started seeing one another and went together for three years. During this time the broker Rex was working with was asked to come out to Diamond Bar because it was horse property and he was a horseman. He knew Rex had a knowledge of horses so he said, "Rex, I'd like you to go out there and represent me. You sit here on this tract and sell all these people home sites." So Rex was driving back and forth each day from Glendale and would stop by a supermarket every night where Shirley was working. "She had the longest line because she had this wonderful feeling for people and they loved to come through her check stand. I'd go in and just stand there and watch till she quit work every night, and that went on for three years."

Shirley's father traveled out to California from Missouri every summer to do assessment work on his Arizona based mining claims, which numbered twenty-three. Shirley asked, "Rex, my father needs some help. Would you mind helping him with his mining claims?" "Sure, and when we get there let's get married," Rex proposed. "And the decision was that quick. I mean, after three years it was that quick," Rex laughed. Being non-residents they could not be married in Arizona, but as soon as they got back to California they were married. "Then all hell broke loose," Rex continued. "She had three girls and I had a boy and a girl. Both were from different walks of life; my son was spoiled, her daughters worked. She had come out from Chicago and worked as a checker to support her daughters, and I admired that. So we came together, took on a foster child, and in 1971 decided to move the office out here." Rex succeeded with Diamond Bar Realty and had it fourteen years before closing it in 1984, and then became a loan broker.

Rex has a brother, Rhodes Reason, who made a career for himself as an actor, appearing in numerous features and television shows, as well as appearing on Broadway as Daddy Warbucks in *Annie*.

We asked Rex if he would sum up his feelings on the acting profession, and he said, "I can't really find anything to say about it except it was meant to be. I just fell into it. Like when I walked down the hallway at the high school and the teacher said, 'I want you for the lead in that thing.' It was a sense of accomplishment I never felt before; getting up there on the stage and getting the applause. That's where it all started. It's a wonderful feeling after a performance – it's like a catharsis; a beautiful feeling. That's what I had when I was on the stage. I loved doing a good performance, and afterwards it's just like you are floating; there's nothing like it. In pictures your audience is the camera; its right here and you can't do much – put it over there and you do a little more. But the stage, it's so full of life. You're using every part of yourself and the whole thing comes to life.

"I had ten years," Rex continued. "I was a young boy in my twenties and never really got into the mature part of the career that I was waiting for. I was in and out, but was lucky to get the roles that I had, so I look at it as another experience in life. You realize it's a phase; that life isn't just the success that you have had in this, but that life is a continual, eternal thing. It's another life; I'm another guy today. I'm glad I made the transition. I'm glad I got out of it and found something else because it's a horrible thing to be caught in the industry as if that's the only thing, waiting for your agent to call you for some work. I'd never experienced that because I've always had contracts, but I wouldn't have liked to be in that position."

Rex concluded by imparting to us this bit of philosophy: "Life is so wonderful, there's so much to it. What you're capable of and able to do, being in the acting field where you can express so much more of your nature and the different sides of your nature that you don't otherwise express. Actually, it's using your emotions; you're pulling from within yourself.

The average citizen just uses one part of his being – look out to get that check, which is security to them. And the bad part of it is that a lot of people start indulging; they don't get no satisfaction so they just go out and indulge, and you get your suicides, murders and rapes because they don't know really who they are. But as an actor you find you have many facets that you can draw on, and you learn many sides of your nature by watching other people because we're different expressions of the same life, which is wonderful to know. As a result you appreciate your relationships with other people because that's where it's all at."

Film Credits: **1952:** Scaramouche; Storm over Tibet. **1953:** China Venture; Salome; Mission over Korea. **1954:** Yankee Pasha; Taza, Son of Cochise; Sign of the Pagan (narrator). **1955:** Lady Godiva; Smoke Signal; Kiss of Fire; This Island Earth. **1956:** The Creature Walks Among Us; Raw Edge. **1957:** Under Fire; Band of Angels; Badlands of Montana. **1958:** Rawhide Trail; Thundering Jets. **1959:** Miracle of the Hills; The Sad Horse.

MARSHALL REED

Marshall's widow was gracious to grant us an interview about her husband and his career in the motion picture business.

Marshall Reed was born May 28, 1917 at Englewood, Colorado. He began his acting career early in life, appearing in children's theater at the age of ten years. Marshall also managed two of his own theater groups during his high school years. After graduating from high school he supported himself with various odd jobs, such as meter reader, horse trainer, bookkeeper, and mail clerk.

"Basically," Mrs. Reed stated, "Marshall started out in the professional theater at the Elitch Gardens Summer Stock Theater in Denver, Colorado. That was quite famous in those days. He started at the bottom building and painting scenery, costumes, lighting, and the whole background of the theater. Then he acted in some of the plays they put on there."

After Elitch Gardens, Marshall began producing, directing, writing, and acting for a variety of theater groups in Denver. He next toured throughout the Western United States with his own repertory group. "They were all young men," Mrs. Reed informed, "and they built all their scenes. They weren't just acting, but did the whole job." Following his acting experience in Colorado and the west, Marshall performed in summer stock in New York and Los Angeles.

"He came out to California in 1942," continued Mrs. Reed, "In order to support his young wife and child he worked nights at Lockheed, and starting in 1943 worked days in films at Republic Studios." Marshall left to serve in the US Navy during the last portion of World War II, and after V-J Day he returned to Los Angeles and resumed his film career.

Marshall's film work consisted primarily of Westerns, often playing the bad man opposite such stars as Bill Elliott, Johnny Mack Brown, Tim Holt, Whip Wilson, Eddie Dean, Lash LaRue, Allan Lane, but occasionally drifted onto the right side of the law in such films as *The Angel and the Badman* with John Wayne or *Oh Susanna!* starring Rod Cameron. He also appeared in over a dozen serials, including playing the title character in *Riding with Buffalo Bill*.

Television also made use of Marshall Reed's talent in many shows, a few of them being *The Lone Ranger, Gene Autry, Roy Rogers, Dragnet, Boston Blackie, Wild Bill Hickok, Range Rider, Superman, Wagon Train, Lassie, Perry Mason, Hopalong Cassidy, Gunsmoke, Bonanza, Kung Fu, Lawman, Marcus Welby, The Six Million Dollar Man* and *The Cisco Kid*. In one of the episodes of the last named series Marshall's quick thinking and horsemanship saved the life of an actress when he stopped a buckboard she was riding from having a serious accident. Marshall also had a regular role as Inspector Fred Asher for four years opposite Warner Anderson and Tom Tully on the television series *The Lineup*. This show was reissued for syndication under the title *San Francisco Beat*. "Marshall enjoyed that show very much," commented Mrs. Reed. "And he enjoyed the location work in San Francisco." Besides acting in these various shows, he also produced and directed several TV documentaries for charitable productions in behalf of crippled children and retarded adults.

Marshall was active in the Masquers Club, a theatrical organization in Hollywood, where he was an officer on the board of directors, as well as serving as chairman of the theater committee from 1965 through 1967. While in this latter capacity he not only designed and directed *Twelve Angry Men* and *The Royal Family*, but also designed settings and executed lighting for nine other Masquers productions.

"A few years before he died," Mrs. Reed stated, "he redesigned the Paramount Ranch out in Agoura, where for years they made many of the Westerns. By that time the buildings were not in the best condition." A production company wanted to shoot a comedy Western, *Shame, Shame on the Bixby Boys* out at the ranch, so Marshall and his crew repaired the needed interiors and designed the whole town for the picture. "Marshall did a cameo part in the picture also," Mrs. Reed added, "but it didn't get much play when it was released.

"He never said how he became interested in acting," Mrs. Reed informed, "but it was just something he fell into. He had a very artistic vein, he drew beautifully, and just had that direction to go, even in his youth. He had the necessary personality for it," she concluded, "plus the looks and the talent."

Marshall Reed passed away on April 15, 1980 in Los Angeles County, California.

Film Credits: 1943: Black Hills Express; The Texas Kid; Silver Spurs; Death Valley Manhunt; Headin' for God's Country; A Guy Named Joe; Bordertown Gunfighters; The Canterville Ghost; Wagon Tracks West; Web of Danger. **1944:** My Buddy; Beneath Western Skies; Tucson Raiders; Range Law; Law Men; Mojave Firebrand; Partners of the Trail;

Marshall Reed

Haunted Harbor; Zorro's Black Whip; Gangsters of the Frontier; Ghost Guns; Marshal of Reno; Headin' for Trouble; Song of Nevada; The Laramie Trail. **1945:** The Tiger Woman; Law of the Valley; The Chicago Kid; Marshal of Laredo; Bandits of the Badlands; It's In a Bag; Colorado Pioneers; Gun Smoke. **1946:** Drifting Along; The Haunted Mine; Shadows on the Range; Gentleman from Texas; In Old Sacramento; West of the Alamo; Gentleman Joe Palooka; The Scarlet Horseman. **1947:** Raiders of the South; Trailing Danger; Angel and the Badman; West of Dodge City; Land of the Lawless; Fighting Vigilantes; Song of the Wasteland; Spoilers of the North; That's My Man; Yankee Fakir; Prairie Express; Stage to Mesa City; Cheyenne Takes Over; Song of the Saddle; On the Old Spanish Trail; Homesteaders of Paradise Valley; Wyoming. **1948:** Sundown Riders; Lightnin' in the Forest; Dangers of the Canadian Mounties; Federal Agents vs. Underworld Inc; The Hawk of Powder River; The Bold Frontiersman; Song of the Drifter; Tornado Range; The Gallant Legion; Triggerman; Dead Man's Gold; Hidden Danger; Back Trail; The Fighting Ranger; The Ranger's Ride; Renegades of Sonora; Mark of the Lash; Check Your Gun; The Denver Kid; Partners of the Sunset; Courtin' Trouble; Overland Trails. **1949:** James Brothers of Missouri; The Invisible Monster; Ghost of Zorro; Cowboy and the Prizefighter; Scene of the Crime; Cactus Caravan (short); Crosswinds; Stampede; Gun Runner; Law of the West; Frontier Investigator; Challenge of the Range; Pioneer Marshal; Navajo Trail Raiders; Square Dance Jubilee; West of El Dorado; Western Renegades; Brand of Fear; Roaring Westward; Riders of the Dusk; The Dalton Gang; Hidden Danger; Range Rogues. **1950:** Over the Border; Rustlers on Horseback; I Was a Shoplifter; Radar Secret Service; The Savage Horde; Rider from Tucson; Six Gun Mesa; Cherokee Uprising; Hot Rod; Six Gun Mesa; Silver Raiders; Outlaw Gold; Law of the Panhandle; Texas Dynamo; Rock Island Trail; California Passage; Covered Wagon Raid. **1951:** Sailor Beware; Oh Susanna!; Gun Play; Hurricane Island; Purple Heart Diary; Vanishing Outpost; Nevada Badmen; Abilene Trail; Montana Desperado; Mysterious Island; The Longhorn; Silver City Bonanza; Canyon Raiders; Texas Lawmen; The Whistling Hills; Lawless Cowboys; Stagecoach Driver; Wanted Dead or Alive; Pirates of the High Seas; Oklahoma Justice. **1952:** Sound Off!; The Lusty Men; The Rough, Tough West; Thundering Caravans; Laramie Mountains; Kansas Territory; Canyon Ambush; Night Raiders; Son of Geronimo; Blackhawk; Fort Osage; The DuPont Story; Montana Incident; Texas City. **1953:** Ride the Man Down; Great Adventures of Captain Kidd; Weekend Father; Arena; Cow Country; Down the River. **1954:** Jubilee Trail; Rose Marie; San Antone; Old Overland Trail; Gunfighters of the Northwest; Riding with Buffalo Bill. **1955:** New York Confidential. **1957:** The Night the World Exploded. **1958:** The Lineup. **1960:** Clear Horizon. **1962:** Broken Lariat; Third of a Man; The Wild Westerners. **1965:** The Hallelujah Trail. **1966:** Madmen of Mandoras (aka They Saved Hitler's Brain); Fate is the Hunter. **1966:** The Long Ride Home. **1967:** A Time for Killing. **1969:** Legend of the Northwest; Support Your Local Sheriff. **1971:** Lawman; The Hard Ride. **1976:** The Day the Lord Got Busted. **1977:** Till Death. **1977:** High Riders; Shame, Shame on the Bixby Boys.

WALTER REED

Walter Reed Smith was born February 10, 1916 on Bainbridge Island, Washington. His father, Major Walter Smith, an Army officer stationed at the now discontinued Fort Ward, had graduated from the Naval Academy at Annapolis, and then moved over to the Army because he continually became seasick. They were transferred from Washington to Honolulu for five years. "My father was in Coast Artillery, and we lived right off Diamond Head. Dale Kahanamoku used to take me out on a surfboard and stand me on the coral reefs nude when I was about three years old and I'd wave at the ships going by. All the drunks thought this kid was walking on water," Walter laughed. Major Smith retired from the Army and they moved to Los Angeles, California, where he owned a large furniture factory and later went into the bond business where he was Vice President of the California Bond and Stock Company. "In 1929 his partner jumped out the window when the crash came and my father was left holding the sack," Walter added. The retired Major turned businessman was pretty clever however. "My dad was a promoter," continued Walter. "He went up and down from being broke to a millionaire."

While attending Hollywood High School Walter had a fight with a kid who turned out to be the principal's son. "That was a mistake," Walter confessed. "I got kicked out of Hollywood High and received one hundred and twenty nights detention." He and his brother Jack Smith (who later hosted the *You Asked for It* television series) transferred over to Beverly Hills High, where they became close friends with Polly Chase, daughter of comedian Charlie Chase, and the daughters of Harry Langdon. "So I grew up knowing all of these famous people," Walter added.

Walter became interested in acting while he was a young teenager. "When I was thirteen I found out that I wanted to be an actor," Walter reflected. "I belonged to the Screen Kiddies Guild – it wasn't like the Screen Actors Guild but it was the start of these kind of things. They sent some of us off to a mass interview and I got into a picture called *Redskins* with Richard Dix." This was filmed in 1929 and turned out to be the last silent film produced by Paramount Studios. The story concerned a Navajo youth (Dix) who is accepted as Thorpe College's first Indian student, where he must face racial prejudice; afterwards, as he returns to the reservation, he is ostracized for his white man's ways. The young man becomes a drifter, shunned by both worlds until he discovers oil and claims it for his people. "It was almost extra work," Walter noted. "You had a line here and a line there. I was an Indian boy. They didn't have any scripts for us; they'd just say, 'Hey you, say this line!' We went out on location to the Southwest by train, which had a club car with a cocktail bar in the rear. In back of the car they had an outside patio where you used to see the President wave," recalled Walter. "I used to love to go back there and one day was drinking a coca-cola; Dix was in there talking to the director (Victor Schertzinger) and said, 'Look, I said if you changed the script I wasn't going to do it!' The director answered, 'Well, it's too late now; we're on the train.' Dix was pretty drunk by now and replied, 'The hell I will,' and opened the door to the balcony and threw his false teeth overboard. We backed the train up and all of us were looking for his teeth because if we didn't find them we didn't have a job. Somebody found them and they were cracked; the prop man had to glue them together."

Walter was also a member of the Amateur Athletic Union where he was a swimmer; he swam with Buster and Buddy Crabbe, Walter Spence and Austin Clapp. In 1929 the Los Angeles Times sponsored a big race from Venice Pier to Ocean Park Pier with eighty swimmers participating. Buster Crabbe came in first place and Walter placed number thirteen – and he was only thirteen years old! "They gave me a cigarette lighter for a trophy," he jokingly remembered. "That was a great thing to give to a young athlete.

"I was brought up at a place called the Beach Club at Santa Monica," Walter said. "It was quite an exclusive club." The swimmers were given honorary membership to the club. Duke Kahanamoka was there. He was the championship swimmer back in 1912 way before Johnny Weissmuller. I spent all week there in the summertime; otherwise we went down there every Sunday." Several producers, directors and actors were members of the club, including Joel McCrea and Edward G. Robinson. "When I was fourteen years old Edward G. Robinson and his wife, when they went out socially, wanted to have someone with their daughter and he used to call me up and ask if I would take Jeanie; he'd pay for everything and we'd go out to the Coconut Grove. I told him I wanted to be an actor and he just smiled at me. When I was sixteen," Walter continued, "Joel McCrea's stand-in became very ill and Joel said, 'Would you like to temporarily stand in for me?'" Walter agreed and went to work with McCrea, whom he had met at the Beach Club. "I put lifts on my shoes because he was taller than me," Walter added.

When the Screen Actors Guild was being formed in 1933, Walter walked in a parade down to Gilmore Stadium and played Aladdin and his Lamp. "Eddie Robinson was in the parade and was very nice to me; he never got so excited that he did anything for me, but I was too young at the time and didn't have any experience. I remember Judy Garland was on top of a piano singing, only twelve or thirteen years old at the time." This was when the actors started joining the Guild to make it possible for better working conditions. "I didn't join it right then," Walter noted. "I joined in New York when I was doing some shorts with Tom Pensacola and Buster West. The Screen Actors Guild started in 1933 and I joined in 1936." Although today (2007) it costs over twelve hundred dollars to join the Guild, Walter told us, "I think I got in for two dollars."

When Walter was seventeen he decided to go on the stage to get the training he needed before he could get into pictures. He began a two-week journey that took him from Los Angeles to New York City, which he described in this way: "I hooked my way on the freight trains. It was pretty rough; had three dollars when I started and had that taken away from me in the shell game in Texas. The shell game is when they'd have the little round peas under the walnut shell; they'd move them around and you'd have to say where it was. I had the three dollars in a little bag around my neck, and I said, 'Hey, I know where it is,' and would put down a dollar and it would be over here. They had a way of doing that; they took me on that," Walter confessed.

"I got stuck in a place called Longview, Texas," Walter continued. "There was this very famous cop there named 'Texas Slim,' and he'd line all the young kids up and he'd boot you, knocking you fifteen feet. He said, 'Everybody get out of here.' The train was going too fast for me. I tried to jump it but it hit me; I bounced away and they picked me up. I was sentenced to thirty days for vagrancy." Walter explained that he, along with other "vagrants," were sent to a work farm, which was "right next to the railway track with just a little fence about two feet high. On the third day, just as the train was coming, the guard says, 'I'm going around the corner to the bathroom. You guys stay here.' About two hundred of us jumped over this fence and onto the train. We found out that was a big racket; they'd get fifty cents a day for you to be there and they wouldn't take you off the books for thirty days. So when they let two hundred guys go over the fence that was one hundred dollars a day for nothing. At night they would chain us to the beds, so I always thought I was a fugitive from a chain gang.

"People were good all over the country," Walter reflected. "You'd get by some of those farms and a guy would come by and see you sitting in the hot sun and say, 'Hey, you hungry kid?' You'd say, 'Yeah,' and he'd take you over and feed you. One time my shirt was half ripped off my back and he gave me a new shirt. I got a bath and then he took me up to where I could get the train again. They were really nice."

Walter explained that in those days of the Great Depression there were many people on the road. "Sometimes when I jumped on a freight train there would be two hundred people on it: bums, hobos and tramps. There was a difference: a bum is a bum, anywhere; tramps would follow the crops; and the hobo never asked for money, he always had a little money here and there. He might have been a bank president, you never knew. It was rough, but at seventeen you don't think it's rough. You eat soup or you go into a bakery at five o'clock in the morning and ask them to give you leavings from yesterday. They always had some stuff they'd give you, or we would always get a night's lodging and some soup.

"I got locked in a refrigerator car one time for forty eight hours," Walter remembers. "It was on the side of the road and I heard somebody come along; I knocked and he opened it up. I could have died in there; they lost a lot of kids, that's why they checked all these cars because kids do stupid things."

"You always kept your shoes," Walter added, "because if you took them off and left them beside you, the next morning when you got up you didn't have any shoes. You're young and it's not tragic. You always think you're going to eat, and you do. Those things are good experiences; they teach you how it is to be hungry. If you ever have to portray somebody like that it helps."

By the time he reached New York City Walter had lost fifteen pounds. He went to see his brother, Jack, who was singing with Phil Harris' orchestra at the Pennsylvania Roof. "I had sent some clothes on to my brother," Walter stated. "I had been on a coal-burner, and boy, when you get in back of one of those it'll get all over you. I had to go down to the barber shop to get a facial to get all those hunks of coal out of my face." Walter spent the night with his brother and Phil Harris dining at the Pennsylvania Roof. One night on a freight train and the next night in luxury.

Walter had a letter from Cesar Romero referring him to a top theatrical agent named Leland Hayward, who turned him over to someone in his office to represent him. Casting auditions just happened to be in process for a couple of military school plays: *Bright Honor* and *So Proudly We Hail*. "I got into the second one the third day I was there, which was about a military school in Virginia," Walter recalled. "It just was fortunate they were casting these shows with someone my age – seventeen." The play lasted only a short time. "I was in nine flops in one season," Walter related. "You got half salary while you're rehearsing so I lived on forty bucks a week for months and months. I roomed with another guy who became a very big studio story editor named Walter Herndon, and I would go to the market where you could get a penny's worth of peas, a penny's worth of carrots, a penny's worth of this, and then I'd go over to the meat counter and ask for a bone for my dog. Well, he'd throw it in and we had stew all of the time. That's what we ate for months and months. But it was fun. You know, when you're young and broke you don't care. I was doing what I wanted to do." Even though these plays had short runs, it opened the door for Walter to join a stock company in Cumberland Hills, Rhode Island, which was run by actress Ruth McDeavitt.

"I did a show called *Father Malachy's Miracle*. A scout saw me and brought me out to Los Angeles to test for a picture opposite Betty Grable, called *Beauty and the Beach*. I was too green," Walter commented. "It was too early for me to be out here. I didn't get the part. I was awfully young for her, so they flew me back to New York and I went back to the stock company." He continued on as the juvenile player at Cumberland Hills, and the next year became co-leading man with Harry Townes at Kennebunkport, Maine, for two years. In between seasons, Walter and Harry got on at winter stock in Chatanooga, Tennessee.

"I did eighty-six weeks of stock," Walter remarked. In Kennebunkport, Walter made two dollars a week plus room and board for his wife, Elizabeth Bryce, and himself. The next year he said, "You have to give my wife two dollars a week," so they put her to work in the box-office. "Those things you think about and wonder how did we do it, but it was fun. We were getting experience and not even knowing it." Among the plays that Walter performed in were *Night of January 16th* and *The Front Page*. Some pretty big stars would come up and play the leads and the stock players would support them. Walter worked with Ian Keith in Shakespeare; Douglass Montgomery was a lead one time; and Elissa Landi starred in *The Warrior's Husband*. "That was fun because you were working with big people and if you kept your eyes open you could learn things. At night," Walter continued, "we'd go out in the pond and catch big frogs and cook them. It's a wonder we weren't killed because they had these black snakes that could ruin you."

When Walter was playing Baby Face Martin in *Dead End* he read in the paper that Joel McCrea and his wife, Frances Dee, were in Kennebunkport. He found which hotel that McCrea was staying and phoned him, saying, "I'm in a stock company here; how about you and your wife coming over and seeing the show?" "We'll do it," McCrea answered. They did come that night, and they loved the show. After the performance, Joel told Walter, "You're ready." Walter replied, "What do you mean?" "You'll hear from me," was McCrea's answer. After the summer season was over Walter received a phone call from Frank Vincent, who was McCrea's agent, who offered to pay Walter's way out to California.

Vincent, who handled some of the biggest stars in Hollywood, turned Walter over to another agent in his office. On his second day in Hollywood, Walter was taken to RKO Studios where he was introduced to the drama coach. He read a scene for her, to which she stated, "This guy's good. He doesn't need me." Walter told us, "I had, as I said, eighty-six weeks of stock plus a couple of Broadway shows, and I was put under contract. It was luck, timing, and knowing somebody. Knowing somebody helps; oh, but you better be prepared when you get it," Walter concluded.

During his career in summer stock Walter had gone under the name that he had always used, Reed Smith. At RKO, however, they said they would change his name. On trying to decide on a name someone suggested Stark Nolan; a woman laughed and exclaimed, "That sounds like stark naked." That was enough for the new contract player, who said, "Let's just make it Walter Reed." So they dropped Smith and he kept his first two names, Reed being for his mother's maiden name. "The first picture I did there was *The Mayor of 44th Street*," Walter noted. "Richard Barthelmess was in it; it was supposed to be his comeback. The leads were George Murphy and Ann Shirley."

Walter followed this with a bit in *My Favorite Spy*, and then graduated to leads or supporting roles in at least six films in 1942 and 1943. When Buddy Rogers went into the Service, Walter replaced him in the final two Mexican Spitfire films opposite Lupe Velez. "I was doing real well,"

Walter informed. "I did a picture called *Seven Days Leave* and played second lead to Victor Mature. When I was doing *Bombardier* I had a pretty big part, and Bob Ryan had a small part compared to me." This last film, which starred Pat O'Brien and Randolph Scott, also featured an actor who was to become a close lifelong friend of Walter named Richard Martin, who played the role of Chito Rafferty in this film before taking on this same name in his Zane Grey and Tim Holt Westerns. After *Bombardier* Walter went into the Army. "That was rough," Walter noted, "because right when I'm the hottest I went in the Service."

While serving in the military Walter toured with many other actors turned servicemen (including Karl Malden, Edmond O'Brien, Damian O'Flynn, John Forsythe, Henry Rowland, and Martin Ritt) in an Army play titled *Winged Victory*. The play, which encouraged people to join the Army, traveled across the United States, and then was performed on Broadway.

When discharged from the military after the close of World War II, Walter returned to his contract at RKO. "RKO wasn't a large studio to start with," Walter noted, "but a very imminent studio and they did some very good stuff. I did a lot of bad pictures there, and I did a lot of good ones. In those days they had double features, so I did shorts, B-pictures; everything they told me to do." Walter considered being under contract at that time a great break for him because you did everything: big parts, small parts; comedy, drama, war and Western films. Upon his return to his contract he had a minor role in *The Bamboo Blonde* and then to co-leads in *Child of Divorce* and *Banjo*. Walter said that these films were not of the same quality as his initial pre-war films, but that he was happy for the work.

In addition to his film roles, Walter obtained work through his studio on radio, including the lead in *Hitler's Children* on Lux Radio. He followed this with a five day sustaining show with Jane Wyman, as well as performing Skippy Peanut Butter commercials on radio. "I'd make extra money for this," Walter added. "The studio would get me these things because in those days they didn't pay very much money under contract."

Speaking of the benefits of being a studio contractee, Walter mentioned, "I played Bob Dalton in a picture called *Return of the Badmen*, and my brother in it was Lex Barker. Well, he's blond and looks as much like me as the man in the moon, but we were under contract so they would use us. That was good experience because it was like doing stock; you did everything. You'd do a Western one week, and a film like *Night Song* the next." Walter would play an outlaw in a Tim Holt Western like *Desert Passage* or *Target*; a doctor in *The Torch*; a stranded airplane crash victim in *Angel on the Amazon*; a fellow with a high hat and coat tails in *Night Song*; and such a variety as this saved you from being typecast to one sort of role for your entire career. This diversity aided Walter when he later left RKO to freelance at the various studios. "I had all this film and when anybody would ask, 'Have you ever played a Naval officer?' I'd say 'Sure,' and call up and get the film so they could see it," he explained.

Walter discussed working in three Tim Holt Westerns, telling us that Tim was a nice guy and that he enjoyed working with his friend Richard Martin again, and that another friend, Robert Bray, was under contract and did a lot of heavies in the Holt films. These Holt Westerns were usually filmed on a two week schedule at Lone Pine in the Alabams, which is the volcanic rock country on the eastern slope of the Sierra Nevada Mountains. "You could shoot in the canyon all day," Walter noted, "because they would always change with the light and shadows. We had a director, Les Selander; he was wild. As the sun would go he'd keep going higher and higher – pretty soon we'd be on top of the highest mountain and somebody would say we're going to quit pretty soon cause we can't go any higher. Six o'clock at night and these guys are way on top of the mountain and it took them forever to get down with the equipment. But he was a good guy; Les probably couldn't have done *Gone with the Wind*, but he sure could do a Western – and they are the ones that made money. The Tim Holt's made a lot of money." Walter would again work for Selander in the Western feature, *War Paint*, which was filmed in the heat of Death Valley.

Walter had a funny story to tell about his early days at RKO. "I did a show that we were doing for the troops called *Goodbye Again*, and I had to smoke a cigar in this. I got so I loved cigars, and I was very young. Charlie Koerner, the president of the studio, called me up to his office and said, 'Walter, I see you smoking these cigars and you're in your early twenties. It looks a little cocky smoking these. I'd rather you didn't do it; it looks bad.' I said, 'Okay, I won't smoke them. I'm sorry, Mr. Koerner.' I went home and when I got there here was a box of dollar cigars for me; he said smoke them at home."

RKO would on occasion loan their actors to other studios and charge ten times the salary they were making. "I was getting three hundred dollars a week and they'd loan me out for three thousand," Walter stated. He was loaned out to Warner Brothers to co-star with Edmond O'Brien and Robert Stack in *Fighter Squadron*. A young actor named Rock Hudson was making his film debut in a minor role. Walter told us that Hudson's line was "Or you got to build a bigger blackboard." After a number of takes of stumbling over this line it was finally given to another actor to say. Years later Walter visited Hudson backstage of a play he was starring in and said, "or you got to build a bigger blackboard," which resulted in a laugh from Hudson as he threw his towel at Walter. Several years after *Fighter Squadron*, Walter was freelancing and played a deputy to Hudson's sheriff in *Horizons West* while Hudson was under contract to Universal. Although Hudson was the star, Walter was making more money per week as a non-contract player. Rock asked Walter, "Gosh, will I ever make that much money?" Walter replied, "Wait your turn, you'll get it." "Rock died a multi-millionaire," Walter noted, "but you have to serve your apprenticeship." Walter also mentioned that they had his character in the film so that in the final showdown he could shoot Robert Ryan (who played Hudson's outlaw brother) instead of having Hudson have to kill his own brother.

Walter was let go from his RKO contract a few days before Christmas, and at the day before Christmas party Walter mentioned to Peter Rathvon (who was then president of RKO) that he had enjoyed working with him and was happy to have known him. "What do you mean?" asked Rathvon. "I was let go," Walter answered. "Today's my last day." Rathvon told Walter that he was very sorry and was not aware that had happened. "That's awful," Rathvon continued, "I'd never let a guy go the day before Christmas. My wife wants to produce a picture; I'll talk to you next week." Walter did get the call and was given a part in the film titled *The Sun Sets at Dawn* at three times the salary that he had received as a contract player. "He gave me that picture," Walter added, "because he thought it was a dirty trick that I had gotten fired." The reason for Walter being let go was that as you go up in salary – and when they decide it's too high – they will either make you a star or terminate the contract. "So that's a par for the course," Walter noted, "you bounce around."

Walter went to work for the production team of Pine-Thomas at Paramount Studio where he appeared in a number of films, among which were *The Eagle and the Hawk*, *El Paso*, *Passage West*, *Caribbean*, *Tripoli*, *The Blazing Forest* (all of which starred John Payne), as well as *Sangaree*, *The Lawless*, and the frontier epic *The Far Horizon*, which dealt with the Lewis and Clark expedition in seeking to find a waterway across the frontier to the Pacific Ocean. Walter and another actor, William Phipps, joined stars Charlton Heston and Fred MacMurray on location along the Snake River as utility actors – which were actors that they could depend on who were on hand in case they needed someone to fill in and say a line here or there. "We were always on the wrong side of the river," Walter smiled. "If they needed someone we were over there. Then they'd put us over here and they'd need us over there. We were on that for weeks and weeks. The only time I ended up in the picture was when I took this jug, put it over my head, drank from it, and said, 'Makes a man feel at home.' We were always fishing somewhere," he laughed.

Walter made several pictures at Republic Studios, one being a Rocky Lane Western titled *Wells Fargo Gunmaster*. Although many actors had problems working with Lane, Walter told us he was a nice man and that he wanted his Western series to be good as that was what was earning his living at the time. As such, he was particular as to how it was done and that turned some actors off to him. Walter later worked with him again when Lane was supplying the voice to the horse on the *Mister Ed* television series. Walter also starred in two serials at Republic, *The Flying Disc Man from Mars* and *Government Agents vs. the Phantom Legion*. He was offered the lead in a third but turned it down as he did not want to become known as a serial star. "Have you ever seen a script to a serial?" he asked us. "It's the size of a phonebook." Walter mentioned that on the serials they set up and took down the shots so fast that one time they asked him to drive a car down Mulholland Drive, a mountain road above Hollywood, and around a bend, and by the time he accomplished this, found a spot to turn around and come back that the crew had already struck the set-up and moved to another location.

When television came in, Walter was one of the actors who said, "I'm going to do it." Some actors criticized those who worked in television in those early days. When a friend asked Walter, "You're not going to do that crazy stuff?" Walter replied, "Yeah, I want to learn it." Walter told us that he had friends who refused to work in television even though they had not obtained any acting roles in six months. "You're only an actor as long as you are working," Walter told us. He began his venture into television by doing a couple of live shows for no pay; a show called

Inspirational Theater was on every week and people like Hugh O'Brian, Hans Conried, and Lauren Tuttle did it free of charge just to learn the new medium.

Walter started with shows like *Fireside Theater, Matinee Theater* and *Front Row Center* – one with Robert Preston just before he went back east to Broadway for *The Music Man*. "Live TV was absolutely scary," Walter admitted. "You'd be saying your dialogue and a guy would be underneath pushing your feet to get you in the right place. It was frightening." Walter once told a fellow actor named Phil Coolidge, "This is wonderful; they have the bathrooms right on the stage. Coolidge replied, "Yes, you could vomit between acts." "When I was twenty or twenty-two, when you're under contract, you think you are God's gift to the business," Walter explained, "and the more you grow up the more you know how little you know, and you get 'scareder.' I didn't know what fright was because you thought you were so good, but now when you look at some of those shows you see how bad you really were."

Walter co-starred in a pilot for an early television show called *Deadline*, in which he was second lead with John Payne. Walter played the owner of a newspaper office and Payne was the reporter. The pilot involved Walter assigning Payne to cover the crime stories and Payne wanting to be a sports reporter; so every time Payne was covering a sports event a crime would take place that needed to be solved. "Payne was the sloppy guy and I was the dandy," Walter commented. "He'd sit on the table and I'd wipe it off; I was the smooth guy with the tie and he was the guy with the old beat-up clothes. It was kind of cute with these guys as best friends, but we were so entirely different." The series, unfortunately, was not picked up even though they had eighteen finished scripts by W.R. Burnett, whose past credits included the classic gangster film *Little Caesar*. "We probably would have done it, but one of the partners, Stephen Ames, died and it was tied up in litigation. It would have been a good series," Walter added.

Walter worked in over eighty different television series in all the various genres that were produced, including Westerns (*The Lone Ranger, Hopalong Cassidy, Annie Oakley, Buffalo Bill Jr., Rin Tin Tin, Wyatt Earp, Gunsmoke, Restless Gun, Zane Grey Theater, Colt 45, Cheyenne, Bonanza, The Deputy, Have Gun-Will Travel* and *Wagon Train*); police shows (*Dragnet, Public Defender, The Line-Up, The Untouchables, Meet McGraw, The FBI, M Squad, 77 Sunset Strip, Arrest and Trial,* and *Peter Gunn*); dramas (*Perry Mason, The Loretta Young Show, The Millionaire, Ben Casey, Waterfront, Superman, Biff Baker, Soldiers of Fortune, Fury, Lassie, Sky King, Sea Hunt, Whirleybirds* and *Men into Space*); comedies (*The Life of Riley, Burns and Allen, Adventures of Ozzie and Harriet, My Three Sons, People's Choice, The Family Affair, Dennis the Menace, Petticoat Junction* and *Hazel*); and supernatural /sci-fi / horror (*The Twilight Zone, One Step Beyond, Voyage to the Bottom of the Sea, The World of Giants* and *Thriller*).

Walter was promised one of the supporting roles in *The High and the Mighty*, but due to certain studio politics the part went to Phil Harris and he was given the much smaller role of the father of an ill boy who was placed on the plane. When another actor in the film, Douglas Fowley, heard of what had transpired he told Walter that he would soon be directing a picture and promised him a part in it. True to his word, Fowley cast Walter in the lead role in a film titled *Macumba Love*, a tale of voodoo that was shot in Brazil.

Walter numbers among his favorite shows a Western in which he co-starred with Randolph Scott, Gail Russell and Lee Marvin titled *Seven Men from Now*. The film was produced by John Wayne's Batjac Productions and directed by Budd Boetticher, a director that Walter had worked for on a number of prior pictures. "I liked it; you just remember something you enjoyed doing," Walter remarked. In the conclusion of the film Marvin has a duel with Scott, and when he is shot he slowly falls and drags his hand across the top of a money box sitting on the ground near him. After the shot was completed, Marvin asked Walter, "When you die, how are you going to beat that?" "I can't," Walter replied, "I'm just going to die." When it came time to shoot the scene where Walter is shot in the back by outlaw John Larch he did just that – he fell to the ground and died.

Practical jokes were a common occurrence on a movie set, and Walter shared a humorous story about Vincent Price receiving the brunt of a joke on the final day of location at Glacier National Park during the filming of *Dangerous Mission*. The special effects man, "Dump" Landon (called "Dump" because whenever you needed a landslide he was the man to call) waited for his cue to approach Price. "Cut! Vincent, you're all through," came the director's voice. "Dump" asked, "You're sure this is the last shot?" "Yes," the director replied. Turning to Price, Landon asked, "would you come over here in this phone booth (it didn't have a top on it) and just look out because we want to take some stills for publicity before you leave." Price went over and stood as directed – and then Landon dumped one hundred gallons of water on him; everyone sat around and roared. Walter related another joke: "We were staying in this very private hotel owned by the North Pacific Railroad. While we were eating dinner one night we had two guys dressed in white coats come in and lift Vincent right out of his chair in the dining room and take him out like he was going to the nuthouse, with all these people looking on. We never brought him back in and he never finished his dinner either. We did a lot of stuff to Vincent," Walter added. "He was a good sport."

Another actor working in *Dangerous Mission* was Dennis Weaver. One day he told Walter that he had just tested for a new television series but didn't know if anything would come of it. Well, Dennis made history in that show as Chester Good, friend and ally of Matt Dillon on *Gunsmoke*.

One director that Walter had the desire to work for was the legendary John Ford. "I had wanted to work for him and could never get in to see him. I knew a guy named Martin Rackin who had written *The Horse Soldiers* and was producer. I knew him when he was assistant writer on *Bombardier*." Rackin got Walter on the film as a rider, so he was on location but didn't really have a part. Three days later, while he was sitting on a mound of dirt by the river, someone called out, "Walter Reed." He answered, "Yo!" Walter told us you always answered something like that because you are in the cavalry. The fellow who had called him came over and it was John Ford, complete with the patch over his eye, and he said, "Rackin tells me you can talk."

Walter replied, "Well, I try." Ford handed him two pages of script and asked him to be ready by that afternoon. "It was a southern colonel part, but I was in a Union outfit so they had to call the wardrobe. In the meantime, he was trying to show me how to use the saber and it hit me; one of the stuntmen told me, 'Keep the cut open, put some dirt in it and make a scar out of it. If he knows he hurt you he'll put you in every show he does.' Anyway, after that I got in the Southern outfit, except I didn't have the beard on, and it got that the wardrobe man would ask, 'Mister Ford, how do you want Walter Reed dressed today?' One day I'd be the Southern soldier and the next I'd do the Union major, so he had me paid double salary. I got to be known as the guy with the reversible uniform."

While relating to the work in the Western shows that he had done, Walter shared one of the first rules an actor should live by. "In all of the pictures they were always the same riders, and you kept in good with these guys because they were real cowboys – and if they didn't like you and you gave them a bad time they could ride you right into the ground and make it look like an accident." Walter also had some good friends who were stuntmen, one of his closest friends being Chuck Roberson. "On certain pictures," Walter continued, "in a big crowd I'd get stuntmen to ride on both sides of me, and they'd protect you from some of those crazy guys." He pointed out an example, returning to *The Horse Soldiers*, where he was the leader of the Second Troop and made a charge across a bridge with his sword raised, and one hundred and forty riders charging close behind him. He had a few stuntmen around him, but the others behind were all local extras with untrained horses. "I went so fast over the bridge, way out in front of them. After we got through, John Ford said, 'You really rode fast across that bridge.' He thought it was great. One of the stuntmen turned to me and said, 'You were scared; you were trying to get away from them.' I said, 'That's right.' I was riding fast trying to get away from those crazy guys behind me; that's why I looked like such a hero."

Walter worked with Ford in three other features: *Sergeant Rutledge*, *How the West Was Won* and Ford's final film, *Cheyenne Autumn*. On the latter film Walter had a part of a lieutenant in the cavalry and had completed his part, along with another actor named James Flavin. Bernard Smith, the producer, was standing next to Ford, and said, "Oh, Jimmy and Walter are through in the script. We don't have to take them to Gunnison, Colorado, because there's nothing else for them." Ford turned to Smith and replied, "Bernie, these are the two most important men I need up there." The next day the company moved to Gunnison and "we were there two weeks and I wasn't called to the set; Jimmy went up there once. Bernie Smith asked, 'When is Walter going out?' 'I have a very important thing for him,' Ford answered. I'm rooming with Mike Mazurki and I'm just sitting there each day; they keep saying 'We'll call you when we want you.' Two weeks later, the last day of the picture, they finally said, 'Walter, you can come out for lunch, we're eating on the set; get your wardrobe on cause you're working this afternoon. The old man said don't worry about the dialogue. Come on out and he'll work it out with you.' At about four in the afternoon he says, 'I don't want Walter on a horse; it's slippery.' It was very cold out there, eleven thousand feet; he didn't tell me or anybody else, but he knew I had had this heart attack and he wasn't about to put me on a horse. He could be very rough with guys or he could be very gentle. I have this one scene with Karl Malden sitting on his horse and the Indians coming in to meet him; I look over and say, 'Cheyennes, sir.' Ford said, 'You don't say it plural, it's Cheyenne.' So the one line I had I blew," Walter laughed. "That's all I say, and that's what he had me up there for two weeks. You don't tell Ford anything," Walter concluded. Bernard Smith's mistake of telling Ford to send Walter and Flavin home cost him a bundle of dollars for two weeks extra work.

After his heart attack in the early 1960's, Walter slowed his work as an actor and went into real estate and was very successful in that field. "I found that you could make money in something else, too. You don't have to confine yourself to one thing." Walter moved away from Hollywood and settled in a fine Victorian home in Santa Cruz, California. He started going back and making films again, but "I found out that I get tired. The sheet would come down and I couldn't remember my lines, so I started taking smaller things in films like *Tora! Tora! Tora!* Or I'd work for guys that I knew, like Bobby Wise in *Sand Pebbles*. I thought, 'Why am I doing this,' so I just decided to quit and took out my pension from Screen Actors Guild." One of Walter's final performances was in an episode of *The Streets of San Francisco*.

Walter told us in our 1983 interview, "I just refuse everything now. Dick Benedict, the director, said, 'Gee Walter, I got a great thing for you. I want you to play a senator,' and I said, 'No way.' 'What? You didn't take a part?' he asked. 'Dick, no way.' He told me, 'You know, you're the first actor that I know that wouldn't say I'll make an exception this time,' and he went away telling, 'You know, I offered Walter a job and he wouldn't take it.'

Walter enjoyed being invited as a guest celebrity to the various Western film festivals around the country and associating with former co-workers and meeting the fans. Walter had many stories to share and enjoyed doing so. In August of 2000 Walter was honored with a Golden Boot Award in recognition of his roles as a heavy in the Western films; on July 14, 2001, the city in which he lived, Santa Cruz, California, set the day aside as Walter Reed Day to honor him, and a local movie house screened *Seven Men from Now* to an enthused audience. Outside the theater, Walter placed his autograph and hand and foot prints in cement next to those of his friend Rory Calhoun (who was so honored several years earlier) with whom he had worked with nearly fifty years earlier in *Yellow Tomahawk*. A short time later Walter passed away in Santa Cruz on August 20, 2001.

Film Credits: **1929:** Redskins. **1942:** Mayor of 44th Street; My Favorite Spy; Seven Days Leave; Framing Father (short); Mexican Spitfire's Elephant; Army Surgeon. **1943:** Petticoat Larceny; Mexican Spitfire's Blessed Event; Bombardier. **1946:** Child of Divorce; The Bamboo Blonde. **1947:** Banjo. **1948:** Night Song; Western Heritage; Return of the Badmen; Mystery in Mexico; Fighter Squadron; Angel on the Amazon. **1949:** Captain China. **1950:** The Lawless; Tripoli; The Young Man with a Horn; The Eagle and the Hawk; The Torch; The Sun Sets at Dawn.

1951: Wells Fargo Gunmaster; Flying Disc Man from Mars (serial); Government Agents vs. the Phantom Legion (serial); Passage West; Go for Broke!; Submarine Command; The Racket. **1952:** Caribbean; Target; Desert Passage; The Blazing Forest; Horizons West. **1953:** The Clown; War Paint; Those Redheads from Seattle; Seminole; Thunderbirds; The Man from the Alamo; Forever Female; Sangaree; Latin Lovers. **1954:** Dangerous Mission; The Yellow Tomahawk; The High and the Mighty; Return from the Sea. **1955:** Hell's Island; Far Horizons; Bobby Ware is Missing; The Last Command. **1956:** Emergency Hospital; Seven Men from Now; Rock Pretty Baby; Dance with Me Henry. **1957:** Three Brave Men; Slim Carter; The Helen Morgan Story; Last of the Badmen. **1958:** The Lawless Eighties; The Deep Six; Summer Love; How to Make a Monster. **1959:** The Horse Soldiers; Arson for Hire; Westbound. **1960:** Thirteen Fighting Men; Sergeant Rutledge; Macumba Love. **1961:** Posse from Hell. **1962:** Advise and Consent. **1963:** How the West Was Won. **1964:** The Carpetbaggers; Cheyenne Autumn; Where Love has Gone. **1965:** Bus Riley's Back in Town; The Money Trap; Mirage; Convict Stage; Fort Courageous. **1966:** The Sand Pebbles; The Oscar; Moment to Moment. **1968:** The Destructors; Panic in the City. **1969:** A Time for Dying; Deadlock (TV); The Monk (TV). **1970:** Tora! Tora! Tora!

FRANK RICHARDS

Frank Richards was born September 15, 1909, in New York City, moving to Fall River, Massachusetts three years later. Frank mentioned that he was the average kid who went to the silent movies for a nickel at the Bijou, and that he especially enjoyed watching the performances of Francis Ford, the actor-brother of John Ford. As Frank was a member of a poor Jewish family, financing his weekly trip to the movies was not as simple as it might have been. "Now how do I get a nickel?" Frank asked. "My father wouldn't give me a nickel on a Saturday, so I used to pick up silver from cigarettes, go to the junk man, who used to give me seven cents; five cents for the movie and two cents for candy."

Frank began working when he was eleven years old, employed for three dollars a week in an oval shop. Next, he went into peddling fruit and had his own horse. "I bought my own horse for seventy dollars," Frank informed us. "Then I went into the wholesale food and vegetable business." Speaking of his school days, Frank told us that he usually was promoted to the next grade on probation. "I think I'm the only one in the United States that ever got promoted on probation. In other words, six weeks before promotion the teacher would say, 'Frank, if you don't try harder you're going to stay back.' So the next six weeks I try hard and get promoted on probation. In those days they didn't have any junior high school; it was eighth grade and then you went to high school. We had a Mrs. Carver that was principal and also eighth grade teacher. She said, 'Frank, no probation. You either get promoted or you stay back.'" Frank studied hard and received the second highest score in the class, receiving a prize of a five pound box of chocolate in addition to his graduation into high school. In high school, Frank received the best marks he ever got in his life.

One day in 1929 Frank decided that he was not pleased with the physical shape that he was in, so began a life-long habit of going to the gym and working out. One day, while thus engaged, a man asked him, "Why don't you box?" "I was taught by my mother, an old fashioned Jewish woman, to be a coward," Frank reflected; "If anyone bothered you, walk away." He went from two hundred and twelve pounds to one hundred and seventy five, and went into training to be a fighter. He boxed for eighteen months in the amateurs in the light heavy class. He fought twenty bouts in 1930-31, winning most of them. "To make a long story short," he explained, "I only had one good eye. I hit him and he falls on top of me and we both go down. We fell down two or three times and they stopped the fight. They thought I had a glass eye; the right eye (my good eye) was froze." Then he went to Providence, Rhode Island, where he had a fight with a guy named Katz. "I lasted three rounds, and all I heard was 'Katz' because that was his hometown. The third fight I knocked the guy out; the fourth time I knocked him out, but then I realized I wasn't going to be very good. You have to have two good eyes when you box, you have to see him with the right eye and you have to see him with the left eye." Looking over his boxing career, Frank mentioned, "It was a good experience, and it gave me one good feeling: I've never quit the gym since 1929, and I've been going regularly."

Asked if watching movies as a child had sparked an interest in a possible acting career, Frank mentioned that the idea never dawned on him until one day in 1932. "I saw a play with Spencer Tracy just before he went to Hollywood on Broadway for fifty cents, titled *The Last Mile*. I thought, 'I could do that, that's easy.'" From this experience watching Tracy perform he decided that this was what he was going to do (twenty years later he performed on screen opposite Tracy in *Pat and Mike*). For seven years, Frank tried unsuccessfully to break into a stock company at Cape Cod. He tried at this particular place because this was where he had had his fruit and vegetable business, and "I knew Cape Cod like my five fingers. One day I went into a non-equity playhouse and auditioned for them; about a week later a Greek in the food store that I had used to do business with, said, 'Hey Frank, they want you at Chatham Theatre. Can you do an Irishman?' I played a small part and got eight dollars. The following week I had a good part in a play called *The Cowboys and Indians*, as a truck driver; got pretty good notices and paid twelve dollars," he smiled.

With this experience, Frank went to New York in 1937, and landed a part in a play, *The First American Dictator*, appearing as a body guard to Louisiana Governor Huey Long. He received no pay for this production, but added another play to his credit. One day Frank was just standing on the corner of Broadway and 44th Street at Walgreen's Drug Store, across the street from the Astor Hotel. An actress named K.T. Stevens, daughter of director Sam Woods, asked him if he had seen her boyfriend; Frank answered that he had not, and she informed him that they were casting a Broadway play called *The Brown Danube*. He went and auditioned, obtaining the part of a Nazi storm trooper. They played Pittsburgh, Philadelphia, Washington and Atlantic City. "I got my first professional show," he said. "We were making forty dollars a week, to me that was a lot of money. I get killed in the second act. Out of twenty four in the cast, I was the only Jew. In Atlantic City I found this Jewish restaurant, seven course meal for sixty cents and no tip. I'm playing poker, and we got guys like Eddie Franz, Dean Jagger and Francis Cleveland (the son of President Grover Cleveland), so I made about sixteen dollars playing poker with them, and I'm going to be a big shot and take eight of them out to this restaurant. They'd never been to a Jewish restaurant. We opened the night before and we got murdered by the Jewish people, and here I am playing this storm trooper with the swastika. As I walk in the door with eight or nine people, the old Jewish woman (who owns the restaurant), spots me. I'd been having fun with her, kidding with her in Jewish. 'You son of a bitch,' she said. 'You Nazi bastard, you!' I said, 'I'm Jewish.' 'A Jew playing a Nazi,' she yelled, 'Get out of my place or I'll call the police!' She wouldn't let us come in; that's how serious it was in 1939. They kidded the life out of me," Frank smiled.

After the close of *The Brown Danube*, Frank returned to Massachusetts and worked on a fruit truck for the summer. Afterwards he returned to New York and read for a part of a laundry truck driver in a Theatre Guild play, directed by Sidney Kingsley and starring Margo. Kingsley said, "We'll let you know." Frank walked up to him, and said, "Mr. Kingsley, you're not the kind of an individual who says, 'I'll let you know,' and then forgets about them the minute you walk out – you either want me or you don't want me." Frank returned to his room, which cost three dollars a day back in those days, and he received the word, "Come to work for rehearsals." Frank told us that even though you reach this stage in the world of theatre, "You're fighting all the time, you never knew because it was five days of rehearsal for nothing, and within five days they could fire you." Frank got the part.

Frank's next credit was the role of a prize fighter in a movie short, and from this was able to join Screen Actors Guild. He received twenty-five dollars for this film work. "Ten dollars for yours truly, two fifty for the agent, and twelve fifty to Screen Actors Guild," he smiled. Frank made several more shorts for March of Time, and then a screen test for Paramount as a gangster in a scene with Cornel Wilde. Frank was asked by one of the stars of *The Brown Danube* if he would drive his wife across the country to California, where this star was testing for a film at Twentieth Century Fox. "He would give me a hundred dollars a week and I'd be his stand-in and chauffeur. When I got there, he said, 'I can't do a thing for you. You're on your own.' I had eighteen dollars; two weeks later I was thrown out of my room. I was broke!"

Frank stayed a week at the YMCA, and then "I met a Samaritan; an old couple took a liking to me. They loaned me money until I got a job at Columbia Pictures in *Before I Hang*, with Boris Karloff, and worked a week. The test I made with Cornel Wilde got me the job." They told Frank that they wanted a New York actor, and he replied, "I'm from New York." He went on to tell them that he was broke and that he would do it for seventy five dollars. "I got three hundred and fifty dollars for the week; I was in seventh heaven." From this salary, he remembers he bought a nice thirty-five dollar sports coat that was on sale for seventeen dollars. Frank started getting small roles in films at Twentieth Century Fox, including *Tall Dark and Handsome*, with Cesar Romero; a German in MGM's 1942 release, *Cairo*; a mechanic in an MGM crime short; a gangster in *Hold That Ghost*, with Abbott & Costello at Universal; and a bit in Cecil B. DeMille's Paramount release, *Reap the Wild Wind*.

Frank entered the Army and served eighteen months during World War II. After his discharge he returned to New York. Continuing in his acting career, Frank obtained a part of a wrestler in a Theatre Guild play with Ethel Barrymore. "She could never be a peasant, she was always the lady," Frank commented. This play flopped on the road, followed by another flop called *Salute To Murder*. Following this he received a call from an agent that the casting was under way for *The Tempest*. "That's Shakespeare," Frank said. "I don't want Shakespeare." Anyway, Frank read for the part of a sailor in the beginning, and they asked, "Would you mind reading another part for us, that of Caliban?" "I did the best I could," Frank told us, "but I didn't get called. They wanted me to go on the road with Canada Lee, who was a black fighter, and understudy as Caliban, but I didn't go." Frank obtained work on some of the radio shows in New York, and always managed to pick up an acting gig somewhere. Frank was hired by a summer stock company in Newport Beach, Rhode Island; reflecting on this portion of his career, he told us, "I've played a Polish character, another time an Italian, and then an Irishman. It's stock, I had to learn forty pages in less than a week; I earned seventy-five dollars a week, you paid for your own room and your own meals. They paid for transportation from New York to Newport. Lots of fun, and the money didn't matter much to us in those days, just the idea to work." He continued to work in various plays, one being the New York production of *Wanlope Building*, playing a sightseeing guide, which ran only two weeks. He always was hustling for a job, and next did a movie in Cape Charles, Virginia, but it was never released. In 1948, he decided to return to Hollywood, and upon his arrival landed the role of a gangster in a film with Paul Douglas.

He continued steadily working, playing a strong-arm hood working for a loan shark in a Los Angeles based play. This performance won him a role of a punchy newsboy in RKO's *The Set-Up*, with Robert Ryan. Following this role came many others: *No Way Out*; thirty some odd films at MGM, including *Across The Wide Missouri*, on which he worked fourteen weeks with Clark Gable, "A wonderful guy;" a "Jewish blue-eyed Indian" in *Sitting Bull*: "We start tomorrow," they told Frank, who replied, "It's a lead and I don't even have much time to learn the dialogue." "We'll make the pay big ... $250 for three days," they responded. "Come on," Frank said. They settled for $350 for three days; went to Rapid City, South Dakota, for Paramount's *The Savage*, with Charlton Heston; *Man with the Golden Arm*, starring Frank Sinatra and directed by Otto Preminger; a chain gang convict in *Carbine Williams*, with James Stewart; and a part in John Cassavettes' *Woman Under the Influence*, with Peter Falk in the lead. Frank had an interesting story to tell concerning his being cast in the 1950 release, *Kim*. He received a call from the casting director, who asked him if he could do an Afghanistan accent; Frank answered, "That's my best dialect." "Would you mind waiting outside, Frank, we want to discuss something," they asked. Soon, he was called back into the office and told that he had the part of Abdullah, a body guard to Errol Flynn. "Now where do I go," Frank thought, "I don't know who to talk to. I don't know any Afghani, and wouldn't know one if I saw one." So he had to concoct his own dialect. "I started fooling around with it and before I knew it I was feeling good about it," he explained. "I got called for my first day. I've never met the director, he's been in India with Flynn." "What is your name?" asked Victor Saville, the director. "Frank Richards." "Oh, you're Abdullah, good. I'd like to hear you read," replied Saville. "I'm going to be shot before I start," Frank thought. He read five or six lines with the second assistant director, and Saville asked, "Habja, what do you think of this man's accent?" "Very authentic," he replied. "I almost fell down," Frank laughed.

In between his work in these, and many other, motion pictures, Frank kept very busy working on television. His credits in this medium include such hits as *Superman, Lone Ranger, Gang Busters, Ramar of the Jungle* and *Death Valley Days*.

One of two performances that Frank is very proud of was an episode of the TV series *Gang Busters* titled "The Case of Carl Boloni," a part in which he had to compete with fifty other actors to play. A review from one of the Hollywood trade papers stated, "Frank Richards turns in an admirable job in the role of a confused and hapless felon who is overcome by inexorable circumstances." The second performance was that of Frank Lovejoy's houseboy in the motion picture, *The System*. "About a week after I got through with the job I got a telegram from Warner Brothers thanking me very much on my job," he added. Frank also received a very nice compliment one day from the noted director, John Huston. He had gone in on an interview for a film at MGM, and Huston happened to watch it. He stated, "There's a hell of a character actor." "He wanted me in *Asphalt Jungle*, but unfortunately I had a call from Twentieth for *No Way Out*, with Richard Widmark," he added.

We asked Frank how he enjoyed the many Westerns that he had appeared in. He answered that he had never been on a horse until he was forty years old, and although he went to the gym three times a week, he was not that nimble sort of a guy. "The wranglers taught me how to ride, so I got to be pretty good on a horse – And did we do Westerns! I worked for Gene Autry and Roy Rogers, and it was a lot of fun. I worked with Joel McCrea and he was a real cowboy; that guy could ride a horse. He was a sweet, lovable guy."

Frank also enjoyed using various types of accents in his roles. "Dialects have always intrigued me," he related. "If I hear a dialect, no matter what it is, and if I like it, I try to listen and pick up the rhythm. The German dialect was difficult for me, but you listen to them and a little while later it starts to flow. There are all kinds, like in America there's three hundred different intonations, but I find it very enjoyable." Frank then illustrated his talent at dialects by telling us several funny jokes, using several various accents.

In reflecting on movies of today in contrast with films made during the 1940s and 50s, Frank stated, "If you watch a movie today you don't see any of the old timers anymore, none whatsoever. Today, if I watch television I don't know anybody. I used to say, 'Oh, I know him,' but not anymore. My wife says these are much better actors now and better written than before, maybe they are, but I'll give you an example: Today a guy's with a girl, and it's got so he's gotta take her clothes off and she's gotta take his clothes off – who the hell cares? I used to like the scenes with Cary Grant or Clark Gable, and all of a sudden there used to be a ruffling of the winds, then they'd go down and you knew something was going to happen, but you didn't have to show it." Frank also mentioned that it is a shame some of the old actors that have perfected their craft over the years through long experience are not able to get work today, but "If you were a doctor or lawyer and know your craft, you've got much more confidence and their talents are used because of their years of experience."

In 1960 Frank entered the real estate business. One day his wife said, "Frank, you're not dying that often; you ought to do something else." "What do you propose?" Frank asked. "Sell real estate," she responded. "You're crazy," Frank said, "I couldn't sell shoelaces!" So, he took the real estate examination and passed. The man who was to teach him how to write a contract for multiple listings, told him, "You know, you're the stupidest student I ever had." "I may be stupid," Frank responded, "but for every buck you make in real estate, I'll make three or four." "And that's what happened," Frank told us. "I went out and was very diligent. I told him, 'You don't have to give me a listing if you don't want to, but if you want someone to work at it, I think I'm your boy.' In one year I took in one hundred and six listings." Frank did terrific in this new field, until in 1984 (due to eye sight) he had to retire, as he was unable to keep his driver's license. "I had to stop driving. So, big deal; I adjust."

Looking over his long career as an actor, Frank told us, "I did so much junk. I was typed, in Hollywood everything is typed – A cab driver had to look like an ex-pug; a gangster had to look like an ex-gangster; it shouldn't be that way, but that's the way it is. I went to the Actors Lab on the GI Bill, and when I came back in 1948 from New York I started to get into it a little more like these guys from New York in the Actors Studio. I'm very happy that in all the years I was never thrown off a set, I was never replaced, I had a lot of fun, and I made a living. There was so much you could do; it was 'Can you use an Italian accent?' 'Yes, I can use an Italian accent,' and it went on and on and on. Then all of a sudden you're not wanted anymore. I use a favorite word today – Adjust. You have to learn to adjust because at my age the most important thing is to keep and feel great. If I get a job, fine; if I don't get a job it's fine too. It doesn't make no difference because I had a lot of fun out of it. I'll give you an example: Working with Gable. We're up in Durango, Colorado, and we're singing the French Canadian song, *Alou Ette Je Te Plumerai*. Clark would say, 'Pomalane.' 'Cut,' director Bill Wellman says, 'Clark, the word's Plumerai. Clark went, 'Alou ette je te pomalane.' It was a mental block with him. Finally, after the sixth or seventh time, he said, 'You know what I'm going to do? The next time I say, 'Je te pomalane,' I'm going to take out my four hundred dollar teeth and sing without them!' I almost peed in my pants," Frank laughed. "Here's a guy who's the star and telling everybody he's got false teeth!

"I worked with Jimmy Stewart for two or three weeks on *Carbine Williams*. They said to me, 'Frank, he's a quiet guy; he doesn't like having people around him.' Anyway, we were supposed to be in the chain gang; it was a wet season, and they were fixing it up, was supposed to be raining. I said, 'Do you want to hear a good joke, Jimmy?' He said, 'I'd like it.' From that time on, every time he saw me he'd say, 'Frank, do you have a joke for me?' It was a wonderful, nice feeling to work with a guy like that. Or the guy I worked with on my first picture, Boris Karloff. I was nervous. Here was a guy who was supposed to be a tough man. It's like you not knowing how to dance and you start to glide. They make you feel like a million bucks; it's a different kind of feeling. I only met two actors I didn't like, but otherwise most of them were nice guys. There was a great guy in this business, George Seaton. He was, without a doubt, one of the nicest men I ever knew. I called him and said, 'George, I'm in real estate now but I want a job.' I got a two and a half week job he did at Catalina (a film titled *The Hook*). There were some nice people, but today you could be talking to the wall. I couldn't go in if I wanted to; I don't feel badly about it," Frank concluded.

About 1989, Frank and his wife removed from their San Fernando Valley home and settled in Las Vegas, Nevada, where Frank passed away on April 15, 1992.

Film Credits: 1940: Before I Hang; Arizona. **1941:** Public Enemies; Tall, Dark and Handsome; Hold That Ghost; The Corsican Brothers; Sky Raiders (serial); Coffin on Wheels (short). **1942:** Reap the Wild Wind; Cairo; A Man's World; Sunday Punch; Alias Boston Blackie; You Can't Escape Forever. **1945:** House on 92nd Street. **1946:** Brooklyn, I Love You (short). **1947:** A Double Life. **1948:** Tap Roots; Appointment with Murder. **1949:** Prison Warden; Cowboy and the Indians; The Threat; The Set-Up; Tough Assignment; Slattery's Hurricane; Thieves Highway; I Cheated the Law; Come to the Stable; Canadian Pacific; The Crooked Way. **1950:** Black Hand; Father of the Bride; The Outriders; California Passage; Wyoming Mail; Kim; Western Pacific Agent; No Way Out; Love that Brute. **1951:** The Scarf; Across the Wide Missouri; South of Caliente. **1952:** Love is Better Than Ever; Stop, You're Killing Me; Carbine Williams; Pat and Mike; The Savage. **1953:** The System; Prisoners of the Casbah; Clipped Wings; Money from Home; I, the Jury; Girls in the Night; The Caddy. **1954:** Destry; The Atomic Kid; Redhead of Manhattan; Tennessee Champ; Bitter Creek; Return from the Sea. **1955:** New York Confidential; Guys and Dolls; Pirates of Tripoli; Gang Busters; A Bullet for Joey; Man with the Golden Arm; Spy Chasers. **1956:** Davy Crockett and the River Pirates; Man from Del Rio; The Killing; Running Target; The Desperados Are in Town. **1957:** Gun Battle at Monterey; The Storm Rider; The Hard Man. **1958:** Escape from Red Rock; The Black Orchid; Teacher's Pet; The Cry Baby Killer; Revolt in the Big House; Lonelyhearts; How to Make a Monster. **1959:** Gunfight at Dodge City; Hangman; Arson for Hire. **1960:** Bells are Ringing; From the Terrace. **1963:** The Hook. **1965:** The Greatest Story Ever Told. **1974:** A Woman Under the Influence.

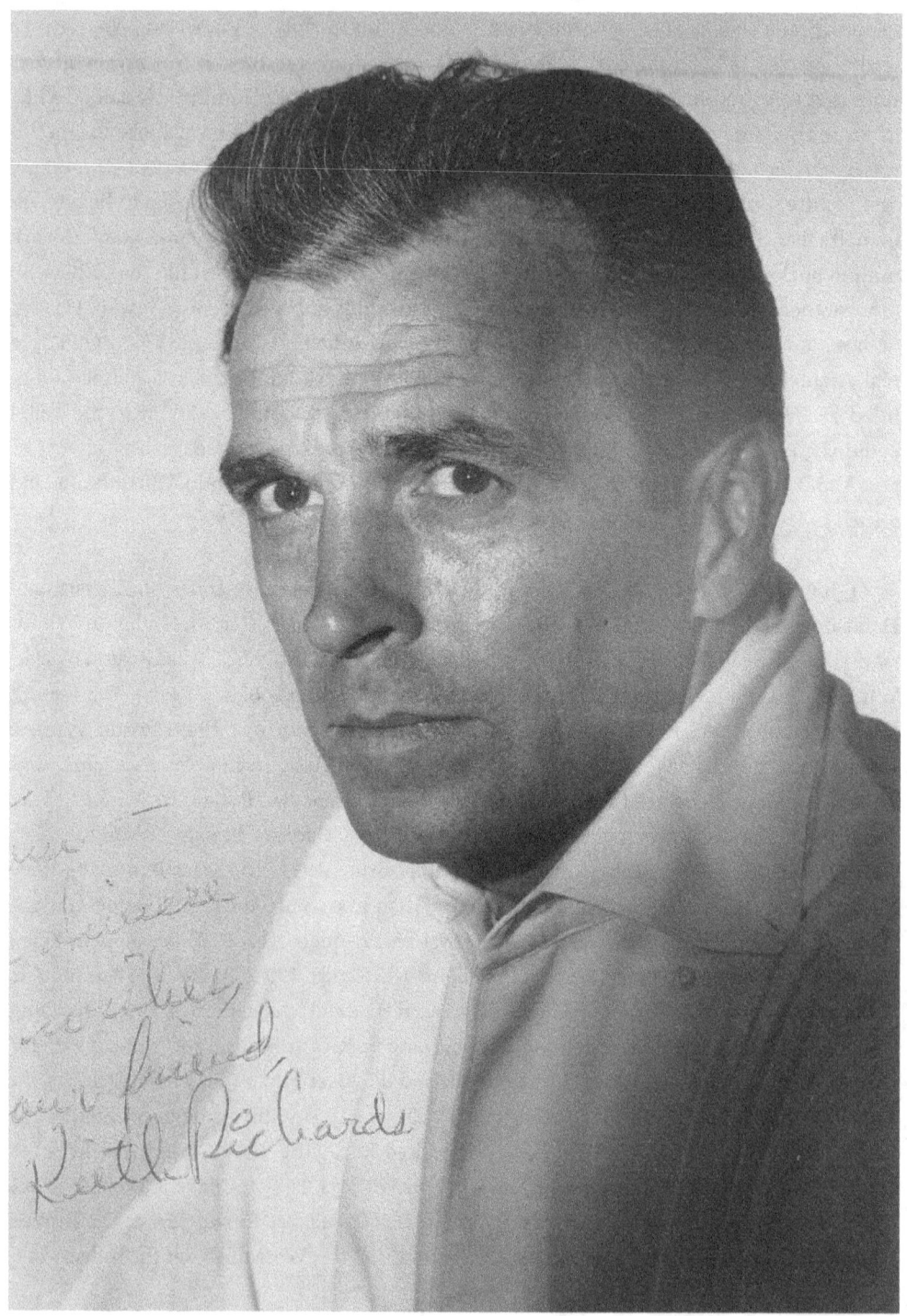

KEITH RICHARDS

Frank and Mary Emma Huish both hailed from England, the former from County Kent and the latter from Liverpool. Frank had been a famous soccer player in his native land before immigrating to America. They had three children: Edith, George and Ted (who later would take on the screen name of Keith Richards). Ted was born July 18, 1914, in Pittsburgh, Pennsylvania, on a Friday afternoon, "arriving in time for the four o'clock tea." Edith, his sister, told us that their brother George died young, and that "our father deserted us. My mother had to raise my brother and I. She took University of Pennsylvania students in for room and board; they had breakfast and dinner and lived right there with us." Edith mentioned, like most young children, her and Keith used to fight all the time. "He was a little devil," she added. He would go out with his friends and swipe oranges from the fruit wagons and come home with an orange in each hand. "Where did you get those oranges?" his mother would ask, and he would reply, "My pal gave it to me." "I know that isn't true," Mrs. Huish would respond. "You know what? You're going to lose something twice as valuable as those two oranges you got there." The next day he lost his most valuable possession, his bicycle; somebody stole it. "He never took any oranges after that," Edith added.

When he was about twelve years old, Keith went to a garage and begged them to let him park their cars and they let him do it. This is how he first learned to drive. One time there was this cab on the street and the driver went inside to get his customer; Keith climbed in and drove it around the block and then parked it in its original spot. "No wonder mother sent him to military school," Edith related, "she couldn't keep up with him and said he got too big to paddle."

I remember her putting him over her knee; me, I used to hide, but poor Ted got caught and she'd paddle him and then he got too big."

Keith attended Osceola Grammar School in Pittsburgh, and in the 6th grade he was enrolled in the Carson-Long Military Academy in New Bloomfield, a short distance from Pittsburgh. It was while attending this academy that he got his first love for the stage in the school plays and as captain of the debating team. Also while attending Carson-Long, Keith became a five letter man in the school's sports program. He was captain of the basketball, tennis and football teams as well as a star pitcher in baseball, having a shut out game to his credit. It is written that "He is an expert at tennis and shines at track events and still holds (as of 1940) the half mile record at Carson-Long and has a cup for winning his academy's mile relay three consecutive years." In 1934, Keith was awarded a special medal as being the academy's best all-around athlete. He had a maple trophy cabinet filled with other cups, medals and clippings he received at sporting events.

After his graduation from Carson-Long in 1934, Keith attended the University of Pennsylvania for one year. He then appeared under the name of Keith Huish with the George Sharpe Stock Company in Pittsburgh at the Fort Pitt Hotel, the same stock company that Ann Harding and Alexander Kirkland had gained much of their training. He met a young man from California, who was attending the University and boarding at his mothers, who told him "You should come to Hollywood with me, I'm sure you could make it in pictures." So he took the man's advice and applied at different places trying to get work.

His fondness for Shakespearian plays led him to employment as assistant business manager with the company that constructed sets for the Laurence Olivier/Vivian Leigh production of *Romeo and Juliet*. He soon attracted the attention of Olivier, who, upon learning of Keith's theatrical background, offered him a minor role in the shows road tour.

A February 1, 1941 newspaper continued telling of this experience, "Huish attracted much favorable comment from the plays leading man Laurence Olivier and was soon advanced to the post of general understudy to the production. Although this was a sizeable task for one so young it offered him many opportunities to display his talents. While with the *Romeo and Juliet* Company he attracted the attention of numerous talent scouts and professional actors who advised him to go to Hollywood, where because of his good looks and talent might find a career. Since his arrival in Hollywood he has changed his name to Keith Richards."

After *Romeo and Juliet* closed on Broadway, Keith returned to Hollywood and was made assistant stage manager for the Noel Coward series of one act plays called *Tonight at 8:30*, which represented at the El Capitan Theatre in Hollywood for the British War Relief and boasted some of the film cities most magnificent names. Jack Easton, an agent, happened backstage and saw Richards and made an appointment for William Michaeljohn, talent director at Paramount, to interview Keith. The result was a test and a contract.

Keith Richards

A Pittsburgh, Pennsylvania newspaper mentioned: "The former Pittsburgh actor, Keith Richards, has been signed a long-term contract by the Paramount Studio and will make his screen debut in *You're the One* with Bonnie Baker and Orin Tucker. Richards was known locally as Keith Huish, for screen purposes he changed his last name." In a Paramount publicity statement we can read the following concerning Keith's attitude toward various activities: "The tall, dark and handsome actor who is in his early 20's reads quite a bit, mostly biographies and prefers pictures dealing with the lives of great men. Someday he hopes to play the character of Paul Revere on the screen. He thinks Bob Hope is the funniest man he has ever met; Ronald Colman the greatest actor; and Paulette Goddard the most beautiful actress in Hollywood. He sketches landscapes and usually uses red paints or pencils in all of his art work. He loves chicken curry but dislikes any kind of fried fowl. His best friend in the movie city is Owen Davis Jr. (an actor who appeared in such features as *All Quiet on the Western Front* and *Knute Rockne--All American*), and his pet pastime is going behind the fountain at the corner drug store and helping the soda jerker mix chocolate malts and other drinks. Richards lives in a modest apartment with his mother and would like to live on a ranch."

Edith mentioned that "he was very close to mother, and she used to help him with all his scripts and cue him on his lines." Dotty Harvey, a longtime friend of Keith, added, "When Keith retired he wanted to live on a ranch and have a horse and a dog. He never got these." Reflecting on his paintings, many of which adorn his sister's apartment, Edith told us that his favorite was the one of a clown."

Another newspaper account reported about the Hollywood Stars Baseball Team and of Keith's invitation to play with them. It stated in part: "Men high in sports have been known to play their way into the movies but comes now a situation in which the order has reversed. Mr. Keith Richards who has been landing himself in a modest way to the betterment of several recent Paramount Pictures lately has received overtures from the Hollywood Stars Baseball Team to come and pitch for them. Mr. Richards is said to have a way with him on the mound and it is for this reason alone and not something unapparent on the surface that he was approached. Thus we would have the business of first a professional actor and then a ballplayer, or the cart before the horse as it were. The feature of this piece is something else. Mr. Richards, who Hollywood snagged from the New York stage, is a Shakespearian actor and there is a rumor that his addiction to the Bard of Avon is such that he frequently recites his lines."

Another reference to Keith's playing with this team states: "Manager Bill Sweeney of the Hollywood Stars Ball Club has decided to give baseball that added cultural lift some folk think is needed. He's offered a pitching contract to 24-year-old Keith Richards, the young Shakespearean actor now under contract to Paramount. Richards won eighteen letters during his days at the University of Pittsburgh, and experts say he has one of the most elaborate assortments of curves and speeds to be seen today. But that's not the most amazing thing about Richards. The boy actually spouts Shakespeare in the pinches! For instance, when Richards decided to hurl a bean ball he grits his teeth and yells, 'Off with his head!' That's from *Richard*

III. If he disagrees with the umpire's decision but admits that argument is likely to be of no avail, he murmurs 'Fair is foul and foul is fair!' That's from *Macbeth*. Then he follows up with 'Play out the play, my friends.' Henry II said that. When a man tries to steal home, Richards catches him off the plate and happily shouts, 'Let the world slide! I'll not budge an inch.' Somebody said that in *Taming of the Shrew*. And when the going is rough and the crowd begins to boo, the pitcher takes sanctuary in his inner self and muses, 'They jest at scars that never felt a wound.' That's from *Romeo and Juliet* – in which Richards appeared on Broadway with Laurence Olivier and Vivian Leigh. Then, when he retires the opposing side in order, our Shakespearian southpaw happily quotes, 'One, two and the third is his bosom.' Romeo said that, too. Richards may not materially increase the intelligence quotient of the mass of baseball fans, but there's little doubt that he will add a certain something to the sport. Just what remains to be seen." The last note concerning Keith's abilities in sports is the fun fact that his role in the feature *Buy Me That Town* was written for both he and co-star Rod Cameron, as they were expert wingmen in ice hockey.

Keith also made many personal appearances at the premiers of some of his motion pictures while under contract to Paramount. One of his closest friends was Richard Arlen, whom he co-starred with in *The Wildcat*. Arlen, Richards and Chester Morris would attend the opening of this show in various places. During his several years at Paramount Keith enjoyed some of his best roles and was being groomed for stardom. One newspaper stated, "THE BREAK FOR RICHARDS. Bill Pine and Bill Thomas clattered along the hallway of the Paramount Publicity Building yesterday stopping long enough to inform Keith Richards, who was there on a press interview, that he's their choice for a top role with Richard Arlen in *Aerial Gunner*. Richards showed to advantage as a radio operator in *Wake Island* who dispatched the films fateful message at the finale of the picture (from which he received a lot of fan mail). This last week he completed *Price of Victory*, a morale short subject produced by Pine and Thomas." Another newspaper account, at the time of his performing in the feature, *Aerial Gunner*, stated of his career during this period: "Keith Richards, the rising young actor, has been cited as the busiest young actor in Hollywood. Cecil B. DeMille, after filming *Reap the Wild Wind*, put him at the top of the list of young actors he thought most likely to succeed in the motion picture world. He has appeared in so many pictures the two years he has been in Hollywood that even he has lost track of the number. Now he is in Harlingen for the filming of *Aerial Gunner* at Harlingen Army Gunnery School. He will play the role of a sergeant in the picture. Since put under contract by Paramount he has been in innumerable pictures, among them *Forest Ranger, Take A Letter Darling, I Wanted Wings, Secret of the Wastelands, Letter from Bataan* and *Henry Aldrich Gets Glamour*. Richards claims he holds the record for the longest shave in the world. Coming to Harlingen on a train he started shaving at El Paso and finished not far from this valley city, and uses an old fashioned straight razor, he said, and was able to shave at stops along the way or else pay the price of a few nicks caused by the rocking motion of the train."

Aerial Gunner was released in 1943 and later that year Paramount did not pick up his option, thus Keith joined the ranks of free-lance feature actors. The next day the studio contacted his agent and hired Keith for the best part to date of his career in *So Proudly We Hail* with Claudette Colbert.

Like so many actors of this time, World War II interrupted his career. Edith informed us, "He was lying on the sofa and had this notice – Greetings! Mother said he got up and said, 'Just in the beginning of my career it's been ruined, but I know I have to go like all the other men,' and he cried. That ruined his career, but he wouldn't have missed doing his part for the country. But that made a bad break in his career. Cecil B. DeMille told him when he got out of the Navy to come and see him. DeMille gave him parts, but the war did stop his career." A newspaper account substantiates this feeling by stating "Keith Richards was beginning to get the breaks before going into the navy several years ago and was chosen by Cecil B. DeMille for a feature role in one of his films…When the war ends he hopes to return to the picture business and resume a career that was leading to stardom when he enlisted in the navy."

Because of his experience at Carson-Long Military Academy, Keith was appointed Chief Petty Officer when he entered the Navy. Edith recalled that "He said the only thing about a Chief Petty Officer is that you got out of your monkey suit." He saw no foreign service, and said "I don't like being at Bathbridge, Maryland, or being in Chicago. Since I am in I want to go overseas." Edith mentioned that he was well-liked by his men and that when he returned after being away over the Christmas holidays that they had decorated his room and gave him a lot of "funny little gifts." After his discharge, Keith returned to Hollywood and resumed his career although it never returned to the heights to which his career had been leading prior to the war. He obtained Lou Deuser as an agent, and Lew Sherrell, and they obtained him parts.

Film roles followed in such features as *Queen of the Amazon* (in which he "gets mysteriously bumped off"); *Seven Were Saved* (he played "the husband she thought was killed by nips in prison camp. Eldredge and Richards both enact their roles satisfactorily. Keith Richards effectively performs his amnesia act"), and *Samson and Delilah*, directed by his old mentor, Cecil B. DeMille, who wrote Keith a letter afterwards stating, "Appreciation is one of the finest things in the world…Thank you for your good work in *Samson and Delilah*. I hope that we work together again." Keith did work for him later in *Greatest Show on Earth* and *The Ten Commandments*.

In 1947, Keith appeared in the first of at least five serials, performing that year in *Jesse James Rides Again* and also *The Black Widow*. Three years later he was the star of *The James Brothers of Missouri*. Dotty mentioned "He did a lot of serials and enjoyed them."

In speaking of his work in Westerns, working opposite such cowboy stars as Roy Rogers, Gene Autry, Hopalong Cassidy, Johnny Mack Brown, Bill Elliott and Whip Wilson, Dotty remarked, "He did most of his trick riding himself in his cowboy films; he didn't use stuntmen." "He liked Westerns more than anything," Edith added, "He loved horses. In *The Greatest Show on Earth* he fell in love with the animals, especially the elephants."

Keith also worked in many television shows, acting in such series as *Lone Ranger*, *Roy Rogers*, *Range Rider*, *Bonanza* and *Highway Patrol* ("He was in a lot of those with Broderick Crawford; he liked that," Edith added). Keith also appeared in a pilot for a show called *Mandrake the Magician* in which he portrayed the title character. Unfortunately it did not sell. Dotty added, "Loretta Young got a little mad at him because he said, 'Oh shit!' She had a little pot and everybody that said a four letter word had to put money in the pot. Keith put a dollar in because he said it's going to happen again."

He also worked in radio and for a long time was the Master of Ceremonies on *The Eddie Cantor Show*. Keith stayed very busy in the various phases of the acting profession, having appeared in "about 129 features films plus TV and serials," Dotty informed. We asked her if Keith ever talked of a favorite film or performance, and she commented "With him maybe if he had a top leading role in some picture it might have made a difference. He did a lot of work, but it wasn't Keith Richards in such and such; but whatever he did he liked. He enjoyed playing one of the Three Musketeers in the feature, *Blades of the Musketeers*. He loved to entertain people; he was a great storyteller and used to keep me entertained for hours at night telling me different little jokes. He'd rather talk about his experiences with other stars than talk about himself."

In the early 1960s acting jobs became very slow and he went to work at the M & K Iron and Metal Company, where they sold aluminum, steel, brass and copper. When the movie work was slow he would go there to help occasionally. He worked hard there and enjoyed it, and for a time worked both in pictures and at M & K. About 1967, he left the picture business and operated M & K, which he finally ended up owning. When the time arrived that he decided to sell the business and was in the process of closing the deal, one day a woman called the office and asked if Keith Richards was in. Dotty, who worked there, told her he was out but to leave her name. The woman responded, "I'll call back." A short time later she called again and was told he wasn't back yet; she said she'll call back. After Keith returned to his office a man called and asked for him. He was a director and offered Keith a part in a series; Keith responded, "Of all times, I'm just in the process of selling my business. I'll contact you after the business is all settled." Dotty told us, "That took a while and he did contact them, but of course the series had already started. They wanted him to be a captain of a ship and I often think it would have been *Love Boat* because he would have been nice in that. The only thing they had, and he wouldn't take it, they wanted his voice for dubbing in some foreign picture. They wanted to use his voice; he had a beautiful voice," she concluded.

After retiring from the M & K Iron and Metal Company, Keith devoted his time to playing golf, a pastime that he truly loved. He often played with movie bad man Bob Wilke, as well as James Garner and Peter Falk. He played at the Chuck Connors Golf Tournament, and as Dotty mentioned, "He even played left handed; he hit the ball opposite of everybody else. He played at the Riviera; it just broke his heart if he saw a little bird that had been killed by a golf ball and that would just ruin his game."

Another talent that Keith had was that of an interior decorator. "He could walk in and look at a place that I thought was a dump," Edith related. "I didn't know how he could do anything to it, and what he turned it in to was just great. Some people have the knack."

Reflecting over his career, Dotty told us "Those were the happiest days of his life. He loved acting." "I remember Keith talking about going into restaurants in New York and ordering a glass of hot water and putting catsup into it and salt and pepper," Edith recalled. "They were starving but they stuck with it; if you love something enough you will stick with it and you will succeed. What I admired about him was singleness of purpose. When you get involved with things like homes, cars and kids it is tough. When business was slow and it rained most of the winter season there was an area here, Garden Junction; he'd go there and cut the beautiful poinsettias. Mother said he'd come home soaked, he'd have to dry everything out and then he'd go back and it seemed to rain every time he was there cutting poinsettias. So he would work; he was a worker. If you wanted to get something done and asked him, he would get it done ten times faster, and I'm sure he applied himself the same way with his career. Everything else was secondary, his career was first. Being correct, being proper, being on cue with his lines; it was uppermost in his mind and everything else came afterwards."

When we wrote Keith requesting an interview he was very ill with cancer. Edith and Dotty told us he was hoping to feel better and was looking forward to meeting with us: "Nothing Keith would have enjoyed more than meeting you two; he would have loved it." Edith remarked about Keith being included in this volume, "Why is it that such nice things happen to people after they're gone." A few days before Keith passed away he said to Dotty, "I'm going to meet a lot of my friends when I leave." Keith died on March 24, 1987 in Los Angeles County, California.

Film Credits: 1940: You're the One; I Wanted Wings; Meet the Wildcat. **1941:** West Point Widow; Nothing but the Truth; Skylark; Midnight Angel; New York Town; a Brad King short; Night of January 16th; One Night in Lisbon; Bahama Passage; Louisiana Purchase; Little Miss Muffet; Secrets of the Wasteland; Among the Living; Hold Back the Dawn; Parachute Battalion; Buy Me that Town; Birth of the Blues; Skylark; Pacific Blackout. **1942:** Lucky Jordan; Wake Island; Reap the Wild Wind; The Forest Rangers; A Letter from Bataan (short); Price of Victory (short); Wildcat; Take a Letter, Darling; Street of Chance; Star Spangled Rhythm; The Lady has Plans; Palm Beach Story; an army short (with Walter Huston); Beyond the Blue Horizon; Night in New Orleans; Holiday Inn; Priorities on Parade. **1943:** Henry Aldrich gets Glamour; Lost Canyon; So Proudly We Hail; Aerial Gunner; Alaska Highway; No Time for Love. **1944:** Texas Masquerade; Miracle of Morgan's Creek. **1946:** That Brennan Girl; Swell Guy; Heldorado; Danger Woman; Lost City of the Jungle (serial); The Mysterious Mr. M (serial). **1947:** Big Town; Seven were Saved; Queen of the Amazons; Where the North Begins; The Case of the Baby-Sitter; Twilight on the Rio Grande; Calendar Girl; Hit Parade of 1947; Road to the Big House; Jesse James Rides Again (serial); The Black Widow (serial). **1948:** Sons of Adventure; Walk a Crooked Mile; The Gay Ranchero; The Far Frontier; Mr. Reckless; Tap Roots. **1949:** Samson and Delilah; El Paso; Dynamite; Duke of Chicago; Flaming Fury; Trail's End; Shadows of the West; Captain China. **1950:** The Blonde Bandit; North of the Great Divide; James Brothers of Missouri (serial); The Invisible Monster (serial); The Damned Don't Cry; Blades of the Musketeers (aka Sword of D'Artagnan); The Du Pont Story; Mystery Submarine. **1951:** Spoilers of the Plains; Up Front; Tales of Robin Hood; When Worlds Collide. **1952:** The Greatest Show on Earth; Loan Shark; Because of You; The Blazing Forest. **1953:** Rebel City; The Great Adventures of Captain Kidd (serial); Off Limits; All the Brothers were Valiant. **1954:** Casanova's Big Night; The Mad Magician; The Snow Creature. **1955:** At Gunpoint; King of the Carnival (serial). **1956:** Yaqui Drums; The Ten Commandments; The Girl He Left Behind; World Without End. **1957:** Untamed Youth; The Buster Keaton Story. **1958:** Ambush at Cimarron Pass. **1959:** Good Day for a Hanging. **1961:** The Gambler Wore a Gun. **1962:** Incident in an Alley.

WARNER RICHMOND

Warner Richmond was born Werner Paul Raetzmann on January 11, 1886 in Racine, Wisconsin, and raised on his parent's farm in Culpepper County, Virginia. The family consisted of his parents, four brothers and two sisters. Being raised in Virginia gave him a terrific interest in the South and the Civil War. As a child he was an athlete, being a very good pole-vaulter, as well as enjoying bicycle racing. He also worked on the family farm and learned to ride horses very well as a boy.

Warner attended a prep school, and afterwards went to West Point, but flunked out. "My dad wasn't too good in math," his son, Warner Jr., told us, "but it was during this time that he developed his feelings for history." In later years he wrote a manuscript for a book he was hoping to have published called *The Man in Grey* that dealt with the Civil War. Unfortunately, it was never completed. Warner loved the subject of the Civil War so much that he later wanted to name his son Robert E. Lee Richmond. At the time his son was born in 1921 he was away somewhere on location and his wife sent him a telegram, "You have a son, Warner P. Richmond Jr." "He wouldn't talk to her for about three weeks because he wanted to name me Robert E. Lee," Warner Jr. laughed.

Warner's oldest brother was named Ewell, and he remained a farmer. His youngest brother, Paul, went on to become a member of the security force at the White House. Will, one of the middle brothers, was considered one of the youngest artist horse drivers at the time. He later worked for Virginia Farms. "He knew his bloodlines so he was always with thoroughbreds," Warner Jr. told us. "He later came to Monterey County in California and worked with horses there." The fourth brother was Al. During the First World War there was a lot of animosity

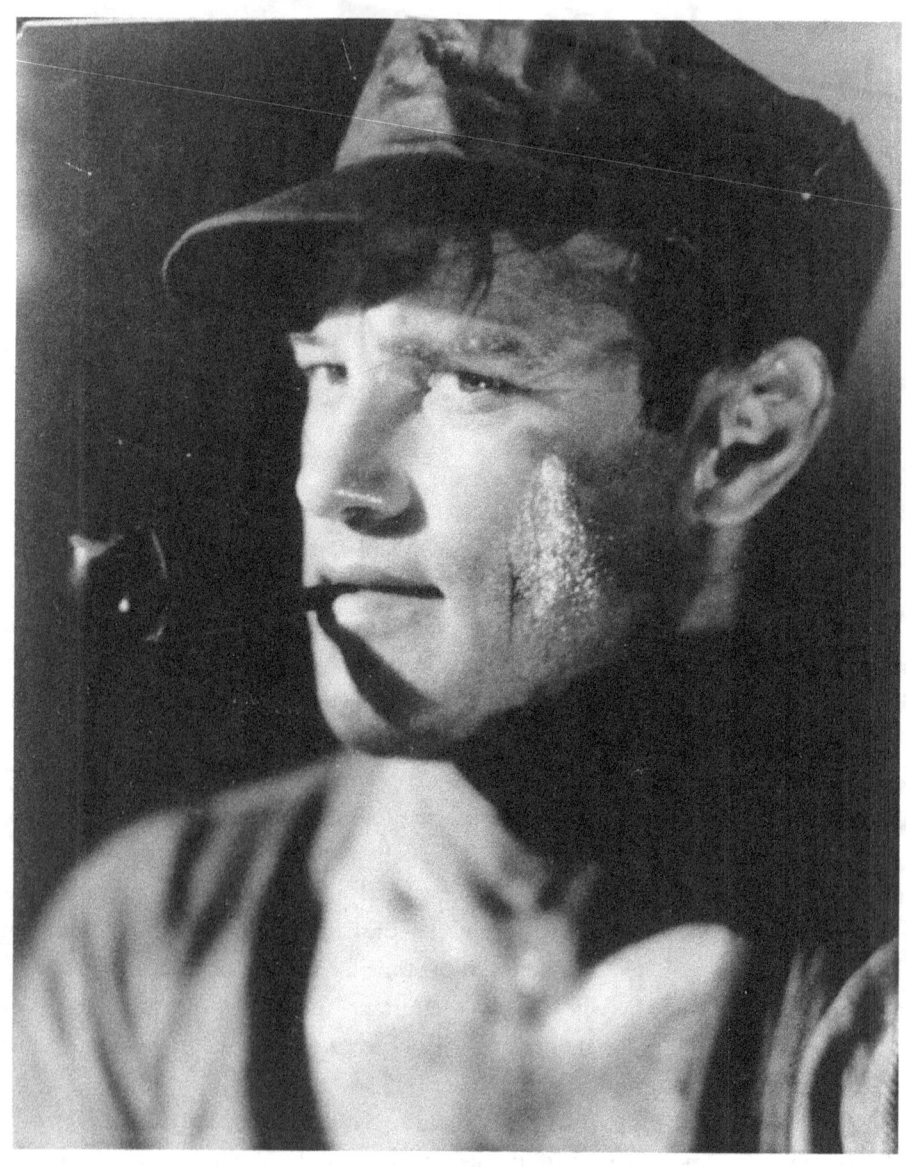

towards the Germans, and as the family name was Raetzmann, both Al and Warner had their name changed to Richmond. "My Uncle Al was in movies years ago," Warner Jr. mentioned. "He was a real cowboy. He had a little spread up in Montana and used to pack up special people every year that he would take out in the woods. One of them was Zane Grey, the writer, and another was an artist, Remington. But he told my dad he didn't like to wear make-up. My uncle just didn't have the training my dad did." He was in *The Courtship of Miles Standish* in 1923 as well as some silent Westerns (including *Border Rider*, *Twisted Triggers* and *Deadshot Casey*).

An early job that Warner held was that of a brakeman on the Baltimore and Ohio Railroad. He pulled the wrong switch one day and spilled a whole pile of railroad rails right in the yard. "I guess he got fired and that prompted him to go into acting," his son surmised.

Warner loved attending the theatre before he ever became an actor, and in so doing this he was very impressed by an old stage actor's performance of Robert E. Lee. It was such a great piece of acting that Warner decided that was what he wanted to do. He obtained work with various stock companies and learned the craft. Under the name of Werner Richmond he was cast as Frank Powers in *The Greatest Thing in Life* at the Fulton Stock Company in Lincoln, Nebraska. He soon changed his name to Warner Richmond, and this is how he is remembered from his countless motion picture credits.

At one point in his career as a stock company performer, work became very slow for a short period and so he took a job in a haberdashery shop in Chicago, selling clothes. "He was always a sharp dresser," Warner Jr. explained. "Not a flashy dresser, but just well-groomed."

Warner moved about quite a bit, residing in Kentucky, Virginia and New York, but it was in the latter spot that he received most of his work. Theatre work was very much in play here, as well as the silent movies. "He worked out of New York in the old Vitagraph Studios," his son said. "He came from the stage and in those days they did everything. They did their own stunts. And they also made educational pictures for colleges." Warner played both Thomas Jefferson and John Hancock in two such endeavors. "In those days it was a combination of stage and stock companies, so they were hustlers," Warner Jr. continued. "My dad had a lot of vaudevillian friends. In those days they were very clannish; very honest people. If they had a nickel they'd give you two-and-a-half cents. And I guess they still do today to a certain degree."

Warner met and married Felice Rose. "My mom was an actress," Warner Jr. stated. "And my grandmother, May Standish Rose, had started the Vagabond Players in Baltimore, Maryland. She used to direct and write the plays and it became pretty well-known so my mother, naturally, played some of the parts. After my father married my mother they moved away and lived on Long Island in New York, so she gave it up. After my father passed away she went back into the movies (*Fighting Vigilantes*, *I Shot Billy the Kid*, *Room for One More*, *Son of Paleface* and *Westbound* are among her features). My father being on the stage was probably why my grandmother liked him so well."

Warner bought a farm in Virginia, where his mother lived and a brother ran it for him. This was before the soil bank. When that came into place the farmers did not do so well, and Warner lost the farm.

Warner appeared with Dorothy Gish and Owen Moore in the 1916 film directed by Allan Dwan, *Betty of Greystone*. The story concerns Gish, who is the daughter of the caretaker of Greystone Gables. She finds romance on the estate but creates a scandal, and the villagers force her to leave. When she returns as the wife of the young heir of Greystone, she is the town's first lady. In those days, the film companies in New York had the choice of filming either in Florida or California during the winter. California won due to the greater variety of scenery there.

Warner's role in the 1921 classic, *Tol'able David* with Richard Barthelmess, brought him to the attention of both the movie makers and the film audiences. "Originally Ernest Torrence was going to play the part that my dad played, but of course he was a big man and meaner looking, so apparently they switched parts," his son related. Several years later after moving to California, Warner Jr. accompanied his father to the Film Art, a small theater on Vine Street that used to show foreign films, when they showed *Tol'able David*. "I was probably seven or eight and he gets his back broke by Ernest Torrence, who holds a boulder over his head and throws it down on him. I'm sitting right next to dad and started to cry because he was dead."

In 1923 Warner starred in *The Man from Glengarry*. "He had to go out and rescue this girl on the logs," his son said. "He was pretty agile and always physically fit, he had to be to be a brakeman and a pole-vaulter when he was younger." When the film was released the review stated, "Whether you have read the book or not you will enjoy this exceptional photoplay. You will want to see Warner P. Richmond in the title role and the death grapple with the bully of the rival camp. Also the thrilling rescue as he risks his life to save his sweetheart who is being swept into the rapids."

"I was up there when I was just a couple of years old," Warner Jr. remembered. "My mother worked on the picture too, just as atmosphere, so I was off on the sidelines. I was looking for my dad and wandered out while they were making the scene. They put the camera on me so that was my first film. That was done in Ottawa, Canada. In those days they used to go to the actual location because they didn't have sound stages; they didn't need sound."

Among Warner's close friends were the Moore brothers, Tom, Matt and Owen. "Tom was the one who talked my father into coming out to the coast. He had come out earlier and my dad came out in 1926," Warner Jr. informed. "So he came out to the coast and stayed at the Hollywood Athletic Club. Apparently he went right to work, I think for Warner Brothers first, where he did most of his earlier work in California. Strangely enough he never went under contract with anybody, he liked to free-lance. It gave him more flexibility. He also worked some for RKO, Columbia and MGM."

Warner starred with Louise Fazenda in the 1929 silent, *Stark Mad*, directed by his close friend, Lloyd Bacon. This was a story about people on a yachting expedition to Caracas, Venezuela. His son was also on this set, and he told us "the fellow that was the gorilla was excellent. He would take pink moulding wax and make a sculpture of you; he was very talented. He also made the gorilla costume and played it."

The final silent movie that Warner appeared in was *The Apache* in 1929. His son related an incident that occurred on the set of this feature. "Dad was sitting down pretty close to a lamp, and instead of the electrician coming over and unplugging it, he jerked on it and tipped over the lamp. My dad put his arms over his face, and it cut him. It took twenty-one stitches, but he finished the picture with his hands in his pockets because he had bandages on them. That's the way they did things in those days."

They lived in a nice colonial style home in Toluca Lake across the street from Lakeside Country Club. Warner's favorite pastime when he was not acting was to work in his gardens. They had seven different lawns at their house, and a Japanese gardener came twice a week, but Warner liked to go out and work in the garden. First thing in the morning he would get up and not even bother to put his clothes on, he'd just wear his pajamas. "He didn't care," his son reflected. "What could they say. He was kind of a solitary man, except when he got with his friends. He did enjoy people and had a lot of close friends." Two of these were Jason Robards and Frank McHugh.

Living on their street in Toluca Lake was an Irish author named Tulle; W.C. Fields lived directly across from the club house; Richard Arlen lived a block away; Warner's son and his friends used to stick pins in Boris Karloff's doorbell, which would cause a continuous ring; Ruby Keeler and Al Jolson lived there, a block and a half away. Near their home was a nice little lake that was fed by natural springs.

Warner Richmond was in motion pictures since its infancy, and had reached the rank of a big star in the silent movies. But fate brought about a change in his life and career. "We lost our home at Toluca Lake," his son explained. "Three things happened: Talkies came in. That screwed up a lot of actors; then there was the Equity strike; and then the Depression. And dad lost the home. Work was hard to get during the transition period."

With the coming of the talkies Warner's career moved into playing character roles in featured parts, no longer the star that he was, and more often than not was cast as the villain. Did he enjoy playing the bad guys? "Yeah, he did," Warner Jr. answered. "In those days, after you're a leading man the next thing is heavies. He could get a lot of meat out of it, he could be real nasty."

His first sound movie was a newspaper film called *Big News* made in 1929 with Carole Lombard. In 1930 he appeared in *Men without Women*, directed by John Ford and featuring John Wayne in a small role. Warner's portrayal of the villainous deputy in *Billy the Kid* with Wallace Beery and Johnny Mack Brown followed shortly afterwards. The next year found Warner appearing as the abusive father in *Huckleberry Finn*.

In 1932 Warner worked his last film ever for his old studio, Warner Brothers, in *The Woman from Monte Carlo*, due to a problem that arose between Warner and director Michael Curtiz. That same year found him appearing opposite Walter Huston in *Beast of the City* and with Richard Dix in the chain-gang drama, *Hell's Highway*. In the mid-thirties Warner began working almost exclusively in the B-Westerns, most often as the heavy.

Reflecting on the 1930 MGM classic, *Billy the Kid*, Warner Jr. told us that he was on the Calabasas set when they filmed it. "It was a pretty unique place with all the boulders. They built that whole town out at Calabasas. That picture was made three different times. Kay Johnson finally ended up with the female lead, but it was made with two other women before that. I can't remember what the reason was."

Warner played a villainous zoo keeper in the 1934 serial, *The Lost Jungle* with Clyde Beatty. His son told us that after the film Beatty invited him and his dad to come to the circus. "My dad and I got to go in and talk to the clowns and watch them put on their make-up. It was really something."

Although he was now a supporting player, the public did not forget him. A newspaper, dated November 5, 1934, stated the following: "Warner Richmond is one of the screen's finest character actors as well as one of the best known. Every man, woman and child knows Warner Richmond. Mr. Richmond will be seen shortly in *East River*, the latest of his features."

Warner made a slapstick Western farce with Roscoe Ates and was the villain named Rattlesnake Pete, in which they made a poster of him with a handlebar moustache. "I wish I had that poster," his son said.

We asked if his dad enjoyed working in the Western films during the last years of his career. "He just liked and breathed acting," Warner Jr. replied. "He was very interested and did a lot of history work on his parts. I would have imagined most of the old time actors were pretty involved in what they were doing. He had a lot of enthusiasm for everything he did. He was a good study. He would read through the script once; then he'd go through and memorize the lines, and then I would cue him. He was a very quick study and always knew his lines."

While filming *Rainbow over the Range* in 1940 in Arizona with Tex Ritter, Warner suffered a serious accident. His son told us what happened. "The wranglers didn't tighten the cinch tight enough so it slipped with him and he fell off the horse and hit his head. He stayed in Arizona for a number of months and then he finally got a little bit better and came home, but after two and a half years the left side of his face was still paralyzed. He had a friend named Art Laskey, an ex-fighter and contender for the heavyweight title, but after his fighting career became a physical therapist. He told my dad that he restored his eyesight partially by just massage. My dad was an avid reader, and while doing so he would sit and pinch his face, and in two and a half years he restored his reflexes except for his eye didn't work as well. He didn't do much work after that accident."

Bob Tansey was an old time friend of Warner's. "He was a jockey at one time and how he got into pictures I don't know," Warner Jr. informed, "but he used to make B-movies. He read the Western pulp magazines and got ideas, then he would get all these different situations together from these pulp magazines and write the script, and he would produce and direct them. They used to go on location and make two pictures at once. You see somebody riding this way and then they would change the position of the camera and they'd change clothes and you'd see the bunch coming back the other way. Anything to make an inexpensive movie. He was responsible for helping my dad get work after his face was paralyzed; he was a lot of help."

Warner spent the last part of his life living at the Motion Picture Country Home in Woodland Hills. "He had his own room, a combination living room-bedroom and bath," his son said. "They made their meals at the dining room. He was only sixty-two when he passed away on June 19, 1948." He concluded by saying, "My dad and I were great buddies. He was serious, had a good sense of humor and never told off-color jokes."

Film Credits: 1912: The Godmother; Song of the Shell; A Modern Atlanta. 1913: The College Life. 1914: Springtime; The Mad Mountaineer. 1915: The Third Commandment; The Seventh Commandment; The Social Law; Lord Audley's Secret; The Great Divide. 1916: Betty of Graystone; Her Maternal Right; Manhattan Madness; Fifty-Fifty. 1918: Brown in Harvard; Sporting Life; Woman; A Romance of the Air. 1919: The Gray Towers Mystery. 1920: A Woman's Business; My Lady's Garter. 1921: Tol'able David; Heart of Maryland; The Mountain Woman. 1922: The Challenge; Jan of the Big Snows; Isle of Doubt; The Man from Glangarry. 1923: Luck; Mark of the Beast. 1924: Daughters of the Night; The Speed Spook; The Declaration of Independence (short); The Eve of the Revolution (short). 1925: The Crowded Hour; Fear-Bound; The Making of O'Malley; The Pace that Thrills. 1926: Good and Naughty; The Wives of the Prophet; The Fire Brigade. 1927: Slide, Kelly, Slide; Finger Prints; Irish Hearts; White Flannels; Heart of Maryland; Chicago. 1928: Hearts of Men; Shadows of the Night; Stop that Man; You Can't Beat the Law; The Crowd; The Redeeming Sin. 1929: Strange Cargo; Voice of the Storm; Little Mother; Stark Mad; Manhattan Madness; Big Brother; The Apache; Big News. 1930: Men without Women; Billy the Kid; Strictly Modern; Remote Control; Vengeance. 1931: Quick Millions; Huckleberry Finn; Stung (short); The Lone Starved Ranger (short). 1932: Hell's Highway; The Woman from Monte Carlo; Beast of the City; Scarface; Strangers of the Evening; Night Court. 1933: Fast Workers; King of the Jungle; Corruption; Mama Loves Papa; The Man who Dared; This Day and Age; Police Call; Life in the Raw. 1934: Happy Landing; Lost Jungle (serial); Gift of Gab; Fugitive Lady; The Scarlet Empress; The Band Plays On. 1935: Under Pressure (aka East River); Mississippi; Phantom Empire (serial); Rainbows End; Smoky Smith; The New Frontier; The Courageous Avenger; Headline Woman; So Red the Rose; The Singing Vagabond; Straight from the Heart; Remember Last Night; The Fighting Marines. 1936: Heart of the West; Peppery Salt (short); Below the Deadline; Hearts in Bondage; The White Legion; Song of the Gringo; Headin' for the Rio Grande; In His Steps; Missing Girls. 1937: Trail of Vengeance; A Lawman is Born; Wallaby Jim of the Islands; Where Trails Divide; The Gold Racket; Riders of the Dawn; Stars over Arizona; Federal Bullets; Child Bride; Doomed at Sundown. 1938: Secret of Treasure Island (serial); Wolves of the Sea (aka Jungle Island); Flash Gordon's Trip to Mars (serial); Singing Cowgirl; Six Shootin' Sheriff; Prairie Moon; Wild

Horse Canyon. **1939:** Trigger Smith; The Oregon Trail (serial); Fighting Mad; Water Rustlers. **1940:**Rhythm of the Rio Grande; Pals of the Silver Sage; Men with Steel Faces; The Golden Trail; Rainbow over the Range. **1944:** Outlaw Trail; Harmony Trail (aka White Stallion); **1946:** Colorado Serenade; Wild West. **1948:** Prairie Outlaw.

CHUCK ROBERSON

Chuck Roberson was born May 10, 1919 in a small Texas town called Jay, near Shannon, Texas. "I don't even think they have a post office there anymore," Chuck said. "Even when I was a kid there was only a general store, one school house, a kind of service station-blacksmith combination with one little gas pump and a cotton gin. That was just about the size of the town. During the war it even got smaller," he added. The Roberson home had three bedrooms and a bathroom. "At that time there wasn't too many houses with bathrooms," he informed us.

"I went to school there for a couple of years and then we moved to Lawton, Oklahoma, where I went to fifth and sixth grade," he continued. "My mom and dad were separated at the time and he moved to Roswell, New Mexico. Then I came out there and went to work on a big ranch called The Flying H during the summertime, and then went to school there a couple of years." But mostly, Chuck worked on the ranch, and then was employed at the Price Ranch for awhile. About 1937 he moved to Hobbs, New Mexico and worked in the oil fields. "I did a little bit of everything," he added. "Then in 1939 I came out to California and had a couple of pretty good jobs."

Chuck obtained work as a policeman for MGM in 1940. His duties included working traffic every morning of every day. "You were sworn in with the Culver City Police Department, so actually you were a policeman. You carried a gun and the whole shebang," he explained. The studio began to have an interest in Chuck as a possible actor but he felt he didn't have what it took for a life in that profession, so he decided to go into military service. After the war Chuck returned to Hollywood and began working again as a policeman, this time at Warner Brothers.

"I worked a big strike there, and, oh man, it was quite a strike," he reflected. "We worked around the clock."

While working for Warners, Chuck was told by several people, "A man with your experience with horses and ranch work should go over to Republic because they don't do anything but Westerns there." So Chuck, still wearing his police uniform, went by there one day after the strike, and told the person in the casting office, "I want to see Mr. Jack Grant." Grant was the head casting director for Republic Studios at the time. He was told, "Just a moment," and then was let in. "If I hadn't had that police uniform on I probably wouldn't have gotten through that door," he informed us. They disclosed to Chuck that "we just signed a guy named John Carroll; you're a dead ringer for him." They sent him straight to Herbert Yates' office, where he was given a letter and told to go to Screen Actors Guild and get a card. "So I came back and went to work the next day," Chuck said.

Chuck worked as a stuntman for Republic for about two years, doubling one cowboy star after another. Rocky Lane, Wild Bill Elliott, Sunset Carson. "I worked on all of them," Chuck reflected. "They just made one little six day Western after another." He also doubled cowboy stars Johnny Mack Brown and Whip Wilson at Monogram. Another actor he doubled in a number of films was feature player, Reed Hadley. "I used to be tall and thin myself," he added. "I even doubled our president (Ronald Reagan) in *The Last Outpost*." He later would double such big Western stars as Joel McCrea and Randolph Scott, the latter in *Seven Men From Now*.

One day he worked on a John Wayne picture called *Wake of the Red Witch*, and then about 1949 he was doing another Wayne feature, *The Fighting Kentuckian*, and they wanted somebody to jump on a horse. Chuck was sitting on the set talking to co-star Oliver Hardy, and said "I can do that." So Hardy walked over to them and told them, "My friend can do that." They were thinking of getting Jocko Mahoney, who was one of the best stuntmen ever to work in the business, but they asked Chuck if he would mind trying the jump. Chuck jumped on the horse, the director remarked "Perfect! Get the clothes on," and so Chuck doubled Wayne in the film.

Within two or three weeks after *The Fighting Kentuckian* was completed, John Ford was ready to begin a film with John Wayne. Wayne told Ford, "You should see this kid who doubled me, he's pretty handy." "So anyhow," Chuck told us, "Old Man Ford sent for me and the rest of it is history. I don't think I ever missed a Ford picture after that, and missed very few Wayne pictures. I doubled him in his last one, *The Shootist*. But I was retiring about that time and did very little in it. Originally, they were going to do a lot of stuff with the horse floundering in eight feet of snow, but on account of Wayne's health they decided not to do it. So they brought everything down from the mountains to Carson City, Nevada, and just had pockets of snow here and there. So I did all of the rehearsing for him and that's about the only thing I did in the picture. There wasn't too much else in it to do."

Chuck continued working in many Westerns performing stunts as well as taking small parts. He worked in B's (many of the Charles Starrett films at Columbia, as well as doubling Monte Hale), and in A's. He worked in many of James Stewart's Westerns. In *Far Country* he played Latigo, the outlaw with a scar, as well as doubling John McIntire ("I really was a bad double for McIntire, but unless you're real close it doesn't make too much difference"); in *Winchester 73* he played Slim, one of Dan Duryea's henchmen; Chuck doubled Robert Ryan in *Naked Spur* as well as doing stunts as various Indians. "Every time Jimmy made a picture I was on the thing," Chuck stated. "Stewart had a double, Ted Mapes, and I told him that I don't know how I get on all of his pictures. Years later, Mapes said, 'Stewart requested you. He likes you.' I said, 'Thank God, I like him too, believe me!' He's my favorite really, he and Wayne. There will never be another John Wayne and there will never be another Jimmy Stewart. They're in a class all by themselves."

The Way of a Gaucho with Rory Calhoun and Richard Boone was filmed in the country of Argentina. "I had to do all the doubling for both guys," Chuck told us. The stuntman that had gone there to double Boone was injured early on while riding a horse. "He wasn't hurt too bad, but a couple of days later when he was barely getting along he went to a saddle shop along a one way street. When he came out and stepped on the street, a guy doing about ninety miles an hour on a bicycle ran into him right between his legs and knocked him out. They had to ship him home, and from then on I did all the doubling. I had doubled them both before and had done a lot of pictures with Boone," Chuck said.

Chuck doubled Gregory Peck on several features, one of them being *How the West Was Won*. He also told us that he doubled quite a few other actors on that film as well as playing one of the train robbers. "I was the first one to be shot off the train, and it was a dangerous spot. Ohhh boy, I had to fall backwards. It was really tight, just one little spot I had to get into. That's where Bob Morgan got his leg cut off. He was a good stuntman," Chuck added.

Chuck told us a couple of funny stories that he experienced in Canada while they were filming the James Stewart Western, *The Far Country*. They were staying in a chalet in Jasper Park, an area that had many bears about. One Sunday afternoon, on their day off, Chuck and several others happened upon one of these bears face down in a five gallon barrel rummaging through some trash for food. "All you could see was his ass sticking out," Chuck related. "I've had a few drinks so I walked up and just dropped kicked the bear in the butt and the barrel fell over. The barrel was old and rotten, so the bear went right out the other end of it and climbed up a tree," Chuck laughed.

The other humorous story he told concerned the night of that same Sunday. Corinne Calvet, Ruth Roman and others from the film went up to Chuck's second floor room and they all started drinking. As the night progressed they started pitching their bottles through the window. The following afternoon the owners of the chalet came and asked why the glass was broken and the screen torn up. "I didn't want to tell him that all these stars were in their drinking," Chuck stated, "so I said that when I walked in last night there was a bear in the room and when I opened the door he just jumped out the window and took the screen with him. The lady half believed me but the husband said he couldn't buy that story. I said, 'Okay, how much is the bill?' 'Sixty dollars,' he answered. So I paid it and that's all there was to it."

A month later the cast and crew were riding a train to Vancouver. Some newspaper people boarded the train and came to see the folks from Hollywood. "Everybody thought they wanted to see Stewart, McIntire or Jay C. Flippen, but no, they said they wanted to see the guy who kicked the bear in the ass. Anyhow, that was a true story," Chuck laughed.

The life of a stuntman can also put a fellow in some dangerous situations at times. We asked Chuck if he had a single experience that he would consider the most dangerous that he performed. He thought for a moment and then answered, "I don't know, sometimes simple little things can be awfully dangerous. There were some close calls on *Hellfighters* because you are handling big equipment, I mean heavy derrick steel, and they're dropping it all around you and you're in mud and water up to your neck practically, you can hardly move, and the fire – there were so many things on *Hellfighters* that were really dangerous."

Another potentially hazardous stunt that Chuck performed was when he was doubling John Payne on *Eagle and the Hawk* in a scene where he was tied between two horses galloping at full speed across an open field. "They tied me between these two horses, and I'm looking up at the sky so I couldn't see where I was going. They would take off and run at least thirty miles an hour. One was a little faster than the other, so I had a piano wire in its mouth and would have to pull on it occasionally to keep him back a little or else they would take me in a circle. I also had a thing that was tied to the horses to keep them off of me. Otherwise, if you are tied in between them and there is any pressure at all when they start running they would just smash you. That was the whole thing. Everybody thought they were going to jerk your arms apart; it's not that way at all. You can take those horses and pull them right into you, but I broke a few ribs on that one."

We asked Chuck how long it took to shoot this scene which lasted no more than two minutes on the screen. "I know I got three hundred dollars a ride, and one day I rode it three times and the next I rode it twice and broke my wrist," he responded. "They just taped me up and went right on with it. We probably shot it for three days. Naturally they had to go in for close-ups on Payne, but of course that was all done on gentle little horses with wranglers on each side leading them. John Payne was a pretty good athlete himself," Chuck added.

Chuck also did his stunts and also worked as an actor on television. He appeared in such Westerns as *Cowboy G-Men, Lone Ranger, Gene Autry, Roy Rogers, Death Valley Days, Zane Grey Theater, Gunsmoke, Wagon Train, The Big Valley, Daniel Boone*, and had a very good part on an episode of *Have Gun-Will Travel* that showed his talent as an actor.

Chuck raised horses for many years, not only for the movies but also raised racehorses. His most famous horse, considered by many to be the best falling horse in the movie business, was Cocaine. Chuck used him in many of the John Ford and John Wayne Westerns that he stunted for. Films like *Hondo, She Wore a Yellow Ribbon, McClintock, War Wagon,*

The Horse Soldiers and *Sons of Katie Elder*, to name a few. Cocaine, who died in 1973, is one of the few animal actors to receive mention in Evelyn Truitt's *Who Was Who on Screen* book. Chuck began raising racehorses in 1950, and when we visited him on his Bakersfield ranch in 1987, he still had descendants of his original thoroughbreds training there. "It isn't a hobby, really, but it gives me something to do," he commented.

Speaking of his horse, Cocaine, he told us that one of the best movies he worked on as far as his salary was concerned, was *A Man Called Horse*. "I don't know how many Indians I played in that," Chuck smiled. "I fell off Cocaine so many times in that thing, they never did use them all, but oh gosh! I sent three horses down to Mexico for that one. I worked on that picture for about fourteen days and made twenty one thousand dollars. They changed my Indian gear and I had one fall after another. I didn't get a scratch," he added.

At the time we interviewed Chuck, he told us that he no longer does any stunts for films, having been out of the business for about ten years. "I'll go down occasionally and work for somebody," he told us. "I'll do a little drive through like *Cobra II*, but no stunts. That vet of mine told me one more fall and I'll be in a wheelchair for the rest of my life, so I'm not going to take a shot at that. I don't even get on a horse anymore."

We asked him about his last film, *Cobra II*, and how the business was then compared to how it was in the old days. "Everything is changed so much now," he reflected. "I went down to do this for Jerry Leonard, the kid who is doing Second Unit on it. I put him in the business. I walk on those sets now and I don't know a soul unless there's an old stuntman or actor around. Most all of the people I knew, the crew and the cameramen, are gone now. I don't mean dead, but retired."

In looking over his career, Chuck summed up his feelings by saying, "I presume if I had it to do all over again I'd do the same thing. Although I might pursue my acting career if I had it to do over because I have so many broken bones and ribs. I went to Ben Bards, at one time a very famous acting school, but I was working so much at the time. I would be in class for a week and then go to Argentina for *Way of a Gaucho*; I'd come back and go to class for another week and then go here or there. At that time I doubled a lot of guys making more money doubling them then they were making although they had a big part in the movie. I don't mean guys like McCrea, but some of the contract players, especially Warner Brothers. I did a film in the Philippines called *Merrill's Marauders* with Jeff Chandler, but there were a lot of contract players in that thing like Peter Brown and Claude Akins. I was on a thousand dollars a week and I know there wasn't one of them making that; not a one. So I presume if I had it to do over again I'd get after my acting a little bit more.

"I've done some awful good parts," Chuck continued. "In fact I had a thing in *Wonderful Country* with Mitchum that they threw at me one day and the next we shot. Unfortunately the picture wasn't any good, but the director on that, Robert Parrish, said, 'Chuck, you should really try to do some more acting. You were outstanding. I hate to say it, but you were even better than

Mitchum.' It was just a small part, but it was a good small part. I stick a bottle in a guy's neck and Mitchum comes in and kills me. But it was really a great career.

"As I said," Chuck went on to reflect, "I was jerked up by the hair of the head in Texas and if it hadn't been for this picture business I would probably still be back there riding horses or some damn thing. I made a lot and I spent a lot. I guess for twenty-five years I was one of the top money makers of stuntmen in the business and that's the reason I never did go into acting because I was happy with what I was doing. I'd kind of freeze sometimes when they put that camera right on me and had to do a close-up, but I didn't have to worry about it when I was doing stunts. You run in and do it and say, 'Okay, let's do it again.' And, of course, in the stunt business you get up and do another one. That's the name of the game. If you get hurt and get laid up for six months that's no good, but fortunately I've worked with broken ribs; I've worked with broken arms; a cracked leg, but I hobbled around and got it done."

It was working on *Hondo* that Chuck broke his ankle on the first shot of the first day, but he kept right on working. He not only doubled John Wayne on that film but also did many horse falls for Indians being shot. "I was doubling Wayne when I fell over with Cocaine. They had Wayne laying right up against the bank of a ditch when I come in and fall as fast as I can with that horse and roll right into him, and he jumps up shooting right into the camera. Wasn't even a cut! Even the studio thought that Wayne fell with the horse because there was no cut away. I had to be so close with my horse that he fell on my foot and I didn't know how bad it was. A few shots later I had to run and jump on that horse and when I took off on that, phew! That's all she wrote. We had a big old tub of ice there with cold drinks in it, so I put my foot in ice water and that night taped it up. I shouldn't of went on, I should have put it in a cast because it's bothered me ever since. I broke this arm in *Chisum*," Chuck added. "I had to fall off a second story into the street and they didn't dig the ground up. Again, I jumped up and went on with the fight. But, as I say, I really don't know of any other business in the world, if I had to do it over, that I'd rather be in. Especially at that time because there were so many great people. Really fine people.

"I did a little speech the other day about the cowboys," Chuck continued. "The cowboys were kind of a breed of their own. Joel McCrea, John Wayne and all of them; you can still take your children to see them. In most cases you can take their word to the bank, and that includes our cowboy who's in the White House right now. It got kind of a laugh because it's getting around about him maybe not telling all the truth about the thing he's been in lately (the Contra involvement), but Ronnie was a nice guy. But, without a doubt, I think the picture business in my time was great. Today, I don't know. You see so many of these TV stars come and go, and they do so many bad things. I don't know, it's a different ballgame today. The support cast is no more. In some of those John Ford pictures, or any picture, they had some of the greatest supporting casts – like *Stagecoach* – Gosh dang, what a great cast they had in that thing! Every one of them was a pro and every one of them was good. Thomas Mitchell, what an actor! You don't see them like that anymore. Of course you got a few good actors today, but they're few and far between. You don't have too many of them left. Paul Newman is one of the all time greats and he's still around, but the hell of it is," Chuck concluded, "is that nobody comes up to replace these people."

Chuck passed away from cancer on June 8, 1988 in Bakersfield, California.

Film Credits: **1946:** The Plainsman and the Lady. **1947:** Calendar Girl; Song of Scheherzade; The Flame; Jesse James Rides Again (serial); The Fabulous Texan*; Wyoming*. **1948:** Homicide for Three; Albuquerque; Wake of the Red Witch; The Three Musketeers*; Angel on the Amazon*. **1949:** Stampede; Western Renegades; Law of the Golden West; Hellfire; Haunted Trails; The Fighting Kentuckian; She Wore a Yellow Ribbon*; I Shot Jesse James*; Bad Men of Tombstone*; Ghost of Zorro (serial)*. **1950:** Rio Grande; James Brothers of Missouri (serial); Trail of the Rustlers; Lightning Guns; The Bandit Queen; Outcast of Black Mesa; Atom man vs. Superman (serial); The Capture; Frontier Outpost; Winchester 73; Cow Town; Eagle and the Hawk*; The Kid from Texas*; Hills of Oklahoma*; Baron of Arizona*; Tripoli*. **1951:** Cattle Drive; Fort Dodge Stampede; Ridin' the Outlaw Trail; Across the Wide Missouri*; The Last Outpost*. **1952:** The Lusty Men; Blackbeard the Pirate; Indian Uprising; The Blazing Forest; The Battle at Apache Pass*; Way of a Gaucho*; Lone Star*. **1953:** Gun Belt; Cow Country; Hannah Lee; Hondo; The Naked Spur*; Calamity Jane*; City of Bad Men*. **1954:** The Lone Gun; Sign of the Pagan; The Outcast*. **1955:** The Far Country; Ten Wanted Men; The Prodigal; Timberjack; The Tall Men; The Man from Laramie*; The Last Command*. **1956:** Rawhide Years; The Searchers; Seven Men from Now; Red Sundown; The King and Four Queens; Thunder over Arizona; The Great Locomotive Chase; Dakota Incident*; The Conqueror*. **1957:** The Hired Gun; Forty Guns; Night Passage; Run of the Arrow; Wings of the Eagles; Hell Canyon Outlaws*. **1958:** The Big Country; Man of the West; The Barbarian and the Geisha; Fort Massacre *. **1959:** The Wonderful Country; Rio Bravo; The Horse Soldiers*; Pork Chop Hill*. **1960:** The Alamo; Sergeant Rutledge; Spartacus. **1961:** Two Rode Together; The Misfits*; The Last Sunset*; The Comancheros*. **1962:** How the West was Won; The Man who Shot Liberty Valance; Merrill's Marauders; Taras Bulba*; Hatari*. **1963:** Donovan's Reef; McLintock; Shock Corridor; 4 for Texas*. **1964:** Advance to the Rear; Cheyenne Autumn; Mail Order Bride; Rio Conchos*. **1965:** Black Spurs; Cat Ballou; The Sons of Katie Elder; The Rounders*. **1965:** The War Lord*. **1966:** Smoky; El Dorado; Nevada Smith*; 7 Women. **1967:** The War Wagon; Welcome to Hard Times. **1968:** The Green Berets; Hellfighters; The Scalphunters. **1969:** The Undefeated; Hard Contract*; True Grit*. **1970:** Rio Lobo; Chisum; The Hawaiians*; A Man Called Horse*. **1971:** Big Jake; The Cowboys*; Shoot Out*. **1973:** Cahill, U.S. Marshal; The Train Robbers*. **1974:** McQ; 99 and 44/100% Dead. **1975:** Rooster Cogburn and the Lady*; Doc Savage: The Man of Bronze*. **1976:** The Shootist*. **1978:** FM*. **1983:** Blue Thunder*. **1987:** Cobra II*. **1988:** Miracle Mile.

* denotes stunt work only.

ROBERT ROCKWELL

Robert Rockwell was born in Chicago, Illinois, and raised in the nearby town of Lake Bluff. His father died when Bob was about four years old, and his mother, who was a school teacher, raised him and his two sisters. "She taught grammar school in Lake Bluff and was principal for a number of years," Bob explained. "So I just grew up there."

Bob reflected on his boyhood in Lake Bluff. He told us that "things were so simple in those days. I had my friends and we'd pal around all the time. We lived across a lane from a ravine that went down to Lake Michigan where we played cops and robbers and had great times. We'd slide down the hills in the winter. And we would listen to the radio. We listened to classical music a lot when we were young. Still do. We didn't have a car. Finally I bought a Model T for twenty-five dollars when I was in high school. That was fun. We'd go out in the country with a little kerosene stove we carted around and cook potatoes, bacon and eggs. Go into the farmer's cornfields and get some corn and cook it. We just did a lot of kid things that were very innocent. I did get thrown into jail one time. One Halloween night, I had four or five of my friends around, we went to the dentist's house, who I didn't like because every time I went there he hurt me. He gave us a bag of apples and it turned out that they were kind of rotten, so I said 'Let's throw them back,' so I threw one back and it went right through the window. Unfortunately, it landed on the table where they were playing bridge. Nobody was hurt. Of course, I knew all of the policemen, and the next thing I know, on each side of the back door, there's a policeman. They said, 'Come on Bob, did you do that?' I said, 'Yeah, I did it.' So they took me up to jail. My sister later came with some candy bars. When they told my mother, she said, 'Well, if he wants

to act that way let him stay there.' About two o'clock in the morning they let us go, and then we all chipped in and bought the new window."

Bob also loved the theatre. "I loved it in grammar school, what little you do, and did everything I could do in high school in the way of shows and plays." Asked what had sparked this love, and he replied "I have no idea. My grandmother on my father's side played the piano quite well, and she was a very good artist. In about 1895, she and her sister went through the missions, starting with San Juan Capistrano, and drew each of them as they were in those days. So maybe that's where I got it, I don't know, maybe it goes back farther than that. I have no idea. I just loved it, that's all."

After his graduation from high school, Bob attended the University of Illinois. "My mother wanted me to go into business so I took business courses the first two years, but I finally told her it was just no good. So I went into the Theatre Arts, and instead of going back in my senior year I came out to the Pasadena Playhouse where I could just concentrate on theatre."

He went to Pasadena for three years. In those days the film studios were placing many young women and men under contract because they knew World War II was coming on and were trying to get as many under contract as they could. "I auditioned and got an agent in 1941 and was ready to sign a contract with Warner Brothers, but I got my letter from the Army in the early part of 1942," Bob stated. "My draft number was quite early, so I decided I'd rather go in the Navy, so I enlisted in early '42, and spent four years there, most of it in Washington D.C."

When Bob was discharged from the Navy in 1946 he decided that he would like to go to New York. One of the women officers that Bob knew in Washington D.C. told him that he could rent their house on Long Island for January, February and March. As Bob told his wife, "I can go into New York and walk the streets and see if I can get a job as an actor." So they rented it for three months. There was a paper in New York called Actor's Cues, which came out every Tuesday morning telling of the activities that were going on for that week, such as shows being rehearsed and where casting auditions for new shows were taking place. "So I would go in on Tuesday morning, get a cup of coffee and go over Actor's Cues, and I'd check off everything I wanted to do during the week," Bob said. "Every day I'd get on the Long Island Railroad, come into town and go to the various buildings for casting, talking and interviewing – even on Saturdays!

"Finally after about six weeks I went up to Radio City where they were auditioning for *Cyrano de Bergerac* with Jose Ferrer. So I got in line. There were fifty guys ahead of me, and when my turn came they gave me a scene to read. Finally I went in to Mel Ferrer, who was directing, and Jose Ferrer, and I read for them. The director said, 'I can see down here that you can fence.' I said, 'I did take fencing in the Pasadena Playhouse, and I can handle myself.' So they said, 'Fine. You're six foot two, that's good, and you make sense out of what you read.' So I got the part. First, because I could fence; second, because I was tall; and third, because I could speak the English so somebody could understand," Bob laughed.

They rehearsed in New York, then went on the road to New Haven and played there for a week or two, then on to Boston and played there for a couple of weeks, and finally to Philadelphia. By this time it was June, and as it was a very heavy, hot show they stopped it for the summer, with plans of picking it back up in the fall. "In the meantime I had to do something," Bob noted. "I had sent my wife and child out to Denver while I was doing the show, so when it closed I came out and got a job as a hod carrier through a friend of mine. So I carried the hod the rest of the summer. But when they sent me a wire to come back to the show in New York, I thought 'No, if I'm going to starve as an actor I'm going to starve out in Hollywood where at least I could pick an orange off a tree. So I came out and have been here ever since."

Arriving back in Hollywood, Bob took a refresher course at the Playhouse on the G.I. Bill. He also obtained the lead role of Robert Browning in *Barretts of Wimpole Street* at the Pasadena Playhouse. It turned out very well. "It was the first good thing I did," Bob added. An agent spotted him in the play and signed him on as a client. The first movie that Bob appeared in was in 1948 with Jimmy Stewart in a Warner Brothers feature called *You Gotta Stay Happy*.

In addition to his film work, Bob also was attempting to break into the tight knit group of people that were performing as radio actors. "I spent two years trying to do this, but you just couldn't get in that group," Bob confided. "Finally, I managed to get some parts. When television came that was the end of radio for the time being. I did the last two years of radio's *Our Miss Brooks*, so I did do that much, although I had done some other shows before that."

Bob signed a one year contract in 1949 with Herbert Yates at Republic Studios. Bob described them as C-movies, but noted that when he recently saw several of them at the Memphis Film Festival they were surprisingly pretty good. One of these was *Red Menace*, which was Yates' expose of communism. "You could see through it pretty well," Bob said, "but that was the time the Un-American Activities Committee was going and there was a big hullabaloo about Hollywood. That was the movie I did first there. Then they put me under contract for a year and I did ten or eleven. They were all detective shows. It was fun, and gave me wonderful experience working that hard, that often when you're just starting out. I had been in two or three pictures before that, but this gave me the opportunity to really learn the business."

Robert had a role in the science fiction classic, *War of the Worlds* at Paramount. He played the forest ranger in a scene soon after the spaceship first arrives. "Of course there's smoke billowing all over, and I am just giving out a lot of orders and commands. I don't think I worked more than a week in it," Bob stated. "It was something a little different, but it was right there on the sound stage. You can always tell by the sound whether it is done on the sound stage or whether it is done outside."

Bob also spent some time working on the sound stage in the popular *Lone Ranger* television series. They did work on location near Simi Valley, riding back and forth or up and down hills, as well as walking out of houses, but for the most part they worked on a sound stage. They built the big rocks on the stage, where the Lone Ranger and Tonto would ride out from behind, dismount and have a campfire or enter into the interior of a cabin and continue with their dialogue. Bob appeared in about twelve episodes, half the time playing a good guy, the other half an outlaw. "The first time I played the good guy and had to deliver the line, 'He's the Lone Ranger.' We were out on the front porch, on the sound stage, supposedly of some house, and you're looking off into the sunset where the ranger's gone. They always wanted it said a certain way, a very special way, and I did it a couple of times and thought it was all right, but they didn't seem to think so. But then I got to laughing over it because I heard it so many times. I just couldn't say the line. Finally, probably about the twelfth take, I controlled myself enough to stop laughing and do it. That was funny. They weren't very happy with me, but it didn't stop them from using me again. But that's the only time I ever had to say that line," Bob laughed.

Another television show that Bob enjoyed working on was *Lassie*. "I did one or two with Jon Provost, June Lockhart and Hugh Reilly. Then when they went with Jed Allen, we did four shows on location at Juneau, Alaska. He had Lassie in the show at that time," Bob reflected. Bob told us that they used two or three dogs to play Lassie, and they were all male! "One they trained to fight; and another to spell the other because when the dog is running over hill and dale, up and down and his tongue's hanging out about a foot, and perspiring trying to catch his breath, they would bring in another one. We had fun up there in Juneau doing those."

Bob is probably best known to many people as Philip Boynton on the *Our Miss Brooks* television show which ran from 1952 to 1956, as well as reprising the role in the 1955 feature of the same name. We asked Bob if he had many fond memories of this show. "Oh, lots of fond memories of *Our Miss Brooks*," he answered. "It was such fun because it wasn't work, it was just fun. We would come into the studio at about ten o'clock on Friday morning. We'd all gather around, producer, director, writers and cast, and other people who were hired for that one week, and read the script. If the writer thought something would work better or if Miss Arden thought something would work better, they'd discuss it, and we would probably read till about eleven-thirty. Then we would walk through the show. The sets were always in sort of an arch. They were permanent sets, but weren't dressed, i.e. they didn't have all the drapes and stuff up, but they had the furniture. So we would go through our positions, entering, talking, getting up, leaving; we'd do the whole show and that would take us no more than a half-hour, so by one o'clock Friday we were out of there. We came back Monday by nine. The cameras were in by that time, and they had crab dollies. A crab dolly has four wheels and, like a crab, can go at all sorts of angles, so it's operator could make it go at oblique angles, front, back, sideways, everything. They had three of those cameras, one was for the establishing shot; one was for someone coming through the door; and one was on Miss Arden or on a two-shot. So all three cameras were working all of the time. And then they would lay down the marks on the floor for each camera. We'd stop for lunch about noon, then come back in an hour and start in again. We would finish working with the cameras, about three or three-thirty. Then the cameras would leave, and we'd get into our wardrobe and have a dress rehearsal and be out of there by five. That was our longest day. Nine to five. Then Tuesday, we would come in at one in the afternoon and have a dress rehearsal for the cameras. And then about five everything would stop and they would cater dinner in. We would have dinner, get our make-up on, get into our wardrobe, and at seven o'clock they would let the audience in, and at seven-thirty we would do the show, and we were out of there usually by eight-thirty or nine, unless something horrendous happened. We had about four hundred in the audience and always used those laughs. I don't think they ever used any canned laughs. There were a lot of fond memories. I think I kissed her three times in a hundred and twenty-nine shows. The audience would scream and yell and whistle and everything else. And then of course when they think I am going to do something – I remember one time, after a dance we're out in Walter Denton's convertible that I had borrowed for the evening and we were watching the moonlight. She said she was getting chilly and wanted to kind of snuggle up, so I said, 'Oh gee, I'm sorry,' and I went back and put my hand behind her as though I was going to put my arm around her, but instead grabbed her coat and put it over her shoulders. Well, the audience had a fit. They booed and booed. It was funny."

Bob added that working with a live audience is fun. "On *Growing Pains*, Jane Powell and I are married and we did about eight together, and that is with a live audience. They're all fun. I did one on the *Sandy Duncan Show*, I think that lasted just a year, and that was with an audience."

Bob did not, however, enjoy the early live shows like *Matinee Theatre* that he occasionally worked on. They had no audience watching in the studio, but as they performed for the camera it was telecast simultaneously across the country. "If you got in a mess you got out of it," Bob explained. "There was no cutting at all. You'd get up from a chair, that chair would be quietly rolled out, the table would be rolled away, somebody would be behind you to take your coat off, put another coat on and you'd walk right through a door, all within ten seconds, and do another scene. I remember Andy Duggan and I did a fight, I hit him, down he went. While I'm standing over him giving my dialogue the make-up man's down there putting blood and bruises on him, then he gets up and knocks me down and they put bruises and blood on me. Then I'd get up and we'd finish the scene. I didn't like that. As far as I was concerned it was nerve-racking and just too hard. I guess I did five or six of those. I didn't enjoy it because it was terrifying to me. The first one I ever did, I guess you'd call it a soap opera, came out here during the summer from New York for about twelve weeks. I'd have my lines on my hands, I had the lines on tables, the lines on the back of lamps, wherever I'd go I'd have a crutch. I finally got over that. To do the best job, you need time and you didn't have time with the rehearsal we got. Nowadays, if you goof everything stops and they back the tape up and start over again. It's not a big deal now; they do it all the time."

Bob has worked on two soap operas, acting for two years on *Search For Tomorrow* and a six month stint on *Days Of Your Lives*. "It's fun; it's hard work," he said, "but you don't really get too much of an opportunity, unless you're a character that has longevity in it and can build something out of it. You just come in and do the best you can do with what they seem to want you to do, that's all you can expect. You have no opportunity."

Columbia decided they were going to make a television series based on the film, *Mr. Blandings Builds His Dream House*. Bob was among many who auditioned for the lead in the series. After about a week Bob received word that the studio decided against making the series and chose to do one called *The Man from Blackhawk* instead. "My agent, unbeknownst to me, had signed me up to do the series," Bob informed. "I never auditioned, but it was fun and that's how I got it. Herb Meadow was a delightful person to work with: he was excellent as a producer."

The character of Sam Logan was that of an insurance investigator during the 1880's in *The Man from Blackhawk* and lasted only one season, 1959-60. "I worked very hard on that," Bob told us. "Stirling Siliphant and some of the best writers in Hollywood were writing for that. So it was going along great guns for the first thirteen or twenty shows, we were doing thirty-nine in those days, but they sent me away to New York on a personal appearance and when I came back Herb was out, his assistant was out, the writers were out. A new producer was in, they cut the budget in half; we had no more location. What had happened, the writers went on strike so all they could do was pull the bottom drawer of a file out where they had all of their Westerns. You see, *Man from Blackhawk* was not a Western, it wasn't supposed to be. Everyone thinks if you wear boots or gaiters or put on a hat and a string tie it is a Western, well it took place all over the country. I was in New England, New York, on the desert, everywhere because we would go on locations. But when they had to bring out these Westerns you just walked down the street and into a building and then you'd be on a sound stage and shoot the scene. Then you go out again and into something else and do the scene or have a fight scene, but it cut the heart right out of the show and it went for just thirty-nine episodes.

"It was a tough show," Bob continued. "I don't do my own stunts. I will let them take a punch at me and I'll take a punch at them, but then if they start to roll and toss around they go into the doubles. Because it's silly, only workmen's compensation if you got hurt, it doesn't make any sense. Just as on a horse, I will get on a horse off camera and ride gently in and get off the horse, or I'd get on the horse on camera and ride slowly away. Now, when they want somebody going hell-bent-for-leather up and down a hill they've got a stuntman. That's their business; it's not my business; if I get hurt I'm through. One time there was a stuntman and I didn't realize he was left-handed. I was getting out of a buggy and he surprised me and threw a punch, it was planned, but I got mixed up and I went to take it from the right side and consequently he hit me. Bam! Right flush on the nose, I bled for fifteen minutes but I didn't break my nose, everything was fine. Another time we were having a fight supposedly in a lake and the water was only about two feet deep in this big pond. Well the stuntman pushed me back and my legs got caught under me and I couldn't go back. I finally was able to slither around and I wrecked my back for about two weeks on that deal. It was a physical show, yet it was fun and I enjoyed it very much. But it was really all business; there was no comedy in that. It started out to be a real good show, but I was disappointed in it because of what happened."

His other television roles ran the gamut from comedy (*My Little Margie*), adventure (*Superman*, on which he played Jor-El, the Krypton scientist who was the father of Superman) to *Gunsmoke* ("I didn't have a very sympathetic role and I just did one episode"). Bob told us about an incident while working on the *Loretta Young Show*. "I'll never forget one time at lunch Clark Gable came on the set, and he and Loretta Young went off in a corner and talked for about a half an hour. It's a thrill seeing people like that, and to work with them they're delightful people. I never worked with Gable, but I've worked with others and they're very nice, helpful people."

Did he prefer comedy over drama? "Drama is fun," he commented. "I enjoy drama, but with comedy you get more or less an instant reaction since you have the audience there. That's what I love about the theatre, whether it's good or whether it's bad you get a reaction. There are people out there breathing, sneezing, coughing, laughing and you know they're there and you get, as I say, the instant reaction. You do a comedy line well and you get a big laugh, it's wonderful. It's also good if you're doing drama, but I have just sort of gone to comedy. People hire me for that. I can't get arrested on *L.A. Law* or those things as much as I've tried."

At the time of our interview Bob was still working in the business. "You do everything in this business that you can do that someone will hire you for. You can't limit yourself," he noted. Whether it be industrial films, commercials (notably the grandfather on the Werthers Candy ad), both on camera and voice-overs. Bob was a spokesman for Pure Oil back in the Midwest and the South. Union Oil bought them out but for the three years before that he was their spokesman. "We'd go down there and do radio and television commercials," he said. "After that ended I thought I would like to continue being a spokesman, but I soon found out that there weren't that many, so I told my agent to just go for anything that comes along."

Bob also continued treading the boards in legitimate theatre. "About three years ago I did the captain, the head of the court, in *The Caine Mutiny Court-Martial*, with Charlton Heston. We played here in Hollywood at the Henry Fonda Theatre for two weeks and then six weeks at the Eisenhower Theatre in the Kennedy Center in Washington D.C. That was fun because you could get out and see all sorts of things and do all sorts of things. I had been in Washington for almost four years in the Navy so I had a good time doing the show. But ordinarily, if you're playing a lot of small towns you do a lot of reading and a lot of listening. I don't say I'd turn it down if the opportunity presented itself and if it was good enough," Bob laughed. Bob worked in another stage show called *Three Men on a Horse*. "Sterling Holloway was the lead in it, and he is a funny man," Bob said. "He could ad-lib; he could make things up. He made up a poem right on stage one night, and we died laughing and the audience died laughing and all of us just leaned on something because we were laughing so hard. He was such a funny man. That's one of the few times, I guess, you can enjoy what's going on instead of just letting the audience."

Bob explained some acting techniques in the various mediums available. "Acting for the radio is one art, one technique," he said. "Acting for the screen is another; acting for television is a third technique. You've got to remember in what medium you're working. It's only your voice in radio, you have to put the people where you are in what you're doing. In television it's mostly close work so you don't project, but it's all in your eyes and mind. If you're not thinking behind those eyes nothing is going to come out. Pictures, they can get farther away and have a little more latitude so it's a little closer to what you do on the stage. The stage of course is the fourth medium where you expand your body and your mind to get across the footlights. All you have there is air between you and the audience. Number one," Bob continued, "you have to listen if someone is saying something to you or if something's happening, you react to that. Your reaction can be in a vocal way or it could be in a physical way. But you've got to first take in what you have been given so you can let out with the right reaction. I just love it. Everything you do with it, whether you work one day or a half a day; whatever, it's great fun."

We asked Bob if he had any favorites, and he answered us, "I worked with Ginger Rogers in a play down in La Jolla called *A More Perfect Union*. Working with her was a great experience for me. Loretta Young did her TV show and I think I did three or four with her. The first time I was on the set I was a stick: I was so terrified because here was this woman, a worldwide actress of great renown. She knew I was, so before our first scene she came up and we sat and talked, and she asked 'Would you like to go over your lines?' so we went over them, we talked some more and she calmed me down and things worked out fine. I was very excited about that and I loved working with her. I think this is true, but it may not be, that we were the first couple to be in a double bed on television. She liked that reality. She did certain shows, maybe she would be in Italy and be romanced by some suave Italian, have a romance here and a romance there, and I said 'Now Loretta, let me be your lover sometime.' She said, 'No Bob, you're my husband.' And I was her husband in four of her shows, but she would never let me do anything else," he laughed.

"I haven't had too many favorites. Most of my work has been in television, you come and you go. Like on the *Bob Newhart Show*, for instance, Bob was very pleasant and you get along, but maybe you work one week and do the show and then you don't see them again for a couple of years. So you just do your job. I'm not a great actor; I'm a craftsman, I guess you might say, with, I hope, some ability to do various things. It was fun working with Charlton Heston, I enjoyed that very much, and the part was fun. At least I made the part fun. I didn't make him a stick, I made him just what I thought would be fun in the somber setting that it was. Working with Bing Crosby, I had very little to do in the picture, but I did have a couple of scenes with him.

"I have also worked with some young people who thought they were great stars and lasted about one season and you never heard of them again because they weren't professional," Bob continued. "They didn't know how to handle themselves, they couldn't discipline themselves. That's what happens if you don't have some training. In the days when I started, the studios were still going, and they would take a person and they would build that person and direct his life in motion pictures, sometimes it was good and sometimes it was bad, they had invested money and they wanted to get their money out, but they had a training ground for these people.

Television doesn't give you a training ground. There is a lot of theatre around town; these young people can work in the theatre, take courses, improvisations, cold readings and so forth. But there are so many thousands of actors. When I used to go out on interviews, I would probably get one commercial for every ten interviews; now it's probably twenty to twenty-five auditions before you get a commercial. There are so many, many, many people.

"I've gotten older now, as much as I regret that, and there are fewer parts," Bob noted. "I'm kind of restricted to judges, lawyers, ministers, executives and things like that, where I would love to do a character, but they don't see me as a character person. After *Our Miss Brooks* I didn't work for over a year, nobody would hire me. They'd say this role isn't like Mr. Boynton. That's how short-sighted some of these people were. For over a year I didn't do one day's work because of that. Today they're young producers, young directors – I'm not putting them down at all because many of them are very talented, but to go in and have somebody say, 'Tell us what you have done.' It does hurt a little bit, but you can't blame them because they don't know me. I'm not doing a big soap or a starring role on something, so I'm caught in-between. They don't see me as characters. It's fun to play a smaller role or a cameo, but they're going to play it safe and bring in a bigger name. Most of my work in the last fifteen years has been on television and on the stage."

In 1995 Bob narrated *Ozarks: Legacy and Legend* for the Imax theatre in Branson, Missouri. This production chronicled the history of the Ozarks.

Hobbies? "I play paddle-tennis twice a week and work out at the gym three times a week to keep fit and active. And I play golf. Life just goes on and is full of things, you never just sit around. And a lot of fixing to do when you have a place this big. I enjoy working on the house." Bob and his wife have three sons and two daughters. One son, Jeff, is currently pursuing an acting career.

In summing up his feelings regarding his career, Bob told us "I'd liked to have done more, that's all. You love to keep busy in this business. I feel I've been retired ever since I started because you don't work all the time. You may work one week here and then you don't work for two or three weeks, then you work another week. In a soap opera maybe you work three days a week. But I love to work and you just don't get enough of it. I would like to do another stage play. We have the California Artists' Repertory Theatre and the California Artists' Radio Theatre, CART, and we do radio shows. We did Shakespeare and *Front Page*. We do wonderful radio shows with great people. I enjoyed doing those very much. Stage is my first love, there's no question about it. That's what I grew up with and I love it simply because of the immediate reaction. I've done summer stock down in Tustin for eight weeks. That's work. It's tough, but it's fun. It's very gratifying. Until the day I'm no longer here I plan to be working if someone will have me. I don't want to retire. People say, 'Are you retired?' and I'll say, 'I'm not working at the moment.'"

Robert Rockwell died from cancer on January 25, 2003 in Malibu, California.

Film Credits: **1948:** You Gotta Stay Happy. **1949:** The Sponge Diver (short); Alias the Champ; The Red Menace; Task Force. **1950:** Singing Guns; The Vanishing Westerner; Belle of Old Mexico; The Blonde Bandit; Destination Big House; Federal Agent at Large; Lonely Heart Bandits; Prisoners in Petticoats; Trial without Jury; Unmasked; Woman from Headquarters. **1951:** Call Me Mister; The Frogmen; The Prince who was a Thief; Weekend with Father. **1952:** The Turning Point; Just for You. **1953:** War of the Worlds. **1956:** Our Miss Brooks. **1965:** A Letter to Nancy. **1968:** Sol Madrid. **1981:** Golden Gate (TV); Murder in Texas (TV). **1982:** Life of the Party: The Story of Beatrice (TV). **1983:** The Kid with the 200 IQ (TV). **1990:** The World According to Straw (TV). **1991:** Hell Hath no Fury (TV). **1995:** Perfect Alibi; Ozarks: Legacy and Legend (narrator).

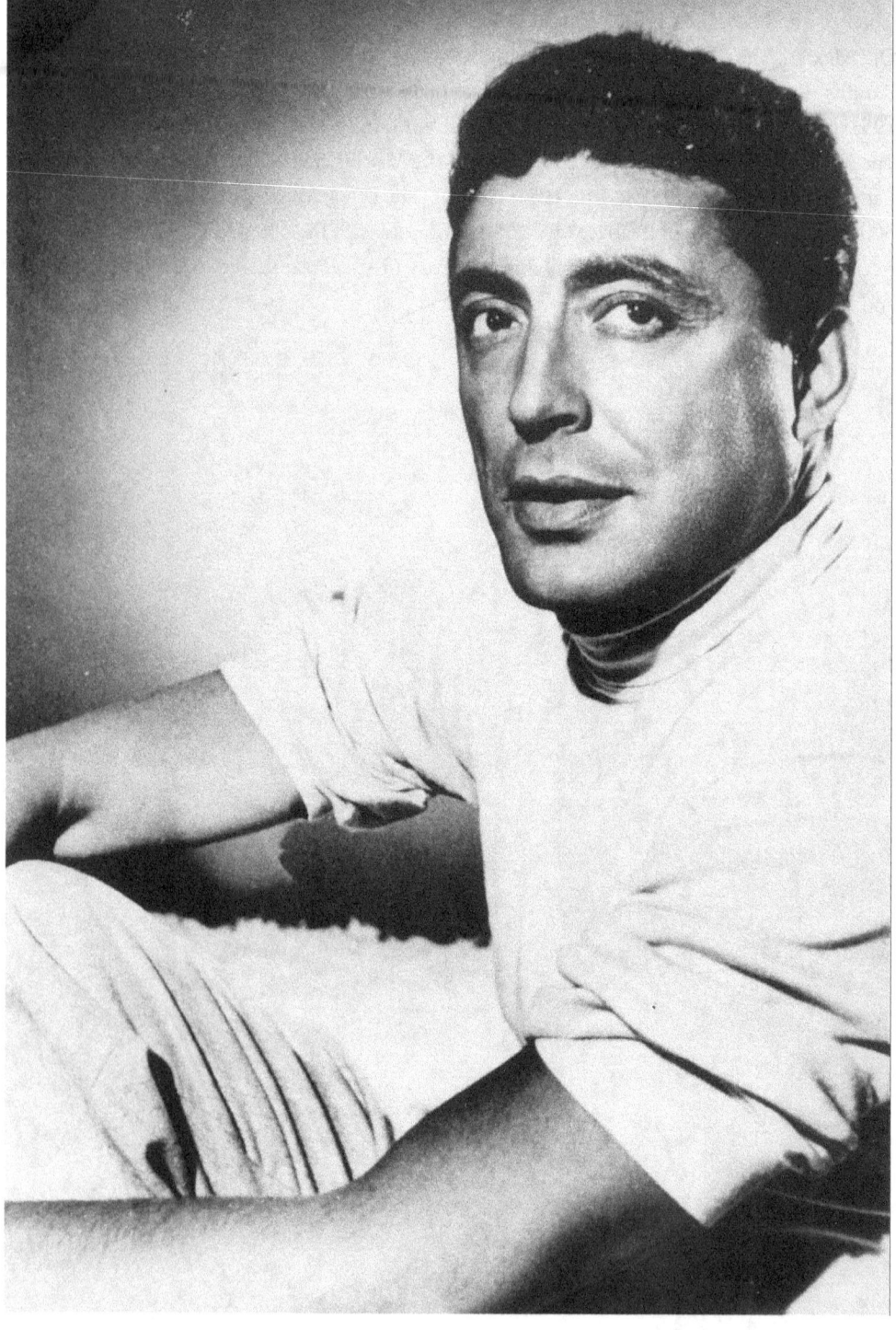

RIC ROMAN

Ric Roman was born September 29, 1916, as Earl Breitbard in Babylon, a little town on the south shore on Long Island out of New York. His younger brother was named William, who later changed his name to William B. Williams. Ric, who was very proud of his brother, told us, "He was the greatest disc jockey that ever lived, and he lived in New York. As Frank Sinatra says in his song, if you can make it in New York, you can make it anywhere. And he made it big in New York. He was with the station WNEW. As an aside, he gave Sinatra the title of Chairman of the Board. Frank was crazy about him, and when my brother passed away Frank said that he lost the best friend he ever had. "

Ric had a rather unusual path that led him to his career as a motion picture actor. He was in the service in Europe during World War II. "I was a private making a hot twenty-one dollars a month, which you got in those days and which you lost the first night in a crap game," Ric began. "I took a test and wound up in Officer's Candidate School and became a Second Lieutenant. The week before I graduated from OCS I was summoned to a hotel to see a Lieutenant Colonel. We did the proper salutes and all that hogwash, and then he said to me, 'Tell me if I'm wrong about this. Your mother was born in Vienna and your father was born in Russia.' I looked at this guy and said, 'How the hell would you know that?' Then I stopped because I was talking to a Colonel. He said, 'You may not realize it but you have a photographic memory and we'd like to send you to Harrisburg, Pennsylvania to Combat Intelligence School.' I went there, and after I graduated from the school they kept me on as an instructor. Finally, I am going nuts in that place and want to get out of there, and they granted my wish and off I went."

Ric was sent back overseas to Europe, but told us "I don't want to go through the war experiences. But after the war was over in Germany, I ran into a Colonel outside of Nuremberg and he said to me, 'There is a job that is going to open up in Paris. I think you would be great for it.' To make a long story as short as I can, I came to Paris and was there for six months and had in my squad a guy named Broderick Crawford."

Crawford and Ric became close friends, and after they were discharged they came to New York together. Crawford asked Ric, "Why don't you come out to California." Ric had reasons for not wanting to go and remained in New York while Crawford went to Hollywood to resume his film career. Ric obtained work in the radio, and told us, "I did about everything there was to do in radio. Two years later I called Brod Crawford up and said to him, 'I'm coming out to California.' He said, 'You stay with me.' "

Ric arrived in Los Angeles in 1949, and roomed with his friend. "His mother was a woman named Helen Broderick. She was retired, but she had been the highest paid comedienne on Broadway, and she took a liking to me. This is how I got into pictures. She said to me, 'You know something? 'You're a long way from handsome but believe me you could make a good buck playing heavies in movies.' I didn't even know what the word heavy meant, but I asked, 'How do you do this?' and she said, 'I'm going to take you to an agent.' She was very big at that point in time, so I went with her. I didn't know anything. I had done radio in New York, but never in front of a camera. She said to the agent, 'If you're smart you'll sign my guy because Moss Hart wants him for a play in New York.' I wouldn't have known Moss Hart, but boom! He couldn't get me fast enough."

Ric decided to change his name for the pictures, and the reason for doing so is best illustrated by the story he told us that happened several years later when he had his name legally changed. "I had to appear before a judge and he looked down and said, 'How do you pronounce it?' I said, 'Judge, if you can't pronounce it that's the reason I want to change my name.' He chuckled, and boom! We were in and out in five minutes." And where did the name Ric Roman come from? "I am one of those people who likes alliteration," Ric answered. "Kirk Douglas was doing a picture named *Champion* with a lady that I thought was something else: Ruth Roman. Where I found Ric I don't know. But that's where it comes from and she doesn't know that to this day."

Ric's agent took him out to Warner Brothers and introduced him to the casting director. He said to Ric, "We're starting a picture with Joan Crawford called *The Damned Don't Cry* and we need some new faces because we're using the same guys over and over." Within a few days Ric received a call to come to Warners, as he was hired to play the role of a gangster named Sam Loman. "I haven't smoked in forty years," Ric informed, "but in those days I had to have two things in the morning or I didn't know what town I was in. I had to have a cup of coffee and a cigarette. The cigarette was fine, I had them with me, but now I walk on stage, and to be very honest with you I was scared, and I didn't know who the hell to ask for a cup of coffee. Guys are running here and there and I don't want to let on that this is the first time that I was ever on a sound stage. A woman walks over to me and it was Joan Crawford. She said to me, 'Young man, you seem to be apprehensive about something. What's the trouble?' I said, 'Miss Crawford, I must tell you something. I'm a guy that if I don't have a cup of coffee in the morning I'm in trouble.' I'll never forget the next thing she said and will always love her for it. She said, 'Somebody get this man a cup of coffee,' and it was like out of the woodwork fifteen flunkies came and brought the coffee over. I sat down next to her and she said, 'Let's run the lines.' All this terminology, 'Let's run the lines,' was brand new to me, but I knew what she meant. Then the director, Vincent Sherman, said 'Let's go,' to all the guys, and then said to me, 'Hit your marks next to Miss Crawford.' I'm in trouble because I don't know what the hell hit the marks meant. I really didn't. So I watched the other heavies and saw them put their feet in the chalk marks, so I did the same with mine and it went very well. She was happy, he was happy, and I was happy. About six months later I ran into Joan Crawford on the Columbia lot, and by that time in my book I was a seasoned veteran. She saw me and said, 'Ric, how are you?' I said, 'Fine.' She said, 'Do you know how to get coffee?' So I've always liked her."

During 1949 and 1950 Ric played bit parts in many films, one being John Ford's *Wagon Master*. When asked what John Ford was like, Ric replied, "Autocratic. You did it his way or you better make sure the door didn't hit you in the ass on the way out. But he knew what he wanted." Years later Ric worked again for Ford in *Cheyenne Autumn*.

Ric talked about his friend Broderick Crawford. "It was Brod Crawford that really got me into the business. But Brod, and I say this with almost a touch of reverence, nobody drank like this man. I mean he and the bottle, it was a wedding. He would drink straight vodka right out of the bottle, and many nights when I lived with him he would not come home, and I'd go out and find him in the bushes. He had fallen down. Later his wife Kay, who was a band singer, threw him out and I lived at a place called the Hollywood Athletic Club, and Brod came and took a room next to me. There was a picture that I worked only because of Brod. He went to the director, Vincent Sherman, the same guy who directed *The Damned Don't Cry*, and asked if I could be on it and he said fine. That's the picture with Clark Gable, *Lone Star*, and with Ava Gardner. She became a very good friend of mine."

Ric reflected on several experiences of working on *The Lone Star*, and of Clark Gable. "In *Lone Star* I had a big scene with Gable," Ric said. "We're doing dialogue and the camera is shooting over me and is on Gable, and I'm entranced because of something that is happening. Very few people ever knew this, but he had a thing that would sometimes cause his eye to tic, which he couldn't stop. So Hal Rosson, the cameraman, came down from where he was sitting on the camera and quietly said, 'Champ, I think we better turn it around so I get you and Ric talking and the tic will be off camera.' They used some kind of crazy excuse to change the shot, and I realized why.

"The second thing about Gable that I loved was that on the old MGM lot he was king, and when he walked into the commissary everybody looked at him. When we made *Lone Star*, Harry Woods, Bill Conrad and myself used to play three-handed poker. But when we would go into the commissary, Gable had a long table at which—and I'm saying this quite appropriately—the king sat on the throne. He would always take Harry Woods, Bill Conrad, myself, and a couple of other guys and sit at the table with us, and always buy the lunch. We did this for ten weeks. He was one hell of a man. Yep."

Ric stated that he loved doing Westerns, but that he was not a very good rider. "Hal Needham use to double me for the real tough riding scenes." Ric's Western credits include *South of Caliente* with Roy Rogers, *Winchester 73* with James Stewart, *Springfield Rifle* with Gary Cooper, *Shadows of Tombstone* with Rex Allen, *Rails into Laramie* and *The Road to Denver*, both with John Payne, *The Duel at Apache Wells* with Ben Cooper, as well as numerous television shows. Ric talked at length on several of the Western features he worked in.

The Last of the Comanches was filmed in Yuma, Arizona, and featured his friend Broderick Crawford, Barbara Hale, Lloyd Bridges, and Martin Milner, who was Ric's roommate at the hotel. "One night the phone rang in my hotel room at about two o'clock in the morning. I answered and it was Barbara Hale, and she said, 'Ric, you better get down here fast. Your boyfriend is on fire.' Brod had bought a lot of gifts and toys that he was going to bring home to his adopted son, and got loaded and fell asleep with a cigarette, and the Yuma Fire Department was now there squirting water. 'You better get down here and get him out,' she said. 'He's incoherent and doesn't know what he's doing.' Barbara was a beautiful lady."

Ric told of one of their pastimes when not working. "It can get hot in Yuma and we were shooting out on the sands." he said. "When we would break for lunch they'd have a crap game at a table. I had a roll, and maybe there was two hundred dollars on the table. I'm shaking the dice, saying all the admonitions you're supposed to say. Maybe one hundred and fifty got covered and slowly there was twenty dollars open, and I said, 'Twenty dollars is open, I'm not shooting until somebody...'and suddenly, boom! A twenty-dollar bill came floating down. I threw the dice and made whatever the point was. I went to collect the money and Marty puts his hand out and took twenty dollars, and I said, 'What the hell are you doing?' because I told him earlier that he was my partner, because we room together. 'Somebody had to cover it,' he said. 'So I did.' I said, 'You dummy, you're covering your own money,'" Ric laughed. "I'll never forget that kid. Whenever I see him we have a chuckle about it."

When asked if he could think of any dangerous situation that he was placed in during the filming of a picture, Ric replied, "I think the most dangerous thing that ever happened to me was when I got on a horse," he laughed. "I can remember one dangerous thing. This picture I was talking about in Yuma, Arizona, the director was a guy with one eye, Andre de Toth. I played a Mexican—one of the few times I played a good guy—and I get killed by the Indians. The other soldiers are looking for me, and see me standing there. But I have an arrow in my back. De Toth wanted a shot where they turn me around and I fall face forward into camera. So Andre said, 'Ric, it shouldn't be tough, but you've got to be careful. We want to catch you as you come face down right passed the camera.' They had mattresses, but he said, 'We'd like it when you go by the camera to just fall; you're dead. Put your hands out to break your fall after you go by camera.' Easier said than done because there wasn't that much separation between where the camera was catching me and where I fell. I thought I broke my nose because I was a little late with my hands. That's the only time. I never really had any dangerous moments."

One of the early Westerns Ric worked on was a story set to Terry Gilkyson's music called *Slaughter Trail* with Gig Young, Virginia Grey, and Brian Donlevy. "We got paid for working six weeks on it, and then Howard Hughes came in and threw one of the leads off the set because he thought he was a communist, so we had to start from day one again. I loved it. I don't care what he was; we got six weeks' salary for nothing. I played Paco, the Indian chief. I always remember that one. I was scared because the guy who produced it called me in and said, 'Ric, do you ride?' I said yeah. He said 'I want you to play an Indian chief, and I want you to shave every hair off your body.' He explained that Indians never had to shave, but I couldn't care less. I was thinking about the damn horse because he told me there was no saddle and that I'd just have a blanket over the horse. I said, 'Fine.' I just wanted to get the money and run.

"To say I was scared in this particular scene, that's a mild word, because I say to all of the cavalry officers that if they don't do something by the time the sun rises, that's all she wrote. Then they have a scene with the sun rising and they cut to Chief Paco sitting on his horse on a cliff scared shitless," he laughed. "I'm supposed to throw a spear down, and I said to the wranglers, 'Listen, what happens if the horse bolts?' 'Don't worry about it Ric, we got him.' You couldn't see the wranglers holding him on the film, but as I threw the damn spear that horse spooked. When I say spooked, I mean he reared up. They should have kept the camera rolling, but they stopped it. We finally settled down, and yes, I was scared with a capital S."

Ric later made another film for Howard Hughes with Jane Russell and Richard Egan called *Underwater*. "I worked in that one for quite some time," Ric mentioned. "Hughes had a big yacht in Catalina and we did a lot of filming there. One of the heavies was Joseph Calleia, and he was supposed to do the diving for the treasure, but Joe, in essence, said he couldn't swim. They said, 'Ric, you do the diving.' They built a tank in the studio and we did it there. When I dove, I got something caught in my thumb and it really gushed blood."

Ric commented about a film role that he considered one of his favorites. It was a film called *Lizzie*, and starred Eleanor Parker. "She was, during the day, a very proper librarian, but at night she used to make it with me. This could have been a breakthrough picture for me. But unfortunately it had a lousy title, and they didn't promote it. There was a particular scene where she's supposed to meet me at a bar, but I get there a little early and there's a little Negro boy playing a piano. In rehearsal I listened to this kid playing and went to Hugo Haas who was directing the picture, and said, 'You got to be crazy. This kid is sensational. You're only giving him eight bars. You should let him play the whole song and revolve the picture around him.' The little boy's name was Johnny Mathis, and the name of the song was *It's Not for Me to Say*. That's the first thing he ever did."

Ric was chosen by his friend Frank Sinatra for a role in the 1958 release, *Some Came Running*. "The only reason was because Frank wanted somebody who knew something about playing cards and would look real doing it. I was on it for two or three days. That was a cute picture only because Sinatra decreed that we were not to start shooting at eight or nine o'clock in the morning, but at eleven o'clock. Then we would break for lunch and they'd have drinks. We broke for lunch and that was the end of shooting for the day," Ric laughed.

Ric mentioned some of the other films that he worked in. *The Ten Commandments* ("You'll never find me. I have a shawl over my head"), *Jet Pilot* ("The only film I did with Duke Wayne"), and *How The West Was Won* ("A very nice stunt man was on there, Red Morgan. That was such a foul up when they rolled the logs on the train and he got trapped under them"). He worked in numerous gangster films such as *White Heat* and *Kiss Me Goodbye* with James Cagney, *Desperate Hours* with Humphrey Bogart, as well as others like *Loan Shark*, *The Purple Gang*, *The Scarface Mob*, *St. Valentine's Day Massacre*, *Hoodlum Empire*, and *The Big Heat*.

Ric worked in *The Buccaneer*, which was directed by Anthony Quinn. Ric was told to wear some very high cowboy boots because the other heavies were all much taller, and when Quinn saw the prospective heavies, one of the first he picked was Ric. Chico Day was Quinn's assistant. "I knew Chico," Ric stated, "and he said to me, 'Every day that you come in, you come in an hour early and go to make-up and have them fix your ear to look like it has been cut open.' They paid awfully good money, and I think for the first eight weeks we never worked, but I came in every day and got an extra hundred dollars for the extra hour because they had to jerk around with my ear. I think I had three lines, but Tony Quinn made sure I stayed on that picture until the cows came home. Those are the guys I remember."

Ric's television credits included such shows as *Superman*, *Tales of Wells Fargo*, *Mr. & Mrs. North*, *Stories of the Century*, *Wagon Train*, *77 Sunset Strip*, *Have Gun-Will Travel*, *The Third Man*, *The Donna Reed Show*, *Batman*, *Zorro*, and *Mannix*. "I think I worked every show that Warner Brothers did," Ric commented. "I was also producer on a television series, *The Racers* with John Ashley."

Ric also served as executive producer on a couple of features, *Bucktown* with Fred Williamson, and *Seniors*, with Dennis Quaid. Stanley Shapiro, who wrote *Pillow Talk*, was one of the co-producers of the latter one.

Ric discussed a humorous experience that happened while working on an episode of *The Lone Ranger* which was shot on location in Sonora under the direction of Earl Bellamy. "I'm playing a priest in this one and I had gone someplace to recover a cross for a church. I told you that I would never be mistaken for a great rider of horses. This isn't a horse I'm on; it's a little mule. The camera is way back and you're supposed to see the priest on his donkey coming over the hill and eventually right to camera. Unbeknownst to me, they (meaning Earl Bellamy and the guys on camera) have it fixed so that they could hear the sound as I come over the hill. I can't move this damn mule, and I hit him and hit him with a switch, and he finally starts to move. Remember I'm playing a priest, and they're picking this up, and I'm cussing and swearing and using every four letter word you're not supposed to use. Well, this mule just stops right on top of the hill and I look down and everybody's breaking up laughing because they're all hearing me. That's what I remember about the *Lone Ranger*. I did a load of Westerns and I hated every horse I ever saw."

Ric worked with Lee Van Cleef in an episode of *Gunsmoke* in which they played a couple of heavies. "Lee was a good guy," Ric said. "My agent's partner, Sid Gold, was Lee's agent, and one Friday night he and I were going to go to Lee's house and play poker together. Sid said to me, 'I'm going to be a little late because I'm going to be at a party where some Italian director named Sergio Leone is at, and I'm going to see if I can get you and Lee a job over in Italy. When he came to the poker game he said you and Lee are going to go on a picture called *For a Few Dollars More*. But only Van Cleef went because I had a work conflict. Biggest mistake in my life because it made Lee a star."

Ric mentioned that the toughest fight scene he ever had was with Roger Moore in an episode of *Maverick*. "Don't ask me why they didn't have doubles, but they didn't. He did it and I did it. I knew a little about fight scenes because part of what I have not told you was that I had worked in New York for Mike Jacobs, the biggest fight promoter that ever lived. I sparred two rounds with a guy named Kid Gavalan in the gym where nobody would get hurt. But he was famous for what they called a bolo punch, which was really an upper cut. We were at the end of the second round with about twenty seconds to go, and I had done fairly well with him. Well, he hit me with a bolo punch and I must have been out for five minutes."

Ric worked in the final episode that Eric Fleming did on *Rawhide*. "We finished work the same time," Ric reflected. "He and I drove back from location in the stretch and we had a nice talk. He said he was planning on going to South America, and that's when he fell off the boat into the school of piranhas."

Ric was in a stage production of *The Clock*. Relating to his work in live theater, Ric said, "Everybody says that's the greatest. I don't think so. I was not enamored. I like the camera much better."

"Let me let you in on something about Ric that you should know," he told us. "That is I was in the business in front of the camera from 1949 to the last picture I did, which was *Nevada Smith* with Steve McQueen in 1965.

"When I went for the interview for *Nevada Smith*, it was with a very famous director, Henry Hathaway. I walked in, and so help me, he looked at me and said, 'You're Italian aren't you?' 'No,' I said. 'Don't tell me. I said you're Italian.' I looked at the old man and said, 'No, I'm Jewish.' He said, 'Bullshit!' I said, 'Have it your way, but I'm telling you, Mr. Hathaway.' Anyway, when we were on location at Bishop, they're setting up a scene. I'm standing next to a tree talking to Karl Malden, and Hathaway is up on a crane way up in the sky and he yells down, 'Hey dago!' I don't turn around. I know he's calling me. Karl said, 'Ric, the old man's calling you, you'd better...' and I said, 'tell the old man to go f--k himself. He knows why I'm not turning around.' Hathaway again yelled 'Hey dago!' and I turned around and said to him, 'Damn you,

you can send me home today, but I told you something in the office.' He got off the crane and started to walk toward me, and Malden said, 'Ric, for your own good, meet him.' So he walked over to me and said, 'You just keep your mouth shut and you listen to me. My grandfather was named Weil.' What this had to do with making *Nevada Smith* I'll never know. He said, 'Weil, that's Jewish. Damn it, you told me you were Jewish. I happen to like you, but you look like a dago and as far as I'm concerned that's my nickname for you.' He put his hand out and shook my hand and then said, 'Now go back and do what you're supposed to do.' When we finished *Nevada Smith* he gave me an autographed picture, 'To the only dago I really love, sincerely Hank.' That's why I love the business."

When Ric left the business, he and a friend from his university days became the owners of the third largest chain of theaters in America. "He was president of the chain and I was vice president," Ric told us. "Between the two of us maybe we could scrape together four dollars, but as we sat in Schwabs one day he said to me, 'Ric, I've got a chance to buy the ABC Theater Chain.' 'What are you going to buy it with?' I asked." He told Ric that he had a friend in Chicago who would give him a million and a half dollars. "Do you know what the Balaban and Katz theater chain was, Ric?" "No," Ric answered. "They were the biggest in Chicago and had eventually sold out to ABC, which was now looking to sell it." He explained that there was a wealthy family in Chicago that wanted to buy it for about fifty million dollars. "As I said, he and I would have trouble putting together fifty dollars," Ric told us. "But he said that they knew he had worked for ABC and knew the business and wanted him to head it. They said they could go to the bank in Chicago and borrow fifty million dollars just like that but needed a million and a half good faith money. My friend said, 'This guy I know will give the million and a half that I need in return for a piece of the action.' When the smoke cleared we bought it. I say we, I didn't put a nickel in. He bought it and became the president and I became the vice-president. I did that from 1975 through 1985."

Ric spoke of several of the people he was able to meet, work with, and become friends with. "Brod Crawford, his wife Kay, and his mother and father had a Thanksgiving dinner, and obviously since I lived with them I was there, and they invited a couple. The man came in with his wife and the evening was just wonderful. Then it was time for everyone to say good night. The man and his wife went to the door, and I looked at this man and couldn't believe I just had dinner with him. I said, 'Mr. Cagney, it's a pleasure to meet you.' He stopped me and said, 'I've been calling you Ric all night. The name is Jimmy.' I've never forgotten that. I must tell you, he was rather short in stature, but to me right then he was ten feet tall. I've worked with some wonderful, wonderful people. Good people. Gable, Brando, Bogart, Wayne. Name them, the legendary figures. All lovely people, but nobody ever stood ten feet tall like Jimmy Cagney did that night."

In summing up his feelings about his career and the motion picture business, Ric said, "I loved the business, every second of it, and if I could repeat it, I would. I have guys call me on the phone and say, 'Isn't it a shame, Ric, what's happening in the business? It's run by kids now.' So what? It's still the greatest business in the world. Sure, just like any other business in life there are some losers and they're going to make it miserable for other people, but by and large I think the people in this business are the greatest. Again, if I had to do it over I couldn't get there fast enough. I thoroughly enjoyed it. Life has been good to me. I worked for it, and now I know where my next cup of coffee is coming from."

Ric Roman passed away in Los Angeles, California, on August 11, 2000.

Film Credits: **1949**: White Heat; Frontier Marshal; Laramie; The Dalton Gang. **1950**: The Damned Don't Cry; Woman from Headquarters; Kiss Tomorrow Goodbye; Between Midnight and Dawn; Broken Arrow; Crooked River; DOA; Last of the Buccaneers; Stage to Tucson; Winchester 73; Wagonmaster; Young Man with a Horn. **1951**: Navy Bound; Mask of the Avenger; The Mob; South of Caliente; Slaughter Trail; The Lady Pays Off; Across the Wide Missouri; Vengeance Valley; Chicago Calling; The Last Outpost; Hurricane Island; Utah Wagon Train; The Hoodlum; Texas Lawman; Hills of Utah; The Racket; Spoilers of the Range. **1952**: Scandal Sheet; Harem Girl; Viva Zapata; Lone Star; Hoodlum Empire; Actors and Sin; Springfield Rifle; Kansas City Confidential; Apache War Smoke; Dead Man's Trail; Wyoming Roundup; Ma and Pa Kettle at the Fair; Laramie Mountain; Kansas Territory; Apache Country; Lawless Breed; Horizons West; Loan Shark; Night Raiders; The Savage; The Maverick; Wagon Team. **1953**: Last of The Comanches; Bandits of Corsica; Texas Bad Man; Scared Stiff; Shadows of Tombstone; The Big Heat; Slaves of Babylon; Son of Belle Starr; Appointment in Honduras. **1954**: Rails into Laramie; Crime Wave; Ma and Pa Kettle at Home; They Rode West; About Mrs. Leslie; River of No Return. **1955**: Underwater; Timberjack; New York Confidential; Wyoming Renegades; Ma and Pa Kettle at Waikiki; The Road to Denver; Wiretapper; Fort Yuma; I Cover the Underworld; Gang Busters; The Violent Men; Kiss Me Deadly; Shotgun; Outlaw Treasure; Apache Ambush; The Desperate Hours; At Gunpoint; The Far Country. **1956**: Terror at Midnight; When Gangland Strikes; The Black Whip; Mobs, Inc.; The Maverick Queen; The Killer is Loose; Thunder over Arizona; Omar Khayyam; Kentucky Rifle; The Ten Commandments. **1957**: Duel at Apache Wells; Lizzie; Gun Duel in Durango; Badlands of Montana; The Wayward Girls; Escape from San Quentin; Jet Pilot; Gunfight at the OK Corral; My Gun is Quick; Gun the Man Down; Up in Smoke. **1958**: King Creole; The Buccaneer; Murder by Contract; Crooked Circle; Quantrill's Raiders; Toughest Gun in Tombstone; Cattle Empire; Ride a Crooked Trail; Revolt in the Big House; Some Came Running. **1959**: Gunfight at Dodge City; Cry Tough; Inside the Mafia; Gunmen from Laredo; I, Mobster; The Scarface Mob (TV). **1960**: Cage of Evil; The Purple Gang. **1963**: Cattle King. **1964**: Cheyenne Autumn. **1966**: Nevada Smith. **1967**: St. Valentine's Day Massacre. **1968**: Five Card Stud. **1970**: Breakout (TV). **1971**: The Trackers (TV).

HENRY ROWLAND

Henry Rowland was born December 28, 1913 in Omaha, Nebraska. His father conducted the Omaha Symphony and his mother was a concert singer. "She sang a variety of songs of all the people," he said. "We used to have such beautiful, lovely songs that were melodic and had nice words like, 'Our love affair turned out to be just another unfinished symphony.' That's a nice piece of sentiment."

When people ask Henry how he got into acting he tells them, "Well, it just never had occurred to me that there was anything other than that which I wanted to do." He started out doing musical comedy and light opera, the first thing he did in California being Victor Herbert's *Sweethearts* at Pasadena Junior College. From there he went to the Pasadena Playhouse in 1934.

Henry worked in many radio shows, including *Lux Theater*. "I had recorded *Lifeboat* with Tallulah Bankhead," Henry reflected. "I played the U-Boat Commander and Jeff Chandler did the John Hodiak part. Chandler was a good actor and did a great deal on radio." Henry continued working on radio later in his career in such shows as *Roy Rogers*.

His first film was a bit in 1935's Boris Karloff horror film, *The Black Room*, and didn't work in another film until 1939, when he began to be cast as German soldiers. The first one was when he was cast as a junior officer in the German Navy in MGM's *Thunder Afloat*. He appeared in 20th Century Fox's *The Moon is Down*, based on the Steinbeck novel about the Nazi invasion of Norway, with Cedric Hardwicke; *Edge of Darkness* for Warner Brothers, starring Ann Sheridan and Errol Flynn; *Escape*, a pre-World War II drama centering on a German concentration camp, starring Robert Taylor and Conrad Veidt. "These were all marvelous pictures; big pictures," Henry noted. "I did *Casablanca* in which I played Conrad Veidt's aide-de-camp; I led them in the singing when we were in Rick's Cafe. It wasn't a tremendous part, but the point was that you were there. It was a tremendous picture and it will always be something to remember. I met Ingrid Bergman, who at that time was just getting started in this country, and I was able to speak with her both in English and German flawlessly. In those days people had abilities; they could do a number of things – You had to be able to dance, fence, and ride. You had to know how to do all of these different things; it was all a part of your education."

In 1943 Henry obtained a role in the feature *Mountain Fighters*, and spent a month on location seventeen miles outside of Leadville, Colorado, at an altitude between nine and twelve thousand feet above sea level. His next project in line was that of another German soldier in *Sahara*, directed by Alexander Korda and starring Humphrey Bogart. Henry had just returned home after completing *Mountain Fighters* when fifteen minutes later the phone rang. Henry answered and the voice at the other end said, "You know you have a commitment with us to do *Sahara*, so we'll send a car and pick you up at 9:15." He quickly threw everything out of his bag and repacked. The car arrived and they drove Henry out to location at Brawley, California, which is about two hundred and fifty feet below sea level. "Here I had been skiing at Tennessee Pass at about thirteen thousand feet, about the highest point in the Continental Divide, and now I come down to do this film with Bogart and it was a tough location. It was hotter than the hinges of hell out there, down by the Salton Sea. This was the same area which Patton had used to practice with his tanks." Henry had to wear a beard stuck on by spirit gum every day and have sand blown into it. After a day's shooting on that location there wasn't a lot to do, so Henry usually would kick back with Bogart and Pat O'Malley for a game of darts.

"Well anyway," Henry added, "I had just come down from up in the mountains so I was fresh, but they had been shooting out on the desert for several weeks around the well. We got to a particular part and someone said, 'We don't know what to do here.' Without thinking I said, 'Well, why don't you just…' Evidently that wasn't one of Korda's better days and he said, 'We don't need any of your advice.' I thought, 'I really put my foot into it now.' Bogart said to Korda, 'The hell you don't! You already used some of us which saved you I don't know how much, and as far as I'm concerned you can sit here till snow flies.' And he got up and walked away. I thought that this was no time to sit here so I got up and quietly left. I'm red as a beet because I'm embarrassed. I'm walking along and pretty soon I hear, 'Psst! Pssst!' I looked around and here's Bogart in back of the well; they can't see him, but I can from the other side. So I stroll over in back of the place and he says, 'How am I doing kid?' So that's my memory of Bogart. As far as I'm concerned he was always a sweetheart."

Henry entered the Service during World War II and toured with *Winged Victory* with the Air Corps. When he was doing the show in New York, Humphrey Bogart came backstage once and talked with him for a while. "That's the last time I had a chance to talk with him," noted Henry. After New York, the *Winged Victory* troupe toured the country, including a stop at Shepard Field in Wichita Falls, Texas. Henry explained the conditions here as "There was nothing between you and the North Pole but a barbed wire fence. This was summertime and if you had a little previous rain you could be standing in mud and the dust would still be blowing." While there, Henry met Bill Karnes, who was a writer and later a director. After getting out of the service Henry acted in the film version of *Winged Victory* and later worked in some episodes of the television series *Dangerous Assignment*, with Bill Karnes directing.

"When we came home after the war there were an awful lot of changes," Henry explained. "There was a time before we had the five day work week that we would work Saturdays too. I remember a director saying when we got the five day work week, 'Sure, five day and night week.' We were still doing the same amount of work, but in five days instead of six – except we were working day and night. It was overtime, but we still had just as much to cover and shoot. How are we going to progress a story? You had to tell it, had to shoot it; and unless it's on film, where is it? You could get away with some of it by having a camera on three of us sitting; telling a certain amount of story through conversation and then switching to the outdoors. They used to do that a lot in serials. You could save an awful lot of time through exposition, but how much of this are you going to get away with in a motion picture? I remember the six days. You'd do all the exteriors the first couple of days of the week; the last couple of days you'd do all the dialogue in the interiors. I remember one Saturday doing the *Kit Carson* TV show with Bill Williams and Don Diamond. Bill was really driving – it was the end of the day and Bill said, 'See, just as I told you. Smur fugglers.' Don looked at him and said, 'Smur fugglers?' The set blows up and it takes five or ten minutes to calm down and finally got out, 'Fur smugglers.' You didn't care at this point of the game. These are cockeyed little things and if it wasn't for these safety breaks at times….I mean you're getting into seven or eight o'clock at night, and when you'd get through you'd go across the street to O'Brien's, have a quick drink, sit down, have a baked potato and a steak, then go home and, after relaxing a bit, go to bed. That one night you wouldn't pick up a script, but you would on Sunday because you'd have something on Monday to do. In those days we'd shoot three in a week. You'd come riding off a thing and they'd have racks of clothes sitting out there in the open. Bobby Rodriguez, the wardrobe man, would say, 'What is it?' and I'd say, 'Don't, I'll get it. If I stop to tell you I'll forget what I'm doing.' I'd dismount and go over to my section of the particular rack, which was made out of pipe, and take off the costume I had and hang it on a section; get the stuff I needed for the next particular show, make the change of dress, handkerchief and hat, and go in and shoot this for scene so and so in episode so and so."

During this busy post-war period Henry was also appearing in a number of A-films, such as *13 Rue Madeleine*, which featured James Cagney; *Golden Earrings* starring Ray Milland and Marlene Dietrich; *Rogues Regiment* with Dick Powell, Stephen McNally and Vincent Price. In this film Powell joins the Foreign Legion and goes to Southeast Asia to track down a sadistic Nazi officer who is in hiding. Henry played a former Nazi who is now a member of the Foreign Legion; *The Searching Wind*, based on Lillian Hellman's play, and starring Sylvia Sidney and Robert Young.

When Henry had attended Omaha High School one of his classmates was Dorothy McGuire, and years later, in 1955, he found himself working with her and Gary Cooper in *Friendly Persuasion*. "That was a picture that took insight and time, and it got back to what Frank Capra always had at his command, and always insisted on: You got to have control of your medium; you got to have control of your product; you got to be the boss, because if there are too many fingers in the situation it dilutes the product to such an extent that it just doesn't function. He insisted that they leave him alone, and that's important because I've been on a number of films that started out going great – like a locomotive going along at a pretty good clip – but you can always tell when sand starts blowing in and they start putting the brakes on. If only they had let it run just a little bit more and kept their hands off the reins it could have been a great picture." In the case of *Friendly Persuasion*, they left the director alone and it has become a great classic.

Henry performed three roles in a stage production titled *Periphery*, in which he portrayed a waiter, an old shoemaker, and a watchman. "The funny thing was," he commented, "was that I got a great notice on the part of the watchman and it was all pantomime. About all the good actors that I have known throughout the years, starting with Lon Chaney whom I had a tremendous respect for and always thought he was the greatest – and this goes back to the 20s when I was just a kid seeing this man. *The Unholy Three* and *The Man who Laughed*, which he did without hands where he was threading needles with his feet, but he had marvelous eyes and I didn't understand until much later that his parents were deaf mutes. These people almost always have very expressive faces, and he may have talked a great deal to them with expression. But all the good actors you can think of have great eyes – Ian Keith and Barrymore. That's one thing I've always loved about pictures, and still do: you can photograph thought. And if someone isn't on the ball, you can pick that up too."

Speaking on the techniques of film acting, Henry stated, "A motion picture is merely one frame after another photographed and hung together. Each one has to be individually framed, lighted and shot – and you got to sustain in between moves, meaning as you move from one room to another and this sort of thing, you got to retain the same tension, the same feeling, the same intensity when you pick it up again. Some have this ability to do it beautifully and others will never get it in a thousand years. The main thing is to know your ability, how to use it, and best of all to know when to get off. You have to be in the scene, that's one of the things that is paramount. If you're in a scene, you got to be in it all the way; you got to be watching, listening, and observing. One of the greatest exponents of that was Spencer Tracy. He was always keeping his eyes on you, and anybody that started fooling around pretty soon would quit it because Tracy would be watching. And if this was one of the yo-yo's from the method school and they'd start picking their nose or scratching their ass he'd better decide to lay off of it, because the camera would be on Mr. Tracy and not on our busy little friend."

In stating his feelings on the difference between the films of today from those of yesterday, Henry made this comment. "Jackie Gleason once said, 'I was in New York on the corner of one of the main streets observing what was going on and I turned around, looked down the street and saw a theater and thought I'd kill an hour or two and catch a picture. So I laid down my four dollars, went in and sat down, and the picture came on and here I was watching what I had been watching down on the corner of 42nd Street and Broadway.' He said, 'The hell with that! I don't have to go to a theater to see that; that's not a picture.' We know how it is; nobody has to show us. This corny bit of 'show it as it is boy,' is so ridiculous that it doesn't really bear any comment. Our main reason for a theater in the first place was for at least a couple of hours we could take you out of this veil of tears and transport you to another place, another time and vestige of a dream. You can sit back and say, 'Isn't that lovely, isn't that beautiful, and the music…' You came out of the place humming and repeating some of the words. You haven't got that today; you'd have to do it with a machine gun if you came out of the place. That's ridiculous! But that was the idea. Today they say, 'That isn't the way it is.' But wouldn't it have been nice if it was. When you take away man's opportunity to dream, that's when he starts to die because you cut off any enticement that there is for sticking around. As long as he's got a dream – as long as he can do that he can lick anything. But if you stop that you don't have a thing. That's the sad part. They used to call this 'The Dream Factory,' and in a sense it was. That was the idea. And to make you laugh – Oh, the comedy. You had the short subject, a comedy and the feature. Like Laurel and Hardy, those wonderful, wonderful guys, and the things they'd get you into. The funny thing was that these were slices of life enlarged, because we've all known someone, somewhere, that were like these two characters who were always getting into something or another. You could write a book from now until the end of time and never cover all the numerous talented people that have given to this medium."

In concluding, Henry said, "When asked what my favorite role has been I say there have been a lot of good ones, but the best is yet to come. I've always left the door open because I always think, 'No, there's got to be another one.' When I first came in as a character actor in '39 I was told by a director friend, 'Henry, the things you do, you're in for lots of heartache because you're years ahead of yourself as a character actor.' Now that I have the years to do it they're doing everything with kids."

Henry Rowland died on April 26, 1984 in Northridge, California.

Film Credits: 1935: The Black Room. **1939:** Thunder Afloat. **1940:** Safari; Escape; Foreign Correspondent. **1941:** A Yank in the RAF; International Squadron; Underground. **1942:** Berlin Correspondent; The Pied Piper; Casablanca; Reunion in France; Desperate Journey; Ship Ahoy; Pacific Rendezvous; Dangerously They Live; Captains of the Clouds;

Phantom Plainsman. **1943:** The Moon is Blue; First Comes Courage; Appointment in Berlin; The Moon is Down; The Desert Song; Paris After Dark; The Mountain Fighters; Sahara; Edge of Darkness. **1944:** Winged Victory; Resisting Enemy Interrogation. **1946:** Rendezvous 24; 13 Rue Madeleine; Gallant Journey; Dangerous Millions; The Searching Wind. **1947:** Golden Earrings. **1948:** Rogues Regiment; I, Jane Doe; To the Victor. **1949:** Port of New York; Battleground. **1950:** Asphalt Jungle; King Solomon's Mines; Bells of Coronado; The Showdown. **1951:** Ten Tall Men; The House on Telegraph Hill; Sealed Cargo. **1952:** Zombies of the Stratosphere; Wagon Team; Operation Secret; Wyoming Roundup. **1953:** All the Brothers Were Valiant; Jungle Drums of Africa; El Alamein; Gun Fury; Captain John Smith and Pocahontas; Vigilante Terror; Rebel City; Topeka; A Perilous Journey; Prince of Pirates. **1954:** The Gambler from Natchez; Ring of Fear; Two Guns and a Badge; Return to Treasure Island; The Forty-Niners. **1955:** Kiss of Fire; Wyoming Renegades; Illegal; The Spoilers; The Man from Bitter Ridge; The Fast and the Furious. **1956:** Friendly Persuasion; Attack; Women of Pitcairn Island; Uranium Boom; Hot Shots. **1957:** Hell on Devil's Island; Ain't No Time For Glory (TV); Looking for Danger; The Girl in the Kremlin; Kelly and Me; The Big Land; Chicago Confidential; Wolf Larsen; Gun Duel in Durango; Shootout at Medicine Bend. **1958:** The Young Lions; The Left Handed Gun; Street of Darkness; International General. **1959:** Cast a Long Shadow. **1960:** Toby Tyler. **1962:** The Four Horsemen of the Apocalypse. **1963:** What a Way to Go. **1964:** 36 Hours. **1965:** Morituri. **1967:** Hurry Sundown. **1968:** Wicked Dreams of Paula Schultz; In Enemy Country. **1970:** Beyond the Valley of the Dolls. **1971:** The Seven Minutes; Diamonds Are Forever. **1975:** Supervixens. **1976:** The Last Tycoon. **1979:** Beneath the Valley of the Supervixens; The Frisco Kid.

HERBERT RUDLEY

"Well, going back a long long way, I was born in Philadelphia, Pennsylvania, on March 22, 1910, and went to school there," Herbert told us. He started Temple University to take pre-law, but by that time he had gotten interested in the theatre, being active in the little theatre group. His instructor was a former actor and had noticed an announcement that Eva LeGallienne was having auditions for her studio group. "She ran the only classical repertoire style theatre in the country," Rudley commented. His instructor suggested that he prepare something and go out and audition, "which I found kind of exciting. I wrote and asked for an interview and received a response. A date was set and I cut school. In the meantime I prepared a soliloquy from Shakespeare, went up and met Miss LeGallienne and was terribly impressed with her, naturally, and then auditioned."

When his audition was over, she had him come down and sit in the theatre next to her and said a very interesting thing to him: "You know, Mr. Rudley, I envy you." He replied, "For what?" She answered, "Because you have an emotional abandon which I have never had in my life. I have always been a cerebral, intellectual actor and I have always yearned to have your kind of emotion, just let it go, which I will never have. So I think you're starting with something good. I think we would like to have you in the studio." Then Herbert said, "I'm very flattered Miss LeGallienne, but I have a problem. I have no money. The money that I earned in the summertime I have already allocated to be paid to Temple University, so I'm broke. I don't have the money to pay tuition." She concluded the interview by saying, "We'll see if we can do anything about that. I'll be in touch with you."

Rudley went home and about a week later he got notification that he had been accepted for her studio with a scholarship. "Well of course I was excited," he told us. "I still had a number of economic problems because I had to be able to live in New York on my own." He scraped together enough money that he thought could hold him through for a while and said good-bye to his family, who were very opposed to the idea. "They wanted me to be a doctor or lawyer, the usual background of the middle class. I came to New York and the studio was a fascinating experience. We had everything: Speech, ballet, fencing; you spent practically twenty-four hours at the theatre because in the daytime you had all of your classes and then you'd watch rehearsals, just by osmosis absorb, which is a very good way to learn. Then you were used as extras in many of the shows. So you were just going all day and all night. But anyway, it was a very exhilarating and exciting period.

"Unfortunately, having very little money to exist on, I began to suffer from malnutrition," he laughed. Rudley was not alone, for there were others in the same financial bind as he was. "You used to go into the cafeterias and they would have these little tables with condiments, like green peppers, relish, red peppers, beets and things. If you bought whatever it was you were buying, you would just help yourself to these condiments," he continued. "We would go in and order a cup of coffee and a roll and then go over and help ourselves three or four times to the condiments table; and that's the way we existed."

After three months of work there, he was taken into the permanent company and got his first paycheck of twenty-five dollars a week. He was given roles that were appropriate for his age and stayed at the Civic with LeGallienne for three years, appearing in plays ranging from *Peter Pan* to Chekhov's *The Cherry Orchard* and plays by France's greatest playwright, Moliere. He graduated from small parts into the young juvenile league, and in course of that did his first Pulitzer Prize play, *Allison's House* by Susan Glasville.

During the summer, Herbert would get a job with the Swarthmore's Talker Circuit, which was a one night touring company performing innocuous little family plays. "When I was doing these things, which many of which were beyond my experience, I began to realize that I was having a tremendous amount of fun, as opposed to what I began to recognize was a sense of anxiety and caution, almost apprehension, once the repertoire season got under way. When I would come back from the summer, I wouldn't have it; I'd feel free. Then as the season progressed, I would become more and more cautious and reserved in my approach to roles and performances. It began to trouble me. I didn't realize it the first year and the second year I became aware of it, but I wasn't able to analyze it; it's a slow study. Anyhow, in the third year it finally came to me that I wanted so much to please this marvelous woman, Eva LeGallienne." He was always conscious of her, even if she weren't in the play or in the scenes, being offstage watching, analyzing, criticizing, which she wasn't doing. "She was delighted with my work, but I couldn't break the cord between pupil / teacher and performer / performer; you know, professional / professional," Herbert told us. "It was just because she was so important to me." Finally with fear and trembling, he went to her and explained the situation. He said, "I don't know what to do, Eva, because I love you and want to be here and maybe you can help me." LaGallienne told him, "Herbert, you're a very, very, almost hypersensitive creative person and you know, of course, that nothing like that is in my mind." "Yes I know, but I can't get it out of my mind," he said to her. "I know, and that's why I think the time has come for you to move on," she responded. "Go up to Broadway, get yourself an agent. If you ever get over this and you want to come back, there will always be a place for you."

So Herbert left reluctantly. "It's kind of like when the time comes, if you're in analysis, for you to leave your analyst and you feel, 'I don't know if I can make it on my own and I need help,' explained Herbert. He obtained the juvenile lead in the Elmer Rice play, *We The People*. "I got the lead just simply by virtue of going to agents, and an agent recommended me and I went in to read for Mr. Rice," he continued. "He gave me the role, which was a very fortunate baptism, but the play was about the Depression and the people who made up the audience were living through the Depression, so though it got very fine critical response the box office was somewhat lacking and we only ran six weeks."

During one of the performances of *We the People*, a man with a cigar and wearing a derby hat came backstage. "He was a real caricature," Rudley told us. "He looked to me like a gangster." He came to Rudley and asked, "Herb Rudley?" "Yeah." "I'm Lee Stewart. I run the casting department at Warner Brothers short subjects out in Brooklyn." Not being impressed with this being theatre oriented and motion pictures not meaning a thing to Rudley, he responded with, 'Oh, nice to meet you.' Stewart said, "You're a hell of an actor, kid, and anytime you're out of a job and need some work, you come out and see me." "Thank you a lot, Mr. Stewart," Herbert replied. "I appreciate your interest," and soon forgot about it.

"At one time it was almost impossible to get a job; there were no jobs. The actors were on relief, as I went eventually. We were working for the Equity Dinner Club, which meant you waited on tables for those few fortunate actors who were working, and by virtue of that you got one meal a day. So everybody ended up with ulcers. You, because of feeling embarrassed, and the poor bastards who were able to work feeling guilty that they were working and you weren't. It was a miserable time." In the Depression, one of the cardinal things that was entirely different from any other phase in Herbert's history was that he found there was no individual enemy. "Your enemy was amorphous; it was the whole world, you see; your whole society. There was no one to take out your frustrations on, except yourself," he explained. One winter evening in a little hotel room, he suddenly remembered Lee Stewart, the casting director for short subjects at Warner Brothers. The following morning he got together a syndicate to contribute ten cents: two cents from one person, a penny from another, one cent himself, as no one had any money to speak of. He did this so he could take the subway ride out to Brooklyn. When he got there Stewart greeted him, "Hi kid. Oh, glad to see you. What do you want, a job?" Rudley answered, "Yes sir, I could certainly use a job." "Well, let's see. What are we doing this week? Oh kid, this is a musical. I don't want to waste you on a musical," Stewart responded. Herbert felt like saying, "Waste me, waste me." Stewart told him to come back and see him on Thursday.

"To make a long story short," Herbert told us, "he had me coming back twice a week or sometimes three times a week for about two and a half months. Each time I would have to refinance the trip and my backers were becoming very dubious about getting a return on their investment, which I had promised them a considerable profit on." Out of this frustration, Stewart now became personalized as the enemy, someone that Rudley could vent his spleen on. "I sat down and wrote him a letter, the essence of which was that he had promised me a job. I had not sought work from him and based on his promise I had gone into debt to a group of people who I must repay. The only way I could repay them was if he would fulfill his promise and I felt he had a moral obligation to do so. I signed the letter and sent it off, never thinking to hear from him, but I had vented my own pent up emotions."

About a week later, Stewart called on the phone. He didn't mention the letter, but he said, "Herb, I've been going over all your credits and I see that you play the piano and sing a little. Do you?" "Oh yeah," Herbert answered, feeling very frightened about saying that. Stewart then said, "Come on out. I've got a great part for you." Rudley rounded up another ten cents and went out to see him. Stewart said, "I'll tell you what this is. This is an exterior scene that we're playing against a flat drop. People are waiting in a bread line. There's a big drum with sandwiches on it and you're waiting in that line for a handout, and you're a young composer. There's a broken down, dilapidated piano there, and while everybody's waiting you sit down and play *We're In The Money*. Do you think you can do it?" "Yes sir, Mr. Stewart." "Okay, you got it." Stewart gave Rudley a contract. About the contract, Herbert told us, "I'd never seen one of these before. By instinct my eye immediately went to the price for the show and it was a hundred and fifty dollars. I thought, 'My God, that's a fortune,' and I signed it with a shaky hand." Stewart told him, "Now kid, you got plenty of time. You got a week before we do this, so get hold of the music and get ready for it. We'll give you a call a couple of days in advance."

Herbert now had a real problem because technically what he had written in the credits was true, he did play the piano and he did sing a little bit, but he had been taught by his brother who was a classicist. "He had taught me and I had been brought up to play only classical music," he mentioned. "He would keep me on one piece, like the Beethoven Sonata, for a year until I was playing it to his perfection, or at least as much as he thought I could do with it, and so I became progressively a poorer and poorer reader of music because you'd memorize it as a gig." Within a week to ten days he would memorize the piece and wouldn't read the music after that, and he would be doing that for a year. The next time he had to start fresh on a piece of music it became almost impossible for him to read. Finally, when he got to be thirteen he gave up the piano, telling his brother why, and he never played again. Herbert's brother was in New York, so he got hold of him and explained the problem he was now faced with. "He had me meet him in a Sherman's music publishing company, got a copy of the song, took me into one of those little cubicles and about three hours later he went screaming out into the night," he laughed. "I had a week's time to learn to play and sing this."

Having no piano of his own, he had to use friends who had pianos, and "I lost a lot of friends doing that." He finally reached the point where, although he was not comfortable with it, he felt he could get through it. The night before, as a result of all the anxiety, he came down with a cold and had no voice. All his backers were plying him with liquor, hot tea and lemon, lozenges and sprays. He wouldn't test his voice until he got there because if there was only a little bit left he didn't want to use it up. "I got there absolutely terrified," Herbert reflected. "There was an assistant director there who said, 'All right kids, everybody upstairs and get out of your own clothes and get into wardrobe.' So they took us up into wardrobe and we took off our rags and put on their rags and we came down looking very much the same as we did before. Then he lined us up and the director came out and said, 'All right, get in line; everybody in line. Now who's the kid at the piano?' I said, 'I am sir.' 'All right, sit down,' he said. So I took out the sheet music and laid it up on the stand. He said, 'What the hell's that?' And suddenly it occurred to me that a composer doesn't have to read music, he plays by ear, and I saw that hundred and fifty dollars just flying out the window. I said, 'Sir, forgive me, this is terribly important. I really can play, but I have to have the music because I can't play by ear. I'm not a director, but couldn't you put the camera some place where you could see me but not see the music?' He said, 'I don't think you could play a note you phony bastard!' and I said, 'Oh yeah, I can. Please just give me a chance.' He said, 'All right, let me hear you.' So I sat down and I was perspiring by this time. I stalled for time by straightening out the music. It sticks to my fingers and falls to the floor; I pick it up and straighten it out, and I look at the sheet music and it's a blur. I can't see anything. I thought, 'Oh God, just remember the first chord; what's the first chord? You get the first chord and it will come back to me.' I remember the first chord and I go to play and it's a dummy piano; all I have to do is mime. It took about five minutes and the scene was shot and I went home, got my check and collapsed. The interesting thing is that nobody was being a heavy. The casting director was doing me a favor, a big favor, but I couldn't appreciate it after going through all that."

Then things got better. The WPA was formed and he got a job in the theatre section of WPA and stayed with that for a couple of years. Then the Depression started to lift and Herbert got back into the theatre again. "I did any number of plays. Some of them were failures, some of them good," he stated. Among them was *The World We Make*, which featured him in the male lead opposite Margo, and he got an award from an organization for the best performance of the year. "I got very good reviews and it was a wonderful experience," he expressed. Rudley played MacDuff in the Anderson / Evans *Macbeth* for a year, both in New York and on the road. His second Pulitzer Prize play in which he appeared was *Abe Lincoln in Illinois*. He also came out to California and appeared in the movie version of that play. Herbert replaced Paul Lukas in *Watch On The Rhine*, which he says was a wonderful experience. He appeared in two plays for Max Reinhardt, one which was a pageant about the

Jewish history. The other was an Irwin Shaw play, which was the last play Reinhardt directed before he died, called *Sons and Soldiers*. It featured Gregory Peck playing the son of Herbert Rudley and Geraldine Fitzgerald. (Almost twenty years later, Herb was again to work with Peck in the Western feature, *The Bravados*). Other productions included *Brother Rat* and *Three Penny Opera*.

Then the conscription had started and Herbert received a 1-A, so he expected to be called up for service. "So I decided before going in, to come out to the coast and have a combined vacation and an attempt to find some work because I was married and had a one and a half year old son by that time," he mentioned. He came out and made the usual round of the agents that other people had recommended to him from back east. He found one whom he liked very much, George Chasin, who became a very big agent. "He was a wonderful guy and was one of the most unusual for an agent because he was completely honest; no pie-in-the-sky stuff," he told us. The first interview he sent Herbert on was for the Gershwin story, *Rhapsody In Blue*, and Herbert got the part of Ira. "It was my first official Hollywood job. The other, *Abe Lincoln In Illinois*, was not really related to the industry. That was my introduction to pictures."

He was very active during the war years; he did thirty-five films. One of them was *A Walk In The Sun*, which was one of his favorites. "I did a picture with Fred Zimmerman, it was his first direction of a feature film, called *The Seventh Cross* with Spencer Tracy, a wonderful guy to work with," Rudley stated. Other pictures included *Marriage Is a Private Affair* at MGM, *The Master Race* for RKO, *Brewster's Millions* and *Hollow Triumph*. Herb told us, "When I signed for *Rhapsody in Blue* I wasn't particularly crazy about the role because it was the nice guy with his hand on his brother's shoulder, reinforcing him and I didn't think it had any great meaning in itself. My contract was on a free-lance basis and Warner Brothers wanted me to do the picture, but sign on a seven year option that they could pick up. I didn't want to be typed in that kind of role, so in talking it over with my agent we decided if they want me badly enough we would not reduce the asking salary; they would have to guarantee me the free-lance salary to start with and then raise it up. Usually it works the other way around. If you were getting fifteen hundred, they would try to sign you for five hundred or seven fifty on a seven year deal, so we turned down the option. In retrospect, I think it probably was a mistake because at that time there was still the whole studio support behind the people they had who were under contract. If you were there and under contract, you would be used for parts because they were paying you anyway. So I would have had a much steadier exposure and a great deal more promotion. However, that was the way I decided to go and there wasn't nothing you could do about it afterwards."

He said that working on *Joan of Arc* was a great experience. "That was with Ingrid Bergman," Herb commented. "I fell madly in love with her, like everybody did. It was not a successful picture, but it was a wonderful experience working with her.

"Then I hit a period which I couldn't understand because I had never went more than three weeks without having a couple of interviews and, generally speaking, I would get one of the parts that I was up for during that period of time." He said that he suddenly woke up one morning during this period and realized that two months had gone by and he hadn't had a call from his agent about an interview for another job. He called his agent and asked, "Hey, what's happening?" "What do you mean," Chasin asked. "Well, it's been two months and you haven't sent me out on an interview." Chasin replied, "Herb, this happens to everybody. You go through cycles." "Have I done something," Rudley asked. "Have I alienated somebody? Has word spread around town that I'm a bad cookie, you know, that I drink or something?" "No, no, everybody loves you," Chasin answered. "You've been used more than once in all the studios and they wouldn't be calling you back if they had any problems about you." Herbert said that he just didn't understand, and Chasin replied, "Herb, that's the business. You've got to understand it and not beat yourself." Rudley told us that this went on and on, and finally Chasin said that perhaps a change of agent would do him good. "Sometimes just that physical thing of making a change, having another face representing you can make the difference," George told him. Herbert said that Chasin was very gracious and told him, "There's something in the wind, that if it works out, don't sign a contract for any length of time."

Rudley signed with another big agency, the Jaffe Agency, and absolutely nothing happened. "I was going to be another Spencer Tracy according to Mr. Jaffe," Herb related. "He was going to handle me personally. It was the whole b.s. After the first time of seeing him and signing the contract, I don't think I ever saw him in six months; never spoke to him either." George Chasin called Herb up and asked him if he was free to leave his contract. He answered, "Yeah," and Chasin replied, "Well come in. I want to talk to you."

Rudley told us, "George had been offered the job at Universal of heading up the free-lance department and said, 'You're the only person I want to take with me if you'll come. Without my being there, that would not be the place for you,' because they have a different method. They sign one person to one or two studios, another person to a couple of studios. So unless everybody cares about you or you're very important, you're not going to be sent up often enough and you're playing percentages in this business anyway, like shooting crap. So I went over with him because he said he could protect me since he would be heading the free-lance. Well, they double-crossed him and after about six months they put him back into being one of those people who only services a couple of studios. So he called me in and said, 'Herb, I don't think this is the place for you anymore,' and he explained. I left and got another agent. By the way, I've always had difficulty changing agents because, again, I'm one of those idiotic people. I suppose from a psychological point of view, the agent becomes kind of a surrogate father and how do you tell your father that you didn't love him anymore? So whenever I had to change an agent, it's always been after great distress on my part. I eventually get the courage and say, 'Hey, it's not working. Let's call it a day.'"

During this very slack period, Herb discovered his interest in writing. "I didn't have any creative outlet; you can't just sit in your home or studio and act for yourself," he said, "so I went into writing to give me a creative outlet." During that period he wrote a play with the woman who was then his wife. It was the first black play that dealt with the problems of the African Americans, not from the point of view from the underprivileged but the central character was the attorney for the NAACP, his wife was a college graduate and they had a seven year old son. They were upper class for the Negro representation. When the play was finished he sent it to Herman Schumland, who read the play and raved about it. He said, "However Herb, I just broke my heart last season doing a play about the Negro and I just can't touch another experience like that. But I think the play is producible and I think you should come back and get it done." So they went back to New York and decided to try and get an independent production to raise the money. They would have readings in their home and Herbert would direct the play. "In starting the preliminary probing for casting, I thought of Josh White because I wanted someone who had the charisma and was very personable as a male," he told us. "He had a son Donny who was perfect for this role, and the idea of having actual father and son play father and son became very intriguing. I was a little dubious about Josh's acting ability because as a folk singer he had never done anything like that, but I worked with him for about a month prior and I saw that there was enough evidence to get a performance out of him. And the kid, Donny, was absolutely marvelous. Prior to our settling on him, he said, 'You know, Eleanor Roosevelt is Donny's godmother and she is very careful about what happens to Donny. I couldn't have Donny do this unless I got Mrs. Roosevelt's approval.' I said, 'Fine, I'll send a script to Mrs. Roosevelt.' 'No!' was her reply. I invited her to one of the readings. She at that time was at the United Nations, and she came down for the scheduled reading. Of course, she was the first one there, still munching a sandwich because she didn't have time to stop for dinner and she was absolutely marvelous. What a magnificent woman, in my opinion.

"We had about twenty people there," Herbert continued, "and she stayed after everyone had gone. She said, 'Mr. Rudley, I think it's a marvelous play. It should be done. I'm very concerned about Donny playing this because as of this time, to my knowledge, he has not experienced prejudice and I'm afraid of what this play might do to him emotionally.' I said, 'Mrs. Roosevelt, I don't want to disagree with you, but I think you should take something else under consideration. I have a child; I know children. And this in no way would be dangerous psychologically for Donny because he knows it's play acting and he knows it's make believe. If anything, it will give him an experience of strength rather than a destructive experience.' She said, 'That's an interesting point I haven't thought about. Let me consider it some more and I'll let you know.'"

About ten days later he got a letter from Mrs. Roosevelt in two sections. The first being purely personal in which she said that she had thought about what he had said about Donny and prejudice, and came to agree with him and therefore gave her consent for the boy to appear in the play. The second portion of the communication was a letter in which she told him what she thought about the play, both from a sociological point of view and from a dramatic point of view. "It was a long glowing letter," Herbert continued. "I wrote back and thanked her for the letter and said, 'I've talked to our publicity man and I'm just wondering, if it be possible, would you give us permission to allow us to use that letter in our pre-production publicity.' She gave her permission, saying 'Why do you suppose I wrote the letter.'"

They opened the play out of town and it received very good reviews. "We still needed more work but we didn't have enough money to stay out of town," Herb related. "We were only out of town for two weeks. We opened the show and three quarters of the critics spent more of their time criticizing Mrs. Roosevelt for daring to invade their sacred area of reviewing a play prior to its production. They resented her intrusions. So actually, her marvelous gesture did not help us and we got luke warm reviews; some very interesting aspects of reviews, some not so good. Unfortunately, we didn't have the capital to keep going and build an audience, which was possible at that time; at that time in the theatre you could do that, use that maneuver. Today, you're either a hit or a flop because it's too expensive to keep going. We didn't have the money in any event, so we had to close the play; but it was a fascinating experience."

While he was back in New York, Herbert did some writing for television, doing a number of adaptations for various dramatic shows. Then he got an offer to come back to the west coast to appear in *The Silver Chalice*, which he did and he stayed out on the coast.

Prior to going out to New York, Rudley started a theatre with Keenan Wynn called The Players Theatre, which he was the director of. "That, again, was before the onslaught of little theatre. We were not a little theatre; we were an Equity theatre," he stated. "Our program was to do a play every four weeks, but only rehearse two weeks like a stock company. I got permission from Equity to waive that clause so we could do it that way. We had a very interesting season, great reviews, but again we were under financed. We made money on the least likely play and lost on the ones that I thought we'd make money on. Example: *On Borrowed Time*. Well, that was one of the plays I happened to love and I decided to do that with off-beat casting, casting Boris Karloff as Gramps. Our theatre at that time had a purpose unlike most of the theatres today. I tried to combine using the commercial aspect using a recognizable Hollywood star in each production, but at least two people in the company would have to be people who either had been typed in certain roles and wanted to get out of that typing (the theatre would give them the opportunity to play a role and be seen by the motion picture industry away from the way they saw them and utilized them), or a beginner who had vast potential and introduced the beginner; so there was a combination of the commercial and experimental theatre. We had a fantastic cast for *On Borrowed Time*, including Margaret Hamilton. It was so well done that the Theatre Guild came out and thought of reviving that play, which they had originally done, using our production, but things happened and it never worked out. We did a production of *Macbeth*, which I didn't direct; I played Macbeth because I hated Maurice Evans in *Macbeth*. We had a young cast; it was quite good. It got a lot of attention. We had producers come out from New York who were thinking seriously of doing it. It didn't work, but the production merited that kind of consideration." We asked Herbert what Boris Karloff was like to work with and he answered, "Boris Karloff was a very erudite man; extremely erudite. Soft, sweet, totally unlike the characters which he played."

After returning to California, when the frequency of employment in feature films started dropping considerably due to television, Herb began to work more in that medium than he did in pictures. "I did a lot of guest things in half hour shows, that type of thing," he related. "Then I got a series, *The Californians*, which didn't last." Later, Herb got into another series called *Michael Shayne*, in which he played Will Gentry, Chief of the Miami Police Department. He said his role in this was just the "ordinary run of the mill type of thing." He had the running part of General Crone in the series, *Mona McCluskey*, which starred Juliet Prowse. Among his guest star roles, Herb played the character, Emmett Egan, in *The Man Who Would Be Marshal* on the popular Western series, *Gunsmoke*. In this episode he played a retired army officer who longs for the excitement he once knew in the service and is desirous of Matt Dillon's job. Convincing Matt to deputize him, he learns that the lack of respect shown to a law officer is vastly different than the respect he received as an officer in the military.

"Then I did *The Mothers-In-Law*, which lasted for two years," he continued. "It was a lot of fun to do. I played opposite Eve Arden. She was an adorable woman to work with; a lovely gal. We had a very nice company. It could have gone on for two more years, except for some political maneuvering on the part of NBC. NBC didn't want our show because they didn't own it. Desi Arnaz and Proctor & Gamble put up the money for it, so NBC had no residual interest in the show and they didn't want us on the air, but Proctor & Gamble forced them to. We were a hit, and we were dropped with a hit rating because they finally prevailed on Proctor & Gamble to go to somebody else." After that, he did the recurring role on *Dallas* as J.R.'s attorney, but he lost the case and his character had to be fired.

Herbert worked in *The Court Jester* with Danny Kaye. He said of this, "It was quite an experience. That was the longest engagement I ever had in motion pictures. It was twenty-three weeks and it was a lot of fun."

Rudley starred with Basil Rathbone, Bela Lugosi, Lon Chaney Jr., John Carradine and Tor Johnson in the 1956 horror feature *The Black Sleep*, which was directed by Reggie LeBorg. "At one time he had been a fairly successful director in the industry," Herbert informed us. "And then, with oncoming age, was considered old fashioned because today if you pick up a script, whether it's a television script or a feature film script, and a character is being described, they will say 'an old man of fifty.' It gives you an idea of how youth oriented this industry has become. The reason is that the industry is completely taken over by youngsters in every phase. I used to tell stories to Spielberg when he was a kid, and Steven Bochco, who produces *Hill Street Blues*. I was a surrogate father to these kids. Our families knew each other and we used to sit around and I would make up impromptu stories for all of them. Well, the whole industry is now inundated with this fresh young blood. And it's fascinating because very often I have heard of people in casting the same way. You go to an ordinary casting director and if a well-known actor or actress of twelve or fifteen years ago comes in, they never have heard of them; they don't know who he or she is."

When we talked with him in 1983, Herbert Rudley had just finished making an independent film titled *Forever and Beyond*. This movie is based on a true story of an eleven year old kid who is found to have leukemia and is dying. Herb had the role of the grandfather who is dying of cancer. "I think it turned out quite well," Herb said. "It's a little downbeat because of the subject matter, but there are some nice performances in it and beautiful photography, and we'll see what happens with it."

In the meantime, Herbert just finished writing a novel. "It's like every other aspect of the entertainment or literary field," he stated. "To create the material is probably the easiest part, but before you can get to sell it, getting representation is the major hurdle. Most of the better literary agents won't accept unsolicited material. Well, how do you get it to them? You remember I mentioned George Chasin; we remained good acquaintants over the years. He has the Chasin-Citron Agency, a large agency which only handles the top stars, top directors, top producers and top writers. They don't read anything else; they don't accept actors in my category. But I called him and told him I just finished a novel. I said, 'I know you're not right for what I want, but can you recommend a good agent. I don't want just a Hollywood agent: I want someone who has literary connections with the publishers in New York.' So he mentioned the name of a very good agency here. I called and spoke to the secretary, saying I had been recommended because George had allowed me to use his name. I explained what I wanted, for him to read the material. She said, 'Mr. Rudley, our policy is that we can't accept unsolicited material unless the person recommending you makes a personal call.' I thanked her and hung up very rejected because I didn't think I could ask George to make a personal call recommending me without having read the material. I didn't want to put him in a potentially embarrassing position. So, reluctantly, I called him back and explained it. 'I don't want to put you in a spot, George.' He said, 'Well, that would be embarrassing.' I said, 'I don't suppose you have time to read it?' 'Oh, no,' he said, 'I got so much of our own clients work. I just can't take the time.' So I said, 'Well, that's nice George. We'll just pass it.' But I just couldn't let it go because it seemed so frustrating. So I called the gal back with a crazy idea. I said, 'Look, I know what your policy is and I know it is a justified one. I can't ask George to take the time to read this, he just doesn't have it. Would it be possible for you, since you must know what their standards and tastes are, to read this off the cuff. Not as a submission to the agency, but just on a friendly basis.' She laughed and said, 'Mr. Rudley, it is a very ingenious idea, but I can't do that because of the liability involved in case somebody comes along and there's a record that I had read this thing, and the office is now involved in a lawsuit, you know.' She went on to say, 'But it isn't necessary for George to know the material. All he has to do is make a personal call.' So I called George back again and talked to his secretary and explained the circumstance. She called me back that afternoon and said, 'Yes, he would make the call.' I haven't yet heard, but that's the first step. If it gets rejected, I'll have to start all over again," Herb concluded.

Herbert Rudley died at the age of ninety-five years on September 9, 2006 in Los Angeles, California.

Film Credits: **1940:** Abe Lincoln in Illinois. **1944:** Seventh Cross; Marriage is a Private Affair; The Master Race. **1945:** A Walk in the Sun; Rhapsody in Blue; Brewster's Millions. **1946:** Decoy. **1948:** Hollow Triumph (aka The Scar); Joan of Arc; Casbah. **1954:** The Silver Chalice. **1955:** Artists and Models. **1956:** The Court Jester; The Black Sleep; That Certain Feeling; Raw Edge. **1958:** The Young Lions; The Bravados; Tonka. **1959:** Beloved Infidel; The Jayhawkers; The Big Fisherman. **1960:** The Great Impostor; Hell Bent for Leather. **1962:** Follow that Dream. **1972:** Call Her Mom (TV). **1980:** Falling in Love Again. **1982:** Forever and Beyond.

BING RUSSELL

Neil Russell, who was born May 5, 1926 in the State of Maine, explained how he picked up the nickname of Bing. "My father was a battler and he figured I'd have to battle, so when I was little he'd get down on his knees and head cuff me, saying 'bing-bang, bing-bang.' I was a naturally sweet kid and wouldn't fight him back, so he got me a punching bag and attached it to the cellar door. I liked that, and when I started working that bag I'd say, 'bing, bing, bing.' I was two years old." That is how he became Bing Russell.

Bing's dad also flew an airplane and Bing learned to fly when he was a kid. They travelled a lot, and through his father's flying he became acquainted with Lefty Gomez of the New York Yankees. "When I was nine years old Lefty picked me up and I travelled with the Yankees for six years," Bing told us. "Five of those years they were champions of the world. From the time I was twelve years old I wanted to replace DiMaggio in center field for the Yankees and to be an actor. How I got that way I have no idea, those were just the two things in life I really wanted to do." His father, who was a hard worker, responded to Bing's life ambitions by asking, "You want to play games your whole life?" and Bing would answer, "That's right! I want to play baseball, I want to play boys and girls and I want to play cowboys and Indians and cops and robbers." That is exactly what Bing has done his whole life. "I belonged to the Yankees and the Chicago Cubs and played on the east coast. I got injured and baseball was over for me. Then I went into show business, and I've been in it ever since," he concluded.

Bing was bartending for a tournament at a country club inn at Rangely, Maine. Winter was coming and Bing had decided to go to New York and attempt finding work on stage or in live television, but before that move was made he was offered a job at the Tradewinds

Club in Florida, so he decided to do that first. While there he learned that a motion picture was being filmed locally called *The Big Leaguer* starring Edward G. Robinson. "I had been a pro-ball player so I set about to get in that damn thing," he confided. "It turned out that Matt Rapf, the producer, was a Dartmouth fan and that was my undergraduate school. I got into the picture as an umpire. That's what made our decision to come out to California rather than go to New York. What the hell, I could always steal oranges, you don't have to buy a lot of clothes and the country stays warm."

Among the guests at his father's hotel in Maine were people like Gary Moore and Perry Como, and they told Bing he was crazy to move to California or to go into show business. "You have here what we all want," they told him. But another guest named Bob Forman, of B.B.D&O., took him aside and told him if you want it go after it. "I think he was right," Bing explained. "I've had more time with my family than any guy I know but career-wise I had to bend it to suit me, to make this business dance to my tune instead of me to it."

When Bing arrived in Hollywood he had ninety-seven dollars, a pregnant wife and two children. "That loft we lived in," he mused, "if you flushed the toilet you couldn't use the bathtub. It took twenty-six hours to drain the bathtub and you couldn't have a plumber because we were living against a zoning area." Bing remarked to his wife that "you better enjoy this because from here we go to east L.A. where I got a room all picked out for five dollars a month." "My one problem was to survive in show business," he reiterated to us. "It was all I had left, and when you have that kind of definition things happen. And they did."

Bing obtained an agent, whom he kept as his sole representative over the years, but became concerned about losing his agent after being sent on a bunch of interviews and not landing a job. He tried to come up with something that would set himself apart from his competition. One night while reading a script up in the loft the idea came to him that he would read against the punctuation and see what happened. "So when I went to readings, if there was a period I wouldn't stop," he explained. "If it was a three syllable word I'd stop in the middle of the word and take statements and end them up like questions, and I'd take questions and end them down like statements. And I ran seventeen jobs right in a row."

One of the shows that Bing obtained by using this approach was in an episode of *Have Gun-Will Travel*, where he played the guest lead and only had three lines of dialogue. The character was a simple-minded man who had been convicted of impaling a very heavy man on a meat hook. A lynch mob wanted to take him out of jail and hang him, so the sheriff sent for Paladin to help protect him. "My only three lines were with the leading lady who brings me cookies," Bing related. The lynch mob takes the guy out of jail and stands him on a wagon and prepares to hang him. "The guy thinks it's just a wonderful party," Bing explains. "He had never had so many people pay attention to him." Paladin rescues him and at the end of the story he is released, but when – out of his jealousy for the girl – he attacks Paladin the audience realizes he did kill the guy. "It's a hell of a role," Bing stated. "Every freak in town was being interviewed for it and I got it with this weird approach to the reading. So those kind of things happened and it led me into playing heavies. I really enjoyed playing heavies."

No actor ever gets all the parts he wants. "I wanted the part of a religious fanatic on a *Gunsmoke*, another great role, but Ainslie Pryor got it," Bing reflected. Bing landed another part in that episode. Another part soon followed in a *Playhouse 90* episode set amongst the U.S. Cavalry titled *Without Incident*, starring Errol Flynn, Ann Sheridan and John Ireland. Bing played the character known as the Star Gazer. The *Hollywood Reporter* wrote that "it was an acting gem." and *Variety* also gave Bing a great review. Speaking of Errol Flynn, Bing told us "He was unbelievable, great. He had ulcers and was in pain, and in this film he had a scrubby beard and was drinking Heinekens from about nine o'clock in the morning. He's sitting out there and takes his teeth out; people came out to see him on the set and here he is with about four Heinekens in him after spending a night in Nogales, and they couldn't believe it was Errol Flynn. But when they called him to go to work, that old son-of-a-gun would slap those teeth in, suck in his belly, slap on his sword, and get on that horse. He was incredible, he could bound from rock to rock and do all that swashbuckling stuff just the same."

In a pilot for a TV show called *Cavalry Patrol*, which was filmed in Kanab, Utah, and starred Dewey Martin and John Pickard, Bing described his role of a man whose wife and son were killed as "possibly the best acting thing I ever had." The pilot didn't go but was later sold as a series called *Boots and Saddles*, starring John Pickard. Other television shoes rolled through the camera lens: "I always wanted to do a *Mickey Mouse Club*," he laughed, "and I worked on three of those shows. I always wanted to do a *Dragnet* but never got to. I was so tickled when I got to do a scene with *Lassie*, who was one hell of an actor," (Bing told us that all the dogs used for Lassie were males, so he was indeed an actor and not an actress). Back in the days of the Warner Brothers Westerns, Bing mentioned that he and Morgan Woodward would alternate as the head of the gang, and "that's where I got to know Denver Pyle and Myron Healey. He's a hell of a cook too, and a more fun guy to have drinks with doesn't live than Myron Healey. I miss that," he concluded.

Other enjoyable television work occurred when he co-starred with his son, actor Kurt Russell. He kidnapped him in a Republic Western with Rory Calhoun, and arrested him in the David Janssen series, *The Fugitive*. In this latter show, as Bing arrested and whacked Kurt, the younger Russell turned to his father and ad-libbed "Police brutality" and they left it in the print. In the TV movie, *Elvis*, Bing played Vernon Presley to Kurt's Elvis; "I never played his father before," Bing commented, "and it was great fun." In later years, Bing has appeared in several of his son's motion pictures such as *Overboard* and *Tango and Cash*.

Because of a mix-up at Screen Actors Guild, Bing appeared in ten or fifteen pictures under his real name, Neil Russell. One of these shows was a television movie called *Yuma* starring Clint Walker. He obtained his part in this film due to his previous baseball experience. "They had this night shot where they wanted this guy killed," Bing explained.

"They wanted him to head for a slide right into the camera and stop on a given spot, it was critical within a couple of inches and it was tough to see. I said, 'I can' and did it in one take, and that's how I got in that one."

Television work followed almost uninterrupted. During the years of 1957-59 there were only six weeks that he didn't appear before the camera. "The old days at ZIV, I'd do two leads in three days. Start off Monday morning on two *Highway Patrol*s and by noon the next morning you were through with that picture and on to the next one. Two half-hour pictures in the can in three days at eighty dollars a day. *Readers Digest, Mr. District Attorney*, about fifteen shows over there. I knew I was finally on the list. About forty of us were on their blackball list from over-exposure. They couldn't use us anymore because they had used us so damn much. It was an awful lot of fun."

Perhaps Bing's favorite TV series he worked on was *Bonanza*. In 1959 he played two heavies on the series, and one week when Ray Teal (who played the sheriff in the series) was on another show, they called Bing to play the sheriff that week. While Teal had a contract with the show, Bing said he would free-lance, so the most Bing appeared in a year was nineteen episodes and the least was three, totaling one hundred and two episodes over the years as Clem Tyson, the deputy, or as Clem Foster, the sheriff. For the ten shows he played Sheriff Clem Foster, fan mail would come to the studio asking where Ray Teal was, did he die? "Then I'd say he was over at Carson City on another deal and get my deputy's badge back," Bing laughed. Bing's first performance as Clem was in an episode in which the Cartwrights wanted to bring a young Indian from the jail to their ranch to try and rehabilitate him. The sheriff, as written for Ray Teal's character, thought highly of the Cartwrights and was not really negative to the idea. Bing gave a new interpretation as a cantankerous sort of guy who was not about to turn over his prisoner without argument. The director took two takes, one as Bing created and one as if Ray Teal was playing the part. David Dortort, the producer, chose Bing's interpretation and thus was born the character of Clem. "I was the damn sheriff, they weren't," Bing told us. "I thought the Cartwrights were good people but a little presumptuous about the handling of the law; as far as I was concerned I was a good lawman. So in the writing of it, if they had one written for Ray Teal but I was playing it, it had to be changed because we were just two different sheriffs."

In reflecting on his memories working on *Bonanza*, Bing told us that "I missed *Bonanza*, after thirteen and a half years when the show died. I was surprised because I was always glad to see the end of a show and go on to something else, but not so with *Bonanza*. I really missed it, just a fun place to be; wasn't like work at all. It was like an annuity, you knew every once in a while they were going to send you a script and you were going to go to work. It fit my scheme perfectly and they knew I was totally dependable, so if I was going to go to work at eleven o'clock, they'd call me for ten. I had the wardrobe here at my house; I'd put it on and go down there. My make-up took about thirty seconds, and so I'd be in front of the camera at eleven and be through by eleven-thirty. One scene in the sheriff's office, and say, 'See you guys next week.' I only worked seven days on one show, *The Pyromaniac*, when Clem's girlfriend tried to burn the town down. That was a fun show. You'd be on other shows so that by the time they were on the second year they'd already be chewing on each other something terrible, like *Rawhide*. That was murder. Other fun shows were *Gunsmoke*, did seven of those, *Big Valley* was a happy show, but most of these shows were unhappy because the players were unhappy and battling with one another. That was what was admirable about Pernell Roberts when he wanted out of *Bonanza*. You never saw that guy when he wasn't ready, always had his lines, never late back from lunch; he was a professional right up to the last day. I was really fortunate to be a part of that show."

Besides his film work, Bing has also enjoyed acting on stage. His all-time favorite role was that of Harold Hill in *The Music Man;* some others he enjoyed were the role of Ben in *The Little Foxes;* and in 1982 while he lived in New York for eleven months, he got the only part he ever auditioned for on Broadway in *The Wake of Jamie Foster* which played at the Eugene O'Neill Theatre. Bing enjoyed that play so much that in 1983 he was starring in and directing it at a theatre in Portland, Oregon. "I love it, a wonderful character and a wonderful play, and Lou, my wife, for the first time co-directed because I want somebody watching me when I'm up there."

Bing has worked in over one hundred movies, ranging from his debut in *Big Leaguer* in 1953 through *Dick Tracy* in 1990. "Sergeant Dunker in *Horse Soldiers* was my favorite," he informed us, "because of the role and John Ford's directing." Other films included leads in *Cattle Empire* with Joel McCrea; *Ride A Violent Mile*; *Barrier*, one of the first films about the end of the world; and said he "co-starred in a picture with Eartha Kitt which was kind of fun because I sang the title song, *Seventy Times Seven*. The song became a hit in Italy and they wanted me to go there with it, but they insisted on me changing my name because they were such Bing Crosby fans. I wouldn't do that so Chuck Connors recorded it."

One of the motion pictures that Bing starred in was an independent film called *Stakeout*. Reflecting on this movie, he told us that "it was a tough film to make in Wichita Falls, Texas, hotter than hell." One night, Bing, eleven-year-old Billy Hughes, the cameraman, and a gaffer were up on the third floor of a building and it was 118 degrees. "The last scene I get shot and killed and am under a blanket totally covered up," Bing continued, "and Billy, who plays my son, comes out and has this scene. I'll tell you he got into it. I've never seen an actor so completely unnerved. Finally we finish the shot and I came up from under that blanket and he grabbed me, hysterical. I picked him up and carried him to this truck. The damn press was trying to get at him and I backhanded this one guy. He was just trembling and crying; so I got him into the cab of this truck and locked the door so they couldn't get at him, his parents or anybody else, because at that moment I was closer to him than anyone else in the world. I tried to talk to him but couldn't get through to him, he was just totally gone. He wasn't going to come out of it, so finally I whacked him across the face. He looked at me and stopped, took hold of me and just cried a little bit. It took about forty-five minutes to get him out of that scene; I've never seen anything like it. I took a great liking to Billy, he was just a dear little fellow. He was a hell of an actor and had the quality of a Bartholomew. I put him with my agent and he had a heck of a career for three or four years. One time I was doing a *Wanted Dead or Alive* at Republic and Billy was doing an episode for *The Law and Mr. Jones* and I went over to see him. A lot of people on crews from different shows would come and watch that kid act. I don't know whatever became of him."

Another motion picture was *Cheyenne Autumn*, directed by John Ford. In this film Bing played seven different parts in the exact same wardrobe. In one shot, Bing played the leader of the platoon coming into the fort with Richard Widmark, and when Widmark goes up front Bing played his Adjutant. "That was in direct sequence," Bing explained, "but Ford was so incredibly perceptive in relation to focus that nobody ever saw it." In another sequence he is shot off a telegraph pole by the Indians and a couple of pages later he plays the soldier who discovers a waterhole is poisoned. "When he shot me at the waterhole, like a damn fool I thought it might of slipped his mind about getting shot off the pole because it was filmed by a second unit director. 'You know I got killed on page such and such,' and he looked at me and said, 'You want to direct this film, Bing?' and I said 'Only if you're tired Mr. Ford.' So I went to the water and discovered it was poisoned," Bing laughed.

As previously mentioned, Bing's favorite movie was John Ford's *The Horse Soldiers*. As both Bing and Ford were natives of Maine, they got on real well together. "I was never more than five or six feet from him," he related. "He allowed me up near the camera and let me cast actors on location. I remember one time he had me rehearsing Strother Martin and Denver Pyle the night they came in and asked me after how they did. I said, 'You'll be very pleased'; chewing on his handkerchief, Ford said 'Really,' and I said 'They're fantastic.'" Bing told us they had a lot of fun on that show "drinking, raising hell and having a terrific time. Strother and I formed the group-haters club; everybody belonged to some kind of group except Strother and me and the only way you could get into our group was to swear you'll never belong to any group, so we were the only two members. That kind of fun."

Bing told us a humorous story concerning John Ford during the filming of *Horse Soldiers*. "Ken Curtis, Jud Pratt, Fred Graham and I are the cadets. We are going south but we think we're going north on leave. Well, the sun's coming up and if we are going north it would come up on the right. If we are going south it comes up on the left. We have six hundred people behind us, the caissons, the horses...the whole thing. They hold the others and rehearse a long dolly shot on just the four of us leading our horses and moving along. So I'm the one that discovers the sun is rising on the left. We are not going north, we are going south, so I point over to the left. After a couple of rehearsals, Ford says 'Bing, can you play the sun on the other side.' For the next few rehearsals I played it over to the right and I knew he'd pick it up. Well, they got ready to roll, and when they roll they would move the whole thing, all six hundred people, and the sun is on the wrong side. I'm just one of these guys that couldn't handle it. Nobody argues with the old man, maybe it's because I'm from Maine that I got away with it, but I just couldn't do the sun on the right. I went to him and said, 'Mr. Ford, if we play the sun over there we are headed north and I'm supposed to discover we are headed south.' Silence, absolute silence on the set. He lifted that flap up off his eye and looked at me. 'You think they'll stop the projector?' and I said 'No sir.' 'You know Bing, I was born on the coast and you're an inlander.' So I said, 'Yes sir,' and I went back and played the damn sun on the right. Okay, they printed it. Five or six days went by and we had in the meantime filmed where we set torches to the cotton storage bins by the railroad. Ken Curtis and I are standing together when the old man walks by and says, 'Bing, Marty Rackin is coming today and I want you to welcome him aboard and tell him you won the bet,' and he walks off. He spoke clear enough for me to understand him, which was pretty rare; that was part of his game, he could speak clear enough but wouldn't. So he left and I asked Ken, 'What the hell was that about?' and he didn't know. We thought it was when we burned the cotton bins and they thought that an airplane probably came in and the cinematographer said 'No,' but it did come in, they've seen it in the dailies and Ford wants Rackin (the producer) to know he knew all the time the airplane might be in – I thought that was it. So about a half-hour later I went over to Ford and said, 'So the airplane was in,' and he mumbled, 'What f---king airplane?' and walked away. I came back over to Ken and told him it wasn't the airplane. Pretty soon the old man came by and said, 'This better be the best scene you ever played' and walked off again. Now, Rackin came up on the set and they are talking together and I know I got to go over there and welcome him aboard, and in the course of the conversation say I won the bet, about what I don't know, and go through some kind of act that's got to sell. So, I go over there; there's nothing I can do because that's what the boss said, so I welcome him and the old man reaches in his pocket and pulls out his money and says, 'Oh, by the way you won that five dollars.' I laughed, and said 'I won it, I can't believe I won it,' and Rackin started to laugh. Ford said he didn't have a five dollar bill, only a ten; so I grabbed it out of his hand and said, 'I'd sooner owe you five dollars than you owe me,' and he knew I was mad about this because I didn't know what game I was playing, so I walked away with his ten dollars. He was mad all day long about me having five dollars of his money, so finally I had the ten changed and gave him the five, he just snatched it out of my hand; I still didn't know what the hell that was all about. Two days later they have the six hundred soldiers, the casons, the horses, and we are headed south again and I play the sun on the left where I wanted to in the first place, and not a word was said. They had picked it up in the dailies, they said I was playing the sun off the wrong side. This was his way of getting me off the hook for having made a mistake. You see, I won the bet so therefore I was the one who said the sun should be over there and he was the one who blew it, and what a wonderful thing for him to do. Marty Rackin knew it wasn't my fault. So we were back here for Christmas and I gave him a compass for a present and, oh, he was mad. He was by far the most exciting director I ever worked for." Another scene in the film called for Bing and others to barrel in on horseback, dismount and come up behind a stone wall. Ford came over to Bing afterwards and told him, "You played that like a Bangor fullback." "That was a real compliment," Bing concluded.

Bing explained one of his techniques that he used in his work. "I was notorious as a bad rehearser," Bing confessed, "but I worked so much that people in the industry got used to it. The reason is that I found a lot of actors left their damn performance in the rehearsal so by the time the cameras rolled they were nailed down. So I began to lay down in rehearsal and throw the stuff away and then hit them in the takes. So I got known as a guy who wouldn't rehearse but don't worry about it because when the cameras roll he'll be there. I did that on purpose, but I remember one time I thought, 'Gee, I'd better do a play because I wonder if this is getting to be part of my bag of tricks.' I never got enough of rehearsal in any play I've done. I went into a play, *See the Jaguar*, by Richard Nash, at the Old Barn. Same thing, I couldn't rehearse enough. The damn thing could run five years and I'd never get enough. The reason is that it is live, the audiences are all different, you're telling your whole story and even the players are different on a given night. I did a bunch of shows with Loretta Young when she was doing her series, and we were in a scene that wasn't going quite right for her. We had a lot of rehearsals and I remember her saying, 'Please dear Lord let me hear these words for the first time.' She was so into it that she couldn't get it to come out like the first time. Of course it did. I remember once off camera to her close-up I got swept up with what she was doing and my cue came and I might as well have been on the moon. I was just looking at her and she realized it and just laughed. She said, 'Was it really that good Bing?' and I said, 'Oh gosh, it was.' You couldn't swear on her set or you had to pay money," he smiled.

Bing mentioned that he learned to rehearse in a small room from Thomas Mitchell, with whom he worked in several *O'Henry Playhouse*s. Mitchell would speak so lightly that everybody in the room would soon be reaching for him. Also when Bing worked with him he noticed that Mitchell would never look straight at him during the filming. Bing wondered about this as he always believed in eye contact to play off the other actor. "I'm a re-actor rather than an actor," Bing told us. "I do my own thing but I really need you in a scene and Tommy Mitchell is playing his stuff off to the side." After filming for the day, Bing and Mitchell went over to the Fomosa for some drinks, and he asked Mitchell why he never made eye contact, and the latter replied, "The reason I do that is because I've never yet worked with an actor who is as good as my imagination." "I later came to know something about that," Bing said, "because I did twenty-six *You Are There* shows and in those you play the lens. Walter Cronkite would be interviewing you as the camera and you look right into the lens. I got to really like the openness of that lens because, like radio, I could make it anything my mind wanted to make it be. Never changed me from being a contact player with other players because I just depended on it too much."

Bing has also done some writing, including the screenplay of the 1966 motion picture, *Eye for an Eye*, and has been modestly successful in that he didn't like to write but was able to sell what he wrote. He also owns a couple of baseball teams, a pro-team in Portland, Oregon, and one back in El Paso, Texas. "So I've always been in those two things," Bing said. "Actually, baseball is my first love and show business is the closest thing to it. You have a home run or you have a scene go well, I like the excitement of it. There is a certain purity in professional sports or in show business because in baseball if you don't help the ball club win you're going to go down the road, and it doesn't really make any difference who you know. In show business as a creative person either you sell tickets or you have an appeal. In my case I've done over seven hundred television shows and got the girl three times and got killed one hundred and thirty seven times, so you know what my appeal was."

In summing up his career, Bing told us "I was in Maine and my baseball was over and now it was time to tackle show business. The two things I wanted when I started out was to replace DiMaggio in center field and win the Academy Award. Well, I never replaced DiMaggio and I think my son is a lot closer to the Academy Award than I am. Like I told you, when I was twelve I knew what I wanted to do so I had no alternative. When I got here the baseball was over, I couldn't fail or my life was over. We lived in a loft over near Pico and Fairchild for twenty dollars a month, so you just hang in there. My career took a turn that I wanted it to take when I picked up *Bonanza*, which was perfect for me because I wanted to grow fat, throw curves, and spend time with my family and we have had fun together. The people in the business have been wonderful, so many have helped us; way back to the beginning to Loretta Young and Mark Hanna, an actor who said to me in the first year, 'Don't worry Bing, you'll get your chance,' and he was so right. You always do. I stayed with the same agent all those years, he's ninety years old now, and he couldn't stand to see me not work and that's why I made so many pictures. He got me up to that category but I didn't like being away from the family, and I told him I'm going to be home from January to August because that is baseball season and Kurt's going to play baseball. I said I've got to live my life the way I want, and he said 'You're either going to have to go up or go backwards,' but that wasn't the case because of *Bonanza*. I said I wanted to play heavies and that's what I did except for Clem, I played one heavy after another and made one hell of a living, and I'm still getting all kinds of residuals from off those hundreds of shows. I can't, of course, say I could have been a star because you'll never know if you didn't do it, but I got to play with my career the way I wanted to in my lifetime. When I was young I'd sit around the set," Bing concluded, "with people like Glenn Strange on *Gunsmoke*. He went back to Republic days of Buck Jones and Roy Rogers, and he'd be telling stories of the old days and I would think that I love this business and hope that someday I'd be fortunate enough and able to contribute enough to one day be sitting around like he was and look back to when pictures were really fun, 'cause that's what he was doing. This was in the early 1950s and he was talking about how great it was in the 1930s. That time came for me now and I was one of the old guys sitting around and I appreciated that I had survived, and I think twenty years from now Kurt will talk about the good old days back in the 1980s."

Our interview with Bing took place in 1983, and in 1991 he wrote us the following note: "Our grandson, Matt Franco, just finished his fifth season in the Chicago Cub Farm System. My wife and I follow him from spring training in March (Mesa, Arizona) through the season's end in September. He's taken us so far to Wytheville, Virginia; Geneva, New York; Charleston, West Virginia; Peoria, Illinois; and Winston-Salem, North Carolina. We're having fun, still playing games."

Bing Russell died at Thousand Oaks, California, on April 8, 2003.

Film Credits: **1953:** The Big Leaguer. **1955:** Tarantula; Cult of the Cobra; Kiss Me Deadly; Crashout; Lucy Gallant. **1956:** Attack!; The Price of Fear; Behind the High Wall. **1957:** Gunfight at the OK Corral; Fear Strikes Out; Teenage Thunder; Ride a Violent Mile; The True Story of Jesse James; Beau James; The Deadly Mantis; Without Incident (TV); Drango; The Land Unknown; Bombers B-52. **1958:** Desert Hell; Cattle Empire; Suicide Battalion. **1959:** Rio Bravo; The Horse Soldiers; Good Day for a Hanging; The Last Train from Gun Hill. **1960:** The Magnificent Seven; The Greatest Impostor. **1961:** Seventy Times Seventy (aka Saint of Devil's Island). **1962:** Stakeout. **1963:** The Stripper. **1964:** Cheyenne Autumn; One Man's Way. **1965:** Hallelujah Trail. **1966:** Incident at Phantom Hill; Madame X; Billy the Kid vs. Dracula. **1967:** Ride to Hangman's Tree. **1968:** Journey to Shiloh; Blackbeard's Ghost; The Love Bug. **1970:** The Computer wore Tennis Shoes. **1971:** Yuma (TV); A Taste of Evil (TV); Million Dollar Duck. **1972:** Now You See Him, Now You Don't. **1973:** Runaway!; Set This Town on Fire (TV); Satan's School for Girls (TV). **1974:** A Cry in the Wilderness (TV); Death Sentence (TV); The Sex Symbol (TV). **1975:** The Apple Dumpling Gang; The Barrier. **1976:** Arthur Hailey's The Moneychangers (TV); The New Daughters of Joshua Cabe (TV); The Lonliest Runner (TV). **1979:** Elvis (TV). **1987:** Overboard. **1988:** Sunset. **1989:** Tango and Cash. **1990:** Dick Tracy.

GENE RUTHERFORD

Robert Eugene "Gene" Rutherford Jr. was born March 4, 1939 in Memphis, Tennessee, but was raised about twenty miles south in Eudora, Mississippi. "My grandfather Rutherford farmed and delivered mail by buggy in Baldwyn, Mississippi," Gene told us. "My dad was rural poor and worked his way through college in eight years and received his Masters Degree from the University of Mississippi in teaching." Gene's mother was Olga Brewer, who died one hour after he was born. When Gene was four years old his dad married Mabel Sims. "She was a very nice woman and also a school teacher," Gene reflected. "I'm very proud of my parents."

Gene grew up in DeSoto County, Mississippi, which was named after the Spanish explorer Hernando DeSoto, and as a boy he enjoyed fishing, swimming, and reading. "One thing that I did I'm not proud of now, but when I was eleven years old I started hunting rabbits, squirrels, doves, bob white quails. I killed a lot of animals. At least I ate the animals I killed, but I'm not proud of it and you couldn't make me hunt now. It's wrong to do it. Animals have rights too. I didn't know any better, and my father didn't know any better. He didn't hunt, but I saw another boy hunting and I wanted to hunt, so he let me."

"The way I got interested in acting was when I was five years old and my father and stepmother took me to a play in Memphis," Gene explained. "I don't remember the name of the play, but it was some kind of costume play outside at night. What they were doing was fantastic and I just knew that I wanted to be an actor. So I had the idea growing up that I wanted to be an actor, although I hadn't done anything." Gene mentioned that he was also inspired by some movies he saw. "When I saw *Broken Arrow* with Jeff Chandler, that film left an impression on

me. *Sitting Bull* made a big impression on me. I looked up to Charlton Heston in some of his films, especially *The Ten Commandments*. I never told him, but he was my favorite film star, and I got to work with him. A great experience there."

After graduating from Tunica High School, Gene attended Northwest Junior College for a year. "I knew I was wasting my time because I couldn't get acting there," Gene confided, "so the next year I went out to California. I was eighteen years old and didn't know anything. I didn't know what a casting director was, a producer or director; didn't know anything about the business. What I did was get a job at a service station pumping gas," Gene laughed. "I asked people about the business and heard about the trade papers, *Hollywood Reporter* and *Daily Variety*, and started sending pictures and letters to casting directors without too much success. Every now and then I got a chance to audition or do a scene for them, and it went like that from 1957 to 1962."

Gene studied with several of the top acting teachers in southern California. "I studied with Barry Cahill, who took over Richard Boone's class, with Clarke Gordon, then with Sherman Marx and then Estelle Harmon. Then I had a break because at 20th Century Fox New Talent School there was a man out of New York named Sandy Miesner who had spent a lot of time at the Neighborhood Playhouse in New York, and I studied with him. That was a great experience because I learned how to act from him. He was the best teacher I ever had."

In 1962 Gene was drafted into the Army and spent two years in the Army Intelligence, stationed in Eritrea, which was then part of Ethiopia, but is now an independent country in East Africa. "When I was in Eritrea there were maybe a thousand Italians living in the town where I was stationed with the Sixth Army for about fourteen months, so I learned to speak pretty good Italian," Gene commented. After Gene was discharged from the service he spent two months trying to obtain film parts in Rome, Italy. "I did a little dubbing in Rome on a film with Gordon Scott, that's all," he said.

When asked how it was working in the dubbing end of the business, Gene replied, "You are seeing what's happening on the screen and then you have the line coming into your ear on a little phone, in Italian. Then you try and say your line matching it with the screen. If your line is 'Prendiamo il treno,' meaning 'Let's take the train,' or 'Ora, che abbiamo l'opportunita,' which means, 'While we got the chance,' you have to try and match these. It's a little difficult," he laughed.

Gene decided he would have a better chance in Hollywood, so after touring Europe for a short time he returned to Hollywood in August of 1964 and obtained a job as a host in an Italian restaurant. "I started pursuing my career and got into a play called *Blues for Charlie*, written by James Baldwin. I played the part of George, and understudied the lead role of Lyle, played by Mike Witney. That play closed down after about a month and I got my job back as host of the restaurant."

Gene obtained his first film work on an episode of *Branded* with Chuck Connors. "I had one scene with William Bryant, who played Grant. 'Mr. President.' He said, 'Huh?' 'The man you're expecting is here.' So I had two lines," Gene smiled.

In May of 1966 Gene heard about the film *Hurry Sundown* by Otto Preminger. "I couldn't get an agent, so what I did was send Bill Barnes, Mr. Premenger's casting director, a letter and he called me in. I played the man in the red shirt," Gene said. "My big scene was in the hardware store when John Philip Law and Robert Hooks come in to the store to buy dynamite. I got about eight lines in the film and loved working with Mr. Preminger, great man and great director. He knew exactly what he wanted and as long as you did your job he treated you with great respect, but if you messed up he would get hot at you."

After Gene finished his work in *Hurry Sundown* he decided that with a good credit and film available he would be able to secure a good agent. "I sent my picture, resume and letter to different agents asking for interviews, and one, Jerry Steiner with General Artists Corp, gave me an interview. He liked my work in *Hurry Sundown* and took me on. That fall I did an *Andy Griffith Show*, *The Monkees*, and tested twice for a spoof on Tarzan called *Tagar, King of the Jungle* for CBS. Mike Henry did the pilot and it didn't sell."

In February of 1967 Gene was hired to work on location at Bishop, California in his favorite role, that of Rufus Quint in *Will Penny*. "This was sort of a big break for me," he told us. "A fantastic experience, I guess the best experience of my life. Donald Pleasence played my father. I tried to learn about acting from him, but he didn't tell me too much. I guess he thought I already knew what I was doing, but I wanted to learn something from him too. Sometimes when it's time for you to do a close-up with a big actor like Charlton Heston they would have to get the dialogue director or script girl to say the lines. Heston was not like that. If he had some dialogue he would stay there with you for your close-up. A great guy. He invited all of us to his house for a nice dinner when the film was being made. It was just a wonderful time. Donald Pleasence and Bruce Dern were so good to work with, as were Ben Johnson and Tony Zerbe. Joan Hackett was absolutely fantastic to work with, and Heston was probably the best of all."

Since Charlton Heston had been Gene's favorite actor as a boy as well as being an inspiration to him in wanting to become an actor, we asked if he was nervous at all working with Heston. "No, I wasn't," he replied. "This teacher I studied with from New York, Sandy Miesner, said you couldn't be intense about being tense. So I learned to relax before the camera. I'm much more relaxed before the camera than I am talking to you here now. I find it easy to relax before the camera, and if I'm not relaxed there are certain physical and some mental exercises I can do to get relaxed and start working.

"I learned something about acting from Bruce Dern. He had a phrase called 'Get your equal sights right,' meaning what the character's doing and what you're doing, make sure they're right—the equal sights. It's a little different than the Sandy Miesner way of acting. The Miesner way covers about ninety-five percent of acting, but not one hundred percent. However, the Lee Strasberg or the Bruce Dern type way does. I never auditioned for the Actors Studio—talking about Lee Strasberg—but I wrote him a letter and asked him to let me be an observer there. He said it's supposed to be for three months, but I hung around for a year just observing him and his students there."

While working on *Will Penny* Gene picked up one of his favorite hobbies, saying, "Every day at lunch time Bruce Dern and Charlton Heston would run down this hill and back up again for exercise. I didn't jog then, but I started jogging in 1967 and ran between five and ten miles a day about six days a week. So jogging was my hobby."

Gene discussed shooting one of the scenes for Paramount's *Will Penny*. "We had to do this scene seven or eight times because something was always wrong with the camera, or Bruce Dern couldn't get his horse. Donald Pleasence is lying on the ground, having been knocked out by Heston when he made his escape. We did one scene, and I forgot Donald was there and ran right over him with a horse. I just said 'Look out Donald' and tried to keep in character, and rode off like I'm chasing Heston. Luckily the horse didn't touch him. Donald didn't move. He laid still because he figured the horse would miss him."

We asked Gene if he had learned to ride horses for the movies, and he replied, "I grew up riding horses and mules in Mississippi, riding without a saddle. I'm not a great rider but I'm a pretty good one. My step grandfather had a farm in Arkansas and a nice horse there that I rode. When I was eleven I had a friend whose father had a plantation and many mules, so I'd ride mules. So I didn't have any problems with that as I was riding since I was eight years old."

The next show Gene worked on was for an episode of *Gunsmoke* titled *The Wreckers*, with Warren Oates. "A great man to work with," Gene commented. "Amanda Blake kissed my cheek after we finished. That was a fantastic experience because it meant she liked me, and I had great fun there. James Arness seemed like a real nice guy. He liked talking about motorcycles. Then I did a *High Chaparral* called "A Quiet Day in Tucson." I played the part of Bart Kellogg, and they brought me back for two more shows as that character. Bart was a big tough guy, but a nice guy. He liked to fight to let off a little energy or a little steam. In this first episode he rides for three days and nights to reach civilization, which is Tucson, and he says he wants a good knock down, drag out fight with no holds barred. I did my own fights in the fight scenes. There was a fight between Cameron Mitchell and myself in *A Quiet Day in Tucson*, and when Cam hits me with a spittoon I say, 'I hadn't this much fun in a dogs age,' and we become good friends. I did it in October of that year and again the next spring, around March or April. I played it twice more. David Dortort (the executive producer of *High Chaparral* and *Bonanza*) saw me in the rushes and put me under option as a semi-regular in seven episodes for *Bonanza*. He put me under option the same time as he did David Canary. My option was not picked up; David Canary's was, but that was also a great experience working in *Bonanza*. All the people I worked with were great. I think there's a reason for that. Actors are glad to have a job, and the ones who are already TV or film stars usually have it made, and they're happy too. So it's really usually a happy time working in a film or a television show. A great time."

Another show Gene worked on was *Mannix* with Mike Connors. "I think that was the best action scene ever filmed in episodic TV," Gene opinioned. "Mike Connors was chasing me on a ledge of a building on Wilshire Boulevard and then jumping out about eight feet to the top of a truck fourteen or fifteen feet high, and then into the cab of the truck and on to the ground. They had a narrow plank with a blanket over it to catch me in case I missed my footing. Mike Connors, who was an extremely athletic person, did the stunt first, otherwise I wouldn't have done it. It was quite a dangerous jump."

Gene confided that he made a mistake in his career in 1968. "I left the agency. Another agent told me he'd do more for me and give me more personal attention, so I left General Artists Corporation and went with this other agent, but he didn't do much for me. From then on my career was just bit parts. I messed up in 1968 at a young age. Then in 1983 my career wasn't going anywhere at all. The last shows I did were *Trapper John, MD*, *Matt Houston* and *Strike Force* with Robert Stack. The very last thing that I did was a *Fall Guy* with Lee Majors. I wrote him a letter and told him that I needed a job and he hired me the next week. He remembered me from *Will Penny*. It speaks a lot for him. You write him a letter saying you need a job and the next week he hires you."

Shortly thereafter, Gene's brother, a civil engineer in Mississippi, offered him a job back in his home state. Gene accepted it and worked with his brother, retiring in 1994.

Gene shared one example of growing up in a small town and not knowing about business or having many dealings with people. "When I did *Will Penny* I didn't have a car. This was my first big money and Tom Gries, the director, sold me a 1959 Chevrolet station wagon he had bought in Wyoming when he was directing an episode of *The Monroes* there for television. He told me, 'If you get tired of the car you can always sell it back to me and I'll give it to my son to surf in.' Well, I drove the car for about six months and it caught fire on me. I didn't know what to do with it, so I sold it to another person at a very low price. Tom Gries called me in to see about a film called *The Hawaiians* with Charlton Heston and I had a great interview. Then he asked me how the car was doing, and I said, 'The car caught fire on me and I had to sell it.' 'What! I told you to give it back to me. I said I'd give it to my son to surf in. You shouldn't have done that.' He turned into a completely different man and got really angry about it, and I didn't work for Tom Gries again for five years. That was about 1970, and he didn't hire me again till 1975 for the part of Juan Flynn, the Panamanian cowboy who lived on the Spahn ranch where Manson was, in *Helter Skelter*. I had a pretty good scene in the beginning of the show, but it looked like police brutality and they cut it out. I'm just in there getting on the bus now; no dialogue or anything. The next show I did for Tom was around February 1976 when he called me in for the pilot of *Hunter* with James Franciscus. It was a small part, but a good part. He told me to use his name and he would recommend me to anybody. He tried to help me, but while he was directing *The Greatest* (1977) he had a heart attack playing tennis and died. Anthony Hopkins gave the eulogy at the funeral. He was a great director and a super guy, but he overreacted about that car. He sold it to me for fifty dollars and it was worth a lot more than that. I should have given it back to him but I just didn't know any better."

When asked how he might advise someone contemplating an acting career, Gene replied, "If someone's interested in acting I'd say good luck to them because luck is what the business is all about. At the same time, develop yourself as best you can as far as your acting abilities are concerned. You learn how to cold read; you learn how to interview. I was never that strong at interviewing. I hate cold readings with a passion, and the reason I hate auditions is that between 1957 and 1962 I did a lot of great scenes. Barry Cahill and I did an absolutely great scene for Lynn Stalmaster, the biggest casting director in Hollywood, but when I got there he asked for my agent. I didn't have an agent so I never got anything from Lynn Stalmaster whatsoever. That turned me against auditions. I did great auditions for agents and couldn't get anything. So I just hated auditions. If you do something for the camera it is there and everyone can judge it. If it is good work, people have to admit it's good; if it's bad work then that's what it is. So I don't like cold readings. If I were a good cold reader I'd have worked a lot more. If I had had to cold read for *Will Penny* I'd never have gotten the part. Luckily, I got the *Gunsmoke* by cold reading, but I know it was just luck. The *High Chaparral* I didn't have to cold read for. I had a five-minute monologue, but the director, Will Paxton, said, 'I don't believe in cold readings. You take the script and come back Monday and read it for me.' Otherwise I wouldn't have got that part. So considering I don't like the auditions and I didn't like the cold readings, I did pretty well."

In summing up his feelings on his career, Gene told us, "I love the business and it has been very nice to me, but I grew up in small towns in Mississippi with less than one hundred people and knew nothing about business. If I had known something about business it probably wouldn't have taken me ten years before I got my first acting job, and I never would have left the agency. I never understood the personal aspect of the business, but what I understand now is that the contacts and the personal relationships are so important in acting. If I had known that back then I could have worked a lot more. A person could be the best actor ever and never work one day in films or television."

Gene Rutherford died in Memphis, Tennessee on September 24, 2006.

GENE RUTHERFORD: 1967: Hurry Sundown. **1968**: Will Penny. **1975**: Candy Tangerine Man. **1976**: Helter Skelter (TV); The Witch Who Came from the Sea. **1978**: Cops and Robbers (TV). **1980**: Beulah Land. **1982**: Love and Money.

JAMES SEAY

James Seay was born September 9, 1914 in the home of his parents on Walnut Street in Pasadena, California. As a young boy his mother would take him every Saturday matinee to watch a stock company performance at the Raymond Theatre. "One day she took me backstage to meet one of the actors," Jim recalled. "We had a long talk about my becoming an actor; he told me acting was a difficult job. He was right."

After James graduated from high school he obtained a job with an insurance company. Commenting on this job, he said, "All I did was answer the phone, it wasn't for me." One evening on his way home on a streetcar, Jim met a friend named Johnny Pelleti and asked him what he was doing. Pelleti answered that he was attending school at the Pasadena Playhouse on a scholarship. Jim mentioned his desires of being an actor at which his friend offered to introduce him to a director who was casting a play. "The next morning he introduced me to Tom Browne Henry, and I got my first part. The play was *Judgment Day*, and I played a guard who led Mischa Auer to the witness stand. A walk on, no lines, but it was a start," Jim concluded.

After the close of *Judgment Day*, James received several small speaking parts. After a time he was approached by Gilmore Brown, the managing director of the Pasadena Playhouse, who accused Jim of being more interested in the girl students than he was in acting. "Well, he was half right," Jim confessed, "but I convinced him I wanted to be an actor." Brown placed Jim in the post graduate class at the school, which class performed plays in a small house in the back of Brown's home. This was called the playbox, where the actors performed not on a stage, but on the same level as the audience. "At the end of the year, a man from the audience came to the dressing room after the play to talk to me," he remarked. "His name was Larry Johns, and he asked me if I'd like to be the leading man in a summer stock company. I said yes, and I was off to Guilford, Connecticut, and the Chapel Playhouse. I did a show a week for ten weeks; a real grind."

After the season closed at Guilford, Jim returned to Pasadena and appeared in two more plays at the Playhouse. He portrayed Essex in *Elizabeth the Queen*, and as Bothwell in *Mary of Scotland*. Because of his performances in these two productions, Jeanette McPherson, who was an assistant to Cecil B. DeMille, obtained a contract for Jim at Paramount Studios. "I worked in six or seven pictures during that contract," he told us, "then I free-lanced for awhile. During that time I did a film for the government; the war was going on and the film I was doing was connected with the Air Force. One of the Air Force officers asked me if I'd like to join their unit. I did, and for the next three and a half years (1942-45) I made training films for the Air Force."

When the war ended, Jim landed a contract with Twentieth Century Fox based on the work he had done in one of his Air Force films. "In a year I did three films," Jim added. Two of the films were *Ten Gentlemen from West Point* and the classic *Miracle on 34th Street*. After his release from his contract at Fox, Jim free-lanced for the remainder of his career, appearing in many features as *Day the Earth Stood Still*, *Vera Cruz*, *Fort Ti*, *Kiss Me Deadly*, *Son of Belle Starr* and *Killers from Space*. In between his many features, Jim was active in television work on such shows as *Superman*, *Fury*, *The Invaders* and as Judge Will Spicer in the Tombstone, Arizona, segments of *Wyatt Earp*.

In 1970 Jim appeared opposite Henry Fonda and Kirk Douglas in *There Was A Crooked Man*, and shortly thereafter retired from his long career as an actor and removed to Laguna Beach, California. He died there on October 10, 1992.

Film Credits: **1939:** Back Door to Heaven. **1940:** Emergency Squad; Golden Gloves; Northwest Mounted Police; Oklahoma Renegades; Queen of the Mob; Son of Monte Cristo; Those were the Days; Way of All Flesh; Women Without Names; Flight Command; I Want a Divorce; The Flag of Humanity (short). **1941:** Mr. Celebrity; Face Behind the Mask; In Old Colorado; Keep 'em Flying; The Kid from Kansas; Two in a Taxi; Meet Boston Blackie; Flying Blind; The Green Hornet Strikes Again (serial); The Mad Doctor; Power Dive; They Died with Their Boots On. **1942:** Ten Gentlemen from West Point; Dangerously They Live; Eagle Squadron; Enemy Agents meet Ellery Queen; Highway by Night; Home in Wyomin'; Man from Cheyenne; Ride 'em Cowboy; Ridin' Down the Canyon; Timber; Vendetta (short); Time to Kill; Tramp! Tramp! Tramp!; Flight Lieutenant; Joe Smith, American. **1943:** Flight to Freedom; Learn and Live (short); How to Fly the B-17 (short). **1944:** Resisting Enemy Interrogation. **1945:** The Return of Monte Cristo; Crimes, Inc.; The Last Bomb (short).. **1946:** Home Sweet Homicide. **1947:** Heartaches; Miracle on 34th Street; T-Men; The Brasher Doubloom. **1948:**

The Checkered Coat; The Cobra Strikes; Don't Trust Her Husband (aka An Innocent Affair0; Secret Beyond the Door; Slippery McGee; The Strange Mrs. Crane. **1949:** I Cheated the Law; Red Canyon; Prejudice. **1950:** The Asphalt Jungle; The Flying Missile; Military Academy and the Tenth Avenue Gang; Union Station; Hunt the Man Down. **1951:** Up Front; Close to My Heart; When the Redskins Rode; When Worlds Collide; Strictly Dishonorable; Day the Earth Stood Still. **1952:** Models, Inc; Brave Warrior; Voodoo Tiger. **1953:** Captain John Smith and Pocahontas; Off Limits; Fort Ti; Homesteaders; Jack McCall, Desperado; Phantom from Space; Son of Belle Starr; Sea of Lost Ships; Problem Girls; War of the Worlds; Torpedo Alley. **1954:** Return to Treasure Island; Killers from Space; Vera Cruz; The Steel Cage; Captain Kidd and the Slave Girl. **1955:** The Kentuckian; Kiss Me Deadly; At Gunpoint; I Died a Thousand Times. **1956:** Friendly Persuasion; Gun Brothers; Man in the Vault; I've Lived Before. **1957:** The Amazing Colossal Man; The Big Land; Man of a Thousand Faces; Pal Joey; Bombers B-52; Beginning of the End. **1958:** The Buccaneer; Street of Darkness; Flood Tide. **1960:** The Threat; The Lawbreakers. **1961:** Secret of Deep Harbor. **1962:** What Ever Happened to Baby Jane? **1965:** Brainstorm. **1967:** The Ballad of Josie. **1968:** The Destructors; Panic in the City; The Green Berets. **1969:** D.A.: Murder One (TV). **1970:** There was a Crooked Man.

To Tom
Best Wishes
Robert Stack

ROBERT SHAYNE

Robert Shayne was born in Yonkers, New York City on October 4, 1900. "I got into show business professionally quite by accident," Bob told us. "I had been a newspaper reporter on a Miami paper; I had been an organizer for the Unitarian Laymen's League in the Atlantic States with offices in New York; I had been a real estate salesman; and a number of incidental things, but I was always active in amateur theatrics whether it was in my church or in the community theatre." Bob's father was in real estate in Miami, Florida, but Bob was not interested in it. However, in need of a job his father introduced him to Vanderbilt Jr and he obtained a job as a copyboy on the newspaper. He was later promoted to the role of a reporter. In reflecting on his time as a reporter for the *Miami Illustrated Tab*, Bob told us of two experiences he had. "I was sent out to go aboard a houseboat berthed on the Miami River to interview a very important political figure. They didn't tell me who it was, so I went down there and got onto the houseboat and who do you suppose it was? Franklin Delano Roosevelt and Eleanor. I had to interview him, he was suffering from his polio condition then, but that was a very interesting experience. Another interesting experience that I had was a policeman was killed in Miami and they finally caught the man who did it up in Palm Beach. We heard about it in the office and the editor said, 'Bob, get on the train and go up to Palm Beach and wait for the train they were going to be on, and then get on and get the story if you can.' So I went up there and got on the train the arrestee was on but I couldn't get an interview. He was in the custody of two deputies and they wouldn't let me speak to him. So I came all the way back to Miami without a story, which was a disappointment to me and to my city editor."

During the years of 1926-27 Bob was in Birmingham, Alabama, and was working as the advertising manager in a woman's-ready-to-wear store. In his spare time he performed with the Birmingham Little Theatre, a local community theatre, and one of the plays he was in was called *Sun-up*, in which he played the lead character. Because of this role he was approached by the director of the local stock company, The Birmingham Players, who told Bob that he was very good as an amateur and would he be interested in working with his group for a one week run. Bob received permission from his employer and accepted the offer. "I did one week with them and got good notices," Bob told us, "and then a week or so later he asked me if I'd do another play and I said, 'Sure.' Well, the Saturday of that week in which I did the second play the firm I was working with went bankrupt and when I went back after the matinee performance to go to work for half an hour or so before coming back for the evening performance there was a foreclosure notice on the door of the store, so I was out of a job. When I went back to the theatre that afternoon I asked if I may stay on with the company, I have no job now. The director said, 'You bet your life you can, I'd love to have you.' So I started with that company the very next week and we finished the spring season together."

Bob left Birmingham and went to Atlanta, Georgia, to the stock company where Sidney Blackmer and Madge Kennedy were playing. "I went backstage and asked the stage manager and asked if I could have a job with them and he said, 'Yes, of course. I need someone.' So that was my second job almost immediately. When that season was over I went to New York and then my trouble really begin because I got there the wrong time of the year and no new jobs were opening up." Bob obtained a job for an agent named Chamberlain Brown pasting clippings in theatrical agency press books. After some months he became fed up with the job and didn't want to do that anymore so he obtained a job on Wall Street selling stocks and bonds. "I didn't know anything about selling stocks and bonds in those days," he informed, "but they put me through a training course; After the Depression of October 1929 I couldn't sell anymore stocks and bonds and either could anybody else, so I told my wife that I'm going back up to Broadway and see if I could get work as an actor." After only ten days Bob landed a job with a company called The Rap and had a very small part of a policeman. "But it was a job," Bob said, "and I was a professional actor now." After the play completed its run in New York, it went on the road to Chicago for another three or four weeks before it closed. During the run of the show Bob questioned his fellow actors on how to go about obtaining future jobs. He was told if you do not know anybody you should write letters asking for an interview. So Bob returned to New York and wrote a letter to the director of the Berkshire Players in the summer stock company in Stockbridge, Massachusetts. The director wrote back that he would be coming to New York soon and while there he would interview Bob. This happened and Bob was hired for the coming summer season and spent that following summer in Stockbridge. "As time goes on you meet more and more people in this business. You talk about what's going on, who's who and in that first company was Walter Connolly,

Netta Harrigan, George Coulouris, Leo Carillo and Frances Fuller." The latter was the wife of a director named Worthington Miner, who was to soon produce a play called *Wild Waves*, which was a satire on the radio business. He gave Robert a part in this play, and, as Bob explained, "One thing leads to another and that's how you get work."

Bob's first real hit as an actor was as the defense attorney in *Night of January 16*. He also appeared in *Both Your Houses*, which won the Pulitzer Prize in 1935. After this show closed, Bob reprised his role in *Night of January 16* all over the New England States in summer stock as guest leading man. "I'll tell you a funny story about that play at Stony Creek, Rhode Island," Bob laughed. "I was a guest star and came on Sunday to rehearsal with the company so they knew what I was going to do, and on opening night on Monday there was a local boy playing the bailiff over at the side of the court room, and when the first act was over he came out center stage and went, 'Sssh! Sssh!' because the audience were all applauding. He didn't have sense to know that was what we were working hard for."

Bob had the usual vicissitudes of a young actor...feast or famine. Most of the plays he did in New York at that time were flops until a chance came along to do *White Oaks* with Ethel Barrymore. He played Rennie Whiteoaks who is the grandson and supposedly the head of the family. They played fourteen weeks in New York, then closed for the summer, and then went on a thirty-nine week transcontinental tour starting in Halifax. They opened there in the fall and finally came down to Boston, where Bob had an amusing experience with Barrymore. The opening night in Boston they were all seated around the family dining room table in the living room. Ethel was at the head of the table and Bob was at her left. The curtain went up and instead of speaking her line she began to babble; the rest of the cast looked at one another and Bob finally jumped in and threw her a cue which she picked up after giving him a baleful look, she then went along and was all right. After the play was over, the stage manager came to Bob's room and said, "Bob, the old lady wants to see you." Bob asked what it was about but the fellow said he did not know, so Bob went down to the stage where Miss Barrymore was seated in her chair. Bob approached her and asked, "Miss Barrymore, you wanted to see me?" "Yes Mister Shayne," she replied, "what was the meaning of that unseemly conduct of yours at the beginning of the play?" "I don't understand Miss Barrymore," Bob responded. She said, "Those words that you gave." "Oh," Bob said, "I thought you had dried and I was jumping in to help you." She turned and gave him another baleful look, and said, "Mister Shayne, a Barrymore never dries."

From there Bob did a number of plays: "Along came a chance to replace Donald Cook in *Claudia* with Phyllis Thaxter," he reflected, "which I leaped at and I had a long run with her at the Saint James Theatre. The following season the Theatre Guild asked me to be in a play called *Without Love* with Katharine Hepburn, and that played all through the winter and on up to February. By February I was tapped on the shoulder by Warner Brothers, and they wanted to know if I wanted to come out and do pictures. I said, 'You bet your life, how much money?' They told me and I was completely satisfied, so on February 22, 1943 I flew to California and arrived there overnight. On Monday I walked out of the Glendale Airport and saw all this gorgeous sunlight and thought, 'Oh boy, this is for me!' and I've been here ever since."

Warner Brothers started giving Bob experience before the cameras with several two-reel Western shorts that were condensations of full-length feature films they had made and released them over the following three years. "I learned to ride a horse at that time," he laughed, "never learned to be very good at it." After the Westerns, the first feature Bob made was *Shine On Harvest Moon* with Dennis Morgan and Ann Sheridan. "That was the first musical I've ever been in." After that, Bob made a picture with Jack Carson and Jane Wyman titled *Make Your Own Bed*; other pictures followed, including playing Bette Davis' lover in *Mr. Skeffington*; a picture with John Garfield called *Nobody Lives Forever,* in which he played the heavy; then opposite Barbara Stanwyck in *Christmas In Connecticut*; and a "small part, which everybody on the lot did, in *Rhapsody In Blue,* with Robert Alda." Then the war was over and Bob figured his career was not going to get anywhere on the lot with some of the leading men coming back from the service, so he asked for a release from his contract to free-lance. The studio honored his request and Bob's agent, Sam Armstrong, kept him working constantly as a free-lance actor.

During this stage of his career he made the first of his science fiction films. His first free-lance feature was a low budget horror film called *Face of Marble*, which co-starred John Carradine. "I went to a preview of that picture at a theatre in East Los Angeles and after seeing the picture I was naturally ashamed that I had been in it. I went out to the lobby with my wife, and as I got to the lobby a couple of girls came out of the theatre and one of them recognized me, saying, 'Mister Shayne, you ought to be ashamed of being in a picture like that.'" Speaking of another sci-fi horror picture titled *The Neanderthal Man,* in which he played the title character, Bob told us "We did the changes in a special performance on a Sunday. The make-up man would make me up and we would take a shot and then we would stop and he would make me up a little more and we would take some more shots, and finally we had what they wanted."

Bob has no favorite films or type of roles, but he enjoyed playing second lead opposite Bob Cummings and Hedy Lamarr in *Let's Live A Little*, and also as the coach of the West Point football team opposite real-life West Point football stars Glenn Davis and "Doc" Blanchard in *The Spirit Of West Point*. "I did anything that came along that they cast me in," Bob explained. "I did the best job that I could do. *Three Strangers* was an odd bit of casting – They cast me as a cockney criminal. I had never played a cockney part in my entire career, but somehow or another I got away with it."

One of the last motion pictures Bob acted in was *Tora! Tora! Tora!*. "I was an officer in the Pentagon who was poo-pooing the idea that the Japanese were going to attack us. I retired from acting after this picture." Bob worked in many television shows in addition to his motion pictures and stage work. He appeared in some of the early live-TV shows, but didn't like it much. "Too much pressure," he stated. "They didn't know the technique of making films for TV in the early days. They learned by experience." Other television roles included work in such series as *Gunsmoke, Lone Ranger, 26 Men*, and in 1990 he came out of retirement to do an episode of *The Flash*. In *26 Men*, filmed in Arizona, Bob commented on the discomfort of the location: "So damn hot the day we were shooting I practically fainted, wearing the heavy woolen Western clothes." Obviously the most well-known series that Bob appeared in was the role of Inspector William Henderson in *Adventures of Superman*. This show ran from 1951 through 1957. Reflecting on this show, Bob said, "My agent called me up one day and said, 'Bob, I have a part for you in a series for TV, do you want it?' I said, 'What's the money?' He told me and I said, 'Sure I'll do it.' He said, 'I have to take you over to the producers office, he wants to see you first before he casts you; he thinks he wants you.' So we went over to the producer's office on the old RKO lot in Culver City. He looked me over and said, 'Do you mind greying your hair, you're a bit young to play opposite George Reeves.' I said, 'How old is George?' He answered, 'Forty-seven or forty-eight.' 'I'm older than that,' I said. He hired me. I didn't think the thing would amount to a hill of beans, I never thought it would be a classic series, and it went on and on for several years. I think the first twenty-six episodes were the best of the whole *Superman* series. They had more variety to them, more conflict. George and I were somewhat of the same temperament, we didn't believe in clowning around on the set. We were there to do our job, and we did it; we were all business, George and I. We were very good friends and his death was a great loss to all of us."

When asked what he has done since he retired, Bob laughed and remarked, "I vegetated. No, I began experimenting with writing. I never solved a crime on *Superman* so I wrote a script for a segment to be on *Love Boat*. The inspector finally gets his man, but just as I finished it *Love Boat* went off the air. I've just written a script that is out circulating now called *An Indian Summer*, which is a simple love story. Writing is harder work than being an actor." When asked if he enjoys writing, he answered without hesitation, "Indeed I do." Bob also organized and ran the Camarillo Community Theatre for three-and-a-half years in the mid-1970s. "I never acted in any of the shows," he commented, "I always directed. I did *Born Yesterday, Little Women, Voice Of The Turtle*; I never had a losing week, always made money." Bob was set to do the play of *South Pacific* in the summer or fall of 1990 for his church in Camarillo. "It got too much for me," Bob commented. "I don't drive anymore and I couldn't function to do all the running around and organizing that needed to be done. I had no organization in back of me like I did in Camarillo Community Theatre that you could draw from for backstage, front office and publicity. I had to build up the whole thing, but it was too much for me so I had to withdraw."

Looking over his career as an actor, Bob told us that he has done ninety-seven motion pictures, three hundred and fifty television segments, forty to fifty stage plays, including stock and some hit Broadway shows. Three of his favorite actresses he played opposite were Bette Davis in *Mr. Skeffington*; Barbara Stanwyck in *Christmas in Connecticut*; and his favorite was Katharine Hepburn in the Broadway play, *Without Love*.

In expressing his feelings on his career, Bob said, "I'd do it all over again if I had the chance. I was struck with the stage and got to love making pictures after awhile. I've enjoyed being an actor and think it's a beautiful profession if things go right for you. I'm not at all in sympathy with the kind of crap that is on television nowadays, I'd be very careful of what I went into if I had a chance of going into something that's being made today. I think some of these young producers and directors are fresh out of drama school and they think they have a brilliant idea and make a bunch of crap. George Kaufman, a famous writer-producer-director in the theatre, told me a good play should have a beginning, a middle and an end. In the beginning you establish your leading man and leading woman and what the situation is; in the second act you throw stones at him, get him up a tree figuratively speaking; and in the third act you get him down. I miss the big studios. All the casting directors in the big studios knew the work of practically every actor in Hollywood. I didn't have to come in for an audition, my agent would suggest my name and they'd hire me. Nowadays you're interviewed by some little girl sitting in a front desk who doesn't know a thing about me or what I've done, and says, 'What have you done, Mister Shayne?' And I'm always tempted to say, 'About what?'" And then he laughed. "A most interesting career indeed."

Robert Shayne died on November 29, 1992 at Woodland Hills, California.

Film Credits: 1934: Keep 'em Rolling; Wednesday's Child. **1937:** See Uncle Sol (short); Off the Horses (short). **1938:** Air Parade (short). **1943:** Oklahoma Outlaws (short); Wagon Wheels West (short); Youth Train for Aviation (short – narrator); Mission to Moscow. **1944:** Gun to Gun (short); Law of the Badlands (short); Rhapsody in Blue; Roaring Guns (short); Hollywood Canteen; Shine on Harvest Moon; **Mr.** Skeffington; Make Your Own Bed; Trial by Trigger (short); I Won't Play (short). **1945:** Christmas in Connecticut; San Antonio; Navy Nurse (short); Frontier Days (short); Escape in the Desert (voice). **1946:** I Ring Doorbells; Behind the Mask; My Reputation; Nobody Lives Forever; Three Strangers; Wife Wanted; Face of Marble. **1947:** Backlash; I Cover Big Town; Smash Up, the Story of a Woman; Spirit of West Point; Welcome Stranger. **1948:** The Swordsman; Best Man Wins; The Inside Story; Let's Live a Little; Loaded Pistols; Shaggy; The Strange Mrs. Crane. **1949:** Forgotten Women; Law of the Barbary Coast; The Threat. **1950:** Dynamite Pass; Customs Agent; When You're Smiling; Rider from Tucson; Big Timber; Experiment Alcatraz; State Penitentiary; Federal Man. **1951:** The Dakota Kid; Criminal Lawyer; Missing Woman. **1952:** Indian Uprising; Mr. Walkie Talkie; Without Warning; Behind Prison Walls; The Ring. **1953:** Flight Nurse; The Invaders from Mars; The Lady Wants Mink; Eyes of the Jungle; The Neanderthal Man; Sea of Lost Ships; Marshal of Cedar Rock; The Blue Gardenia; Prince of Pirates. **1954:** Tobor the Great; The Desperado; Trader Tom of the China Seas (serial). **1955:** Murder is My Beat; Double Jeopardy; The Eternal

Sea; King of the Carnival (serial). **1956:** Accused of Murder; Dance with Me Henry; Rumble on the Docks; The Indestructible Man; Hot Shots. **1957:** Kronos, Spook Chasers; Footsteps in the Dark; Death in Small Doses; The Giant Claw. **1958:** How to Make a Monster; War of the Satellites; Revolt in the Big House; The Lost Missile; I, Mobster; Teenage Caveman. **1959:** North by Northwest; Battle Flame; The Rebel Set. **1960:** Valley of the Redwoods; Toby Tyler; Cage of Evil; Why Must I Die?; From the Terrace. **1961:** 20,000 Eyes. **1963:** Son of Flubber. **1964:** A Tiger Walks. **1966:** Runaway Girl. **1969:** Winning; The Arrangement. **1970:** Tora! Tora! Tora! **1971:** $1,000,000 Duck; The Barefoot Executive; The Priest Killer (TV). **1972:** Cool Breeze. **1975:** The Specialist. **1976:** The Four Deuces. **1977:** Never Con a Killer (TV).

To Jim —
Health and happiness to you! My blessings and love always
Marion Shilling

MARION SHILLING

Marion Shilling was born December 3, 1910 in Denver, Colorado. Her father, Edward Schilling, and his partner, O.D. Woodward, operated a stock company at the Empress Theater in Saint Louis during the 1920's. In addition, they also operated simultaneously companies in Kansas City, where Shirley Booth was leading lady, and in Cincinnati, where Amelia Bingham was the star. Other reliable players in the company included four actors that later became familiar faces on the movie screen, those being Bradley Page, Selmer Jackson, Frank Jacquet and Erville Alderson.

"My grandparents," she told us, "were pioneers of Colorado. My mom's father, David Connelly, was born in Albany, New York, just a week after his immigrant parents had arrived from Ireland. As an adult he learned of the possibilities in the new state of Colorado so he traveled there and purchased a lot of land."

David was a strong Democrat and supporter of Grover Cleveland. There hadn't been a Democratic president since before the Civil War. One night in the fall of 1884, David, campaigning for Cleveland, joined a torchlight parade, caught a cold that developed into pneumonia, and died.

"When his sons grew to manhood," Marion continued, "they wanted cash and the three of them insisted on selling the land their father had acquired. Despite my mother's protests the land was disposed of and this very property later became the heart of Denver's business district."

Marion went on, "My mother's mother was born in Cork, Ireland, emigrated to America, and later met and married my grandfather in Denver. My dad's father, Peter Schilling, was born in Alsace- Lorraine. He and his family came to America when he was three years old and settled in Western Pennsylvania. Grandpa was a drummer boy in the Civil War. His older brothers fought in the first battle of Bull Run. After the war the family moved to Colorado and the boys worked as coal miners.

"Grandpa served as a timber boss and was outraged at the unjust treatment the miners suffered. When the mine owners temporarily shut down the mines, the miners and their families would almost starve. There were no provisions set aside for these dry periods. The working conditions were deplorable. This was true also in Wales. Throughout the world workers were downtrodden. Fortunately a few enlightened people like Eugene V. Debs saw the injustice and did something about it," Marion explained. "Grandpa was one of the organizers of what was called the Knights of Labor. This later developed into the American Federation of Labor.

"In those days the miners were terribly exploited," Marion informed us. "They worked under inhuman conditions, while the mine owners thrived. Unions were highly important in our country's history, in our national consciousness. But later the pendulum swung the other way. And ironically in the turnaround my father was affected adversely. In Saint Louis, when daddy was operating a legitimate theater, the unions were very strong and were actually run by gangsters. For instance, an orchestra played an overture and furnished music between the acts. The union would dictate all the terms, who the particular director would be and how many musicians would have to be employed. There was considerable variation in the talents of the musical directors, but the theater management would have no choice in the matter.

"A set number of people had to be employed backstage. One man was employed merely to turn on the lights initially before each performance. He was paid a substantial salary to do this. On union terms, of course. One night he happened to show up late and someone else turned on the lights. The next day, during the matinee performance, a stink bomb was thrown into the theatre and the audience had to leave. The union boss would occasionally come by the theatre to check things out. He had a sinister demeanor and a holstered gun was clearly visible.

"When my dad and his partner eventually came to California to operate theaters, open shop prevailed. There were no unions to worry about in those days. Canned music was even permitted. The need for unions has surely been well indicated in the unfoldment of our country's history, but if everyone were fair-minded, practiced the Golden Rule, unions would not be necessary.

"Daddy and Mr. Woodward were able to secure the rights to produce the play, *Dracula* on the West coast. They brought the original cast, headed by Bela Lugosi, and all the scenery to California. It was an exceedingly profitable venture. All up and down the coast, Los Angeles, San Francisco, Seattle, Portland, and so forth, every theater in which the play was presented was filled to capacity. Every last seat even in the second balcony had to be dusted off. The theater was packed for each performance."

When Marion's father first read the script of "Dracula," he was crestfallen. "Good heavens, what have I done, investing in this silly play," he thought. But produced on the stage, it was entrancing. The public adored it. Bela's part was only fifteen "sides" long, but he commanded the entire performance. "What presence he had," added Marion.

"In Los Angeles at the old Biltmore Theatre, it was exciting to see the many movie stars and notables trooping into the theater. Clara Bow, then at the peak of her fame, attended at least two performances a week during the two months run. She'd sometimes come directly from her beach house wearing a fur coat over her bathing suit. The play's attraction for her? Bela Lugosi! She had a terrific crush on him. Bela liked to tell my father that if I were a bit older, without question he'd marry me. I'm certain this was a bit of blarney. In competition with the scintillating Clara, what chance would poor green little Marion have had! I was a very unsophisticated seventeen. I had an exceedingly protective mother. I was naive, even by the standards of that long-ago period. In those days, well-brought up girls almost without exception lived at home until they were married."

Marion shared an amusing side note concerning Bela Lugosi. "Lugosi told my dad that when he first undertook the role of Dracula he was fresh from Hungary and spoke no English. He had to learn all of his lines in the play phonetically. One line in the play continued to puzzle him. It is brought out that the only way Dracula can be done away with is for a stake to be driven into his heart while he is sleeping. In his limited English, the only stake he was familiar with was beefsteak. For at least the first six months of the play he simply couldn't figure out how a steak could be driven into his heart, and how that could kill him.

"My father and his partner brought several other distinguished plays from New York and London to the West Coast - *The Play's the Thing*, *Her Cardboard Lover*, and *The High Road* - and then sound came to the movies and this sensational novelty made its advent in spectacular display. Everyone wanted to witness the talkies. And, alas, the legitimate theaters were deserted.

"My father's health had been failing him and things began to look rather gloomy for our family. Then, suddenly, Fortune smiled, and our Fairy Godmother touched us with her wand. I had a small part in *Dracula*, a top Hollywood agent happened to notice me and one day I got a surprise call from him," Marion explained. "Meet me in my office in half an hour," he said. "MGM is looking for a young actress and you seem just right for the part." Marion was tested for the part, got it and a term contract at MGM.

Kempy had been a top Broadway hit and was transferred to the screen as *Wise Girls*. It was MGM's very first film made exclusively for theaters wired for sound. "I had the leading ingénue role, appeared in nearly every scene and had the pleasure of working with Elliott and J.C. Nugent, Roland Young and Clara Blandick," Marion said. "Then came the leading ingénue role in the MGM musical, *Lord Byron of Broadway*, and a cameo appearance in a Buster Keaton feature, *Free and Easy*.

"Then I was put under contract to Paramount and enjoyed the privilege of playing opposite William Powell in *Shadow of the Law*. I was lent out to Fox studios for *On Your Back* and then was signed by RKO-Pathé. There followed *Beyond Victory* opposite Lew Cody, *Young Donovan's Kid* opposite Richard Dix and Jackie Cooper, and a good part in *The Common Law* starring Constance Bennett. Then came my first Western, *The Sundown Trail* opposite Tom Keene."

Leading or starring parts followed: *Forgotten Women* for Monogram. This with Rex Bell; the top role in *Shop Angel* for Tower Productions, also *The County Fair*. Allied Artists featured her in *A Parisian Romance* with Gilbert Roland and Lew Cody, and *A Man's Land* with Hoot Gibson. Then Marion kept busy in a long string of Westerns with Buck Jones, more with Hoot Gibson, Tom Tyler, Big Boy Williams, Tim McCoy.

There were also two major serials, *The Red Rider* with Buck Jones and Grant Withers, and *The Clutching Hand* with Jack Mulhall, Ruth Mix, Rex Lease, Mae Busch, and a long roster of stars from the silent days of pictures.

"A most exciting privilege was granted me in playing the role of Helena in Max Reinhardt's magnificent stage production of *A Midsummer Night's Dream*," Marion stated. "Olivia de Havilland made her professional debut as Hermia, Mickey Rooney played Puck, Leif Erickson was Oberon, and Bottom's country folk were all played by little people, all of whom were movie character actors who on returning to Hollywood were used by Walt Disney as models for the Seven Dwarfs. We toured throughout the Midwest and an entire train was needed to transport cast, crew, a large ballet and a chorus. The leading symphony orchestra of each city we played furnished the music.

"I had no acting lessons to prepare for all of the above. My only experience had been several child parts in my dad's company in Saint Louis, and these roles had to be played in accommodation to my studies at school. In an aside, may I remark that one of the best preparations for an acting career is reading aloud. Lillian Elliott Fontaine, mother of Olivia de Havilland and Joan Fontaine, as well as a coach and scholar, had her girls reading Shakespeare aloud from the time they learned to talk. This helps to account for their clear diction and the rich resonance of their voices.

"My career thrived as long as John Lancaster was my agent. But during the period at Pathé when things looked most promising for me - I was even accorded the honor of being chosen as Wampas Baby Star of 1931 - Mr. Lancaster suddenly had a heart attack and soon afterwards, died. An actor needs a strong agent or interested director or producer to act as guide and mentor. I was too young and not smart enough to be able to manage my professional life by myself.

"It's an advantage for an actress to be seasoned, a bit toughened up to cope with life's vicissitudes. My parents, with the best of intentions felt they should keep me innocent, ignorant. In a number of movies, for instance, I was supposed to have slept with a man. I have a vivid recall of many of the scenes I played, the lines I spoke, and years later, the implications suddenly hit me, and in retrospect gave me some good laughs. In *Beyond Victory*, Lew Cody is about to go off to war. We have an ardent love scene and I plead with him with deep emotion not to leave me. We walk into his bedroom. I, then, had no idea what was going on! Poor little Marion.

"Sophisticated actors, especially the great kidders, had a ball with me. Cliff Edwards, who later supplied the voice for Disney's Jiminy Cricket, teased me unmercifully, as did Tom Keene and Nick Stuart. But these wags, bless them, helped me to cultivate a keener sense of humor and to develop some snappy comebacks. I must admit that being an actress enriches one as a person. What fascinating people I had the privilege of meeting! Right off hand, I knew Madame Ernestine Schumann-Heinck quite well, I chatted with Giovanni Martinelli at a party, danced with David Sarnoff, S. A. Rothafel, of theater fame was a good friend of my family … and all those movie icons I met! During my first movie, Greta Garbo walked up and down by my dressing room every morning practicing her lines for her first talkie. Joan Crawford talked with me a number of mornings while I was having my hair done. John Gilbert, well aware of his good looks, sauntered by each morning as I was putting on my makeup. During those movie and stage days my eyes, my life, were full of stars!

"Reminiscing a bit," Marion continued, "William Powell was a superb actor and most ingratiating person. He sensed my insecurity and tried to put me at ease. He gave me valuable suggestions to help me feel more relaxed in front of the camera and told me little jokes on himself, recounted times when he had stumbled, forgotten a line, indicating that he was a fallible, fellow human being. Bill was lacking in vanity, not at all prepossessed with his importance. He lived modestly, I don't believe he owned a car. A studio limousine picked him up each morning. You would never realize, the way he lived, that he was one of that era's top movie stars.

"A contrast Powell was to Richard Dix, who played the role of 'movie star' for all it was worth. He'd make his entrance on the set each morning followed by a parade of retainers: stand-in, secretary, valet, and several musicians prepared to put him in the proper mood for his scenes. Richard was very aware of his star status, but perhaps he felt it necessary to create an image. He was always courteous and pleasant to me. I remember him urging me to gain some weight. He was trying to be helpful.

"Gilbert Roland was a great tease. His humor was a bit rough, suggestive, he liked to embarrass me, bring forth some blushes and giggles, but he was lots of fun.

"I did several films with Lew Cody, the distinguished star of the silents, whose long stage experience aided his second career in sound pictures, but, alas, he died an early death. His home was within brief walking distance from ours, and one Sunday afternoon all his personal effects were auctioned off on the front lawn of his home. My folks and I walked over to see the well-advertised excitement, but we were appalled by the crude remarks made by the auctioneer. I can still recall his jeering jokes about Lew's rather garish sports jackets. Lew was an immaculately dressed man, who could wear his Rodeo Drive wardrobe with a flourish.

"A thrill it was for me to know Pola Negri in person. I had a teen-age crush on her, never missed one of her movies, and prized a large scrapbook of her pictures. We were both under contract to Pathé at the same time and my scream was substituted for hers on a soundtrack. I did a scream backstage during the run of *Dracula* and was known in Hollywood as an expert, letting out a terrific yell for many a star.

"Jackie Cooper had a prominent part in the Richard Dix film, *Young Donovan's Kid*, following Jackie's big hit as Skippy," Marion continued. "He was a remarkable little actor. His grandmother usually accompanied him on the set and when he was required to do a crying scene, she'd take him on her lap, talk quietly to him for a few moments and he'd produce copious tears and do the scene in one perfect take.

"Boris Karloff played a bit part in that picture. Supposedly a drug addict, he lurked in a dark alley and grabbed me as I walked by. Then Richard Dix came along and rescued me. Boris was a charming polished man, whose fresh-from-England accent enchanted me. Soon after that film Boris was signed by Universal Pictures and went on to his great fame.

"In a number of movies some famous character actor played a prominent role. Invariably he'd seek me out between takes to flirt, help me with my lines and regale me with anecdotes about his career. The actor would revel, I'm certain, in my rapt attention. I specially enjoyed knowing H.B. Warner, Hobart Bosworth, Frank Sheridan. Such fascinating lives they had had. H.B. Warner told me, for instance, that when he portrayed Jesus Christ for Cecil B. DeMille in *The King of Kings* extra women would come to him, kneel, and kiss the hem of his garment.

"The movie with H.B. Warner, *On Your Back*, which also starred Irene Rich, sort of derailed me from a role I would have preferred – opposite John Wayne in *The Big Trail*. John had been a football star, then, trying for a movie career, he became a prop man for Fox. Someone recognized his good looks and decided to give him the leading role in *The Big Trail*. Guthrie McClintic, New York's most distinguished stage director, had been brought to Hollywood by Fox to direct *On Your Back*. The leading ingénue role in this required an actress who could handle long speeches. My stage experience had equipped me for this. Mr. McClintic tested me and I got the part. Meanwhile I had tested for *The Big Trail*. Fate is fickle. Who could ever have guessed that *The Big Trail* would launch the career of one of the screen's greatest stars. I had no say in the matter, of course, but in hindsight one can imagine which part I would have chosen. John was so pleasant, warm, genial, he'd have been great fun to work with."

Reflecting on working in *On Your Back*, Marion told us that "I played the part of a chorus girl and my side kick in the film was a wise-cracking comedienne. The director asked me to spend half a day helping him test an up-and-coming young actress for the part but he finally decided against this actress because he found her 'too tough.' Her name, Carole Lombard. David Manners was tested (again I helped) for the male lead that eventually went to a New York actor, Raymond Hackett, who never made it in Hollywood. David later starred at Warners, RKO and Universal. George Brent played a bit part in this film, then was discovered by Warner Brothers and made a star. This movie, as I mentioned, was directed by the great New York celebrity, Guthrie McClintic, who was the husband of Katharine Cornell. He knew nothing about movie-making, however, and he really messed up this picture and it bombed.

Isn't it interesting to note how some geniuses, like Alfred Hitchcock or Frank Capra, can take a simple story and, with their magic, turn out a classic.

"Joel McCrea was another nice guy. I played in *The Common Law* with him, Constance Bennett, Hedda Hopper and Lew Cody. Joel and Connie were being teamed together in a number of films. She at that time was one of Hollywood's most important stars, for a while earning twenty thousand dollars a week, in those Depression days, a staggering sum. In later years, Joel became much more famous than she. Connie had a tremendous crush on Joel. During filming of *The Common Law* as soon as a scene was completed she'd yank Joel into her dressing room. She'd let no one else near him even to talk to him. She gave his career a big boost though.

"When my son, Ned, was in the Army Reserve, he and Joel's son, David, were in summer camp together. Ned said he seemed a fine person, like his dad. Then years later, as a defense attorney, Ned needed a character witness for one of his clients. Joel McCrea's name was given Ned. Joel spoke well of the man on trial and he was acquitted. Joel subsequently wrote a charming note to me. This was sometime in the late sixties. He said movies weren't as much fun to make as they had been in former years and that the values had deteriorated deplorably.

"Another very fine man I had the pleasure of working with was Buck Jones. *Stone of Silver Creek* and the serial *Red Rider*. I did a considerable amount of riding in this serial and also in lots of Westerns. I was terribly awkward and scared on a horse at first, but I learned fairly quickly and I can boast that eventually I learned to make a flying mount. There was a double, usually a man in clothes like mine, for the very dangerous scenes, but I shudder now remembering some of the chances I took. Galloping over rough countryside with so many gopher and snake holes was certainly hazardous. If the horse had happened to stumble on one of those holes it would have been disastrous. My horse on one occasion was stung by a yellow jacket and I was thrown. I got right back on again and continued with the scene. I saw it in the rushes the next day, and decided that for sure I had a guardian angel watching over me.

"One day while making *Red Rider*, I thought it was a good idea during a long wait between scenes to go off by myself and practice riding a bit. I became aware of someone following me, I looked around and there was Buck Jones. As I caught his eye, he started laughing and said, 'Marion, that's the best example I've ever seen of a horse riding a girl!'

"Buck, over a period, gave me some excellent tips that were very helpful. Buck was a dear person, thoughtful of everyone. He told me one day that he wanted to introduce me to someone," Marion recalled. Buck guided her to an old Indian sitting in the corner of the set. "Marion," Buck said, "I want you to meet Jim Thorpe." "Not THE Jim Thorpe," Marion exclaimed. "The very one," Buck answered. "I'm certain that Buck staged this incident more for Jim's benefit than for mine," Marion told us.

"What a completely different experience it is to act on the stage rather than appear before a camera. There's an excitement about the stage; you get an electric *something* from the live audience. The very smell of a theatre is enchanting. Once you've walked upon a stage, you'll forever carry fond memories. The muse who wrote the script of my life blessed me with a cherished favor in permitting me to be associated with the great Max Reinhardt in his production of *A Midsummer Night's Dream*. Reinhardt must be considered one of the leading theatrical entrepreneurs of the twentieth century. Like many noted achievers, he was of diminutive size. He was modest, gentle, kind. To meet him casually, one would never suspect he was a genius. But what an imagination he had! What an artist he was!

"Mickey Rooney as Puck dominated the show. He squeezed the last drop of possibility from that part. How delighted Shakespeare would have been with his performance. Mickey was a longtime friend of mine. Every night while I was applying my makeup, Mickey would come to my dressing room and hold the hair dryer over my hair; and he'd never fail to get me laughing about something. In 1931, he and I were the first people to ride up Hollywood Boulevard leading the Christmas Parade. Mickey was a small boy then. I recall his mother boosting him up onto the float."

Later, Marion's husband, Edward Cook, played tennis with Rooney at the Los Angeles Tennis Club. She told us that sometime back in the 1950's as they were driving to the East Coast, they stopped off the first night at Las Vegas and Rooney happened to be headlining at the Sands Hotel. "We were fortunate to get a ringside seat for Mickey's dinner show," she informed us. "His act was sensational, the audience loved him. After the performance we went backstage and were flattered by the reception he gave us. He hugged both of us several times and introduced us to his current wife, a tall, gorgeous brunette. Mickey well deserved his fame. He's so full of talent, enthusiasm, love."

When asked to sum up her feelings on her acting career, Marion stated, "How deeply I appreciate the tremendous privilege I enjoyed being in the fascinating world of the theater and participating even modestly in the Golden Age of Hollywood. That prestigious period brought forth films of highest quality, films that carried excellent values. Movies then achieved their appeal through character, genuine human interest, common sense, rather than in violence and explicit sex.

"I'm grateful for the joy of sharing in the magic of that fabled period. I'm grateful for having known and worked with such worthwhile people. My chief regret is that I can't play those parts all over again! As the years progress we grow as persons. We unfold as human beings. I'm so much wiser now, so much smarter than was that unripe young girl.

"Such directors as William Wyler and Charlie Chaplin are said to have made innumerable shots of a scene until a perfect result was achieved. Perhaps fifty or sixty repetitions. A contrast indeed to the quickie Western where the first attempt, good or bad, was printed. Alas, life, like the low budget films, is strictly a one take production! All that we stumbling, bumbling humans can do is to do our best – and leave the rest to God."

Marion passed away at Torrance, California on November 6, 2004.

Film Credits: 1930: Wise Girls; Lord Byron of Broadway; On Your Back; Shadow of the Law; The Swellhead. **1931:** Beyond Victory; The Common Law; Sundown Trail; Young Donovan's Kid; June First (short); Easy to Get (short); Take 'em and Shake 'em (short). **1932:** Heart Punch; A Parisian Romance; The County Fair; Forgotten Women; A Man's Land; Shop Angel; A Woman Commands (Voice only); Only Men Wanted (short); Gigolettos (short); Rule 'em and Weep (short); Niagara Falls (short); Screen Snapshots (short). **1933:** Curtain at Eight; Not The Marrying Kind (short); Elinor Norton. **1934:** Inside Information; Thunder over Texas; Fighting To Live; The Red Rider (serial); The Westerner. **1935:** Keeper of the Bees; A Shot in The Dark; Society Fever; Stone of Silver Creek; Blazing Guns; Captured in Chinatown; Gun Play (ala Lucky Boots); Gunsmoke on the Guadeloupe; Rio Rattler; Gun Play (aka Lucky Boots). **1936:** The Clutching Hand (serial); Romance Rides the Range; I'll Name the Murderer; Idaho Kid; Cavalcade of the West.

RICHARD SIMMONS

Richard Simmons was born August 19, 1913 in St. Paul, Minnesota. When he was only fourteen years old, Richard learned to fly airplanes. Being raised there, he attended the University of Minnesota. While going to school he worked as a radio announcer, "simply to make some money," he commented.

Richard and a friend decided to come to California, not with the idea of getting into the picture business, rather it was during the Depression era and as a result there were not any jobs at home. "We were young," he recalled, "so we got on a freight train and came to the west coast. The trip took over a month; every so often they'd stop and shake all of us bums off and make us fight forest fires."

After arriving in Los Angeles, Dick started into radio announcing, and also announced the bands at the Palladium, "All the big bands," he added. He began to do some little theater and then appeared in small parts in several films, the most notable of them being *Sergeant York* at Warner Brothers in 1941. "I was on the picture quite a while, but didn't have much of a part in it," he noted. "I couldn't make enough money at it so I went back into flying." Dick was flying airlines when the war came along and as he had a reserve commission in ROTC, he was pulled into the war right away. "I was a fighter pilot in the war," Simmons continued, "and stayed in the Air Force reserve for twenty-nine years."

Just before the war, Richard had been riding in a rodeo at Palm Springs and was spotted by L.B. Meyer, who invited him to the studio where he gave him a screen test and hired him. "I did *Stand by for Action* with Bob Taylor, Walter Brennan, Brian Donlevy and Charles Laughton. It was an all-men story," he added.

After the close of the war, Simmons went back with MGM, where he was placed under contract and put through their school. "I was in everything," he reflected. "Diversification is the hallmark of how good you may or may not be."

During the fourteen years he was with Metro, Dick appeared in such films as *Love Laughs at Andy Hardy*, with Mickey Rooney; *The Three Musketeers*, with Gene Kelly; *Battle Circus*, starring Humphrey Bogart; and *Lady in the Lake*, featuring Robert Montgomery. Of the last film, Dick comments, "It was a picture done in an unusual way. The camera was the star of the show, shot from its point of view so that you didn't see Bob Montgomery unless he was reflected in a mirror. I was always talking right at the camera."

"Action films were more fun than anything else," Dick commented. He appeared in several serials at Republic Pictures, and in 1954 played the title role of *The Man with the Steel Whip*, a character who was quite similar to Zorro. "I was one character during the day and another at night," Simmons stated. His last two major feature films were action-comedies entitled *Sergeants Three* and *Robin and the Seven Hoods*, both films starring his longtime pal, Frank Sinatra. "I've known Frank since he was singing with Dorsey," he said. "I told you I used to announce the bands at the Palladium. Frank's a very good friend of mine; a fantastic guy. We had lots of good times together."

For years, Dick would be the MC at all of MGM's premiers and he also had a couple of MGM radio series. The first was titled *Good News from Hollywood*; Lucille Ball and Desi Arnaz were on it once, and Dick remembers they came in and said, "We almost spent our last dime for gas. This better be good." "Look where they went from there," Dick said. The other radio show was in 1950, and was called *At Home with Lionel Barrymore*. It was about two guys sitting on Lionel's front porch gossiping about the neighbors who were imaginary characters that would pass by the street in front of his house. Lionel would say something like, "Well, there goes so and so again. I wonder what he's going to do," or, "Did you know what he said?" Dick mentioned, "Barrymore was like a father to me. He was fantastic. We had great, wonderful fun."

About 1954, the picture business began to ebb somewhat and Richard got into television. "You did everything you could," said Dick. "I did those *Hallmark Hall of Fame* shows; I don't know how many. I did them opposite Sarah Churchill, Winston Churchill's daughter." Other television shows followed, such as *Mr. & Mrs. North*, *The Loretta Young Show*, *My Little Margie*, *Kit Carson*, *Stories of the Century* as bad man Ben Thompson, and in 1955 the title role of *Sergeant Preston of the Yukon*, a weekly series which lasted until 1958. Speaking of Sergeant Preston, Dick reflected, "At the time I didn't really want to do it because I thought I was going to get stuck doing this thing, but I did it and it turned out to be one of the top shows on the air at that time."

Speaking of the busy schedule that one can have as a television actor, Dick continued, "One year I made fifty-two Preston shows, ninety-three shows for the Pacific Power and Light Company, making them at night and on weekends, and eight shows with Loretta

Young. They do not waste any time: seventy-two set-ups a day; pretty tough. I'll tell you, I was hanging on the ropes, but that's the way it is with this business. It's either feast or famine."

After *Sergeant Preston* concluded, Dick did a daytime show for CBS titled *Clear Horizon*, a soap opera about Cape Canaveral. Other television roles included episodes for *Perry Mason*, *Gunsmoke*, *The Munsters*, *Richard Diamond*, *Rawhide*, *Leave It to Beaver*, *Ripcord*, *It Takes a Thief* and *The Brady Bunch*. From there he went into a show called *Daring Venture* for his longtime friend, Bob Stabler, who was a veteran of the television series *Death Valley Days*. "I made a lot of those with Ron Reagan and Bob Taylor," Dick commented. In the process of making *Dark Venture*, Dick was involved in a helicopter crash. "We weren't shooting the picture at the time," Dick mentioned, "but I was flying the helicopter and the rotary came apart and we hit the side of a mountain. I broke my back and both legs and was laid up for about three years. So I thought, well, why not just hang it up."

They sold their large home in Encino, as their children were no longer living with them, and moved to a mobile home park where he became manager of the complex until recently. "Now I'm retired again," Dick related. "I play golf and take life easy."

In describing his career as an actor, Dick summed it up this way: "It was a great experience. It was something that led you into areas and through doors that no other occupation would probably allow you to do. When I was doing the Preston show, I was in New York one night at a big dinner and was sitting at the speakers table between the Duke and Duchess of Windsor. All I could think about was here was a guy who abdicated his throne for a woman; gave up his kingdom for a woman." Another time, when Ronald Reagan was campaigning for Governor of California, "I was the guy who introduced him and put him on the air; then Ron came on and made his speech. So, you get into things where you meet kings and queens or presidents, or whatever. If I had it to do all over again, I'd do it all over again. It's been very good to me and I don't have any complaints."

Richard Simmons passed away on January 11, 2003, in Oceanside, California.

Film Credits: 1938: Million To One. **1939:** Dead End Kids on Dress Parade. **1940:** King of the Royal Mounted; One Million BC. **1941:** King of the Texas Rangers; Pirates on Horseback; Sergeant York. **1942:** Yukon Patrol; Stand By for Action; Dr. Gillespie's New Assistant; Keep 'em Sailing (short); Seven Sweethearts. **1943:** Pilot No. 5; The Youngest Profession; Thousands Cheer. **1946:** Love Laughs at Andy Hardy. **1947:** Lady in the Lake; This Time for Keeps; Undercover Maisie. **1948:** Act of Violence; On an Island With You; The Three Musketeers; Easter Parade; A Southern Yankee; The Pirate; Three Young Daughters. **1949:** Look for the Silver Lining; The Great Sinner; Neptune's Daughter. **1950:** Duchess of Idaho; Dial 1119; To Please a Lady. **1951:** The Well; No Questions Asked; I'll See You in My Dreams; Three Guys Named Mike; Angels in the Outfield; Mr. Imperium. **1952:** I Dream of Jeannie; Glory Alley; Desperate Search; Thunderbirds; The Sellout. **1953:** Woman They Almost Lynched; Flight Nurse; Battle Circus; Three Soldiers and a Girl; Above and Beyond;

Easy to Love; So This is Love; Remains to be Seen. **1954:** Men of the Fighting Lady; Man With the Steel Whip; Rear Window; Rogue Cop; A Star is Born; Brigadoon; Tennessee Champ. **1955:** You're Never Too Young; Love Me or Leave Me; Interrupted Melody; It's Always Fair Weather; The Scarlet Coat. **1962:** Sergeants Three. **1963:** Lassie's Great Adventure. **1964:** Robin and the Seven Hoods. **1965:** A Letter to Nancy. **1968:** The Devil's Brigade. **1969:** Don't Push, I'll Charge When I'm Ready. **1971:** The Resurrection of Zachary Wheeler.

MICKEY SIMPSON

Mickey Simpson was born Charles Henry Simpson on December 3, 1913 at Rochester, New York, the son of an ex-policeman. "Dad made seven dollars a week raising three kids," Mickey reflected. "I shined shoes for five cents." He had a spot at Rattlesnake Pete's, a local saloon, and if a client was drunk enough he would throw a dime in for a tip. "A big tip in those days," Mickey added. He later did some boxing.

When Mickey was seventeen years old a friend named Doug asked him, "Why don't we take a run out to the coast and work in the woods?" "Why not?" Mickey replied. He talked it over with his dad, who gave his blessings for the trip. A skeptical uncle, however, said, "You'll never make it. Tell you what I'll do – I'll give you fifty dollars if you make it in fifty days." "Doug," Mickey asked, "can we do it?" His friend answered, "We'll have to ride express trains."

Their destination was Marshfield, Oregon. "Furthest point west from New York State," Mickey informed us. They hitchhiked to Cleveland, Ohio. "Not many cars on the road in those days," he explained. "Hopped our first train out of there. I had fifteen cents in my pocket, a can of sardines, and a change of clothes. We didn't look like hobos, we were clean and we kept clean. So we started out and, by golly, we made Marshfield in three weeks, right to the day, through all kinds of rainy and snowy weather." Marshfield was a quiet little seaport town with a booming logging business. "First thing, I bought a postcard, sent it to my uncle, and he sent me the fifty dollars," Mickey noted.

Mickey spent some time in Marshfield before heading south down the coast to Los Angeles via a short stopover in Eureka, California. He met a girl in Los Angeles and they

The Encyclopedia of Feature Players of Hollywood

were married, and then he joined the Navy and expected to be sent overseas at any time. However, the Service had a different idea on what to do with the six-foot-five-inch recruit: They placed him in the shore patrol. "They put me on duty at the Hollywood Canteen when it opened," Mickey stated. "Naturally I was gaw-gawed when I saw those beautiful starlets and famous actors. I never dreamed that one day I might be rubbing elbows with them and working with them because acting, at that time, was the furthest thing from my mind."

While working at the Canteen, Mickey's physical stature must have attracted the attention of some movie people as he began to be cast in bit parts as guards, cops, toughs, and other various strongmen. His work included two serials, *Gang Busters* and *Sea Raiders*, and a Johnny Mack Brown Western, *Boss of Hangtown Mesa*, but he never harbored any serious aspirations of being an actor.

Also working at the canteen in charge of the hostesses was Mary Ford, wife of director John Ford. Normally officers were not allowed in the canteen as they had their special room upstairs, but one day Captain John Ford came in to see his wife, and as Mickey happened to be there she introduced him to her husband. "I was a third class bosun mate," Mickey noted, "and naturally I saluted him." Ford said, "I hear you're doing a pretty good job here." "Well," Mickey replied, "I'm doing the best I can, sir. Just following orders." "How would you like to go to China with me?" Ford inquired. "I'd love to," Mickey replied, "but you'll have to check with my skipper first." Ford approached C.H. Fogg, Mickey's skipper, with the question, and was met with the response, "No. We want Mick here. Bette Davis asked for him personally. He's doing a good job, and there's been a lot of undercover work going on here and he's handled it. So we are going to keep him here." Ford returned to Mickey and told him that "when this shindig is over, look me up." "Fine, look him up. What can he do?" Mickey thought to himself. "Maybe I'd get a job driving a truck on the studio or something."

When the war ended and Mickey was discharged from the Service he remembered what Ford said so decided to try and see him. Ford was preparing to direct *My Darling Clementine* when Mickey stopped by his office. "Can you grow a beard," Ford asked him to which Mickey answered in the affirmative. Ford told him to go home, grow a beard and to come back in three weeks. Mickey obeyed orders, wondering why a beard was necessary to drive a truck, and returned three weeks later. "Yeah, you don't look like a baby now," Ford remarked, and turned to his assistant, Wingate Smith, and told him to take Mickey over to get some clothes. As they left, Mickey asked Smith, "What is this all about? What kind of clothes? What's the scoop here?" "You're going to become an actor," Smith informed him. Mickey was startled for a moment, and then remarked, "I can't act." "Either can half the guys going into pictures," Wingate explained. "He'll make an actor out of you." Mickey was fitted for costume and then they returned to Ford, who said, "You look the part. And from what I hear you are as mean as you look, so let's go on." Mickey told us, "and that's what happened."

Mickey played the part of one of the Clanton brothers and went with Ford on location to Monument Valley. "Being a green kid, I was eyes and ears and had brains enough to just sit back and listen and learn," Mickey told us. "When the picture was over I asked Mr. Ford, 'Pappy, would you suggest that I go to an acting school?' He answered, 'Do you have any trouble with learning your dialogue?' 'No, sir.' 'Stay away from them,' he said, 'they ruin more actors than they do good.'"

During the filming of the picture Mickey heard many stories about Ford in the past. Things like everyone being equal on a Ford picture, there are no stars whatsoever. And it was true. "Hank Fonda was just as common as the little green man that sets up the flowers around the set," Mickey explained. Another story was that he heard that Ford used live ammunition on some of his shows, that he had two sharpshooters named Duke Lee and Cap Anderson. "The first thing I saw about this was the shot where Hank is coming down at dawn toward us with the sun behind him; there are shots of his feet where the guns are shooting at him and he stopped. 'What's wrong, Hank?' 'Nothing Jack.' Ford replied back, 'Let's do it over again, and if you don't want to we'll let a little green man get your outfit and put it on.' So we went and did the shot over again, and it was perfect: the dust kicked up in the sunlight and it was a beautiful shot." They are now preparing to shoot the gunfight at the OK Corral and it comes time to film Mickey's death scene. Ford tells him, "Mick, Hank and Doc Holliday are to come in and start firing at you; I want you to land right in that water trough headfirst, and I want you to stay there until the water runs out." Mickey was preparing for the scene when he noticed Duke and Cap up on the edge of a building aiming their rifles at the water trough. "It made you a little scared," Mickey told us, "but I figured I gotta just fall crookedly because there's where the hole is going to be." He fell where Ford instructed, the bullets were fired, the water ran out and "that was it."

Mickey told the story of Walter Brennan's big scene at the end of the film when he is left standing there alone with all his sons lying around him dead. Right before the filming of this scene began, "Walter was kidding and joking around with us and he wasn't in the right mood for this scene, so Mr. Ford started working on him. He did a take, but he doesn't have a quiver in his voice like he just lost his whole family. 'Is that the way you want it?' Ford said. 'I thought you could act! You are the lousiest, stinkinest actor I've ever seen in my life. Where the hell did you ever get all your reputation in Hollywood? This is the first time we ever worked together, but oh…Come on, we'll try this crappy thing once more and if you don't do it, that's it!' Walter was just shaking, and when he started to talk his voice was just quivering. He did the whole thing, and Pappy came up and gave him a slap on the butt."

From this film, Mickey became a member of Ford's stock company, appearing in six other Ford films: *Wagonmaster*, *She Wore a Yellow Ribbon*, *Fort Apache*, *When Willie Comes Marching Home*, *What Price Glory?* and *The Long Gray Line*. While on the Ford set he heard and experienced some classic funny moments. Mickey shared some of these stories with us. One concerned Alan Mowbray while filming *My Darling Clementine*. "Mowbray didn't have much to do in the Monument Valley shooting, most of his scenes was to be shot back at the studio. He said, 'Well boys, I'm leaving tomorrow morning bright and early. While you colonial peasants are out here in the hot sun and red sand I'll be sitting at the Masquers Club sipping a martini down thinking about you. But before I leave come up to the clubhouse tonight and I'll tell you a few ditties.' So Ford sent the runners out and let everyone know that the first person who laughs is going to be on the plane going back with Mowbray. So he gets up there and starts, 'Have you ever heard about the Englishman who went out to the...' Silence. He tried others. Finally he said, 'I can't take it,' and ran out the back crying his eyes out. Ford got back at him for what he said. He's a funny guy," Mickey concluded the story. "He'd wait for things to happen."

Another story Mickey told us concerned the big fight scene between himself and Victor McLaglen in *She Wore a Yellow Ribbon*. "I had my sledgehammer with me. I slung it and supposedly hit the bar and broke it; then McLaglen grabs me and shoves my head in a barrel of flour. Francis Ford was there, and said, "Mick, you're working with flour, so take some cotton and shove it up your nose so you don't inhale it because you can choke and cough on that stuff." I thanked him, went over to the make-up man, got a couple of wads of cotton and shoved it all the way so you can't see it in the camera. Ford spotted it, and asked, 'What the hell have you got there?' I said, 'Putting some cotton up my nose.' 'What the hell for?' he asked. 'So I won't inhale that flour when my head goes in the barrel.' He said, 'You don't have to worry about going into the barrel. After you swing that sledgehammer and McLaglen takes a swing at you, I want you to back up clear to that wall back there and just sit down. Don't move.' I was shocked. You remember the shot? I just backed up and backed up and sat down. He didn't want anybody to do something that he didn't tell them to do."

A couple of other examples that Mickey told us illustrated the fact that you don't tell John Ford what to do. On one set, he didn't remember which film, there was a large courtroom scene. "John Ford asked for seventy-five extras, but they gave him only twenty and told Ford to scatter them around. He sent them home and shot with an empty courtroom. The producer saw it and asked what was wrong. Ford said, 'I asked for seventy-five extras, you sent twenty – what can I do?' The next day he had his extras and re-shot the scene." Another incident took place on the stage where they were set to shoot the big dance scene for *Fort Apache*. "We were getting ready to do the dance," Mickey reflected. "There must have been seventy-five actors and extras standing around waiting for the shot, and through the door walks the producer. Ford is sitting there chewing his handkerchief the way he does, the whole company just standing around. So the producer asks, 'Everything all right, Jack?' 'Oh fine, fine.' 'What's wrong with the shot, what are you waiting for? Everybody seems to be ready.' 'We're waiting for you to get your ass off the set; soon as you do we'll roll 'em.' So the producer walks out and we film," laughed Mickey.

Practical jokes were a common occurrence on a John Ford set, and when one is pulled on a stock regular they will more likely than not get back at the perpetrator, even if not until several movies later. Mickey told us how Frank McGrath got John Ford back one time. Coming back from Tucson where they had been location filming, we all had big beards and needed haircuts. Frank ran in and said, "The old man says we can all shave and get haircuts; leave it a little long, but get it trimmed nice and even, we're all through with that crap out there." "We go back to the studio in a couple of days, clean shaven and hair trimmed all nice. Ford went absolutely out of his mind. Ford had played a trick on him and I think that's why McGrath did this," Mickey laughed. We must flashback two or three years to *My Darling Clementine* to find what Ford had done to McGrath. "If you remember, John Ireland was making a play with Linda Darnell and came running on the balcony, jumped off to the ground, mounted his horse and took off. McGrath was going to double him. They broke for lunch and Ford said, 'I want you to go over and cover the soft ground and make it as hard as you can, because I owe him one. So McGrath goes off the roof and bounces like a rubber ball," Mickey reflected.

One last Ford story that Mickey shared with us had happened years before he had become a member of Ford's stock players. Ford and George O'Brien, who was then a star out at 20th Century Fox and had starred in Ford's silent classic of *The Iron Horse*, were very close friends. One day Ford invited George out for lunch on his boat and started pouring them some Jack Daniels; several drinks later and O'Brien looked out the porthole and saw no land – they had taken off for Hawaii. There's an all-points bulletin issued as Fox couldn't find the star of their show. Ford had kidnapped him, and naturally he has to get even with him. So sometime later after Ford made a new film and was going to San Francisco for the premier he was met with a surprise. As he was disembarking from the train with a large group of people he was confronted by a hysterical woman pointing at him, while yelling to nearby policemen, "That's him! That's the man that killed my husband!" A stunned John Ford is jerked off the train, thrown into a jail cell for three days and is being denied any phone calls. "George O'Brien's father was the Chief of Police in San Francisco," Mickey laughed. "That's how he got even with him. There were laughs in those days; today you can't have any laughs."

Mickey had some classic fight scenes in the movies and on television. "With my fighting experience," he remarked, "these movie fights I had to do were nothing compared to what we did in the ring. They'd always ask me to do my own and I finally got smart and said, 'Yes, but you got to pay me for it. Anything real dangerous, naturally, like falling off horses, they'd bring in a double because I did none of that stuff, but falls and fights I'd do myself."

The first film that Mickey made at Warner Brothers was a Western titled *Carson City* starring Randolph Scott. "I was the leader of a bunch of miners and had a great fight with Scott. That was only supposed to be a one day job, the fight wasn't even in it, but the director said to the writer, 'First time I ever worked with Mick, write something in there for him to do.'" So the writer wrote in the fight scene, and the director, Andre de Toth, approached

Mickey and explained, "Mick, this is going to be a good fight. I got it set up for a whole day, eight or nine hours; take your time." In the fight scene, stuntman Red Morgan doubled for Scott. "We fought," Mickey told us, "and it looks pretty good." The last shot of the fight shows Scott up against the bar; Mickey picking up a chair and then throwing it at a big mirror hanging up behind the bar. "Hit it right in the middle," de Toth instructed Mickey, "because it's the only one we got." "I took that chair and it hit right in the middle, and of course it breaks and the shot is over. They gave us one thousand dollars for that scene."

Perhaps Mickey's classic motion picture fight scene took place in George Stevens' epic, *Giant*, which starred Rock Hudson, Elizabeth Taylor and James Dean. This famous fight scene was first planned to be performed by stuntmen instead of the actors, but after three weeks rehearsal Stevens and the camera crew came in and he said, "All right boys, let's see what you've done." The stuntmen went through the fight routine and Stevens stated, "Thanks a lot; I appreciate what you've done. It looks exactly what it is, a rehearsed fight. That's what I don't want; I want a fight where these two guys are mad at each other." Stevens took Simpson and Hudson aside and explained the concept of the scene, and why the fight occurs. Mickey's character, Sarge, hated Mexicans because he had a Mexican lieutenant that rode him during the Service, so he's going to be picking on Mexicans and refusing them service in his restaurant. Hudson figures he owns the whole damn world and is angry at Sarge because he now has a daughter-in-law that is a Mexican. "They get real mad at each other," Stevens noted. "They go after each other and away they go. That's what I want, and I don't care if it takes a month to do it or two months to do it; we're going to get it right. So I want you two boys to do your own fight. If we do two or three scenes a day, perfect; one a day, perfect; if we do five a day, perfect; but take your time, don't get hurt, and let's do it."

The filming of the big fight scene began. "I did this and thought it was perfect," Mickey told us. "Mr. Stevens took me, put his arm around me and walked me over, saying, 'The reason I haven't printed you – there's nothing wrong with you; don't get me wrong. If I didn't think you could do this thing you wouldn't be here doing the part. We tested every big fellow in this town; you got it. I picked you. I know that you can give me what I want. It's up to me as a director to pull it out of you. So don't worry, you just go ahead and do what you're doing, but let me pull what I want out of you.' At this point you feel so good – he blew me up so great that nothing could bother me, everything just flowed. He got what he wanted. 'Print it!' And that's the way he worked with his actors; he would just go on and on and get what he wanted."

Gordon Douglas called Mickey in late 1963 and asked if he would like some Christmas money for a small fight scene in a film he was directing called *Rio Conchos*. "I get my head slammed on a bar for refusing this black guy a drink. It was shot in one take and I got a few hundred dollars for it," Mickey noted.

In summing up his screen fights, Mickey said, "I've broken my wrist, been hit a hundred times, cut eyes, cut lips, and was having gallbladder trouble at the time I did *The Great Bank Robbery* with Clint Walker." Mickey went on to tell of the terrible experience making that film during his final screen fight. "I'm supposed to be jumped by six Chinamen, and taken and thrown in a cell. I asked the first assistant, 'Isn't there a stuntman around to do this?' 'Oh, these guys are all right. They're just little piss ants, you could eat them alive.' You know," Mickey continued, "you get six guys and they don't know what the hell they're doing. The first thing you know they grab me, push me, and shove me to the ground. One guy's got a foot on my neck, another one on my back, and another gives me a perfect right smack and splits my eye open. So the shot wasn't any good and I get up with blood running down my face. 'First aid,' the director yells, 'get him a doctor.' 'Just give me a Kleenex,' I said, 'let's do it over again.' I held up the Kleenex and said, 'We couldn't have it better, we have our own blood.' I got my rifle and two guys get a hold of my wrist and shove it between the bars and push me, breaking my wrist. Down on the floor again – they don't kick me, but they shove my head down so hard that my eye bursts open again. All this on the second day of the picture and I got six more weeks to go. This was my last film."

Mickey played opposite James Cagney in *A Lion is in the Streets*, and enjoyed working with him. "He's a great guy," Mickey remarked. "One of the few men who was short and loved to work around tall men. If there was a fight to do, he wouldn't rely on hitting you in the chin to knock you out, but he would rely on his judo. Most of the other short actors would not give you a chance to do that."

Mickey had high regard for the many stuntmen that he worked with, people like Billy Jones, Chuck Roberson, Fred Kennedy and Jocko Mahoney. Speaking of Mahoney, Mickey said, "I would call him the most flexible stuntman there ever was. He could stand two feet behind a horse and spring and leap right into the saddle without a trampoline."

Besides motion picture work, Mickey was kept busy on almost every television Western show, such as *Cisco Kid, Annie Oakley, Gunsmoke, Maverick, Sugarfoot, Rifleman, Have Gun-Will Travel, Bronco, Colt 45, Yancy Derringer, The Deputy, Bonanza, Bat Masterson, Rough Riders, The Dakotas, Big Valley,* and *26 Men*. "I did a lot of *Lone Rangers, Cheyennes,* – Clint and I were very close – *Range Rider, Buffalo Bill Jr.*; so many of them. We would do three pictures a week, and get script after script." Mickey's agent told him, "Some day they are going to pay you for these old things on television. Keep doing them; if something good comes along we'll take it, but in the meantime do these things." Mickey explained that these old TV shows paid practically nothing, saying, "You'd do three shows for two hundred and fifty dollars. Sure enough, the residuals came along but they didn't pay anything until after 1965; all the stuff prior to that you didn't get a dime for." Mickey's television work also included non-Western shows in such diversified series as *Mister Ed, 77 Sunset Strip, Thriller, Richard Diamond, Rocky Jones,* and *Superman*.

Mickey also co-starred as Boley the Bosun with Maxwell Reed and Tudor Owen in the television series *Captain Grief*, based on Jack London's sea stories, where each week their boat *The Rattler* sailed the seas of the West Indies in search of adventure. They had several exciting experiences on this show, which was shot on location in places like Cuba and Mexico. One episode was being filmed in Mazatlan and the scene called for the police to pursue Mickey as he ran down a street and fire his gun. "Out in the corner of my eye I saw someone with a shotgun holler, 'I'll get him!' He let go with the gun and I hit the ground," Mickey related. "I told the director after that he should have an assistant go around and tell these idiot people that we have some guns going off and to keep their real guns in." On some other episodes they filmed in Cuba during the revolution and it got a little rough at times. "You'd get pinned down in places and couldn't get out; damned near got killed a couple of times. One time we're coming in to Cuba on this seventy-five foot, three mast schooner and it's loaded with people on the deck. One of the girls says, 'Oh, look at those pretty flying fish out there.' Those are bullets! They forgot to run the flag up," Mickey laughed. "Here we are pulling into harbor and they got fifty-caliber machine guns going tat tat tat."

When asked if he had a favorite film, Mickey responded, "I think *My Darling Clementine*, being the first, and what I think is the best story." Another film that he enjoyed was Ford's *Wagonmaster*. While on location with the latter film, Mickey and fellow actor Fred Libby, both being interested in the Indian culture, would go to the Indian camps and talk with them. "We'd just come into our camp, dropped our bags off, and heard the Indians – they were having a Yipishay dance group going on; so Fred and I decided to go over and see. It was coal black, didn't have any flashlights with us, but they had fires over there so we could see them. We were walking along in the sand and we heard a voice, 'How are you, Mick? How are you, Fred?' It's an Indian right out of nowhere. How he got there I'll never know or how he knew it was us, I'll never know. It was so dark we couldn't see our shoes, but this guy knew it was us. We saw the dance and made acquaintances again; greatest bunch of people."

On summing up his feelings on his experiences in the film business, Mickey stated, "I enjoyed it immensely; it's been the greatest. The only place they can pay you for being mean. The meaner, the better. Back in the sixties I had a road show called *The Badmen of Hollywood* that I've taken out to various towns. Rand Brooks, Jay Silverheels and others – we'd shoot up the town, put on little skits, and you'd find that back in the east they like the badmen as well as the good guys.

"I took out my retirement at sixty-two because I could see the handwriting on the wall," Mickey told us in concluding the interview. "It was all changing. The old gang wasn't around; a lot of them quit and went into something else. The directors are all different and I thought I might as well get out of this thing while I still have my health. Years ago, when Lauter, Wilke, George Barrows, Elam and all of us were working they never asked anything, they'd just say, 'Go pick up a script,' or 'You're going to work tomorrow on this or that.' None of this interview stuff or readings. They knew your work, they knew you could ride, chase, fight or do anything they wanted and that would be it. Today you have to read for every single part. The motion pictures today are run by supermarkets, oil companies, and so on; not by movie people – and that's part of the problem. Before I took out my retirement I went out on a few interviews, but it takes the heart out of you. I have a book of stills from some of the pictures

I've done, but you go into an office and some twenty-three year old asks, 'What have you done?' I say, 'I've worked in seven pictures for John Ford.' They say, 'Who's he?'

Mickey Simpson passed away in Northridge, California on September 23, 1985.

Film Credits: **1939:** Panama Lady. **1941:** Honolulu Lu; Abbott and Costello in the Navy; Keep 'em Flying; Obliging Young Lady; A Date with the Falcon; Swing it Soldier; Sea Raiders; Tight Shoes. **1942:** Arabian Nights; The Falcon Takes Over; Boss of Hangtown Mesa; Swingcopation; Timber; The Spoilers; Gang Busters; Lady for a Night; Highways by Night; Behind the Eight Ball. **1943:** No Time for Love. **1946:** My Darling Clementine. **1947:** Tarzan and the Huntress; The Wistful Widow of Wagon Gap; Slave Girl; Sons of Scheherazade; Case of the Baby Sitter; Road to the Big House; The Fabulous Texan; The Spook Speaks (short); The Bachelor and the Bobby-Soxer; Trail Street; Calendar Girl. **1948:** Fort Apache; River Lady; The Argyle Secrets; That Wonderful Urge; The Three Musketeers; Joe Palooka in Fighting Mad; Wake of the Red Witch; The Adventures of Don Juan; Are You With It?; Half Past Midnight. **1949:** She Wore a Yellow Ribbon; The Fighting Kentuckian; It Happens Every Spring; They Live by Night; The Judge Steps Out; A Woman's Secret. **1950:** When Willie Comes Marching Home; Surrender; Wagonmaster; Wabash Avenue; Kill the Umpire; Southside 1-1000; Cargo to Capetown. **1951:** Roar of the Iron Horse; His Kind of Woman; Kentucky Jubilee; Drums in the Deep South; The Lady Pays Off; The Red Badge of Courage; Mask of the Avenger; Ten Tall Men. **1952:** Bela Lugosi Meets a Brooklyn Gorilla; Lone Star; Leadville Gunfighter; Hellgate; Gents in a Jam (short); The San Francisco Story; Outlaw Women; Apache Country; What Price Glory?; Carson City. **1953:** Star of Texas; A Lion is in the Streets; Salome; Saginaw Trail; Devil's Canyon; Man in the Dark; Three Sailors and a Girl. **1954:** Prince Valiant; Rose Marie; The Bounty Hunter; Demetrius and the Gladiators. **1955:** Tall Man Riding; I Died a Thousand Times; Seven Angry Men; The Long Gray Line; New York Confidential. **1956:** The Lone Ranger; Giant; World without End; The Houston Story; The Steel Jungle; Toward the Unknown; The Ten Commandments. **1957:** The Gunfight at the OK Corral; Undersea Girl. **1959:** Warlock. **1963:** Donovan's Reef. **1964:** Rio Conchos; He Rides Tall. **1965:** The Greatest Story Ever Told; King Rat. **1968:** More Dead Than Alive. **1969:** The Great Bank Robbery.

JEREMY SLATE

Jeremy Slate spent the first nine years of his life in Margate, New Jersey, where he was born on the 17th of February, 1926, the year before Lindbergh flew the Atlantic.

"I've been a gypsy ever since then," Jeremy stated. "I grew up on a dairy farm in Vermont and during World War II joined the Navy at sixteen. Just after I turned eighteen, I found myself off Omaha Beach at Normandy on D-Day. My ship (the Destroyer U.S.S. Murphy) made it through, but by the time we got to bombard Cherbourg and invade southern France, we were the hardest hit Destroyer squadron in the Atlantic Fleet."

After three years in the Navy, Slate entered college under the G.I. Bill and graduated from St. Lawrence University in 1952 with honors in English. He was also president of the student body, editor of the literary magazine, football player and coach, member of the Honor Society, and morning personality on local radio.

After graduating, Jeremy became a sportscaster and DJ at WWNY in Watertown, New York and at WSTC in Stamford, Connecticut, eventually winding up behind a desk for six years with W.R. Grace & Co., where he became travel manager for the president, J. Peter Grace. He was then sent to Lima, Peru, where he spent two years establishing and operating a public relations department for the Grace Steamship Line. Jeremy had married his college sweetheart in his senior year and by now they had three children, Jefre, Jamie and Jeremy.

"I thought we might be staying down there a long time," explained Jeremy, "so I started a local bi-lingual program of news and entertainment on one of the local radio stations during the three hour siesta each day." From that show, Jeremy was invited to join a semi-professional

The Encyclopedia of Feature Players of Hollywood

English language theater group and within two seasons was awarded the Tiahuanaco, the Peruvian Tony Award, for his performance as *The Rainmaker*.

Convinced he should pursue acting as a career, Jeremy returned to New York with his family. By early 1958, another son, Jason, was born and Slate decided to become a full-time actor. He left W.R. Grace in June and by October was in a Broadway play, *Look Homeward, Angel* at the Barrymore Theatre. The play starred Ed Begley, Miriam Hopkins and Andrew Prine. "That's where I met Victor Kilian. We shared a dressing room and he was a great educator for me; he was my mentor," added Jeremy.

Jeremy also had met Sally Perl, the head of Central Casting, which was the largest extra casting company on the east coast. Sally was especially helpful to struggling actors and put Jeremy to work as a "visible extra" in *That Kind of Woman*, starring Sophia Loren and directed by Sidney Lumet, and *North by Northwest*, directed by Alfred Hitchcock and starring Cary Grant.

After a year and a half in New York and on the road, Jeremy decided to try Hollywood. On the 29th day of July, 1959, he arrived in Hollywood, knowing almost no one in the industry. His friend, Victor Kilian, had told him "My apartment is sitting out there on Ogden Drive, you can use it for as long as you want."

"I got a good job in a play, Arthur Miller's *Enemy of the People*," Jeremy informed us. "It was directed by John Marley and starred James Whitmore and David White. In the play was also a tall, gangly, sweet striving actress about eighteen. Her name was Sally Kellerman and we became close friends." An agent came to see Sally and signed up Jeremy, too.

He was interviewed by Ivan Tors for a co-starring role in a TV series Ivan was developing for CBS. *Sea Hunt*, created by Ivan, was then the most popular show ever in syndication, and Jim Aubrey at CBS asked Ivan to create an hour long show with two characters. Jeremy was signed to play opposite Keith Larsen in *The Aquanauts*, which was slotted for Wednesday nights at 7:30 opposite the most popular network show at the time, *Wagon Train*.

"*Wagon Train* ran over us," Jeremy laughed. "Half way through our first, and only, season, CBS even changed the name of our show to *Malibu Run* and replaced Keith with Ron Ely, but nothing helped." In fact, Jeremy worked in thirty-two one hour episodes, more than likely a record never equaled since by an hour long action/adventure series in one season.

Jeremy's first television role in Hollywood was two days work at ZIV on *Men in Space* with William Lundigan. His first speaking role in a motion picture was in *G.I. Blues* with Elvis Presley, directed by Norman Taurog and produced by Hal Wallis.

For the next ten years, from 1960 to 1970, Jeremy found work nearly every week, appearing as guest star in nearly two hundred TV shows as well as over a dozen feature films.

Hal Wallis put Jeremy under contract after *G.I. Blues* and he co-starred with Van Johnson and Janet Leigh in *Wives and Lovers*, with John Wayne in *The Sons of Katie Elder* and *True Grit*, and again with Elvis in *Girls, Girls, Girls*. In addition to the Wallis pictures, Jeremy also had top roles in *I'll Take Sweden* with Bob Hope and in a number of "biker" films, one of which he also wrote the screenplay, *Hell's Angels '69*. Speaking of this last film, Jeremy told us "That was an incredible adventure. It was the only film of all the biker films, or any films at all, in which the Hell's Angels were actually starred."

Reflecting on his work with Janet Leigh in *Wives and Lovers*, Jeremy smiled and said, "One of the sweetest things I remember about this film was after I did the seduction scene with Janet Leigh, Edith Head – the great costume designer – came up to me and said, 'That's the best seduction scene I think I've ever seen.' Janet was wonderful and such fun to work with."

During his decade of work in TV, Jeremy appeared in *Gunsmoke* seven times, *Alfred Hitchcock Presents* five times, *Bonanza* three times, *The Virginian* twice, *Run For Your Life* in six episodes, *Combat* two episodes (one directed by Robert Altman), two episodes of *One Step Beyond*, *Perry Mason* twice, and in such other show as *The Untouchables*, *Empire*, *Naked City*, *The Defenders*, *Ozzie and Harriet*, *The Magician*, *Dr. Kildare*, *Have Gun-Will Travel*, *The Deputy*, *Bat Masterson*, *Mission: Impossible*, *Man From U.N.C.L.E.*, *Route 66*, *Checkmate*, *Bearcats*, and starred as Willie McGee in an unsold comedy pilot titled "A Man Called McGee" about a man who inherits an entire California town from his deceased uncle.

When asked if he has a preference for working on stage or in film, Jeremy has an unusual answer due to the eight years he spent working in daytime television, mostly as Chuck Wilson on *One Life To Live* from 1979-86.

"I actually prefer daytime over anything else, as a separate genre from film and stage work. The use of time is so much different," he explained. "In TV and films, it's always 'Hurry up and wait,' but in daytime you have to utilize every available moment and I enjoy that challenge." He hastens to point out that while contemporary series don't produce more than twenty new episodes a season, soap operas pound out two hundred and sixty one shows during the same period. "Quite a difference," he added.

Jeremy also reflected on his work with John Wayne in *The Sons of Katie Elder* and *True Grit*, both of which also featured Dennis Hopper, who became a close friend. On the first one, he told us that the location shots were scheduled to be filmed in Durango, Mexico, and the remainder back in the states. While on location they heard that there was a threatened cameraman strike, so Hal Wallis decided rather than risk losing his entire camera crew to make a deal with Traesco Studios in Mexico City to film the interior shots there. Jeremy, wanting very much to do a good job on his first John Wayne feature, drove himself to Durango about two weeks before he was scheduled to begin work there, and was given the Mexican cow pony he was to use in the film. "The pony and I hung out together for two weeks, so I could ride well in the movie," Jeremy added.

The first scene of the day found Jeremy on his Mexican cow pony. He was to gallop in as fast as he could up to the wall of the sheriff's office, dismount and run inside. "Action!" Well, Jeremy came galloping in, and within twenty feet of the wall said, "Whoa!" He got ready to dismount, the horse suddenly stopped and Jeremy went sailing over its head and right on to the ground. He got up in a daze and muttered, "What the hell was that all about?" "That was all about because you were riding a cow pony," Duke answered. "Well, I've been riding him for a month," Jeremy responded. "Yeah, but you don't know what they do," Duke replied. "What are you talking about?" Jeremy asked. "Come here and I'll show you," Wayne advised. "Now when you get on a horse they work on a system, and the system is the instant you rope your calf you want to put pressure on the line so the minute your foot hits the stirrup like you're going to dismount that horse stops on a dime. What you got to do is trust the horse and you got to ride right up until your nose is up against that wall before you do this, because otherwise he's going to stop and throw you." "You want him to throw me right into the wall, is that what you want?" Jeremy asked. "No, no, just believe me, it'll work." And sure enough, the next time Jeremy did the scene he waited and waited and the horse stopped like Wayne had said it would and he was able to do the scene.

Working on *True Grit* was an enjoyable experience. "I had a good time on that, and so did Dennis," Jeremy reflected. "Again, working with Duke was a lot of fun. He used to kid Dennis and me all the time because we were pot smokers at the time. One morning we were coming out on location and were standing there with our horses ready to do a scene. Duke looked over at Dennis and me and said, 'I bet I know what you guys got in them there saddle bags.' Dennis said, 'What do you think we got in our saddlebags?' 'I bet they're full of grass,' Duke answered, 'and you know what kind of grass I'm talking about, don't you?' He used to kid us all the time."

Jeremy's first love is actually music. "My three sons are musicians and my two daughters are dancers," he smiles. "On the farm I grew up playing the harmonica and now specialize in Appalachian music."

During the sixties, Jeremy also owned, with two partners, a demo music producing studio. As a song writer, he composed Tex Ritter's last hit, *Just Beyond the Moon*, and while he and Glen Campbell were working together on *True Grit*, he co-wrote *How Come Every Time I Itch*, which appears on the *Galveston* album, sung by Campbell.

In Big Sur, California, where Jeremy lived a number of years, the most well-known band ever to come out of there was *Canyon*, founded by his three sons and still performing after nearly twenty years.

Jeremy also directed theatre for the Big Sur Players theatre group for eight years. The company was founded by his son Jeremy and his partner (and the mother of his granddaughter, True Slate) Kim Candler. He has also directed for the Pacific Repertory Company and for the Kitchen Ensemble Company at the Coronet Theatre in Los Angeles. Jeremy has also taught acting at Santa Cruz studios and at Monterey Peninsula College.

"I'm very happy about how my professional life has been conducted," he says with gratification. "I worked hard for ten years, dropped out for ten, then got into it again for another eight. That way, I got a taste of retirement right in the middle and became well adjusted to living a gypsy life." By that time, he says, "I knew how much fun I could have without having to work, so now that I'm officially retired, I can do dozens of things I've always wanted to." He's busier now than ever before, and he can choose everything he wants to do.

"What a life!" he exclaims from his logger's cabin far up among the giant redwoods in Big Sur. "I have lots of lively friends everywhere, and always come home to the redwood forest. Couldn't ask for anything more!"

Jeremy moved to Malibu in his last years and reestablished himself as an actor. His last role was in an episode of *My Name is Earl*. He died on November 19, 2006.

Film Credits: **1959:** That Kind of Woman; North by Northwest. **1960:** G. I. Blues. **1962:** Girls! Girls! Girls! **1963:** Wives and Lovers. **1965:** I'll Take Sweden; Sons of Katie Elder. **1967:** The Born Losers; Wings of Fire (TV). **1968:** Devil's Brigade; The Mini-Skirt Mob. **1969:** Hell's Angels '69; Hell's Belles; The Hooked Generation; True Grit; **1971:** The Cable Car Murder (aka Crosscurrent) (TV); Drag Racer. **1972:** Curse of the Moon Child; Alligator Alley. **1973:** The Man Who Died Twice (TV); Return of the Big Cat (TV). **1974:** The Centerfold Girls. **1975:** Stowaway to the Moon (TV). **1978:** Stranger in Our House (TV). **1979:** Mr. Horn (TV). **1988:** Deadlock; A Whisper Kills (TV). **1989:** Goodnight, Sweet Marilyn; Dead Pit; Trenchcoat in Paradise (TV). **1990:** Stolen: One Husband (TV). **1991:** Dream Machine; Voyage of the Heart. **1992:** The Lawnmower Man.

PAUL SORENSON

Paul Sorensen was born on February 16, 1926 at Kenosha, Wisconsin. His debut on stage occurred at the age of three years in a local church production, and he just continued on performing on stage during his years in elementary, junior high and high school. "I guess I always had an interest in theatre," Paul added.

When World War II was in full swing, Paul failed the physical exam for the military due to a perforated ear drum. At the age of eighteen he became a member of the Kenosha Little Theatre. Of this experience, Paul related to us that he was fortunate in a way at the time because so many of the young guys were off to the war, saying, "So I played many roles that chances are I never would have played." Paul was also an avid reader of the Theatre Arts magazine, and he said the words "Pasadena Playhouse School of the Theatre, home of the stars" always jumped off the pages at him. "Of course I was interested," Paul commented.

We asked Paul if there was any certain event that sparked that interest in acting and he answered, "I don't think there was any specific thing. I'd like to say that I saw one play or one movie, but I think it was just...Well, go to any part of mid-America and ask anyone if they'd like to be in movies, wouldn't they just love to? I suppose it was the same thing with me. As I said, I read Theatre Arts and envisioned myself performing in the theatre. I initially didn't have that great of a design for the motion picture industry, I considered myself primarily a stage actor because of my voice, my stature and my training. My family background is creative in that my mother played the piano, my father sang, I have two brothers and two sisters and there were six of us singing in the church choir all at one time. My sister played the piano, studied and taught piano. My oldest brother was a very successful singer, he appeared on Broadway with

Kitty Carlisle; he did *Guys and Dolls* for three and a half years on Broadway. He did the first production on television of an opera, Arturo Toscanini directing *Madame Butterfly*, and was a regular on Jane Froman's musical variety television show. I sang for awhile, I did *Lil Abner* in San Diego; I sang in my church as a soloist for a number of years; I studied voice for a number of years; but my primary interest was the theatre. So, I don't know, what can I tell you? Another brother was a radio announcer, another sister sang, so we were musical and creative from that point of view, but there is no family tradition in the theatre or anything of that nature. I have two sons and neither gives a hoot about show business."

Paul told us as a boy growing up in Wisconsin that he loved Errol Flynn and the other swashbucklers like Tyrone Power and Laird Cregar. And Olivia de Havilland. "I thought *Robin Hood* was just terrific," Paul added. "I grew up at the time with Tom Mix, Ken Maynard and Buck Jones, and I remember having seen Tom Mix in a circus as a youngster, and that's going way back."

Paul worked in an aircraft factory plant during the war, saved his money and headed west to Pasadena in 1945 to the Playhouse. He graduated from the Pasadena Playhouse in 1947. Some of those that he met while studying there were Lenny Freeman, who was later to become the producer of *The Untouchables* television series; John Mantley, the actor-writer who eventually became producer of the hit TV series *Gunsmoke*, as well as *How the West was Won*; and character actor Gene Evans. "A number of guys who went on to make a successful living in the business," he noted. After his graduation, Paul went back to the mid-west where he performed for a season in summer stock in an old log theatre in Excelsior, Minnesota.

Paul returned to California at the close of the summer stock season and became a member of a theatre group called the Orchard Gables Repertory Theatre. "We were located in the heart of Hollywood," he explained. "About twenty-four guys and gals rented this large estate that was like a city block on the corner of Wilcox and Fountain. We all lived there and chipped in and paid the rent and built a theatre in this big home, and we did the classics: Moliere, Jonson, Ibsen; just wonderful things. In fact we were reviewed in *Time Magazine* one time and they called us an oasis in the heart of Hollywood. We were really quite the ensemble, playing together and living together. We had a director who was of the Stanislavski School of acting, and we learned a lot. It was a wonderful background," Paul added.

Paul next returned to the mid-west again to appear in theatre there when the Korean War began. "Uncle Sam beckoned me," he stated. "He wouldn't take me in the Second World War because of my ear drum, but as far as the Korean conflict goes I guess it didn't make any difference. So I wound up in Korea in 1952 and I left there in 1954."

When Paul returned to California after his discharge there was a show going into production of *Born Yesterday* at the Sartu Theatre in Hollywood on the corner of Hollywood Boulevard and La Brea. "I went down and read for the thing a couple of weeks after I was out of the service and I was cast in the role of Brock," Paul mentioned. "An agent by the name of Wally Middleton saw the show and wanted to know if I would sign with him, and of course I did.

He assured me that there was a place in the television and motion picture industry for me and in November of 1954, that same year, I got my first job in a show called *Stories of the Century* about a railroad detective, with Jim Davis." He played bad man Billy Stiles in the episode about Burt Alvord. "And from then on I never stopped. I did all of the early shows," Paul added.

Paul's television credits included such shows as *Highway Patrol, Rin Tin Tin, Gunsmoke, 26 Men, Broken Arrow, Black Saddle* and a number of *Big Valley* episodes, as well as *Flamingo Road, Dynasty* and *Dallas*. On the latter show he played the reoccurring character Andy Bradley of the oil cartel for nine years. Paul mentioned that his character was more involved in some of those seasons than others, "so over the years I imagine I've appeared in thirty five shows," he added. "But in recent years it has dwindled to nothing, there were absolutely no segments in the last season at all. And that's the way that goes. I suppose if I counted them up I've done over 500 television shows and probably about fifty or sixty movies," he concluded.

In reflecting on his work in two of the aforesaid series, Paul told us on *Highway Patrol*, in all the years the show was on the air, that the star, Broderick Crawford, was hit by a bullet only twice. "I did one of the very first *Highway Patrol*'s, and I did one of the very last, and both times he was hit by my shots. That was just strictly coincidence," he remarked. During the height of the Westerns he just would go from one to another. Paul had learned to ride for the Westerns, but never considered himself an expert rider. "I was good enough to ride into the scenes and ride out," he added. "In the series *26 Men* they had to have a double for me. They just rode like crazy in that thing over arroyos and through cacti; that was too much for me. That was a real rough show. I remember once we were working in the summer and it was one hundred and seventeen degrees; I had a woolen shirt, leather jacket, hat and gloves. We had to close down shooting because our leading lady was completely dehydrated. They sent her to the hospital and pumped in two gallons of glucose. But you just kept going; you kept cranking those things out." Paul mentioned that the producers were so happy with one of the episodes he did for them that it was their selection for the Emmy consideration.

Paul reflected on several humorous experiences that happened while he was performing before the camera and on stage. He mentioned that because of all the lights that he usually wore his dark glasses when they were setting up the shots. "Once when I was doing a Western they were setting up the shot shooting over my shoulder at somebody," Paul smiled, "but in the take I had to turn around to the lens and of course you know what happened. I still had my dark glasses on." Paul then told us his most embarrassing moment on stage. "As I walked out I was wearing a dark navy blue suit and a pink shirt, and I left my fly open. I walked out on stage with my shirt tail sticking out of my fly. Well, the audience was howling. I knew something was wrong and the other actor on stage was saying, 'Your fly! Your fly!' At that stage of my development as an actor I could not justify reaching down as the character and zipping up my fly, so I continued on. Never mind I should stop and get out of character for a moment and zip it up. But I could not justify that so I walked around for half that scene with the audience laughing."

On the other side of the coin an actor can also be placed in dangerous positions while performing. Paul talked about two experiences, one of the scariest times being on the Schlitz Malt Liquor commercial with the bull with the big horns. The scene was shot in a small room of about ten feet by twelve. "This was the day when the actors remained in the room with the bull," Paul explained. "They used an electric prod to get this thing to come charging down a ramp into the room, and when he comes roaring in he is just looking for something to take out. I was the police officer and I had this guy in tow, so when the bull came into the room they had devised it in such a fashion that we jump on the booking judge's desk. They had things for us to hold onto while we were standing there and this bull was running around the room. If we moved and he saw us move he would have crashed into this thing we were on. Well, I don't know how many takes they had but I want you to know that that had to be one of the scariest things. I later learned one guy was seriously injured because there is no such thing as a trained bull."

The other incident still gives Paul nightmares at times. He was doing a pilot in Santa Cruz, California titled *The Flim Flam Man* with Forrest Tucker and a young kid. Paul played a police officer in the show, and in one scene Tucker and the boy are coming down the railroad tracks on a hand car, while Paul is sitting in his patrol car blocking the tracks in an effort to stop them. Well, that isn't going to stop those guys, so at the last second Paul is to step on the gas and get that car off the tracks as they go shooting on by. "Now it had snowed the night before," Paul related, "and I'm sitting on those tracks and here comes those guys down the hill lickety split on this hand car. I go to step on the gas and the wheels start spinning and spinning, and these guys are getting closer and closer and just at the split second before colliding, the car moves off the tracks and those guys went on by. And, as I say, my stomach just cringed telling you that; those guys would just have splattered."

When we asked Paul if he had any favorite show that he had worked on, he answered "Yea, I think I liked *Hang 'Em High*. I liked the character, I liked the people I worked with and worked for, it was a successful picture. And then I liked what I did. I thought I was successful in creating a role." In television Paul enjoyed playing a character that he described as "a crummy sort of guy that would not put his cigar out in an elevator and had a fight with the lady of the show."

Many of the characters that Sorensen portrayed were the villain of the show. Many people would ask him, "Don't you find it difficult because you're such a nice guy?" "It didn't bother me," Paul told us. "It's sure a lot easier than playing nice guys. You have a chance to do something. To play yourself is very difficult. I admire some of these leading men who get up there and do themselves, you have so little to work with opposed to the bad guy. To play somebody who is the antithesis of your personality will force you to get lost in the character."

Paul became interested in the Church of Religious Science in 1963, started taking classes in 1965 and continued taking classes until he became a professional practitioner in 1973. He then started in the school of the ministry in 1976, graduated in 1979, and had his first church in 1980. At the same time Paul was also busy as an actor, 1980 being his busiest year. "Strangely enough," he told us, "the first year I had a church I served as an interim minister for six months, but during that period I did the first two or three shows of *Dynasty*, I did the first five shows of *Flamingo Road*, and I had the re-occurring role on *Dallas*, on which I did five or six shows at that time. They all dove-tailed, there was no conflict, so for the first six months I was totally busy as a minister and totally busy as an actor on those shows; it was the most productive time of my entire career. It was really, really incredible."

Paul mentioned that through the 1970's as a free lance actor he worked an awful lot. "Not that they were all starring or co-starring roles, but feature roles," he stated. "In one season I did twenty five different shows, and that's a lot of shows; that's the same as a guy being a regular on a series at that time. So, there were seasons that I was very, very busy and the business was good to me.

"In recent years I know that the roles aren't being written for my type," Paul continued. "I'm not the young heavy anymore, I'm not the father, I'm not old enough to be the grandfather, and I'm not the dog heavy that do the fights and falls that I used to do, so I feel that I'm in an interim period at this stage of the game which I found myself early in my career. I was neither beast nor fowl from the time I got out of high school until the time I started working in my late twenties; I was not a juvenile, I was not a leading man, I wasn't really much of anything, it was just a growing period. I compare that training period of about ten years to that of a lawyer or a doctor or anything in that I worked constantly as an actor; not paid, but I worked on the stage working and developing my craft constantly, and for which I have no regrets."

When Paul was growing up back in Wisconsin, which he described as a "Wonderful outdoors state," his favorite pastime was hunting and fishing. He loved this sport so much that when he went to Korea he obtained a shotgun from the supply sergeant and went hunting for the Mongolian Pheasant. "That was really a dumb thing to do," Paul confided, "because there were still a lot of land mines which had been sown around there and which were undetected, and occasionally in the *Stars and Stripes* you would read where some guy was doing what I was doing and got blown up. But that's how much I enjoyed hunting." Upon his return to Southern California he got married and started to raise a family during the fifties and there were just not that many places to go, so he didn't hunt at all for ten years. Then in 1963 Paul met a man who had a place in Grass Valley up in Northern California, and he invited Paul up there, so Paul hunted with him for about thirteen years. In 1976 Paul had a hunting accident when he brought two boys, his sixteen year old son and a friend, on an expedition. A rabbit ran down a hill and Paul's son's friend fired at it, hitting Paul who was standing at the bottom of the hill. "So that was kind of scary and I wound up with one hundred pellet holes in my body," Paul related. "My body is still loaded with lead shots that never came out, but I obviously survived; but that somehow took the sting out of the desire to hunt. And also in my philosophy now, being with the Church of Religious Science, we believe in the sanctity of all life, that the spirit or God or mind, whatever you choose to call that power, expresses itself through all living things whether it's a bird, a beast, man or a tree. So from that standpoint we respect the divinity of wildlife."

Paul still enjoys occasionally working on the stage. His son has a large church in Ventura, and for the last two or three years they have been doing Dickens *Christmas Carol*, in which Paul plays the role of Scrooge. "I get a big kick out of doing that," Paul added. In 1984, he did a show called *A Conflict of Interest* with one of the local equity houses. Ken Mayer, a very good friend of Paul's, co-starred in the play. "We did that show in October and November and the following January he passed away," he stated. "I belong to the local ANTA, which is the American National Theatre Association. I don't have the time now, but I love theatre. We have the Globe Theatre in Hollywood, they've done all the Shakespeare shows, and in recent years I did *Much Ado about Nothing* there. I guess I'll always consider myself an actor. I haven't pursued it as vigorously as I did in the early years."

Paul's first motion picture role was that of a sentry in the 1955 Universal movie with Rock Hudson called *Battle Hymn*. Paul mentioned that it was filmed in Arizona and had a wonderful cast. He obtained the part in there due to his appearing opposite Robert Horton on stage in *The Rainmaker*. One of Paul's latest motion pictures is *Star Trek III: Search for Spock*, in which he plays a space pirate that is killed off by the Clingons.

Paul also enjoyed working with Bud Abbott and Lou Costello in *Dance with Me Henry*. "I was kind of happy to have done that," he said. "I think it was their last picture. They were real characters, and were as unalike as night and day; two entirely different guys."

Sorensen talked about the difference between movie making in the fifties and sixties as opposed to the eighties and nineties, saying the one big thing is the time element. "They just don't have the time or take the time like before," he informed. "I did *The Greatest Story Ever Told* and was on that for a number of weeks. George Stevens would sit there for maybe a whole day waiting for the right light. They just don't do anything like that today. That was an incredible piece of work." Paul played one of the rabble rousers, along with Mickey Simpson and Joe Sirola, running around getting the crowd stirred up, saying "Crucify him." "Michael Ansara and I shared dressing rooms throughout the whole thing," Paul added. "But times have changed as to taking time. The dollar factor is just so great."

In summing up his feelings about the motion picture industry and the part he has played in it over the years, Paul said, "I love and respect the industry because, needless to say, through the years people have approached me and said, 'What can you tell me about so and so' or 'I hear that so and so is such and such,' and I have truly always made it a point to say 'that as far as I am concerned my experience with them,' and this is the truth for the most part, 'is that they have been very professional as they come in. They'll do their work, they know their lines, and it is a job for them, a profession for them, and they come to work and when the day is done they go home. Now what they do with their personal life is their business. It doesn't concern me at all.'

As far as the business goes I think it has been very, very good to me, and thirty some years in the business is certainly a roller coaster. I have never known from one month to the next how the bills are going to be paid, how much money I am going to have, but that's the way it is with a free lance actor, and fortunately I married the kind of a woman that is willing to accept and understand that. There have been lean times and there has been wonderful times, and I never would have been able to experience those grand wonderful times had I the regular job. You know with an actor you can make that fantastic money and do wonderful and fantastic things. Now the guy that goes along with that steady salary, he never has those glorious moments, he's stuck in that little spot all of his life, so one learns to live with the hard times, and the good times by far make up for the bad times. So I say the industry has been very good to me and I am very grateful. I feel that I have somehow brought some joy, some happiness, lifted the person somehow out of their otherwise mundane world; the shut-in, whether it's an elderly person in this country or somebody abroad somewhere that my contribution has entertained them and made their life a little happier at that moment. And I would like to suggest that I have contributed in that fashion, perhaps not in a grand scale, but all parts constitute the whole and it's kind of fun to think at any given moment I might be seen by millions of people across the world in a given day in the shows that I have been involved in. So that's my feeling about the industry. I respect it and think it's a wonderful medium and I think it can do and has done wonders for the world and mankind."

Paul later moved to the California seaside community of Cardiff-by-the-Sea, where he passed away on July 17, 2008.

Film Credits: **1955:** To Hell and Back; Las Vegas Shakedown; Inside Detroit. **1956:** The Brass Legend; Revolt of Mamie Stover; Dance with Me Henry; The Women of Pitcairn Island; Glory. **1957:** Battle Hymn; House of Numbers. **1958:** The True Story of Lynn Stuart. **1960:** Seven Ways from Sundown; The Great Impostor. **1961:** The Steel Claw; Tammy Tell Me True; Flower Drum Song. **1962:** Kid Galahad. **1963:** Captain Newman, MD. **1965:** The Greatest Story Ever Told; The Satan Bug. **1966:** Hawaii; Torn Curtain; Chamber of Horrors; Scalplock. **1967:** Guide for the Married Man. **1968:** Hang 'em High; Jig Saw; Madigan; Live a Little, Love a Little; Shadow on the Land (TV). **1969:** Support Your Local Sheriff!; Grasshopper; The Big Bounce; Trial Run (TV). **1970:** Monte Walsh; Suppose They Gave a War and Nobody Came. **1971:** The Resurrection of Zachary Wheeler. **1972:** Evel Knievel; The Heist (TV); Lapin 360. **1973:** One Little Indian; Westworld; Executive Action; Girls on the Road; Money to Burn (TV); The Alpha Caper (TV). **1974:** Earthquake; A Cry in the Wilderness (TV); The Elevator (TV). **1975:** Return to Witch Mountain; The Hindenburg; The Missing are Deadly. **1976:** Sherlock Holmes in New York (TV); Dawn: Portrait of a Teenage Runaway (TV). **1977:** Freaky Friday; Smokey and the Bandit. **1980:** Kidnapping of the President; First Family; The Return of Frank Cannon (TV); Flamingo Road (TV). **1984:** Lassiter; Star Trek III: The Search for Spock. **1989:** Cage.

ARTHUR SPACE

Arthur Space was born in New Brunswick, New Jersey, on October 12, 1908, the son of Charles Augustus Space and Isabelle Barrett. He attended the city's grammar and high schools, playing on the football team. He had a rather rebellious education *per se*, and hit upon a drama class in high school during his junior year, where he was highly acclaimed and scared to death, but had a wonderful drama coach. He was truly interested for the first time to study. In his senior year in high school, Arthur was picked to play the male parts in the New Jersey College for women, which is now called the Douglas College. They needed men for their shows. He appeared in their plays for some ten years and then went into summer stock, a road company and various New York plays. His film career began with MGM in a Wallace Beery movie and now has to his credit fifty stage productions, one hundred and fifteen movies, and three hundred-fifty television shows. He was the regular on two TV series: *Lassie* and *National Velvet*. Arthur had some interesting "firsts" in his career. He made the first Lassie picture, *Lassie Come Home*; the first Rock Hudson movie, *Fighter Squadron*, which Hudson only had one line of dialogue; and he did the first television program in New York City in 1935, during experimentation. Arthur Space passed away on January 13, 1983, in Los Angeles, California. Here is his story, from his writings, newspaper accounts and letters:

When I was about eight years old, I started a magazine route, selling *Ladies Home Journal*, *Country Gentleman* and *Saturday Evening Post*. I have forgotten the profit I made on each sale, but that wasn't the important item. The important aspect was the prizes you won when you sold over a certain number; yes, the prize was prizes. Just listen to this: Boy Scout

knives, hunting knives, lanterns, scout axes and a sack of agates. Agates, you know, are the gem of marbles. I sold the magazines from door to door. In those days when you knocked, people welcomed. Some friends and relatives bought and I'd stand on corners outside of airplane factories, rubber factories, Johnson & Johnson Medical factory; anyplace I figured I could make a sale. I sold them from wagon, bicycle, sleigh and scooter. I always liked the sack they gave us to carry them in. To get my wares I sold, I had to make a trip to the lower part of town; Bennet Street along the Raritan River. The river would overflow and flood every year. This part of town was quite old and run down, and like today, the poor foreigners lived here: the Italians, Poles, Jews. There were no blacks as I recall; there was only one black boy in the whole school. Anyway, I loved the smell when I walked into where stacks of brand new, clean cut, shiny just off the press magazines were kept. It was a pretty heavy load pulling up that hill back toward home. I was allowed to keep the money I made and spent it on movies, marbles, candy, cream puffs, sodas and milkshakes. The covers of the magazines I always had a feeling for, but of course I didn't notice who painted them. It was Norman Rockwell, of course. The *Country Gentleman* was the one I felt closest to; it appealed to the rural folk, the farmer. The *Ladies Home Journal* was for women, which I didn't know anything about. I was told the *Saturday Evening Post* had some good stories in it, but I was never one to read much.

There were a few other playthings that were a part of me. The pea shooter, magnifying glass, sling shot, marbles, hoop, sleigh, scooter, bicycle, wagon, ball and bat, and my first shotgun I got when I was fourteen years old. Oh yes, steel traps and water pistol and nip – don't forget that. The pea shooter was nothing but a twelve inch tin metal tube. If it was a luxury model, it had a wooden mouth piece to prevent you from cutting your lips. A mouthful of peas and you had it made. There were a lot of ways a young boy could apply this weapon, much of which could get you into trouble. Using people for targets was one way; aiming at windows was another. I remember once I was taking a walk with my dog and wound up in back of the high school. There must have been hundreds of small pain windows spread across the back of that school. I was still in lower grammar school; I knew little about this high 'echelon." I happened to have the old shooter with me. Well, it didn't just happen; I was in a period where I was hooked on the shooter. I carried it with me at all times, plus an ample supply of ammunition. Within shooting range of those windows glistening in the afternoon sun, was a big tree with a trunk that could easily hide a small boy if he stood behind it. I sort of let the dog pull me towards the tree, which was a natural instinct on his part. I found myself behind the tree out of sight of those glistening windows, realizing I just happened to be in an advantageous position. With haste and anticipation, I proceeded to feed the ammunition into my mouth; dry peas that is. That accomplished, I drew my weapon from my pants belt. Slowly, ever so slowly, I protruded my head around the circumference of that large trunk, put the weapon to my mouth, took a deep, deep breath and let one go. Phutt! A very quick withdrawal; a fraction of a second wait and a clear distinct "ting" reached my ears. A direct hit. With success making my head swim with accomplishment, my whole being engrossed, I did it again and again, "tinging" most every time. Oblivious of the outside world, completely engrossed in what I was accomplishing, and – Yam! A big hand with a firm grip had me by the shoulder. It was the janitor, sent to see what was causing the "tings." With great fear, I was taken to the Principal's office.

Now this is high school, big time stuff; big, big, way above my class standing. My dog and pea shooter, of course, went along with me. Being as I was a good boy, a boy that was being brought up with Victorian church standards and values; one who a hundred percent was taught to respect elders, teachers, ministers, parents, lawyers, doctors, etc. – not only respect them, but fear them. Well, this must be like people who go to the gallows. I don't recall what punishment was handed down, but that's not important. I vividly recall the feeling. It was like death. You know how the saboteur was exposed? It was my pal and buddy, my closest friend: my dog, straining on his leash from behind the tree trunk. Oh well, one tends to get careless when one is flushed with success. Then again, my dog didn't have much experience in this sabotage work.

The magnifying glass. This was real magic to me. Usually I'd get this glass from one of the flashlights I had won by selling magazines. Holding this magic glass toward the sun and adjusting the sunlight rays that filtered through it down to as fine a dot as you could get on your hand, a rag, a dried leaf, or corn silk wrapped in toilet paper. Holding the tiny spot of light as steady as you could for just a minute – and magic! The leaf would start to burn and smell good. On your hand it would suddenly feel as though a bee had stung you. The corn silk would start smoldering and quickly you would put the homemade cig to your mouth and puff hard. Yes, that was what I called real magic.

There was plenty of snow in New Brunswick, New Jersey most of the winters, so a sleigh was an important part of a child's equipment. I started out with just a regular sleigh; it was all right, but it didn't compare to the flyer I got later. That flyer was really something. The old one was all wood. It didn't steer very well and was heavy. But the flyer's front end was designed with steel bends, making it lighter and much more flexible in its steering. There was a good hill right in front of our house. That is important, because a sleigh without a hill is like a wagon without a horse. It can be used, but not efficiently. A couple of blocks away in either direction there were two more hills. One was steeper, gave you more speed, but it was a short hill and gave you a short ride. The other hill in the opposite direction was steeper and longer and faster, but near the bottom of it was a cross street. In the middle of that street there were tracks used by the new invention, the trolley car. Needless to say, one was always taking a chance going down that hill. Even if the kids took turns warning, sometimes you couldn't hear them or they weren't conscientious about their job. A lot could go wrong. No, that was too dangerous. Oh, once in a while you would give it a whirl on a dare or when things got a little dull on your hill. It was a thrill sliding down those hills. You and the sleigh were as one, shimming down at high speed six inches from the snow, the white stuff flying up in your runny-nosed red face, feeling and hearing the soft solid rumble of your vehicle bumping along on the hardened street snow. It was a thrill all right. It was a thrill.

My first bike was given to me by my parents when I was lucky enough to bring home a report card that was good enough to promote me to the next higher grade, probably in later grammar school. A lot can be accomplished with a bike. With it, one can deliver magazines, take a half dozen steel traps down to the Raritan River and try and catch a muskrat; take a real adventure ride to our Morgan Beach shack fifteen miles away; ride to the silent movies every Saturday; peddle to a patch of woods five or six miles away in a light snow, discover rabbit tracks, follow them to an old overturned barrel. Stoop down, look inside: see a cottontail rabbit; work up courage to put my hand in there and pull him out. Put him in a big pocket that ran across the whole width of my mackinaw; get on my bike and ride home. It's snowing harder now. On arrival home, in order to incarcerate him, I turn a bushel basket upside down, put him in it; stake it down. He'd never get out. The next morning there was a three inch hole near the bottom edge of the basket. He had gnawed his way out wisely. Good for him. Other uses for the bike were: ride three or four miles to the canal or Weston's Mill and go canoeing; get your glove and ride over to a friend's house and catch a few; run errands and maybe make a dime; ride out to a small rural town and pick cherries; ride out to another friend's house outside of town, venture into a patch of woods, find a hollow tree trunk, discover two flying squirrels in it and try to bring them home. They too escape. Oh well, to try is the thing. A bicycle fights back, too. When pumping hard up a steep hill, the chain breaks just as you are standing up on the peddle, your full weight comes down on the crossbar, nearly cutting you in half. Summer vacation. Set free, pardoned, released, escaped. That's the feeling I had when school closed in the middle of June and we went to the shack on Morgan Beach for the summer. The relief I felt from those ten month periods of school, that ten months of putdown worry. I sweated out every year. How good it felt to be rid of that burden. There is so much that I felt, so many happy sensations, so many happy moments, time would not allow me to elaborate, although each moment deserves a chapter.

While in high school, I was a member of the New Brunswick football team. The same night that I graduated from high school, I left New York City to board an old tramp steamer that lay in the harbor of 22nd Street. It was the last of the coal burners and carried a crew of nine sailors and nine stockers. We sailed to Rio, Buenos Aires, Montevido, the east coast of South America. Quite an adventure for a home boy.

From 1927-35, most of my little theatre plays were done at New Jersey College for women at New Brunswick. One play was for Princeton University for the Triangle Club. I usually played the leads in these plays. Some I recall were: *Mrs. Moonlight* (Mr. Moonlight); *Seventh Heaven* (Chico); *The High Road* (Lord Trench); *Behind Red Nights*, *Wild Duck*, *Royal Family*, *Milky Way*, *Death Takes a Holiday* (in the role of Death), and more. I was leading man at the age of twenty-six in the East Orange Stock Company.

We lived on 52nd Street between 5th and 6th Avenue for about two or three years. All night clubs were on this street called "Swing Alley." It was a four story old brown stone building. We lived on the fourth floor. If you went up on the roof for some air during the summer, the Radio City building a block away would tower over us. During my stay here, I worked in shows like *Awake and Sing, Three Men on a Horse, Red Lights, Night of January 16th*, and others.

In 1940, Arthur Space received a letter from the Television Division, Dumont Television, which said:

> I have your letter of December 17th and want you to know that I am certainly keeping you in mind for some television activity, once we get our station on the air. I share the belief with you that television has a marvelous future and feel certain once the wheels of the industry begin rolling, we'll move along at a great speed. Feel assured that I have not forgotten your stage and television work in the past and that I will call you on some active participation when the time for program presentation arrives.

A letter from Metro Goldwyn Mayer in January of 1941, when Arthur Space was still living in New Jersey, stated:

Dear Arthur:

> Believe me that I got quite a thrill out of receiving your letters, even though it was written in yearly installments. I waited to answer it until I saw your pictures and it seems to me you haven't changed much in appearance in the past few years. With reference to your future in motion pictures, I'm really hesitant to give you any concrete advice, because it's such a haphazard business and even more "catch as catch can" than Broadway. In the first place, I don't know how you would photograph nor can anyone tell, until they get you before a camera. Economically, you'll have quite a struggle here, because although I might be able to give you a day or so work in a picture, I only do four or five pictures a year and that wouldn't keep you alive. Frankly, I have always believed that you have a great ability and would be willing to give you every opportunity to do something for me in a picture, but even if the opportunity would present itself, I don't believe it would be enough to keep you going. You would have to have enough money in the bank to last you at least four or five months, so that an agent could take you from one studio to the other and get you started in bit work. At the beginning, such a career is tough, so you must be prepared for a stiff grind. But as you have the ability, I think you can get somewhere and I for one will do everything in my power to help.

This letter was from Sylvan Simon, whom Arthur had worked for in a stage play in New York. The following August, Simon wrote him again:

> Dear Arthur:
>
> Just a hasty note to let you know that I have received your letter and that I'm starting a picture with Wallace Beery entitled *The Steel Cavalry* on Tuesday, September 2nd. If you were to get out here within the next week or so, I could offer you a few days work at about $50 a day in the picture. The part might run a few more days, but I can't promise more than an initial engagement of a few days. But at least it will be an opportunity to be seen. Of course, you know the Screen Actors Guild requires a payment of $55.
>
> Sylvan Simon

I came to Hollywood alone, straight from two or three years of beach combing along the Raritan Bay, New Jersey. One good suit and enough money for a month's sustenance. I was staying in a big house on Vine Street, two blocks up from Hollywood Boulevard, living in a room that slept four people, one meal a day, for twenty dollars a week. The only future I had was three days work at seventy-five dollars a day in a Wally Beery picture at MGM studio (*The Steel Cavalry*, which title was changed to *The Bugle Sounds*). Since that time, years have slipped by and so has a hundred pictures, three hundred TV shows and one stage show. Sometimes ignorance is a great help in succeeding; if one were conscious of the odds against him, he never would venture. What happened in Hollywood is another story, another era in my life, another world to be written about. Right now, I would like to mention Pop's part in it. I needed more money to prolong my Hollywood effort and increase my chances of succeeding, so I got in touch with Pop. He's in Lima, Peru now. I told him what I was up to and asked for some money. I'm sure he felt I was still drifting like the wood in the bay. Nonetheless, he staked me with a hundred dollars or two hundred; I have forgotten the exact amount. So you see, he did come through. I realize now, with that money a thirty year old man straight from the beach with only a suit and a hat, with connections in the same portion, had less than a chance of conquering the almost unattainable place called Hollywood; but he did. Thank you, Lord.

The following article appeared in a New Brunswick, New Jersey newspaper:

> Arthur Space, a former local thespian who several times stood on the threshold of fame in the dramatic world, is again offered the opportunity to go to places in the acting profession. This time to Hollywood. Space is one of the best known actors in this section about five years ago, appearing regularly in performances of Miss Jane Inge's little workshop theater at New Jersey College

and getting several good assignments in stock companies in New York and road companies.

After many years of effort for recognition on legitimate stage, he now has made a start in motion pictures. He was offered the opportunity to go to Hollywood by Sylvan Simon, a movie director who held the same position with Bide Dudley's Player group in New York City in which Space appeared and at that time made his acquaintance. He writes of his experiences as follows:

I arrived on a Thursday night and on the following day received word to go out to the MGM studio. That afternoon I was introduced to the producer, J. Walter Ruben and everybody else that had any interest in the picture. When I had finished meeting all these people that had to give me the "okay," things didn't look so bad nor did they look so good. First thing that I knew, I was called to be fitted for my wardrobe, which consisted of an old soft hat, old leather jacket, pants and hunting shoes. When I arrived on the set, I found most of my scene was to be shot in an old barn. Hank was the name of the character and he was to be part of a group plotting against the US Army. *The Bugle Sounds* is the name of the picture and the job turned out to last nine days, instead of three days as was intended. I have a fight scene with Beery and a short scene with George Bancroft and Beery at a gas station. I'm the villain that rushes over to the detonator and stands poised, ready to blow up the bridge over which a trainload of army tanks will be crossing any minute now. But much to the satisfaction of the Saturday afternoon kids, Beery comes to, wrenches a gun from Bancroft's hand, and shoots me in the back. I fall dead over the handle of the detonator, pushing it down and consequently blowing up the bridge before the tanks reach it.

Space reveals in his letter that he does not want to give the impression that he is a full fledge star and that the trail ahead is a long one. He says, "If you have the habit of blinking when you go to the pictures, you had better get rid of it before you go see this one, because it may be while you are blinking, one of the blinks you might miss seeing me."

The former actor was given his second part in the picture *Torpedo Boat*, with Richard Arlen. He was given only an hour's notice. He describes the scene as follows: "Had about eight speeches and regretted that the scene was shot across my back, because I feel that I would have shown up very well in the part. I do face the camera at the end of the scene, though." He warns, "I have been lucky and may not have another part for the next six months." Space is still exhibiting the same persistence and confidence which marked his earlier dramatic career. The day after he wired Hollywood accepting an offer, he received a return wire telling him to stay home. He was stunned, but was so determined, he left anyhow and took his chances which thus far have been good.

From a 1942 newspaper article:

> From the New York stage comes Arthur Space to appear as the villain in Metro Goldwyn Mayer's *Rio Rita*, which stars comedians Abbott and Costello. Space came to Hollywood after a successful role in *Night of January 16th* for a role in Wallace Beery's *The Bugle Sounds* and *Riot Squad*.

I have just finished eight days in Joan Crawford's new picture, *Reunion in France*. I took a chance on this job: by that I mean I shaved off my moustache, cut my hair around the ears and played the part of a nasty Nazi. I only had a couple of speeches, but the work was done in the company of Miss Crawford, Albert Basserman and John Carradine. I figured it was a good idea to find out in the beginning of my career just what I looked like with and without hair. If I show up well as a Nazi, it's possible that I will have a much better chance at getting similar work.

You know, it's funny playing a Nazi. When you put on a Nazi uniform, you immediately notice the difference in the attitude of your fellow workers. At noon hour, as you walk through the lot on your way to the commissary, you have all kinds of remarks thrown your way by studio workers. Most were in a joking mood, but I could detect a real emotional disturbance on their part. Most of them would just hiss; others would go as far as to say, "I don't like you." They were people whom I had never seen before. As I walk into the commissary towards my table, I could hear a dozen hisses before I seated myself. After the first day in uniform, I decided to do something about it. Before going to lunch I'd return to my dressing room, take off the top part of the uniform and put on my street clothes. Why, I even felt like a Nazi when I had the darn outfit on. Well, that's just a little proof the feelings of Americans toward those things that are giving us all so much trouble. With that kind of spirit, we can't lose this fight.

Concerning life in Hollywood, Space writes that he experienced his first earthquake:

"I was awakened out of a sound sleep about one o'clock in the morning, being bounced up and down in bed. When you suddenly realize that there isn't anyone there to make you bounce and you notice the doors on your room swinging back and forth in slow rhythm, you get what some people call a thrill, but I was just plain scared."

Arthur Space worked with the Spotlighters, a well organized group of professional actors, writers, directors, producers and executives banded together to aid the Youth Foundation in every possible manner. The Spotlighters believed that if you give the teenager a place to enjoy, the teenager will give you the pleasure of having served.

The Encyclopedia of Feature Players of Hollywood

In 1954, the *Hollywood Reporter* wrote:

> Arthur Space stars in *The Rainbow Chaser* for *Death Valley Days*. It is the first for the new season and the last one to be filmed by Flying A. *The Rainbow Chaser*, teeing off the new series, deals with the wastrel who is always grubstaking prospectors; completely irresponsible of his family's duties. Dreaming of that gold mine in the sky, he finally goes off looking for one himself. Years pass and it is assumed he is dead. Meanwhile, his family goes to work and has a happy life, until one day the characterless character ambles in, ready to resume his head-of-the-house position, but not to work. The old bum creates a lot of friction, as he can't understand why he isn't loved; just cause he took a few years off chasing rainbows. Happy ending in this yarn comes when the wised-up wife grubstakes her hubby to hunt for a mine she knows doesn't exist and this time he never does return. Arthur Space turns in a convincing portrayal of the ne'er-do-well.

In 1955, Arthur Space starred in an episode of the television series *Medic*. A Los Angeles paper wrote:

> It is the story of Dr. Halstead and his associates. A group of dedicated scientists, they were seeking an effective antiseptic. Their joy at the discovery of cocaine soon was dispelled by the further discovery that continued use did more harm than good. *Medic*'s treatment of the discovery of that was well handled and in the best of taste. Director Worthington Miner said it was the first time he discovered "a good actor who's been around for years," referring to Arthur Space who portrays Dr. William Halstead. Space is destined to become one of the better TV actors of the year in this drama, according to insiders.

A 1955 New Brunswick, New Jersey newspaper printed the following article about Arthur:

> Youth who played reluctant stage role here in 1927, visits city as successful TV actor. A research scientist who developed cocaine as a pain killer, only to discover it was habit forming, stopped here the other day to visit boyhood friends. If you are one of the countless television viewers who enjoy the weekly *Medic* series, you'd recall the story some weeks ago about Dr. Halstead and his associates. A native of this community where he entertained thousands of people in amateur productions during the early 1930s, Space dropped into town for a few hours the other day. He was returning from the Virgin Islands where he has a role in the multi-million dollar Universal International production,

Arthur Space

Away All Boats. He was on his way home to Hollywood and decided, more or less on the spare of the moment to stop over in his hometown. He chatted for a few hours with friends, made a few telephone calls, then left for Middlebush where he intended to spend some time with relatives of his wife, the former Mollie Campbell.

Finished character actor of today, now forty-four years old, is a far cry from the sixteen year old boy who was prevailed upon in 1927 to accept a male lead in the NJC production of *Seventh Heaven*. Then a student at New Brunswick High School, Space had no particular aspirations for the stage. The NJC group needed someone for the lead and Space's English teacher, Miss Anna R. Nelson, prevailed upon him to undertake the role, since he previously appeared in several minor school plays. When he graduated from high school, Space gravitated into various odd jobs, but the theater became his primary love. He worked with Jane Ingle in a little theater workshop. He recalls that for a while, he worked on a Pennsylvania railroad construction gang from dawn until noon, then joined the workshop group, remaining there until midnight. During this time with the workshop, he appeared in many plays. Then followed years of summer stock and more years in road companies. In 1939, Space played a leading part in a production staged by the late Sylvan Simon at a resort in Schroon Lake, New York. When Simon became a producer in Hollywood in 1941, he sent for Space and they became close friends. The producer considered the young actor his talisman and insisted that Space be given a role, however small, in every picture he produced. As a result, Space appeared in some forty films over the next five years. When Simon passed away a few years ago, Space continued his work in Hollywood, and with the advent of television, was offered many minor video parts. But it was the performance in *Medic* that boomed his stock. As a result of his fine characterization, Space was asked by Ray Milland to take a role in Milland's first independent production, which Milland directed. The picture entitled *A Man Alone* will soon be released. His next job was in *Away All Boats*, now being filmed in the Virgin Islands. Space was there for two weeks and has about six more weeks of work to complete in Hollywood. Space is still the modest person that endeared him to many people in this community years ago. "Acting is all I've ever known how to do and I love it. And if you write anything of my visit to New Brunswick, I hope you will express my deep regret at not being able to spend more time here and see a lot of other friends that I just won't have time to see." Space was wed to Mollie Campbell in 1936. They and their two daughters live in Hollywood.

I have learned through past experience that you do not count on anything in this business, until you are actually working or have signed a contract. The rigorous routine of an actor isn't so much the physical strain as it is the mental activity. If he's as serious about his job as an actor should be, that's the part that really tires him out. It's probably much harder on the wife of an actor than on the wife of an average worker. I guess a woman has to spend something getting used to the irregular schedules and hours. After that, it's not really too bad.

Another article on Arthur, reported:

> Arthur Space goes over his scripts before and during breakfast. Sometimes he's studying several at a time and he gets to the studio about eight o'clock. After some time in makeup and wardrobe, where he's made to look like the roles he's playing, he goes to the set where he may briefly run over the script again or discuss the day's sequences with the director. Sometimes he doesn't get home until seven or seven-thirty, in which case he usually gets a casual dinner, reads the script again and goes right to bed. He uses his spare time to refresh his mind from the acting routine. "I like to hunt and fish, spend time outdoors. Most people think that an actor has all kinds of money to spend, but the average actor's salary is almost the same as anyone else's. I fix my own fences, mow my own lawn, and work on my car. Very few of us can afford to job out everything that needs doing around the house."
>
> How does one get to be an actor? Arthur answers the question, "Hard work and determination; same as any other job."

I'm very proud of my accomplishments, considering what I have just reviewed; a hundred pictures and three hundred and fifty TVs and a face that is known over the world. It sure didn't look that way back in the third grade.

Film Credits: 1941: The Bugle Sounds; Riot Squad. **1942:** Rio Rita; Quiet Please, Murder; Torpedo Boat; Andy Hardy's Double Life; Grand Central Murder; Salute to the Marines; Tortilla Flat; Random Harvest; Tish; Reunion in Vienna; Don't Talk; Enemy Agents Meet Ellery Queen; Tennessee Johnson. **1943:** Lassie Come Home; The Dancing Masters; The Heavenly Body; Whistling in Brooklyn; A Guy Named Joe; This is the Army; They Came to Blow Up America; The Man From Down Under; Appointment in Berlin; Swing Shift Maisie. **1944:** Wilson; Rationing; The Big Noise; Thirty Seconds Over Tokyo; The Woman in the Window; Ladies Courageous; Wing and a Prayer; The Ghost That Walks Alone; Dark Shadows (short); Strange Affair; The Mark of the Whistler; Gentle Annie. **1945:** Leave Her to Heaven; Our Vines Have Tender Grapes; Abbott and Costello in Hollywood; Music for

Millions; Leave it to Blondie; Twice Blessed; A Gun in His Hand; The Great American Mug; The Seesaw and the Shoes (short); Son of Lassie; This Man's Navy; The Crimson Canary; The Clock. **1946:** The Magnificent Doll; Black Beauty; The Mysterious Mr. Valentine; Child of Divorce; Secret of the Whistler; Boys' Ranch; Home in Oklahoma; The Cockeyed Miracle; The Man Who Dared; Bad Bascomb; That Brennan Girl; Courage of Lassie; The Great Morgan; Our Old Car; Black Beauty; Gentleman Joe Palooka; The Secret of the Whistler; Magnificent Doll; Lost City of the Jungle. **1947:** The Guilt of Janet Ames; The Red House; Big Town After Dark; Rustlers of Devil's Canyon; Millie's Daughter; The Crimson Key; Her Husband's Affair; Mr. District Attorney; Heartaches; I Love Trouble; The Invisible Wall; Key Witness. **1948:** Tap Roots; Walk a Crooked Mile; Silver River; A Southern Yankee; Fuller Brush Man; Fighter Squadron; The Paleface; Homecoming; Return of October; Joan of Arc. **1949:** The Lone Wolf and His Lady; Any Number Can Play; Mr. Belvedere Goes to College; Shockproof; El Paso; Sorrowful Jones; Miss Grant Takes Richmond; Chicago Deadline; House of Strangers; Lust for Gold; Mary Ryan, Detective. **1950:** Father is a Bachelor; Fuller Brush Girl; The Good Humor Man; The Killer that Stalked New York; The Happy Years; The Vanishing Westerner. **1951:** Tomahawk; Up Front; Her First Romance; Night Riders of Montana; The Barefoot Mailman; Three Guys Named Mike; Utah Wagon Train; Government Agents vs. the Phantom Legion. **1952:** African Treasure; Red Ball Express; Sudden Fear; Sound Off; Rainbow 'Round My Shoulder; Here Comes the Marines; Jet Job; Jumping Jacks; Because of You; Feudin' Fools; Fargo. **1953:** Back to God's Country; The Man from the Alamo; The Eddie Cantor Story; So This is Love; Confidential Connie; Battle Circus; Last of the Pony Riders; Clipped Wings; Canadian Mounties vs. Atomic Invaders. **1954:** Target Earth; Yankee Pasha; The Silver Chalice; Pride of the Blue Grass; The Admiral Hoskins Story; A Star is Born; Panther Girl of the Kongo. **1955:** Rage at Dawn; Foxfire; A Man Alone; The Spoilers; Wyoming Renegades; The Eternal Sea. **1956:** Away All Boats; The Killer is Loose. **1957:** The Spirit of St. Louis; Twenty Million Miles to Earth. **1958:** Twilight for the Gods; St. Louis Blues. **1959:** A Summer Place; Day of the Outlaw. **1960:** Gunfighters of Abilene. **1964:** Taggart. **1968:** The Shakiest Gun in the West. **1971:** Shoot-Out; Bedknobs and Broomsticks. **1973:** The Folks at Red Wolf Inn; Frasier, the Sensuous Lion. **1974:** The Bat People; Herbie Rides Again; Ma and Pa (TV). **1975:** The Strongest Man in the World. **1976:** Mansion of the Doomed; The Lindbergh Kidnapping Case (TV). **1978:** The Swarm; On the Nickel. **1979:** Promises in the Dark; Hot Rod (TV).

PEGGY STEWART

Peggy Stewart was born June 6, 1923, in West Palm Beach, Florida, and moved to Atlanta, Georgia when she was five years old. "In my movie going I would go on Saturday to the matinees and catch all the cowboys and Tarzan," Peggy reflected. "I caught Katharine Hepburn as Little Jo in *Little Women*, and Hepburn has been my total inspiration. At Christmas time our grammar school was doing a little scene, and I wanted to faint like Little Jo did—the heck with the dialogue. I just wanted to twirl and flop on the floor like Hepburn did. We did that little scene, and I thought, 'Someday I'm going to be an actress.' I didn't know when, where, or how, and didn't pursue it in my thoughts anymore after that."

When Peggy was twelve, she accompanied her mother and two sisters to Los Angeles to join her grandmother for her mother's brother's wedding. "While we were out here for that summer I asked Grandmama if I could go to a dramatic school," Peggy noted. "This was when schools were in full swing rather than workshops. She said, 'Sure,' and I went to a school called Newly Dictions, which I loved. I said, 'This is it—I want to stay.' I asked Grandmama if she'd stay with me and she said to ask my mother if it was all right, which I did. Mama called Granddaddy in Florida and he said okay, so everything was go for me to stay. My sisters and mom went back to Georgia, and I stayed with my Grandma and continued on with dramatic school."

Peggy and her grandmother lived in an apartment complex in Hollywood where a character actor by the name of Henry O'Neill also resided. He was a Warner Brothers contract player who had been loaned out to Paramount to work on a Western called *Wells Fargo*. "He knew that they were looking for a young teenage girl with a slight Southern accent to play

Joel McCrea and Frances Dee's daughter," Peggy informed. "He told the director, Frank Lloyd, about me, and they tested me. That was my very first part, so Pop O'Neill got me that."

After *Wells Fargo*, Peggy worked in three films at Universal Studios. The first one was with Deana Durbin in *That Certain Age*, then two with the Little Tough Guys (*Little Tough Guy* and *Little Tough Guys in Society*), some of whom were the former Dead End Kids that later graduated into the East Side Kids and the Bowery Boys. Peggy next worked with Henry O'Neill at Warners in *Everybody's Hobby*, followed by another at that studio titled *All This and Heaven Too*. She next returned to Universal for *Back Street* with Margaret O'Sullivan.

Peggy shared her feelings working with her Little Tough Guys co-stars, saying, "They were fun; they were wonderful; and they were wild," she laughed. "They'd drive the crew insane because they'd come tearing in on the set very seriously, yelling, 'Fire! Fire!' and these guys would clear out. They would especially scare Marjorie Main to death. She was hyper anyhow. But they were really fun to work with. I think all of them except Frankie Thomas are gone now. I loved Gabe Dell, he was really the stable man of it all."

Peggy stated that she loved being a child actress. "I had no problem with it whatsoever. I went to a special junior high school, the Mar-Ken Professional School, where everybody there were professional kids like Jackie Moran and the Mauch twins. When we worked, we would take over on the set our homework or whatever they had given us at school to do. Miss West was the schoolteacher on the set at Universal, but there was no break in our schoolwork. I found that the work you would be doing while on the set was what you'd be doing in the school." Peggy finished her last two years of school at Hollywood High, but stated, "That was a different set-up. They were not really equipped to let you go for however long it took you to make a film, and to come back it was kind of different there."

Peggy married an actor named Don Barry in 1939 and was out of films for almost three years, appearing in only one during this time at PRC titled, *Girls in Chains*. In 1944, when Peggy and Don were separated and headed for divorce, Don went to Herbert Yates and recommended Yates take Peggy under contract at Republic Studios. "Don told Pop Yates that I had been an actress and almost a professional rider (when I lived in Atlanta I had showed horses for the Keene Stable), so Pop Yates said all right," Peggy noted. "Republic was a small studio so didn't have the budget that the larger studios had to make a test film, and used the Westerns as a screen test." Peggy's first film was a Red Ryder Western with Bill Elliott, titled *Tucson Raiders*. "Pop Yates said, 'Fine,' put me under contract, and I just rode into the sunset." During her three years at Republic, Peggy worked in two-dozen Westerns, six of them during her first year there. She worked in eight films with Sunset Carson; seven with Bill Elliott; five with Allan Lane; and one each with Roy Rogers and Gene Autry. She also starred in two serials, *Phantom Rider* and *Son of Zorro*. Only on a few occasions did Republic allow Peggy to climb off her horse for a non-Western, one of those being *The Vampire's Ghost*. "That was a terrible picture," she laughed. "I so hated that picture that every chance I had I was off the set visiting with Elliott or

Sunset or whoever was working. The first assistant was running back and forth: 'Peggy, get back on the stage.' I really didn't like that film at all."

Peggy mentioned that she had been riding horses since she was six years old, but only English style riding. Polly Burson, one of the great stuntwomen of the movies, did all of Peggy's stunts. Polly and Peggy used to ride through the hills in back of the Hudkins Stables, across the wash from Warner Brothers where Forest Lawn is now located. "Polly had to exercise her trick horse, so I would go and get Smoky – who I always rode in the Westerns. We'd throw an old halter on them, lead them out, and take a brown bag with us for lunch. Wherever they took us that's where we went and we'd sit under a tree and eat. Polly also took me down on the river bottom where the sand is nice and soft, and said, 'Gal, you've got to loosen up a little bit.' So we got rid of some of the English look. But I still rode very stiff from the waist up, elbows in, not flopping – which I liked and was my choice."

In 1944, Republic released a John Wayne picture titled *Tall in the Saddle*, with Ella Raines. The Ella Raines part resulted in a big change for Peggy at Republic. "After she did that part they started writing more things for a stronger woman for me being able to handle myself." Peggy mentioned that one of her favorite films was *Days of Buffalo Bill*, in which her role was inspired somewhat by the Ella Raines character. "I wore chaps and ran my own ranch," she stated. "I liked that."

Peggy worked in a serial, *Son of Zorro*, and told of a humorous incident that occurred during the filming of an ending to one of the chapters. "We were always playing jokes with each other," Peggy smiled. "Everybody was like a big family, it being such a small studio. We'd pop in and visit each other on the sets all of the time, and we were always playing jokes on the crew and cast. In this serial they had to pull me up by a rope and drop me down into a huge galvanized tub of water. They had handles on the bottom of this tub, and Bud Thackery, the cameraman, said, 'Peggy, listen. There's dialogue going on up here a little bit after you hit the water, so grab those handles, because your clothes will make you float to the top. We don't want to see you, so hang on there. We'll kick the tub when the dialogue is finished and you can come up.' So they dropped me into the water, I got down there, and I am hanging on and hanging on. My, I turned as blue as my blue jeans, and thought, 'Heck, nobody's kicking this bucket. I've got to come up.' I came up and nobody was on the set. I looked out through the big barn door, and everybody was standing with their arms crossed because they were all waiting, wondering how long was that idiot going to sit there under water," she laughed.

Peggy mentioned also that she had to watch Thackery very careful. "I had the V-shaped rather than the round-shaped boots so they didn't fit tight to the leg. I had to always watch it, and I'd buy into it every time even though I knew better. Buddy Thackery would always come up on a close-up outside, especially at Iverson Ranch, and he'd say, 'I have to tell you this one thing because of this reflector over there…' and as he was talking, he'd get a handful of gravel and put it down my boot. I'm telling you, if you ever tried to get out of boots with gravel down them, they're horrible. It smarts. I'd say, 'You son of a gun…' It was either water or gravel."

Of the cowboy stars she has worked with, Peggy named Sunset Carson and Bill Elliott as her favorites. "Sunset, I loved him. He was like my big brother. I loved working with him and Bill Elliott. Bill just had a wonderful aura about him—the gentleman of them all. He befriended me. When I left Republic, Bill was the first one I ever knew to keep a timecard. They didn't have them at the Guild yet, and he kept on me, saying, 'Now you keep a timecard.' I'd say, 'Billy, I don't need one.' Anyhow, about three months before my three-year contract was up, they wanted me to do a serial, but I didn't want to do another one. So they said, 'We'll have to suspend you.' I said, 'Why don't you just let me go?' Wilson, who was the vice-president, said that Yates was out of town and wouldn't be back until the next day. So the next day I talked to Poppy Yates for about an hour and a half, and he told me how cold the world was out there, but they had no intention of moving me out of so-called B-Westerns into more of the A-films. They said that I saved them money as far as riding and all of that was concerned. I couldn't see myself going anywhere, and said, 'I'd rather leave and just take my chances.'"

Robert Newman, of Republic's accounting office, sent Peggy a letter stating that she owed the studio something like one hundred and ninety-eight dollars. "My contract was prorated, where you work twelve months rather than being off," Peggy told us. "You know, a contract says you're off three months a year. So I had my contract prorated to where I was paid each week, and it was from that they said I owed them money. Well, I didn't have a hundred some odd dollars. I went to Billy Elliott, and I'm crying. He asked, 'What are you crying for?' I said, 'I don't have my timecards.' Bill took the letter, and just from his timecards on the Red Ryder's that I had done with him – I had made nine Westerns in eleven weeks (not all of them Red Ryder's) when the set directors and carpenters were on strike, so I was putting wardrobe on lunch hour, working after dinnertime, and all these crazy hours – Bill found from the shows that I had done with him that Republic owed me about four hundred dollars in overtime and penalties. He sent that to Newman, and I got back this beautiful envelope, not like the first one at all. It said, 'Dear Peggy: We found that we made a mathematical mistake. Love, Robert Newman.' That was the last I heard of it, so I thanked Billy very much. But he was like that. He had a charisma about him that never came across on the screen like it did in person. He was really a charismatic person."

Peggy left Republic in an attempt to break the chain of Westerns and serials, with hopes of going back to where she had started with films like *Wells Fargo* and *Back Street*. "Evidentially I had made a reputation in town, which I was unaware of, with the Westerns. So my calls all came in on Westerns. The first one I did was with Sam Katzman at Columbia, a serial: *Tex Granger*. Then I did three Westerns with Lash LaRue, a couple with Jim Bannon (as Red Ryder), one or two Charley Starrett's, and then Bill Elliott. He had left Republic and went to Monogram, and I did one of those (*Kansas Territory*). Then came the TV stuff."

These shows were on episodes of *Gene Autry*, *Cisco Kid*, *Wild Bill Hickok*, and *Roy Rogers*. Reflecting on *The Cisco Kid*, Peggy stated, "Leo Carillo was serious, kind of a grouch like old Gabby, but Duncan Renaldo and the crew loved him. I didn't bother to get to know him very much. I was very immature as far as he was concerned—just a young girl. But Duncan, what a sweet, sweet man he was."

In 1953, Peggy decided to leave the film business for a while in order to break her reputation of working primarily in Westerns. "Live television was coming in, and it was all New York people that didn't know me from Adam," Peggy related. "I thought I would just get out of the business for a couple of years and then come back with a brand new name and use my real name, which is O'Rourke (Stewart was my stepfather's name). My husband, Buck Young, is an actor, and he had been doing a lot of things at NBC in live television. NBC didn't have a casting office, but Buck was very good friends with Jane Leff, production secretary for Jimmy Durante, who was trying very hard to organize a casting office for NBC. Buck had introduced me just quickly one day at lunch, but nothing was said about the casting office. I didn't know anything else but acting, so I went to Los Angeles and took a three- day schooling to become a salesgirl at the Broadway Hollywood. The morning I was going to begin work in the glove department I was rescued, because that business and I couldn't get along. I had my hand on the doorknob fixing to leave my apartment when the phone rang. I answered it and a woman said, 'This is Jane Leff.' I said, 'Hi Jane, Buck is not here.' 'No, no,' said Jane, 'I've gotten an okay for an opening for an NBC casting office. Do you want to do it with me?' I said, 'That's wonderful. I'd love it, but I never have worked in an office. I don't know protocol.' 'That doesn't make any difference,' she said. 'All you have to know is some actors, I'll take care of the rest.' So I went to work that morning. Jane worked all the contracts, and I had to learn payroll because at that time you had to be on the set when they were shooting and figure out the hours and how much to pay the actors. We had to make up our own payroll. So that was seven days a week back when live TV was a baby. CBS had *Playhouse 90*, and we had *Hallmark* and *Matinee Theater*. Our office grew as we got more shows, and we wound up with five casting people and finally had our own accountant. We started the careers of six directors there, including Boris Segal, Walter Grauman, and Lamont Johnson."

Peggy stayed with the NBC casting department for three years, and then quit. "I'm happy I saw that side of the desk," Peggy stated, "but it certainly wasn't for me. The last year there was a lack of time, and time pressure. And I began to categorize actors as they come through the door before they read or I even had the chance to meet them—and I hate that! I literally could feel sensitivity leaving, and I didn't want to lose that. So I said no more, that's for somebody else, not for me. I quit and went back to acting, and wouldn't you know, on my very first call I was right back up there on the buckboard again in *Have Gun- Will Travel*."

Peggy acted in numerous Western television shows during this portion of her career: *Wyatt Earp*, *Gunsmoke* (five episodes), *Yancy Derringer*, *The Rebel*, and *Hotel de Paree*. She also began obtaining work in a few other shows, such as *National Velvet*, *Peter Gunn*, and *The Twilight Zone*. "When I left Republic," Peggy stated, "outside of Frank McDonald – who I never worked for at Republic – no director from Republic ever used me. It's an odd thing that happens – when you are out of context, away from the studio, they don't think of you. You're a different person. At NBC they all saw me as casting in their office, and I never worked for any of those directors when I went back to acting except Lamont Johnson."

Peggy finally was able to make the transition into character parts. Television shows such as *Emergency*, *Taxi*, *Seinfeld*, *Quincy*, *Beverly Hills, 90210*, *Popular*, *The Norm Show*, and *Yes, Dear* have come her way. "I really can't remember what my first character part was," she noted, "but around the first was when George and Andrew Fenady were doing a film called *Terror in the Wax Museum* with all British actors: Maurice Evans, Ray Milland, and Elsa Lanchester. George called and asked if I could do a Cockney accent. I said, 'All I can do is try.' So I played a charwoman. An English girl named Carol, who had a grandmother that was a charwoman, gave me a lot of wonderful hints about them. She also helped me with the dialect. They had an actress from South Africa playing my partner as a charwoman, and she bought the fact that I was Cockney. About three days on the set Elsa Lanchester was resting in a group of chairs on the stage for the cast to use. I had a break and went over to sit down and rest, too. Elsa is an absolute perfectionist as far as the dialogue is concerned, and as I started to sit down, she said, 'What's the accent?' I thought, 'Oh dear, I'm caught now.' I looked at her, and said, 'Contrived.' She laughed, and then said, 'No, really.' I didn't know what to tell her, so I said, 'All I know is that I'm split right down the middle. My father is Irish and my mother is Scottish.' She said, 'That's what it is, it's Scots.' I said, 'Oh, really,' but I left well enough alone," Peggy laughed.

Later Peggy obtained a wonderful character part on the soap opera, *Days of Our Lives*. "I had to go dressed as the person or they wouldn't buy me as the character. All I knew was that she was an old mountain woman, so I rigged up the costume at home: the hair and a horrible old snow cap, some of Buck's old boots, and long skirt. I went over and did the mountain lady and they laughed up a storm, and I got the part over the character women who were doing those parts a long time and were older than I am. After I got her, I came to find out that she was really a detective who was sent out as an undercover woman as these different characters, and the mountain woman just happened to be one of the characters. The second one I was in disguise of a Russian royalty. That was a fun thing to do."

Asked if working on a soap opera was harder to do than a normal show, Peggy replied, "I wouldn't find it so because it was a mixture of film and stage to me, and I do both. It seems to me that the most fear in doing a live show is what if I can't remember my line? But that isn't so with the soap. They tape those shows, so if you forget it, you can do it over."

Peggy Stewart

In the mid-1960's, Peggy spent a couple of months in Oregon working in *The Way West* with Kirk Douglas, Robert Mitchum, Richard Widmark, and her old Republic co-star, Roy Barcroft. "We had a great deal of fun," Peggy stated. "I think we traveled every way there was to travel, except submarine. We were in Eugene first, and crossed the river there on rafts. Then we got down to Bend and stayed there for most of the rest of the time. I loved that little town. It's so pretty with that river going through. We had to have some snow, which was fairly close by, so we took a ski lift up to the snow. We had a ride on the helicopter every morning for about a week to get to the desert part; I think it was on the way to Burns. Then we went to a place where they built a tent fort for *Rooster Cogburn*, and we used that fort in the forest on those funny puddle jumpers that you use when going into mountain territory. So we traveled every which way there was," she laughed. "By bus, by stretch-out, by motorbike, by wagon, of course, but I had a wonderful time up there. I loved the territory. And again, when you're there for that length of time the company becomes family. I had a great time with Roy Barcroft. We had a lot of fun, and we'd go to the market together. He had his little camper and would stay in there. And in that camper, the whole sides of it were lined with boxes of 8x10 production shots. He had shots from long ago from Republic, and even prior to that. It was so great to see those of all the crew and people that I knew. A lot of them have passed."

Peggy worked for a producer-director named James Conway for Sunn Classics, based in Utah. "I had a wonderful time, and a great relationship with James Conway. He left the Sun-Shick banner and became Lorimar, and I worked again with him down here on the television series, *Paradise*." In Utah, Peggy worked with him on several made-for-television movies: *The Fall of the House of Usher* with Martin Landau ("I was a barmaid with a slight English accent"), *The Adventures of Nellie Bly*, *The Time Machine*, *Donner Pass: The Road to Survival*, *Behind Death's Door*, *In Search of Historic Jesus*, and *The Capture of Grizzly Adams*.

Peggy also worked in theater, her latest being *Hell Bent for Good Times* with James Best. "Jim and I got along great. He wrote, directed and produced it, and was hoping to showcase it for a possibility for a series. Jimmy's comedy is a mixture of burlesque and farce. It's broad, and he likes a good punch line. So I picked up some knowledge of comedy from him. Timing. Because I've done very little comedy, actually. But I had a natural feel for it, which I didn't know. You get out there and try a couple of things and, whoa, I can do that."

"I love working on stage," Peggy continued. "I can see where if you haven't got yourself a hit it can get darn boring, because it runs every night. But, if you've got a hit, for me if I had a *Peter Pan* or something like it, there would be nothing to playing it for two years. Because I love acceptance and applause, but I think any actor does. And you'll get it if you have a hit show. The audience feeds you energy." Other plays that Peggy performed in include, *John Brown's Body*, and *Picnic* with Nick Nolte, for which she was nominated by the LA Drama Critics as best supporting actress, with a theater company run by James Gammon, Timothy Scott, and two other actors.

When not working, Peggy loves gardening. "That teaches me a lot, too. It's a wonderful way of thinking when you get out there in the yard and watch the flowers when the business has got you irritated or a little stressful for the moment. You just go out and see those buds, and it's like the Bible says—they don't sweat or toil, they just unfold. What I'm trying to say is that they sort of keep your feet on the ground, and put things in the right perspective. I'm also an avid tennis fan and enjoy watching the US Open tennis matches."

When asked if she noticed much of a difference between the Hollywood of today and the Hollywood of the 40's and 50's, Peggy responded, "A big difference. People don't have fun anymore. They work for the check. I would imagine if you look closer, it's probably the regulars on the shows that have the fun. I did a *Seinfeld* and I've done soaps, and on both of those shows the ensemble is very tight. They help each other and are a wonderful ensemble. If you are part of that, you probably feel a lot better. And believe me, Jerry Seinfeld was fast to come up on the set the first moment that he saw you and welcome you. It's not because of any phoniness on the regular's part, but even there they don't have the time, so you don't see the closeness between the ensemble and crew. It's a business association relationship; it's not the fun family relationship that was warm. We were literally a family in those older days; we worked six days a week. You had Sunday off, and that's the only time you saw your family. The rest of the time it was the crew and the cast, because make-up call was six in the morning and you may work till ten that night. So they became literally your aunt, your uncle, your brother, and your sister."

At the time of our interview, Peggy had just completed work the previous week in a comedy television series with Martin Short. Shortly before this, Peggy performed in a television pilot called *Last Chance Detective*, which is similar to what the Hardy Boys and Nancy Drew used to be. This pilot emulated Disney when he first started out, focusing on family films. "We shot it in Kingman, Arizona," Peggy noted. "James Callahan and I played the grandparents who own a diner called the Last Chance, because it's the last chance for food and gas on old Route 66. Beside the diner is a great big B-17 that my husband flew at one time. My grandson and three other kids, two boys and a girl, form a detective company and make the B-17 their office, so the stories evolve from this. The first one was called *Mystery Lights on the Mesa*. The producers are in the process of selling it now, but outside of that I can't say where or when it is going to be on. I hope it goes." Peggy has also worked in various commercials. "They have been great as far as your bread and butter," she added.

Peggy and her husband, Buck, played husband and wife in the 1972 feature, *Pickup on 101*, and their son Greg played their son. Buck, who was an avid golf player, performed in numerous films (*The French Line*, *Suppose They Gave a War and Nobody Came?* and *Death Wish II*) and television series (*Official Detective*, *Steve Canyon*, *Gunsmoke*, *The Real McCoys*, *U.S. Marshal*, *The Rebel*, *How the West was Won*, *Kojak*, and *Dallas*.) during his career. He passed away on February 9, 2000. Peggy's sister, Patricia O'Rourke, played Mahala in Sabu's *The Jungle Book* and was married to actor Wayne Morris.

In summing up her feelings on her career thus far, Peggy told us, "I just enjoyed every minute of it. All the learning processes—at the time it's pain when you are learning. One of the biggest pains to learn is that there are no rejections. I've taught acting, and Buck has too, with Lieux Dressler. We started with about ten of us, and then had to move to a bigger place because we grew and grew. We taught strictly techniques. I really stressed to all the kids of finding a way of thinking, and would suggest the way that I had to help me weather through thinking there's rejection—Wondering, 'Was I reading right?' 'Why was I not right?'— Because it begins to rip like a Japanese torture chamber. It's like war out there. Especially commercials. I think statistics are now that when you go out there, there will be seventy-five tries before you get one. So you have all those seventy-four times thinking, 'Why?' And then you see that commercial on the screen that you went to read for, and it's very obvious why. It's nothing to do with you or your talent."

Peggy continues working in television in such recent shows as *My Name is Earl* and *The Office*, and had the running part of Cherien's mother in *The Riches*.

Film Credits: 1937: Wells Fargo. **1938:** Little Tough Guy; That Certain Age; White Banners; Little Tough Guys in Society. **1939:** Man About Town; 5th Ave Girl; Everybody's Hobby. **1940:** Star Dust; All This and Heaven Too. **1941:** Back Street. **1942:** Sleepytime Gal. **1943:** Girls in Chains. **1944:** Tucson Raiders; Silver City Kid; Stagecoach to Monterey; Cheyenne Wildcat; Code of the Prairie; Firebrands of Arizona; Sheriff of Las Vegas. **1945:** Utah; The Vampire's Ghost; Oregon Trail; Bandits of the Badlands; Marshal of Laredo; Rough Riders of Cheyenne; The Tiger Woman. **1946:** The Phantom Rider; Days of Buffalo Bill; California Gold Rush; Sheriff of Redwood Valley; Alias Billy the Kid; Red River Renegades; Conquest of Cheyenne; The Invisible Informer; Stagecoach to Denver. **1947:** Son of Zorro; Trail to San Antone; Vigilantes of Boomtown; The Rustlers of Devil's Canyon. **1948:** Tex Granger; Dead Man's Gold; Frontier Revenge. **1949:** Ride, Ryder, Ride!; Desert Vigilante. **1950:** The Fighting Redhead; Cody of the Pony Express; Messenger of Peace. **1951:** The Pride of Maryland. **1952:** The Black Lash; Kansas Territory; Montana Incident. **1961:** When the Clock Strikes; Gun Street; The Clown and the Kid. **1967:** The Way West. **1971:** The Animals. **1972:** Pickup on 101. **1973:** The Stranger (TV); Terror in the Wax Museum. **1975:** Trained to Kill. **1976:** Bobby Jo and the Outlaw. **1977:** Black Oak Conspiracy. **1978:** Donner Pass-The Road to Survival (TV); The Time Machine (TV). **1979:** In Search of Historic Jesus; Beyond Deaths' Door. **1980:** Beyond Evil. **1981:** The Adventures of Nellie Bly (TV). **1982:** The Capture of Grizzly Adams (TV); The Fall of the House of Usher (TV). **2007:** Hollywood: It's a Dog's Life. **2009:** Operating Instructions (TV). **2010:** The Runaways; The Bag (short). **2011:** Dadgum, Texas. **2012:** That's My Boy.

HAROLD J. STONE

Harold Jacob Stone was born in the Manhattan area of New York City on March 3, 1913. His father was a famous actor, owner and stage manager in the Yiddish Theatre. When Harold was a young boy, he would accompany his father to the theatre every weekend. "Although, as I grew up I was a very shy kid and had no more thought of going into the theatre than the man in the moon," he commented. "My father was not like ordinary fathers because I had to learn the piano, and I was going to be this and that kind of thing, and if I didn't practice the piano all hell broke lose."

Harold wanted to study medicine, taking pre-med at New York University, received his B.A., and went on to the University of Buffalo Medical School. "By this time the Depression was on so great and my father had died in 1931," he told us. "I finished two years and then I had to leave because there was no more money." His mother was very ill, so Harold, being the only child, started searching around for work. "I had a job here and I had a job there. I could have taught, but I didn't have no interest in teaching because if I couldn't fulfill my ambitions of becoming a doctor, I just said, 'The heck with it,'" he noted.

He started looking around the theatre for work after he left school. "We had a co-operative theatre in New Jersey in 1936, and we starved and finally gave that up after the summer," Harold stated. He continued seeking work again and received a call from a cousin, asking if he would come to Torrington to help them out for the Christmas week at their store. "I was supposed to be there for a couple of weeks and I stayed on for a year and-a-half," he said. Seven miles from Torrington was the Litchfield Theatre Playhouse, where Harold did some stock. He also did some radio work at WTIC, where Harold met Ed and Maude

Begley and George Petrie. In 1938, he returned to New York City and looked for work, going from one casting office to another. "In those days," Harold said, "your fellow young aspiring actors would say, 'They're casting up at 57th Street,' and we'd run from 44th Street to 57th Street. Then we'd go in there, and little did I know, they would say to me, 'What have you done?' I would say, 'Well, I was a walk on in this and a walk on in that.'"

Finally in 1939, through a relative, Harold obtained a job with George Jessel's *Little Ol' New York* at the World's Fair, as a ground cop. They rehearsed several weeks at the Nora Bay's Theatre on 44th Street. "I just sat there. As I said, I was shy; finally they were going to have a night clerk and didn't even pick me for that." They opened on May 27, and Jessell asked Harold to stand by Eddie Cantor, George Burns, and Gracie Allen to see that people didn't pester them as they did a couple of stints on the stage outside the boxing ring. The next day they were starting the night court sketch, the judge being played by a famous straight man from burlesque. Up to this point, Harold's only duty was as a ground cop to help keep everything orderly and flowing smoothly. So Harold approached the actor playing the judge and said, "I have a story to tell you about this Pollock who kills his wife." The judge asks him, "Why did you kill your wife?" "I get up in the morning and then go to work and I work like a dog. I come home at six o'clock and there's no supper on the table." "Why did you kill your wife," the judge repeats. "Six o'clock must be supper on the table!" The actor playing the judge said, "I don't know. Let's have a go at it; let's try it." Harold then recommended instead of killing the wife, let's say he wants a divorce, and picked out a name by looking at the last page of the telephone book: Zygnevskie. The actor playing the judge was quick enough to pick it up – he couldn't pronounce it. "Anyway," Harold told us, "from a two minute sketch it blew to be eight minutes. They were going to fire the four of us who were ground cops because they (the fair) had ground cops, in fact there was a good actor, Richard Reeves, who was one of the ground cops with the fair. So I saved the contracts of the other three people and I stayed until the very last day of the World's Fair and got a raise every week." This night court, which was a small courtroom that had a jury box which was reserved for the celebrities who came in from California or New York, built up to a tremendous impact, playing nine shows a day and thirteen on weekends.

An actor friend called Harold in August and told him that Sidney Kingsley was doing a play with Margo, called *The World We Make*, and there was a part of a Polish father that Harold should go down and try out for. Stone immediately went to see Kingsley and read a scene for him. Kingsley said, "Thank you very much." "Then I went home, and it's the only time in my life that I ever did this," Harold reflected, "I wrote a letter to him telling him of my aspirations and my talents and that I was good at dialects." About two weeks later he received another call, and again Harold went in and read for him, Kingsley replying, "Thank you very much." On October 29th, as the fair was ending, they gave a huge party, which Harold

Harold J. Stone

attended, and it lasted long into the night so he didn't go home. The next evening at five pm his mother phoned him, saying that the Kingsley office called and they want him to be at the Nora Bay's Theatre at six o'clock. This was the last night of their performance at the fair, and Harold asked the stage manager if he could go and that he would be back. "I went and read another scene for Mr. Kingsley and he said, 'Thank you very much, you'll hear from us.' Twelve o'clock the next night they called me and offered me the part. I found out the other actor who became my understudy was getting eighty-five dollars a week and they offered me seventy-five, so I said I want one hundred and twenty-five. They could have gotten me for forty dollars, which was the minimum at the time, and Kingsley said, 'If you don't want the part, get out.' On Saturday morning they called him, and "I started rehearsing and I did my first play with Thelma Schnee. We made our debuts. Her brother, Charles Schnee, was the famous writer who won the Academy Award for *The Bad and the Beautiful*, and then he became a producer and did *Somebody Up There Likes Me*."

This play was followed by another titled *Morning Star*, which Harold received the Richard Watts Award for one of the ten best character performers of 1939 and 1940. He then went on to do *Mr. and Mrs. North* on the road, and *Counter Attack*, which featured Morris Carnovsky, Sam Wanamaker, Karl Malden and Richard Basehart. Harold did *One Touch of Venus*, with Mary Martin and John Boles, and from there he went into *A Bell for Adano* with Fredric March, for which he received the Italian Artist Member of the Italian Society. They thought Harold was brought in from Italy because of the part he played. At the close of this play he was going to do a picture at Warner Brothers in 1946 called *Cloak and Dagger*. "I came out and Fritz Lang said, 'I have no time to teach Broadway actors moving picture technique,' so I didn't do it," Harold commented. "I got three weeks compensation for it, and finally I stayed out here with George Tobias, who was sort of a relative. In fact, his parents were my godparents. My mother and father were married in their home, so it was sort of a family kind of thing. I was out here for nine months and I couldn't get a job. I didn't have any film footage on me, and maybe I was lucky because in those days (even to this day) the idiots who are the so-called casting directors would type you. You play a cop and you're always a cop. Anyway, I went back to New York, and I wanted to get married to my childhood sweetheart." Harold did, however, manage to play one minor role in a movie titled *The Blue Dahlia* in 1946.

Back in New York, Harold had an appointment to meet a friend after a show and had arrived a few minutes early. Across the street from where he was waiting was the Mansfield Theatre, where *Anna Lucasta* was playing, and standing out in front of the theatre was John Wildburg and Nick Volpe, who were the producer and business manager of *One Touch of Venus* at the stock company in Mapleton, New Jersey. "I had done *Room Service* with Jackie

Cooper there. Anyway, for a gag, I said, 'Do you need an assistant stage manager?' They said, 'No, but how would you like to take it out on the road as stage manager? We'll be open here for three weeks and then we'll close for three weeks, and then we'll open in Philadelphia.' I said, 'Great! I need a hundred dollars; I'm going to get married.' 'Be at the box office tomorrow,' they said. Anyway, I was assistant stage manager to learn the ropes. I learned and remembered, and of course it was a very great experience because we did plays every other day. Every night they did a different play and on weekends they did one play. We opened in Philadelphia in Christmas week and I was gone for nine months. By this time I had gotten married and this was our honeymoon," Harold smiled.

At the close of the run, Harold came back to New York and he and his wife got an apartment through Ted Newton, an actor friend. "He got us that coal flat down in the village, 128 Charles Street," he told us. Robert Emhardt, Richard Carlyle, and Henry Jones also lived there, and James Edwards would come stay with Newton. "We had an awful lot of fun," Harold added.

"Years ago in '39 when I was with the William Morris office," Harold reflected, "there was a young office boy who is now one of the vice presidents, Sam Weisbord. I saw him before I had done *The World We Make*, and we are talking, and he said, 'You'll never do pictures because you got a big nose.' In those days they wanted the Clark Gables and Tyrone Powers, and it wasn't until television came in that they began to see the character actors and the odd ball faces not like the pretty boys, where you get the Ben Gazarras and the Rod Steigers; you know, people like Tony Caruso and myself."

Harold did a couple of plays at the City Center with Jose Ferrer, which included O'Neill's *Long Voyage Home*. In the beginning of the 1940s, he worked in Bucks County, Pennsylvania, doing plays, not as a resident member but always receiving tremendous notices no matter what he did. "I did The *Road to Rome*, and I played the sergeant of the army with John Fiedler. It was a small part, but I played it as a Brooklyn sergeant and it was funny. The scene between the two of us was just great," Harold told us. "Acting to me, no matter what you say, you cannot go to school to be an actor. You got to have talent. You can't become a great composer unless it's there. I mean, there are many great composers but they just don't have the Brahms or Beethovens or Rogers or that type of people. They said to me one day, 'What school did you go to?' I said, 'The streets of New York, because I would go to the Polish section and sit there and watch and observe, and I would go to the Italian section, and I would go to the Russian section of the town. There was this great melting pot, and there you learn. I've always said that acting is self conscious mimicry. The only one who is the creator is the writer. When I came out here in later years, I went to a couple of writer dinners and four of them would come over to me and would say, 'Harold, you've brought out things in the script that we never knew was there.' Perhaps this is my misfortune, because directors like to be directors, but when they give me leeway and let me go we'd work and have a lot of fun on the set, because if I can't have fun on the set I don't want to do the thing."

Harold J. Stone

When television came in, Harold began to do a show here and there, and "they finally discovered me," he stated. "But still, things were pretty rough. My daughter was going to be born in April, and I needed ready cash so I got a hack license and drove a cab for about four weeks. This way I could get money every night." Harold's daughter, Jennifer, was born in 1949. Finally more television work began to come his way on *Kraft Theatre*, appearing in *June Moon* and *Torch Bearers*. He also landed the part of the Handyman in a weekly television series called *The Hartmans* in 1949 that lasted a brief time. They were still living on Charles Street, but there was an apartment building being constructed in Queens. Harold picked up the plans for it and they chose an apartment to move into when it was completed. In the meantime, he went on the road in the Clifford Odets play *Golden Boy* with John Garfield. Stone played Garfield's father, Papa Bonaparte. The play closed its run in Princeton, and Harold was told it was the best Papa Bonaparte performance ever seen. Next Harold got a call from Jose Ferrer to replace Robert Strauss in *Stalag 17*. "I did *Stalag 17* on Broadway, and was doing the *Ed Sullivan Show*. At that time they did biographies on the Sullivan show; I was doing that with Bea Lilly and Reginald Gardiner."

Harold was truly an all around man. In 1951, when Frank Sinatra was in New York, Harold did the Sinatra show for a whole year. "They used to call me 'Tripling Tom,'" he reflected. "We worked with Jack Benny, Basil Rathbone and many of the stars from Broadway, but no rehearsals. You just got the script and 'Don't worry, we'll go over it in the dress rehearsal.' But these guys were frightened to death, which reminds me of the story of Alfred Lunt. In '52, I'm doing *The Goldbergs* (a weekly television series) and doing *Stalag* and having conflicts. My wife used to say to me, 'Why don't you stop making so much money and smile?' because she never saw me. We went to rehearsals for *The Goldbergs* every other day and we'd do the show every other day, and I was doing *Stalag* and had a matinee on Wednesday and Saturday. Finally in '52, I got a call to do the Sherwood biography with James and Pamela Mason doing a scene from *The Road To Rome*, Raymond Massey doing a soliloquy from Abraham Lincoln, and Helen Hayes doing a soliloquy from a play called *Acropolis*, and then I played the part of a Polish character with Alfred Lunt in *There Shall Be No Night*. We get there on a Thursday and they give us a script, we read it, and they say 'Goodbye, see you Sunday.' Well these guys were frantic. Actors want to rehearse and it's the first time these have been on television. Anyway, Lunt clung to me like a little pussycat; all that Sunday he was frightened to death. That night we do the show and he was marvelous; the whole show was great. Anyway, now I go to London to do *Stalag 17*, and while we were rehearsing I went to see the Lunts in a play called *Quadrill* by Coward. I sent him a note during intermission, maybe he'd remember me, and about three minutes later a note comes back that says, 'Dear Harold, do come back, but please forgive me if I can't spend too much time because Lynn and I are having supper with the Queen.' I've never forgot that and I will always try to instill that in young actors that you've got to have humility, which a lot of them don't have anymore."

Sometime after the Stone Family had moved to Long Island, Harold was doing a live-TV show with Eddie Bracken and Hope Emerson. From this he got a call from Max Arnold to come see him about a picture called *The Harder They Fall*. Mark Robson and Philip Yordan wanted him to do a screen test for them. Harold received the part of the Jewish sports editor, the only sympathetic character, and worked with Humphrey Bogart in the film. Harold later heard that Bogart had a tremendous admiration for him as an actor.

After this, he was invited to come to MGM and meet Leonard Murphy to discuss a picture to be titled *Somebody Up There Likes Me*, about the life of Rocky Graziano. Three weeks later, Murphy contacted Harold and told him that since he was in a fight picture they didn't think he was right to do another one. "If that's the way you feel, fine," he responded. "But the one is black and the other is white. I played the only sympathetic character in *The Harder They Fall*, and the other part was a drunken, frustrated bum of an Italian father." About a week later, Harold received word that Charles Schnee, the producer, and Robert Wise, the director, wanted to see him at MGM and he was given the part.

When he got back to New York, Harold got a call that Warner Brothers wanted to see him for the Alfred Hitchcock feature, *The Wrong Man*. They started filming this in March and it was freezing cold. Hitchcock wanted Stone to be built up a little bit so he would be as tall as Henry Fonda, so they put wooden blocks in his shoes. "Can you imagine walking on the pavement in wooden blocks, and freezing cold in March in New York?" he asked us. Harold mentioned some of the problems on this picture were: Hitchcock had a cold; the police department did not want to co-operate; the actor who was hired to play the judge had had a stroke, so he couldn't remember his lines, and they had to send for someone else from California to replace him; Warner Brothers wouldn't let Hitchcock use the projection room in New York, so they had to send the film to California, only to find that they were using a slow camera and had to re-shoot it. "I wasn't about to go over and talk to Mr. Hitchcock and say, 'Top of the morning to you,'" he laughed. Harold became pretty good friends with Hitchcock's story editor, who told him that "Hitch is a great director, a wonderful guy, but if you don't know your lines, or if anybody doesn't know their work, he will cut whoever it is to ribbons with jokes." "Well, that's all I had to hear because my big scenes were out in California," Harold noted.

After coming out to California, just before doing his big scene where he interrogates Fonda, Harold went on to the set to get a cup of coffee when they were filming a scene with Anthony Quayle and an actress. As he stood there watching the filming, the actress after delivering her line made a gesture, and Hitchcock called out, "Again!" And again, the actress said her line and made the same gesture, to which Hitchcock replied, "When Eleanore Duza was a young child, she never made a gesture like that!" The actress was cut out of the whole picture. The next scene to be filmed was the twelve page scene between Harold and Fonda, and Harold told us, "I'm shaking in my boots, and if I blow it I'm going to get killed." The scene is done in one take, and Hitchcock remarked, "Anything Mr. Stone wants, he can have." Harold went on to tell us, "Then we got to be very good friends, and he said to me one day, which is a great story, 'Harold, that picture you made, *The Harder They Fall*, isn't doing very well is it?' I said, 'No, Hitch.' (You got to call him Hitch, like Walt Disney – You had to call him Walt). 'You know, Hitch, there's no sex in the thing, and it's a fight picture, they had all these great fighters, and it's very very bloody.' He said, 'What do you mean?' I said, 'Well, take for instance the scene where the Indian has to take a dive, getting a thousand dollars for it. They come out to Oklahoma and they find out that his whole tribe is out in the audience and he refuses to take the dive. They cajole, they beg, they plead, everything, and he refuses. So they finally decide to use a piece of chicken wire and put it in the mouthpiece. He gets hit in the mouth, and blood runs profusely, and they stop the fight.' He says, 'Well, I see. It must be a picture of old world charm.'"

After completing *The Wrong Man*, Harold went back to New York and appeared on stage in *Will Success Spoil Rock Hunter* in summer stock. He was called that they wanted him back on the west coast for a film about *Confidential* magazine with Steve Cochran, titled *Slander*. He traded in his three year old Victoria Ford for a Chrysler Imperial, and he, along with his wife and two children, came out to the coast in their new car. "Then I sent my family back. I said, 'Look, I'm not going to commute anymore because I'm gone for four weeks, six weeks, eight weeks, and I miss you.' They went back and sold the furniture and brought back a few things. We rented a home in North Hollywood, and then the following year we rented in Beverly Hills," he told us.

Harold got work in a number of pictures, which included *The Garment Jungle*, with Lee J. Cobb; *The House of Numbers*, with Jack Palance; *Showdown*, with Audie Murphy; and *The Chapman Report*, for which he received the Global Award, which is the Hollywood Foreign Press Award. "I've always found in any kind of work: Simplicity...simplicity," he told us. While filming *Spartacus*, Harold got a slipped disc and couldn't finish the last three days of the picture. "I had the thing operated on, and then it was great," he mentioned. "Then my wife got rheumatoid arthritis. By this time we bought a home in Brentwood, and the following year she passed away." Harold re-married in 1962, and found himself once again commuting to New York, doing the television shows, *The Defenders* and *The Nurses*. For his work in the latter series, he received an Emmy nomination. While doing a particular episode on *The Defenders*, Harold told us, "At eight o'clock in the morning I was in a cab going up Third Avenue and it was freezing cold in January, with the beautiful blue sky and the snow. All of a sudden there's a horn honking and I look over and there's a squad car, and I said to the cabby, 'What did you do, pass a light?' He said, 'No, no, no. They told me to pull over.' Well, I'm concerned, and I'm sitting there freezing with a Kashmir spring coat, no tie, and with the script in the corner. He pulls over to 79th Street, and the next thing I know I see him and the blood has drained down his face. The door opens and the biggest .38 you ever saw in your life is in my puss, and the partner has his gun out. The cop looks at me and says,

'Oh my God, it's Harold Stone. We thought you were Joe Bananas.' That was at the time he was kidnapped, if you remember the story of Joe Bonaninos."

In between his features, Harold had a full schedule working in television, guesting on such series as *Gunsmoke*, *Alfred Hitchcock Presents*, *Route 66*, *The Twilight Zone*, *The Voyage to the Bottom of the Sea*, *The Big Valley*, *The Rifleman* and *The Untouchables*. He did several episodes in the last named show, telling us the first was *The Rusty Heller Story*, with Elizabeth Montgomery. "The first part I didn't say a word; I played this Greek mafia head. Finally she comes to the office, she wanted a hundred thousand dollars from the FBI, and a hundred thousand from me. She was an informant playing one side against the other. I finally come around the desk, and I grab her and kiss her. Liz was the most wonderful gal, she didn't fool around; when you kiss, you kiss. And Wally Brauman, who was the director, did twelve takes; then we did the close-ups. By that time my jaw was coming out. If anybody thinks it's all romance and sex – it's a lot of baloney! Anyway, I did that, and I did the manager with Viveca Lindfors playing my wife; then I did *The Tommy Copeland Story,* and then I did the one I played the Jewish banker. I think I guest-starred in seven of them."

The last feature Harold had appeared in when we talked with him in 1983 was *Hardly Working* with Jerry Lewis. His latest television at that time had been an episode of *Lou Grant*. Harold told us that although he has many credits, things had been very slow recently. His final work was in an episode of *Highway to Heaven* in 1986.

We asked if he could sum up his feelings thus far on his career, and Harold answered, "I feel I get compliments. I think the greatest compliment I get from people is that you do me more good than doctors, and I always say it is one of the reasons that I went into this. I would have loved to have been a physician or a doctor, but it's got to be the way it's got to be; Que sera, sera. I get compliments all over. In fact, I was in Scotland a few years ago and when I was coming back, I was on the bus taking me to the plane from Heathrow, this little Scotsman said, 'How come you play the rough guy?' Every award I got was for the good guy. It's always been a revelation. I love doing it and I love entertaining people. I loved working and I always had fun on the set. I was always there on time and knew my words. The wardrobe people would ask me, 'How come you hang up your stuff?' And I said, 'That's my background.' That's the theatre training; you don't have wardrobe people hang up your clothes. I used to say to myself, 'Gee willikers, if I died I think they'll close the studios.' Now I can't even get into the studio, but still I'm very happy with what I did. And I made an awful lot of people happy. So, that's my story."

Harold J. Stone died on November 18, 2005 at Woodland Hills, California.

Harold J. Stone

Film Credits: **1946:** The Blue Dahlia. **1956:** The Harder They Fall; Somebody Up There Likes Me; The Wrong Man; Back from Eternity; Slander. **1957:** The Garment Jungle; House of Numbers; Man Afraid; The Invisible Boy. **1959:** These Thousand Hills. **1960:** Spartacus. **1962:** The Chapman Report. **1963:** X – The Man with the X-Ray Eyes; Showdown; Recoil (TV). **1965:** The Greatest Story Ever Told; Girl Happy. **1966:** Operation Razzle Dazzle (TV). **1967:** The Big Mouth; St. Valentine's Day Massacre; Ready and Willing (TV). **1970:** Which Way to the Front?; Breakout (TV). **1971:** The Seven Minutes. **1972:** Pickup on 101. **1974:** The Photographer. **1975:** Mitchell; The Wild McCullochs; The Legend of Valentino (TV); The Werewolf of Woodstock (TV). **1976:** McNaughton's Daughters (TV). **1981:** Hardly Working.

LIAM SULLIVAN

Liam Sullivan was born in 1923 in Jacksonville, Illinois. "My family builds Ferris wheels," Liam stated. "My grandfather started the factory in 1900, and when he retired in 1927 my father took over, and when he retired in 1966 my brother took over. I was supposed to have gone in there after graduating from Harvard with a degree in Economics and take over the business." He did go back for six months to the office and update everything in the accounting system, and then said, "Pop, get the boys in here to run this." Liam had a friend who was working in CBS Radio in New York and was being promoted. He told Liam that if he wanted to come out there he could get him the job that he was just leaving. Liam decided that was what he would do. He went to tell his father, who had just gotten through paying for an expensive Harvard education. His father replied, "Well, if you're going to be sitting here staring out the window wondering what it's like in New York, you're not going to be much good for either one of us. So maybe you better go and find out, and if you don't like it come back and we'll dust off the desk. If you do like it, I'll get somebody who doesn't stare out the window."

So Liam went to New York and worked at CBS for a year or two. "Actually what I did," Liam explained, "was start working in radio in New York on *Theatre Guild of the Air* and shows like that, and while I was at CBS I got to know some of the engineers who let me in to watch the other radio shows. I started getting the bug about maybe wanting to be an actor. I had been an actor while I was in college and high school, but I never thought about trying to make a living out of it." Liam then went back to Harvard to talk to the man who was head of the theatre department, who made an appointment for him to go see Jasper Deeter at the Hedgerow Theatre outside of Philadelphia. "This little theatre had been there since 1923 and had about ninety-nine seats, and was built from an old mill that used to grind corn in the days of the civil war," Liam added.

Deeter had gone there and started this theatre and had managed to survive all those years. In 1946 Liam went to the Hedgerow Theatre and had an interview with them, and they decided they would take him on. "I was down there for two years," Liam told us. "It was interesting and I learned. There were acting classes, I was taught how to run the lights and set them up. It was a repertory theatre and they had a different play every day, so I climbed up those sixty foot ladders to change the lights every morning for the different plays. I never bothered to tell anybody I had a fear of heights, I just thought if that's what I have to do, that's what I have to do. I also learned how to build props and had to build sets. I was a carpenter before because my father was a great builder and showed my brother and me how to build things. So, I wound up helping to construct sets, build props, do the lighting and work in the box office part of the time. And I was in some plays as an actor. It was an all around education in the theatre and I don't think that there is any place in California where kids can get that kind of training. When young people ask me today, "I want to be an actor, what do I do?" I look at them blankly and think, "I don't know what to tell you because the facilities that were available when I was growing up and becoming an actor aren't around anymore."

After leaving the Hedgerow Theatre, Liam went to Saratoga Springs, New York. A girl friend in New York, who was working for the producer up there, got Liam an interview to go there for the summer playing parts in the plays. He passed the interview and was accepted into the summer stock company. He also helped build the scenery after they discovered he was skilled in that area. "It was sort of like if you want the acting jobs you will also build scenery," Liam noted. One of the plays they produced was *The Man Who Came to Dinner*, in which Monty Woolley, a resident of Saratoga Springs, came out of retirement for one last reprise of the title role. "I had a marvelous time," Liam concluded.

Liam returned to New York City and acted in several plays with a group called the Equity Library Theatre. It was a thing that Equity, the actor's union, set up so that actors could be in plays as a showcase for other producers to review their work. He noticed an audition for a scholarship to the Royal Academy of London. Liam thought he would try for that and learned a piece from Shakespeare. The judges consisted of a stage producer named Margaret Webster, Gertrude Macy, who was general manager for Katherine Cornell, and Lucille Watson. After the audition, the actors were encouraged to go around and talk to the judges, and as Liam spoke to Margaret Webster, who was the chairman, she said, "You don't really want to go to London. With the background you had with Hedgerow Theatre you've done all that already, you're wasting two years. On the other hand, I'm sending out a Shakespeare Company and if you'd like to come out with my company there's a couple of small parts left if you want to get some experience here. Think about it and let me know tomorrow." So Liam thought about it overnight and decided that "a bird in the hand might be better than an England full of bushes." And although both Webster and Macy had told Liam if he wanted the scholarship it was his, he told us "Since I've been offered a job, let's get started. So I did and went off on tour for a year with Margaret Webster's Shakespeare Company doing *Julius Caesar* and *Taming of the Shrew*." Between the two plays Liam understudied thirteen parts, and right near the end of the tour one of the actors became ill and Liam wound up playing Tranio in *Taming of the Shrew* and Decius Brutus in *Julius Caesar*. Reflecting on the tour, Liam said, "That was a grind. It was on a bus or in a truck and we played a different place almost every night. You got up in the morning, got out of the hotel and into the bus, drove somewhere and got there by six o'clock, you got off, carted your own costumes to the dressing room at the theatre, went off to get a bite to eat, went back to do the show, fell into bed and got up the next morning and did it in a different city. It was not a lot of laughs, but it was a lot of good experience."

When Liam came back to New York he worked again in some of those Equity Library Theatre plays and also in live television. One of his favorite television series he worked in was called *Light's Out*, a rather spooky show. "The reason it was one of my favorite shows was because I played a young sailor, and there was this adorable little blonde girl who I played opposite, and her name was Anne Francis. That was her last television show she did in New York before she came out to California. We have kept in contact and she is one of my best friends today."

Liam would send Gertrude Macy a card about the various television shows he was appearing in. "I knew she didn't have a television set, or even watch it, but this went on for a year or so, and one day out of the clear sky I got a phone call from her," he noted. Macy told Liam that "Katherine Cornell and Brian Aherne are taking a production of *The Constant Wife* out to Central City, Colorado, and there is a part of a butler. It's not a very big part, but it's there, and I could also make you assistant stage manager so you can be paid full salary from the first day of rehearsal. Are you interested?" Liam was. She told him to send some pictures that she could show Guthrie McClintic, Cornell's director-husband. "I never met Guthrie McClintic or Miss Cornell until the day I showed up for rehearsal because Gertrude Macy, who had seen the audition and had gotten this endless series of postcards from me, said 'He'll be fine.' So I wound up spending a year in *The Constant Wife* with Katherine Cornell. The most wonderful time of my life. She was such a gracious lady." They played in Colorado for the summer, where it went so well they decided to do it in New York. So after a break for a month, the company went to Cleveland, St. Louis and Kansas City for an out-of-town trial and then on to New York where it played. At the end of the year they took it to Boston, Philadelphia and Washington D.C., where they met President Truman.

Asked if playing the same part for a year ever became boring? "Never got boring, but it was never exactly the same twice," Liam replied. "And the audiences, of course, were never the same. Sometimes you got laughs on a very funny line, and the next night nobody laughed. Couldn't figure out why, but the next night they'd laugh again, so you say, 'Well, it isn't anything I did wrong.'"

Liam appeared in a production of *Romeo and Juliet* on Kraft Television Theatre in the days of live TV. Liam played Romeo and fifteen-year old Susan Strasberg played Juliet. "I had gone to audition for another show that had some Shakespeare in it. I read that and they said, 'Would you mind reading for Romeo?' Well, somebody had clued me in before I went in for this first reading that they were going to do Romeo, and actors will do anything for a part like that, so I had gotten the play down and I had memorized much of it. I went in for this audition and they said, 'Hmmm, very good. We're doing *Romeo and Juliet*, would you care to read for that?' 'Sure.' They said, Here's a copy of the play, why don't you take it in the other office, pick a scene and work on it, then come back.' I had to be young, nobody would have the guts to do this unless you're very young," Liam laughed. "I said 'If you can do Shakespeare, you can do Shakespeare.' I flipped open the book, which fell open to the balcony scene. I said 'Why don't we do it.' 'Don't you want to look at it?' 'No.' So I gave a performance of the balcony scene that I had been rehearsing for two weeks. And guess what? I got the part," he laughed. An agent in California saw *Romeo and Juliet* on the air and suggested that Liam come to California. "And that's what got me out here," he added.

Two things happened when Liam arrived in California. He played two parts in television that had pieces of Shakespeare in them, and then a friend of his, who was a casting director, cast Liam in a *Gunsmoke* as a psychotic cowboy who Marshal Dillon finally kills. "All of a sudden all I got called for was cowboy heavies," Liam said. "When you got a call, the first thing they made you do was ride a horse. Fortunately, when I was growing up in the small town of Jacksonville, my father had a couple of ponies in a fenced back lot behind the Ferris wheel factory, so I started riding when I was about eleven years old. So, I had no problem with that. After the *Gunsmoke*, it was *Have Gun Will Travel*, *Tombstone Territory*, *Bat Masterson* and a dozen at Warner Brothers where they had a whole series of Westerns like *Cheyenne*. So during this whole period of time when nobody knew about the Shakespeare I wound up doing cowboy heavies."

Liam enjoyed playing heavies because the parts were more interesting, and they gave him a chance to play a variety of characters. "You can get away with playing nice guys and leading men really just kind of playing yourself, which is what Gary Cooper, James Stewart and a lot of those people did," Liam explained, "but to reach out to something which is not a part of your own experience, like a murderer or a guy that's really mean, I think stretches you as an actor. Otherwise, if you keep doing the same thing the way you behave walking down the street or whatever, you're not going to grow that much as an actor. I have been very fortunate because I have had a chance to play a lot of different kinds of things."

Liam spoke of an episode called "The Silence" on *Twilight Zone*, which was directed by Boris Segal and co-starred Franchot Tone and Jonathan Harris (with whom he later worked with in an episode of *Lost in Space*), saying of all the series he has appeared in that this and a *Star Trek* episode have been rerun more than any other. Liam mentioned that on *Twilight Zone* the part was originally written for George Grizzard, who was in a play in New York and wasn't available, so they auditioned thirty-two people before the casting director called Liam. At that time his hair was beginning to go grey, so Liam was told "I think you got a crack at this. They're tired and want to set somebody, but do me a favor and get something to take that grey out because the character's supposed to be about thirty." So Liam did. He went into the reading and Segal, who didn't want him for the part, reluctantly cast him. "So everyday before I went to the studio to the make-up department I had to put this stuff in my hair so the director would never see that I had any grey," Liam laughed. On *Twilight Zone* they rehearsed three days and then shot three days. On the first day of filming they shot the scene in the men's club that opens the show. "It was totally a monologue for three solid pages where I just keep talking," Liam noted. They rehearsed it and the opening sequence did not work to the director's satisfaction. "Going faster doesn't seem to do it, I don't know what's wrong with it, but it's just not working," Segal stated.

Liam told us that the night before they were to start shooting "I remembered a Bob Hope television show I had seen that week and I got to thinking back about the technique that Hope used. He never stopped at the end of a sentence; he tells a gag and then goes three words into the next sentence and then stops to wait for the laughs, and then picks it up and goes on. I thought, if I get to the end of the sentence and keep on going as though it is supposed to be longer and then take a breath in the middle of the sentence, I will never actually be stopping for a breath at the end of a sentence and it will sound as though those three pages are one long sentence. So I worked on that." Liam went in the next day and Segal said, "Okay, let's rehearse." Without telling him what he was going to do, he did it. "That's exactly what I was looking for, what did you do?" Segal asked. "Did it work?" "Yes." "Then don't ask," Liam said. So they rehearsed it and were just ready to shoot when Rod Serling, who was on the set watching, came over to Liam and said, "Hold on. I love what you're doing. In fact, I'd like to cut away from you to Franchot Tone's ear and then back to your mouth to build up the fact that this is driving him crazy, but I didn't write enough dialogue for that. If I write another page can you learn it?" Liam told us, "I was not as young as I was when I played Romeo, but still young enough to say, 'If you can write it, I can learn it.'" Serling laughed and went over and wrote another page of dialogue while they set up the lights. He handed it to Liam, who went over in the corner and learned it and came back and they filmed it. "This really set the tone for the whole piece," Liam mentioned. "If Rod hadn't been on set and if I hadn't watched Bob Hope – It's strange how things like that happen."

Discussing that episode brought to mind another *Twilight Zone* that he appeared in with Donald Pleasence. "Sort of a *Goodbye Mr. Chips*," Liam noted. This then reminded Liam of another show on television that he had later acted with Pleasence in called *Final Eye*, which took place in the future. "It was not a very good show," Liam noted, "but I played a billionaire in a wheel chair who built a city which was to be the perfect retreat for artists, scientists and so on; everybody there was chosen as the peak of their race. No matter what happened anywhere else, the best of the world was going to continue in this area. Donald was my evil assistant in this town who was determined to get rid of me, and had gotten together with some scientists and figured out how to clone people. They cloned me and there was this series of six coffins with glass covers with liquid in them, and these six clones of me were inside them. At one point I happened to go into the room where they were. I knew nothing about them, and all of a sudden the camera panned and there were six Liam Sullivan's in glass faced coffins except the hair was black; they hadn't cloned long enough to look as old as I did." On the first day of work Pleasence kept looking at Liam, and said "I know you; we've worked before." "*Twilight Zone*," Liam answered. "Of course, you fired me," Pleasence replied. "He said that had been the first thing he had ever done in America," Liam added. "I liked him a lot. He was a funny man with a weird sense of humor."

Liam co-starred with Michael Anderson Jr. in a television series called *The Monroes*, a Western set in Wyoming about five orphaned children attempting to claim their dead father's land title on land being used by an English cattle baron named Major Mapoy, which was the character Liam played. The entire series was filmed on location near Jackson, Wyoming and the Grand Teton Mountains. "That was one of my favorite times," Liam said. "We went up there in November of 1965 to do the pilot. It cost six hundred thousand dollars and took three weeks to film. Bernard Kowalski directed it more like a feature."

The original intent of the show which they tried to preserve the best they could was the relationship between the major and the kid. The major really didn't want anybody on the land; he didn't want these kids there or have to bother with them, but he couldn't very well kick them off because their father had planted his belt buckle as a sign that he was taking possession of that little piece of ground. On the other hand, the kid didn't want to acknowledge that he needed any help from the major. So Liam played it, "I'm not going to help you because I don't want you here," and Anderson played "I don't need your help." "But it wound up that we did, we helped each other," Liam informed. "I loved that show. I think the look of that, especially the pilot, was one of the most beautiful pieces of film I have ever been in. The cabin was actually constructed on the banks of the Snake River. One side of it was on kingpins and they could pull the pins out and lift the side of the cabin away, so when you rode up to the front and hitched your horse and opened the door and went inside the camera moved on past the end and kept on shooting as you walked into the interior."

Liam mentioned an outdoor sequence around a campfire that they began filming one afternoon. Liam had finished his scene and left, but there were several more pages to go when it became dark and so they knocked off for the night. During the night it snowed. They returned the next day to pick up the scene, but it would never match. "It's not a very heavy snow. Let's knock off for a couple of days and do some interior shots, maybe by then the snow will melt," the director decided. Next night it snowed again. They were beginning to panic because there had been some people in the earlier part of the scene that had been dismissed and gone back to California. They became concerned that they would have to re-shoot the whole thing. The cinematographer said, "Why don't we put Ben Johnson (who played Liam's foreman) up on a horse, put the camera down low and shoot against the sky and have him look around and say,

'I have a funny feeling; I bet there will be snow before morning.'" "They did and inserted that, and when they picked up the scene the next day, what do you know? It snowed," he laughed.

Liam played a villainous knight in *The Magic Sword*, a film with Basil Rathbone and Estelle Winwood, directed by Bert Gordon. As he reflected on his two co-stars, he said "Basil Rathbone was a funny man. A story teller. Every time the camera stopped Basil had another story to tell. He was just wonderful. And Estelle Winwood was a funny, witty, charming lady and as sharp as a tack. Don't ever play bridge with her; she was a killer bridge player."

As far as his memories of the film, Liam mentioned that it was shot in about three weeks, but after the first four days he came down with laryngitis and couldn't talk above a whisper. "Bert Gordon, a man that did things as cheaply as possible, was not about to replace me and go back and re-shoot four days," Liam told us. "He said, 'talk as loud as you can for the soundtrack and we'll dub it all later.' So I did that for the rest of the picture. Then they gave me a week to get my voice back, and I went back and dubbed almost the entire thing."

Liam had one other story to relate about an incident in the making of *Magic Sword*. There was a scene out on the Twentieth Century Fox ranch that they had to film one night which was a ride-through with the nine knights that had gone on the quest with Liam. They had three horses for Liam to use in different scenes, all of which looked alike. One actually had what looked like a dark star on his forehead; the others were white faced with the dark star painted on. One was a walking horse; one was a running horse; and one was a rearing horse. "The night we were to do this ride-through they made a mistake and brought the rearing horse instead of the walking horse. I'm trying to get this horse to walk in a quiet way," Liam stated. "Well, this horse wanted to get on his hind legs and do all kinds of things. I said, 'What's wrong here. I had no trouble with this horse before. It's not that I've never been on a horse before, but all of a sudden I can't make this horse do what I want him to do.' The wrangler came up and said, 'We made a mistake. We brought you the wrong horse.' So there are a couple of scenes in which the horse reared up and I managed to get him, on his hind legs, to go around in a circle. After these nine guys have ridden past me I brought up the rear because otherwise there was no way I could hold that horse in one place," Liam laughed. "But again, do you think we're going to stop shooting and go back into town to get the right horse and bring him out there? Not with Mr. Gordon. You'll lose too much time. So instead of my leading this group of guys, I supervised their getting off on to their ride while I did this turn on the horse and finally followed them off."

Liam returned to New York to appear on stage in *The Little Foxes* with Geraldine Chaplin. They performed there and then went on tour with it. After the play closed, Liam stayed on in New York and did an off-Broadway production of *Anna Karenina*. Upon his completion with that project, he returned to Hollywood and worked for a time in the soap opera, *General Hospital*.

Liam also has several other interests in the film and entertainment business. At the time of our interview he had written several screenplays that were being optioned or read by several important people in the industry. He was also working on a fictional novel based on some historical facts and possibilities concerning the question as to whether William Shakespeare authored the many plays he is credited with. The reasons for this feasible theory that Liam has incorporated into his story and how it could have been accomplished are very interesting, and the political intrigue involved therein would make fascinating reading.

Liam has also written the lyrics for numerous songs, several of which have been used in movies. He had been introduced by Ben Cooper to an organization called The Thalians which helped raise money for emotionally disturbed children, and through this met a singer named Margaret Whiting. They began talking about some lyrics she had hired someone to write for her night club act and was unhappy with. Liam offered some suggestions and wrote several songs for her. Whiting encouraged Liam to attend a lyric writing course at UCLA, which he did, and thus started his side career as a lyricist.

Ethel Winant, a friend of Liam's as well as the associate for John Houseman, called one day and asked if he could come out to MGM and listen to a Greek folk dance that Manos Hadjidakis had written for a film produced by Houseman called *In the Cool of the Day*. Someone had decided that if they could write English words to this tune they could use it to help publicize the movie, and she wanted to ask Liam if he could come up with those lyrics. "I went over to MGM and listened to it," Liam reflected. "I told her to make the music match the title of the picture, I needed two short beats followed by a long beat occurring twice in the music for *In the Cool of the Day*. But there was no place in this music in which there are two short beats and a long followed by two shorts and a long. However, make me a dub of this and let me take it home overnight and play it and think about it. She did. I phoned the next day and asked about the rights to this music and if we could change any of it. 'If I add two short beats at the beginning it will work.' She checked and found that they owned that tune outright, so I added two pick-up notes in the beginning. Then I cut some, tightened the rest and wrote the lyric."

Liam made up the lead sheets and handed them to Houseman, who responded, "Unfortunately you're dealing with a producer who can't read music. Would you mind playing it for me." "Mr. Houseman," Liam replied, "unfortunately you're dealing with a lyricist who can't play the piano. However, do not despair. We will meet here again tomorrow at the same time at which point I will have a demo record for you." He called a friend of his who had a recording set-up, and they made a slow and fast version of the tune on a tape. He then went to a place in Hollywood and cut an RPM record, one version on each side. "I went back to Houseman and played it," Liam told us. "He loved it and said he'd do it."

A couple of days later Liam received a call from Jesse Kaye, head of MGM music. He has been described as a rather arrogant man that ran that department with an iron fist. Nothing happened that he didn't know about in advance, but he got a call from John Houseman to phone Liam and make a deal on a song that he didn't know anything about. Houseman said, "Dear fellow, we already have the song, just make the deal." Kaye called Liam and said, "You're going to have to split the royalties from the lyrics with a Greek friend of Hadjidakis, who was his arranger. There's no money in the budget to pay an arranger so the only way to pay him is to split the lyrics money with him. So that's the deal." Liam told us that "I figured five hundred bucks up front and half of the money on the royalties of the lyrics, who knows? The thing might do well. Besides I get a screen credit and I'm now a professional song writer. So I said okay." Kaye then told Liam, "I don't know who we'll get to record this. I don't like the tune myself." They couldn't find someone to do it so finally the president of MGM, who liked the tune, called Nat King Cole, who also liked it and said, "I'll do it." Liam was invited over to the studio when Cole recorded it over the opening credits. The deal was also made for Cole to make a record of the song and it was placed on the flip side of *Lazy Hazy Crazy Days of Summer*. "*In the Cool of the Day* got a respectable air play, but *Lazy Hazy Crazy Days of Summer* went crazy, it hit the top ten," Liam noted. "You don't get royalties in terms of air play, but when they sell records they can't sell half a record, so if you're on the flip side of a hit you get the same money as the guy who wrote the top side. And believe it or not, every six months I still get a royalty."

Liam also wrote the lyrics of *Laura Lee*, a folk ballad used in the Western feature, *Major Dundee*. Through an association with musician Bobby Darin, this song was recorded by such artists as Eddy Arnold, The Young Americans and Wayne Newton.

Liam played the king of the underground people in a science fiction feature titled *What Wait's Below*, which was filmed a quarter of a mile under the ground in a huge room in a Tennessee cave. Liam explained that a track had been laid in the tunnel heading down to this room on which tourists would ride in little golf carts for their trip down. The film company decided to lay their cable down this tunnel for the lights. When they saw they did not have enough cable they set up a generator in the cave, and to avoid paying for an electrical one and stringing all the wires, they got a gasoline generator. Everyday they had that running to make the lights go to shoot the movie they were pushing carbon monoxide into the cave, and after about ten days somebody almost passed out. An official was sent for and brought a machine to register the air quality. "Everybody out of the cave," he ordered. "Carbon monoxide alert." Liam told us that "the tunnel we had to go through to get out was where that stuff was really concentrated. By the time we got out (I was wearing this crazy make-up. My face was not just painted white, it was all pieces of foam rubber glued to my face) by the time we got out of there people were having to be dumped onto these little golf carts and taken out because they were just wanting to collapse. It was decided that the last half-dozen of us that had gotten out of the cave were to be taken to the hospital. By three o'clock in the morning when it was determined we had enough oxygen and were going to be okay and taken home, I still had this stuff glued to my face." They had to wait three or four days for the fans placed in the cave to clean the air, and were by then way behind schedule.

"What happened to that picture shouldn't happen to a dog," Liam commented. "So they were behind schedule, running over budget and the bond company, that makes sure the picture is done on time, sent a man over that said 'You're taking too long to film this. You don't need that scene, cut it!' So they cut a bunch of scenes and some of the script never got shot at all." But two nice scenes that were filmed included one between Liam and the woman scientist who tried to converse with him. They could not speak each other's language, but found a way to communicate in sounds and the scene built to the point where they each put their hand out and touched them together. "A very lovely little bit that we improvised and worked on ourselves," Liam informed. The director said, "I love it; we will shoot that." In the second scene, which came near the conclusion of the film when the military turned on the generators in the cave which put out a sound that was deadly to the underground people, there was a sequence where the sound was killing a little boy, who was Liam's grandson. "I had my hands over my ears to keep the sound out, and when the kid ran over to me and was clutching me I took my hands away from my ears to put them over his to save his life and I died," Liam explained. "The last thing in the movie was of the underground people carrying me away, like Hamlet on a litter further into the cave to bury me in a place that the army would never discover." The distributor viewed the film, and exclaimed "The Army's the bad guys in this, they're doing all the destructive things. The underground people are only trying to protect themselves. That won't do. You have to cut all that. The underground people have to be the bad guys and the army the good guys." "So they cut all this lovely stuff about my dying at the end, all the nice stuff between me and the scientist lady; it was all gone," Liam stated. "When I went to see a screening of it, I said 'What happened to the end of the movie?' It all disappeared."

Reflecting on this last experience, Liam said "It's like the cutting room floor. You never know. Lots of times if you're a young actor and you're playing the scene with a star and the star decides that you're too good your footage is going to get cut. This only happened to me once. In *The Twilight Zone* with Franchot Tone, not only did he not do that in the scenes we had together, but in the sequence where I have the confrontation with him the first time where he is telling me off and I was mostly reacting to him, they shot his part of the scene and then they called lunch. They said, 'Mr. Tone, you can go back and rest because we're going to do Liam's close-up and we'll have the stage manager read your dialogue to him.' He turned to his valet and said, 'When they begin again, call me.' And he came back and played the scene. But I did several episodes of *Falcon Crest* playing a lawyer, which culminated in a trial scene. Mel Ferrer, who was directing the episode, also played the opposing lawyer. Mel had been very complimentary on what I was doing and said 'You're really surpassing me in this sequence.' I said, 'The words are here; the words are not there.' So we shot the whole thing, but when it was cut and put on the air most of my best scene was a voice-over while you saw a close-up of Mel Ferrer. It happens, but after you've been in the business for a number of years it's not the end of the world. Tomorrow's another day."

Asking Liam to sum up his feelings as he reflects back over his career, he mentioned some of the things that he liked best as well as some parts he would love to play in the future. "There is a lot of stuff I did because it was part of my growing up as an actor and part of reaching out and trying to stretch and do different kinds of things. So it's not all terrific parts that I loved doing and there have been a couple of things that I thought I wished I hadn't done because of the way it turned out. *Romeo and Juliet* worked out pretty well. I loved *The Monroes*. I loved the character. It's too bad they didn't get a second year because they had written story lines for the major. The fiancée he had left behind in England came to America to try and get him to go back and he wouldn't because he hadn't finished what he had set out to do. There was a whole back story about his father. The major was a bastard and he had determined to come to America and make enough money so he could go back to London and meet his father, who was a wealthy man and had never acknowledged him, on an even basis: toe to toe, dollar for dollar and pound for pound, and say to him 'You never acknowledged me, I don't need you anymore because I have made it on my own.' And that was all for the second season which we never got to. Also an episode of *Bonanza* that I did with Michael Landon. A lovely part of an Irishman who was supposed to be hanged for murdering somebody. I claimed I hadn't done it and escaped jail. Little Joe was on the jury and my plea that I did not commit murder was so strong that he begin to wonder if they made a mistake in condemning me. It was really justifiable homicide because I had found this guy beating his wife to the point that she would be killed, and the only way to stop the beating was to kill him. The wife was a lady I had left at the altar twenty years before. The whole last scene of that picture was between the wife and me, my trying to explain why I had run off twenty years ago, and realizing that they were going to string me up because I had killed someone and she wanting to run away with me. I knew I was going to get killed and didn't want her to get killed. So we had this long scene, at the end of which I went out the front door and slammed it behind me and left her inside. I heard the posse coming so I fired in the air to attract their fire and they killed me, but she was free. It was written as a three scene with Michael, and we rehearsed it. Michael said 'I can't be in this scene, this is too intimate between these two people, they wouldn't say that before a third party. We've got to write me out of this and I'll come back at the end of the scene.' The production manager thought we would be here a long time while he rewrote the scene, but we broke for lunch and the three of us worked out the scene. While we were rewriting we were rehearsing, so when the crew came back from lunch and said, 'How long will it be?' the director answered 'I think we're ready to try one.' So we did and they loved it and it worked. That scene was about eleven minutes long. It turned out to be one of the best things I ever did. There were also a lot of other things I did because I liked doing it.

"But I don't know if an actor is ever satisfied," Liam continued. "There will always be more things that you would like to do. There are a lot of things yet that I would like to do. One day, simply because it's unplayable, I would like to try *King Lear*. I would love to play King Henry in *The Lion in Winter* because it's a great part. And *Foxfire*, a play about an old couple. It is mostly on the front porch, and he is dead and comes back as a ghost, and he appears and talks with her and she talks to him. The cabin where they are is in the middle of a housing development and their son is trying to talk her into moving off to a home someplace. She doesn't want to go because she is afraid her dead husband won't know how to follow her. It's an interesting play. Kathleen Nolan went to North Carolina to do it and wanted me to come do the other part with her, but the people there wrote to somebody who was on a soap opera in New York at the time. That would have been fun. Like I said, there are still a bunch of things that I would like to do.

"And I think dissatisfied," Liam went on, "but only to the extent that there are a lot of things that I would have liked to have done that I am now too old to do. I have seen a lot of versions of *Hamlet*, and I have some ideas on how the thing ought to be played. I'm glad I got to do Romeo when I was young enough to do that. If I were to act in Romeo now I would do it differently than what I did then. I would play it much looser and more relaxed because I think that Shakespeare allows itself to be done that way now, which was much more formalized forty years ago when we did it. The great thing about working on the stage is that you can grow while you're working on it, and you have enough time. I did a play called *The Browning Version* in summer stock and we only played for a week, but it was one of the best growing experiences as an actor that I ever had. In the doing of that play I learned to do things I hadn't been able to do on the stage before. The reach, I think it's called. I did a play out here called *The Bedroom* about a recluse, a man in his seventies who lived alone and his whole social life was with ghosts. He had rematerialized the ghosts of his dead wife and the girl that he had been in love with when he was nineteen. He materializes them from the bedroom; the play takes place in the living room and there's the door into the bedroom, and whenever the ghosts appear the door opens and light comes out. He could materialize the two of them at will. It's a very exciting concept. His daughter kept coming to him, and saying 'Get out of this awful apartment and do something else.' He said, 'What? I'm happy here and there's nothing in the world that I relate to anymore.' One day when she came to see him, she sees the ghosts and is terrified. At the end the daughter is going to Paris, and he says 'Why are you so interested in dislodging me. I can't come live with you because you're going to be in Europe. I can't depend on you. I depend on these ghosts.' She insists that he exorcise the ghosts because it's just unhealthy; and he does. He realizes he doesn't need the ghosts, or the daughter either, and decides to get back into the world. It's a terrific part and I had a wonderful time playing this old man. Despite the fact that the guy who wrote the play could not make up his mind, he kept rewriting while we were rehearsing. We rehearsed for about seven weeks, and the director was fired and the producer took over the directing. The producer was fired and the author took over the directing and kept rewriting. Finally, the morning of the day we were going to open, he came to me and said, 'I had an inspiration last night and have rewritten the whole opening scene.' The opening scene was a monologue, I was on stage all by myself. I said, 'You've done what?' 'Well, I've rearranged some of it and written some more.' 'Okay, maybe we'll be ready to open next week,' I said. But he wanted to open that night. So I spent the rest of the day memorizing a new scene for opening night. It's the only time I ever got an adequate – not really a bad – but an adequate review on a play I was in. I was really upset about that, but when the author-director lays down the law there's not too much you can do about it. You can't say, 'I won't play tonight.' You can't do that.

"Like I said, there's still things I'd like to do," Liam concluded, "and I don't think I have to apologize for anything I've done so far. George Burns is ninety-two and still going, so there's still time."

Liam Sullivan passed away on April 18, 1998 in Los Angeles County, California.

Film Credits: **1962:** The Magic Sword. **1964:** One Man's Way. **1965:** That Darn Cat. **1972:** Particular Men (TV). **1979:** The Best Place to Be (TV). **1981:** Isabel's Choice (TV); The Five of Me (TV). **1982:** Computercide (aka The Final Eye) (TV). **1984:** What Waits Below; Ernie Kovacs: Between the Laughter (TV); The Cowboy and the Ballarina (TV). **1985:** A Death in California (TV). **1986:** Wisdom; Dreams of Gold: The Mel Fisher Story (TV); Free Ride; North and South: Book II (TV). **1987:** Nutcracker: Money, Madness and Murder (TV); Daniel and the Towers (TV). **1990:** Jury Duty: The Comedy (TV). **1992:** In the Arms of a Killer (TV). **1997:** George Wallace (TV).

LYLE TALBOT

Mr. Hollywood had come to America with his family from Ireland, entering into this country through Ellis Island. He was a poor man, a coal miner, and settled near Pittsburgh, Pennsylvania, because they had surface coal mining there for the steel mills. They eventually removed to the west, leaving part of the family behind, and resided at Thermopolis, Wyoming (near Yellowstone Park), where they also had surface coal mining. One of the Hollywood daughters married a Mr. Talbot, and the Talbot's daughter married a Scotchman named Henderson. Henderson was a farm boy from Nebraska, and was twenty years of age when he married the eighteen year old Miss Talbot, who was from Brainard, Nebraska, and they removed to Pittsburgh, Pennsylvania, where their son, Lysle Henderson, was born February 8, 1902. Even though Lysle was born here, he told us that "I always call Nebraska my home because that's where I spent most of my time. My mother became very sick and they thought they better come back to Nebraska, and she died four months later. So my grandmother raised me. She was an old Irish lady, and felt that my dad was somewhat to blame for taking my mother away and would not let my father see me or even be near me. She took me to the county seat and adopted me and gave me the name Talbot; then it became my legal name."

Lyle never saw his father to really know him until he was about fifteen years old, and by this time his dad had married Anna Nielsen and gone into show business. They were actors and toured all through the mid-west, primarily Nebraska, Iowa, South Dakota, Oklahoma and Kansas. In the summertime they would perform dramatic shows in tents, and in the winter they would perform inside theatres. As a matter of fact, in most of those companies the actors were married because if a husband and wife worked as a team the managers could hire them for less money than two individuals. As a team they would be paid about forty dollars a week, as opposed to twenty-five dollars a week per individual. Lyle's parents and Roy and Hazel Hilliard (parents of Harriett Hilliard, who later became Harriet Nelson, wife of Ozzie Nelson) traveled together in those old shows for many years. "So when I started in show business in 1919, those were the kinds of shows I started in because those were the kinds of shows that existed around the Middle West," Lyle told us.

Lyle described the atmosphere that surrounded these types of traveling theatres in the early days. His father told him about situations that arose when a company would run out of money on the road, leaving the actors broke and stranded, often the only way to get back home being to ride the rails. Actors were looked down on in those days, they were taboo; they became the lowest form of men after an actor named John Wilkes Booth assassinated Abraham Lincoln. People used to say, "When the circus comes to town grab your wash off the line because they would come and steal the clothes right off the clothesline." Actors were viewed in the same manner. "So along came the unions and gave us some respect, as they have through the years, and developed into SAG and AFTRA to protect us," Lyle said. "But in those early days there was none." Before the unions came in, the actors were expected to do everything. If you were in the tent shows you'd have to help put up the tents, or if you were in what was called "a blow down," if you had a cyclone or tornado, and the tent was ripped up some, you would have to sew it. "That happened a couple of times in my career," Lyle reflected. "We'd sit there all day, the actors and everybody, sewing the tent up so they could put it back up for the night's show. So those were part of the experiences we would go through in those days." An actor in these little traveling companies played many parts. One may be a magician, a juggler, a comic, a musician or any number of various forms of entertainment. Some tent shows carried with them a band of ten or twelve musicians to make up an orchestra, many of whom were actors or the roustabouts who worked in the show. And every company had the Toby character. Toby was a country bumpkin and always had a girlfriend named Susie. He always wore a red wig, red nose, big freckles that he would put on with a pencil, and a couple of blacked out teeth. Many of the plays were melodramas, and many were written by the actor playing the Toby character. In the first two acts of the play he was a comic and would always be the butt of all the jokes, but in the third act he would foil the villain's foul deeds. Several of the Toby characters owned their own company, one of the most famous being Harley Sadler, who had his own tent show and owned two railroad cars, painted white with gold etchings on the outside. He had the Harley Sadler Comedians, and was headquartered in Austin, Texas, and was so popular that at one time the people wanted to run him for Governor of the state. Each of the comedians had a following, and each company had a regular circuit that they played year after year. "I was with one company that always played Aberdeen, South Dakota, at Christmas time," Lyle added.

Lyle started in 1919 as an amateur magician and toured with a traveling hypnotist. They had what was called hypnotic shows and volunteers from the audience would come up on stage, get hypnotized and be instructed to do various comic things. "I traveled with the guy to fill out the show," Lyle told us. "It was usually a two hour show; he would be the last half of the show, and the first half would be singing, comedy or whatever. I sang, did a little magic and a couple of sketches. We toured little towns in Iowa, and that was my first kind of experience." Lyle eventually branched out into a little higher type of show and toured all through Colorado, playing at such towns as Holly, Florence and Sterling. From here, he moved on up into the resident stock companies, working in Sioux Falls, South Dakota, for two years. At Sioux Falls, "I played forty weeks a year, a different play every week. I did eighty plays in two years. I've played in over a thousand plays during my life," Lyle stated. "In the old days the plays were longer. Today most of the plays, outside the musicals, are one set plays because it's too expensive to have a two set play. In the old days each act was a different set, and that's why they would have specialties or acts in between to be continuous. So if the actor could sing or do something else, they would drop the curtain and he would come out and do a specialty while they were changing the scenes."

Lyle opened his own stock company in Memphis, Tennessee, and operated it for a few years. "A lot of actors had their own companies if they got to be important enough, and I had built a good reputation as an actor and was able to find someone who would back me. In those days it didn't cost as much to do something like that, and I had a following in Memphis because I had played there before." Lyle became a part of the community there, joining the Kiawanis Club and belonged to a Shrine there. He mentioned that he had twelve resident actors that were professionals, and if he had a big cast like in the play, *The Front Page*, he would use local people. Lyle hired his father and stepmother, who had retired, to come to his theatre and play the character roles.

From Memphis, Lyle went to Dallas, Texas, where he performed in theatre, but the theatres were beginning to die in the early 1930s as a new form of entertainment was opening in the cities and towns across the country – the talking pictures. As the theatres closed down, many of the actors migrated to Hollywood because many of the silent film performers were unable to make the transition to sound. Lyle told us, "Those of us that came from the theatre naturally came into the movies because they had to have actors who could talk." Some of the silent actors as William S. Hart, Douglas Fairbanks and the Barrymores had come from the theatre, but they were not required to use their voices; they generally ad-libbed and never learned lines like you would in a play or a script. "So when talkies came along you had a situation out here," Lyle reflected, "You had to have a script and you had to talk, and it replaced theatre as the form of entertainment; plus it took the actors into the pictures. The thirties was the Depression era. People were in breadlines, in New York people were selling apples on the streets, but everyone could go to the movies for fifteen cents and forget the woes and cares, and be entertained. So we all were working in Hollywood and making what was then pretty good money as opposed to what other people were making. We were three thousand miles from New York; nobody flew in those days; five days away by train, so Hollywood was another world completely. We never had a home, we lived in hotels or rooming houses. We all came from homes, most of us were middle class; very few of us were college graduates as usually you went into show business early. I was lucky to get out of high school, I just decided I wanted to be an actor." Thus Lyle arrived in Hollywood and began his career in motion pictures.

Lyle made a test at Warner Brothers and was signed to a seven year contract (which was what all contracts were in those days). The casting office told him they were going to change the spelling of his name, Lysle, to Lyle and drop the "s," as it sounded too much like Lysol, which is a disinfectant. "So they dropped the "s," but Lysle was the original English spelling of the name," he noted. During these early days in Hollywood, several of the actors became the nucleus for forming an actors union, which eventually became Screen Actors Guild, and Lyle was one of the organizers. "There are only two of us left from the original twenty-four; Leon Ames is still around," Lyle informed. Lyle mentioned that the catalyst of the movement was a New York actor named Clay Clement, who was known as the women's leading man as he appeared opposite the likes of Katharine Cornell and Ethel Barrymore in plays that the woman was the star of. He had come out to Hollywood but didn't much care for it because it was not the theatre. The hours were miserable, six days a week, all hours of the night, and Clement used to say that there was no time for enjoyment. "And it was true," Lyle concurred. So a small group of actors, including Clement, Lyle, James Gleason and his wife, Ralph and Frank Morgan, Boris Karloff, Charles Starrett, Bradley Page, Ames, and others (totaling twenty-four) would meet at the Masquers Club. Clement stated, "Hey listen, this is too much! We ought to do something about it. Why don't we have a film actors' union like Actors Equity?" Lyle told us that Actors Equity had tried to organize in 1929 a film actors union but they failed, primarily due to certain actors like Lionel and Ethel Barrymore. "Ethel was a great supporter of Actors Equity and had fought for it in the famous strike of 1919 when they first organized, and George M. Cohan refused to produce anymore," Lyle said. "The actors had to fight the producers and finally won out. In Hollywood, the Barrymore family was at MGM and influenced by Louis B. Meyer and became very loyal to him. Meyer did not want a union, none of the producers wanted the actors to have a union, so Lionel and Ethel went right along with them." Thus the 1929 attempt to organize had failed but Clay Clement now gave new birth to the idea of forming a union, and this time it did become a reality. Of the twenty-four actors initially involved, Lyle was the only one under a contract to a studio, all the others were free-lancing. "I used to take a lot of guff from the studio for what I was doing," Lyle said. The studio manager would call him into the office and ask, "Lyle, what are you guys doing? What's this with the union?" "It's simple, we need a union," Lyle answered. Lyle explained that one studio would raid another studio by attempting to talk their actors in leaving and joining with them. He told the studio manager that this practice would stop. He also said, "We work six days a week, and these hours are ridiculous; we work fifteen hour days and are back in make-up at eight a.m., and the women, because of their hair, have to be there at seven in the morning." ("Joan Blondell was the first actress to get the idea of wearing a wig," Lyle told us). The studio manager replied, "We'll give you a little more rest." Lyle told us that was the big thing, it had nothing to do with money "because we were all making what was considered pretty good money in those days for what we were doing, so there was no gripe there. But the studio contracts were all one sided; the only thing that made them legal was the fact they had options in them, and in each option period they had to pay you more money and if they didn't, that was your only out. You couldn't get out of a contract any other way. If you refused to do something you'd go on suspension, which **meant** you went off salary, and when you came back that time period was added on. If you were off five weeks it would be added on, so conceivably you could be there forever! I went through that one time myself, and Bette Davis lost everything. She tried to fight it and ended up in England, and they (Warner Bros. and the courts) wouldn't let her make movies there. So anyway, that's how the Guild was started," he concluded.

Lyle was under a seven year contract but it lasted six years. He played mostly gangsters in his films at Warners, which he described as being generally interesting characters, but he became a little tired of them. He would be loaned out to other studios and appear in features like *One Night of Love* at Columbia, or *No More Orchids* with Carole Lombard, and be allowed to do light comedy. Lyle enjoyed doing these other roles more than the gangsters that Warners typed him in, and he started asking to be loaned out quite often, which didn't sit well with the studio brass. "So they finally gave me a release and let me out after six years, and I never worked there again until television came in and did one of the *Mavericks*," Lyle said.

Lyle mentioned that after his release from Warner Brothers that "I was never under contract again for anything. As a matter of fact, I worked with Ozzie Nelson for almost fourteen years and was doing the Bob Cummings show at the same time, and neither one knew about it at the time." He was doing *Love That Bob*, appearing in about every sixth one, playing his pilot friend who had a romance with his sister. "It was a great character to play and I had a lot of fun doing it," Lyle added. He was coming to work one day, and right next to where his show was made there was Stage Five, which was where Ozzie and Harriet was produced. "I never ran into Ozzie there, and Harriet I had known long before Oz did. As a matter of fact, Harriet and I had a little romance that was mostly by mail and telephone; we never actually got together too much, but her mother and father and my mother and father were good friends, and traditionally they were thinking wouldn't it be wonderful if Harriet and Lyle could carry on the tradition. When I first met her she was still going to girls' school in Minnesota somewhere that her mother had put her in, and I was traveling with the Winninger Players. Charley Winninger had gone on to be a big star, but I was with his brother John. There were four brothers from Warsaw, Wisconsin, and each one had his own company. I was the juvenile and Hazel McNutt (Harriet's mother) was the leading woman; Harriet asked to come and visit at Christmas time, and that's when I first met her and we traditionally fell in love." Harriet eventually went to New York and became the first mistress of ceremonies at a night club where she sang. She finally became Ozzie Nelson's girl singer, and eventually he fell in love with her. Lyle was going from one place to another and was only going to be in New York for one night, so he called and arranged to see her. The band was playing at the roof garden of the Roosevelt Hotel; Lyle knew that Harriet was Ozzie's girl singer but did not know about the romance that had started. "I'll never forget," he reflected, "I was down in the lobby and she was going to come down between sets to see me and I only had a short time. I was going to try and talk her into coming out to Hollywood. She came down alone first, and we were talking, and then down comes Oz. I didn't think anything, and we meet and that was that. We say good-bye, and the next thing I know is that she and Oz were married. So all through the years in Hollywood I never saw her again." One day on the studio lot when Lyle arrived early to work with Bob Cummings, he happened to park next to Ozzie, and Lyle said, "Hello." The two started talking as they walked to the stages, and Lyle mentioned how much he enjoyed watching the *Ozzie and Harriet Show*. Ozzie responded that they have a new set and that he was just going in to check it out, as they didn't start shooting his show until ten a.m.; he asked, "Would you like to see my set?" So Lyle did. "He was a perfectionist," Lyle explained. "If you lined up a shot and there was a picture behind you, they'd say, 'Don't worry about it,' but if you're doing a close-up it had to be there. He would never use fake flowers in a set, they all had to be real flowers. Even the grass around the house outside was real sod things, and all the plants outside the house were actually in buckets that would be concealed; his plants had to be real." "It would be a lot of fun working on this," Lyle said to Ozzie. "Would you like to do a show?" Ozzie asked. "Yeah, I'd like to do a show with you sometime," Lyle replied. So Lyle left and went to work on the Cummings show. Two weeks later his agent called and said, "Ozzie wants you." Lyle came into the show as a non-descript neighbor, not the Joe Randolph character into which his role would develop, and it worked well. "I saw Harriet," Lyle said. "It was a strange kind of a thing, it wasn't as though we hadn't known each other, it wasn't meeting somebody for the first time, but we were both diplomatic; you couldn't help but remember that there had been something, even if it was a high school girlfriend or sweetheart. So anyway, this went on for fourteen years." Lyle mentioned that he had been doing the show for a long time, and Ozzie said to him one day, "Hey, I saw you on the Bob Cummings show." "Yeah, I've been doing it since...." "Oh really." Ozzie had not known that Lyle was also working the show on the neighboring soundstage, not that it made any difference because Lyle wasn't working under contract. Then one day Bob Cummings said, "Hey, you're doing that Ozzie show too." "Well sure, I'm not in every one of yours," Lyle responded. "So I was the only actor in two top shows at one time," Lyle added.

    Lyle told us that he worked with Harriet one other time after Ozzie had passed away. David Nelson, their son, called Lyle one day and told him that he was doing a picture for the Lutheran Church. They had a show called *This Is the Life* that was on television every Sunday morning. "They were semi-religious and had very good stories that had a moral," Lyle noted. David said, "I'm going to do it with mom, and there's a great old character in it. Would you do it?" Lyle answered, "I'll be happy to do it." "It was a good little film, and that was the last time I worked with Harriet," Lyle added.

We asked Lyle if he enjoyed working in the Westerns, to which he responded, "Yeah, I'm a lousy horseman though, horses hate me. Horses are stupid but one thing they can tell the minute you approach them is that I got a greenhorn here, I'm really going to let him have it! You sit on them and they wouldn't move until the clappers, and then they take off. Oh, another thing was I had this back injury and I couldn't mount. They used to say you got to drop a little rope ladder for me, or mount on the high side of a hill or from off a porch, just step off the porch and into the stirrup. Otherwise I had to be pre-mounted or I'd play the banker in the little wagon, that was great. So I was the only pre-mounted cowboy," he laughed.

Lyle had a friend who was a stage manager from his theatre days named Frank MacDonald, who directed a lot of Westerns. He was directing an episode of the *Wild Bill Hickock* television series in which Lyle was appearing in. A particular scene had Lyle with a posse, and as the others rode off in one direction Lyle was to go the opposite way. "Well, I'm on a horse that's not going to be left alone, he goes with the posse; that's part of his job. He's a posse horse. A good cowboy would get him going but I'm not a good cowboy," he chuckled. "So we got five takes on this, and Frank is saying, 'Lyle, please, we don't have all day.' I say, 'I know, and I want to go as much as you want me to go. I want him to go but he won't go.' He said, 'Make him go!' So this is the fifth take, and I do something and I fall off. Now I'm not planning to fall off, I'm not protecting myself, and I fall flat and it knocked me out. They thought I was dead. They rushed me to the nearest hospital in Newhall, and I finally come to, but they had to stop shooting for the rest of the day. It had knocked the wind out of me and I thought I was dead too," he laughed.

Lyle said that he enjoyed working with Johnny Mack Brown, and had a funny story he wanted to say. "I'll never forget working with him one day – this I got to tell on him. God love him, he's up there and probably hearing us. I'm this banker and we have this big wad of money. Now we had rehearsed this scene but hadn't used the prop, so now we're getting ready to shoot it and they don't want more than one take in these five day Westerns, with a director who's trying to save time and make it even faster than that. I'm to hand this money to Johnny and he's supposed to take it, mount and go. I hand it to him and he has no place to put it, and he's got to mount. He hadn't planned on where to put it, so he rips open his shirt, shoves it in, and it's sticking out; now Johnny's got a tummy on him at this time, so he looked like he had a goiter on. He got on the horse and I could hardly keep from laughing, fortunately I held it in. Johnny thought it was funny too. They printed it; I'd love to have that film."

Lyle worked with the legendary director, Mike Curtiz, and had this funny thing to say about him. "He used to have a direction for me, and would say, 'Talbot, now in this scene you come when I don't say stand still.' So I'd say to myself, 'What does he want me to do?' and then think, 'Oh, he just wants me to come.' Okay Mike," he laughs.

When asked if he had any favorite roles, Lyle answered, "Not really, they would be various ones for various reasons. One of the first good acting parts I got, the first ones never required any great acting, I think *Three On A Match* was a good film for its time; *20,000 Years In Sing Sing*; and I liked others for different reasons: *No More Orchids*, I liked it because I was madly in love with Carole Lombard, but she was married to Bill Powell at the time so it was no touch; I think the really good things I've done as an actor has been in the theatre. As an actor I did a lot of things that were all right, but I wouldn't say any great performances like I've seen others have a chance to do. I knew my craft; we were all good actors really, I think. I worked a lot because I liked working. I did some real dogs – one that became famous, and the poor guy died a pauper, was Eddie Wood that made *Plan Nine from Outer Space*."

Talking about various techniques that actors use to learn their crafts and ply their trade, Lyle had this to offer: "You can't learn to act in a school, I don't believe in any methods. I think you can only learn to act by acting, I don't think there is any other way to do it. You can stand in front of a mirror all night, and if you have to start sitting down and theorizing it's too late. You don't have time to tell the audience what you're thinking; you can't say, 'Look, when I say this line here's what I really mean.' You got to do whatever the script is, and it's got to immediately have an impact with the audience if you're going to act for an audience, and I don't know why else you would act – You don't act for yourself. I mean if you're an actor it's a job; you are an actor and that's why you're called an actor, because you're acting. These things about getting lost in a part to me is so much crap. In the first place, you can't get lost in your part because if you get lost in your part you have no control over it. You have to have control. If you're driving a car you have to know what you're doing, don't you? If you're acting you have to know what you're doing. So you can't get lost. Yes, you can get emotional, and you can get caught up in it, but you can't get lost; you got to control it. There are so many theories but that's mine, and most of the guys that I knew, Spencer Tracy and Bogart, they all felt the same way and that to me would be the consensus. But whatever your bag is, you do it," he laughed.

Lyle continued appearing on stage up through the late 1980s, playing in dinner theatres at such places as The Showboat Theatre near Clearwater, Florida; toured the country in various plays; and more recently in Sacramento, California, in such hits as *My Fair Lady* and *Camelot*. Speaking of the latter show, Lyle said that he played Pelanor, the old king who comes in with the sheep dog. "It's a great part and I love doing it; I've done him in a lot of places other than Sacramento." Of his role in *My Fair Lady*, Lyle said, "It was a very good character for me. Of course, I had sung a little. As a matter of fact, at one point I was pretty good at pop type stuff." Since the mid 1970s, Lyle would go to Sacramento about every third year doing one of these plays, and also a version of Schubert's *Rosalinda*, and *Kiss Me Kate*

("That wasn't a singing part, it was a straight part in it"). Another play that Lyle enjoyed was *On Golden Pond*, "long before Henry or Jane Fonda ever heard of it." He told us that he believes it is one of the finest plays ever written. Ernest Thompson was an actor who couldn't get a job in Hollywood, and in desperation he started writing; he wrote some one acts and then this play, and the story is actually about his own parents and grandparents on Golden Pond. It was produced twice in New York, receiving good reviews but was never a success. There were two people in Kansas City that had two dinner theatres, one was called Tiffany's Attic which is in a gay 90s motique, and the other was a former movie theatre located on Waldo Street, so they called it the Waldo Astoria. "I started doing plays for these two guys and they were always looking for plays for me," Lyle said. "They had seen *On Golden Pond* in New York, and said, 'That's the play for Lyle.' It was simple to get the rights, the author was happy to have somebody do it, so they sent me the script, I read it, and I said, 'I've got to do this play.' So we set a date, and Thompson was going to come out, when I suddenly had this heart thing. I woke up one morning and couldn't sleep, couldn't lie down as a matter of fact, but then I seemed to be all right. I said to my wife, 'It was nothing.' It happened the second night the same way; after I sort of get to sleep I suddenly have to sit up, I couldn't lie down. My wife said, 'That's it, you're going to the hospital.' I was due to leave in about ten days for Kansas City for *On Golden Pond*." Lyle's nephew came over and drove him to emergency at the hospital. They called his doctor, took Lyle in, and put him on the table and started making some tests. Lyle told his doctor, "You know doc, I got to get out of here. I'm going to Kansas City." "You're not going to Kansas City," he replied, "You're staying here." They discovered that Lyle had an irregular heartbeat, deciding that medication would be all that was required. He gave Lyle his blessings on going to Kansas City on condition he contact a doctor there, which was carried out. He went back and did the play, which was a great success. "I did it in a lot of places, and then it came out as a movie that Jane saw as a vehicle for her father," Lyle concluded.

The longest time that Lyle has ever been in one play was with Glenda Farrell and Alan Dinehart in a little farce comedy called *Separate Rooms*, which in 1939 and 1940 had a sexy connotation. The title was originally *Thanks for My Wife*, which they were playing it under in Chicago. They were planning on closing it down because the reviews were not good, and the play itself just basically needed too much work to get it right. However, there was one good scene in the second act that was funny and they would receive laughs from the audience. One of the Shuberts happens to come to Chicago, and just happened to enter the theatre one night during this particular scene. Benny Stein, the company manager, was standing with him, and Shubert asked, "Why are you closing this for? You have a great show here," "It needs a little work," Benny replied. "No, it's great. Come on, bring it to New York; I'll give you a theatre." Lyle told us, "The two week notice was up, and we thought we were all ready to go back to Hollywood. Benny goes backstage, takes the notice down, and says, 'We're going to New York.' So we closed there and went to New York. We brought in a director that sharpened up the show, and we opened. We were all three from Hollywood, the first actors from Hollywood with any kind of names to be doing a play on Broadway. One of the critics referred to us as three sun-kissed actors from Hollywood," he laughed. "We got panned but we had the opening night crowd at our theatre. There was another play opening that was by a known producer, and here we come in with a play that nobody ever heard of and we got the whole New York crowd. We were sold out opening night and the audience loved the show. I remember we went to the Stork Club, which was the place to wait for the morning papers, and the New York Times was the first paper to come out and it blasted us! But the thing caught on; we were the Hollywood actors and people wanted to see Hollywood actors. Finally the Shuberts gave us a better theatre right in the heart of town, the Plymouth, a great theatre to play in and we played there for two years."

Lyle was asked if there were any funny stories to relate on his experiences in this show. "Dinehart had no shame, and I didn't have any shame about getting a laugh," he responded. "We did not moon the audience but we did just about everything else, and we would try to top each other in the scenes we had. I would say that we did ridiculous things that worked. I remember the war was coming on and they started rationing, and gas stations were only open a certain time. The butler runs through with something, and I said, 'He has to get to the gas station by eight o'clock,' and they howled. We had a matinee on the Fourth of July and somebody shot, of all places, a firecracker out on 45th Street, and Glenda had just made an exit. I said, 'She just left with a bang!' and they howled. We'd do shameless things, simply awful," he laughed. Lyle said that the play lasted three years, from 1939 to just before Pearl Harbor; "We were on tour and were in Detroit on Pearl Harbor Day," he concluded.

In addition to the Broadway play he was appearing in, Lyle was the first actor to do a Hollywood gossip show on WHN, a half-hour show three times a week. The show was sponsored by National Shoes, and Lyle started the phrase, "The most walked-about shoes in town." On the show, Lyle played one record; the material he was to talk about was written for him at first, and then said, "What the hell, I'm going to get my own material." "I'm now a newsman," Lyle told us, "and all the clubs I've been paying to get into I now get in free. I would interview friends of mine. Danny Kaye was just Danny Kaye and he was very popular in a place called La Martinique, a small night club in the basement of a big place on 59th Street, and I was a big fan of his. He had a regular following but wasn't generally known outside just the following he had. He was doing the fast talking songs that he became famous for, and Sylvia, his wife, was his pianist. I had him on for an interview, and just by coincidence about six weeks later, he always gave me credit for it, he got *Lady in the Dark*, which was his first show, starring Gertrude Lawrence and Ginger Rogers; it was a big musical. I did that radio show for about a year."

The last two acting appearances that Lyle made were in a couple of television comedies. He did a cameo with Tony Danza in his show, and then he played a hundred-year-old character in *The Bob Newhart Show*. Speaking of the latter one, Lyle told us that you rehearse it for a week and then it was done live. In this scene he is at his birthday party and they bring in this huge cake with a hundred candles on it, and he is supposed to blow them out and then drop dead. So the day of shooting the show arrived, and Lyle thought of a brilliant idea. He asked Newhart, "Bob, why don't I, when I blow the candles out, just fall in the cake?" "You're kidding," Newhart responded. "No, that would be funny!" Lyle said. So Newhart asked and they wouldn't let him do it. "That would have been wonderful to just fall into the cake," Lyle told us. "Anyway, those are the last two things that I've done."

During his career of upwards of seventy years in the acting profession, Lyle has had many interesting experiences connected with the business. As a matter of fact, he had considered doing a book literally on just this one following once-in-a-lifetime story. In short, Warner Brothers had backed the Franklin Delano Roosevelt presidential campaign. As a result, after his election, the studio was invited to come to the inauguration, which was then in March (up until after 1932 they were always held in March). The head of the publicity department at Warner Brothers had met a fellow on a train one time coming back from New York, and he happened to be with General Electric. They got drunk together and were saying, "Oh boy, wouldn't it be great to do something about a train," and they devised this whole thing in a drunken moment; but then along came this situation where Warners was invited to come to Washington as a studio, and, of course, the heads of the studio: Harry Warner, Jack Warner, and the Major. So what was conceived through the two publicity departments was a train that would go back to the inauguration tied in with the movie *42nd Street*, which was the big musical that they had made with Busby Berkeley. They put together this fourteen car train covering the outside of it with gold and silver tinfoil, which was glued to the train on either side with an electric sign that had letters about three feet high running the full length, reading "Warner Brothers General Electric Forty-Second Street Special." On the train, there was one car equipped with all of General Electric's latest equipment of that period. The idea was that the kitchen was where they prepared the food of the stars, actually it was never used except for the tourists. The public could come down to the railroad station and go through it. Lyle, Bette Davis and Preston Foster were chosen to be among the stars on this special cross-country train, but Lyle told us, "Why I don't know; we were new on the lot." Others included well-known stars as Joe E. Brown, Leo Carillo, Tom Mix and his horse, Tony, and, for a portion of the trip, Jack Dempsey. Also included were fifteen Busby Berkeley girls, three musicians, publicity men, and two wranglers were along to look after Tony, who had a special horse car for himself. "You could imagine this thing going through the countryside at night all lit up and scaring the hell out of the farms," he smiled. The rear car was called the Malibu Beach Car, and in it were General Electric sunlamps so the stars could keep their tans while they were away from Hollywood. The inside of the car had one side painted like the homes that were there at Malibu Beach; the other side the artist had painted what the ocean looked like that day; and on the floor were two truckloads of sand that actually came from Malibu Beach! They didn't want anything phony. The train had the right-of-way over every train in the United States, all of the others had to get off the tracks and let them through. They had their own Pullman cars, and each celebrity had their own compartment.

When the train arrived in the major cities, Denver, Colorado, being the first one, they would be met at the station by the local General Electric representative and the mayor. Lyle explained the reception at the cities along the way. "It generally was planned for us to arrive at noon and we'd be met by a contingent representing us, get into the cars and parade up to wherever our luncheon would be. Every band that was available was there, and the parade went down the full length of the town. They'd take us to a hotel in each town where we could shower, and that night we would appear with the picture at the Warners Theatre and do an hour show. The Berkeley girls would dance, and Preston Foster had a beautiful voice, an operatic voice, he sang and I sang and we all did a little sketch." They stopped at Kansas City, Saint Louis, and Chicago, where Lyle remembers they were just building the Worlds Fair, where Sally Rand danced out on that big pier, "and we went out to just sort of dedicate that." They stopped in Cleveland, which in those days was the home of General Electric. Lyle mentioned, "Incidentally, the train was always stationed not in the back with the freight cars, but was always the closest to the station. That train stayed there so that when you literally stepped out of the station you were on your train. It always had the best place it could be put so the public could go through that one car. It was like you were in a world all your own. The bank holiday had come while we were on the trip and none of us had taken any money, and I remember in Toledo (which was Joe E. Brown's hometown) Joey arranged to get our laundry washed and charged to him. I'll never forget that," he laughed. "We didn't have any dough because there wasn't any reason to take any money; we had a little change but we didn't need any money because everything was paid for."

They also stopped at Pittsburgh, Pennsylvania, which was Lyle's birthplace. The owner of a big hotel there was from Omaha, Nebraska, and was an acquaintance of Lyle's dad, who told the man that Lyle was going to be there. "We'll have a special suite for Lyle," the man said. "Now it's prohibition, and the only guy that had any real booze on the train was Tom Mix," Lyle told us. "Tom wouldn't drink anybody's but his own; he had to know that it was real. We arrive in Pittsburgh and I go up to my suite, and here is a big fruit basket – had more booze than you could imagine. I never saw so much in my life. In the basement of the hotel was a big nightclub, and there were big marble steps that went down into the nightclub itself. This was the night before we were to arrive in Washington D.C. for the inauguration. So the train had to leave at a certain time to be in D.C., so all the tracks are cleared. Anyway, they decide that they are going to have to give me a birthday party. Mix and I had become pretty good pals on the trip, and Tom said, "I'm going to be there Lyle, and I'm going to bring Tony." I said, 'You're going to bring Tony?' and he said, 'Well, sure I'll bring Tony.' 'You can't bring Tony into the club,' I said. 'Don't worry, I'll be there.' Mix goes down to the train and he gets Tony. He had special shoes for Tony, like rubber – they weren't metal **horseshoes**, because he always rode him in the parade. Anyway, he – in a cab – led Tony (naturally on the outside, he didn't sit in the cab), and Tom's loaded of course by now, and it's about eight o'clock at night, and up comes Mix leading Tony through the streets of Pittsburgh. The train station wasn't too far away, actually, and he gets on him and rides him down those steps onto the floor. All I can think of is Tony taking a, you know, having to go to the can. That's the only thing I could think of. We were all at a big table, and there is Mix in an outfit – he had a white outfit, hat and boots; it was just the most beautiful thing you ever saw. White and trimmed in different decorations, and the material was the finest; his outfits were gorgeous without being a lot of phony stuff. He was a great character. The party went on and on and on, and finally they were saying, 'This things got to stop! We have to get to Washington D.C.!' That train went through like a bat out of hell, and fortunately we didn't have any accidents. Most of us had heads this big when we arrived in Washington D.C., and had to be in the inaugural parade to begin with, and that night all the parties in town. They spread us out to several hotels throughout town and some of the Roosevelt family would be at each one. We sat at the daughter's table at the Willow Hotel. So that was a trip I'll never forget."

Lyle concluded this most interesting story by saying, "It could never be duplicated now; it was a one of a kind. That was almost my second year in Hollywood and I just happened to be a part of it. Those are the kind of things you remember; it didn't have anything to do with acting but it is part of my experience in life."

In summing up his feelings, Lyle told us, "I've been very fortunate and have had a good life. My wife and I were married for forty-two years and had a happy marriage and four wonderful children. So I have been very fortunate. My sons live in San Francisco, so when it became necessary to sell my house in Studio City, where we had lived for forty years, I moved up to San Francisco after my wife passed away. I've been in San Francisco a number of times and liked it, played in theatre here many times, so they found this condominium for me to live in so I could be near them. So I'm up in San Francisco and I'm happy," he smiled.

Lyle Talbot died March 2, 1996 in San Francisco, California.

Film Credits: 1930: The Nightigale (short). **1931:** The Clyde Mystery (short). **1932:** Unholy Love; The Purchase Price; Big City Blues' Three on a Match; Stranger in Town; Klondike; Love is a Racket; No More Orchids; Miss Pinkerton; The Thirteenth Guest. **1933:** 20,000 Years in Sing Sing; Ladies They Talk About; 42nd Street; College Coach; Life of Jimmy Dolan; Parachute Jumper; A Shriek in the Night; Girl Missing; Mary Stevens, MD; She Had to Say Yes; Havana Widows. **1934:** The Dragon Murder Case; Mandalay; A Lost Lady; Fog over Frisco; One Night of Love; Registered Nurse; Return of the Terror; Murder in the Clouds; Heat Lightning; And She Learned About Dames (short). **1935:** Broadway Hostess; While the Patient Sleeps; Party Wine; Page Miss Glory; Chinatown Squad; Case of the Lucky Legs; Red Hot Tires; Oil for the Lamps of China; It Happened in New York; Our Little Girl. **1936:** Murder by an Aristocrat; Trapped by Television; The Law in Her Hands; Mind Your own Business; The Singing Kid; Boulder Dam; Go West, Young Man. **1937:** Second

Honeymoon; Westbound Limited; Three Legionnaires; The Affairs of Cappy Ricks; What Price Vengeance. **1938:** Gateway; Change of Heart; I Stand Accused; Call of the Yukon; One Wild Night; The Arkansas Traveler. **1939:** They Asked for It; Forged Passport; Second Fiddle; Miracle on Main Street; Torture Ship. **1940:** He Married his Wife; Parole Fixer. **1942:** They Raid by Night; She's in the Army; Mexican Spitfire's Elephant. **1943:** A Night for Crime; Man of Courage; Meanest Man in the World (scene deleted). **1944:** One Body too Many; Dixie Jamboree; Are These our Parents; Up in Arms; The Falcon Out West; Gambler's Choice; Mystery of the Riverboat (serial); Sensations of 1945; Trail to Gunsight. **1946:** North of the Border; Murder is My Business; Strange Impersonation; Gun Town; Song of Arizona; Chick Carter, Detective (serial). **1947:** Danger Street; The Vigilante (serial). **1948:** Shep Comes Home; Appointment with Murder; Joe Palooka in Winner Take All; The Vicious Circle; Parole, Inc; The Devil's Cargo; Thunder in the Pines; Quick on the Trigger. **1949:** Highway 13; Sky Dragon; Fighting Fools; Mississippi Rhythm; Batman and Robin (serial); Wild Weed; Joe Palooka in the Big Fight; The Mutineers; Ringside. **1950:** Everybody's Dancin'; Border Rangers; Atom Man vs. Superman (serial); Cherokee Uprising; Revenue Agent; Big Timber; The Jackpot; Champagne for Caesar; Triple Trouble; Lucky Losers: The Dalton Women; Johnny One-Eye; Federal Man; The Du Pont Story; One Too Many. **1951:** Abilene Trail; The Man from Sonora; Jungle Manhunt; Purple Heart Diary; Fury of the Congo; Fingerprints Don't Lie; Hurricane Island; Gold Raiders; Vanities on Parade; The Stage to Blue River; The Scarf; Blue Blood; Lawless Cowboys; Colorado Ambush; Texas Lawmen; Oklahoma Justice; Mask of the Dragon. **1952:** The Old West; Sea Tiger; With a Song in My Heart; Son of Geronimo (serial); Kansas Territory; Montana Incident; The Pathfinder; Outlaw Women; Desperadoes Outpost; Feudin' Fools; African Treasure; Texas City; Untamed Women; Wyoming Roundup. **1953:** Tumbleweed; Down Among the Sheltering Palms; White Lightning; Clipped Wings; Trail Blazers; Mesa of Lost Women; Wings of the Hawk; Star of Texas; Adventures of the Tucson Kid (TV-short); Glen or Glenda; Six Gun Decision. **1954:** Tobor the Great; The Mad Magician; There's No Business Like Show Business; Captain Kidd and the Slave Girl; Jail Bait; The Hidden Face; The Steel Cage; Two Guns and a Badge; The Desperado; Trader Tom of the China Seas (serial); Gunfighters of the Northwest (serial); So You Want to be Your Own Boss (short). **1955:** Jail Busters; Sudden Danger. **1956:** Calling Homicide; The Great Man. **1957:** She Shouldn't Say No; Guns Don't Argue; God is My Partner. **1958:** Hot Angel; The Notorious Mr. Monks; High School Confidential. **1959:** Plan 9 from Outer Space; City of Fear. **1960:** Sunrise at Campobello. **1986:** George Carlin: Playin' with Your Head (TV).

STEVE TERRELL

Steve Terrell was born December 6, 1929, in La Jolla, California. When Steve was six years old his parents divorced and he moved to East San Diego with his mother and stepfather, and later during his teenage years, moved to Burbank, and attended high school there. "This was really traumatic, and ever since I was a little kid I just had this urge to act and perform," Steve explained. "I think I was looking for my folks to take an interest in me because I was shuffled from aunt to uncle while they were in this divorce thing, and for years while I was living with my father he couldn't take care of me. So I was with different people and I think I was just looking for somebody to take notice of me. In high school I flunked out of algebra, and I flunked out of Spanish, and was always very unsure of myself as a person. The only thing I thought I could do well was to act. I enjoyed it, and I think the reason that I did was because somebody was paying attention to me."

After high school Steve decided to study at the Pasadena Playhouse, and after graduating from there went into the service for a year. "After the service I decided I had gone to school long enough, so I tried my luck over in Hollywood. I got a montage of myself of all the work I had done at the Pasadena Playhouse and took it around to agents. After many months of trying to get an agent and doing little theatre around Hollywood, I was doing a play at the Pasadena Playhouse, *Life With Mother*, and these two agents came to the play. One came backstage and said, 'I won't sign you, but if I hear of anything you can do I'll let you know.' I was running my car on fumes at the time and it was just really a hassle, but about six months later he phoned and said, 'I got a three line bit for you.' It was in a thing called *Talk of the Family* with George Nader. You know, you can't get a part till you join the union, and you can't join the union till you get the

part. The agent said he would go to bat for me and get me this job, and, like I said, I was running my car on fumes, but I went out and scrounged up this money. I paid the SAG dues which was about one hundred and seventy-five dollars, and I made about seventy-five for the show."

Steve's second show had him cast opposite Rod Cameron in a *Schlitz Playhouse* production titled *Gold Mounted Guns*. "Rod Cameron was an undercover sheriff looking for the outlaws, and I was playing a Billy the Kid type. It was kind of fun, but it was real spooky having a lead role," Steve confessed. He told of a scene where he is trying to impress Cameron on how bad of a guy he is, telling him of money hidden under the floorboards in a ranch house, and saying he would steal it and then they could go south of the border. "So my game plan was to tear the place apart, and when I hear a buckboard coming outside to dash into the bedroom and wait until they come in. When they come in I was supposed to come in, but as I do and see this old man and girl, I'm supposed to have a change of heart and have five pages of dialogue. I run through my lines, and then slowly say 'You think five hundred dollars means anything to me?' and pick it up and throw it down on the floor, jump out through the door and ride off on my horse. So I did the whole thing. I acted like Marlon Brando and did the whole thing and really made a mess of the place. When I heard the buckboard I jumped into the next room and stood their panting and scared to death, because I'd always wanted to play a cowboy, and here I had these big guns on me and high heeled boots. I thought, 'Man I'll make a big entrance when I open that door and just really blow them away.' So when they came in, she said, 'Oh papa, this place is terrible. Somebody's been in here,' I threw open the door and as I did I slipped on the cables on the floor and landed on the back of my neck and knocked myself out. When I came to, they asked, 'Kid, do you think you can carry on with this?' Boy, I was shook, but said, 'Yea, I'll try.' So we went through this whole thing again and I'm seeing these five pages of dialogue going down through my mind and just getting happier and happier inside. When I came to the final line, 'Do you think five hundred dollars means anything to me?' and threw it down, as I jumped out the door I hit the door jam and knocked myself out again. They called me the confused cowboy out there for a number of years after that," he laughed.

Steve mentioned that having not really performed for the camera before he would ask a fellow co-worker, "Did I do all right?" And when they said "Cut," he asked, "Is it my fault?" because when he first got into films he thought they just filmed the whole show straight through. "I wasn't really aware that they cut the thing up in a million tiny pieces and put it all together later," he confided. "Finally, after I did a few of them I realized this was pretty simple. You just shoot four or five lines and then sit back and learn the next line, shoot those, and let them do the other work."

Steve mentioned that his initial experiences in the picture business were tough, but after the *Schlitz Playhouse*, things looked better. "They liked me out at Revue, and as time went on they found that I was a fast study and could pick up on a thing quickly so they kept me working. Then a series, *Pride of the Family*, with Natalie Wood came up where I played her boyfriend. I would go back about twice a month and work for them, but they never gave me a contract.

It was just on a show by show basis kind of thing, so I left when *Life with Father* came up with Leon Ames and Lurene Tuttle, and I did that for two years."

When Steve auditioned for the role of Clarence Day Jr. on the *Life with Father* series he was one of five hundred actors that showed up to play the children in the family. "It was a cattle call because it looked like a big show," Steve said. "CBS had paid five million dollars for the rights to the show from Warner Brothers, and it was the longest running show up to that time on Broadway so they really thought they had a winner. They lined us up with different guys they thought would play the father, and then with different women they thought would play the mother. Then they lined us up with different combinations of boys and had us read just gobbly goo to see how you read. It just went on and on and on. After going through our marital status and our draft status I was their second choice and Ralph Reed got the part. Well, three weeks into the show Ralph got drafted and I had already been in the service so they took me. Ralph had all the pre-publicity for the show so any book that comes out on *Life with Father*: there's Ralph. But I did get the money," Steve laughed, "and I got the part."

This series was the first live color series for network television shot in Hollywood. The show was set in 1880's New York City and dealt with the Day family: The stern father, his wife and their four red-headed sons, played by Steve, B.G. Norman, Harvey Grant and Malcolm Cassell. The show lasted only two and a half years because, as Steve said, "It wasn't a good show. The kids jumped when father spoke, and the scripts weren't particularly razzmatazz. You know, there weren't any car chases or anything in it so we lost our sponsor to Red Skelton, but they kept us going for a year on film because they thought it would pick up. We had special costumes for fast changes when we were in live television the first year of it. All the shoes had zippers in the back, and we had zippers in the back of our vests and coats too, so we could take them off quickly."

In reflecting on live television work, Steve said, "It was awful. It was hair-raising because with live film you don't get very much rehearsal time, but it was like stage because you go right through the thing in one big shot. And there were no mistakes because you couldn't go back like today. You had to go through it and you had to be perfect. We would come off after a show just ashen faced, every one of us." At CBS, where *Life with Father* was shot, there was a long row of seats where they had the audience come in because they didn't have laugh tracks in those days. "The problem is that you had to play to the audience to get the laughs," Steve explained. "So you mugged it like crazy so you could project the laugh to them, but you had the camera right in your puss and if you did that you messed up because you're overacting. Today I understand they just add a little laugh track and if the guy misses you just stop and do it over again. I would have loved that," Steve laughed.

"One time I had to make a clothes change where I did one scene over here in the barber shop. I had to get all the shaving stuff off my face, have a complete clothes change, and come into a garden scene with a girl over there. During the change people are pulling at your clothes while you're running across the stage and people in the audience are laughing at you. It looked terrible, but that's the only way you could do it in those days. They didn't have it where you go back and change your clothes and come back out again. So what the camera would do is come in on the girl and she would have the beginning dialogue, and then they'd pull back from the table where she would take a glass and have two or three sentences to give you a little more time to get there. Then you come in on your marks and you're panting and glad you made it."

After the series closed in 1955 Steve free-lanced for the remainder of his career, working in a number of television series including *Thriller, Dragnet, Perry Mason, The Millionaire, Climax, Navy Log* and *Richard Diamond*, as well as in features for Alex Gordon at American International. The bulk of his work, however, was in the TV Western shows of that period. These shows included *Gunsmoke, Have Gun-Will Travel, Trackdown, Tales of Wells Fargo, Tombstone Territory, The Texan, Man Without a Gun, Bat Masterson, Bonanza, Maverick, Death Valley Days*, and *Stagecoach West*. When asked if he enjoyed working in Westerns, Steve replied, "Yes. During the fifties when I did most of my stuff is when the TV Westerns were really big. When I started realizing I was going to do a lot of Westerns I went out and started taking lessons. I learned to ride a little bit. I wasn't a real hand, but I could hang on. When they did *The Wild One* with Marlon Brando I had never ridden a motorcycle either, so I went out and took some lessons so I could do that. I didn't make it in that one, but later on it helped me because when I did *Motorcycle Gang* for American International I could ride a bike. The problem was I never got to ride the bike. You could do the dialogue, get on the bike, put your helmet on, get the glasses down, and they would cut and go to the stuntman. He would come with his hands on the glasses like he was putting them down, stomp on the bike, and take off with it. So I was very disappointed," Steve laughed.

"So even though I had some riding lessons I was no accomplished rider," Steve reflected. "By the time I did *The Restless Gun* I had done quite a few Westerns; this was maybe three-fourths of the way into my twelve years in Hollywood. I got on this horse, and as soon as he heard the clapper his ears pricked up and I knew I was in trouble. He took off and I could not stop him. I was going head bent for hell when we started and then realized that I had no control over this horse. I was pulling back on the reins and leaning back in the saddle and even in the show you hear me say 'Whoa...Whoa!,' " Steve laughed. "What they did was send a stuntman out who grabbed the reins and got him. I would have been into tomorrow with this horse. I was really scared...scared to death."

"Things like that don't happen very often," Steve continued. "And that was another thing. Because budgets were short in those days they let the actors do a lot of things that they don't let actors do today. Pay was terrible in those days. You could do a half-hour show and maybe get $750 if you were lucky, and that would be a lead part in a half-hour show. But it was fun. I look back on it and it was twelve years of real interesting stuff and, of course, I came out of it with nothing. I could have if I had paid attention. I was just a dumb kid, but if I had paid attention I could have moved into directing or something when I got too old and couldn't play juveniles any longer. No, not me. I had to be horsing around on the set and talking to everybody or playing cards instead of watching the director and seeing what was going on. Foolish kids, you know."

Steve mentioned that one of his favorite shows was an episode titled *The Open Cell* for *Zane Grey Theater* with Dick Powell. "I played a tough kid who he had taken into his house and was trying to rehabilitate. I really liked that part. It was really a meaty part because I could chew the scenery a little bit. I always took a part, and liked everything I did because it shows in your work if you don't like what you do. So no matter what I did I liked it, and when I got through with it I forgot it and went on to the next one. It was exciting, and it was fun. People look at it as being glamorous. It wasn't really that glamorous back in those days. It was hard work. You'd get your script the night before and learn the next day's work, then you go do that day's work and hopefully do it in one take so you didn't have to go to a second take, because everybody would be saying 'That kid can't do it.' Then you go home and memorize the next day's lines and then come back the next day and do the day's work, and it was just really hard. You get there at five or six o'clock in the morning and put on your makeup and sit around for hours trying to study your script and trying to get ready to go. Then they put you on for five minutes and you go back and study your script for awhile. So it was really hard work in those days. I don't know how it is today, but I found it really tough. And then I wasn't really a Hollywood person. I wasn't into the parties and that sort of thing. I had a nice wife and a nice little house out in the San Fernando Valley, so when I got through work I went home and stayed home and waited for my agent to phone me again. It was that kind of life," Steve smiled.

Steve was the star of the American International cult classic, *Invasion of the Saucer Men*. When asked for his reflections on this film, Steve remarked, "I understand that a poster for it sold for $2,500 last year. I was paid $500 for that show," he laughed. "Mr. Arkoff's brother-in-law did the script for it and he couldn't write scripts for beans. He didn't know how people talked, and he couldn't get a plot. I think what really saved that show was the fact that they did it in very low light, and the little people that they used, strapping those big rubber heads and long fingers on. That's what really kind of saved the picture because it was, for those days, really weird. I enjoyed it but it was like I never knew my lines as it went so fast, and finally they were writing lines on the script and handing them to you and you were expected to do them. For the big scene, when all the teenagers surround the saucer men and at my command were supposed to turn on all the lights and zap these little guys, I had this big speech in the car. I tried it a couple or three times because I hadn't seen it, I was just sort of winging it, and they said, 'No, do it on first take.' I said, 'Okay, I'm trying.' No rehearsal. I just tried it and was very unhappy about it, but they took it and used it. Edward Cahn, the director, was a good guy, but he was just trying to get them out. It was done in five days and I got a hundred dollars a day. I had a contract for seven years with American International to do three pictures a year in starring parts, but after four pictures with them I decided this just wasn't my cup of tea. I wanted out. So I went up to Mr. Arkoff and Mr. Nicholson, who were the big moguls of the thing, and said I just really would like to get out of my contract. They thought I had a better offer from somebody else so they grilled me for about a half an hour and finally said, 'Well, okay Steve. We'll let you out of your contract.'"

Steve finally retired from the business, saying, "I became a Christian. During 1960, films started to disintegrate as far as morals were concerned, and I was asked to do things in pictures that I just felt as a Christian I couldn't do. At that time there were four casting agents in town and they all knew me as a different type. One, you'd play a cowboy; another, you'd play a tough guy; another, a lead kid. So when I'd say, 'No, I don't want to do a part for you' to these four guys, they started calling somebody else. There's a long line of guys standing outside the room who look just like you and can do the part just as well as you can, so you better not say no. But I just started turning down parts and finally I found myself with my nose up against the glass looking in and I was on the outside. The old movies had something to say and there was a moral to it. Everything is anti-hero today. It's really depreciating to our kids today. Anyhow, that was my reason and I don't regret it. I also had another problem. I'm short and I have a high voice. I don't have one of those deep voices. So I saw the handwriting on the wall, and had I not had that conviction I probably would have stayed in, but probably would have fumbled around and not really have made it had I stayed because I had that high voice."

After leaving the business Steve went to school to earn his Bachelor of Arts Degree. His interest was in books, particularly selling Christian books. "I thought that was a great avenue of producing a message rather than preaching because I never saw myself as a preacher. So I went to school. I ran out of money and had to come back to the picture business again. I made a little money, and finally decided I just couldn't do it. It wasn't good for me. So I went to work as a Christian education director at a church in Burbank for two and a half years and attended night school, and finally went to Loyola College and got my BA in Christian Education. Then they asked me to teach drama and speech there so I had to get my Masters Degree. I went to Cal State Fullerton and got my Masters in Theatre and taught six years college level.

"You remember the San Francisco Mime Troupe in the 1970's?" Steve asked. "They traveled to campuses dressed with capes, big shoes and masks. I thought, here are Marxists reaching the kids on the college campuses, and the kids were just coming out of the woodwork to see these guys, and I thought here I'm a Christian and I got a good message, and these guys take the ball and run with it. So I went back to Bethel College and taught for three years, and developed a group called Lambs Players, which was a theatre group in San Diego, and traveled around the country doing renaissance type plays. They were actually Christian plays with a message, but we were dressed in medieval renaissance. We set up in parks and had a little parade and did these plays, and they were free. If you liked the play, give us a donation. I thought, how could we support ourselves, because we were sort of limping along. I thought we needed a theatre so we could make money using community people. We would let them make our money for us in the theater and then we'd use the money to go out and do our plays in the parks and on college campuses. It didn't work that way because the kids decided they wanted to be in the theater too and not go out, because that was a lot easier. So it didn't fizzle, it just turned into something I didn't vision it to be. So now the Lambs Players have the Coronado Theatre in San Diego and they're doing theater down in Horton Plaza. It's a real big thing but it's all inside theater. It's just Christians in the theater; it wasn't my idea of what it was all about. So we got out and moved up to Sonora."

When Steve moved to Sonora he thought he would semi-retire, but went to work at the state prison near there as a guard for five years. "That was the most eye opening thing that I have ever done. It was a good job for me because I learned something about the other half, and also it gave us a little pension plus a paid-up medical policy. So with that and what I get from the motion picture retirement fund we were able to make our retirement." In 1994 Steve also wrote a book about bible prophecy. "I'm very excited about it because it's completely different than anything that anybody's ever written," Steve concluded.

Film Credits: **1956**: The Naked Hills; Tea and Sympathy; Runaway Daughters. **1957**: Dragstrip Girl; Invasion of the Saucer Men; Motorcycle Gang. **1961**: Posse from Hell.

RUTH TERRY

Ruth Terry was born Ruth McMahon on October 21, 1920, in Benton Harbor, Michigan. "My mama played the piano, so we'd sing along and have a nice gathering," Ruth said. "I could remember lyrics easily, so mom and dad thought I wasn't too bad at singing. When I was about ten years old they put me into a contest where the one that got the most applause would win." This contest was held at the local movie theater, where they would have amateur night. The contestants would perform, and then a dollar was given to the winner. Ruth realized that a dollar was ten movies at ten cents a movie, and she loved movies. In fact, she would go to see a movie at the matinee, and her dad would send the police down at eight o'clock at night to pick her up and bring her home because she would stay and watch the same movie over and over.

Ruth loved to sing, but neither she nor her mother could read music. Ruth's mother played the piano by ear and Ruth sang by ear. Every week Ruth would go to the amateur night and win a buck, and after she had won four or five times they told her that she couldn't enter the contest anymore. Ruth would also go to a dancehall on Pawpaw Lake where her dad was a guard, and when the bands played she was often asked to perform, unrehearsed. After that, Ruth's parents entered her in the amateur contest at WLS in Chicago, which was a very big radio station. She won the amateur contest and received a contract with the Paul Ash Theater Orchestra. "When I was about twelve I started singing with them, and I sang with them at the Chicago World's Fair in 1933." The Paul Ash Orchestra advertised her as the youngest blues singer in the country.

Ruth later traveled with Clyde McCoy, a famous trumpeter of the time. "Mama went along with me on buses, with one-night stands, mostly at dance halls. You'd sit on the stage, and

when they played your tune you'd just get up, sing your song, then go back and sit down again. Everybody danced around you. I did that with the old marathon dancing, and the band would play. They danced all night long and all day long, trying to earn money. In those days, it was really rough."

Ruth mentioned that her schooling came mostly from boys who had just graduated from high school. "I would have some lessons and they would tell me what to do. Later on, when I was fifteen or sixteen, my uncle in Chicago, who was a lawyer, got me a fake birth certificate (stating she was older than she was) so I could play in the dance halls and theaters." When any authorities came backstage and said, "You don't look sixteen to me," Ruth would respond by showing the birth certificate that her uncle had furnished. "That's the way we got away with that," Ruth laughed. While on the road, Ruth was chaperoned by her mother and aunt. Her aunt would often relate a story about Ruth when she was under age and singing in the nightclubs back in those old speakeasy days. She would tell about Ruth getting up to sing, and the bartender would clear a space under the bar where she would go to sleep during the next set. So as far as her schooling was concerned, Ruth only went through the fourth grade in formal schooling because she was traveling all of the time. So she got her education on the road, and later, when she got to the studios, she went to school at 20th Century Fox. When Ruth was on the road doing the one-night stands, we asked what she did when not performing. "We played baseball," she replied. "We were young, and we would go shopping at different dime stores. I made maybe twenty to thirty dollars a week, so we didn't do much spending. I don't really remember that much about what we did. Remember, when you're working like that, you are doing five or six shows a day so you really don't have much time. You might have time to see a movie, and then it was right back on stage again. So it was that kind of a routine. We would be booked for a week and do five or six shows at the same place. Then we would take a bus to another town and do it for a week, and so on."

Ruth related an exciting experience from those days. "There was one speakeasy where I worked that was a very nice club, but it was owned by gangsters during the prohibition. One night I was singing late and they bombed it. They closed the club until they got it cleaned up. But that was the kind of environment. I never knew any gangsters, but Chicago was full of them."

After Ruth completed her tours with the Paul Ash Orchestra, there was a family her folks were very friendly with named the Capps Family. "They were vaudevillians, they were acrobatic dancers," Ruth informed. "They said, 'Ruthie, why don't you come travel with us? You can sing and we'll do our acrobatic dancing, in two separate acts.'" She traveled with them for about two years, performing at state fairs and in many theaters in between the movies. "It was fun because we all got along so well together that it was very enjoyable. I loved it."

One of Ruth's aunts worked as a private secretary for Irving Berlin, so Ruth went to New York and worked at his studio. "They had individual rooms that were all glass, and people would go into a room with a piano, someone would play the song, and I would sing it, and then they could buy the sheet music. I did that for a few months." It was here that Walter Winchell said that Ruth McMahon was not a good name to sing under, so he took Ruth from Babe Ruth (though that was her real name), and took Terry from Bill Terry, both very famous baseball players, and she became Ruth Terry.

After Irving Berlin, George Wood, an agent in New York for the William Morris Agency, approached her. "He had heard me sing, and said, 'I'd like to book you and put you under contract. I get ten percent of whatever you make.' My dad said that was fine, so Wood would book me into nightclubs and theaters. I was on my own then (not with any other act), and I went down to Miami, Florida (singing at Jack Dempsey's), to the Chez Paree in Chicago, and nightclubs." Ruth's cousin had married Joe Patterson, who owned the *New York Daily News*, and Ed Sullivan was a columnist there before he got into television. Sullivan would write about Ruth in a lot of his columns. It was during this period, when she was fifteen years old, that she was singing at Jack Dempsey's Vanderbilt Hotel in Miami. That's where 20th Century Fox first saw her. They didn't sign her there, but her next engagement was when George Woods booked her into the Chez Paree in Chicago, and 20th followed her there, sat in a couple of nights and listened to her, and then said to her dad that they would like Ruth to go to Hollywood for a screen test. "My dad said, 'No, we can't do that. If you want her, you sign her up here and then we'll go to California.' So they did. They signed me and we went out on the super train. My mama, my dad, my brother, my dog Patsy, and me – we all headed for California."

The William Morris office met them at the station and took them to the Roosevelt Hotel in Hollywood, which was where they stayed when they first arrived. "Then they took us out to 20th Century Fox and I was introduced to Zanuck," Ruth noted. "They had singing lessons, acting lessons, dancing lessons, and they just groomed all of us. That was very nice, but you worked every day."

When asked if she noticed much difference between working for a camera in her first film and working on stage, Ruth answered, "The first thing they put me in was on a big stage with an orchestra behind me. It was just a big production number. There were three gals that sang, and then I came out and sang a song, so it was just like being on stage again. No problem. The camera didn't bother me at all. Once you're in front of the public and you're on stage, it doesn't bother you." Her first film was *International Settlement* with Delores Del Rio and George Sanders, which was followed immediately by *Love and Hisses*, which starred Walter Winchell as himself. Although *International Settlement* was filmed first, *Love and Hisses* was the first released. Other early films at 20th Century Fox include *Alexander's Ragtime Band* with Tyrone Power; *Hold That Co-Ed* with John Barrymore; and *Wife, Husband, and Friend* with Loretta Young and Warner Richmond. Speaking of working with John Barrymore, Ruth said, "He was an actor. I wasn't anybody, so I didn't even get a chance to talk to him. You just don't approach those people. I would never do that. But that poor man was never sober. I remember one time they were trying to keep him sober and they couldn't figure out where he was getting the vodka. They finally found that he had the water cooler filled with the vodka and was always going over to take a drink of water. Pretty soon he was just bleary-eyed and falling down drunk. But he was a beautiful actor."

Ruth remained at 20th Century Fox for two years. "They wanted to keep me at the same salary," Ruth related, "and my dad said no. He said that I should have more than four hundred dollars a week. I should have seven hundred and fifty. They said, 'We can't do that,' and my dad said, 'Okay, we'll leave and go somewhere else.' So then I did some free-lance with studios, in bit parts in pictures. Then Howard Hughes came into the picture. He was signing up a lot of girls, and would loan us to other studios. He was getting me seven hundred and fifty dollars a week, but he charged them twelve hundred and fifty. Finally I didn't want to be under contract to Hughes anymore because you played his way or you didn't play at all. So I left."

Ruth worked in her favorite picture during this period at United Artists opposite Pat O'Brien, Broderick Crawford, and Eve Arden, in a picture titled *Slightly Honorable*, which was a mystery comedy that was shot under the working title of *Send Another Coffin*. "That was a fun picture because I had an important part, which I didn't know at the time. I thought Eve Arden was the star, but I turned out to be the lead, really. That was a thrill, and I really enjoyed making that picture." In *Slightly Honorable* Ruth has one scene where she is in a slip, on her tiptoes, kissing Pat O'Brien on the cheek, but the Hayes Office said they couldn't put that in the movie because she had just a slip on. "It's gone a long way, hasn't it?" Ruth asked. When the movie was released to the theaters, Ruth had the opportunity to go back to doing Vaudeville again. "I went on the road with the picture for a while, doing a stage show where the movie was being shown."

This film was followed by Universal's *Appointment for Love* with Charles Boyer. Of all the actors she worked with, Ruth said that it was Boyer that she was most in awe of.

While Ruth was under contract to Hughes, she was also loaned out a number of times to Republic pictures. "That's how I got at Republic, because I was doing so many Republic pictures," Ruth told us. The reason Republic wanted Ruth was because of the Broadway musical hit, *Oklahoma*. They decided that they needed to get into the musical business and come up to some response to *Oklahoma*, so were looking for someone who could sing and had acting experience. They thought that since they paid her seven hundred and fifty dollars a week, that if they put her under contract they could get her for four hundred a week. So they hired her at that. Then they made *Hands Across the Border* with Roy Rogers. In the finale they have Mexican dancers, cowgirl dancers, violin players, the three Wiere brothers. "You name it, they got it. It was like a big production number, and that was their response to *Oklahoma*."

Ruth worked in five Westerns for Republic, one with Gene Autry, one with Robert Livingston, and three with Roy Rogers. "I only did the one picture with Gene Autry, and never even talked to him. We'd just do our scene and then I was with the crew or my group. He was a nice man, but he was a businessman and he didn't have time to sit around the set and fool around with us. He wasn't interested. He didn't even say hello to us. Roy Rogers was something else. He was always a good guy. He would be with all of us. It was like a family. Bob Livingston was a very nice man, and we got along very well together. Very easy, and we always had a lot of laughs on the set. I didn't really enjoy the Westerns that much. But what can I say? They were all good people. That's one thing: Everybody on a Western was absolutely perfect, really nice people. I rode very little, and when I did there was always somebody hanging onto the reins out of range of the camera," Ruth laughed.

Ruth shared one experience while working with Roy Rogers on location in Lone Pine, on one of her Westerns. "Roy and I were on horses riding away from the scene, and were then supposed to ride into camera. We got way out there, and Trigger reared and nearly threw Roy off, but, of course, he was such an excellent rider that it didn't faze him at all. We looked down and there was this rattlesnake that had frightened the horse. Roy jumped off his horse, pulled out his pistol, and shot the rattler. These were blanks, but the blanks scattered the rattler. He took the rattler, held it up, skinned it, laid it up on a rock, and had it around his hatband the next day. So, that's Roy. He's just that kind of guy."

Ruth stated that she did not enjoy working on location. "It's rugged. You're up at five o'clock in the morning and still working at six or seven o'clock at night. Working with the horses, the cattle, and the dirt," she laughed. "It was fun, though, as far as that was concerned."

Ruth married in 1941 to a test pilot. "I had known him for about three weeks," Ruth stated. "I thought, 'That's what I'm going to do. I'm going to get married, settle down, have a family,' and that's exactly what I did. My family was very upset with me. I had a baby right away, which was nice, but was still under contract to Republic, so that didn't work out very well. Anyway, we divorced."

John Ledbetter, Ruth's present husband of fifty years, inserted, "Remember, all of her life she had been chaperoned by her mother, her father, and her aunt, and was never a teenager. She had performed all of her life and had fun doing what she was doing, but a lot of it was being encouraged by others to do it. She finally came to feel that she really didn't have a life of her own. She was not a Hollywood person ("I didn't really have any friends at all") and wasn't one to go to all the big parties. She was home and in bed, learned her lines, up at four in the morning to get her hair done and into make-up, shot all day, went home and into bed. So she wasn't really a social Hollywood type and thought so many of the big actors were phonies. Not so much at Republic, but before that. She just always worked and supported the family. So it was very easy just to pick up and chuck it, and say I've done my thing, now I'll do something different. So she decided it was time to make a change, and on the spur of the moment she got married."

Ruth worked in a number of non-Western features at Republic, such as *Affairs of Jimmy Valentine*, *Mystery Broadcast* (considered by many to be Republic's best mystery film), *Goodnight Sweetheart*, *Tell It To a Star* (both featuring Robert Livingston), *The Cheaters*, a Christmastime tale with Joseph Schildkraut, and *My Buddy* with Don Barry, in one of his favorite pictures.

Some years after her divorce, Ruth met a Canadian, and they were married in 1947. "That's when I went to Canada. I decided that's what I wanted – to get out of the picture business. I didn't need this anymore, so I went to Montreal, Canada, and settled there for ten years. We had a kennel and raised about forty dogs. I did that for a while, and then I got a radio show, which was nice, and was a disc jockey for about a year. My family did documentaries for the Canadian Travel Bureau, and my family was my life. By then I had two more children, so that meant I had three – two boys and a girl. I lived there for ten years and never got back here to California. So after my divorce, my family decided it was time for me to come home. I packed up my kids and never went back."

After Canada, Ruth returned to California and lived in an apartment building that her brother, Stewart McMahon, built for his parents and Ruth and her children. Stewart was a pilot with the Flying Tigers from 1949 until his retirement in 1976. About ten years later Ruth married John Ledbetter, and they have been married for fifty years. William Morris didn't really want to sign her under contract again because she had been gone ten years and they had all of these new young people coming up. "By then TV was in," Ruth noted, "and it wasn't that easy to get back into the business again. I tried to do a few little things, and got some TV Shows (*Donna Reed Show, Ben Casey, Cheyenne, Maverick*), but I knew that it was another world." Ruth also performed for two months at the Riviera Hotel in Palm Springs. She had been a friend for many years of Mousie Powell, wife of actor William Powell, and Mousie's sister Maxine booked acts into the Riviera Hotel. In 1963 she asked Ruth if she would sing for a couple of weeks – they had a band coming in and they needed a singer – so Ruth said sure, and they booked her for two weeks. She stayed two months.

Ruth's final film role was in the 1962 20th Century Fox release, *Hand of Death* with John Agar. "I screamed in the movie," Ruth smiled. Ruth had a friend named Gene Ling who wrote the screenplay for the movie, and he called Ruth one day and asked if she would like to be in the film. She said, "What do you want me to do?" And this is all she did: John Agar played a scientist who was working in his laboratory when it exploded and turned him into a monster. All Ruth had to do was come out of a drugstore with a handful of packages, see him walking down the street as the monster, scream, throw her packages, and run. That was her part. Gene called her one day after they did the shooting, and said, "You'll be glad to know that your scream was so good that they put it in the Hollywood Scream Library so people could borrow it if they need a scream."

On May 24, 1996, a star honoring Ruth was dedicated on the Palm Springs *Walk of the Stars*. "The Dusty Wings Girls, all flight attendants, got that for me," Ruth stated. "They put on a function and raised twenty-seven hundred dollars for me to get the star. I thought that was pretty nice. They had a 1934 Ford convertible with a rumble seat that I rode in. It pulled up in front, I got out and people applauded. It was a very nice day for me, very special."

Today, Ruth said, "My house is my life. I also enjoy putting. I don't play golf, John's the golfer, but we have putters who just putt. We go up to the clubhouse every Tuesday and putt eighteen holes right there on the putting green. Other clubs come here and we go to their clubs and have tournaments, and it's very pleasant. Then with the Dusty Wings Girls, I go out to lunch with them and that sort of thing."

John said of Ruth, "There's a thing that I have learned. Ruth never thought of herself as a star ('I'm not,' she inserted). She just did it. It was a living for the family. She enjoyed it, it was fun, but she never thought of it as an extraordinary career. She was always in awe of the people she worked with. She thought they were the big stars, and they were. She worked with Ronald Reagan, John Barrymore, Pat O'Brien, and on and on. But she never thought of herself in that category. So consequently, she was never one to push. Today she's very happy being a grandmother, a mother, a wife, with two dogs, two cats, and living where she lives. She's reached a point in her life where it's more than she wants to do to go to film festivals in North Carolina or Knoxville. She's turned them all down. She doesn't understand that fifty-eight years after she made her last movie why people seek her out for her autograph."

In summing up her feelings about her career, Ruth mentioned that she has never felt that she had sacrificed her childhood by working all of the time. She also said, "Singing in nightclubs and theaters, before a live audience, was what I enjoyed doing the most." With her career in Hollywood, Ruth stated, "It was a good experience; it paid well; I met a lot of very nice people; and it's something that I will always have and enjoy. I never really had any bad times, nothing ever really bad happened to me, and that was good because you hear about so many bad experiences. You learn to avoid any mishaps. For instance, Boyer: Anyone new on the set he would invite for lunch in his dressing room, and you knew from then on that's where he starts playing around, and so you avoid all of those things."

Film Credits: **1937**: Love and Hisses. **1938**: International Settlement; Alexander's Ragtime Band; Hold That Co-Ed. **1939**: Wife, Husband and Friend; Hotel for Women. **1940**: Angel from Texas; Sing, Dance, Plenty Hot; Slightly Honorable. **1941**: Appointment for Love; Blondie Goes Latin; Rookies on Parade. **1942**: Sleepytime Gal; Affairs of Jimmy Valentine; Call of the Canyon; Youth on Parade; Heart of the Golden West. **1943**: Man from Music Mountain; Mystery Broadcast; Pistol Packin' Mama; Hands Across the Border. **1944:** Jamboree; Goodnight Sweetheart; Three Little Sisters; Sing Neighbor Sing; My Buddy; Brazil, Lake Placid Serenade. **1945**: Steppin' in Society; The Cheaters; Tell It to a Star. **1947**: Smoky River Serenade. **1962**: Hand of Death.

FRANK M. THOMAS

Frank M. Thomas was born July 13, 1889, in St. Joseph, Missouri. When he was young he ran away from home and sailed down the Mississippi River. "It wasn't that his home was unhappy," his son, Frankie Thomas, told us. "It wasn't. He just always liked the water."

Frank returned home, where he and his older brother, Calvin, became interested in the theatre. When Frank was about eighteen he joined the Van Dyke Stock Company that was playing in their town. Afterwards they both obtained jobs going on tour with theater companies that performed one-night stands. The show that Frank traveled with was a melodrama called *The Hidden Hand*. They played fifty-two weeks of one-night stands, and then returned to St. Joseph.

Frank then obtained work with one of the largest touring companies in the country. "They didn't do one-night stands," Frankie explained. "They came into a town and played a week, and when they moved they moved by train. It was a big outfit. Dad was cast in this show because he had a good voice and a good laugh. The villain always needed that."

Frank finally made his way to New York where he obtained work in plays on Broadway rather rapidly and was in some big hits. He played opposite Laurette Taylor, who at that time was considered the finest actress on the New York stage. Then he played opposite Lenore Ulric, who was David Belasco's biggest star, in *Aloma*, which was one of her bigger hits.

Frank enlisted in the Navy during World War I. After his discharge, he returned to New York and was hired to play the lead in a play written by Sinclair Lewis. Frankie related an interesting story concerning this play. "Dad came to rehearsal a little early and the theatre was locked. He went around to the stage door and it was locked too. He found Mona Bruns, a young

leading lady, waiting there, like he, a little early. That was mother, and that's how they met. They got married about a year later. Mother eloped to Chicago where dad was playing with Holbrook Blinn, who was then the leading male star." This was about 1920, and Frank played there for about a year. Blinn was playing the Mexican bandit in *The Bad Man*, and Frank was playing the young leading man. Judith Anderson was playing in Chicago at the same time in *Cobra*.

The following year, Frank and his wife, Mona, returned to New York. About this time Frank worked in a few films for a producer named Samuel Goldfish, who later changed his name to Goldwyn. "They were doing films around Forest Hills, and dad played with some well-known leading women in pictures," Frankie stated. Frank continued with the stage, and was very fortunate. He, his brother Calvin, and Sidney Blackmer were known as the three best looking leading men on Broadway.

At one point in their careers, Frank and Mona were signed to play the leads at the Denham Theatre in Denver, Colorado for the winter stock season, playing a new show every week. They lived at the Brown Palace Hotel, which was near the theatre and situated across the street from a nice restaurant. "It was customary after doing a legitimate play to have a bite to eat because you don't eat too much before the performance," Frankie said. "The whole company used to go to this restaurant after the show. One night they were sitting there telling tales, as actors will do, when suddenly dad looked around and there wasn't anybody else in the restaurant. The waiters were still standing there, so dad called Andy Dillon, the owner, over, and said, 'Andy, I'm awfully sorry. We've kept you open, you were ready to close.' He said, 'Mr. Thomas, you couldn't have done me a bigger favor if you tried.' Dad asked, 'What do you mean?' Dillon replied, 'Sitting in the next booth to you were Mr. and Mrs. Swift of Swift Meat Packing Company, and they came to me and said they had never spent such a fascinating evening in their life listening to the stories of those actors.'"

In 1934 Frank's son, who was starring on Broadway as a child actor in *Wednesday's Child*, was hired by RKO, a Hollywood film studio, to recreate his role in the movie version. The studio people were so glad that Frank and Mona were not the typical parents of some child performer that they gave them parts. Mona was given the part she created in the original show, a part of a nurse, and they wrote in a part for Frank just so he would be in the picture. However, they changed his name to Tom Franklin so there wouldn't be any confusion with his son, Frankie Thomas.

After *Wednesday's Child*, the family returned to New York where Frank's son was cast in the lead part in a play titled *Remember the Day* at the National Theatre. The producer, Philip Dunning, asked Frank, who was a leading man on Broadway at the time, "Now look Frank, this part of Frankie's father is not too much, but would you consider doing it just to be with him?" Frank answered that he would do it. "So I had the extreme pleasure of appearing with my father," Frankie told us. "Our director, Melville Burke, was an old hand and he had the good sense to let a performer of dad's caliber interject things that came to his mind. By the time we opened, his part was a jewel. Sam Briskin, President of RKO, attended the opening night because I had just starred in two pictures for his studio. And what did he do? He signed dad to a seven-year contract at RKO. And dad came out to Hollywood and did over three hundred pictures, starting out at RKO and then going free-lance." Needless to say when he returned under contract, he came back under his own name, that of Frank M. Thomas, and not, as was his previous case in *Wednesday's Child*, as Tom Franklin.

Frank spent about ten very active years in Hollywood before returning full-time to New York. His film credits include *China Passage*, *Brigham Young – Frontiersman*, *Chad Hanna*, *Life with Henry* and *Talk of the Town*. Frank also worked in a number of Westerns during his stay in Hollywood. "Dad was in the first starring picture Roy Rogers did when Republic signed him," Frankie remarked. "It was called *Saga of Death Valley*, and that was a very good Western. Dad played the heavy and his part was better than Roy's. He worked about two other Westerns with Roy and about three with Gene Autry. In fact, one year before the war Jane Withers and Gene Autry were two of the top ten draws in the country, so they put both of them together. Twentieth got Autry from Republic and did a picture called *Shooting High*. I went on the set to see dad, and that's where I met Jane Withers. We had never worked together and it was the beginning of a long friendship."

In making these Westerns, Frank was no stranger to horses. "He was practically born in the saddle and could talk to horses," Frankie stated. His father, Jesse Thomas, was in the meat business in St. Joseph, Missouri. He had been a cowboy and was on the first big cattle drive out of Mexico to Kansas City. Being a resident of St. Joseph, he had played poker with Jesse James every week. When Frank was twelve or thirteen, he used to deliver newspapers riding down the streets bareback. He had two saddlebags, one on the left side and one on the right, and he'd ride down the street flipping one paper with his right hand and another with his left.

We asked Frankie if his dad had any favorites among his theatre and film roles. "He always liked *Remember the Day* because we played together," he answered. "I guess *Aloma* was one of his favorites. He did a picture of no importance called *M'Liss*. If you want to see a case of outright theft you ought to run that. Dad played a barber and Douglas Dumbrille played a gambler, and the two of them walked out the front door with that picture. I run it every so often just to see how smooth you can be. They were marvelous. That was one of <u>my</u> favorites."

Frank and Mona played together on Broadway in *Chicken Every Sunday*, which was a hit. Frank also worked in live television in New York, appearing with his wife in *Hallmark*, and performed an outstanding piece of acting in *Street Scene* on *Philco Playhouse*. Another early live show was called *The Black Robe* for NBC. Frank, who was the only actor in the program, played the judge of a night court. The rest of the cast was made up of non-actors who worked without a script. They just told their story to the judge in their own words. That was quite a job for Frank because some of these people would arrive from the bowery intoxicated and he had to control them so they wouldn't run over the time limit. After *The Black Robe* he played Captain Burke on *Martin Kane, Private Eye*. That was a long run, and Frank saw them through four Martin Kane's. First there was William Gargan, Lloyd Nolan was the second, Lee Tracy the third, and Mark Stevens the fourth. Mona had worked a number of years as Aunt Emily on *The Brighter Day*, and the producers decided to write in a romance for her, so they created a character named Adolph McClure and Frank played it. "The organist was absolutely inspired," Frankie added. "Whenever they did a scene together he would play as a musical background *September Song*."

After *Martin Kane*, Frank did about four or five plays. There were no long running hits, but one was *Lizzie Borden*, in which he played her father. It was during this time in New York that Frank worked in his final movie, *Eye Witness*, which starred Robert Montgomery.

After Frank and Mona retired, they lived on their farm in New Jersey, which kept him busy. He enjoyed golf, but his principal love was sailing. "He was born on fresh water so he loved salt water. That's very common," Frankie explained. "He had a number of sailing boats and won the Bermuda Race in 1928 with the *Yankee Girl*. Dad was just in love with sailing. We had a boat in California called *The Mona*, named after mother. Later we had another one in New York called *The Mona #2*." Mona wrote a book titled *By Emily Possessed* about *The Brighter Day*, and her career. In 1962, they moved to Los Angeles and lived there for the rest of their days. Frank died at the age of one hundred years in Hollywood, California on November 26, 1989.

Film Credits: 1934: Wednesday's Child. **1936**: Special Investigator; The Ex-Mrs. Bradford; The Last Outlaw; Grand Jury; M'Liss; Don't Turn 'em Back; Mummy's Boys; The Big Game; Without Orders; Wanted-Jane Turner. **1937**: We Who Are About To Die; Criminal Lawyer; Racing Lady; They Wanted to Marry; We're on the Air; Don't Tell the Wife; Crime Patrol; The Man Who Found Himself; The Soldier and the Lady; The Outcasts of Poker Flat; You Can't Buy Luck; Super Sleuth; The Big Shot; Hideaway; Forty Naughty Girls; Breakfast for Two; Danger Patrol; High Flyers; Crashing Hollywood. **1938**: Quick Money; Everybody's Doing It; Bringing Up Baby; Night Spot; Maid Night's Out; Joy of Living; Go Chase Yourself; Law of the Underworld; Vivacious Lady; Blind Alibi; The Saint in New York; The Marriage Business; Strange Faces; Crime Ring; Smashing the Rackets; The Renegade Ranger; Mr. Doodle Kicks Off; A Man to Remember; The Wrong Way Out. **1939**: Disbarred; The Mysterious Miss X; Burn 'em Up O'Connor; Idiot's Delight; Secret Service of the Air; Society Lawyer; They Made Her a Spy; The Rookie Cop; Grand Jury Secrets; Bachelor Mother; They All Come Out; Death of a Champion; $1,000 a Touchdown; Scandal Sheet; Beware Spooks!; Saga of Death Valley; Geronimo. **1940**: City of Choice; High School; The Man from Dakota; Women Without Names; Shooting High; Lillian Russell; Queen of the Mob; Maryland; Brigham Young – Frontiersman; Chad Hanna. **1941**: Wyoming Wildcat; Life with Henry; Arkansas Judge; The Monster and the Girl; A Shot in the Dark; Sucker List; Three Sons o' Guns; Sierra Sue; Among the Living. **1942**: Henry Aldrich, Editor; Obliging Young Lady; Wild Bill Hickok Rides; Dangerously They Live; Reap the Wild Wind; Sunset on the Desert; The Great Man's Lady; A Desperate Chance for Ellery Queen; Flight Lieutenant; The Postman Didn't Ring; The Talk of the Town; Sunset

Serenade; Apache Trail; Eyes in the Night; Mountain Rhythm. **1943**: City Without Men; No Place for a Lady; Hello, Frisco, Hello; The Desert Song. **1950**: The Sleeping City. **1976**: Killing of a Chinese Bookie.

HARRY TOWNES

Harry Townes was born September 18, 1914, in Huntsville, Alabama, a town that was founded by his ancestor, John Hunt. "It was then just a small sleepy little southern town," Harry recalled. "My father died when I was seven years old and left my mother with four children to raise. I had a sister, a brother and a baby brother that died when he was quite young; my mother also raised a cousin of mine whose mother had died, so that was my family." Harry's growing up years were spent close to home helping his mother with the work she had elected to do. "She was a southern gentlewoman," he explained, "who had no training in any kind of business, and all she could do was to prepare good food, as all good southern gentlewomen could, so she became a caterer. She did it in the home so she could keep an eye on us, and I helped out what I could." Harry's formative years were very normal, going to grade school, high school and taking part in the social life of the town, which was quite extensive.

When asked what attracted his interest toward acting, Harry replied, "I do not know how I wanted to be an actor, I just always did. It was a surprise to everyone in the family, including me, when I found that deep desire because I had never seen anything professional until I went to the University of Alabama." Harry was about nineteen when he left home to attend the university, which was made possible by his winning a scholarship, where he stayed for three years. While here he saw such stars as Walter Hampden and Katharine Cornell perform on stage as they travelled through the area on tour. "I wanted to study drama, but there was no drama at the school," Harry reflected. "All I could study was Shakespeare, and that was pretty dull because I wanted to act in it, not just study the text." They had a drama

club there, but Harry was rejected the first year from joining that group. In his second year he was accepted as a member of the club and by the third year he was elected President of the drama club. During his term at the university Harry acted in a number of plays which impressed the head of the English department, who sent a letter of reference to a summer stock theatre on the east coast. The theatre accepted Harry as a student actor. "I accepted that and went to Westford, Massachusetts, and never went back home except to visit," he added.

After the summer season closed and fall descended, Harry went to New York City and obtained several small jobs there. "Then I got into *Tobacco Road* and toured with that for two years. I played the owner of the plantation, who was called Captain Tim," Harry stated. "During this time I worked very hard on loosing my accent; I had an outrageous, really awful southern accent. It took me several years of hard work getting rid of it." So with *Tobacco Road*, Harry began his career (and could have stayed with that show much longer), but decided the time had come for him to leave for his return to New York and concentrate on working there.

Upon his return to New York, Harry performed many types of odd jobs to keep a roof over his head and food on the table while he attempted to land a stage play. "I worked at the Strand Theatre as an usher," he told us. "And I was a doorman, and a telephone operator; I'd go back to them every time I would close in a play. I'd always go back to the Strand, and they'd keep trying to make me assistant manager; I had to fight them off and say, 'No, no, I don't want to be a manager. I just want to come back and work so I can leave when I get a job.'" Every summer he would leave to go to various summer stock companies and work there. "That's where I met Walter Reed at the Kennebunkport Playhouse, and we became good friends. I played there for four different seasons. That's where I really learned the tricks of the trade," he commented.

Harry was back on Broadway performing in a play called *Mister Sycamore* with Lillian Gish, when he was drafted into the Armed Forces during World War II. "I didn't volunteer; they ran me down and caught me," he interjected. "I never thought they'd take me as I wasn't hardly the picture of health; I had several things wrong and they said they would never take me, but they did." Harry tried to get switched over to Special Services, but it all moved so fast and he found himself in India before the transfer could take effect and served his time in the Air Corps Intelligence. "I was qualified for Special Services, and could have worked on *Winged Victory* for the Air Force or *This Is The Army*, but that didn't work and I stayed in the Oriental theatre for four years." Harry told us of the misery, disease and malnutrition he witnessed while stationed in Calcutta. "It was just awful. The cholera epidemic of 1943 where every morning a death cart would come through the city and pick up the dead bodies from the night before; they would have a wagon full of bodies from disease and malnutrition. They stacked them along the Hooghly River, seven feet high for half a mile, burning at the burning ghats. So the whole thing was very unsettling." Harry commented that he would like to return to India someday and witness all the positive changes that have occurred since he was there. "I loved India and the Indian people. I had a chance to meet a few, not many as they didn't allow us to associate with the Indian people because of the disease. A beautiful country and so kind, sweet people, they were all so pacifist. You could hardly stir them up to do anything; the Hindu religion wouldn't allow them to kill, except now the Hindu's are fighting the Sikhs. That's terrible," he added.

After his discharge in 1946, Harry returned to New York and was discouraged, as he thought, "I'll have to go through all that again to get started again." That fact did not appeal much to Harry, so he decided the heck with it, he will give the acting idea up and go to the Columbia University and finish college. He took some courses in Political Science, thinking his acting experience might be helpful in that field, with the idea of obtaining employment with the State Department. While attending this school, Harry obtained a part in a play there and was spotted by a New York producer named John Golden, who invited him to return to the New York stage. "Well, he didn't have to beg long," Harry smiled, "and I auditioned for a replacement in *Finian's Rainbow*, which was a very popular musical-comedy. David Wayne had left the part and had gone into another big hit, so I auditioned and they accepted me. I played the part of the leprechaun for a long, long time on Broadway, and that established me as a featured Broadway player. I never had a problem after that; that was really the foundation of my establishment as a serious actor."

Television had become very popular by this time and Harry obtained work on such important live shows as *Matinee Theatre* and *Studio One*. This started after he was asked to do an interview for an episode of *Studio One*. He did not receive the part but the producer, Washington Miner, told Harry, "That was a fine reading and I promise you I will have a part for you in the future. I don't think you are quite right for this one." Harry left very dejected, thinking that was a polite way of saying no, but within a couple of days Miner's office called him, saying there was another story and would he do it. "I certainly well," Harry responded. It was a story called *The Little Black Bag* about the Governor of New York, and was a big hit. "I found myself a television star and went from one *Studio One* production to another, and from there I branched out into all the shows that were being done in New York. About every other week I'd be doing a starring role on one of the popular TV shows; I then suddenly found myself a celebrity. Walking along Fifth Avenue, for instance, and having people recognize you...It was quite a startling thing. It's not so much that the money was big, but the fame was big," he reflected.

As Harry continued to work on stage and television, he was offered the starring role in a motion picture to be filmed in Canada, titled *Operation Manhunt*. He played the real-life character Igor Gouzenco, a Russian spy that defected to the Canadian Government. This film opened up a career in motion pictures for him. "Pretty soon I was getting calls to come to Hollywood to audition for pictures," Harry commented. "I did *The Brothers Karamazov*; *The Mountain*; and a whole series of them. In between my TV work I must have done twenty films." Harry worked constantly on television, several of the shows he performed in were *Rawhide, Thriller, One Step Beyond, Death Valley Days* (as Edwin Booth), *Twilight Zone, Bonanza, Falcon Crest*, and seven episodes of *Gunsmoke*. "I enjoyed television a lot," Harry concluded.

Harry did very well in his acting career and bought a house in the Hollywood Hills off of Laurel Canyon Boulevard. "Then I don't know what happened," he said, "but I decided I wanted a little more in my life than what I was experiencing; it all seemed to be kind of futile. I didn't really appreciate what I was doing and thought there must be something better. I wanted to find out the answer to a few questions, questions that we all have: Who am I? Why am I here? Who made me? Where am I going? What is there to life that is important? I thought, 'Where will I find that out?' and said, 'I'll go to the seminary,' and I did." Harry returned to college and completed his education in order to enter the Episcopal Seminary; attending UCLA at night and performing his acting jobs during the day. His courses needed for his objective included Old and New Testament, Psychology and Philosophy. After completing this he was allowed to enter the seminary. "I was there for about four years, and the reason it took so long to complete was that I would stop in the middle and take a job in Mexico, Canada, Hawaii or someplace, and would have to leave and come back and repeat that work. So it was really a tough job and I don't know how I managed to keep at it, but I did." Harry was ordained a Deacon in 1973, and, in the same year, went to Houston, Texas, and performed on stage at the Alley Theatre. About six months later he was raised in the Priesthood by the Bishop of Los Angeles, staying in the work there for about six years, working at various places as Good Samaritan Hospital in Hollywood; St. Mary's in Culver City; and St. Stephen's in Hollywood as an assistant. He never accepted any money for that, it was all volunteer; so he was acting at the same time to make a living. Reflecting on this period, Harry told us, "Really, I was doing too much. I had a heart attack and the doctor advised me to give up one or the other. Well, I have to make a living so I gave up the Priesthood and went back to acting full-time and have been doing that ever since." From 1987 to 1989, Harry assisted at St. Thomas the Apostle Episcopal Church in Hollywood. Harry appeared in the 1986-87 season of television's *Knot's Landing*, and in 1987 told us, "I am always on call for jobs when the agency calls me. I do enjoy acting, but I don't really care an awful lot anymore, I mean I don't need to do it."

Harry's true love has always been performing on the stage. In reflecting on the importance that theatre plays in our society, Harry has said "I like the freedom of the art. I think that it's inclined to get a little pornographic at times, the pictures today and even television. I don't particularly enjoy that and have never taken part in anything that I thought was the least bit pornographic. But at the same time, I thoroughly approve of freedom in the arts because I think they are portraying our society as it is. The theatre should reflect society in all of its facets, its bad and its good. It would be ridiculous to show society in just pink and blue. Its written in bold colors, life is; and unless theatre reflects life in its entirety, it's being not true to itself and to society either. That's why theatre is exciting to me, it's dynamic. It changes with society. It sometimes even points the way that society should go. It should show us as we are truthfully, honestly, explicitly, thoroughly; and if it's ugly, it's up to us to change, not the theatre." Harry had to give up the stage because he had trouble with his hearing and felt very insecure and uneasy on stage because often an actor would turn upstage or just not project, and he was constantly fearful he wouldn't be able to hear his cue. It became too much of a strain and stress, so he had to turn down the stage offers that came his way. "They said that is part of the strain of this heart business," he said referring to his past heart attack. "The last thing I did on stage was Tennessee Williams' *Eccentricities of a Nightingale*, and the reason I did it was because the whole company was top notch and Tennessee Williams was going to direct it. Perry King, Nan Martin, Sandy Dennis and I were the four stars; I played that for weeks and weeks," he concluded.

Referring to his stage experience when asked if he ever had any mishaps or scary times, Harry told us, "Fortunately, I've never had any really tragic things happen like forgetting my lines in any sensational way. Of course all actors make little slip-ups, but I never got into any deep trouble. An actor always has that deep-seated fear that one night on the stage he is going to go completely utterly blank and not know how to get out of it. Well fortunately that never happened to me, but I guess that's every actor's nightmare."

Harry's last motion pictures was the 1986 release, *Check Is In The Mail*, which he described as "A big flop; I don't know what went wrong with that picture but it was a big disappointment to everybody. It was done carefully and done well, but it just wasn't funny and you wonder why." Harry mentioned that he has done about a half-dozen features for video release, saying, "They turn them out rather carelessly, I can't even remember the name of the last one I did." He went on to say that "I've never really had a big hit in pictures; I've always been working but it has just never been my good luck to find a real blockbuster success in pictures. It's just the way the cookie crumbles."

Speaking of cookies, the most recent acting job that Harry has performed was the role of a harried business traveler on an airline. After a long day, he is unhappy to be seated next to a small boy. The boy offers him an Oreo cookie, and after first refusing, he takes one. His dismay turns to delight and he asks the flight attendant to bring them two milks. This plot was for an Oreo cookie commercial. Harry remarked with a smile that he will probably be remembered as The Oreo Cookie Man.

When asked if he has a favorite role that comes to mind, Harry responded, "I think *Finian's Rainbow*. It's not that I like that role so much, I liked it because it was such a stepping stone for me. It was successful and I enjoyed that role because I was featured on Broadway for the first time. I can think of numbers of roles; I did a play on television one time which I didn't think was going to be successful because it was a grim subject called *One Left Over* for *Kraft Theatre*. I thought at the time I was doing it that this was going to be a real bomb because people were not going to go for this. It was about a man, myself, whose wife and two boys were killed in an automobile accident and I was left with one little girl. The whole play dealt with his sorrow, grief, shock and the funeral. That was what the play was, three or four days in the life of a grief-stricken man. Well, it went over with such success. People identified with it; everybody goes through a grief of that kind and they're interested to see how a person deals with that real traumatic thing. So it was a big hit. I got immediate mention all over the country in all the major magazines and newspapers, so that is kind of a favorite of mine although I didn't realize at the time it was going to be as good as it was." Harry went on to mention that working with Spencer Tracy on *The Mountain* was fun; he enjoyed such stage productions as *Eccentricities of a Nightingale*; a couple of George Bernard Shaw plays; Eugene O'Neill's *Ah, Wilderness*; and Shakespeare's *Twelfth Night*. "So I have favorites," he concluded, "but actually the thing I enjoy most is the one I'm doing at the moment."

Harry mentioned that he also enjoyed the Westerns he has appeared in, particularly the role of Pezzy Neller on *Gunsmoke*; working with his old friend Lorne Greene on *Bonanza*; and the two movies (*Heaven with a Gun* and *Santee*) he co-starred in with Glenn Ford. "The Westerns were lots of fun," he commented.

"I used to find more enjoyment on the stage and never intended to be a movie or television actor. I never wanted to be anything but a stage actor, that's why I went to New York and was a stage actor for many years. It was accidental that I got into pictures. Then I found that pictures were so easy and paid so much more money than the stage that I very quickly became adjusted to working in pictures and liking it very much," he laughed. Working in live television also came about accidental but due to his long experience of stock theatre, where you rehearse one play during the day and perform in another at night, he had no trouble doing these shows. "That little red light went on and you were being watched by five million people; didn't bother me at all because my training had prepared me for that kind of thing. But as you grow older it doesn't come easier, so I enjoy the lack of tension of working in pictures; you know you can do it again if something goes wrong, so I enjoy being a movie actor."

Harry told us that he has one confession to make about his life as an actor. "One of the few things in life I can look back on and say I'm really ashamed of is that I should have answered every letter I got. I know so many actors that do that, they answer letters and send photographs. I guess I just never thought of myself as being so big that people would write and want my picture. I'm very sorry about that, so you can write that I should have answered all my fan mail and didn't."

In looking over his career as an actor up to this point, Harry told us, "Yeah, I had a lot of fun in my career. Made lots of friends; I enjoyed the work and I look back on it and think I wouldn't change anything. I wouldn't even want to have been more successful; I dealt with what little success I had and it may have been bad if I'd gotten too rich and too famous. I don't think I could have handled it. At least I'm happy to have had what I had."

In 1989, Harry left Hollywood and settled near his hometown of Huntsville, Alabama. "My sister and her husband and my two nieces live here, so I thought it was time for me to slow down and take it easy to see if I enjoyed vacationing. I have three dogs and a cat; when I lived in Hollywood I had chickens, a goose, a duck, dogs, cats and a garden," he remarked. "So now I'm pretty much half-retired I guess you'd say. I've had a couple of calls from Hollywood to come back, but I'm refusing all offers at this time to see if I really like what I'm doing. Also, it depends on what they call me to do. If it appeals to me, I'll do it; if not, I won't. I probably will go back and do something. You know, an actor never has to retire; he can work as long as he can walk and talk."

Harry Townes died in Huntsville, Alabama, on May 23, 2001.

Film Credits: **1954:** Operation Manhunt. **1956:** The Mountain. **1958:** The Brothers Karamazov; The Screaming Mimi. **1959:** Cry Tough; Destination Space (TV). **1961:** Sanctuary. **1965:** The Bedford Incident. **1969:** Heaven With a Gun; Strategy of Terror. **1970:** The Hawaiians; The Andersonville Trial (TV). **1971:** They Call It Murder (TV). **1973:** Santee. **1975:** The Specialists (TV). **1979:** The Last Ride of the Dalton Gang (TV); Backstairs at the White House (TV). **1980:** Condominium; Casino (TV). **1984:** The Warrior and the Sorceress. **1986:** The Check is in the Mail.

VIRGINIA VALE

Virginia Vale was born Dorothy Howe on May 20, 1920 in Dallas, Texas. Her education there was in a little private school followed by a grammar school and then high school. "I was always the first one up to volunteer to sing a little song or do a little dance or recite a poem," she related. "But I didn't come from a theatrical family at all, so I don't know where I got this urge to get up in front of people. In high school I was in nearly every play or every musical. I studied dancing when I was a teenager – I think I was thirteen, but I always looked sixteen or seventeen. I just did anything to get up in front of people. I graduated from high school in 1936 when I was fifteen. I went right to work in an office and did anything theatrical that came along." That same year Virginia was in a play, *Night of January 16th*, in the Dallas Little Theatre, in which she played the important role of the wife of a man the defendant in a court trial was accused of murdering. "Well anyway, I did that play and the director of the Dallas Little Theatre – which at that time was one of the best in the country – asked me if I would like to audition for Oliver Hinsdale, Paramount talent scout and also the dramatic coach on the Paramount lot." Virginia said that she would, so got an audition piece together. Afterwards, Hinsdale asked her if she would send some photos out to Hollywood and, if they liked the photos, if she would be willing to come out for a screen test. "Of course I said yes."

Virginia received word from Paramount to come to California for the screen test. "I was sixteen when we left Dallas," she reflected. "So I started in the business pretty young. My mom and I came out – my dad had left home several years before. We just packed everything up because we swore that we weren't going to go back to Dallas. We were going to go to California and we were going to stay. So that's how I got started."

Virginia spent a year and a half at Paramount under her name Dorothy Howe. Her first film was a bit part with John Barrymore in *Night Club Scandal*, followed by bits in *True Confession* and *The Buccaneer*. "My first feature part was in *Big Broadcast of 1938*; that was Bob Hope's first film. He had three wives and I was one of them. A rather small part, but I got to wear beautiful clothes and was with Bob Hope. That was my introduction to the feature world." Virginia's second feature role came in *Her Jungle Love*, which involved flyers Ray Milland and Lynne Overman stranded on a tropical island. J. Carrol Naish played the heavy, and Virginia played second female lead to Dorothy Lamour. "I did the three big ones at Paramount: *Big Broadcast*, *Her Jungle Love* and *Cocoanut Grove*, all in 1938, and then the option was dropped. I don't know why but I guess they didn't have any plans for me," she explained.

Virginia's final film for Paramount was a small role in *Unmarried* starring Buck Jones. He played a boxer, Donald O'Connor played the little son of Buck's manager, and Helen Twelvetrees was the lead actress. "I had the part of a singer in her nightclub," Virginia related. "I got to sing again. I was invited to the Buck Jones festival in Rochester, New York a few years ago. I had to tell him that I did work with Buck Jones, but I probably worked with the man personally for about fifteen minutes. He said that's all right, just as long as you were in his presence," Virginia laughed.

Virginia's next break for her career came in July 1939 with *Gateway to Hollywood*, and then RKO. "My agent called and asked if I would like to enter the Jesse Lasky *Gateway to Hollywood* radio contest for acting and singing," Virginia stated. "I said sure, and I won that particular thirteen week series. The fellow that won was Kirby Grant, and he had to take the name Robert Stanton (he later resumed his real name and starred in features and as *Sky King* on television). That's where I got the name Virginia Vale and the contract at RKO. I was there for two years and I never regretted one minute of it." Her first film at RKO was the featured part in *Three Sons*.

"After I finished my work in *Three Sons*," Virginia continued, "they put me with George O'Brien in the first of his last series of six Westerns. I guess we worked well together, or looked good together. I was nineteen and he was forty, but I always looked older and was rather tall and statuesque. So I guess due to the way he looked and the way I looked, we worked. It was fun and I enjoyed it very much. He was a real nice guy."

Virginia mentioned that when she was a little girl there was not any actor or actress that she was inspired by, but in her early teens she thought that Jeanette MacDonald and Nelson Eddy were just wonderful together. "Of course I always loved to sing," she noted. "I thought, 'Oh, if I could just have the opportunity to do what she's doing I know I could do it.' Anyway, I never got that opportunity. I sang on the Jesse Lasky radio contest, but that was blues type singing. But in *Three Sons* I sang a Strauss Waltz in soprano, which was fine. I was in the commissary one day and we were getting ready to make the number six O'Brien – his last one. I was sitting next to the director at the counter and said 'I've got to take a voice lesson this afternoon.' He said, 'Oh, do you sing?' and I said, 'Oh yes, I sing.' So Ray Whitley wrote a little song for me to sing in *Triple Justice*. I faked playing the guitar and sang the song."

Having appeared in a number of Westerns in her career, we asked Virginia if she learned to ride horses for the movies. "No, I didn't learn it for films," she replied. "The only time I ever rode in Texas was back when I was about ten or eleven years old, when I spent a week on a friend's ranch. When I came out here I started riding in the stables, but I rode English. I'd ride once a week so I was a pretty good rider, but I did it just for the fun of it. That was before I went to RKO and before I did a Western. So when I was in that Western saddle you're not supposed to post – you know, take the bounce out of the trot. I was bouncing all over the place, so after the first picture they sent me out to Fat Jones farm to better learn to ride Western. So I knew how to ride, but I'd never ridden Western. I loved to ride."

Virginia made the six Westerns with George O'Brien, and then did one with Tim Holt, *Robbers of the Range*, as well as eight shorts with Ray Whitley. Speaking of the shorts, Virginia laughed and said, "One of them was the silliest thing. I played a girl attending an exclusive girl's school. We were out camping for the week and we danced around in Grecian type dresses in a circle on the lawn. When I looked at it the other day, I thought, 'Oh my, that is the silliest thing.' But they were made for fun; just twelve minute things." Virginia also performed in two shorts with Leon Errol in which she played his wife. "He was a very good comedian, I thought. He was fun to work with."

Virginia spoke to us about her work in the George O'Brien films, saying, "They were pretty well done. It wasn't a three or four day shoot. We shot about eight or nine days. We didn't have a lot of retakes because we knew our lines and we were told where to cross; there was nothing terribly involved. Not that we had to do it in one take – but if it was nice we did – and sometimes we'd do it three or four times. But of course George was such a wonderful actor. I wish I could see him in things other than Westerns. He didn't have to have much direction as far as the dramatics were concerned; there aren't a lot of dramatics in a Western. I didn't have to have any real dramatic character direction either, because usually the scenes were just three or four lines. But of course nowadays they put the camera on the girl's face or the man's face and all they do is stare at the camera and nothing happens, but they still move you. But I really never had a part that was long and involved that had deep character involvement. They were always easy to play or the scenes were very short and not really heavy, so it was quite easy. And we would rehearse. We'd run through it two or three times, but, again, the lines were never long or involved. They moved pretty fast. Generally we shot locally in the valley, but I did get to go up to Ivarsons and in that general area where the rocks and the trees are. Of course I loved it, too. To get paid for having fun," Virginia laughed.

"I thought George O'Brien was a magnificent horseman, the way he could sit a horse. He was just glued to the saddle. When I was working with George I thought he was really something. If I hadn't been raised the old fashioned way and if I hadn't been shy, and if he hadn't been married, had a family and been twenty years older than I was, I'd probably have flirted with him," Virginia laughed. "He was just so nice, just a prince of a fellow, at least as far as I was concerned.

"As far as working with Tim Holt," Virginia continued, "I think the total hours I worked with him on the film might have been one, because it could have gotten along very well without the girl even being in the picture. That's true with a lot of the Westerns because you don't have to have a girl in it, but it does lend a certain something to the film. But I only had four very short scenes with Tim, and it's so easy to shoot one in fifteen or twenty minutes. So, at the most, maybe it was two hours that I worked with him. He was fine, but I didn't talk to him very much. I was rather shy and really didn't know him. And I never played the social scene in Hollywood either. I was a pretty old fashioned girl. I was brought up that way, so I never had the Hollywood chase, sort of speak. I don't mean that I was a recluse when I was a teenager or young woman, but I had very few friends in the business. I don't know why, maybe it is just because I wasn't too good of a joiner," she chuckled.

Virginia expressed her feelings on several of her favorite films that she worked in. "I liked *Stage to Chino* as far as the Westerns were concerned. I liked it very much because this girl had more to do in it. In this case, my part was more or less vital to the story. And then I liked *Marshal of Mesa City* because that was the first Western and she was vital to the story there as well. So those are my favorites as far as the Westerns are concerned. When I worked at PRC I had the leads, so I think *South of Panama* (a 1941 film which also featured Roger Pryor, Duncan Renaldo, Jack Ingram and Hugh Beaumont and involved enemy agents) because I was an important part of the film. It makes a difference if you have more to do. I sang a song in that too. I did another at PRC with Ralph Byrd called *Broadway Big Shot*. It had nothing whatsoever to do with Broadway; it was a prison picture. The shooting title was *The Warden's Daughter*, and I was the warden's daughter. For some reason they decided to change it to *Broadway Big Shot*. It was about a reporter who gets himself sent to jail so he can uncover the true culprits."

When asked if she had any humorous things occur while working in a film, Virginia replied, "I have to say no, not that I can remember. I just reported to the set and did my job and that was it. I'm basically a shy person so I never sat and talked with the people on the set, I'd just get my book and go sit. I was not a good conversationalist and thought they were not interested in me. So nothing really funny happened." When questioned as to if any dangerous or exciting events happened in her career, she answered, "One thing. When I was making *Blonde Comet* I was under contract to RKO, but they loaned me out to Producers Releasing Corporation, a small independent. The film was released in December of 1941 and concerned a female car racer who, having established quite a reputation in Europe, comes to America where she meets another racer, played by Robert Kent, and a state of rivalry is created. So I played the Blonde Comet. We were shooting at the Ascot Race Track one day and they had me in a car so they could shoot some close-ups going around the track. They had to start the car because I didn't know how a race car started, I had no idea. What they did was put a rope on the front of it from a tow car and started it up and said, 'When it gets to speed you can put on the exhilaration.' Well, I didn't know what speed was, whether it was a mile an hour or ten miles an hour, so I stepped on the exhilarator a little bit too soon. It almost turned the car, but didn't. They yelled

'Halt! Stop! Stop!' So everything stopped. They said, 'You stepped on it too soon. The rope was just about to wind around the axel or wheel.' That was a little bit close. But as far as the horses were concerned, no – nothing, because I was always very comfortable on a horse."

Virginia's career slowed to a crawl in 1942 and she decided to leave the business. "In that year I only worked three weeks," Virginia noted, "and I said, 'I'm not going to take this anymore.' So before I was completely broke I freshened up my shorthand and typing, and mother freshened hers up too. After we came out here mom didn't work till the business and I parted. She went to work as a clerk for the OPA (the Office of Price Administration) during the war and I went to work as a stenographer at Lockheed. I stayed at Lockheed for thirty-four years and decided to retire as soon as I could handle things more or less how I wanted. So I took early retirement and now all I do is play," Virginia laughed.

Virginia did not completely quit the business when she began work at Lockheed as she made two exceptions. She returned to RKO for a Ray Whitley short, titled *Range Rhythm*. "I took two days sick leave from Lockheed and did the short. But nobody ever sees these things anymore. They used to play them on television in 1986 on American Movie Classics in-between movies." The final return to films occurred in 1945. Virginia didn't remember how she obtained this role as she was no longer seeking any work in the business and no longer had an agent working for her, but she made her final bow on the screen in the PRC picture titled *Crime, Inc.*, a mystery drama directed by Lew Landers and starring Leo Carrillo, Tom Neal, Sheldon Leonard and Lionel Atwill. This film, in which Virginia had a smaller role, concerned a crime reporter who goes out to expose a gang of racketeers only to fall in love with the sister of one of the hoods. "I also got to sing in that one," she added.

Virginia only had one regret in her career. "I wish I could have made a big location trip," she confided. "I think that would have been a lot of fun. The biggest location trip I ever had was on *Her Jungle Love* at Paramount with Dorothy Lamour and Ray Milland. We went over to Catalina Island for some long shots. But it was a great life."

When asked if she had a preference between performing on stage before a live audience or in front of a camera, Virginia said, "I've never been asked that question. I didn't do a lot of stage, just in Dallas, and then Paramount put me in a couple of plays in a theatre here (including a co-star role with Lee Bowman in *Two on an Island*). That's all I've done. I guess I'd have to say I prefer films because I had more experiences in the film part. Oh, I don't know. It would be kind of fun to do a play or a musical again. Take me back to my teens for sure," she smiled.

Virginia remained very active in her retirement years. "I'm a figure skating judge. I've been doing that since about 1947. I still judge competitions – the singles, the pairs and the dance. I've been invited to judge all over the country. Judging figure skating is a responsibility. These kids spend so much time and their parents spend so much money, especially when they get up to where they can win any kind of title, whether it be a sectional, a regional or the national. They spend thousands and thousands of dollars. So when you're placing them or passing or failing the tests, you've got to think about those things – but you can't let it influence your judging of the skating itself. It is a responsibility, but I enjoy it very much. I do that, and for the past five or six years I've enjoyed going on high sierra trail rides. They're great fun. You can't call them trails because it's over rocks and stones and the poor horses slip and stumble. It's very hard, but it's so beautiful. You can sleep in a tent or sleep outside and they do all the cooking. I'd like to do it more often, but I try to get away four or five days at least once a year. I go with a commercial pack station out of Bishop and usually start out at Rock Creek. I also love to do white water rafting, but I haven't found anybody to go with the last two or three years. I could go alone because you always go with a company, but it's more fun if you have somebody to go with you. I love to do the Colorado and the Tuolumne – they're exciting. So that's about what I do with my time. And if I don't want to do anything, I don't have to. That's one nice thing about being retired.

"People often ask me, 'Wouldn't you like to be back in the business?' and now that I've been going to film festivals for the past four or five years and I'm around the people, it would be fun to get back in, but I wouldn't have any idea how to go about it. I don't know if I would want to tie myself up, but as they say you can take the girl away from the movies but the movies never leave the girl. That's true. You always love it. But I'm satisfied with the way my life is going. I'm as busy as I want to be and I've met some wonderful people going to the festivals. At my first one I didn't know what to expect. There's so many fans and they're so appreciative of what you've done and that you're there. It's just marvelous."

Virginia Vale died in Los Angeles, California on September 14, 2006.

Film Credits: **1937:** Night Club Scandal; True Confession. **1938:** The Buccaneer; Big Broadcast of 1938; Her Jungle Love; Cocoanut Grove; King of Alcatraz. **1939:** Disbarred; Ambush; Persons in Hiding; Unmarried; Three sons; The Marshal of Mesa City. **1940:** Legion of the Lawless; Bullet Code; You Can't Fool Your Wife; Prairie Law; Corralling a School Marm (short); Millionaires in Prison; Stage to Chino; Triple Justice. **1941:** The Fired Man (short); Prairie Spooners (short); Repent at Leisure; Redskins and Redheads (short); Robbers of the Range; South of Panama; A Panic in the Parlor (short); Musical Bandit (short); The Gay Falcon; California or Bust (short); Blonde Comet. **1942:** Keep Shooting (short); Broadway Big Shot; Cactus Capers (short); Range Rhythm (short). **1945:** Crime, Inc.

RUSSELL WADE

Russell Wade was born June 22, 1917, in the little town of Fairline, in Oklahoma. "I was an adopted child, and my family moved to Ada, Oklahoma for a while," Russell said. "Then we moved to Fort Worth, Texas, where I was a leader of a little gang. We had a donkey and a cart and would go around and do things like selling papers. We would steal them on Sunday and go to another part of town and sell them," he laughed. "My grandfather had a farm: sixty acres of citrus in Chatsworth, California, and we moved there in 1929. The Depression came on and things were pretty rough, so there was very little time for me to have fun. I've been working since I was eight years old. I remember getting up at five o'clock in the morning, wrapping my feet in burlap because it was so cold, and going out and delivering papers. Like I said, we stole them on Sunday and took them to the other part of town."

After Russell got out of school he was able to land a job, working in the lab at Universal. "I had worked in the lab for a couple of years, when a friend of mine, who was going to read for a part for a play called *The Family Upstairs*, invited me to come along. So I went—they asked me if I wanted to read for the part, and I said sure. I read for it and got it, and from there I went back to Universal under contract." Russell was put in his first picture in 1935: *Fighting Youth* with Charles Farrell.

After about a year and at least five films later, Russell's option was not picked up. "I started working extras and bits for a while," Russell commented. One of the films during this period was *You Can't Cheat An Honest Man*. "W.C. Fields was a fantastic guy," he told us. "A kick in the pants. You never knew what he was going to say. He adlibbed, and would leave you standing there with egg on your face," he laughed.

Russell continued working bits and extras at various studios until 1941 when he was performing in another stage play, titled *Where Do We Go From Here?* "I used the name Russell Lee as an extra, but was working on the stage as Russell Wade. A talent scout saw me in the play and signed me at RKO." The motion picture, *Mr. and Mrs. Smith*, was the first of at least twenty three pictures that he would appear in at RKO during his six years at that studio.

"I worked in whatever they wanted me to do," Russell noted. "When you're under contract, you are at their command, and if you don't do it they put you on suspension. So I was eager to do it. I got to work in a lot of pictures; many I didn't get screen credit on because the part wasn't that important. I got a good background of doing everything they wanted me to do, which was wonderful. They were grooming me."

Five of the early films at RKO were Tim Holt Westerns, *Bandit Ranger*, *Sagebrush Law*, *Pirates of the Prairie*, *Fighting Frontier*, and *Red River Robin Hood*. "Westerns were a lot of fun. It was like playing cowboys and Indians," Russell commented.

Russell related one experience when he was almost injured on a picture: "Once on a horse we were doing a chase. My horse stumbled, and I damn near went on my head. That could always happen on those Westerns."

In 1944, Russell had a featured role in the John Wayne Western *Tall in the Saddle*. Reflecting on John Wayne, Russell stated, "He wasn't my favorite. First of all, he didn't want me in the part. He wanted his buddy Don Red Barry, but why should the studio promote Don Barry when they had me, who they were already paying? They didn't want to pay another actor from the outside if they could help it, and they thought Ella Raines and I looked like we could be brother and sister. So Wayne made it kind of tough on me. In one scene, Gabby Hayes took my gun, brought me up to his room in the hotel, and handed my gun to Wayne. Wayne handed it back to me and I put it in my holster. He says, 'Talk.' I don't say anything, and he slaps me. I said, 'Wait a minute. This is wrong. I'm supposed to be a hotheaded young man. I pulled a gun on you earlier in the movie, so I wouldn't stand there and let you slap me, because a gun is an equalizer. You're six foot four and I would have grabbed the gun.' The director said, 'That's right.' Wayne said no. So we're arguing over this, and Wayne calls the head of the studio to close the set down. The headman came down, and when it was explained to him he said, 'That's what Russell would do. He's right.' But Wayne's going to do it his way. So we start shooting. He hands me my gun and I put it in the holster. He says, 'Talk.' I don't say anything, and he hit me so hard with his hand that it knocked me clear across the set, and his handprint started to swell on my face. We go at lunchtime and start up a baseball game. I'm pitching and Wayne wants to bat. That's all he wants to do. So I fanned him out. I fanned him out every time he got up," he laughed. "So I got something out of it. When the picture was over they had a party at the commissary, and Wayne said, 'I want to talk to you. Get a drink.' He poured himself a big drink and poured me a glass of straight liquor, and said, 'Come on, let's go.' I don't know if he was trying to ease his conscience or what. We walked around, and I kept drinking and he kept talking and talking, and I don't remember a thing that he said."

RKO loaned Russell out to do several shorts for a director named Ben Holmes, and Russell became a friend with Alan Stensvold, who was the cinematographer. "Alan shot this in 16mm Kodachrome color, which is real nice, and he could blow it up to 35mm. We wanted to make a Western, and my next door neighbor, Rodney Graham, who was a writer, named it *The Sundown Riders*. I borrowed myself from RKO to make it, but they put in the agreement that we couldn't blow it up to 35mm. Now we needed twenty-five thousand dollars to make the picture." It was shot in 1944, and concerned a trio of cowboys known as the Sundown Riders who go up against a gang of outlaws. The cast included Russell, Jay Kirby, and Andy Clyde as the Sundown Riders, as well as veteran Western performers Evelyn Finley, Marshall Reed, Jack Ingram, Steve Clark, Henry Wills & Bud Osborne. The Director was Lambert Hillyer, who had directed one of Russell's early Tim Holt Westerns. "Jay Kirby's father put up the money," Russell continued. "We shot it in the hills at Chatsworth for under twenty-five thousand dollars, in color, which was quite a trick because we lost two days due to the weather. We got terrific reviews, but nobody would touch it because we couldn't blow it up. So we had an idea to show it in schools. And we were going to do locations like Yellowstone and the Grand Canyon for an educational travelogue deal for kids, but it didn't work. It was a flop. It got good reviews saying that it was very interesting, but that was so much for that."

At one point during his career at RKO, the studio ran a survey where they showed pictures on trial runs in Los Angeles, Chicago, and New York in which the audience had a device in their hand that they would press when a performer they liked came on screen. It was a way for the studio heads to see who the audience believed had potential. "I had the highest of anybody at the studio and that's why they kept me around," Russell informed.

Russell thought very highly of producer Val Lewton, who put him in three of his productions: *The Leopard Man*, *The Ghost Ship*, and *The Body Snatcher*. He mentioned that on these films, more time was taken to set the lighting for the right mood. Lewton's series of eight gothic motion pictures have since become cult classics. Reflecting on *Ghost Ship*, Russell told us, "I have always admired Richard Dix. I saw him in *Cimarron*, and here I am the featured player with him. It's funny how things work. In the beginning I was somewhat in awe of working with him." He also stated, "We had a big boat on a soundstage that rocked."

Russell also commented on working with Boris Karloff and Bela Lugosi in *The Body Snatcher*. "There was a little bit of jealousy going on between them, so it was kind of a strange feeling. But Boris Karloff and Bela Lugosi were both very nice to work with. I became ill on *The Body Snatcher*, and they had one day's shooting left of a rain sequence between myself and Boris Karloff," Russell continued. "And if they didn't finish with him they had to pay him seventeen thousand dollars. They asked me if I wouldn't go in the rain sequence, and I said, 'I'm running a temperature of 103 and just don't feel like doing it. Can't we do it tomorrow or the next day?' 'No,' was the reply. 'We have to do it because he has a previous commitment and the studio has to pay him.' I told them I would do it if the doctor said it was okay. Well, the studio doctor said it was okay, so I said, 'Put it in writing.' He wouldn't do that, so I said I had a wife and two children that I had to protect, because I felt terrible. But I finally said okay, and they put me in a rubber suit and all kinds of clothes underneath my regular clothes that I was wearing in the movie, and we finished it.

"The studio appreciated it and sent my wife Jane (who had been Olivia de Havilland's stand-in) and I down to Indio to a thousand acre ranch that belonged to the owner of RKO," Russell informed. "I started feeling better because of the dry air. We stayed there for a week, and I felt really good. There was nothing to do so we would drive to Palm Springs for dinner and meet some friends from Hollywood. We stayed with a friend one night and then moved into Smoke Tree Ranch. At this time there was nothing much out here, and Palm Springs only had about thirty-five hundred people living there. I said, 'This place has a future. I'm going into the real estate business.' I asked my wife if it was okay with her, and she said, 'Why don't you try it for a year.' The contract at the studio stated that you worked forty weeks a year with twelve weeks off to do whatever you liked. So I got into the real estate business in the Valley on my twelve weeks off. I'd buy a little piece here and a little piece there, and sell it. I thought this place had a great future because the sun is here and the weather is great, and I thought we could make something out here. So we'd come down on weekends and made a go of it."

Russell decided to leave the picture business and go into full-time real estate due to the very precarious nature of the former. We asked if RKO tried to persuade him to stay on when he told them he was leaving. "No," Russell laughed. "Because the fellow who liked me and was head of the studio had passed on, and the new one, Sid Rogell, fired me. We didn't see eye to eye because I worked for Val Lewton. I thought Lewton had taste with his pictures and had lot of talent."

Russell had made his final film at RKO in early 1946 in a film titled *The Bamboo Blonde*. Afterwards he moved to Palm Springs where he started full-time in real estate. He made his final three films while living there. "I made two films after I came down here. One was a Western called *Renegade Girl* in 1947 and the other was *Shoot to Kill* in 1948." Both were directed by William Berke for Screen Guild. Russell was the star of the latter one, playing a reporter who goes up against gangsters that attempt to control the town.

Russell's final film performance was in *Beyond Glory*. One of the producers that Russell had worked for at RKO was Robert Fellows, and he was now at Paramount. Russell went to see him and told him he was planning on leaving the business but was wondering if there might be something in a picture for him to do. Fellows said, "I'll be happy to have you in a picture, but it's up to Alan Ladd, who was the star. If he says it's okay, then it's okay with me." So with that, Fellows walked into the office and told Ladd that Russell was there to see if there was a part for him in the picture. He asked, "Would it be all right with you?" "Sure," Ladd replied. "It'll be fine." So Russell went to work in his final film. "We got on a train and went to West Point and worked there for a couple of weeks," he noted. "Then I came back here and was on the picture for fourteen weeks, but was also down here selling real estate and getting paid."

Since Russell had also performed on stage, we asked the common question: if he preferred one medium over the other. "I liked them both," he noted. "They are completely different. You get to do it over in the pictures," he smiled. Russell also performed a couple of times on radio.

Russell mentioned several of the directors that he particularly enjoyed working with. "I thought Bob Wise was sensational, and I liked Mark Robson very much. I also liked Richard Wallace, who directed *Bombardier*. We had a lot of fun on it. We were in Albuquerque, New Mexico. It rained for about a week, and it was cloudy the next week. We were all just sitting there, and around the corner of our hotel was a little pub where they served draft beer. We'd all be drinking beer, and when we went back to work a call came in from Hollywood, saying, 'What the hell is going on? All of the actors look like they gained twenty pounds.'"

Russell told us that he had no particularly favorite picture he worked in. "They were all good for me," he stated. "I had a lot of fun in pictures. I didn't take it too seriously, but tried to make it light and have fun with it. Be serious when you are supposed to be serious, but on the set I tried to be jovial and cheerful and lift everybody up if I could. After all, it's only a film."

When we interviewed Russell in 1999, he was still working in real estate, saying, "I have some good people working for me."

In summing up his feelings on his acting career, Russell said, "I have very fond memories. I felt kind of badly leaving, but I couldn't see any future in it. It was trying times with television coming in, and they didn't know what to do with it. Everybody was mixed up. The studios were boycotting television. Bill Boyd was the only one who bought his own pictures. He could show them or sell them or do anything he wanted to. The only thing I disliked was the cheating that was going on—trying and get you out, like when Wayne wanted the part for Don Red Barry. But I thought it was wonderful, and it opened a lot of doors for me."

Russell Wade died on December 9, 2006.in Riverside County, California.

Film Credits: 1935: Fighting Youth. **1936:** The House of a Thousand Candles; We Went to College; Postal Inspector; Yellowstone; Ace Drummond; The Girl on the Front Page; Flying Hostess. **1937:** Music for Nadine. **1938:** What Do You Think (short); It's in the Stars; Fugitives for a Night; Spring Madness. **1939:** You Can't Cheat an Honest Man; Three Smart Girls Show Up; Sorority House; These Glamour Girls. **1940:** Broadway Melody; Star Dust; Flowing Gold; One Night in the Tropics. **1941:** Mr. and Mrs. Smith. **1942:** A Desperate Chance for Ellery Queen; The Big Street; Bandit Ranger; Highways by Night; Dear! Dear! (short); Army Surgeon; Rough on Rent (short); Pirates of the Prairie. **1943:** Red River Robin Hood; The Great Gildersleeve; Fighting Frontier; Sagebrush Law; Ladies' Day (short); The Leopard Man; Bombardier; Gildersleeve's Bad Day; The Falcon in Danger; The Iron Major; The Ghost Ship; Higher and Higher. **1944:** Prunes and Politics (short); Marine Raiders; Tall in the Saddle. **1945:** The Body Snatcher; A Game of Death. **1946:** The Bamboo Blonde; Renegade Girl. **1947:** Shoot to Kill. **1948:** Sundown Riders; Beyond Glory.

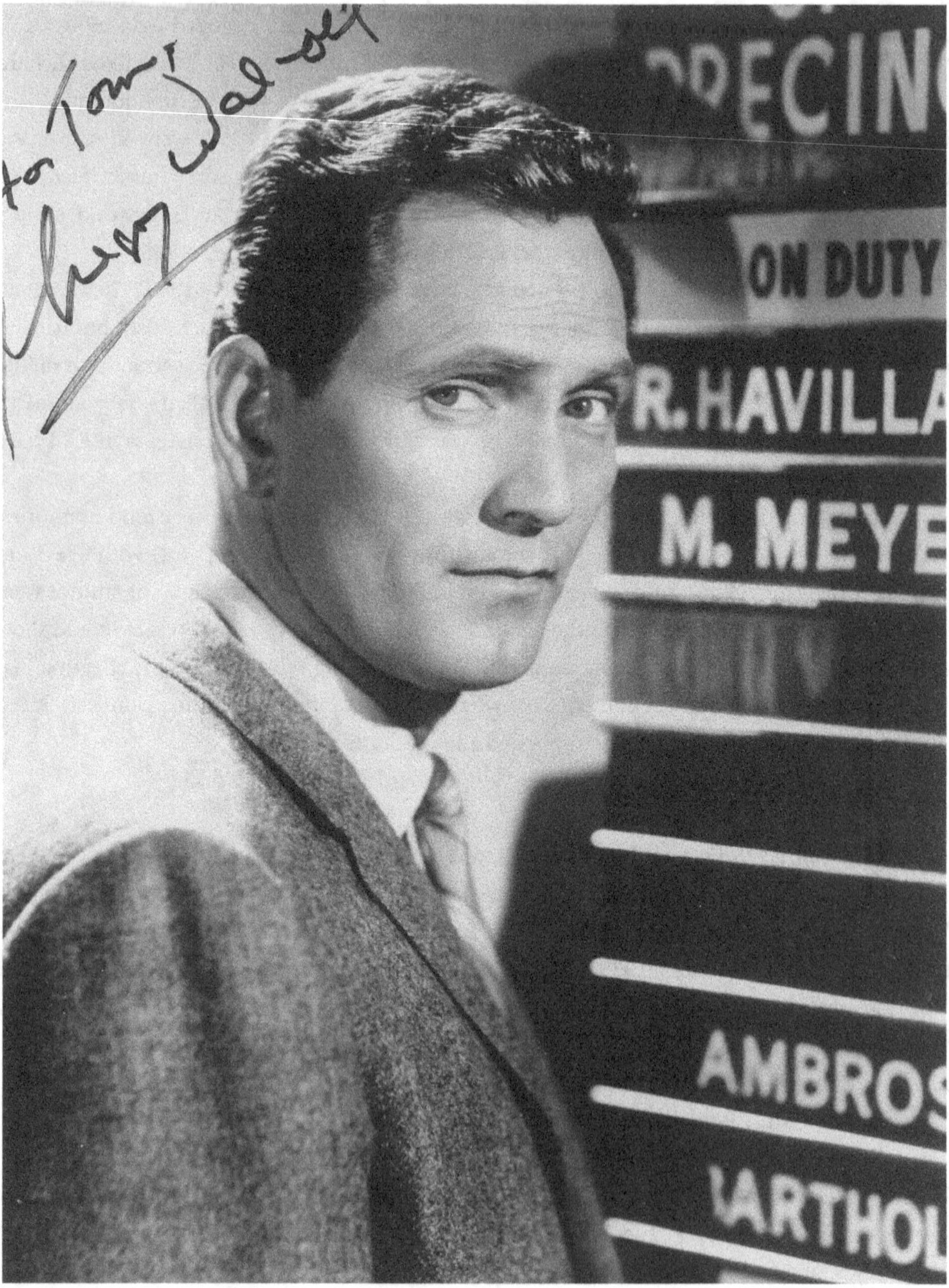
to Tom!
ON DUTY
R. HAVILLA
M. MEYE
AMBROS
ARTHOL

GREGORY WALCOTT

Gregory Walcott was born Bernard Mattox on January 13, 1928 in Wendell, North Carolina, and raised in nearby Wilson. "I was a child of the Depression era and things were very difficult in those days," Greg told us. "My father worked long, hard hours as a salesman and my mother, to make ends meet, rented out rooms to college students and widow ladies. My oldest sibling was my brother five years my senior, and after school he worked at the A&P." Greg and his brother would also rake up a big bundle of leaves on Saturday and sell it to the florist for a quarter, and for a dime apiece they would go to the movies. "We had a nickel left over to split a Powerhouse candy bar," Greg added.

We asked Greg what inspired him to want to become an actor, and he replied "The first movie I ever saw in my life when I was six years of age fascinated me." The film was Robert Louis Stevenson's classic *Treasure Island* with Wallace Beery and Jackie Cooper. "I related to that little kid," Greg continued. "I was rather shy as a child and I lost myself in the darkened cavern of the movie theaters. That silver screen became a wonderful world of adventure for me and I projected myself into those colorful characters. I was Johnny Mack Brown, I was Tarzan, but I was also Nelson Eddy singing those beautiful romantic duets with Jeanette MacDonald who was the love of my life. So I think in my childhood I had such an identity with the screen that after I had a hitch in the army I said, 'I'm going to go to the west coast and try to make it in films.' It had been in my genes for a long time."

Greg left North Carolina in September of 1949 and hitchhiked all the way to California. He had about a hundred dollars with him and slept in the YMCA for a dollar a night. Reflecting on this experience, Greg noted "In the morning I would get up, put on a clean shirt and shave, wear a bright smile and carry a tennis racket. Anything was interesting to a twenty year old kid who had never gone past Knoxville, Tennessee. So it was all very fascinating to me to see the Grand Canyon, the Mississippi and the mountains and deserts. I had a very easy trip, and got along just fine."

On the sixth day he arrived in Pasadena, California, knowing absolutely no one at all. "The next morning when I got up I left the YMCA and started walking around Pasadena. I noticed at city hall there was a crowd of people out front behind police roped barriers and it looked like a parade was going to go on," he stated. "I asked someone what was happening and he said they were shooting a movie starring Clark Gable. Naturally I was curious and wanted to see Gable, and pretty soon he came out, and on my very first day in California I saw the biggest star in Hollywood."

Several days later Greg took a bus to Hollywood and stayed for his first week in the YMCA. "I was very lucky," he recalled. "There was a sweet motherly lady from Kentucky who owned a very beautiful Victorian home and rented out rooms to retired people and a couple of old actors. She made me an offer, and that was to do the lawns, trim the hedges, take out the trash and hang up the laundry, and for doing that she would give me a room free of charge. I grabbed at the opportunity and lived there for three years."

Greg attended a drama school on his G.I. Bill, and began to appear in such plays as *Yellow Jack*, *Men in White* and *My Sister Eileen*. Greg also had employment in various jobs such as parking cars, waiting on tables and singing for weddings and funerals to supplement his income while attending school. Greg appeared as the young leading man on stage at the Showboat Theatre in Hollywood which performed the old-time melodramas. "That was my first paying job. Ten dollars a week," Greg added.

Greg's next door neighbor was the character actor Richard Gaines (*Enchanted Cottage*, *Brute Force*, *Drum Beat*), who came one night to see him in a play. "He was a bit amused at my antics on stage so he introduced me to his agent, and on the recommendation of Gaines he took me on as a client," he noted. At this time Otto Preminger was preparing to open his west coast production of *The Moon is Blue* with David Niven, Scott Brady and Diana Lynn. Niven was to play a southern gentleman, and Greg was chose to teach him how to use a southern accent. Niven couldn't quite master the art and Preminger dropped the idea of having him use one, but he decided to keep Greg on as the understudy for Scott Brady and serve as assistant stage manager.

Greg's agent introduced him to the head of casting at Twentieth Century Fox, who in turn brought Greg to the attention of the producer and director for *Red Skies of Montana*. "They were looking for a young southern guy to play a smoke jumper, and they liked me. On my very first film interview I was cast in a fairly decent role in a film at a major studio," Gregg said.

With that type of a role in a major film one would think Greg was on his way to a nice movie career but, to the contrary, only a few bits during a long dry season transpired. Greg joined an acting class to learn additional skills and techniques during this period, as well as working out in a gym. "Within a year's time I went from a skinny one hundred-and-seventy pounds to a two hundred pounds, and the casting directors began to see me in a new light," Greg informed.

Greg also had to again work at various side jobs while waiting for his break in the business. At one time he was a delivery man for the Railway Express. Greg's agent called him, saying, "They want to see you over at Republic. Somebody had to drop out of the Younger Brothers episode on *Stories of the Century*." "So I managed to work my route around to Republic Studios, park my truck out on the side street and rush in," Greg explained. "They read me real fast and said, 'You'll be fine.' So I went to work the next morning. *Stories of the Century* is what started things going, because on the second day of that show Herbert Yates came on the set and introduced himself. He said he would like to talk to me about a contract and, of course, that thrilled me to death. My agent said 'Let's wait just a little bit and not rush into it.' Amazingly enough, somewhere within a week's time I was with him at Warner Brothers when he was there to pick up a script for somebody. I was just sitting there waiting, and Solly Baiano, who was head of casting, came down the hall. He saw me and introduced me to Raoul Walsh, who asked me to read for the tough drill instructor. He liked what I had to say and cast me in *Battle Cry*, which led to a contract. So by waiting and going to Warner Brothers I was put into a major studio category."

The first picture Greg appeared in there while under contract was *Strange Lady in Town* with Greer Garson. It was a Western, Mervyn LeRoy's first and only Western. Greg had never been on a horse in his life until he came to the west coast. Bill Orr was the head of talent at Warners at that time. Orr asked, "Greg, can you ride?" Greg replied, "Sure." Orr looked at Greg and said, "I think I'll get you some brush up lessons." So he called a riding stable over on Riverside Street in Burbank and Greg went there and got his instructions on how to ride. "I didn't know how to ride a horse, but I learned. I went there about every day for two weeks and when the film started on location in Arizona I was doing pretty good," he stated.

Greg worked with John Ford in *Mister Roberts*. One morning Greg received a call from casting at Warners, telling him that there had been some production changes on the film and they wanted him to come over right away to do a role. "About an hour later I walked on the sound stage still bleary-eyed, not knowing what was going on," he stated. "They put a uniform on me and thrust a script into my hand. I was really confused, but fortunately Henry Fonda could see my dilemma and he invited me into his dressing room where he patiently described the character to me and what the scene was all about." Asking what Ford was like, Greg responded that "by that time in his life and career he was regarded with awe and reverence, everybody kowtowed to him. I never got that close to him, but he seemed to get along all right with me because he liked tough guys, he didn't like a mamby pamby. Although I was apprehensive about working with him I kind of put on a facade of being tough and he respected that. But it seemed like on every show John Ford did he had to have one whipping boy and he would treat that person merciless, and unless you could take it you would crack under it. I can't say that John Ford was the most pleasant person to be around, but he was great in what he did."

Greg next discussed an embarrassing moment for him while appearing with Claudette Colbert in *Texas Lady*. One scene called for him to step into the dance hall where all of this dancing was going on. "She eyes me and I eye her back," Greg recalled. "I thrust my hat into somebody's hand, walked over and took her into my arms, and I'm supposed to swirl her around the dance floor. I was a good dancer, but I had never learned how to waltz, and it was a waltz tune. Everybody thought I was kidding. Claudette said, 'I bet you can do a wicked tango,' but I simply could not. I was good at ballroom dancing, twirling and dipping and all of that, but I simply could not get the hang of waltzing. I guess we spent two hours trying to get that scene. Claudette was trying to show me a few simple steps while a crew of eighty stood around yawning, and extras were laughing and giggling. I felt like an idiot. And to this day, whenever that film comes on, I avoid that scene because I look like an ox out there. It was very embarrassing."

Greg continued working steady in Warner Brothers pictures, including *The McConnell Story* and *The Court-Martial of Billy Mitchell*, as well as for other studios in such features as *Thunder over Arizona*, *The Steel Jungle* and *The Lieutenant Wore Skirts*. His credits on television included such hits as *Cheyenne* and *Perry Mason*. Then about 1957 along came a film called *Plan 9 from Outer Space*.

Greg belonged to a little church near Beverly Hills, which also counted among its members a man named Ed Reynolds. He was a great fan of Cecil B. DeMille's *The Ten Commandments*, and felt he was divinely called to make biblical epics. A director of low-budget pictures named Ed Wood contacted Reynolds and convinced him by making a few exploitation films he could earn the bankroll to do his epics. As a favor to his fellow church member, and after unsuccessfully attempting to talk him out of investing his money in Wood's project, Greg reluctantly agreed to star in it. "He came to me one day and said that he was going to make a film starring Bela Lugosi, and that he wanted me to play the young male lead. I said to him, 'But Ed, Bela Lugosi's dead.' He assured me that a very ingenious writer-director named Ed Wood had written a screenplay around the existing footage of Lugosi and that he would use his chiropractor, who resembled Lugosi, to be his double. But it was a mistake," Greg noted. "The film was atrocious, and the dialogue was abysmal. The special effects you can't believe: Hub caps were used as space ships and the gravestones were made out of cardboard. The film was so overwhelmingly bad that it was funny, and years later it became an international cult film.

"Ed Wood always had an entourage of people hanging around him," Greg told us. "Astrologers, masseuses – just a kind of an odd bunch of people. So Ed Wood began to go to this church to give Ed Reynolds a feeling he was interested in his faith. When Wood's entourage – I call them his menagerie – found out there was a guy going to this church who was going to bankroll some films they began to show up on Sunday morning. It was quite an odd sight to see these people come in with pasty faces and dressed in strange clothing sitting there amongst little old ladies. To convince Ed Reynolds he was sincere, Wood wanted to be baptized. Tor Johnson thought it would be a good idea too, but he was too big to get into the baptistery. The minister, being an enterprising fellow, got one of the ladies in the church to loan her swimming pool for the baptismal. I happened to be there that day. Wood was duly baptized in a white robe, and they had to make one for Tor Johnson because they couldn't find one big enough for him. He weighed four hundred pounds. The little preacher was quite small and had to push him down and somehow got Tor just beneath the surface of the water and he came sputtering up like a beached whale. But it was so amusing to see. There were several others of Wood's entourage who were baptized that day, and to see them come up out of the water, with their eye shadow running down their faces, smiling very sweetly. I tried not to doubt their sincerity in their religious demonstration, but amazingly enough when Ed Reynolds no longer had any more money to produce films these new devotees no longer showed up. There were so many funny things around the making of that film," Greg concluded.

An interesting side note here is that Greg played a potential investor in the 1994 motion picture, *Ed Wood*, which was the story of this director. Martin Landau won the Academy Award for his portrayal of Bela Lugosi in this film.

After *Plan 9* it was difficult to get going again in bigger budget films. Greg worked in lower budget pictures like *Badman's Country* and *Jet Attack*. He decided to become more aggressive and do his own footwork to push his career. He began a routine of trying to see at least four people a day that could move his career in an upward path, and after about six months he started to see results. Greg began to obtain decent roles in television shows, such as *Wagon Train*, *Bat Masterson* and *Laramie*.

In 1961 an important event happened that resurrected Greg's career. He was again cast as a drill sergeant, this time in *The Outsider*. This film led to a contract at Universal, which loaned him out to Paramount for a nice role in *On the Double* with Danny Kaye. "It was enjoyable working with Danny, he was a comical genius," Greg informed. One film at Universal was *Captain Newman, M.D.*, with Gregory Peck, who Greg referred to as a "consummate professional, a superb actor." Universal then placed Greg in the role of Detective Roger Havilland, one of the leads, in the television series, *87th Precinct*.

In 1966 Greg had the opportunity to go to Hong Kong to play the title role in the motion picture, *Bill Wallace of China*, which he also produced. This was based on the true story of a Tennessee doctor who served as a medical missionary in China. We asked Greg whatever became of this film? "It was released on the east coast and played in Texas and throughout the Midwest, but it never did get to the west coast," he answered. "It did pretty good. We were shooting at the time of the Red Guard riots and apparently they knew that our film had some indications that Dr. Wallace had died under the hands of the communists. Our editing room was moderately sabotaged one night so we had to have a guard there all of the time. And when we were shooting on location out in the regions of Hong Kong we could tell we were not getting the co-operation from merchants. Like we would hire a store or pay merchants along a street there, and we would give them a nice fee to let us use the front of their store. At first they were very cooperative, but later on we found they were being apprehensive and a little fearful, and they didn't cooperate with us. What we had to do, and I made this suggestion myself, I said the scenes we wanted to get that they would interfere with, we would put a long lens on the camera and put it in a second story hotel room and shoot the action from a distance. And we really got a lot of that. So the Red Guard did give us some trouble, but we were able to manage and finish it. It was a nice picture which gave me a great deal of satisfaction."

The 1970's brought choice roles in films like *Prime Cut* with Gene Hackman and Lee Marvin (a film in which he gained thirty pounds and shaved his head); *Sugarland Express*, directed by Steven Spielberg, who, because of the part in *Prime Cut*, invited Greg to play the role of a highway patrolman. He asked Greg to take the script home and read it, and if he liked the part he could have it. "So I took the script home and read it, and I liked it," Greg added; the Clint Eastwood films *Thunderbolt and Lightfoot*, *Joe Kidd*, *The Eiger Sanction* and *Every Which Way but Loose*. "Eastwood is very clever. He would tell you as an actor basically what he had in mind for a role, and then he would leave it up to you," Greg noted. "I rather like that because it makes it a collaborative effort"; *Norma Rae* with Sally Fields; and an Italian Western titled *A Man from the East*, as well as zany Italian comedies. Of these latter films, Greg commented that these pictures took him to Italy, Holland and Yugoslavia. "It was like going to a circus every day," he added. "It was great fun." An additional treat was that he brought his wife, Barbara, and his children with him and they traveled throughout Europe. He also continued being busy in television on up through the 1990s, working in shows such as *Airwolf*, *Simon and Simon*, *Alice*, *The Quest*, *High Chaparral*, and *Murder, She Wrote*. All told, his credits include about fifty features and three hundred TV shows.

Greg told us that he enjoyed playing the villain roles he's performed over the years. He remarked that "the villains always seemed to have a little more dimension, a little more color, a little more character." As far as having a favorite role, Greg mentioned that would be difficult to say. "I get certain satisfaction out of different roles. It might be the director I work with or the people or the location, but there are other roles which forces me to stretch my range as an actor. I rather feel challenged by doing a role that is not me at all, and it's kind of fun too."

Greg mentioned that actors he has looked up to include Spencer Tracy, Gary Cooper and Henry Fonda because "they did things with such a naturalness, such an effortless economy." Of the classical actors he admires Richard Burton, stating the best Shakespeare he has ever seen was Burton's *Hamlet*. Others include Jack Lemmon, Gregory Peck and Gene Hackman. Of actresses, Greg stated that Meryl Streep can do anything, and Angela Lansbury is the "quintessence of professionalism, and a real jewel of a lady." He considers the two directors who stand out above the others to be David Lean (*Lawrence of Arabia*), saying "he was a perfectionist and that every detail of his film was planned," and George Stevens (*Gunga Din*), and noted that Stevens "understood the human condition and depicted it vividly through the lens." One of the greatest regrets of his career was missing out on working with Stevens in *Giant*. He gave Greg a nice part, but another film in which Greg was working in at the time went over schedule thus this great opportunity slipped by and they had to recast him in *Giant*.

The other disappointment that Greg talked about was "when a producer or a director or a writer want you for the role and the thing is set to go, but at the last minute some studio boss or some network executive overrides their decision. That's happened a number of times and it's very painful."

When asked if he noticed much change in the motion picture industry over the last forty years, Greg replied "Well, I think so. It has always been a very difficult, competitive business, but in those days it seemed to have more style, more dignity, more class. Studios had their own crews, they had their own actors that they kept under contract, and it was like a family. You got to know everybody on the lot. The family feeling, but now it's so big. You've probably heard this worn out cliché that it's now run by accountants and lawyers and that's basically true. And in those days the casting people were great guys and women like Hoyt Bowers, Ralph Winters and Joyce Selznick. They were very discerning; they were courteous and very professional; they did their homework. They knew who the actors were, what their portfolio was, what their background was. So when they called you in it was for a specific role, but now the casting people don't quite have the class and discernment and the training that the old timers had. They might call up an agent and say send me so-and-so and then maybe have twenty actors there basically for the same role without ever really studying their background. So unfortunately in this day and time it's changed and doesn't have the style, class and dignity of the old days."

Greg described a typical day for him going to work. "That all depends on when your call is. When it is an early call and the show is being shot in Los Angeles I have to get up about four-thirty. I'll get up and shave and shower, have a little breakfast and feed the dogs. I have a little physical program that I go through each day. I try to get limbered up, do my walk and exercises which make me come alive and get my blood circulating. That's important. Then I get in my car and drive to work to try and avoid the traffic. In my last show on *Murder, She Wrote* we were shooting in Hollywood Park for a couple of days and had to be there at six-thirty. That's about a forty mile drive, so you have to plan your day to get there at a fairly decent hour."

Greg appeared in about nine episodes of *Bonanza*. On one episode he played the happy-go-lucky guitar playing friend of Little Joe who turned out to be a fugitive; on another, Greg was an ex-confederate captain who leads a band of terrorists that burn ranches. Greg referred to *Bonanza* when responding to the question if it was common to receive script changes at the last minute on the set. "It's not common to get script changes during the production, but it does happen occasionally. On *Bonanza* a number of times Michael Landon didn't like the way something was written and he would rewrite the thing right on the set. You had to learn these lines as he rewrote them and if you were not a quick study you'd be in trouble. Fortunately, I was a quick study. I will have to say this in defense of what Michael did. For example, there would be dialogue that Little Joe wouldn't say like that, or there would be a scene that just wouldn't work, and having been on that show so long he could sense what was not right, and he would rewrite that whole bloody scene while the actors went to lunch or something."

If You Blink You Die is an eighteen minute short that Greg wrote and directed, and was planned to be presented to various film festivals in 1991. It's a spoof on the spaghetti Westerns. His son-in-law played a gunman, while another actor played an ex-gunfighter with a wooden leg, who became a monk at a monastery. His companion was a three-legged dog (based on a three-legged dog that lived next door to Greg). The monk must remove his shroud when the gunman comes looking for him and put a gun on one last time and face him in a duel.

Greg discussed some of the things he enjoys doing in his time away from the camera. One is writing. He mentioned that he often is working on a screenplay idea or writing an essay or short story. What type of writing does he like? "Things that I write are the stories about a man who is under a great crisis, his life is filled with perplexities and distresses and somehow he manages to overcome it. I particularly liked the film *Save the Tiger* with Jack Lemmon. I like to see stories where men are struggling to overcome their problems. That's most of my type of writing."

He also enjoys his framing studio which allows him to work with his hands, working with wood and design and coordinating colors. "It's very relaxing," he added. He finds satisfaction in attending the annual Oscar Awards. "It gives me a chance to mingle with those people that I have worked with, to congratulate them on their achievements. It's also a time of defining and affirming my role in my chosen profession. It's really very nice," he said.

Greg mentioned that as he is getting older he enjoys a quieter, more reflective life. His books, journaling, good music. He and his wife collect a little art. Greg is also very concerned about the environment, ecological concerns. "I try to do my share in saving planet Earth," he commented. Greg added that he finds pleasure in sitting out on the patio late in the afternoon reflecting over the events of the day with his wife, planning the things that they want to do. He enjoys his dogs. "I especially enjoy that time of day, long shadows and soft sunlight filtering through the leaves," Greg noted. "I think if I should ever direct a movie I would schedule scenes to be shot at that particular time of day, I really like that time of day."

We asked Greg how he would like to sum up his feelings thus far about his career. "Well, I came to the west coast without knowing a single person here, without one contact, and had about a hundred dollars. I was naive in many ways," he replied. "I have not reached my life-time goals, but I have taken a big bite out of life. I've made some mistakes. I have not used the best judgment at times, but I have lived and I have not done too badly. My work in films has taken me all over the United States, Europe on several occasions and Asia on a couple of occasions. I have been married to the same wife I was married to when I first started in the industry. I have three terrific kids, five grandchildren, they're such a delight. Time flies so rapidly and they grow so fast. So I haven't reached my goals, but I haven't done too badly either."

Film Credits: 1952: Red Skies of Montana; Above and Beyond (scene deleted); Fearless Fagan; Ruby Gentry; Battle Zone. **1955:** Court Martial of Billy Mitchell; The McConnell Story; Mister Roberts; Strange Lady in Town; Texas Lady; Battle Cry. **1956:** The Lieutenant wore Skirts; The Steel Jungle; Thunder over Arizona. **1957:** The Persuader. **1958:** Jet Attack; Badman's Country. **1959:** Plan Nine from Outer Space. **1961:** The Outsider; On the Double. **1963:** Captain Newman, M.D. **1967:** Bill Wallace of China. **1969:** Changes. **1972:** Joe Kidd; Prime Cut. **1973:** The Last American Hero; Who Stole the Shah's Jewels? **1974:** A Man from the East; The Sugarland Express; Thunderbolt and Lightfoot. **1975:** The Eiger Sanction. **1976:** Midway; Gemini Man (TV); The Quest (TV). **1978:** Donner Party: Road to Survival (TV); Every Which Way but Loose. **1979:** Norma Rae; Tilt. **1980:** To Race the Wind (TV); The Contender (TV). **1987:** House II. **1994:** Ed Wood.

GEORGE WALLACE

During a break in the shooting schedule of a TV movie titled *Child of Rage*, in which George Wallace played the role of the Grandpa, we had a chance to meet with him and have this interview. Because it had been raining for two weeks solid in Vancouver, British Columbia, where the show was being filmed, and due to the fact that the lead child actor came down with chicken pox, they took a break in the production and George was able to return for several days to his southern California home. George remarked that they had a twenty one day shooting schedule, and even with this production delay they only were coming in one day over the schedule.

George Dewey Wallace, named for his great-great grandfather Admiral George Dewey, was born June 1917 in New York City. His mother was divorced when George was five years old, and when he was thirteen she re-married a coal miner from West Virginia, and they moved there from Long Island to the town of Wheeling, West Virginia. George had just graduated from the eighth grade in public school and that was the end of his schooling. He mentioned that this was during the Depression and the important thing was to get a job, saying "At thirteen I began working in the coal mines and I've been working ever since."

George worked in the mines ten hours a day, six days a week. "It was just go to work, go home to bed, and eat Polish Kabooska, which my stepfather used to make every Sunday. It was just a soft coal mining town; lived in company houses. They were all little bungalows, all covered with black soot. You've heard the expression stick in the mud? Well, that's a game we used to play going to work in the morning because it was at the foot of the Appalachian Mountains and all the water there from the Ohio River just saturated the area, it was covered with mud. We'd have two sticks with points on them, and as you walked to work in the morning for a mile or so I'd throw the stick and stick it in the mud and then you'd throw a stick to knock mine down and make your stick stick in the mud, and that's where 'stick in the mud' came from."

In 1935, George joined the Civilian Conservation Corps, which he described as the opposite of the Works Progress Administration. "The CCC was for the sons, the WPA was for the fathers," he explained. "We went off into the mountains and built roads and cleared streams."

George joined the navy in 1936 and planned on being a career man because all of his people had been in the Navy. He was shipped out to the west coast and served until 1940. He boxed in the Navy, and was light heavyweight champ of the Pacific fleet for two years, 1939-1940. George re-enlisted when World War II began and served in the Navy until 1945.

George commented that "acting was the farthest thing from my mind; I had no thought about it." George worked a variety of jobs in California, saying "I used to knock steers in the head at Wifford Meat Packers in Los Angeles; then I became a lumberjack in the high sierras; Then I began cutting Christmas trees; I worked for a tree wrecking company in Los Angeles at forty five cents an hour; washed cars; became a bouncer on skid row for two years. We had twelve b-girls selling champagne, and if guys got mad and started slapping them around and started big fights we'd have to throw them out; we had big fights all the time. In 1946 Mickey Simpson and I were bouncers at a nightclub called the Florentine Gardens on Hollywood Boulevard. It was a big nightclub like Earl Carroll's. Yvonne DeCarlo was in the chorus, and the Mills Brothers and Allen Jones performed there. Then I got a job in Hollywood as a bartender at a place called the Sanbar because the owner had two daughters named Sandra and Barbara.

"I had always liked to sing," George continued. "During the war I even had a guitar aboard ship and would sing away with it. When I was a bartender, the owner had a juke box and people would come in and play the old songs and I would sing with the juke box. People would throw down twenty cents and I would sing along with the juke box while I was fixing drinks, having a great old time. One night a man came in and had a drink and when he left he gave me his card, and said to call him tomorrow. It was a man called Jimmy Fiddler, the famous west coast columnist. I went to see him and he asked how I would like to sing in the Jewish benefit. I said I'm not Jewish, and he said who cares. So he introduced me to a man named Mickey Katz, who is the father of Joel Grey, and he played a wonderful wailing clarinet. I learned a couple of songs with him and sang for the Jewish benefits like The City of Hope, and those were always good for ten or fifteen dollars."

George next became a laborer at MGM. "I was what they called a greens man," he explained, "because of working on tree wrecking I knew all about trees and bushes. As a greens man you build trees for a set and bring in hedges, bushes and plants." While George was there he worked on such features as *Sea of Grass*, *The Kissing Bandit* and *Green Dolphin Street*.

Jimmy Fiddler sent George to a singing teacher. He knew a fellow who paid for his lessons for three months, and after that time he said, "Okay, let's go out and make a lot of money."

George told us that after these three months passed he was worse than when he started because his singing teacher had taken all of his bad habits that he had away, and so he was starting over from scratch. So his benefactor threw his hands up and said forget about it. The singing instructor had noticed the potential in his voice and offered George a proposition. She told him that her husband was getting old and **if** he would take care of the garden, paint the house and take her shopping, she would continue to give him two or three free singing lessons a week. George agreed to the deal.

"I was working down at the corner of Sunset and Fairfax at the Richfield service station from midnight till eight in the morning," George reflected. "I went to Ben Bard's Dramatic School. Stuart Whitman and Harry Guardino were in class with me, from nine in the morning until three in the afternoon; went to my singing teacher, took care of the garden and took her shopping and did what I had to do till seven at night; went home and then to bed for four hours; got up and went back to work again. I did that for about a year and a half."

George began appearing in films about 1950 when he made his debut in *The Sun Sets at Dawn*. He appeared in minor roles in features until he landed the lead in the 1952 Republic serial *Radar Men from the Moon* which he considers his first real motion picture role. "When I was still going to dramatic school I got a call one day to go out to Republic Studio at ten o'clock in the morning to audition in a new series about Commando Cody in *Radar Men from the Moon*," George recalled. "So I went out there and auditioned for the part of a heavy. The producer and director asked me if I had any film on myself. Well, I had done a couple of shows on *Fireside Theater*, and they said that they would call my agent because they wanted to see it. They said to hang around, and I hung around for lunch and then about three o'clock I was getting damn upset because just to go out and play a part of a heavy in the thing wasn't worth this. Anyway, they called me in about four o'clock and said they saw the film and asked, 'How'd you like to do the lead as Commando Cody?' So I did the twelve chapter serial that used to play every Saturday afternoon in the movie houses. That was really the first thing I did for the movie theater."

Another serial that George worked in was for Sam Katzman in the Columbia serial *The Great Adventures of Captain Kidd* with John Crawford. Crawford played Captain Kidd and George played his sidekick, and the pirates were played by old-time wrestlers like Mr. Moto, Gorgeous George, and Killer Karl Davis. "They put wigs and ear rings on them and made them look like pirates," George laughed.

Reflecting on the dozen or so Westerns that he had appeared in, George said that he worked opposite such stars as Joel McCrea in *Border River* and *Lone Hand*; Rock Hudson in *The Lawless Breed*; Wayne Morris in *Star of Texas*; Kirk Douglas in *The Big Sky* and *Man Without a Star*; Wild Bill Elliott in *Vigilante Terror* and *The Homesteaders*; Randolph Scott in *Man in the Saddle* and *Rage at Dawn*; and Audie Murphy in *Destry*, *Drums Across the River* and later *Six Black Horses*.

Reflecting on working with Howard Hawks in *The Big Sky* with Kirk Douglas and Dewey Martin, George smiled and said, "I played a heavy in that. There was a scene where Kirk Douglas was new in town and I'm in this hardware store sort of hanging around. He walks in, and Howard Hawks said to just walk up to him, look him up and down like 'What are you doing in town?' and then walk away. It is the beginning of a threat. I said okay. There were brooms and pots hanging around; we rehearsed it a couple of times, and just before the take I took off a piece of broom and I started sucking on it. 'Action!' I walked over to Douglas, looked him up and down, turned around and walked away. 'Cut!' Kirk Douglas went over to Howard Hawks; conversation. Howard Hawks called me over and said, 'George, the business with the piece of straw, that's great; leave it in. Only this time after you suck on the straw take about a three count just staring at him and then walk away.' Well, Kirk Douglas had around his neck a piece of leather with a saber tooth hanging on it. 'Action!' I go over, look at Douglas and suck on the straw; he took up the saber tooth and sucked on it while I'm counting my three. He used my business and I just had to walk away," George laughed.

George told us of a humorous event while working in one of his early movies called *Japanese War Bride* with Shirley Yamaguchi and directed by King Vidor. "It was my start in the business and I was full of theatre and the whole baloney at the time," he smiled. The dialogue director came around and asked, "George, do you know your dialogue?" George reflected that he was so full of himself in those days that he answered, "Not only do I know my dialogue, I know the meaning of my dialogue." So the dialogue director passed George's response on to King Vidor. "In that case you need no rehearsal," Vidor told George, "because you're just dancing with Marie Windsor." "No, I don't need no rehearsal," George replied. "Action!" Vidor directed. "I couldn't tell you where I was," George laughed. "I couldn't tell you my name. I knew nothing; I was in outer space, I was frozen. I just didn't know a word. And they just kept right on going. Finally I looked around very sheepishly and said, 'Cut'"

Some of the stars that George mentioned he worked with are Clark Gable (*Soldiers_of Fortune*), Jane Russell (*The French Line*) and William Holden and William Bendix (*Submarine Command*). In talking of the last film he mentioned that a lot of his dialogue was like he had said many times while in the Navy, which came out the way it should be: Navy-sounding. William Bendix, whom George had always admired, walked over to the director, John Farrow, after they had completed the scene and talked a little bit. Farrow then called George over and told him that because of the story line and the way the story was set up he thought it best if this other actor took those lines, that it fit his character. "He took away half of my dialogue," George stated, "convincing the director that it would be better if he said it than my saying it."

George mentioned that last story reminded him of an incident when he was doing a scene that was filmed right after lunch in *The Lawless Breed* which starred Rock Hudson as John Wesley Hardin. George was playing a heavy, and in this scene he was screaming at Hudson, "I'm not afraid of you Hardin!" George commented that he was just screaming and carrying on like mad. Raoul Walsh, the director, said "Wait a minute George, just because you had hot pastrami for lunch, don't let it get the better of you." Well, he kept picking on George and it started getting to him. George was growing angry, and although he was delivering the line to Hudson he was meaning it for Walsh. George delivered the line "I'm not afraid of you" in a low growl instead of the scream. And that's what Walsh wanted, that low inner thing, not screaming and hollering. After they finished the scene, Walsh approached George and said, "Pretty good, ain't you." "I'll never forget that," George told us.

George did a Western called *Strange Lady in Town* with Greer Garson and Dana Andrews, and directed by Mervyn LeRoy. "This was after I had done all the Westerns," George related. "I had a fast action scene where I ride into town and tell the sheriff this and that, and they were so amazed that an actor could make fast mounts and fast dismounts in a feature film, because always doubles did that, that they carried me over for an extra week or two to do something else, but in television you did that eight times a day; it was just another job."

On television, George appeared in such Western series as *Hopalong Cassidy*, *Stories of the Century* (as outlaw Cole Younger), *Wyatt Earp*, *Zane Grey Theater*, *The Virginian*, *Walker, Texas Ranger* and *Gunsmoke*. On the latter series he worked in the pilot and told the producer that this show would never work because Jim Arness was so big and there were only so many big actors in town that he could fight, that if he beat up on a little guy it wasn't going to mean anything and it wouldn't last. "It lasted twenty years," he chuckled.

George told us that Edgar "Buck" Buchanan was a dentist before he became an actor, and that every morning while working together on *Destry* he would bring his little black bag on the set. "When we were in between takes, Buchanan would sit you down and scrape the tar off your teeth and say, with his short stubby cigar sticking in your face, 'I think you need a filling back there,'" George laughed. He went on to tell us that Buchanan and William Boyd did not get along together while making the *Hopalong Cassidy* television series. "As a matter of fact," George told us, "Hoppy wanted me to be his sidekick for a while because he and Buck just didn't make it, and Bill and I just got along great. There was something about the chemistry and he was a sweetheart of a guy, but he would have had to buy out the contract and it didn't work out."

We asked him if he learned to ride horses for his Western roles, and he answered, "My mother used to be a waitress in resort hotels, and in the summertime she worked in a big summer resort on Long Island, and in the winter time she worked in Lakewood, New Jersey at a winter resort. I got a job there as a kid in a riding academy shoveling out manure and currycombing the horses. Finally I got to where I could lead people through the woods on the trails for an hour or two ride. So I learned to ride there, but it was English saddle. When I came out here there was nothing but Westerns, that's about all there was on my end of it because television was starting about that time. A friend of mine called Three Finger Eddy (he used to play the guitar with his three fingers, but he could play the hell out of it) was a friend of Jock Mahoney. Three Finger Eddy, Jock and I used to go out to the riding stables on Riverside Drive on the weekends and exercise the horses. We'd be in the corral and rake up the horse shit about so deep, button up our collars and button up our coats, and learn how to fall. That is where I learned Western riding. In those days when you went in for a part the director would ask, can you ride? and can you fight? If you could then you got the part."

George said that he loved doing the Westerns and had his own fast draw holster that he used. It was made so that when you reached for it and pulled the hammer back on the revolver that the cylinder could turn in the holster so that you could fire it as soon as you had it out. "Yeah, I enjoyed the Westerns. In the old Hoppy's I played the sheriff quite a bit, and when I rode down that street sometimes I thought I should have been born in 1880 because of that man and the elements type of thing.

"In the early days the Westerns were wonderful," George continued. "There was a wonderful director named Tommy Carr that I worked quite a bit with. In the old days they had a budget of sixty thousand dollars; ten thousand a day for a six day week. You shot it, rain or shine, in six days. We'd go out in the morning and the sun would be shining, everything would be great. We'd be shooting on location at Ivarson's Ranch and in the afternoon it would cloud up and start to rain. Tommy Carr would set up so the camera would stay dry and we would keep on shooting. He would say to me, 'Okay George, take the line,' so maybe I'd be sitting there with the guys by a campfire with a hood over us saying, 'when I get to Abilene I'm going to get the best steak,' and then, 'I told you it's going to rain,' and keep right on shooting. And then, so many of the guys in the early days were just learning how to ride, and maybe they'd be the heavies that just robbed the bank. They run out of the bank, mount up, go down the street about half a block and make a hard left turn and get the hell out of town. There would always be one or two guys that would fall off accidentally. Tommy Carr would say, 'Okay George (I played the sheriff), take the rifle and take a couple of shots.' It looked real because it was real," George laughed, "and they wouldn't have to pay anybody for a fall because you see me go boom and you see a guy fall off. They used everything. To me, those were the real Method days, not the Actors Studio; method is using what is there. If it rains, it rains, there's no way you are going to cover it up. Use it."

All told, George appeared in at least twenty five motion pictures before landing a role in the 1955 MGM sci-fi classic, *Forbidden Planet*. "I was the boatswain mate of the rocket ship. Leonard Murphy, who was head of casting, knew when I was in the Navy I was a boatswain mate and when he was reading *Forbidden Planet* he thought about me," George said.

While George was working on *Forbidden Planet*, Murphy came down to the set one day and said, "George, when you were a laborer here a couple of years ago, every time you went by the truck or by the set I would always hear you singing. You sing?" "Yes," George replied, "I sing." Murphy asked him where, and George responded that he had been doing the Jewish benefits for the City of Hope. Richard Rogers was on the studio lot at this time doing *Oklahoma*, and Murphy set up an audition during the lunch hour for George with Rogers. "I auditioned for Dick Rogers and he took me to Broadway in 1955 for my first play called *Pipe Dream*, from a book by John Steinbeck called *Sweet Thursday*," George related.

George worked with David Niven on an episode of *Zane Grey Theater* shortly before leaving for New York. In this episode, George had the townspeople locked up in a bar because they had killed his brother in a bank robbery attempt and he planned on killing them. George told us that "David Niven is supposed to have a big fight with me, and I weighed about a hundred and ninety then. He couldn't get over the fact that he was going to beat me in this fight and kept saying this is ridiculous. He was such a sweet man. I told him that when I finish this I'm going to New York to do my first play, and he said that he was going to England in about two months and if he had time he would drop by and see it. Do you know that he came by way of New York and saw the play. That was the type of a guy he was."

From *Pipe Dream*, George went on to replace John Raitt in *Pajama Game* for six months, when Raitt left to make the movie version. The lead in a musical about the life of Anna Christie titled *New Girl in Town* with Gwen Verdon came next; then another Broadway play appearing opposite Mary Martin in *Jennie*. So, in addition to his motion picture and television work, George has had a very successful career on the New York stage. He also did many commercials in New York to supplement his income, as theatre never paid as well as films. "I was there for about five years, one show to the other," George added.

George came back out to Hollywood about 1959 to appear in Disney's six-part television show set in the Revolutionary War called *The Swamp Fox*. There was an accident during the making of this show and he broke his back. George spent three months in St. Joseph's Hospital, followed by at least a half year wearing a back brace. "I ended up driving a yellow cab out in the valley because I couldn't get a job for a good year and a half," he said. "It was very hard to get going again – It was a good year and a half or two years."

His first offer of work after that came from Disney to play a ranch foreman in *Texas John Slaughter* with Tom Tryon. The first day he reported for work he had a scene at the corral with the horses. They knew this was George's first time back after breaking his back two years before, so they had a three step built for him to get up on the horse. George became very angry inside because of the idea that he was thought to need this aid to mount a horse. The macho thing, he called it. "I kicked the hell out of that three step and got up fine. Came home that night and I had a broken big toe," he laughed.

After *Texas John Slaughter*, work picked back up again, one of the first features being the villain in *Six Black Horses* with Audie Murphy and Dan Duryea. Speaking of this last one, George smiled and said, "I was a mean one in that one; I was so mean I scalped Indians."

George told us a story of how he first met Dan Duryea, his co-star on this last named feature. George had gone on an interview for a show, and when leaving the office he noticed about twenty men standing in a line that led to another upstairs office. "What is this?" George asked. "They're interviewing guys for a part of a sailor in a new series called *China Smith* with Dan Duryea," he was answered. Well, he just stepped in line. When it was his turn to enter the office he was told, "Okay, you're a sailor. You've been all over the world and you collect sea shells. One night some big guy stomps all your sea shells and you choke him to death. Now, what I want you to do is to pick up a sea shell and listen to it." George lifted one to his ear and, after a short pause, said, "That's the Pacific Ocean." Duryea said, "That's the guy." "That's how I first met Duryea," George told us. "Then I did *Six Black Horses* with him. Dan Duryea was a sweetheart of a guy. A wonderful smile and glittering eyes all of the time. Nice man."

In playing the good guys as opposed to playing the villains, George said that he enjoyed the heavies. "You could bring so much to the heavy," he related. "You can bring a limp, you can bring one eye, you can sneer and do a lot of things instead of being the straight leading man. I'm very lucky because in films and TV in the early days I was always the heavy, but on Broadway I was the leading man; now, as time went on in my older years, I become the judges. Last year I had a series at Paramount, which unfortunately didn't go too well, that was called *Sons and Daughters* with Lucie Arnaz and Don Murray. I played Grandpa Hank in that one. We were pre-empted so many times, three times with the Gulf War; once with George Burn's birthday party; another time for the Miss America Pageant; so it just went down the tubes. And then I did a television movie of the week called *The Haunted* with Sally Kirkland for Fox Network." Other television work followed in such shows as *The X-Files* and *Star Trek: The Next Generation*, as well as work in features that included *The Stunt Man* with Peter O'Toole; *Punchline* with Tom Hanks; and *Defending Your Life* with Albert Brooks.

Since George has worked so much in film and on the stage we posed the question as to if he preferred one medium over the other. "It's a tough thing to say," he replied, "because it's a financial thing that gets in the way. Theatre doesn't pay anywhere near what television or film does. A wonderful thing about stage is that you start at the beginning and go through it to the very end, and if you somehow or another don't get it right you say, 'Tomorrow night I'll do it again and try it this way.' Another thing is the great reaction of laughter that echoes up; or the applause, and no matter how good on camera you do a scene all you get is 'Cut! Print!' That's it. I remember many, many years ago I worked for a director and I thought I had done a good scene and when I finished I went to him, and I've never done it since then, and asked, 'Was that all right?' His answer was, 'When it's not I'll let you know.' I love doing both of them.

"I'm lucky I can do the transition from the theatre to film," George continued, "because you can't be as big as you want to on camera." He explained that on stage the actor reaches up to the balcony, but in a close-up on camera you cannot. On camera they take the master shot which is a group of three or four people; then they come in for the close-up. An actor must remember when he is doing the master shot he cannot make broad movements or gestures, because when they come in for the close-up he cannot do that or else he will be out of camera. "So you're restricted to a certain extent," George added, "but I really like both. I just like to do – just to do.

"It gives me a chance to be someone else than George Wallace," he stated. George explained that it is basically no different than a little kid out in the backyard in a cardboard box pretending to be a racecar driver, when his mother says, "Willie, come in!" and he answers, "I can't mom, I can't." "You're somebody else," George disclosed. "And the transition is great. I remember in Dramatic School one time I did a play called *Clash by Night*, and I played the Paul Douglas role. We played for a couple of weeks and during that I became remorseful, I put on weight, I didn't want to see anybody because that's the way I was in the show. I ended up choking this guy to death in a projection booth because he was flirting around with my younger wife. Doing a play, the character stays with you more." George gave an example from the time he played King Arthur in the National Company's production of *Camelot* with Arthur Treacher and Kathryn Grayson. Off stage, when he would go into a restaurant, people would ask him, "What part of England are you from?" because "I became Arthur to a certain extent, speech-wise and mannerisms. I loved doing Arthur," he concluded.

After his tour of *Camelot*, George obtained a role of a policeman in a film at Fox called *Caprice* with Richard Harris before Harris did *Camelot*. "He found out that I had just done a year or two as Arthur and he picked my brains about *Camelot* every second that he could because he was going to do it," George added.

George told us that in the theatre the cast became like a family. In the old days, they had three or four week's rehearsal in New York City, and then they would go to Boston for four or five weeks, followed by another month in Philadelphia. "During that three or four months before opening on Broadway I'd know when you hurt your big toe," George reflected. "I'd know when you got your girl pregnant; I mean you become a family. Really a family. You see everybody every day, they're there when you rehearse, and you realize what you've gone through together to make it what it is, and you meet every day at the theatre – You become a family."

George contrasted this with working in Hollywood, where you go in and do a show and say "We'll be in touch." "Baloney! You leave, that's the end of it," he said. "You get back to your agent and get the next job and you're off on something else. You don't become as close as you do in the theatre. The TV series becomes more like a family, but on the average job, two weeks here and two weeks there, you're gone and..."

George had just recently completed a feature titled *Diggstown* with Lou Gossett, James Woods, Bruce Dern and directed by Michael Ritchie. It's a fight story, in which Wallace played Bruce Dern's southern lawyer. Before starting the film, Ritchie sent the actors two cassettes of talk shows from Atlanta so they would get the authentic southern flavor when they talked. The jail scenes were shot in Colorado, the exterior shots were in old Sacramento, and the interior was in an old theatre in downtown Los Angeles that they converted into a boxing ring. "Lou Gossett's a nice man," George said. "I went to Mexico and did one of those *Gideon Oliver* episodes with him. They put a lot of money into that series but it just didn't go."

George is married to actress Jane A. Johnston. They met in Long Beach doing a play called *Most Happy Fellow*. George was hired to replace a young actor in the role of Joey. Anne Jeffries, the female lead in the show, was described by George as "a beautiful, wonderful lady, but she was just too much woman for this young man, so the director (George Berkeley) called me and asked if I wanted to do the show. So I went down and that's how I met Janie." Later they appeared together in *Company* on Broadway with Jane Russell. They did it for six months on Broadway and then they toured all over with it for the National Company. They also toured with *Kiss Me*

Kate and several others. "We get along so well together," George remarked. "Janie's got a great sense of humor." They were in Honolulu doing *Funny Girl*, which has a dance number where Nicky and Fanny are dancing and he start's singing, "I want to be seen, be seen with you in my arms..." He has the hat and the cane in the scene, and part of the choreography called for George, as he began singing, "I want to be seen with you," to throw Jane the cane, and she would catch it and sing, "With you in my arms," and then throw the cane back to George. "This one night we're doing the show and I threw the cane, and somehow it got hooked up in my fingers and it fell on the floor in front of her," George recalled. "She picked it up and started her song and just threw it back on the floor in front of me," he laughed. "That's the kind of relationship we have on the stage."

When not working in a film, George keeps busy around his Hollywood hills home. We asked what hobbies he enjoys; he answered, "My first hobby is keeping my wife happy." "Working around the house is his hobby," Jane added. "He can fix anything. He does plumbing, electricity, he has saws that cut anything that go in different directions. He's constantly busy; he's never at rest. He doesn't really know what relaxation is." "Yeah," George continued, "and I love to work in the garden, and during the springtime out in the back I grow tomatoes. I have a '64 Buick Riviera that I bought brand new; I gave birth to it and it is in mint condition in the garage, and I tinker around with that and keep it up. But I like to create things."

George considers himself very lucky to be able to continue working in his chosen field so often. He stated it is feast or famine. "You can have a great year and the next you're zilch and for no unknown reason; you just never know," he stated. "No more of a reason then I know why I get half the parts I do anyway. You go out and for two days you don't hear and you think that's it, and then they call and say come out for wardrobe, you got the part. When I go in and there's twelve to fifteen guys there I look at them and think those three guys are really right for the part. It's like when I got the *Matlock*. They're looking for the part of a farmer. Well, I'm not a typical farmer – farmer type as they put it – I go out, there's about fifteen guys with the boots, the Levis, the bib overalls, looking like real farmers. I went in and read for them, and they called the next day and I got the part. Why I got it I'll never know," he confided.

Twenty years ago an actor that was established in the business seldom had to go before a casting director and read for every part, but in today's Hollywood that is no longer true. "I find lately everybody's insecure," George told us. "Would you believe that when you go out for a part now, just in a television show, maybe you just have six or eight lines, that there are eight to ten people that you have to audition for. You sit down and you have to read for the casting person, who sits there and reads with a monotone voice, and you have to give something to the meaning, and you have to please eight or ten of these people. Nobody wants to take the responsibility until the very last second because they're forced to because they're going to start shooting tomorrow morning. And then you get home at nine o'clock and they say 'You got the part.' It's that type of thing. In the old days you would walk in to the director and producer, that's it. This part I'm doing now I didn't have to audition for because I have this seven or eight minute tape of different shows that I have done that you send to the studios for them to look at. They looked at it, called the agent and made the deal. That is the way it was done in the old days; they knew who they wanted and took the responsibility for it."

George mentioned, like so many of the other performers that we have talked with, that most of today's casting directors are girls in their early twenties. He had a strange encounter with one of these on an interview. She asked what has he done and, among others, he mentioned he was in *Strange Lady in Town* with Greer Garson and Dana Andrews. The casting director asked, "Dana Andrews? What series was <u>she</u> in."

Jane continues to perform on stage in Southern California, having appeared in four plays in the 1991-92 season and was leaving in a few weeks to play Vera in *Mame* in San Jose. Jane has also appeared in such features as *Fandango* with Kevin Costner and *Corvette Summer* with Mark Hamill. She says of her film work, "I've not done very much, not like George has. I haven't transferred very well to it, I am very animated. It's almost negative when I go into film work because I have to cut back on everything. But I'm doing a Movie of the Week, a small part but a very interesting role of Farrah Fawcett's mother in *Looking for Harry*. I don't think more than twenty television shows over a long period of time," she laughed.

We asked George how he feels about his career thus far. "I feel great about it. I'm here," he laughed. "I don't want the big mansion on the hill. I just want to do what I enjoy doing, be able to pay the rent, take my wife on a vacation now and then, and be together and that's about it. I never thought of being an actor in the first place, it just all happened. I have said to Janie that I'm thankful now that I am in this business because when you read in the paper about all these big corporations folding, and all the intrigue in the corporations of people almost reaching retirement age and getting fired and if you don't have the weekend with the president you are nowhere in the company; there's none of that in this business. As long as you walk and talk and behave yourself, age makes no difference. You can keep right on going as long as the good Lord's willing. So as long as we can pay the rent and be happy together and keep our health, and we have that, that's what we want."

Since our interview in 1992, George continued working in television (such as *Chicago Hope* and *The Practice*) and motion pictures (such as *Bicentennial Man* and *Forces of Nature*). His final performance in a motion picture was in *Minority Report* with Tom Cruise, and his final television work came in an episode of *Joan of Arcadia*. While on vacation in Pisa, Italy, George had a fall and died July 22, 2005 of complications from this accident after returning home to Los Angeles.

Film Credits: 1950: The Sun Sets at Dawn. **1951:** The Fat Man; Submarine Command; Inside the Walls of Folsom Prison; Up Front; Man in the Saddle. **1952:** The Big Sky; Japanese War Bride; Kansas City Confidential; The Lawless Breed; Back at the Front; Sally and St. Anne; Meet Danny Wilson; Ghost Buster; Million Dollar Mermaid; Yankee Buccaneer; Radar Men from the Moon (serial). **1953:** Arena; The Homesteaders; Star of Texas; Vigilante Terror;

Francis Covers the Big Town; Lone Hand; Great Adventures of Captain Kidd (serial); Pardon My Wrench (short). **1954:** Border River; Destry; Drums across the River; The French Line; The Human Jungle. **1955:** Man Without a Star; The Second Greatest Sex; Soldier of Fortune; Strange Lady in Town; Rage at Dawn. **1956:** Forbidden Planet; Great Day in the Morning; Star in the Dust. **1962:** Six Black Horses. **1966:** Dead Heat on a Merry-Go-Round; Texas across the River. **1967:** Caprice. **1971:** The Skin Game; In Search of America (TV). **1974:** The Swinging Cheerleaders; The Towering Inferno. **1976:** Lifeguard; Return to Earth (TV). **1977:** The Private Files of J. Edgar Hoover; Billy Jack Goes to Washington. **1978:** Deadman's Curve (TV). **1980:** The Stunt Man. **1982:** Things are Tough All Over. **1984:** Protocol. **1985:** A Death in California (TV). **1986:** Native Son, Just Between Friends; Fresno (TV). **1987:** Nutcracker: Money, Madness and Murder (TV). **1988:** Punchline; Hot to Trot; Prison; Terrorist on Trial: the United States vs. Salim Ajami (TV). **1990:** Postcards from the Edge; People Like Us (TV); Working Trash (TV). **1991:** Defending Your Life; The Haunted (TV); The Boys (TV). **1992:** Child of Rage (TV); Diggstown. **1993:** Miracle Child (TV). **1994:** My Girl II; Schemes; Almost Dead. **1996:** Seduced by Madness (TV); Multiplicity. **1997:** Meet Wally Sparks. **1999:** Forces of Nature; Deal of a Lifetime; Bicentennial Man. **2000:** Nurse Betty. **2002:** Minority Report.

DAVID WARNER

David Warner was born July 29, 1941, in Manchester, England. "When I was a kid, without going into any details, it was really rough. I was moving about, went to seven different schools, and I didn't have much of an education. I was insecure because of various domestic problems. I was isolated and didn't have a lot of friends because I didn't stay in one place long enough. I had no interest in theatre or acting until I realized at school that I wasn't really very good at anything," David recalled. "I wasn't an athlete, I wasn't an intellect, and so it was really the school play that got me interested in theatre or acting. I left school without any kind of exams at sixteen or seventeen years old and sold newspapers and books in a bookshop. I didn't want to go home much because of the various domestic problems, so I needed a hobby, or just hang out on street corners. My hobby was joining a local amateur theatre group, painting scenery, doing stuff for stage management, and I got a few tiny parts with them. Then I tried for the Royal Academy of Dramatic Arts while I was still selling newspapers. Quite to everybody's surprise I managed to get into the drama school, and it was great to get away from home. So acting was really basically a hobby. Again, I played just small parts and didn't distinguish myself particularly playing fantastic roles. Then gradually I sort of graduated, I suppose the word is, and got small parts, extra work, stuff like that."

There were a couple of actor's performances that first impressed David with the idea that acting might be an interesting field to examine. "When I was a kid I went to see, in one day, *Great Expectations* and *Oliver Twist* with Alec Guinness. The reason being I couldn't believe that in *Great Expectations* there was this young guy, and an hour later I saw in *Oliver Twist* this old guy, and they were made in two or three years of each other. I thought this is very

interesting. So seeing Guinness was really the spark that sparked me into thinking about it as a hobby, which was basically what it was before I went to the Royal Academy Theatre. And on stage I saw Paul Scofield in *Ring Around the Moon* and thought there was something interesting there. So it was the combination. And I worked with Scofield once on stage in *The Inspector General*."

David was working in a small role in a stage production of *A Midsummer Night's Dream* at the Royal Court Theatre. "Tony Richardson was directing that play and it just came about that I was asked to read for *Tom Jones* too, and I got the part," David stated. "That's because I knew, and was working with, Richardson. So that's how I got the part in that. It won the Oscar for best picture, and *Titanic* won thirty-five years later, so every thirty-five years I'm in the best picture," David laughed. "*Tom Jones* was the first speaking part I ever had."

The Royal Shakespeare Company had an experimental theatre, not at Stratford-on-Avon where the main base was, but at a very small theatre. "I had seven lines. Somebody saw me do this part and invited me to audition for leading roles at Stratford-on-Avon. The desire to be a movie star or anything like that was never an issue back then. All you did in England was radio and stage."

After performing with the Royal Shakespeare Company for two years, David was asked if he would like to play Hamlet. "I thought it was a joke," David noted. "I said, 'No, no, no. He's got to be good looking.' 'No,' I was told. 'I want you to play it.' The hardest thing for me was learning the lines and understanding it because I was not a scholar, even though I had been doing Shakespeare, and I'm still not. I was twenty-four when I played Hamlet, which nowadays is old, but then it was quite a thing to be that young to play that role because I had the responsibility. Guinness was the same age when he played it. It was just a fantastic opportunity. It was amazing to be asked to play that part at such a prestigious theatre. That was wonderful. I did it for two years, not every night, but over a period of two years."

During this time David was also asked to star in the black and white cult classic, *Morgan*. "During that time, after *Morgan* came out, there were offers from Hollywood to come and do various things, but I was committed to doing theatre. A lot of people say to me, 'After *Morgan* what happened to you? We look at your resume and you didn't do anything.' Well, I was doing theatre."

Another early film for David was *The Fixer* for director John Frankenheimer. "Again, Frankenheimer just called and asked if I would do it. It was with Dirk Bogarde, Alan Bates, and Ian Holm. Ian and I had done a lot of theatre together because he was at Stratford too. He had been at Stratford since I was at school playing small parts. He played Richard III while I was there; he's a wonderful actor. I was on *The Fixer* for two weeks and only had two scenes in it, but it was great to be a part of that."

A few years later David was invited to come to Hollywood by Sam Peckinpah to co-star with Jason Robards in *The Ballad of Cable Hogue*. "He had seen *Morgan*," David informed. "That was my first trip to the States, and then I went back to England and carried on doing stuff there." One of his films was *The Omen* with Gregory Peck. Although it was based in England and shot there, as well as in Italy and Israel, it was an American film. "It was a successful movie, and as a result of that you get on the list and then you get invited over." David came to Hollywood for a film called *Nightwing*, and then *Time After Time* came shortly after that, followed by *The Man with Two Brains*, with Steve Martin. "So rather than looking for work, I was actually asked to come over," David added.

David reflected on *The Omen* and *Time After Time*:

The Omen: "Working with Gregory Peck was just wonderful," David noted. Speaking of the graveyard scene where he and Peck are attacked by vicious dogs, he said, "They were so well trained and docile that we actually had to put meat underneath our raincoats and in our pockets so that they would attack us. They really didn't want to go for us. We had to hold their necks towards us while pretending to push them away because they weren't dangerous at all."

Time After Time: "It was great working with Malcolm McDowell again. He had been at Stratford-on-Avon when I was playing Hamlet and he had a smaller role. So it was really nice. By then he had done *Clockwork Orange* and all those others, so he was a big star. I wasn't a star, I was a character actor; there's nothing wrong with that. It was great to meet up with Malcolm again and to work side by side with him, and also to work with the director, Nicholas Meyer, who was really a very clever and intelligent man. It was great to be working on a very interesting movie too, which is kind of a cult film now."

David worked three times for director Sam Peckinpah, in *Ballad of Cable Hogue*, *Strawdogs*, and *Cross of Iron*. "Peckinpah has a reputation, and I'm sure you read about him. He asked me to work with him three times and I chose to work with him three times, so he was very loyal. Whatever stories you hear, and I won't go into them now, I would have always worked with Sam. He was difficult and he was strange and weird, but he was somebody that I felt was on my side. He was very supportive of me. I mean, even if somebody didn't want me in one of those movies, he fought for me, and that's a sign of friendship."

David spoke of an experience that happened while filming a scene in *Ballad of Cable Hogue*. In the movie, David's character was supposed to be afraid of the rattlesnakes that he had gathered for food out in the desert. "I had a bag full of rattlesnakes and they kept falling out of the bottom of the bag, then I have to run away because I was afraid of them. But in order to do the scene, I actually had to hold in between each finger, by the tail, these rattlesnakes because I had to let them go one by one so they'd fall out through the bottom of the bag. Everybody was so scared, and I had no fear of them. Because of living in England I really didn't know anything about the danger of rattlesnakes. I had to hold about ten of those things as they were winding themselves around me."

David played as the Frankenstein monster in a 1984 made-for-television movie. "The makeup was a three hour job," David recalled. "It was just great having the opportunity of doing that character, and meeting John Gielgud again. We had made another film together called *Providence*, which was directed by Alain Resnais, the French director, and written by the man who wrote *Morgan*. What was extraordinary about that film, from a screenwriter's point of view, was that David Mercer was asked to write it for a group of actors. Normally you'd write a script and then they'd cast a star, but this director said to David, 'We have the money. Write it for Dirk Bogarde, John Gielgud, Ellen Burstyn, David Warner, and Elaine Stritch. Will you write this film for these people?' Scriptwriters don't get that opportunity unless it's for Tom Cruise or somebody like that, but to write for a whole group of actors is very unusual."

David enjoyed working in the classics, two of his films being based on plays by Anton Chekhov. "To have the opportunity of doing *The Sea Gull* and *Uncle Vanya* was wonderful. Konstantin and Vanya weren't heavy characters, and they were wonderful characters to play: And Ibsen's *The Doll House* with Jane Fonda, was really great, but it wasn't successful. It's not always successful to try and translate the works of people like Chekhov, Shakespeare and Ibsen to the screen. It's not always easy, but it's great to have the opportunity."

David worked in several of the *Star Trek* movies. "I didn't really know anything about *Star Trek*, and suddenly I got a call," David informed. "I think Nicholas Meyer had something to do with it. William Shatner directed *Star Trek V*. The role in itself wasn't very big, but it was fun to be a part of. Nicholas Meyer directed *Star Trek 6*, and I had a bigger part in that. I played a human being, I played a Klingon, and I played a Cardassian in one of the television episodes of *Star Trek: Next Generation* with Patrick Stewart. So I played all sorts of races and aliens. The Klingon makeup took three or four hours to put on in the morning—and that was four o'clock in the morning—but I knew that beforehand."

One of the more recent films that David worked on was the Academy Award winning *Titanic*. "That was more of a technical movie, and I don't mean that to put it down, but so much was dependent on mechanics, weather, and things that could go wrong that it was just a relief to get a scene done. Nobody knew that it was going to be the big monster that it was at the box office, because all we would hear was how expensive it was. On a daily basis, the *Variety* or the *Hollywood Reporter* would have a daily *Titanic* budget watch, saying it's gone up another five million. So we were making this movie and could see people getting nervous about how much it was costing, so when it became the biggest movie ever it was a very pleasant surprise. Because of the technical things, it was a relief to get scenes finished and completed."

David has worked in a few Westerns during his career. Reflecting on this genre, David stated, "It was great for somebody who hadn't anything to do with the west to be suddenly asked to be involved in stuff like that. *The Blue Hotel* was one of the first two or three American short stories that PBS did, and it was lovely playing in that."

In addition to his motion picture roles, David has also employed his voice for animated features and radio. "I had great fun narrating the *Winnie the Pooh* videos for the kids—that was very nice. A gentle story-telling narration for Disney. I also do radio here in town—I've done Shakespeare, Shaw, and Oscar Wilde, which is great because you don't have to shave," David laughed.

Having worked on stage and in film, we asked David if he had a preference of one over the other. "I haven't done stage for a long time," David responded. "I'd like to do stage in a small setting. It would be great to go to Broadway or something, but that's not a dream. I've been in the West End of London; I've been in one of the best companies of the world in the Sixties. I'd like to do theatre, but it would have to be the right part. I stayed in Hollywood basically because I married. My wife is American, so it's just the way life works."

In Hollywood, many actors are typecast into a certain kind of role. David has played his share of villain roles during the course of his career, but is quick to point out that he has also played sympathetic parts as well. "I've been playing villains, but I can do other things. People don't see or remember that. People that know movies think of *Time After Time* or some of the heavier stuff I've done rather than knowing the whole body of work, which really is that I have done more less villainous roles than villainous roles. Films like *Tron*, where I played kind of a villain, so I was sort of seen as a heavy. A couple of television mini-series that I did, *The Holocaust* and *Masada*, playing the heavy there again. So you get clipped into that and you fight desperately to try and make people see you do something else. I enjoyed working, I've always enjoyed working, but I always hoped that one day somebody will see me in other roles. You don't bite the hand that feeds you, I mean you accept whatever is there. In *Titanic* I was a villain, that's just the way it is. And in *Time Bandits* I was a comedy villain. But I was in *A Christmas Carol* with George C. Scott, in which I played Bob Cratchit, who is a very sympathetic character. And it was interesting to be a part of *Wild Palms*. I wasn't a heavy in that one either, which was great. So it's nice when mini-series people remember those."

David has worked in various locations around the world. One of his favorites was on a film that was shot in Sardinia, Italy. "It was on a film you have never heard of and nobody ever will, but that was wonderful," David noted. "I went to the Caribbean to do a movie called *The Island*. The whole idea was that it was an island in decay, and so it was really quite unpleasant filming there. Unfortunately we had to shoot a lot of it at night and on really rather unpleasant parts of the island. But it was nice to be in the Caribbean. I had the good fortune of filming in Israel on a couple of occasions; Italy; Sri Lanka was very beautiful; and Africa. That's one of the bonuses."

Looking over his numerous acting roles on film, David was asked if he had a favorite among them. "I'm very self-critical," he answered. "I hardly ever look at anything that I've done. So it's really the memories of the people. I loved working on *The Sea Gull*. That was a wonderful experience. I don't know if the film was any good, but I loved working on that. While we were making *The Ballad of Cable Hogue*, the locations were kind of remote for me. I couldn't drive and was stuck in a hotel and had lots of days off. It was quite difficult, but when you look back you forget all about the difficult stuff because it was such a memory. Again, I don't like looking at my work, so it's hard to say, 'Oh, that's the best,' because I'm always looking for all the things that I could have done better.

"The thing that I remember most of all is the number of wonderful people I had the opportunity to work with. To work with people like Gregory Peck, Jason Robards, Simone Signoret (who was in *The Sea Gull*), James Mason (who was also in *The Sea Gull* and *The Cross of Iron*), and Trevor Howard (who was in *The Doll's House*). All these kind of wonderful solid names."

David worked on a number of television mini-series, made-for-television movies, as well as some episodic television. Contrasting the series with the movies, David said, "*Perry Mason* was a formula. You come in and it's *Perry Mason*. *Wild Palms* was a whole thing where you didn't know what it was going to be. It's what I first heard James Mason call a jobbing actor. It's a job: you get offered a *Perry Mason* script and you do it because you like working. It's like being a workaholic sometimes; you just have to work. *Perry Mason* is *Perry Mason*. *Wild Palms* is a whole new script and a whole new thing, and it was also a lot of visual effects. It wasn't successful I don't think, but it was a fascinating piece to do."

David spoke candidly about different elements of the motion picture business pertaining to what an actor might face in the various aspects of his profession. "I don't know how to talk about acting. I couldn't be an acting teacher because I don't really know what it's about. I'm an instinctive actor, not an intellectual actor. It's just stuff that happens without me being able to write or talk about it. When you play a villain do you dredge up some terrible...no, it's written on the paper, and that's basically it for me. I do talk a lot to a director if I have a responsible role to play and I usually try to explain what I'm doing rather than asking him how to do it. I tend to do kind of a natural thing. Whatever works for whatever actor, as long as it doesn't harm another actor.

In talking about auditions, David said, "When I met James Cameron (director of *Titanic*) I didn't audition for him, because he knew everything I'd done. He knew I had done another Titanic film (a mini-series) years ago. He knew all my work. He offered me the role. What happens now is you have to audition for a first-time director who doesn't really know who you are – that's fine. Except you would hope that people who love film would know a little bit about things before *Jurassic Park*. It's tough if you haven't been used to the audition technique. It's tough to go in there and convince people. If I was going to be a director, I would do some research and find out about the people who are going to be in front of the camera. So that's the irony. An experienced director like Cameron knows who you are. You have to audition for somebody who doesn't really quite know what he wants, so he wants the character to walk in through the door. Now, Alec Guinness, who was a great actor, would never have been able to walk in, I don't think–unless he really wanted the role so badly–as the character. He would just have said, 'Look, this is me, and my work is thirty-five years of movies. Now you want me or don't want me. It's not an ego thing. I'm an actor, but I can't necessarily do it in this room for you.' I love meeting directors, but as I said, it's the directors who have never worked who insist on auditioning you, and you always feel that they're never quite sure what they want.

Any movies that you have ever seen me in, I think I can safely say, except for *Morgan*, where I did a screen test, I never auditioned for. I was offered the part."

With so many of today's movies relying on special effects, we asked David if he thought there was a danger of it getting in the way of the characters. "There are scripts out there and films being made that don't rely on special effects," David stated, "but I think the emphasis is on special effects. People want that thrill. I've done so many special effects movies, but I think that there is a danger of the special effects, the visual effects, and computer animation swamping character, so you have to do movies that don't have any of those things. I mean, it would be great one day to be able to make a picture about character with those things as well, but that needs somebody who is very sensitive to the human condition and also to the technical condition."

In contrasting the moviemakers of earlier years with many of today's, David stated, "It's quite simple. Take *Morgan* for example, which wasn't a big box-office, but has been well remembered by a lot of people. You have the director, the writer, and the producer. The money's coming from somewhere, but you assume that the people who are giving the money to these people trust them. Trust their judgment, trust their talent, and trust their taste. 'We'll give you the money; we trust you.' Therefore they can come and ask me to screen test and cast me without the money men saying 'absolutely not.' I'm sure that they did it in certain instances, but there was more power to the creative side before. Nowadays I don't think that's true unless it's someone who is really in control, like James Cameron. I think you've got to go through a committee of a hundred to approve a casting decision or a writing decision or whatever. Then, the people who hired the creative people trusted them, and that's something that's different now."

Once upon a time in the world of motion pictures there was time taken to rehearse the scenes and to stay with the written word of the screenwriter. Today, on many occasions, maybe due to budgetary concerns or whatever, rehearsals are not as complete as they were in the A-films of former days. Also, there are certain actors who choose to ad-lib the scenes instead of staying with the script. We asked David what he thought of this. He told us, "In *Morgan* we rehearsed, rehearsed and rehearsed. That was a very dialogue-driven piece. But, in the main, now most films are action oriented so you don't have a lot of rehearsals." As far as if there is much ad-libbing in the movies, David responded, "No. Even if the script is really bad you have to say it word perfect. You can't change a word. There is, I'm sure, in some, but I'm not a very good improviser, I really have to have it written down." When we mentioned someone like Red Skelton as having a reputation as a notorious ad-libber, David said, "Well, he was doing comedy to get the laughs. But if it is a well-written script or a well-written play, that's why it's made—because it's a well-written play. You don't have to alter it because somebody has been sitting there for a year. Now, if you have an actor on television, and somebody's been sitting there for a week, or it might be overnight, it's a whole different thing, and they have a tough job. There were the days when Frankenheimer and Penn were doing the live plays on TV. Those were crafted plays that were being done and they had time to rehearse. Now there's no time for that because it all has to go fast, there's commercials, sponsors, and all that, but that's the system under which we live. And again, you can't bite the hand that feeds you."

There are well-known legends amongst the motion picture directors such as John Ford, William Wyler, Henry Hathaway, William Wellman, and Raoul Walsh who were very exact in their task of directing a picture. We asked David what the role of today's directors is. "In episodic television or in movies?" he asked. "They're different at times. On a series, the directors are hired to be in control of the whole thing because of the format, the stars, and just the way it's all done. So from what I can see it is quite difficult for directors to have too much control of anything because they're not in control. Because, as I say, the directors like Cameron, Spielberg, Lucas, and Zemeckis, those guys are in control. It's their business. So I think there are some directors that create the thing, and there are some that are just hired to be there as a controller, but I would never know the difference, except the director who is in control can hire you, and the director who isn't in control can't. That's basically what my experience has been. I know a lot of writers, directors and producers who say there's a wonderful role for you in this picture but unfortunately your name's not big enough and what have you done lately? And that's the way the business has always been."

In looking over his career thus far, David summed up his feelings by saying, "It's been a very fortunate career, because I'm one of over eighty thousand members of the Screen Actors Guild and I've been working constantly. As you get older there are less opportunities in certain things, but to still be in the game, I mean that's basically all I can ask for. I didn't set out to try to be a big star, but just to be a working actor, 'a jobbing actor' as James Mason said, is basically all you can ask for. This has been the way I've been able to earn my living and I just want it to continue that way. It's not a question of ambitions; it's just staying in there and being a part of the game if possible. It's not easy, but you do your best."

Since our interview, David has returned to England where he continues to perform as an actor in films as well as such television series as *Conviction, Sensitive Skin, Wild at Heart, Doctor Who: Dreamland,* and *Wallander.*

Film Credits: 1963: Tom Jones. **1966**: Morgan; War of the Roses (TV). **1967**: Work is a Four Letter Word; The Deadly Affair. **1968**: The Sea Gull; A Midsummer Night's Dream; The Fixer; The Bofors Gun. **1969**: Michael Kohlhaas. **1970**: Perfect Friday; The Ballad of Cable Hogue. **1971**: Straw Dogs. **1973**: From Beyond the Grave; A Doll's House. **1974**: Little Malcolm. **1975**: Mr. Quilp. **1976**: The Omen; Victory at Entebbe; Summer Rain. **1977**: The Blue Hotel (TV); The Age of Innocence; Cross of Iron; Providence. **1978**: Silver Bears; The Thirty-Nine Steps; Clouds of Glory (TV); Holocaust (TV). **1979**: Nightwing; The Concorde - Airport '79; S.O.S. Titanic (TV); Time After Time. **1980**: The Island. **1981**: The Disappearance; Time Bandits; The French Lieutenant's Woman; Masada. **1982**: Marco Polo (TV); Tron; The First Time. **1983**: The Man with Two Brains. **1984**: Frankenstein (TV); A Christmas Carol

(TV); Charlie (TV); Nancy Astor (TV); The Company of Wolves. **1985**: Love's Labour's Lost (TV); Hitler's S.S. (TV). **1987**: Hansel and Gretel (TV); Desperado (TV). **1988**: Waxwork; Spies, Inc; Hostile Takeover; My Best Friend is a Vampire; Mr. North; Hanna's War. **1989**: Magdalene; Grave Secrets; Star Trek V-The Final Frontier. **1990**: Tripwire; Mortal Passions; Perry Mason-The Case of the Poisoned Pen (TV); Secret Life of Ian Fleming (TV). **1991**: Drive; Blue Tornado; Uncle Vanya (TV); Teenage Mutant Ninja Turtles II; Cast a Deadly Spell (TV); Star Trek VI-The Undiscovered Country. **1992**: Oeil qui ment L; The House on Sycamore Street (TV). **1993**: The Lost World; The Unnamable II-The Statement of Randolph Carter; Taking Liberty; Quest of the Delta Knights; Piccolo grande amore; Body Bags (TV); Perry Mason-The Case of the Skin-Deep Scandal (TV); Wild Palms (TV). **1994**: Return to the Lost World; Tryst. **1994**: Necronomicon; Loving Deadly; Inner Sanctum II. **1995**: Zoya (TV); Naked Souls; In the Mouth of Madness; Ice Cream Man; Final Equinox; Signs and Wonders (TV). **1996**: Felony; Rasputin (TV); Beastmaster III (TV); Seven Serpents; The Leading Man. **1997**: Pooh's Grand Adventure-The Search for Christopher Robin (voice) (TV); Money Talks; Titanic; Scream 2. **1998**: The Little Unicorn; Houdini (TV); The Last Leprechaun. **1999**: Shergar; Winnie the Pooh-A Valentine for You (voice) (TV); Wing Commander. **2000**: Cinderella (TV); In the Beginning (TV). **2001**: The Code Conspiracy; Planet of the Apes; Hornblower (TV); Back to the Secret Garden; Superstition. **2002**: The Investigation; Dr. Jekyll and Mr. Hyde (TV). **2003**: Kiss of Life; Hearts of Gold (TV). **2004**: Cortex; Ladies in Lavender; Avatar (aka Matrix Hunter); What Mrs. McGillicuddy Saw (TV). **2005**: Straight into Darkness; The League of Gentlemen's Apocalypse; Sweeney Todd (TV). **2006**: The Battle of Rome (TV); Hogfather (TV); Perfect Parents (TV); Mr. Loveday's Little Outing (TV). **2008**: In Love with Barbara (TV). **2009**: Albert's Memorial (TV). **2010**: Black Death. **2011**: A Thousand Kisses Deep. **2012**: Shakespeare's Daughter.

PEGGY WEBBER

Peggy Webber was born September 15, 1925, in Laredo, Texas. She was a member of a dancing school when she was selected at the age of two and a half years old to perform during the intermission in a silent movie theater. "From then on I was constantly put into various things, and also modeled," she related. "I did a number of radio shows and started producing and directing my own programs when I was eleven, at WOAI in San Antonio, Texas, and also did stage productions as well. Then we moved to Tucson, Arizona when I was thirteen and I created my own dramatic radio show on KVOA, which was sponsored by the Tucson Light and Power Company. I also did announcing at the station while I was going to high school." When Peggy was sixteen, two events happened in her life. "My father died and I graduated from high school, at which time I came to Hollywood with my mother and went to USC."

Peggy began making the rounds seeking employment and before long she was working on network radio. "I think the very first show I did was for *Main Line* for Ted Wick, Selznick's promo-producer, then *Sherlock Holmes* with Basil Rathbone and Nigel Bruce," she reflected. "My very first big break in radio was on an NBC series, *Dreft Star Playhouse*, as Ilsa in *Casablanca* right after Ingrid Bergman had done the film." She won the part over forty of the most respected actresses in radio. "I was about eighteen and did it for thirty episodes, five days a week on NBC." Peggy then obtained work for Selznick doing Bergman's voice for promos, etc., thanks to Ted Wick.

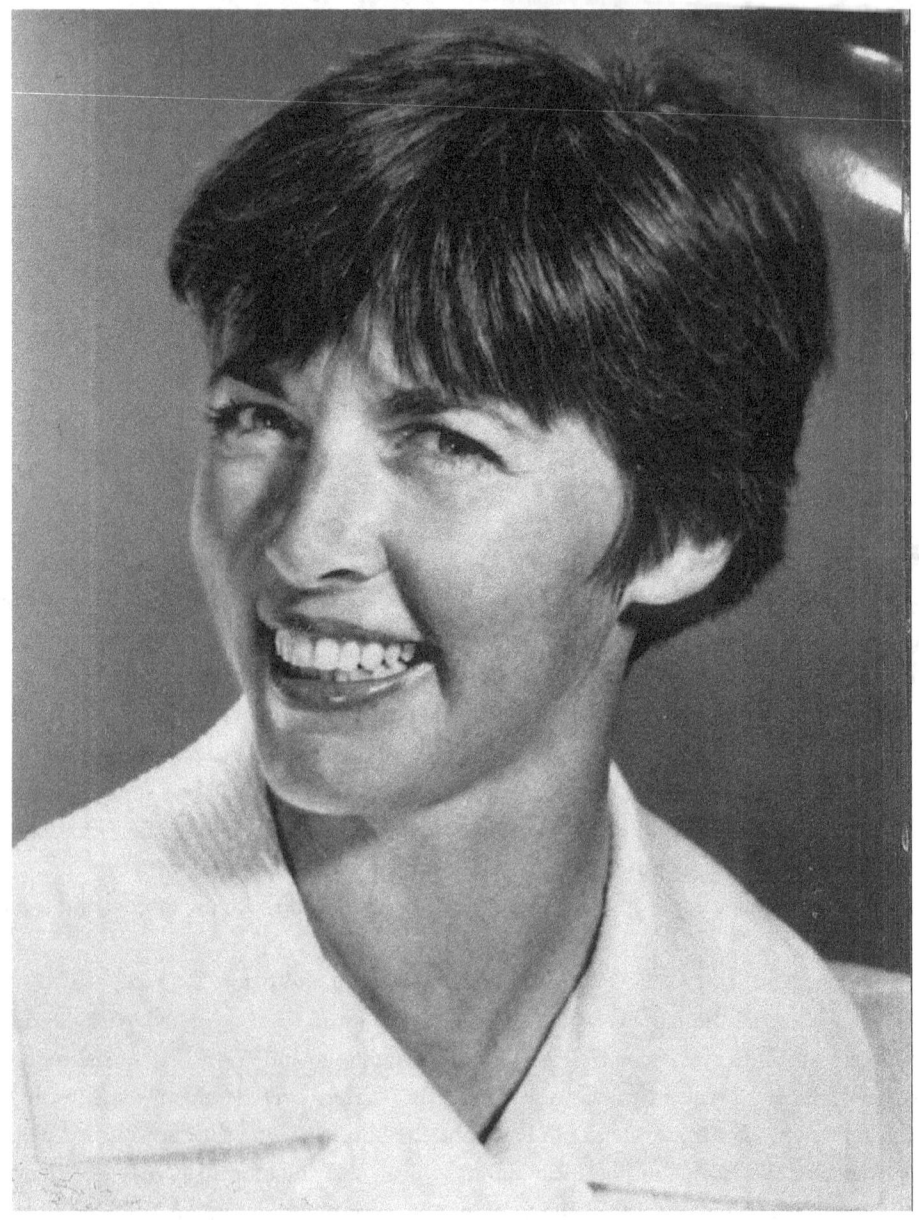

Peggy did hundreds of Carlton E. Morse's radio shows, such as *One Man's Family*, *I Love Adventure*, *The Upper Room*, a running part in *Woman in My House* as the counterpart to Claudia, who was the regular female romantic lead in *One Man's Family*. "There were many series that Morse wrote at that time, and I was in almost all of them. Then I was with William Spier on *Sam Spade* and *Suspense*, and for three years I was Herbert Marshall's leading lady on *The Man Called X*. I was doing twenty-one shows a week during this time. I had three soap operas and the evening shows."

Time Magazine followed Peggy for a week and wrote a feature story with pictures on her. "My experience with *Time* Magazine was also very special," Peggy noted. "It was not customary to have their reporters follow any other actresses at that time, in radio or films, for a full week, watching every performance in twenty-one shows." *Time*'s summation: "She picks up accents as quickly as Arthur Templeton picks up a tune." It created a whole career for me in network radio," Peggy added. "I was eighty-five times on *This Is Your FBI*, and I was on *Dragnet* from its inception. I played Joe Friday's mother, but I also played many other parts. Jack Webb used me more than any other female until I left to go to Japan, which I did in latter 1951." Peggy returned to Hollywood four months later in time to appear in the third episode of the *Dragnet* television series, and continued on the radio show as well until February, at which time she returned to Japan for two years.

Peggy married, in Japan, to an American doctor who worked with the Atomic Bomb Casualty Commission. "He wanted to stay there, so we lived in Hiroshima and Nagasaki," Peggy remarked. "While there, I was the entertainment person for the British and Australian Officers Club, where I did shows. I also presented children's programs, but I was there primarily because I was newly married. After a year and a half my first child was born. Then we came back to America and I did about thirty-one leads on television. After doing these shows I went with my doctor husband to Duke University while he finished his residency, and had another child there. I then came back in the middle of 1954 and began to work network TV programs."

Peggy mentioned that before she was married she created a series on television which was probably the earliest dramatic series from the West Coast. "This was an experiment in television in the early days and we did twenty shows. I wrote and directed it and often played the leads. It was called *Treasures of Literature*, and was like an early *Masterpiece Theatre* where we did all of the classics such as *The Doll's House*, *Wuthering Heights*, and *Oliver Twist*. I cast mostly radio people, but some film stars. TV was new and we were novices at what we were doing, but ambitious. I had three cameras and usually five or six sets, and I worked with the set designer, Serge Krizman, on this, and I did all of the costuming. I used to go down to Western Costume. They made a deal with me that I could pick out anything I wanted and they would charge us ten dollars an outfit. So in many of the shows I had Scarlet O'Hara's entire wardrobe from *Gone with the Wind*, a very effective costuming for very little money. In one of these shows Lou Krugman, a dear friend, was shot, and the camera sees him die. He drops to the floor and we dissolve on the dead body. Then we pick up the next scene on the next set. Well,

Lou opened the door to go out to the dressing room, but instead he walked into the next set, and said, 'Thank God that's over.' He thought he was in the dressing room, but the cameras were right on him for the next shot," Peggy laughed. She won an award from the new *Academy of TV Arts and Science* for most popular program in January 1949, which was presented on air to Peggy in person by the President of the Academy, Charles B. Brown.

Among Peggy's three hundred television shows are *Cavalcade of America, Dragnet, Mr. District Attorney, Kings' Row, Climax, The Millionaire, M Squad, Cheyenne, Medic, Wanted Dead or Alive, The Rebel, Big Town, Law of the Plainsman, Matinee Theatre, I Spy* (which performance she was very proud of), *Whirlybirds, Jane Wyman Presents, Gunsmoke, Wagon Train, Ford Theater, Trackdown* (in the role of Robert Culp's sister in two episodes), and her latest was in an episode of *The Inside*.

The television show that Peggy received the most attention for was an early episode of *Dragnet*. "This episode (which was the second episode Jack Webb filmed, but the third aired) was the first time on television that a show was done totally on close-up on the leading character," Peggy remarked. "It was Jack Webb's idea. He thought since the screen was so small on most people's sets that it was a smart idea to just focus in on the face. I was playing a young Spanish woman who had lost her baby in childbirth and had stolen another baby from the nursery and taken it home where they were having a party for its christening, and they arrested her during the festivities. So it is a very moving piece. We had done it on the air as a radio piece before I went to Japan, and after I came back Jack told me he wanted me to do it on television. So when that came out, every studio in town called for me. The cameraman was Ed Colman (who was nominated for the Academy Award for *Mary Poppins* and *The Absent Minded Professor*). He did a beautiful job, and Jack did a very sensitive job of direction. Jim Moser was the writer, and everything he wrote for *Dragnet* was classic, with many layers of thought and sensitivity. I don't think he ever got the proper acknowledgment for his ability. Jack and Jim split up about the time *Dragnet* became a huge success. After that, Jim went on to write *The Doctor* for radio, which I worked on, and I talked him into making it a TV series, which was titled *Medic*. I did maybe twenty-five of the *Dragnet* television shows over the years."

Peggy also worked on the *Medic* television series and knew Richard Boone very well. "I helped Dick establish his workshop," Peggy stated. "In fact, I met him on *Dragnet*. He was a very great talent, but he had never done a radio show and had only become a professional actor about a year before. I was sort of a regular on the show and he kept watching me. One day he came over and asked, 'Did you study with Strasberg?' I said, 'No.' 'Didn't you go to the Neighborhood Playhouse? You remind me very much of Lee Grant the way you work, and I don't know how you could have developed this technique unless you went there.' I said that I had started so young that I developed my own technique. We dated and went out to dinner a number of times and each time he told me a little more of the story of his background, which was very colorful and which prepared him to be a good actor. It was very simple to help him understand what we were doing in radio. He was applying all of his techniques that he had learned from the Neighborhood Playhouse (with Lee Strasberg and Elia Kazan) and teacher Sandy Meisner. He was applying sense memory. He would touch cloth and wood and different things to give him sense memory, and he would apply that to radio, which worked for him. Anyway, we did some radio shows together, and when Jim Moser and Jack Webb put together *The Doctor* for radio, we did the first episode of an hour-long show. Dick wore a rubber glove that would squawk while he was doing surgery because it helped him feel like he was cutting and getting into the intestinal track. His technique, and the technique of Marlon Brando and all of the actors coming out from the east at that time, was very sense oriented. And Jack Webb, who had come out of a different era, wanted the truth and perfect sound. So it all kind of meshed and was the right thing at the right time for Boone. And I've always felt that Jack was the right time for me. He did great things for me. He gave me a wide array of parts to play and allowed me to do more than he allowed a lot of other people. He'd step on people and say, 'Read the script' or 'Keep your eyes this way.' Every once in a while he'd cut loose and let me do whatever I wanted to do. I also worked with Richard Boone on *Wuthering Heights*, on *Matinee Theatre*. He played Heathcliff and I was Cathy. And on stage I worked opposite him in *Man with the Golden Arm*."

Peggy worked in many Westerns and had to learn to ride a horse for those. "There are a lot of funny stories about that," she smiled. One was for a lead in an episode of *Frontier* called *Mother of the Brave*. It was a story about a woman whose husband was killed by Indians and her two sons were stolen, and for the rest of the story she's hunting for her two sons. "After we finished the filming, Worthington Miner, who was one of the producers, came out from the east and wanted to do some pickups and close-ups on some scenes, and one of the pick-ups was to put me bareback on an Indian horse at the top of a hill. When they hit the clapboard down below, that controlled the horse. It paid no attention to me whatsoever; he was only interested in the trainer. Well, somehow a hornet's nest was activated there at the top of the hill and these hornets begin swirling around the horse's head. I had nothing to hang onto, and every time the clapboard would go this horse would try to get rid of all the hornets. It would rear up and then go down the hill lickety-split with the hornets chasing after us. And this went on for I don't know how many takes because of this, and I thought I was going to die. Every time we went back the hornets were all over," she laughed.

A short distance away they were filming a different episode of *Frontier*, and one of the actors, Sean McClory, saw Peggy going through all of those routines. "At one point they had me off the horse, marching across the top of the hill, and coming on down," Peggy commented. "I was getting ready for the close-ups by doing the emotional preparation because it had been about a month since we shot the rest of it. I thought I needed to get back into that person who was absolutely heartbroken and worn out, but Sean came over to me and said, 'Don't you realize you're about a half an inch tall on the screen? Don't you know that they don't care how you're acting? Here you are acting your heart out coming down the hill and you look like a flyspeck on the screen." That was in 1955, long before Sean and I ever got together, and I must say that he wasn't my favorite person after that," she laughed. "But I had to do close-ups shortly thereafter and I thought that was the only way I could get emotional and tearstained."

The man that inspired Peggy when she was very young was Orson Welles, and the time came for her to realize a dream of working with him. "He was always my idol," she reflected. "I just adored Orson Welles from about the time I was eleven, which inspired me to do the radio work in San Antonio. I heard him in 1937 doing his show from CBS in New York (he was not famous yet), and I said, 'That's what I want to do for the rest of my life. I want to be like that and have my own dramatic radio program.' From then on it was my dream to work for Orson Welles, and when I was about seventeen I suddenly got a call while I was working on another show, telling me that Orson Welles wanted me on his radio program before a live audience. So I got over to the CBS Studio and played the romantic lead of a Russian girl. He was so amazing. At one point he gave us all a glass, and the whole cast of eight or ten were to throw them against the wall in the Russian dinner scene at the end. He also did a trick because he once had an experience where he dropped his script and the audience went crazy. So just before airtime he would come to the microphone and say, 'Thirty seconds,' and then his script went all over the stage. He was pulling a trick to get the audience all on edge just before we went on, because somebody else had a script for him. Another thing he would do was cut the script just five minutes before airtime. The red light's going to go on any minute and here he is taking twenty pages and nobody knows if they are on those pages or not, but he's busy trying to mark it up and it's really very unnerving. But he liked to do things like that.

"Then one day he called me and asked me to come out to Republic because he wanted to hear me read Lady MacDuff for his film version of *MacBeth*. I had been under a sunlamp, which I had never used in my life before, and had fallen asleep. My face had swollen up and I was red. I thought, 'Here's the dream of my life and I've done this to myself.' Anyway, I went up to the projection room at one of the big sound stages and he was there. He had me read, then said, 'That's it. Go down and record it.' So I went downstairs and recorded all of Lady MacDuff. Two weeks later we started filming. Welles had a loud speaker playing the recording back to all of us so we had to act to our own voices, which I found very difficult because by that time you may have had a different concept of what you were going to do, but you were wedded to this first reading. As it turned out, for three years we dubbed and re-dubbed and looped and re-looped, so it didn't matter what we did with that first reading because it was all different by the time it was finally put together. The film was released after about two years, then it was pulled back and parts were redone. I also did the Witch's voice with two or three of the people in the company. Orson was in Italy, and they would send him the recording on a glass disc. He would select what he liked, and then would record a message, saying, 'Peggy, I liked the reading on this. Now if you could do it again and add that other line.' He'd give you all the directions, but it was long distance. After that was done he would re-record other comments, then you would come back and do it a different way, so this went on and on."

Dick Wilson, who was Welles' assistant, managed some of the direction. "He handled one of my close-ups in the film. Orson said that he would come over and direct my scene, but he wanted to get a close-up of me first, so for Dick to take the close-up while I'm wandering through the corridors. My wig had slipped or something, and Dick, who was a dear sweet man, didn't notice it, and it looked so bad I will never forgive him for that close-up," she laughed.

Welles also hired Peggy on two or three other pictures. "I did all of Valentina Cortese's part in *Black Magic*. That was her first role, so I was her voice throughout that. Then I did some other bits and pieces for him after that, so I continued being in touch with him for quite a few years." Peggy also dubbed other famous stars during her career. "I've dubbed Ingrid Bergman, Audrey Hepburn, Barbara Stanwyck, and many other big stars. Audrey Hepburn had left for Switzerland; Ingrid Bergman was in Italy somewhere. Those are the times I'd get called in," she added.

Peggy appeared on screen in twenty-one motion pictures. "They were all in a block of four or five years," she informed. Some of the movies that Peggy appeared in were *Submarine Command* with William Holden: "I had the second female lead in that." *Journey Into Light* with Sterling Hayden: "I played his drunken wife who commits suicide. I did all of these things before I ever lived. I had never been drunk before I played the drunk and I didn't know how to play it," she laughed. *The Greatest Story Ever Told*: "I didn't get screen credit and was promised by the casting director that everybody in Hollywood was doing this and that they were giving stars one line parts. It's a woman praying in the temple and we'll put your name on the credits, but they never did. So I had a nice little scene, but they never gave me any credit for it." *Space Children* with Jackie Coogan: "I was thrilled to work with him. But to be very honest with you it was a boring picture because this blob—the thing from outer space that the children were going to fly away with—was just dumb. Those kind of pictures don't do very much for you," she laughed. *The Wrong Man* with Henry Fonda, and directed by Alfred Hitchcock: "I was the girl who put the finger on him and sent him to prison. Hitchcock was fun if he liked you. If he didn't like you he would embarrass you and make you hate the whole experience. He said actors were children, like cattle. But he liked you if you worked hard. What he did with me in a scene where I'm supposed to be frightened half to death was to keep the stage very cold. He loved it because I was trembling, thinking I was going to be killed by Henry Fonda. He was very good to me. He made jokes all of the time, and Fonda would go in his dressing room and fall asleep, and they'd say, 'You're in the next shot Mr. Fonda,' and he'd come out and be wiping the sleep out of his eyes. He was so relaxed and was a very sweet man." Peggy did repeat the fact that it was a real treat to work with Orson Welles on *Macbeth*.

Peggy did not work with Charlie Chaplin in *Limelight*, but she was considered for the role that eventually went to Clare Bloom. "It was just before I left for Japan, and Chaplin sent me to his photographer. We spent the entire day up at his house, and we walked all over his estate up in the hills above Hollywood. He was the most unassuming, warm, sweet, funny fellow. He read the whole script aloud to me, and as he got to each song he would jump to the piano and play the music, which he composed himself. I was very thrilled to have that opportunity to spend that day with him."

When asked if she had a favorite among her films, Peggy paused a moment. "*The Screaming Skull*," her husband, Sean McClory, loudly proclaimed with a laugh. "Do you remember that one?" she laughed. "I was three months pregnant when we started the picture. I remember I was supposed to fall down a flight of stairs and I had to tell the director I couldn't do that because I was pregnant. But I never felt that any of the movies I did were really great. Alex Nicol directed *The Screaming Skull*. He was in Richard Boone's workshop with me. I helped Dick form this workshop about 1950. He asked me to suggest West Coast actors with serious intent or training. I suggested Jeanette Nolan and Lamont Johnson. Included in the workshop were James Whitmore, Kenneth Tobey and other people who all came from the Actor's Studio or Neighborhood Playhouse."

Peggy listed some of the stars she had the opportunity to work with on radio. "I played with Humphrey Bogart on *Bold Venture*. I did some other shows with Bogart and Lauren Bacall. He was a very shy, sweet man who never spoke up, and his wife was very dominant. She spoke up for him all the time. The James Mason's did the same thing. I worked with he and his wife Pamela, and she used to take all the notes, and told him what to do, and the director sometimes wished she would disappear. I was on *The Saint* with Vincent Price. He was so darling. He had a great sense of humor and never forgot anything. I saw him twenty years later when I went backstage (after a show Price had appeared in) with some friends and wasn't going to introduce myself, and he rushed over and grabbed my hands and said, 'Peggy, I'm so glad you came.' He was always like that. We went to the Pioneer Broadcast because they were paying a tribute to him before he died, and he did the same thing. He remembered me. You don't expect that in radio; you think they'd forget you. There were so many big stars in those days that I got the chance to work with: Jimmy Stewart, Charles Laughton, Sir Cedric Hardwick. I think the only big star I didn't work with was Clark Gable."

Many humorous things, both intentional and accidental, occur when performing before the microphone on a radio show. Peggy shared a couple of these humorous events. "One of them was when I was on *The Peter Lorre Mystery in the Air*, where I was his leading lady for a full season. At one point we were doing "The Horla," and he got so excited. He always got very excited. These were live shows with an audience, but he was practically foaming at the mouth, doing all of his business, and on this one he accidentally dropped his script. It was all over the floor. I had my script, but there's no point following it because he's not following it. I would say something to him and he would go into a conniption fit – We were ad-libbing on a live show to New York and the West Coast. It was a very scary performance until the music cue ended our predicament. But the thing that was probably the funniest that ever happened to me was when I was doing a soap opera called *Doctor Paul*. In that, I was a vicious and terrible woman who had inherited a construction business from her father. I was a crook, and didn't put enough cement in the construction of buildings, so when I would build an orphanage or a hospital I would cheat on the cement and they were collapsing and killing people. I was only about eighteen when I first started playing this woman, and she was in her mid-forties. The director, George Fogel, used to take me outside into the hall and tell me how a person at forty would feel about these things. Anyway, in one episode I was having a baby and was in prison for my sins. I was Doctor Paul's wife and I'd been committed to twenty-five years in prison. So this whole show I had to do all of the narration, and she's going into labor pains. It's just one of those horrendous scripts, with me alone on the mike for fifteen minutes. After the show has begun and the red light has gone on and I'm really into it very intense, the director comes out, and over my shoulder takes a red pencil and slashes the page. This terribly throws you because you're doing a monologue and trying to figure where does this connect, and I'm on the air and the only one talking. Then I turn that page and he slashes the next page. I think, why is he doing this to me when I'm on the air. I knew he was a perfectionist. He had directed *Ma Perkins* in Chicago and was a very fine director. Pretty soon he knocks over the big screen that protects the actors from the organ so the organ music doesn't override us, and I'm thinking, 'My gosh he's clumsy, he's doing this while I'm on the air. What's he doing this to me for?' He made some other terrible noise knocking over a music stand, and by this time I'm absolutely beside myself. It's just one big noise after the other, and then he goes back into the booth and the door slams behind him. Well, finally the red light goes off and the horrible thing is over with. They're laughing their heads off in the control booth and I'm getting very angry wondering why they picked this script to do this? Then the director says, 'You were pre-empted. Truman made a speech.' So I wasn't on the air at all."

Comparing work in radio, film, and on stage, Peggy said, "Actually, if you do it completely there is a delight in each one. Generally speaking, I always found that in early television at the end of the day I was very empty. I never felt that the director allowed you the time to do what you should do, but when you do a film they usually take the time. They keep shooting until they get exactly what they want, and usually the director was sensitive, and he cared. Whereas in television, often you would have a director who hadn't even read the script. It used to drive me crazy when you would come in with a beautiful script and that would be the reason that you were doing it, and the director hadn't even read it. He would just skim over it and forget the key scenes that were the most important, and it left one very frustrated. I started a theater at that time because I couldn't stand coming home feeling like this. I thought at least in the evening we could read a play or start working on one so I wouldn't have this feeling. And that helped."

Peggy started the Rustic Canyon Theater in 1957. "I was working with Dick Boone in his workshop altogether for about seven or eight years. For a short time we tried to raise money to build a theatre when I was starting the Rustic Canyon." She had a group of actors that included Lee Marvin, James Whitmore, Paul Fix, Lamont Johnson, Bob Denver, Doris Lloyd, John Dehner, Jocelyn Brando, Betty Hartford, and Lou Krugman. "At that time there was almost no theater in Los Angeles," Peggy informed, "and people had to travel all the way out to Rustic Canyon, which was quite a long way to go in those days. As Margaret Hartford, a critic, used to say, 'It's hard to find and a long ways to go, but it's well worth it.' We toured with Shakespeare to colleges and high schools, and opened the Bing Auditorium at the LA Art Museum. We were the very first to perform in there." The play we opened with was *A Midsummer Night's Dream*, and the cast included James Whitmore, Lou Krugman, Ford Rainey, Ted Cassidy, Marvin Miller, Bob Denver, Richard Hale, Clancy Cooper, and Peggy as Puck.

"Then after I was divorced," Peggy continued, "which happened in the middle of all this, I opened a dinner theater called *The New Hope Inn Dinner Theater*, and Ted Cassidy was my partner. We proceeded to present the same roster of stars at the dinner theater. We did serious shows, and as a result, when the Old Vic came to town with Laurence Olivier and the other wonderful people in that company, we entertained them with *Under Milkwood*. They came twice to our homes, and one time we had a party that went on for three or four days. Lee Marvin and I lived next door to each other with a gate in- between, so the party went on in both houses. The yards were huge, so these people were all tripping around in the gardens. It was such an unbelievable party. They had never seen an American home in those days with dishwashers and garbage disposals, so all of these English actors were playing around with that equipment. They just thought it was the greatest thing in the world. When everybody had gone, Bette Marvin and I were cleaning up Lee's playroom out behind the house and this English gentleman came out of the men's room, and as he was straightening his tie, said, 'Cheerio.' Everybody had left already – the Old Vic was gone – and he was still asleep in there," Peggy laughed.

Peggy mentioned that she hasn't pursued television or film work since the mid-1980's, but keeps busy with radio and theater. "I've had six theaters," she stated. "And when I married Sean we opened with my incorporate name for my last theatre The California Artists Repertory Theatre in North Hollywood and did a number of plays there. Sean won the best actor award from Critic's Circle for *Shadow of a Gunman* in which he played the old beggar, and he was excellent. He also did *The Importance of Being Earnest* for me. I also have a series of radio shows that I write, produce, and direct. We're on National Public Radio and now XM radio. We do the shows here, then they select the ones they like and broadcast those on the *NPR Playhouse* and XM Sonic Theatre. We've won numerous awards with the radio theater," Peggy continued. "I won two Gold Awards in 1992 for the radio version of *Macbeth* which I did with David Warner and Jeanette Nolan. I produced a show in December 1993, with Norman Corwin, who wrote and directed it, called *The Plot to Overthrow Christmas*. My company, California Artists Radio Company, which Sean acts in, did the program. I was able to get that on three networks, and locally it played on seven stations, so we're hoping that will get some kind of an award at the end of the year. We're starting a whole series that we'll be broadcasting from the Hollywood Roosevelt beginning the end of April 1994, doing a dramatic show. Now we have spent nine years at The Cine Grill and, after that, five more years at the Beverly Garland in North Hollywood. We have recorded approximately one hundred and fifty ninety minute shows." Peggy has won over thirty national and international awards for her shows.

In summing up her career at the time of our interview in 1995, Peggy stated, "I think the best is yet to come. I'm so excited about all of the radio shows that I'm doing. For instance, the six or eight months that I just spent with Norman Corwin was one of the highlights of my life. To spend that much time with a genius really changes you. With these kinds of experiences I hope to maybe evolve into directing some film. As a young person I did. I directed the first *Colgate Comedy Hour* on film when I was about twenty-one, and had at that time a great ambition to be a director. To me, the greatest joy is in making the whole shoe. I really love that. I'm having probably the best time in my life right now just writing and directing these scripts, and getting great actors to play in them."

Peggy's husband, Sean McClory, died in December of 2003, and outside of a memorial she did no shows in 2004. In 2005, Peggy recorded five new programs, and in February 2006 she prepared to record a new production with William Windom, Samantha Eggar, JoAnn Worley, Peter Dennis and a cast of ten in *Anatol*s, and, at eighty years of age, had four new shows in preparation. She said, "I am beginning to focus after his death, but not really. I am still in a state of quandary. I continue to work, but not at my full energy."

Film Credits: 1946: Her Adventurous Night; Little Miss Big. **1948**: MacBeth. **1951**: Journey into Light; Submarine Command. **1956**: The Wrong Man. **1958** The Screaming Skull; The Space Children. **1960:** Flap(voice); Caliostro (voice). **1965:** The Greatest Story Ever Told. **1966:** Chimes at Midnight. **1967:** Bonnie and Clyde (voice); Tarzan and the Great River (voice). Wait Until Dark (voice) **1968:**Tarzan and the Jungle Boy (voice). **1973:** Well of the Saints. **1979:** Going Steady (voice). **1984:** Smurfs (voice). **1999:** Chameleon. **2001:** 8MM (voice).

JACQUELINE WHITE

Jacqueline White was born November 26, 1924 in Los Angeles, California, and raised in neighboring Beverly Hills. "From the time I was a little girl I've always wanted to be an actress," Jacqueline began. "What I loved most of all growing up was anything to **do** with the theater. I used to love doing little plays at home. We had two steps going into the living room and the two steps up above the entrance hall was always my stage. So as a little kid I was always getting some kind of a show and my folks got a kick out of it. Sometimes a bunch of us kids would go to a movie and we would watch it a couple of times and then go back to see it the next week if it was something that we really loved."

When Jacqueline attended high school she became involved in theater there. "I did plays in high school, and also, Beverly Hills High School was kind of avant-garde in a lot of things," Jacqueline reported. "We had programs we would do for television and, of course, television was really quite new. That was fun to do. My best girlfriend was Ann Connolly, and the two of us planned to go to college for a year or two and then see what we could do on the New York stage." Ann, who was daughter of character actor Walter Connolly, joined a USO show after her first year in college, and Jacqueline went under contract to a famous motion picture studio.

"What happened," Jacqueline explained, "was that I went to UCLA and was in a play there, playing Muriel, the ingénue, in *Ah! Wilderness*. From that play there were three studios that contacted me. I was tested at MGM, 20th Century Fox, and Warner Brothers, and offered a contract by both MGM and Warner Brothers. I took the MGM contract."

Jacqueline signed in May of 1942 at MGM and her first job there was for a film titled *Tish*. "Right after I was signed they called me and said, 'Come out. We have something for you to do. We need you out at the studio immediately.' I thought, 'Oh my gosh! It's a part. This is wonderful.' So I went dashing out there all excited, but what it was they wanted me to do was to sneeze on a soundtrack for ZaSu Pitts. So that was my very first job."

Jacqueline worked in small uncredited parts in a number of films, including *Dr. Gillespie's New Assignment*, *Reunion in France*, and *A Guy Named Joe*. "There were so many that I don't even remember the names of because they were small parts, and then I started to get a little larger parts." These films included *Thirty Seconds over Tokyo* and *Swing Shift Maisie*. Soon larger feature roles came her way in pictures like *Song of Russia* and a lead opposite Laurel and Hardy in *Air Raid Wardens*. Another thing that Jacqueline enjoyed doing at MGM was volunteering to act in screen tests opposite new people they wanted to test. "One time they were screen testing a guy that sang," she informed, "He was very short, very fat, and very uninteresting, but he had a beautiful voice so I did this screen test with him. It was a love scene and he certainly was not my ideal of anybody I'd want to do a love scene with. The next week they called me in and said they have a guy from Mexico to do a scene with and I came out and it was Ricardo Montalban. That was a big difference. He was delightful to work with and just one of the sweetest people you could ever meet."

Speaking of Stan Laurel and Oliver Hardy, Jacqueline said, "They were both delightful men. When working on camera they were real pro's to say the least and knew what they were doing. They were so wonderful on the screen and very enjoyable to work with, but once the scene was over they were very serious and it wasn't a constant patter of humor like it was when I worked with Red Skelton. I did *The Show-Off* with him and he never stopped being funny. One of the things that kind of tickled me was that Marjorie Main was in the movie and she evidently took a lot of pills. One time she was taking this very large pill and Red said, 'Marjorie, the last time I saw anybody take a pill that big he won the Kentucky derby.' He was just funny all of the time. It was just a constant amusing time with him. So Laurel and Hardy were really quite different than Red Skelton."

Jacqueline continued her contract at MGM until 1946. "I was kind of unhappy at MGM and was somewhere when I ran into a casting director. He said, 'We would love to have you at RKO if you ever decide to leave.' I felt I needed a change so I talked to MGM and it was a mutual agreement that I leave and that was fine." So Jacqueline left MGM and went under contract to RKO in 1946 and continued there until 1948.

When asked why she was unhappy at MGM, Jacqueline replied, "I lost a couple of parts that I really would have loved to have done. One was *The Yearling*. Jane Wyman was not available so they gave me a test with Gregory Peck and Claude Jarman, Jr. and they seemed to think it was really great. They sent me to Florida and we shot a couple of long shots. My father died when I was there and I came home for that, and then Jane Wyman became available and I lost the part. So that was difficult. Another thing was with Bob Walker in *Till the Clouds Roll By* about the life of Jerome Kern and I was all set to play Mrs. Jerome Kern in that. The director had selected me and they took a lot of publicity shots for it and then when it started they switched directors and he had someone he wanted to use in the part. So it was disappointing and I went over to RKO and was very happy there."

While under contract at RKO Jacqueline had lead roles on such films as *Banjo, Seven Keys to Baldpate, Crossfire, Night Song, Return of the Bad Men,* and *Mystery in Mexico.* As she reflected on her work in a dog story titled *Banjo,* she said, "We had so many complications working with the dog. It was a stupid dog, and I guess they didn't give it a brain test first," she laughed. "This dog just wouldn't do anything that they wanted him to do. In one particular scene he was supposed to run into the room and jump up on me and almost knock me down. Well, he comes running into the room and he sees me and just stops dead and backs up a little. So they got this stuffed cat and waved it over my head on the end of a fishing pole and the dog came running into the room, got close to me, jumped up into the air and did a complete summersault. They finally put a meatball on a pin that I was wearing and had the dog realize what it was, and finally got the dog to jump up on me."

Another incident that happened in *Banjo* was a scene in which Jacqueline falls into the water off of a bridge. "This was a dirty, murky, filthy pond and in order for me to be thrashing about I had to sit down in there because it was so shallow. If I stood up it would only have been up to my knees," she laughed. "So I was thrashing about and trying to stay under a very shallow pond that was really filthy. They said we'll only do one or two takes because we only have two dresses, but we did it in one take so it was fine."

Jacqueline was hired to star opposite Randolph Scott, Anne Jeffreys, Robert Ryan, and Gabby Hayes in her first Western, *Return of the Bad Men.* "I really wasn't a horse person so when I did a Western I went out and worked with people on my riding. The Westerns were fun and all very informal and it was a nice thing to do. I just thought all the people I worked with were great, delightful people. Randolph Scott was a wonderful man. Anne Jeffreys was delightful. I can't say anything mean about anybody because I don't have anything mean to say."

Jacqueline had the opportunity to go to Mexico to star in the drama *Mystery in Mexico,* which co-starred William Lundigan, Ricardo Cortez, Walter Reed, and Tony Barrett, and directed by Robert Wise. "It was just a wonderful troupe," Jacqueline reflected. "I had never been to Mexico before and didn't know what to expect at all, and it was so different than anything I had seen. To see some of the people going down the street with burros and with jars on their head was quite unusual. It was really fascinating. We drove to Puerto Vallarta and to Taxco, and I was completely enchanted with the country. We all had a great time there. An interesting thing on this picture was that we had to have a Mexican equivalent to whatever we had in an American person. So we had a Mexican director, a Mexican producer -- none of which did anything -- but their union was such that we had to have an equivalent. The photographer we had was married to a Mexican girl so they considered him to be one of them, so they only needed one of him. We had a lot of Mexican actors on it, but we didn't have to have people standing by for the American actors."

Walter Reed was Jacqueline's co-star in four of her pictures at RKO (*Banjo, Night Song, Return of the Bad Men*, and *Mystery in Mexico*), and she said of him, "He was so funny. He had a marvelous sense of humor. He just had us in stitches all of the time and I have often thought he missed his call because he would have been so good in comedies. He had this natural flair and his timing was great. Maybe he did some comedy, but I never saw it."

Another one of Jacqueline's credits was playing Mary Jordan in the 1947 version of *Seven Keys to Baldpate*. "Eduardo Ciannelli played the villain in it. I had known him since I was a little girl and that was nice because I always thought he was a wonderful villain. He had that sinister look about him. When he would look sinister he was sinister."

That same year Jacqueline performed in the film noir classic, *Crossfire*. "That starred the three Robert's," she related, "Robert Young, Robert Mitchum, and Robert Ryan. They were all outstanding actors. And Gloria Grahame was in it, a delightful girl. It was a fascinating film to do because we knew that it was a subject (race hatred) that was not really used before, and it was nice working with those people."

Jacqueline left RKO in 1948. "I met Bruce Anderson in August, 1948, and married him in November, and then I didn't care what happened. He was in business with his dad, and while we were gone on our honeymoon his dad sold the business so we were on our own. He had to go to where the work was and we ended up in Casper, Wyoming. I didn't have enough of a name to say 'Send me a script and I'll see if I'll do it.' I did do three movies after we were married, however."

Jacqueline worked with Tim Holt in *Riders of the Range* and with Lew Ayres in *The Capture* before she moved to Wyoming. Speaking of Tim Holt, she said, "Tim was a very nice person. He was fairly newly married and his wife had a Doberman pinscher that hated him. Every time he walked in the room, if the dog was there it would start snarling and growling, and unless she was there to protect him he couldn't go in because I think the dog might have killed him. He didn't like Tim a bit. I presume, after that somewhere down along the line, that dog had to go."

Jacqueline appeared in her final film, *The Narrow Margin*, opposite Marie Windsor and Charles McGraw after she had moved to Wyoming. "I came back to Los Angeles when my first child was born and went out to RKO to show off the baby pictures. Richard Fleischer was there having lunch with Stanley Rubin, and he came over to the table and said, 'Jackie, we have something we'd love to have you do if you're available,' and mentioned *The Narrow Margin*. My husband was already back home, so I said, 'Let me check with my husband and see how he feels about it.' It was fine with Bruce so I stayed and did that. Then I went back to Casper, and that was the last I did."

Jacqueline returned to Los Angeles for the birth of her second child and while there was asked by Arch Oboler if she would star opposite Robert Stack in the first commercial 3-D motion picture titled *Bwana Devil*. "He called me up and said he was interested in me for the lead," she stated. "But when I talked to my husband about it he was undone because we did live in Casper and it would be difficult. I called up Arch and said there is just no way. So that was just kind of the end of it when I had that interview."

We asked Jacqueline if she missed acting, and she replied, "No." After a short pause she continued, "I say no, but I see a movie that I think, 'Gosh, wouldn't that be fun to do. I wonder if I had stayed on if I could have done this or that.' But I ended up with five children, wonderful young people, so my life is very busy and very full, and we had an exciting life going on. My husband was starting from scratch and we built up a nice company together and four of our children are involved in the company. It's a little oil company called Anderson Oil, in Houston, Texas."

Of all the films she worked in, we asked if she had a favorite film. "It is difficult for me to say a favorite, but I think I would say *Mystery in Mexico* because we went to Mexico and it was such a fascinating experience for me, being the first time to ever be in Mexico and not having any idea of what it would be like."

Today, Jacqueline has a number of activities that keep her busy. "We love to fish, but usually go to Alaska or British Columbia because salmon fishing is my favorite," she stated. "So we take a trip up there most every year, and I caught two twenty-eight pound salmon. That was exciting. And then I'm a docent at the Ima Hogg House museum, which is connected to the Museum of Fine Arts in Houston. It has twenty-two rooms, and the Hogg family did a great deal for the state of Texas. Jim Hogg was the first Texas born governor. It's a fascinating thing to do. I'm involved with my children and grandchildren, and we have a lot of friends. It's a fascinating life and one that I have really enjoyed."

In summing up her feelings on the motion picture business, Jacqueline said, "I think it's a fascinating profession and that it's a wonderful thing to do. I enjoyed it tremendously when I was doing it. My feeling about it is that I think it's up to the individual. Our daughter had quite a bit of talent for that sort of thing, but after high school she decided on other things. It's changed tremendously since I was there so I can't really say much about what it's like now because I don't know. I think they could use some good writers down there," she laughed. "You don't get the nice stories, just the horror, killings and sex. I think that movies have a tremendous impact on the public. We wonder why things are going awry the way they are with our young people, and if you look at what's on television and what's at the movies it's understandable why these things happen. And they try to excuse it and say it has no connection, but it does. They say you should watch what your children watch. Well, you can't be with them over at their friend's house or be with them twenty-four hours a day and be able to talk to them about everything that they're seeing. It's a hard thing raising children today compared to what it was. Back then you might have *Frankenstein* and it might scare you, but that was different," she concluded.

Film Credits: 1942: Tish; Reunion in France. **1943**: Dr. Gillespie's New Assignment; Air Raid Wardens; Three Hearts for Julia; That's Why I Left You; Swing Shift Maisie; A Guy Name

Joe; Song of Russia. **1944**: Easy Life; Thirty Seconds Over Tokyo; Dark Shadows. **1946**: Our Old Car; The Show-Off. **1947**: Banjo; Seven Keys to Baldpate; Crossfire. **1948**: Night Song; Return of the Bad Men; Mystery in Mexico. **1950**: Riders of the Range; The Capture. **1952**: The Narrow Margin.

ROBERT WILKE

Robert Joseph Wilke was born in Cincinnati, Ohio, on May 18, 1914. "I had a wonderful mother and father; a great family," Bob reflected. "I had five brothers and two sisters, all older than me; I got a kick in the ass by each of them every day so it didn't amount to too much fun," Bob laughed. He attended the Catholic school and church, and performed in skits at school. "Then I went to Catholic high school where I stayed one year **before** they threw me out," Bob confided. "I hated school; just couldn't get interested in it." Bob later had training at a business school, "which I didn't care for."

Besides school, Bob kept busy pulling a cart delivering groceries for a local grocer. "Cincinnati is all hills," Bob informed, "and most of the houses were way up. You'd carry a crate of groceries up those hills and it wasn't much fun." After quitting this job, Bob went to work keeping books at his father's hay, grain and feed store. The extra hours away from school and work were usually taken up with football, baseball and a lot of swimming. "I used to go down to the Ohio River and dive off the derrick, which was about seventy-five feet high. Crazy things like that trying to kill yourself," Bob added. This practice would eventually lead to a movie career for him, but for the moment it took him to Illinois. "I was at the World's Fair in Chicago in 1934 doing diving exhibitions," stated Bob.

The next job to come Bob's way was that of a lifeguard. He worked in Cincinnati; at New York's Coney Island; and then south to the humid oceanfront city of Miami, Florida. While in the latter locale, he and a friend used to gather coconuts, fill them with gin and place them in the icebox. One day they ran out of coconuts. "I had a few," Bob confided, "so I climbed this coconut tree and when I was twisting the coconuts off I got dizzy and fell out of the tree

and broke my shoulder. The friend of mine said, 'Let's jump in the car and go to California,' and that's how we got here."

One day Bob met the assistant cameraman that was working on the MGM movie *San Francisco*, and he invited Bob out to watch him film. "They were shooting the earthquake sequence and I saw these guys falling out of windows into these nets," Bob related. "I asked, 'What do you get for that?' They said about a hundred dollars a fall. I said, 'Where do you sign up?' because that was right in my line. So that's how I got started. I did stunts for quite a few years, but it was different in those days because you'd do stunts but also they'd give you a little speaking part in the picture. That was to keep you around in case they needed you to do another stunt. Those were the days when you got fifty dollars a day for falling off horses," Bob added, "and today a stuntman won't walk on the set for fifty dollars. It's completely changed. After sticking my head in the ground for a few years I got tired of that and just went into straight acting, and have been doing that ever since." Bob's first picture that he performed in strictly as an actor only was at Republic. "How I got out of stunts was I was working with director Lesley Selander and we were sitting there having lunch and he said, 'Bob, why don't you get out of stunts; you're going to get killed one of these days. Go into straight acting, you're good at it.' So I did. Although he had worked in many films at that studio as a stuntman, and continued doing so as an actor, Bob told us "I never signed a contract with anybody. I always free-lanced."

Although he occasionally sidetracked to different types of films, the majority of Bob's pictures were in the Western genre. "I enjoyed making Westerns," Bob commented, "That's all they used to make; it was Westerns or nothing, so knocked them out one after another. The way we used to make the Westerns there was no way that you could keep track of them – I've went on two at the same time, but they don't do that anymore. " In the 1940's the studios had their own theater chains; they knew when and where their films would be shown and exactly how much they would get back. So when Republic Pictures paid out an average of one hundred thousand dollars per feature, the film was already pre-sold and there was not any gamble on whether they would recoup their finances. This no longer applies today. "Those were rough days," Bob went on to say. "Calls at four o'clock in the morning, be ready to start at five-thirty, drive to location, eat a terrible box lunch, and work fourteen hours a day. But we had fun – that was the important thing. We used to start at Iverson's Ranch," Bob noted. "We'd start down in the flats as soon as the sun got up; then we would just keep getting higher and higher, and by the end of the evening we're on top of the mountain getting the last of the sun."

Asked if he had to learn to handle horses for the Westerns, Bob replied, "I had a little experience with them. My dad had horses and we used to take them out and exercise them, but I got a lot more experience out here. These horses were smarter than we were," Bob explained. "The minute that they say, 'Roll 'em,' those horses would perk right up; 'Action,' and off they'd go; the guy hollers, 'Cut,' and they stop. You just sit there."

Even though the hours were long and hard, the movie set was not all work and no play. "We had so many humorous experiences on the set," Bob recalled. "Why, we would go to work and spend half the day figuring out ways to play tricks on people." The jokes were many: rubber reins on horses, rubber stirrups – like "when a guy makes a running mount and it goes all the way to the floor," Bob laughed. "Just gags like that they would dream up. Work all night to fix up a saddle to get somebody. I'll never forget this one day. We were shooting water into each other's face with water guns, and this one stuntman grabbed a hose and started running after a guy – the only thing he forgot is that he's going to come to the end of the hose, and when he did he did a pratfall; I've never seen anything like it; it just jerked him right off his feet," Bob laughed.

Bob's acting career included his years as a stuntman, bit parts in numerous B-Westerns and serials, finally graduating to featured roles in films like *Best of the Badmen*, as outlaw Jim Younger, with Robert Ryan, and opposite Tim Holt in a number of films (*Overland Telegraph, Gunplay, Road Agent*), but his big break came when he was cast as Jim Pierce, one of the three outlaws waiting for Frank Miller's arrival to face Gary Cooper in the Academy Award winning classic *High Noon*. From this point on Bob became a top character actor working with some of Hollywood's top stars of that period in numerous Westerns, such as James Stewart (*The Far Country, Night Passage,* and *Cheyenne Social Club*), Charlton Heston (*Arrowhead*), Rory Calhoun (*Powder River* and *Raw Edge*), Gary Cooper *(Man of the West)*, Joel McCrea (Wichita), Greer Garson *(Strange Lady in Town)*, Yul Brynner (*The Magnificent Seven*). Bob also worked in such non-Western classics as *From Here to Eternity, Twenty Thousand Leagues Under the Sea, Written on the Wind,* and *Spartacus*.

In reflecting on his work in *Night Passage*, Bob stated, "that was interesting. We made that up in Colorado; it was shot in Silverton up in the mountains at fourteen thousand feet, which didn't make it too easy to breathe."

Reflecting on his work in *High Noon*, Bob stated, "Working on *High Noon* was a pleasure. Fred Zinnemann was the director; a great person. Cooper was a very good friend of mine and I always enjoyed working with him. Spent a couple of weeks on location and the rest of it was shot out at Columbia Studio on a back lot. I guess I was the only guy that was ever shot by a princess; shot me in the back through a window. Yep. Grace Kelly was wonderful; a magnificent person. Cooper was great; Lee Van Cleef's done very well in those spaghetti Westerns; Sheb Wooley always was a singer and songwriter; and Ian MacDonald is dead. He had Parkinson's disease. It was a great film; I guess one of the best Westerns that was ever made.

Asked if he had a favorite role that he had played, Bob laughed and said, "Well, I played so many different roles that I really couldn't pick one that I really would say was a favorite. I think my favorite picture was *High Noon* without a doubt. *High Noon, From Here to Eternity* and *Twenty Thousand Leagues Under the Sea,* those were the ones I enjoyed best as far as films are concerned. In talking to us about the latter film, Bob remarked, "When we made

Robert Wilke

Twenty Thousand Leagues Under the Sea at Disney's it was a great place to work; it was a family studio and you knew everybody. You started at ten o'clock in the morning and finished at five o'clock in the afternoon. You had a wet dressing room, a dry dressing room, and a big dressing room; they couldn't treat you well enough. It was fantastic." Referring to the scene in which a giant squid attacks the submarine and its crew, Bob said, "The scene with the squid was scary. It was all hydraulic and that thing could pick you up and throw you thirty feet. It was really a piece of genius. I think they still have it down at Disneyland." Bob had an interesting side note to add about Disneyland. "I saw Disneyland before it was ever built. Walt had it in miniature: He took the walls out between three offices and had the whole thing in this big room, and everything worked just exactly like it is down there."

Bob's acting career also included television, where his credits included such Western series' as *The Lone Ranger, Roy Rogers, The Range Rider, Gene Autry, Cisco Kid, Cheyenne, Tombstone Territory, Jim Bowie, Man without a Gun, Colt 45, Tales of Wells Fargo, Rifleman, Lawman, Have Gun-Will Travel, Bat Masterson, The Texan, Zorro, Wanted Dead or Alive, Laramie, Bonanza, Wagon Train, Rawhide, The Virginian,* and *How the West Was Won.* Bob was Ben Tilton, a regular on Disney's limited series of *Andy Burnett,* and co-starred as Marshal Sam Corbett on *The Legend of Jesse James* television series during the 1965-66 season. "I was disappointed that it didn't keep going," Bob stated. "ABC took it off because they said we were glorifying a criminal. I mean, Jesse James is a piece of American history." Bob's other television credits included *The Untouchables,* which reunited him with Robert Stack whom he worked with a number of years early in the heat of Death Valley on a picture titled *War Paint.* In *The Untouchables,* Bob portrayed gangsters Bugs Moran and Legs Diamond, "those two characters were historic too," Bob added. Other television shows included *Superman, Court of Last Resort, Four Star Playhouse, B.J. and the Bear, Dallas, Tarzan, My Three Sons, Perry Mason, Sam Benedict, Checkmate, Peter Gunn,* and *A Man and the Challenge.* Bob guest starred on seven episodes of *Gunsmoke,* a series he enjoyed working on, having worked in prior years with James Arness in *Hellgate* and *Gun the Man Down.* "Arness is a very good friend," Bob added. In his first episode, titled *Matt for Murder,* he portrayed Marshal Wild Bill Hickok. In his final episode nine years later (*The Cattle Barons*) Bob played Luke Cumberledge, a cattle baron who was feuding with a rival cattleman performed by Forrest Tucker. "That was fun doing that with Tuck. Tucker's a good friend; I play a lot of golf with Tuck. They just don't make that stuff anymore; now it's all like *Dukes of Hazzard* and stuff like that. That makes you sick watching stuff like that; all it is is just a car chase. No story; no nothing. "

Talking about what it would take to produce a Western today, Bob said, "You can't afford to make Westerns anymore. I think a rider costs you two hundred dollars a day; a horse will cost you a hundred dollars a day; and there's no location out here where you could make them anymore. That means you've got to go out of the state and you got to keep everybody and feed them; it's just exuberant. That's where you get into these thirty million dollar pictures like *Heaven's Gate*. I think they made *High Noon* for a million and a half.

Bob spent six months on location in India where he was associate producer for a children's film titled *Monkeys of Bandipur*, but released as *The Great Monkey Rip-Off*. This 1978 feature co-starred Bob and Alan Hale Jr. The rest of the cast were all Indian. "I taught the boy how to act," Bob explained. "He did very well. There's some beautiful things in India: the Taj Mahal – That's fantastic. We filmed in the Taj Mahal and at the castles and walled cities of Jaipur. I just couldn't believe it was absolutely beautiful; but then right on the other side is the poverty with people sleeping and dying in the streets. It's beautiful, but yet it's ugly. It leaves a bad taste in your mouth really, but I would like to go back just for a visit. The mountains and Kashmir are beautiful. I came back very sick, but that's a part of India – sickness. They've got diseases down there that's never been heard of. And I don't need any of that. I have enough trouble staying healthy." Returning to the subject of the film he made there, Bob added, "It's a good little film, but they haven't done much with it. It was fun, but an awful lot of hard work."

Bob spent four months on location in Canada for *Days of Heaven*. "That's a long, long time, believe me. Food was terrible; the Holiday Inn was the worst I've ever been in. The first day that I went into my room there was a piece of Kleenex rolled up lying under the heater; the day I left it was still under there. It was no fun. I went to work one morning and it was about seventy degrees and all of a sudden it started snowing and the wind came up, and I hadn't been in snow in years since I left Ohio. I didn't realize that snowflakes actually could hurt you, it was blowing that bad.

"That was the scene where the two were out there on the hay pile." When we mentioned to Bob that he had a really great part in that film and thought it had the potential for the Supporting Actor category of the Academy Awards, Bob acknowledged that it was a good part, but added, "I don't believe very much in those awards; I think you buy them most of the time."

Bob's final film was in the Bill Murray comedy, *Stripes*. "That was an interesting little effort," Bob mentioned. "They sent me to Louisville, Kentucky; I get to the airport and they got a reservation for me but no one has paid for the ticket and I have to write a check for the ticket. I get to Louisville and they said it was Holiday Inn East. There was no one to meet me so I get a cab and they drive me over to Holiday Inn East, which was in Indiana. The cab fare was about twenty-five dollars. I go into the hotel and they don't know anything about a movie company, so now I think, 'what the hell do I do now?' First of all I call my agent but nobody was in – they were all out working – then I talk to the girl behind the desk and she called the Holiday Inns around. They finally found it – I had to go about fifty miles to a little town this side of Fort Knox. I didn't get to the hotel until about nine-thirty that night. I was furious. Just so much stupidity, that's what irritates me about the business now.

The production manager on the company is a good friend of mine and he raised holy hell with everybody, but it was too late then; all the damage had been done.

"Another thing I don't like about the picture business," Bob continued, "is they call you in at seven o'clock in the morning and you work at five o'clock that night. It takes all of the sharpness out of you; just sitting around with nothing to do. They say as long as we're paying you, you got to be here. It isn't fun, believe me. Hollywood was great, but it's sure a changed business now. It was different in those days. I look at cast sheets and I don't know anyone in the cast. And there's so much of this method acting; it drives you up the wall. Getting up into the method routine – these guys that have to run around the set a couple of times to get themselves set to go in and do it. That's not my idea of acting. I talk to fellows in the business and they just cannot believe that it could deteriorate the way it has. It's just not fun, so I'm going to take it easy. That's all behind me now," Bob continued, "so I'm not going to worry about it."

Commenting on his favorite pastime, Bob said, "I enjoy golf. They asked me if I wanted to turn pro but I was making too much money in pictures. I belong to the Riviera Country Club near Pacific Palisades, so I get over there three or four times a week and play a little golf. Have to do something; can't just sit around." When asked the question on what type of movies he enjoys as a viewer, Bob replied, "I enjoy comedy very much." What he doesn't like is the gory psycho type films ("if you pick up the newspaper or turn on the TV you get it all you want.") and the attitude that if it doesn't have sex in the first three pages of the script then the pictures no good. "To be very truthful with you," Bob confided, "I haven't seen a picture since *Days of Heaven* and I went to see that because my wife wanted to see it. And I haven't been in a theater in years; I saw *Days of Heaven* at the studio at MGM. There's just nothing around that I want to see. It's just psychos and killings, who wants to see that."

Asking what his future holds concerning his motion picture career, Bob remarked, "If something good comes up, I'll do it; if it doesn't, I won't. I'm not going to abuse myself anymore; I'm too old for that. If I'd known I was going to live this long," concluded Bob, "I'd of taken better care of myself."

Robert Wilke died March 28, 1989.

Film Credits: 1936: San Francisco. **1937:** Decatlon Champion (short); San Quentin; SOS Coast Guard; That Man's Here Again. **1938:** Come on, Rangers' Fighting Devil Dogs; Heroes of the Hills; Prairie Moon; Down in Arkansaw. **1939:** Star Reporter; In Old Monterey; Daredevils of the Red Circle; Woman Doctor; I Was a Convict; Street of Missing Men; Man of Conquest; SOS Tidal Wave; Jeepers Creepers. **1940:** Adventures of Red Ryder; In Old Missouri; The Crooked Road; Grand Ole Opry; Girl from Havana; Hit Parade of 41. **1941:** Dick Tracy vs. Crime Inc; Country Fair; Arkansas Judge; Tuxedo Junction. **1942:** Spy Smasher; Shepherd of the Ozarks; The Old Homestead; Johnny Doughboy; Bells of

Capistrano. **1943:** The Masked Marvel; California Joe; Mountain Rhythm; Overland Mail Robbery; Pistol Packin' Mama. **1944:** Captain America; Zorro's Black Whip; Haunted Harbor; Beneath Western Skies; Hidden Valley Outlaws; The Cowboy and the Senorita; Yellow Rose of Texas; Rosie the Riveter; Marshal of Reno; Bordentown Trail; The San Antonio Kid; Cheyenne Wildcat; Code of the Prairie; Sheriff of Sundown; Vigilantes of Dodge City; Firebrands of Arizona; The Big Bonanza; Faces in the Fog; Stagecoach to Monterey; Thoroughbreds; Sheriff of Las Vegas; The Fighting Seabees; Call of the Rockies. **1945:** The Topeka Terror; Great Stagecoach Robbery; The Tiger Woman; Corpus Christie Bandits; Santa Fe Saddlemates; Trail of Kit Carson; Rough Riders of Cheyenne; The Man from Oklahoma; Bandits of the Badlands; Lone Texas Ranger; Sunset in El Dorado; The Purple Monster Strikes; The Daltons Ride Again; Hitchhike to Happiness; The Chicago Kid; Bells of Rosarita; Earl Carroll's Vanities. **1946:** Daughter of Don Q; The Crimson Ghost; The Catman of Paris; Passkey to Danger; Rendezvous with Annie; Badmans Territory; White Tie and Tails; King of the Forest Rangers; Out California Way; The Inner Circle; Traffic in Crime; The El Paso Kid; Roaring Rangers; The Phantom Rider. **1947:** West of Dodge City; Blackmail; The Michigan Kid; The Pilgrim Lady; The Black Widow; Twilight on the Rio Grande; Law of the Canyon; The Vigilantes Return; Last Days of Boot Hill; Buck Privates Come Home; The Ghost Goes Wild; Web of Danger. **1948:** Six Gun Law; West of Sonora; Carson City Raiders; Sundown in Santa Fe; G-Men Never Forget; Dangers of the Canadian Mounted; Daredevils of the Clouds; The River Lady; Out of the Storm; Homicide for Three; Desperadoes of Dodge City; A Southern Yankee; Trail to Laredo; The Wreck of the Hesperus. **1949:** Federal Agents vs. Underworld Inc; Ghost of Zorro; Laramie; The Wyoming Bandit; Coyote Canyon (short); The Blonde Bandit; James Brothers of Missouri; French Fried Frolic (short); San Antone Ambush; Post Office Investigator; Flaming Fury; Death Valley Gunfighter. **1950:** Outcast of Black Mesa; The Desert Hawk; Kill the Umpire; Mule Train; Twilight in the Sierras; Beyond the Purple Hills; Across the Badlands; Frontier Outpost; Traveling Saleswoman. **1951:** His Kind of Woman; Best of the Badmen; Saddle Legion; Gunplay; Cyclone Fury; Pistol Harvest; Overland Telegraph; Vengeance Valley; Hot Lead; No Greetings Asked. **1952:** The Las Vegas Story; Road Agent; Laramie Mountains; Carbine Williams; Wyoming Roundup; Fargo; Cattle Town; The Maverick; High Noon; Hellgate. **1953:** Arrowhead; Cow Country; Powder River; From Here to Eternity; War Paint. **1954:** The Lone Gun; Two Guns and a Badge; Twenty Thousand Leagues Under the Sea. **1955:** Smoke Signal; Shotgun; Strange Lady in Town; Far Country; Wichita; Son of Sinbad. **1956:** Backlash; The Lone Ranger; Rawhide Years; Canyon River; Raw Edge; Gun the Man Down; Written on the Wind. **1957:** Night Passage; Hot Summer Night; The Tarnished Angels. **1958:** Man of the West; Return to Warbow; Never Steal Anything Small. **1960:** Spartacus; The Magnificent Seven; The Slowest Gun in the West (TV). **1961:** The Long Rope; Blueprint for Murder. **1963:** The Gun Hawk. **1964:** Fate is the Hunter; Shock Treatment. **1965:** Morituri; The Hallelujah Trail. **1966:** Smoky. **1967:** Tony Rome. **1969:** The Dangerous Mission (TV). **1970:** The Cheyenne Social

Club. **1971:** A Gunfight; Resurrection of Zachary Wheeler; Dangerous Mission (TV); They Call It Murder (TV). **1972:** The Rookies (TV). **1973:** Santee; The Boy who Cried Werewolf. **1978:** Days of Heaven; The Great Monkey Rip-off; Wild and Wooly (TV). **1979:** The Sweet Creek County War. **1981:** Stripes.

SCOTT WILSON

Scott Wilson was born March 29, 1942, in Atlanta, Georgia. "I was in sports and I particularly loved basketball," Scott began. "There was a little recreation center down the street from us and all of the kids would come there and play sports. When I was a kid I used to play out in left field on a baseball team. Someone hit a shot off the bat and I thought it was going to go way over my head. I took off running backwards, but I looked and it was way in front of me," Scott laughed. "I had to reverse, and made a diving catch on my belly. Probably if I stayed where I was it would have come right to me. That's when I knew I wasn't going to be much of a baseball player."

Scott's father, who died when Scott was only thirteen, was a building contractor. "His dream was T.H. Wilson & Sons with me and my brother," Scott said. "He wanted one of us to be an architect and one to be an engineer. I kind of half-heartedly tried to follow through with it in a way. My mother had moved us to South Georgia after my father died in my junior year in high school because her brothers lived there and she wanted us to have some male supervision. The day after I graduated from high school I left town to go to Cincinnati, Ohio, to go to work laying brick with a friend of my dad." On his way, Scott stopped in Atlanta to see his old friends, and one day while he was playing basketball with them, a man approached him and said, "Where are you playing ball?" "I'm not," Scott replied. "You're not in school?" Scott said, "I just graduated." The man then told him that if he could pass the entrance test for Southern Tech, which was a branch of Georgia Tech, that he could play basketball there for him. Scott passed the exam and was accepted there on a scholarship. "I ended up in the infirmary with hepatitis. They said I couldn't play basketball anymore and that a relapse would be fatal, so I started thinking I wanted to see some of the world."

When Scott was released from the infirmary, he returned to his mother's home in southern Georgia. While he was at Southern Tech, Scott had met a songwriter who was going to go to California and write songs. "So I wrote a couple of songs and was thinking about California," Scott informed. "Then a friend of my mother who was living in California came back to Georgia to visit and have dinner, and she was talking about California. While they were both talking about California, I said 'What the hell, I'm going to California.' So when I was healthy enough I hitchhiked out here, and that's how I got to California."

Scott had forty dollars when he left Georgia, and upon arriving in California, he said, "I did a little serious going hungry. When I first got out here I paid eight bucks for a room about the size of a broom closet, in a rooming house. I had thirteen dollars left. That lasted me for about a week and then I was flat broke. For six weeks I didn't have a penny to my name, but I had a lot of adventures in those six weeks. Then I got a job as a mail clerk at the Superior Oil Company. Two other guys and I rented a small house. One of them, Bill, was looking at the want ads in the newspaper and saw an ad that said Actors Wanted. He said, 'Let's go see about getting an acting job.' He had an old car so we drove up to the place, and we saw a girl walking down the street. He said to me, 'You go on in,' and he picked this girl up, drove off with her, and I'm left standing in front of this door. I tripped over the door walking in and fell on my face, embarrassed as hell. I got up and they started talking to me about giving them my money. I said, 'I thought you were going to give me money.' So that didn't work out."

Bill kept telling Scott that he should go to an acting class, so he finally called the Theater of Arts and made an appointment for the weekend, when he was off work. "I got drunk and didn't go," he told us. "Then I made another appointment for the next weekend, got drunk again, and didn't go. That happened about three times. Then one weekend Bill happened to be there. I was four sheets to the wind, really drunk. He physically carried me through the front door of this acting class, set me down on the couch, walked up to the counter, and said, 'Who's in charge here? I have a movie star for you.' So I sat through this class and the teacher came up to me and said, 'I don't know what your problem is, but don't come back in the class drunk.' Probably if he hadn't done that I would never have gone back. I felt that this was something that was important to him, so I went back the next week sober to apologize to him, and he gave me a scene from a Eugene O'Neill one-act called *The Long Voyage Home*. I went back the next week, did the monologue in front of the students, and I knew then that's what I wanted to do. It was like magic. I was hooked from that point on."

Clint Prentiss, the teacher, and another associate there named Elliott Fayad, broke away from the acting school and started their own place, and Scott followed them. "I did theater," Scott said. "We'd do one play while rehearsing another. I was involved working for five and a half years either doing plays or scenes or building sets, doing lighting or whatever was needed to be done to get the thing going. The first play I did was *The Importance of Being Earnest*. It was a pass-the-hat production. My mother has my check framed on the wall for fifty cents. That was in 1962. The last play I did was a Tennessee Williams play. He came out and worked with us on it for about two weeks. It was a play that he kept re-writing, and he was never happy with it. It was called *Outcry*. There were about two or three different versions of it that he kept rewriting. After opening night he came backstage with tears running down his face, and said, 'At last I've seen the play done properly.' That was a thrill."

While Scott was involved with the acting class he was also still working with Superior Oil as a shipping clerk. "The personnel called me in one day and said, 'We are very happy with you. We want to send you to college at USC or UCLA, but you have to work for us; you just can't promise to work for us an x amount of time after you're through with school.' I said, 'I'm going to school.' They said, 'You are? We're thrilled to hear that. Where are you going?' 'I'm taking acting class.' Shortly after that they fired me. Then I was working as a shipping clerk at an educational film place, and also at Ralphs as a box boy. So I had two jobs going, and classes. I was very ambitious in those days. At Bailey Films they kept giving me raises, so I gave up the Ralphs job and had more time for acting. Before I took the job at Baileys they agreed that if I needed to take off for an interview it would be okay. I was there for a year and a half and never had an interview. Then I had one to read for a play. I told them I needed to go for it, but they said I couldn't go. I said that was part of the deal when I started to work there, and they said, 'Yes, but you made yourself too important to us.' I said I'm going, and left anyway, and they fired me."

Scott next met a man in a poker game that worked alone at a gas station, and he hired Scott. "At the gas station I met one of the producers of a TV show called *Mr. Roberts*," Scott said. "He got me into the Screen Extras Guild. I was a stand-in on that show and I did get two words, 'The galley.' I thought I was an actor. I didn't know the difference between an extra and an actor. On my first day on the set I was a sailor on the ship. I had never been in the service and didn't know the protocol, so I'm listening to him talk to the actors and he's saying that when the flag reaches half-mast, salute. So I'm in the line with the sailors, my back is to the camera, it's half mast, I pop a salute, and I'm the only one saluting," Scott laughed. "I guess that's only for officers to salute. The director went absolutely ballistic. He turned purple in the face and started screaming at me. It was brutal. I was called over to the corner of the soundstage, and he said that he never wanted to see me again. I crawled off and was crying, but I survived that and did extra work for a while for different places."

Scott obtained extra work in *Three on a Couch* with Jerry Lewis. "There was a silent bit that the assistant director gave me to do," Scott related. "He had me standing in front of a brownstone waiting for a girl, and when she comes out I walk off with her. So I'm standing in front, pop my sleeve and look at a watch, only I don't have a watch. I start up the stairs and then go back to wait. I start up again and then go back. Then she comes out and we walk off. The next day the assistant director called me at home and said, 'Mr. Lewis wants you to be his stand-in.' It's kind of a legend that he treated his stand-in's pretty good, and a lot of them went on to become producers or assistant directors. I said, 'Tell Mr. Lewis I'm flattered and I appreciate it, but I just stopped doing extra work.' I was making better money than I had ever made, but I felt it was a trap, that I was going to get hooked into a life style that I had to support, and it wasn't in the direction I wanted to go in. So I quit doing that and went to work parking cars for two bucks an hour," Scott smiled.

One night Scott was hitchhiking to his acting class and a man stopped to give him a ride. "I thought he was an actor," Scott said. "We were talking about acting and about an actor named Michael Parks. A few weeks later I'm in class and I get a call from Michael Park's agent, and he said a friend of mine at MGM wants me to come out for an interview. I said, 'I don't have no friends at MGM.' 'Then you don't want the interview?' I said, 'I'll take the interview.' In the meantime I had bought a '53 Kaiser and was driving to the interview on the freeway when it threw a rod through the oil pan and the motor caught on fire. So I walked down the freeway and climbed a fence, thinking who can I call to get me to the interview. I called Michael Parks, who this guy and I had been talking about (it ended up this guy was Joe D'Agosta, a casting director), so Michael, who I had met when I was going to class, came out, picked me up, and took me over to the interview. I went in and gave a reading for the role and they liked me, but I didn't get it. But as a result of that reading I had an interview for a *Ben Casey*. It was a terrific lead guest role, and they said, 'Great. If we can't get a name, we'll go with you.' They got a name so I didn't get that role, but Joe D'Agosta called me back, gave me a part in a show, and I got my SAG card.

"Three and a half years later I got my next interview," he laughed. "That was interesting too. They hired a guy named Dick when I was working at Bailey Films and I found out that Jack, his stepfather, was an agent, and that his mother was Whitney Blake, an actress. So, Dick and I used to play basketball when we had time, and I would go up to his house. I never talked to his stepdad or his mom about wanting to be an actor. I felt like they would think I was trying to get to them through Dick, and that wasn't the basis of our friendship. I didn't want to tamper with friendship by trying to hoist myself as a user. Ultimately, I was doing a thirty minute scene in my acting class from *A Hatful of Rain*, and I called Jack—this was after knowing him for a long time—and I said, 'Listen. I've never talked to you about acting, but you know that I'm an actor, and I'm doing a scene I want you to see. I know that I'm ready to work, and after you see the scene if you don't want to represent me, that's fine. But I would like you to represent me if you like it.' So he sent a sub-agent down, and the sub-agent went crazy, went back and was telling Jack how great I was. His partner came down to see me and they signed me up. I went by to pick Dick up to play some basketball one day and Jack was on the phone. He said, 'Just a second. I have one more guy I want you to see.' And that was my first interview, and it was for *In the Heat of the Night*. Jack went with me on the interview, and Lynn Stalmaster (the casting director) asked, 'Can he do a Southern accent?' and Jack said, 'Let him read.' So I read the scene, and then I went in to read for Norman Jewison, and he asked, 'Can you do a Southern accent?' Jack and Lynn Stalmaster started laughing, and said, 'Let him read.' So I read the scene, and then went in to meet Walter Mirisch who was the producer of the show. Walter asked, 'Can you do a Southern accent?' Norman, Lynn, and Jack started laughing, and said, 'Let him read.' So I got the role, which was a huge break. I knew I was ready to work. If I hadn't started working I don't know what would have happened to me. I think I would have ended up in the nuthouse somewhere. I felt like I was ready to explode. I would tell anybody I could act. I was cocky, more so than I am now."

Next Scott landed the role in *In Cold Blood* with Robert Blake. There is an interesting story of how he came to be considered for the part of Dick Hickock, one of the two brutal murderers of a Midwest family in that film. "I was talking to Sidney Poitier on the set of *In the Heat of the Night* one day, and he asked, 'Are you up for *In Cold Blood*?' and I said, 'What's that?' He said, 'It's something you should be up for. Tell your agent to get you up for it.' So I mentioned it to my agent and he said, 'You're not old enough and you don't weigh enough.' I said, 'Okay, Sidney suggested that I tell you to put me up for it.' And I forgot about it. Without my knowing about it, Norman had been letting Richard Brooks look at the dailies. On the last day of shooting *In The Heat of the Night*, the assistant director came over to me and said, 'Go over to Columbia and see Richard Brooks for *In Cold Blood*.' I called my agent. He wasn't in, so I didn't go. I figured it took me five and a half years to get an agent so I'm not going to do anything unless he knows about it. Sidney came on the set, and said, 'What are you doing here? You're supposed to be over at Columbia talking to Brooks.' I said, 'I was waiting for my agent to get into it.' He said, 'The hell with your agent. You get over to Columbia right now and talk to Brooks.' He walked me out to the car and really pumped my ego up. So I walked through the door feeling like Godzilla."

Scott met Brooks, who said, "We need a combination of Montgomery Clift, Gary Cooper, Clark Gable, Burt Lancaster, Humphrey Bogart, and Spencer Tracy." When he was through naming the biggest stars ever, Scott replied, "I'm afraid you have the wrong boy. I can't play one of those guys, let alone all of them. But I'll tell you what, I'm one hell of an actor." Tom Shaw, who was Brooks' production manager, was in Scott's corner from the word go. He said, "You're the one; I'm going to be pushing for you. Don't sell that short. I think you're the guy." And he did keep pushing for Scott. In the meantime, Scott read the book by Truman Capote that the film was taken from. He thought to himself, "Why am I telling him I can't do that? Of course I can do that." Brooks called Scott back and asked him to do a scene. He was walking from his desk to the couch with his pipe in his mouth, and asked, "What scene did you decide to do?" Scott answered, "*Hamlet*," at which Brooks almost bit his pipe stem into. After Scott completed the scene, Brooks asked, "Where have you done Shakespeare?" "At home in my living room, by myself," Scott replied. Scott then reflected on his first monologue he had done years before from O'Neill's *A Long Voyage Home*, and said, "I've got something else I can do," and performed it with an Irish accent. After this, Scott left and was later called by Tom Shaw, who said, "You were great."

"In the meantime, weeks were going by and I was so nervous I wasn't able to sleep," Scott confided. "Then they called me back in and Brooks gave me some scenes to do from *Night Must Fall*. I did those, and then I did them for the head of the studio. After doing the scenes they called me back to do a screen test, and I got the role."

Other films followed. Scott worked with Burt Lancaster in his next two films. In *The Gypsy Moths* he played one of a trio of daredevil parachutists with Lancaster and Gene Hackman, and in *Castle Keep* Scott appeared in his first film shot on a foreign location. Then came the lead in *The Grissom Gang*, followed by a co-starring part opposite George C. Scott and Stacy Keach in *The New Centurions*. Scott next worked with Rod Steiger and Robert Ryan in the tale of two feuding backwoods families in *Lolly Madonna XXX*. Another good part, as George Wolson, the vulnerable garage owner who murders Robert Redford in *The Great Gatsby*, followed. He appeared in the Israeli film *The Passover Plot* opposite Harry Andrews and Hugh Griffith. In 1980, Scott's performance as Captain Billy Cutshaw, the mad astronaut, in *The Ninth Configuration* earned him a best supporting actor nomination at the Golden Globe Awards. "After that I went for four years without working," Scott added.

Scott's career took him to a number of foreign locations—such countries as Yugoslavia, Hungary, Poland, Spain (*La Cruz de Iberia*), Germany, Austria, and Japan. "I've seen a lot of the world," Scott mentioned. "In 1968 I was in Yugoslavia on *Castle Keep* when the Russian tanks rolled into Czechoslovakia, and that was quite a big world event at that time. We were sitting there with communications not as they should be and wondering what the hell was happening. There was a special effects guy, Lee Kavitz, on our picture (he did the burning of Atlanta in *Gone With the Wind*), and every time I'd go out with him he'd have a couple of drinks and kept saying how much he hated this castle and couldn't wait to blow it up, because in the film the castle is blown up. This was in Novi Sad, and I'd been to Belgrade one night. I came in about two or three in the morning, and everyone was up. I thought, 'Oh shit! I wonder what happened. I wonder if the Russians rolled in or something.' I went to Lancaster and asked, 'What's happening?' and he said, 'Lee blew up the castle.' He had blown the castle up before it was supposed to be blown up. It was an accident, but they had to rebuild the castle to shoot the rest of the movie. So that was quite an experience."

Another film on foreign soil was in Japan, called *Puraido Unmei No Toki* (American title is *Pride*), based on the war crimes tribunal in Japan after World War II. "I played the prosecuting attorney," Scott noted. "It is a controversial film, and if it plays here there will be a lot of protests. But researching it, I think there is a lot of accuracy in it. I think it was kind of victor's justice in a way. Not that there weren't atrocities committed in the war, but these were people put on trial who were really pacifists that were opposed to the war. Some of them were found guilty and hanged, and shortly after six or seven were hanged, twenty-eight people were put on trial. Two or three years after the trials, the ones that weren't hanged had their sentences commuted. So that tells you they must have known the trials were not really up and up."

After his work in *The Ninth Configuration* it seems the bottom fell out from under Scott as far as his career went. For some unexplained reason, work in the business eluded him. "I got a job with my old buddy that I had worked for at the gas station who was now a painting contractor," Scott explained. "I went to work for him doing manual labor. I lugged the paint cans around, did the cleanup, set up shop, and did the grunt work. He was painting an art gallery one day and the guy who owned the gallery kept walking by and looking at me. Ultimately he came over to me and said, 'Aren't you Scott Wilson?' I said, 'Yes, I am.' 'What are you doing here?' 'I'm trying to make a living.' 'Well,' he said, 'you can go to work with me here at the art gallery.' That may have been in an earlier period when I went a year and a half without working. Yeah, I had some down times. If you knew up front that you were going to have that 'down time' you could go to college, become a doctor, and get into a profession that you could make a living," Scott laughed. "I feel that in this business you don't know that when you first start out. You think it's art, and you should always feel that way, but in reality it is a business. You can be very professional, but I don't think you are in a profession. Any other profession that you were in, if you were a dentist, a lawyer, a doctor, an architect, or even a craftsman like a bricklayer or a painter, you can say you have a profession. I don't think you can say you have a profession as an actor. You can be professional, but there are too many variables. It isn't like if they were constructing a building they'd probably need carpenters or bricklayers or painters or electricians to go out, and ultimately you're going to get a job. It doesn't have to happen in acting."

When asked why he thought that four years would go by without a job after being nominated for the award for *The Ninth Configuration*, Scott answered, "Who knows. I am constantly amazed. You think you've seen everything and you haven't. Why did I start working after five and a half years? It was just a break. Who knows? Maybe it's the alignment of stars, just luck. I think you have to be prepared to work when that opportunity comes. If you're not prepared, then how many more opportunities are you going to get? And during the course of your life as you go through different phases with ageing and everything, you constantly have to redefine how people perceive you. Now he fits into this age, and now he fits into that age. So I know in that four-year period I just took whatever was there so that people would know that I was alive. I was fortunate enough to get a little part in *The Right Stuff* and I realized that I took the role even though it was smaller than any role I've ever had. I took it because it would be months before it would come out and people will know I'm in it, and they will assume I have a larger role and maybe I'll get some work off of that. So, it worked out that way: I did get a bigger role, and it afforded me the opportunity to do *A Year of the Quiet Sun* in Poland. I didn't make any money off that film but I wanted to do it, and I could afford to do it because of the couple of jobs I got before we were able to shoot that. Now, I don't know why I'm working. People call, and sometimes they just give me an offer and sometimes I have to audition. I don't audition that much anymore because I don't think I'm good at it anymore. I was when I first started, but I had to do it for such a short period of time. In *In The Heat of the Night* I went in and gave a terrific reading, but now I don't think I could give a good reading because I realize what happens in that office is not what happens on a set. It's just difficult for me to go into an office, mainly because I've done so much work now I feel that people should know who I am. They should know if I can act or not, and if they don't think I can act then why are they interviewing me? I'm not going to convince them with a reading," Scott laughed. "I suppose you can, but look at some of my films if you want to see what I can deliver."

Scott's next important role after *The Ninth Configuration* took him to Poland to star in *A Year of the Quiet Sun* for Polish director Zrzystof Znussi. "We shot it during martial law in '84," Scott noted. "I met the director in Los Angeles, was talking to him, and didn't know that he knew I was an actor. I was asking him how you become an actor or director in Poland. The next day this mutual friend, who had introduced us, said that Znussi wanted to do a film with me. I said that I didn't know he knew I was an actor. He said, 'He's seen everything you've ever done.' So we met again, and he had two outlines that he gave me. One took place in Poland and the other in Ireland. He did most of his films with an actress named Maja Komorowska, and I said, 'Let's do this one. I want to work with your actress.' Znussi and I talked about it for nine years. When he was here we'd meet in airports, talk about the characters, and had good collaboration. So nine years later we got to make the film; it took that long to get it off the ground. It is a partially subtitled film and I'm the only American in it. It's a love story with an American GI at the end of World War II who doesn't speak Polish and a Polish lady who doesn't speak English. So it presents an interesting challenge: How do you do a mature love story without a common language and keep it from being me Tarzan, you Jane?" The challenge was met effectively, and it garnered the Golden Lion Award at the Venice Film Fest.

Other films followed, including *The Tracker* with Kris Kristofferson. "That was fun," Scott stated. "It was really the first full fledge Western that I have done where I could ride a horse and shoot a gun. It was like being a kid playing cowboys and Indians. I rode when I was a kid, but I had to refamiliarize myself. I'm not a great horseman, but I can ride a horse. They had a special saddle made for this little girl that my character kidnaps so that she could ride in front of me. There was one scene where we're supposed to be tearing down the road and the camera car is going to be riding right beside us, filming us. I was a little apprehensive about it because I didn't feel I was a great horseman. I talked to one of the stunt guys and he assured me that I could do it. I didn't want the girl to know I was apprehensive about it so I acted like I was a real horseman for her. I said to her, 'If you get scared just tell me and I'll stop.' Well, the horses are smart. Once they hear 'Action,' and get spurred, they know they're supposed to run. And every time they hear 'Action' they'll run because they don't want to get spurred. So they said 'Action' and we took off. The first take was great and they said fine. So great, we could leave. It was done. We rode back to the camera car and the director said, 'We'll do one more for coverage.' So I said, 'Okay, but you've got it, right?' He said, 'Yeah.' So we did it again. I was right in the process of leaning back and shooting when I heard the little girl say, 'I'm scared.' She had lost her grip a little. I turned around, put my arms around her, trying to rein the horse in. She was bouncing up and down in the saddle and I was afraid she was going to hurt herself, so I pulled the horse up and stopped." This turned out okay because the first take was great and they decided to keep that one." *The Tracker* was filmed in the four corners area and in Mesa Verde.

Scott continued working in films such as *Young Guns II*, *Geronimo -- An American Legend*, *Flesh and Bone*, *The Glass Harp*, *Judge Dredd*, and *Dead Man Walking*, before obtaining the role of the antagonist Judd Travers in the film *Shiloh*. Scott was cast in this film due to the recommendation of the film's co-star Rod Steiger, who Scott had worked with earlier in his career a few times. "Steiger promoted me to the producer and director," Scott related. "They were familiar with my work and liked me, but Steiger was relentless and wouldn't give up, and ultimately they hired me. I thought it was a very nice, smooth children's book about a boy and his dog, and it was required reading in lots of 4th and 5th grades. I had a lot of fun doing the film, and the director was a lot of fun to work with. I didn't think that much about it, and then the reviews came out and a lot of the critics just loved it. Although it had a limited theatrical life, it was very successful because it did great on cassette." The critics wrote, "Wilson helps us to understand a man who is almost too easy to hate;" "Scott Wilson is superbly nuanced and unexpectedly complex;" "Best of all is Scott Wilson as Judd, whose meanness is unforgivable but at the same time understandable." Gene Siskel wrote, "I want to credit Scott Wilson's performance. He is a real powerhouse character." Roger Ebert penned, "Wilson has just produced one great supporting role after another." There was also a movement afoot to push for his nomination as best supporting actor for an Academy Award. Scott was called back to play the same character in the sequel, *Shiloh Season*, and in 2005 was back in a second sequel called *Saving Shiloh*.

After *Shiloh*, Scott worked in Poland in *Our God's Brother* in January of 1997, followed by *Clay Pigeons*, and in January of 1998 he was in Japan for *Pride* ("This was with a Japanese director and a Japanese cast"). The next film was the second *Shiloh* movie, which was followed by a Western with John Cussack and L.Q. Jones for Showtime called *The Jack Bull*. "I played the Governor of the territory of Wyoming," Scott added. Other subsequent films included *Pearl Harbor*, *The Last Samurai*, *Don't Let Go*, *Open Window*, *The Sensation of Sight*, *Junebug* and *Big Stan*.

Scott has also worked in several television shows, such as *The Twilight Zone*, *The X-Files*, *Karen Sisco*, *Justified*, and as Sam Braun in fourteen episodes of *CSI: Crime Scene Investigation*.

Scott mentioned that when working in films, sometimes the actors stick with the written word and other times there is quite a lot of ad-libbing. "It depends on the script, on the director, and on the style of the film," Scott explained. "Some scripts you don't want to change anything, other scripts there is improvisation. The film we did in Poland (*A Year of the Quiet Sun*), there was a lot of improvisation; that was a unique situation where the director gave a lot of leeway. This last film that I did with Znussi (*Our God's Brother*) based on the play the Pope wrote, there was no improvisation because we wanted to stay faithful to the Pope's dialogue. He was an actor and a playwright prior to going into the church, and wrote it in his late twenties. It's about Adam Chmielowski, who was his inspiration for giving up the world of art and going into the priesthood. Chmielowski was born in 1845 and died in 1917. He was a successful artist and was well respected, and in his forties he came into contact with the poor and the homeless and it changed his life. He was conflicted as to whether he should pursue his art and painting or devote his time to the homeless. He felt he couldn't do both, so ultimately he gave up the world of art, became a monk, and changed his name to Brother Albert. After the playwright became Pope he canonized him, so I guess maybe it's the only time in history that the playwright has sainted his protagonist. It's not your traditional movie. It's very wordy; very talky. I met the Pope in Krakow before the premier and asked him if he would sign my script. He was great. I introduced him to my wife after that, and he said to her, 'Oh, you play your role as well,' which was very astute to realize that you (the actor) need support. And I think you do. If you're going to survive in this business you have to have someone who believes in you. You need to believe it yourself, but you need someone to prop that belief up. And I do," as Scott motioned to his wife, Heavenly.

When asked if he had a favorite among his film roles, Scott responded, "There were some films that I'm better known for than others, like my first lead role in *In Cold Blood*. *In The Heat of the Night* was a great first role. The film *The Grissom Gang*, which I loved but very few people have seen, is another one. Robert Aldrich directed it. It was a terrific role and happened to be one of the last pictures that ABC Pictures was making, so it never got the attention that it should, and it never got the release that it should have had. That still happens to this day because of turnovers in the administrations or a demise of a studio. So some of these films aren't promoted or nurtured like they should be, and that is unfortunate, but it happens.

"Actors should have the opportunity to fail and never be afraid to fail. Sometimes you may misfire on a role, but even if you do, you look at it and think, 'Maybe I missed there but I know what I was trying to do. I don't think it worked,' but you say it's a learning experience. But missing in the business costs a lot of money. I don't usually have the weight of carrying the movie on my shoulders, so it must be very tough for people who are super stars that realize that if they tank it, it's going to impact their income. Also, I don't think the stars are overcompensated. I think they deserve every penny they get and maybe more, but they've really depressed the income of actors below star level. It's really difficult for an actor to make a living if you're not a star, and it didn't use to be that way. They used to take care of the supporting players. You could have a lifestyle, you could have a house, and if you had kids you could send them to school, but that is not as much the case now. It's much tougher, and I think a meaner spirit in business than it was. And I'll say that to anybody.

"It's much tougher now," Scott continued, "and I think ultimately it's going to be bad for the business at large. If the supporting actors and the character actors are unable to make a living and unable to support their lifestyle—and I don't mean an elaborate lifestyle—but if they are unable to send their kids to school, if they're unable to pay their bills, or buy a house, actors are not dumb and they'll find other ways to make a living. You have too. So if they're not able to do that, ultimately they're going to be causing the producers to go look around and say who can handle this role? But they won't have anyone, and it will hurt the quality of the product. And if the quality of the product starts hurting, then the big bucks that are being made off a lot of the films now are going to be diminished. So ultimately it's bad for the business at large. Maybe I'm wrong, maybe they'll get robots to do what we're doing, but I think they feel that way about actors a lot. Unfortunately, the people who call the shots are not necessarily filmmakers. They don't know the first thing about making films. They may like to go to movies, they may like the power that comes along with calling the shots. But to be quite truthful, they don't know the first thing about making a movie—most of them don't. They don't know how to read a script; they don't know what a good script is. And you have a lot of directors now who don't know how to direct. Not everyone of course, that's a very general statement I just made. There are still some people who are talented. But I don't mind saying that. I know what it is out there."

When not working as an actor, Scott has had various side interests or hobbies to keep him busy. "At different times I used to play tennis; I've given that up and started kind of late playing golf. I burned out on golf and stopped playing that. I always thought golf was a ridiculous game when I was a kid and I went back to thinking that, but it was fun and it occupied me for a long time. Maybe one day I'll play it again. I think it's ridiculous, but if you start playing it you really get obsessed with it. I got involved playing chess for a while, and backgammon. I enjoyed poker. Nothing really all that constructive," Scott laughed. "But I read, and then burn out on that for a while, and then go back to it again. Recently I wrote a script with a couple of buddies called *Don't Step on the Ants*. It took us about two and a half years to write it, not a steady two and a half, but when none of us were doing anything else we'd get together and work on it. So we are in the process of getting that together, and we'll see what happens."

Scott had a couple of scripts on his couch that producers were interested in him performing in. He said, "There's a couple of low-budget scripts that I may do. I don't care what the cost of the picture is if I like the role. It doesn't matter. I'm on the Foreign Language Committee at the Academy this year and have really seen some terrific foreign language films that otherwise you might not get to see." On June 20, 1998, Scott was given an award at the Florida International Film Festival. "They were going to give me a Lifetime Achievement Award, but I said, 'Wait a minute. I don't think it's over yet,' so they changed it to an Acting Achievement Award.'"

In summing up his feelings about his career to date, Scott stated, "I feel that I have been very fortunate. Like the little thing in *Tall Tale*, I felt like I came up with a little character that was fun to do and I enjoyed it more than ever. I've worked in different countries and have been exposed to different cultures. When you work in different countries you work with people who do the same thing you do. It's amazing how universal a lot of things are. Being an actor, I have been exposed to things I never even thought about. It's just amazing how your life can lead you down these roads, like that Robert Frost poem, 'Two roads diverged in a yellow wood.' It's been exciting. I hope it continues, but there's no guarantee. I suppose that I haven't been as smart of a businessman as I could have been, particularly when I first started: I thought talent was the only thing that was needed. If I was teaching a class, I would insist that there was some time devoted to the business side as well, because it is a business. As a young person you don't think of that, and maybe you shouldn't dwell on it. But you should be aware of the fact that you have to play businessman at times. It's important, because at one time the studios took care of a lot of things that now actors have to take care of. If you were under contract to a studio, you worked, got your paycheck, they took care of the press for you. You could go to the bars or go fishing or whatever you were doing and say the hell with this business. You could do that because they were taking care of business for you. And they would come in and say here's a role you're going to do. So they pretty much popped the wheel, and in the meantime they took care of the business for you. After the demise of the studio system, there was good and bad with everything. The bad is that now the actors have to take care of those business aspects that the studios once took care of. It's caused the loss of certain types of actors. I'm not saying that one is better than the other, but the extroverted person doesn't mind going out and promoting himself. The introverted personality resists that stuff and has someone else do it, maybe to the point of not getting someone to do it at all. Truthfully, that was part of my problem. I've never promoted myself, but I think it should be done, even if you are an introverted personality. You have to integrate some business sense into your pursuit of being an artist. If you don't, you have to be very fortunate, which I have been. When I started, it was not long after the demise of the studio system, and a lot of the actors that were working that were the stars were people who were the stars in the studio system, so it took a while for new stars to develop. There was a period of time where there wasn't very many young actors developing. When I did *In Cold Blood* I was one of the youngest serious actors around working. I didn't handle it properly, but a lot of it was also due to the time that it came out in the 60's. You know, you don't trust anyone over thirty. To hell with big business, you didn't trust them. I was a product of my generation and had all the slogans that you had in those days, justly or not. Now I say, don't trust anyone under thirty," Scott laughed.

In February 2006, Scott was invited as a guest to the Floating Film Festival that was held aboard ship as they sailed through the Panama Canal. Roger Ebert had suggested Scott, and at the festival he was awarded the Exemplary Achievement Award for his work in motion pictures.

Film Credits: **1966:** Three on a Couch. **1967:** In the Heat of the Night; In Cold Blood. **1969**: Castle Keep; The Gypsy Moths. **1971**: The Grissom Gang. **1972**: The New Centurions. **1973**: Lolly-Madonna XXX. **1974**: The Great Gatsby. **1976**: The Passover Plot. **1979**: La Legal. **1980**: The Ninth Configuration. **1983**: The Right Stuff. **1984**: On the Line; A Year of the Quiet Sun. **1985**: The Aviator. **1986**: Blue City. **1987**: Malone. **1988** The Tracker (TV); Jesse (TV). **1989**: Johnny Handsome. **1990**: Young Guns II; The Exorcist III; La Cruz de Iberia. **1991**: Pure Luck; Femme Fatale. **1993**: Geronimo-An American Legend; Elvis and the Colonel-The Untold Story (TV); Flesh and Bone. **1995**: Tall Tale; The Grass Harp; Dead Man Walking; Judge Dredd; Soul Survivors (TV). **1996**: Shiloh; Mother. **1997**: Our God's Brother; GI Jane. **1998**: Puraido-Unmei no toki; Clay Pigeons. **1999**: Shiloh II: Shiloh Season; The Jack Bull (TV); The Debtors.

2000: South of Heaven, West of Hell; Way of the Gun. **2001**: The Animal; Pearl Harbor. **2002**: Don't Let Go; Bark! Coastlines; Guide Season (TV). **2003**: The Last Samurai; Monster. **2005**: Junebug; **2006**: Open Window; Saving Shiloh; Behind the Mask: The Rise of Leslie Vernon. Come Early Morning; The Sensation of Sight; The Host. **2007**: Big Stan; The Heartbreak Kid. **2009**: For Sale by Owner; Bottleneck; Saving Grace B. Jones. **2010**: Radio Free Albemuth. **2011**: Dorfman. **2012**: B4TM.

MARIE WINDSOR

Marie was born Emily Marie Bertelsen in Marysvale, Utah on December 11, 1919. "I first became interested in acting when my grandmother used to take me to the movies in a little tiny theater in a little tiny town of less than three hundred people," Marie explained. "They just played one movie twice a week and I fell in love with Clara Bow, and I decided I wanted to be just like her." Marie also expressed interest in dancing when still a young child. "So when I got to be about eight years old my mother used to drive me thirty miles over a dirt road for dancing lessons. That's how it all started."

Marie attended Brigham Young University in Provo, Utah for two years studying Drama. "I was ambitiously aiming toward two degrees, majoring in Art and Drama," she reflected. "They had a very good drama department but I only stayed two years." Doctor Pardoe, in a conversation with Marie about her goal of becoming an actress, reaffirmed her own thoughts that if it was her desire to make a living in this profession that she wasn't really going to get into it by staying at the university. "This isn't quite true nowadays," she added.

Her parents began to investigate various dramatic schools where Marie could obtain the proper training, and in so doing came across an ad in the Cosmopolitan Magazine for Maria Ouspenskaya's School of Drama in New York. "About that time my grandmother took me east to a Postmistress's convention and investigated this school and found that they had moved to Hollywood. So not too long after this they sent me to Maria Ouspenskaya's school in Hollywood and I lived at the Hollywood Studio Club. They paid the tuition for six months and then the folks couldn't afford to keep me there any longer," she remarked.

Marie saw an ad on the Hollywood Studio Club bulletin board for a job as cigarette girl at the Mocambo Restaurant. "Three of us girls went over there and got the job," she continued. "I was there for about six weeks when I decided it wasn't up my alley, selling cigarettes to people expecting tips so I didn't. I used to say to people, 'Look, only give me ten cents because the concession gets it anyway.' Actually, they were almost ready to fire me when I quit." The actual event that transpired on Marie's last night of work there was when she was helping people on with their coats. The head cigarette girl was an alcoholic, and Marie burst into tears and was crying all over her cigarette tray. The fellow she was helping with his coat, Arthur Hornblow, a film producer, said "It doesn't look like you're happy with this job." "No," Marie responded. "I guess you want to be an actress, is that why you're in Hollywood?" he asked. "Yes." "Well, what are you doing about it?" Marie told him about her attending Ouspenskaya's drama school. "Well," he opinioned, "I can see you're not happy here. Why don't you call my secretary and make an appointment and let's see if we can help you." Marie quit the job and went back to the club.

The next morning came and Marie told us "I got too shy to call him. The secretary tracked down where I lived and called me, so I went over there. He told me that LeRoy Prince was casting a show on Stage 20 called *All American Co-ed*, a little movie at Hal Roach, and needed some young high school age kids and some show girls in it. I went over and LeRoy Prince hired me and that's how I got my SAG card. I had a two week contract at sixty dollars a week and that was the beginning."

Many small parts followed, including an interesting MGM short titled *The Lady and the Tiger*, as well as features like *Parachute Nurse*, *The Big Street*, a Pete Smith special and *Call Out the Marines* at RKO in which she had a nice little part with Victor McLaglen. After about two years in Hollywood, 1941-43, Marie heeded the advice of many people saying "You're not going to make it any place until you make it through New York." Marie told us that "Somebody tipped me off that they were casting a stage show that was to open in Detroit, so I went to see this producer and I got into the show. It was called *Henry Duffy's Merry-Go-Rounders*; it was a high class Vaudeville show. They cast me as a show girl and a straight woman in it. We opened in Detroit and played Washington and Buffalo and then we folded." While they were performing in Washington, co-star Jay C. Flippen introduced Marie to a friend who had a friend named Jerry Devine who did radio in New York City. "They gave me a letter to give Jerry Devine and when I got to New York I contacted him and he started giving me parts in radio," Marie continued. "Then I got on a soap opera that I was on for eight months, that's how I paid the rent." Marie's work in radio consisted of over four hundred shows between 1941 and 1946. Marie also appeared on stage as the narrator for a fashion show for the New York Times.

Her next stage appearance came in 1945 on Broadway when she replaced Karen Stevens as the heavy in *Follow the Girls*. "I was in that for about three months, and in that time somebody from Metro had seen me and put a good word in and said they wanted to test me at MGM." As Marie was coming west to visit her parents for Christmas she continued on to Hollywood, where they tested her. Marie was put under stock contract and was there for two years. During her stay there she appeared in such films as *Song of the Thin Man*, *The Hucksters*, *The Romance of Rosey Ridge* and *The Three Musketeers*. "When they dropped my contract at MGM my career started to bloom," Marie added.

At this time of her career Marie began to freelance opposite such stars as John Garfield (*Force of Evil*); George Raft (*Outpost in Morocco*) in which she had to learn to dance bending her legs to appear shorter than her partner, Raft; Joel McCrea (*Frenchie*); and Rod Cameron (*The Jungle*). Many of her features were for Republic Studios.

Marie who appeared in three films with John Wayne, reflected on a humorous experience in one of these features. "I was a very bad woman in *The Fighting Kentuckian*, I was his bitchy wife in *Trouble Along the Way*, and finally I got to be a nice lady in the third movie I made with him (*Cahill: United States Marshal*). I ran a boarding house and was taking care of his kids in the movie. My boarding house, which was way up on the top of a hill, was quite a distance from the town. So there was this shot where I was driving a wagon with these two kids, and it was quite a shot because it included horses and people crossing the street. A long shot, picking us up at a distance coming from the house; so we started down the hill when Andy McLaglen yelled 'Action.' We got half way down when Andy yelled 'Cut! Marie, take off those damn sunglasses,'" she laughed.

Due to her many Western roles, we asked Marie if she learned to ride horses for the movies and she answered, "I learned to ride in Utah. I got my first horse at age ten. I learned to ride without a saddle." Anyone that watched her films can attest to the fact she looked very natural on horseback.

When asked what her favorite film or performance was, if any, Marie answered "*Hellfire*, *Narrow Margin* and *The Killing*." The reason for these choices was "because they were great parts."

When asked about any feelings on *Cat Woman of the Moon*, her comment was "an awful movie." Concerning any reflections on her role in *Outlaw Women*, she said "Not necessarily, but it was fun to play." On her role in *Story of Mankind*, Marie mentioned, "I liked doing a scene with Dennis Hopper."

On her memories of the making of 1953's *The Tall Texan*, Marie remarked, "It was a very hard movie to make. We made it in New Mexico in an area where the dust was so fine that when we drove to location, even though the windows were wound tight, we'd be covered with this fine dust, and breathing it." Lloyd Bridges was the star of the film, and his wife and two young sons were there on the set also. Marie reflected that "His wife was there with Jeff Bridges, who at that time was wearing 'heavy diapers.' It was twenty years later I worked in *Hearts of the West* with Jeff, and I reminded him that I knew him well when he was still in diapers," she laughed.

Marie also appeared on television in such series as *Waterfront, Public Defender, Science Fiction Theatre, Climax, Line-Up, Cheyenne, Lawman, Maverick, 77 Sunset Strip, Lassie, Wyatt Earp, Perry Mason, Bonanza, Barnaby Jones, Marcus Welby, MD, Fantasy Island, Charlie's*

Angels, Lou Grant, General Hospital, Simon and Simon, Rawhide, Target, Gunsmoke and played Belle Starr in an episode of *Stories of the Century*. Television movies included *Wild Women* and *Stranded*. Her final performance came in 1991 on an episode of *Murder She Wrote*.

In looking over her long career as an actress, Marie summed up her feelings thusly: "Well, I hope I never completely quit acting, but there isn't a lot I can look forward to at my age," She laughed. "I had a wonderful career. I mean it wasn't as wonderful as I would have liked but it has been quite fulfilling. I've gotten to know some wonderful people and I'm just generally a happy lady with my husband Jack Hupp and my son Rick."

Marie died on December 10, 2000 in Beverly Hills, California.

1941: All American Co-ed; Playmates; Weekend for Three. **1942:** Parachute Nurse; Call Out the Marines; George Washington Slept Here; The Big Street; Smart Alecks; Eyes in the Night; Flying with Music; Four Jacks and a Jill; The Lady or the Tiger (short). **1943:** Let's Face It; Three Hearts for Julia; Chatterbox; Pilot No. 5. **1944:** Follow the Leader. **1946:** I Love My Husband But! (short). **1947:** Song of the Thin Man; The Hucksters; The Romance of Rosy Ridge; The Unfinished Dance; Living in a Big Way; I Love My Wife But! (short). **1948:** On an Island with You; The Kissing Bandit; Force of Evil; The Three Musketeers. **1949:** The Beautiful Blonde from Bashful Bend; Outpost in Morocco; The Fighting Kentuckian; Hellfire. **1950:** Dakota Lil; The Showdown; Double Deal; Frenchie. **1951:** Little Big Horn; Two Dollar Bettor; Hurricane Island. **1952:** The Narrow Margin Japanese War Bride; The Jungle; The Sniper; Outlaw Women. **1953:** The Tall Texan; City that Never Sleeps; Trouble along the Way; So This is Love; Cat Women of the Moon; USSR Today; The Eddie Cantor Story. **1954:** Hell's Half Acre; The Bounty Hunter. **1955:** The Silver Star; Abbott and Costello meet the Mummy; No Mans Woman; Two-Gun Lady; Swamp Woman. **1956:** The Killing. **1957:** The Unholy Wife; The Girl in Black Stockings; The Story of Mankind; The Parson and the Outlaw. **1958:** Day of the Bad Man; Island Woman. **1962:** Paradise Alley. **1963:** Critic's Choice; The Day Mars Invaded Earth. **1964:** Mail Order Bride; Bedtime Story. **1966:** Chamber of Horrors. **1969:** The Good Guys and the Bad Guys. **1970:** Wild Women (TV). **1971:** Support Your Local Gunfighter; One More Train to Rob. **1973:** Cahill, U.S. Marshal; The Outfit. **1974:** Manhunter (TV). **1975:** Hearts of the West. **1976:** Freaky Friday; Stranded (TV). **1979:** Salem's Lot (TV). **1981:** Lovely but Deadly; The Perfect Woman (TV). **1985:** Humanoid Defender (TV). **1987:** Commando Squad.

MORGAN WOODWARD

Thomas Morgan Woodward was born September 16, 1925 at Fort Worth, Texas, the son of Dr. Valin and Frances (McKinley) Woodward. His father was one of seven brothers, all of whom were doctors. Morgan's grandfather was also a doctor as was his grandmother's father. "One hundred and seventy-five years of doctors," Morgan remarked, "and I have a brother that's a doctor. I was the black sheep; I became an actor."

Speaking of his childhood, Woodward recalled, "I was raised in Arlington, Texas, with two older and two younger brothers. Raised a lot of hell, especially with no girls in the family. We had a lot of fun times – we fished in the creeks and hunted in the fields. I can remember the early 1930's during the depths of the Great Depression when people were really poor. People who needed medical treatment bartered with my father; very few had money so they brought vegetables, chickens, eggs or milk. So I learned very young what it is to be poor."

Morgan attended grade school in Arlington, and while in high school he did the usual things that most kids in Texas did: "We were not big baseball fans and we were not big basketball fans," Morgan reflected. "We were football people there. I played football with the Arlington High School team." Another of Morgan's interests was flying. "I've always had an interest in aviation," Morgan informed. "Would have been perfectly happy to be a professional airline pilot and would have been a senior captain by this time if I had gone with Continental Airlines which I started to do after the Korean War, but I changed my mind. I started flying when I was sixteen years old and continue to fly today." As a matter of fact, Morgan's chief hobby is restoring, rebuilding, and flying antique airplanes. In aviation circles, Morgan is recognized as an authority on early American aircraft and has received

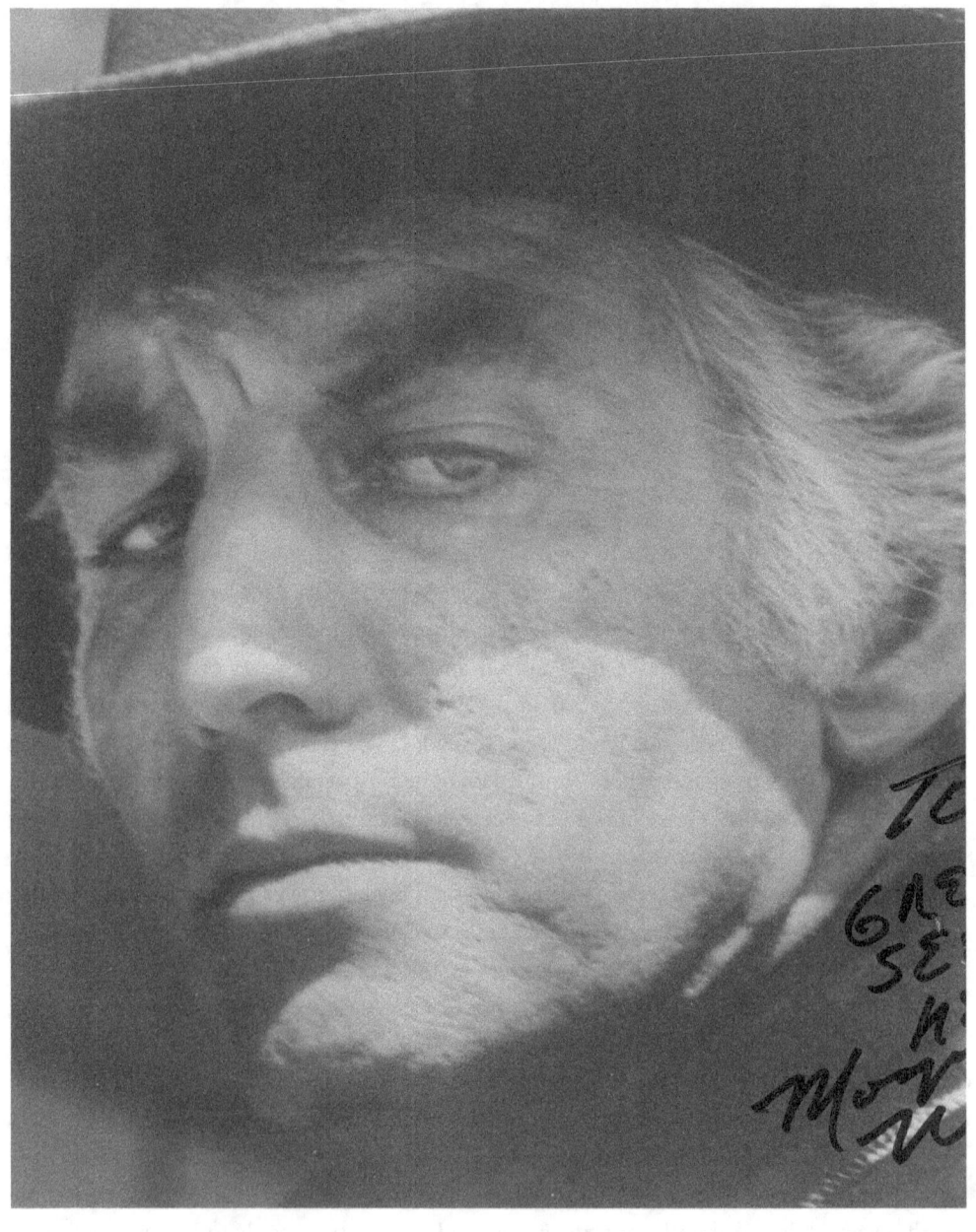

some seventeen awards for his restoration projects from the Antique Aircraft Association of America.

After graduating from high school in 1944, Morgan went into the Army Air Corps during World War II and stayed until December 5, 1945. He arrived home just before Christmas and started junior college at Arlington State in January of 1946. While here, Morgan was introduced to the theater. "I was with Margo Jones Repertory Company in Dallas when I was in college. We were doing the only theater-in-the-round in America. My goal was the musical theater, and I sang light opera." Morgan had hopes of joining the Metropolitan Opera, but due to the decline of grand opera in America he transferred in 1948 to the University of Texas and changed his major from music and drama and graduated in 1951 with a BBA Degree in Corporation Finance. Afterwards Morgan attended Law School at the same university. While attending the university he was unable to get completely away from the world of entertainment. He told us, "I had an hour variety show on radio station KTMX on Sunday afternoons on which I was the host." Morgan also had a dance band with a barbershop quartet. Among his classmates were his close friend Fess Parker, as well as Jayne Mansfield, Rip Torn, L.Q. Jones and Pat Hingle. His fraternity, Pi Kappa Alpha, named Morgan the recipient of the Distinguished Achievement Award of 1981.

Morgan's law schooling was soon to be interrupted by the outbreak of the Korean War, at which time he was recalled into the Air Force with the Military Air Transport Command and spent about two years overseas. When he returned home he went to work with the Lone Star Steel Company in Dallas as a junior executive. "I couldn't stand that," he mused, "so I decided I'd do the thing I really wanted to do – to be a singer and an actor. So I went to California."

Morgan left Texas in 1955 and came west to Hollywood where his fraternity brother, Fess Parker, had become a big star playing Davy Crockett. "He got me inside the gates at Disney and I did a test for him which led to three pictures. Disney was a terrific guy," Morgan noted. "The first day I was on the set he came down and introduced himself." Morgan's first picture was in November of 1955, and was titled *The Great Locomotive Chase* starring Fess Parker, Jeff Hunter, and Jeff York. The film was based on a real life account of the Andrews Raiders who hijacked a Confederate train during the Civil War. This picture was followed shortly by a second, *Westward Ho, the Wagons*, which also starred Parker and York. The third film for Disney in March of 1956 titled *Along the Oregon Trail* completed Morgan's initial phase in Hollywood.

The period following the Disney films was a rough time. Morgan recalled, "Since these pictures were almost a year away from being released I had nowhere to go after Disney. There was a long period of time where I had to try and support myself with odd jobs. I exercised, groomed and trained horses at stables in Griffith Park and did every other kind of odd job I could to stay alive."

Eight or nine months later the Disney pictures were finally released. "Fortunately there's some interest shown in a new face in Hollywood and I began to do some small parts," Morgan stated. This period was followed by a couple of episodes on the *Wyatt Earp* television series, and being impressed with his work they signed him up as a regular to co-star with Hugh O'Brian, his part running from 1958 through 1961. "Then there were some very lean years because although the Earp series was a very high rated show nationally, it was not high rated in Hollywood," Morgan explained.

After leaving *Wyatt Earp*, Morgan mentioned, "I almost literally had to start over again because every time my agent would submit me for a part they'd say, 'Oh, the old guy that rides the donkey.' 'Well, no – He's a Western actor.' I was about thirty-one or thirty-two years old, so apparently I played the part very well because they thought I was an old man at the time."

Morgan considers the role of "the man with no eyes" in the 1966 feature *Cool Hand Luke* as the turning point of his career. "It was a giant step forward. I was told by people who know that I came very close to being nominated in a supporting role for the Academy Award. My co-worker in the picture, George Kennedy, got the nomination and won, so it was certainly a giant step forward for him; but the picture helped me a great deal."

In addition to *Cool Hand Luke*, the television series *Gunsmoke* was an important factor in the advancement of his film career. "I did my first episode in 1965," Morgan stated. "Pam Polifroni, the casting director, had me in to read for a part, and in the next ten years I did more *Gunsmoke*'s than any other actor in the world. I did more than even Strother Martin, who worked over the twenty-one year period. I did sixteen in ten years which is some kind of record, and it still remains my favorite show. I enjoyed it because if you were a guest star you better be able to cut the mustard because if you couldn't you never appeared on that show again. I think John Mantley and Leonard Katzman did a great job on that show. The regulars – Jim, Amanda, Milburn and Ken – in the last years they had very little to do with it, they were the thread that tied it together. They invited you into their setting to do your thing. If you break the law then Jim comes in to warn you, and if you do it again then he arrests you. If you get hurt, Doc takes care of you; Festus usually muddles things up. So it was really a great idea and ran very well."

Morgan has been nominated for three Emmy's during his career – two were from episodes of *Gunsmoke*, one titled *Lobo* and the other *Vengeance*; the third Emmy was for *Daggers of the Mind*, an episode from *Star Trek*. Every year the Western Heritage Foundation have the networks submit their best Western fare for the Golden Spur Award, and in 1969 Morgan was in two of the three submitted. *Lobo* from *Gunsmoke*, and *The Buffalo Soldiers* from *High Chaparral*. In the same *Newsweek* magazine issue that announced the fact that we have landed on the moon also appeared an article called *The Dirty Half-Dozen*. It had a full page spread of six of the meanest, dirtiest heavies in motion pictures and television at that time. "Being included in this didn't hurt either," Morgan informed.

Morgan Woodward

With the temporary demise of the Western, Morgan has remained busy on television, including the recurring role of Punk Anderson on the then popular series of *Dallas*. Referring to this show, Morgan said, "We just finished my third season on the series and I'm sure I'll be on the show next year. We film June, July and August in Dallas. I like the chance of going back to Texas; that is home." Other TV series that Morgan has worked in include Westerns (*How the West Was Won, Wagon Train, The Restless Gun, Bonanza*) dramas (*Matlock, The Waltons, Murder She Wrote, Perry Mason*); sci-fi (*The X-Files, Millennium*), comedies (*The Lucy Show, Pistols 'n Petticoats*) and soaps (*Days of Our Lives*).

Morgan has also appeared in recent motion pictures such as *Girls Just Wanna Have Fun* and *Battle Beyond the Stars* have kept him before the movie house going audience. Speaking of the latter film, Morgan jokingly referred to it as "the high point of my career. I played a lizard." The feature starred George Peppard and Richard Thomas in an updated *Magnificent Seven* theme set in outer space, and had Woodward's lizard character being the sidekick to the hero. He stated that his experience in this film as "sheer agony because that mask was molded to my face. One time I worked seventeen hours and the costume was very uncomfortable – webbed feet, my hands were claws, and the mask literally glued on so that the mouth and eyes would move. I couldn't eat, drank liquid through a straw. Very uncomfortable."

Morgan summed up his career to us in 1985, saying, "It's been really fine for the last twenty years. I was lucky enough to come out because of Fess and get started. Of course, I died after I did those for Disney, but I was only dead for a few years. I came back. It's an exceedingly difficult business and you really are no better than your last picture. I'm still alive and I survived so far and intend to continue that way. I said that I worked very hard; sometimes I think I have and sometimes I think I really haven't, that I could have done more, but I guess we always think we could have done more. On hindsight, I would do a few things differently which might have possibly enhanced my career. I would have paid more attention to production because I find now that I have a great interest in that. I think I might be a pretty good producer and I intend to try that in the next year or two. I would like," Morgan concluded, "to be instrumental in bringing back the Western."

Morgan has served on the board of directors of the Golden Boot committee which honors those who have spent a portion of their career working in the Western movies with an award and dinner ceremony each August, with all the funds derived from this activity going to help support the Motion Picture home. In 1988 he was awarded the Golden Boot himself, and has appeared as a celebrity guest at numerous Western film festivals across the country. Morgan is now retired from the picture business and serves on the Golden Boot Award committee. He spends his time between his home in Hollywood and his ranch in central California.

Film Credits: **1955:** The Great Locomotive Chase. **1956:** Westward Ho the Wagon; Along the Oregon Trail. **1957:** Gunsight Ridge; Slaughter on Tenth Avenue. **1958:** Ride a Crooked Trail. **1962:** The Gun Hawk; The Devil's Bedroom. **1965:** The Sword of Ali Baba. **1966:** Gunpoint; Cool Hand Luke. **1967:** Firecreek. **1969:** Death of a Gunfighter. **1969:** The Wild Country. **1971:** Yuma. **1972:** One Little Indian; Running Wild. **1975:** The Midnight Man; Ride in a Pink Car. **1975:** The Killing of a Chinese Bookie; A Small Town in Texas; The Last Day (TV); The Hatfields and the McCoys (TV); The Big Rip-Off (TV). **1976:** Moonshine County Express; The Quest (TV). **1977:** Supervan; Walking Tall – The Final Chapter; Which Way to Go; Deadly Game (TV). **1978:** Speed Trap; The Other Side of Hell (TV). **1979:** Centennial (TV); A Last Cry for Help (TV). **1980:** Battle Beyond the Stars. **1985:** Girls Just Wanna Have Fun. **1988:** Dark Before Dawn. **1992:** Gunsmoke: To the Last Man (TV).

HANK WORDEN

"Well, I was born a long time ago, that's for sure, because I'm past seventy-five," he began. "Hank was a nickname that I got at Stanford; Norton is my first name. They remember Hank. The bottom line there is to have a name they remember." His father had been an engineer on the Denver & Rio Grande in Colorado and would go from Salida to Gunnison over Marshall Pass, which at the time was a narrow gauge. His father had a sister who lived in Missouri, and when she died, her last wish was for him to come down and take charge of her farm until her oldest daughter turned twenty-one. "So we lived in Missouri for two years," Hank stated. "Then we moved up to a homestead in eastern Montana and I suppose that's where I remember most things." His mother taught him *Twinkle, Twinkle, Little Star*, which he used to recite at the ranchers and homesteaders picnic. "People seemed to like it and I always enjoyed entertaining people," he noted. Up there in Montana, horseback riding was the only means of transportation, and Hank grew into a good horseman.

Hank, who was born July 23, 1901 in Rolfe, Iowa, attended the University of Nevada in Reno and tried out for the campus players but was unsuccessful. After this, he went back to New York and rode in the rodeo at Madison Square Garden. At this time, the New York Theater Guild was casting *Green Grows the Lilacs*, in which he and some of the other cowboys, including Tex Ritter, were chosen. They had a cowboy for the lead part who turned out to be a poor actor, so they cast Franchot Tone, an understudy, in the lead role of Curly. Helen Westler, who was one of the six original founders of the Guild, played Aunt Ella. The play opened at the Fremont Theater in Boston and after two weeks they brought it to New

York. After the New York engagement, they took the show on the road. Later the Guild disbanded the show; Hank went back to a dude wrangling job in Cody, Wyoming, and Tex Ritter stayed in New York and got a radio show going. "Four years later, the Guild took the original book and made it into the musical *Oklahoma*," Hank mentioned. "I guided a couple of years in the Grand Canyon during the Depression. You had to be able to entertain, so I used to sing *The Old Chisum Trail* and that sort of thing, and I did a little jig. People used to tell me I ought to get over to Hollywood, and I finally did."

His first picture was Cecil B. DeMille's *The Plainsman*, with Gary Cooper and Jean Arthur. Hank was an extra in this 1936 film. "I got that because I had been working on a dude ranch, Smoke Tree Ranch down in Palm Springs. Billie Burke, the wife of Ziegfield, was there and she thought I was good," Hank explained. "So when I came up to Los Angeles, she called up Bert McKay over at Paramount who was casting extras, and so I got on that way. Then Tex Ritter came out and I was comic relief for him, and it went on and on."

In Tex Ritter's first two or three films, Hank Worden went under the name of Heber Snow. "That was Edward Chatham's idea," he mentioned. "When we were rodeoing up in Idaho, I was riding saddle broncs and he was roping, and he said, 'If you have Heber Snow, all the Mormon people would go and see him,' but I soon got tired of that."

Asked if he had any favorite parts, Hank answered, "I didn't know that people would remember old Mose Harper from *The Searchers* too well, but when I come over here (to the restaurant where we met with him) for breakfast, people sometimes come over and ask, 'Do you work in Westerns?' I say, 'Yeah,' and they ask, 'John Wayne Westerns?' 'Yeah,' and they turn around and say, 'I knew it. That's Mose Harper, I remember him.' Sometimes they don't know my name at all, but they remember the character's. So sometimes I think that must have been the best part I did. I was the parson in *The Alamo* and the deacon in *The Horse Soldiers*, but that's the one most people remember."

In the script of *Wagonmaster*, it originally called for three nephews of the Charles Kemper role, and they decided to have a fourth, and that Hank would play the part, making him the oldest and smallest of the nephews. "There was Jim Arness who was six foot seven, Mickey Simpson was six foot five, Fred Libby was six foot four, and I was the runt; I was only six foot one," he mentioned. "That was the first picture, I think, that they made up in Moab, Utah. Ben Johnson had been working as a stuntman on Ford's *Fort Apache*, and then Ford put him under contract."

Asked what it was like working with John Ford, Hank answered, "Ford was a very good director. He knew exactly what he wanted, and he could read the parts better than any of the people playing them – man, woman, or child. He seemed to understand the psychology of the viewers, and only offered them things that they enjoyed. I think he kept away from too much dialogue when he was doing an action picture, because the action got slowed down to first gear and didn't hold the interest. If it's an action picture then he would keep it going, just tie it together with a little dialogue here and there."

"Hawks was a very good director, too," he continued, referring to Howard Hawks. "He also knew exactly what he wanted. He also rewrote the script right on the set. I remember he was writing some new dialogue for Duke, Brennan and Montgomery Clift on *Red River*. He kept his dialogue compressed, concise and to the point. When they finally got it the way Hawks wanted it, the script girl would go away and pound out four or five copies. In the meantime, they're lighting the set, so they had to do a fast learning job."

"I liked the scripts I've been fortunate enough to work on, and you just read it over and memorize the lines, and expect the director to tell you if you're not playing it right," he added. "That's what the director's for. He's studied the script and in the back of his mind he knows how he wants everything to fit together. Anyway, I'd hate to be a director, because all the weight is on his back."

In talking about the difference between working in a Tex Ritter movie and a John Wayne Western, he mentioned, "Tex's were being made in 1936-38, and they were made in six days. These were probably only one or two takes and if the second take wasn't good, they would cut it out and go on to the next. Whereas in an A-picture, they keep shooting until they get exactly what they want. So there's a lot of difference. If you take your time with something, one would probably end up with a better product than if you shoot seventy-five set-ups a day, and only maybe eight or ten on an A-picture."

In *The Big Sky*, Hank played an Indian character named Poor Devil, and he said that his best line in that film was, "No got whiskey." It was filmed up in Jackson Hole, Wyoming. "That was kind of fun," he noted, "but it had its problems. I had to spend an hour and a half in makeup every morning for the false nose, the scar, and the black-out teeth. Then we get out to location and there were a lot of mosquitoes and I didn't have much protection so I was pretty mosquito-bitten, but you live through all this."

Among his later films are *UFOria* which is a semi-science-fiction about a woman who dreams about the space people who are coming to take her away; *Please Don't Eat the Babies*, which he stated, "That's a blood murdering thing. Granny and I lure people up to our cabin. We're supposed to be down in the Caribbean region, and Granny makes herbal tea that kills people. She and I finally get killed, so it comes out to a better ending." Hank plays Old Geezer, who talks to the alligators in *Soggy Bottom, USA*, which starred Ben Johnson, Dub Taylor and Anthony Zerbe. In 1990 and '91, he also appeared as a senile waiter in four episodes of the television series *Twin Peaks*.

In summing up his feelings about his career, he said, "I enjoy working in pictures very much. I enjoy the people behind the camera as much as I enjoy the people in front of the camera with whom I'm working, because they're all great guys, they're all pros; the sound crew, the camera crew, the truck drivers, the wardrobe, makeup, all of them. I certainly like all the stunt guys. They're my best friends; they do some wonderful stuff. I enjoy all of these great people. I like to be with them."

Hank Worden passed away on December 6, 1992 in Los Angeles, California.

Hank Worden

Film Credits: **1936:** The Plainsman; Ghost Town Gold; For the Service; Come and Get It. **1937:** Sing Cowboy Sing; Riders of the Rockies; Trouble in Texas; Riders of the Dawn; Moonlight on the Range; Hollywood Roundup; Boss of Lonely Valley; Sudden Bill Dorn; Mystery of the Hooded Horsemen; Hitting the Trail. **1938:** Tex Rides With the Boy Scouts; The Singing Outlaw; The Last Stand; Flaming Frontiers; The Cowboy and the Lady; Frontier Town; Western Trails; Rollin' Plains; The Stranger from Arizona; Where the Buffalo Roam; Ghost Town Riders. **1939:** Sundown on the Prairie; Rollin' Westward; The Night Riders; Stagecoach; Timber Stampede; Bandits and Ballads; Reno; Cupid Rides the Range (short); Oklahoma Frontier; Chip of the Flying U. **1940:** Gaucho Serenade; Mollie Cures a Cowboy (short); Ride, Tenderfoot, Ride; Triple Justice; Beyond Tomorrow; Winners of the West; Viva Cisco Kid; Rancho Grande; Riders of Pinto Basin; Shooting High; Prairie Law; Cross-Country Romance; Brigham Young – Frontiersman; Northwest Passage. **1941:** Border Vigilante; Mad About Moonshine; Robbers of the Range; Love at First Sight; Dude Cowboy; Ride, Kelly, Ride. **1942:** Code of the Outlaw; Just Off Broadway; Valley of Hunted Men; Cowboy Serenade; Riding the Wind. **1943:** Tenting Tonight on the Old Campground; Black Market Rustlers; So Proudly We Hail; Jack London; National Barn Dance; The Woman of the Town; Canyon City. **1944:** Lumberjack; Wyoming Hurricane; Forty Thieves; None Shall Escape; Forty Thieves. **1945:** The Bullfighters; Abbott and Costello in Hollywood. **1946:** The Missing Lady; The Shocking Miss Pilgrim; Frontier Gunlaw; Undercurrent; Lawless Breed; Duel In the Sun. **1947:** Prairie Express; Angel and the Badman; The Sea of Grass; The High Wall; The Secret Life of Walter Mitty. **1948:** The Sainted Sisters; Red River; Three Godfathers; Yellow Sky; Fort Apache; Lightning in the Forest; Tap Roots; Slippy McGee; Hazard; Feudin', Fussin', and A-Fightin'; Whispering Smith. **1949:** Hellfire; The Fighting Kentuckian; Cover-Up; Streets of Laredo; Red Canyon. **1950:** Wagonmaster; Father is a Bachelor; Curtain Call at Cactus Creek; Frenchie; When Willie Comes Marching Home. **1951:** Joe Palooka in Triple Cross; Sugarfoot; Comin' Round the Mountain; The Man With a Cloak. **1952:** The Big Sky; Apache War Smoke; Woman of the North Country; Boots Malone; The Story of Will Rogers; Sky Full of Moon; Ma and Pa Kettle on Vacation. **1954:** The Outcast; Ma and Pa Kettle at Home; Crime Wave. **1955:** The Indian Fighter; The Road to Denver; The Man from Texas; The Vanishing American. **1956:** Accused of Murder; The Searchers; Davy Crockett and the River Pirates; The Warrens of Arizona; Meet Me in Las Vegas; Thunder Over Arizona. **1957:** Spoilers of the Forest; The Quiet Gun; Dragoon Wells Massacre; The Buckskin Lady; War Drums; Forty Guns. **1958:** Toughest Gun in Tombstone; Bullwhip; The Notorious Mr. Monks; Sing Boys Sing; Bullwhip; Wild Heritage. **1959:** Horse Soldiers. **1960:** The Alamo; Sergeant Rutledge. **1961:** One-Eyed Jacks. **1962:** The Music Man. **1963:** McLintock. **1967:** Good Times; The President's Analyst; Hondo and the Apaches (TV). **1969:** True Grit; Big Daddy. **1970:** Chisum; Rio Lobo. **1971:** Big Jake; Black Noon (TV); Zachariah; Bedknobs and Broomsticks. **1972:** Rolling Man (TV). **1973:** Cahill, US Marshal. **1974:** The Hanged Man (TV); Eve of St. Agnes. **1975:** Sky Heist. **1976:** Flush. **1977:** Which Way is Up?; Smokey and The Bandit; The Legend of Frank Woods; Every Which Way But Loose. **1978:** They Went That-a-way and That-a-way; Big Wednesday; Sgt. Pepper's Lonely Hearts Club Band. **1980:** Bronco Billy; UFOria; Soggy Bottom USA; Hammett; The Outing. **1981:** Please Don't Eat the Babies. **1984:** The Ice Pirates. **1985:** Scream; Space Rage; Runaway Train. **1988:** Once Upon a Texas Train (TV). **1990:** Big Bad John; Almost an Angel.

THAN WYENN

Than Wyenn was born on May 2, 1919 in New York City. "It was the lower east side with Jewish, Italian and Irish neighborhoods," he informed us. Growing up there was an intense experience for him and wasn't the happiest time of his life. "I wasn't a battler, a street fighter, and there was a lot of that going on; I mean kids to kids," Than told us. "Some kids from one block would see kids from another block and question you, give you a punch in the stomach if they didn't like you, and then you go chasing after them."

One of the good things in that area was the Madison House, a center for kids. Near this center was the Henry Street Settlement which produced some of the great actors of the Group Theatre. "And there was the Educational Alliance, and these were excellent things. Those were happy experiences," he stated. The Madison House had a boys club called the Heroes, and their counselor was a man named Arthur Solomon, who later became a counselor in a prison. The Educational Alliance had wood workshops with plenty of benches and wood vices where the kids could make things. They had basketball and also a roof garden, which during the hot summers was covered and a boy could buy milk and crackers, and play ping pong and checkers. It was a great place for kids to socialize. The Educational Alliance also had a camp called Surprise Lake Camp. During the summer it was sponsored by them, and during the winter sponsored by Eddie Cantor. "Now this was for kids who were undernourished or poor. About sixty kids," Than mentioned. "I was anemic at that time and I had the privilege of going there for six months or so, and going to school there when I was in about Grade 7B, and I skipped 8A to 8B. I can still smell the pancakes in the morning. We slept dormitory style and collected stamps. I still collect, when letters have festival

stamps, anything that isn't the usual stamps. I'm tearing them off and I take a quick glance and I put it in a box and I give it away to somebody, but it's a hangover from the stamp collecting. They had a marvelous lake there and we would do things like bird watching, so for a kid from the city it was a marvelous experience. I used to love it so much that I would walk in the empty lots in New York and close my eyes, and if there were any weeds at all there, I would try to imagine I was back in this camp." Years later Than appeared as a union organizer in a *Playhouse 90* titled *Sizeman and Son* which starred Eddie Cantor. For lunch the cast went out to Farmer's Market on Third Street, and as he was going up in an elevator Than mentioned to Cantor that he had been the recipient of one of his grateful gestures. "He was very fragile at that time, he would have to rest for many hours," Wyenn stated, "but I did have a chance to communicate how grateful I was."

When entering his teenage years, Than celebrated his Bar mitzvah. "That's when you reach the age of thirteen, in the Jewish faith, you are declared a man," he informed us. "You go through certain blessings and rituals and the rabbi gives you a tap on the shoulder and says, 'Now it's all ahead of you young man.'" Than's father was a tailor who worked for Howard Clothes which was a clothing factory. He eventually had his own store and Than would deliver the garments.

During the early part of the WPA days, the time of the Depression when they were paying professional actors twenty-four dollars and fifty cents a week, a theatre group under the direction of Harry Coultoff was using the auditorium in the Madison House for rehearsals. Than commented, "I became involved accidentally by walking in and they needed a kid, so I was in that particular production. I came in and they were throwing in snow, which was a detergent. It got into my eyes and I remember wandering around in the scene for a while." Wyenn was intrigued, and Coultoff asked him, "Why don't you come and take a look at the classes?" Harry Coultoff was doing classes in body work, such as dancer's training and stretching. Than was attracted to it because it was different, and was invited to join the class. "I was about fourteen and began to work out. They began doing scenes, little bits," he stated.

After the WPA ended, they moved to Carnegie Hall and Coultoff created his own school. Members of this group were both actors and writers who were given acting training which helped them visualize their characters. "There was a studio there and he gave me half a scholarship," Than stated. The full tuition was fifteen dollars a month, and Than went on to say, "My father wasn't too happy I was doing that career wise, so my mother would secretly give me half of the fifteen dollars. So that's where my interest started to grow, with Harry, who was a brilliant hard master. But he studied with some of the finest in the world, so what he was able to impart was always useful. That was my interest. It satisfied, it gave me a place, gave me a purpose."

When he began working with Coultoff, Than's club leader from the Madison House told him he would never make it in the theatre because of his heavy New York accent. "That of course made me mad," he told us. "That's when I pushed that aside. I began to work –

Actually, I didn't work too much on the speech; the resonance eventually came with the work. Then I studied speech with Margaret McLane and others, and I studied voice."

While studying acting with Harry Coultoff, Than became deathly ill. "I went swimming one day in the Atlantic Ocean. My resistance was low and a very bad staph bug got into my nostril and affected my whole sinus. It was deadly because I had septicemia. I was about sixteen and I was down to sixty-six pounds. It infects your entire body, and I had fourteen blood transfusions over a period of a month. The family prayed. I learned to get in a wheelchair, get back into function. I never thought of death; I thought only of exercises, life. Eventually when I got out of the hospital, it was about four months later."

Harry Coultoff had changed his surname to Colt, and the group formed a stock company during the time that Than was sick. The following year they went to Cape May, New Jersey, and Wyenn played the young roles or the very old roles, and was also the stage manager at the Cape May Playhouse. "I was recuperating then," he explained. "Illness, as you know, can beat you up spiritually as well as physically, and I couldn't find the original freedom and spontaneity that I had. But by the hard discipline of doing whatever I did to the best of my ability, whether it washing dishes or collecting props, it slowly regenerated my confidence and faith in myself. We did several plays there and cleaned up the theatre. It was a thrilling experience to be part of a professional theatre. That was my first professional production." One of the things Harry Colt always pointed out to Wyenn was to sustain his characterization between the scenes so he wouldn't have to rebuild it by the time he went back on stage. He also landed some narrating jobs on occasion, and they performed the play *Johnny Johnson* in Greenwich Village where Than acted as stage manager.

He heard about a company performing Shakespeare, doing one night stands. At this time stock companies were going out of fashion. Than thought to himself, "Maybe they'll accept me," and auditioned as Romeo, doing the death scene from *Romeo and Juliet*. He heard nothing from them for two weeks. Then he got a call saying, "We'd like you to come join with us and be an actor and assistant stage manager." He was told they were doing four plays with a company of ten. "I had to memorize about ten roles in two weeks, which you could never do unless you were eighteen," he informed us. Wyenn went to live at his acting teacher's house. In learning the ten parts he told us, "Even though we had rehearsals, there's too many plays going on. It was like touch and go. I said, 'I don't know which play I'm memorizing it from.' They said, 'Don't worry. Once it rolls, it rolls,' and that's what happened. They were so experienced."

Than went on to tell us about this Shakespeare company and his experiences with them. "They were the declamatory theatre. You know, the sound of the voice. They were part of the old school, and they had good make-up techniques. An elderly gentleman named Jim Coburn in the cast, knew how to apply a couple of highlights and change your character just with some powder. So you learn from those things. It was a tough and wonderful few months. One morning the chauffeur of the company and I hired a guide and we took a rowboat to go fishing, we practically drifted out to sea and almost lost our lives. We rowed like hell to get back. We finally made it, and the next day the paper had an article, 'Actors battle tide and wind so that the show may go on.' This was in Galveston, Texas, in the big gulf.

"We opened, I think, in Maryland," he continued. "We played for universities, and there were young people there with the book watching to see if we skipped a word, and we'd meet with them and it was very delightful. We covered many states and we were always very warmly received. We eventually came back and I wound up in the hospital. We thought my kidney was infected, but it wasn't. It cured itself. It was just the weariness."

After coming back, there was not much work. Than would get an occasional narrating job and he continued to study. "I studied with Eugene Morgan at the Salmaggi Opera Company in Brooklyn," he commented. "It's like the mini-Met. Just to give a shading, so my voice could go up and down, to widen out the range. I worked on speech and worked on body movement. In fact, while on the tour in Abilene, Texas, I was invited by one of the universities to teach body work there, but I didn't feel like I wanted to live down south."

After the tour was over, Than came back to New York City. This was at the time when unions were beginning to do little things in drama. "I heard that the International Ladies Garment Workers Union (ILGWU) had been doing a play which was touring the country called *Pins and Needles*. It was of union life. I heard that Lee Strasberg was teaching there. Although I used to work as a stock boy, I wasn't working then, I phonied up some kind of excuse and got into the class and eventually became narrator for a pageant they produced titled *I Hear America Singing*.

"My teacher, Harry Colt, had a student named Dick Campbell; he was married to Muriel Rahn who was the star of the musical, *Carmen Jones*," Than stated. Campbell was directing in Harlem in an Equity waived theatre and decided to do *Booker T. Washington*. He invited Wyenn to play Baldwin, one of the great railroad magnates.

After this plays run, Than auditioned for *The Merry Widow* which was being produced in New York on the subway circuit. "That isn't directly on Broadway. It's in the big theatres in Brooklyn and Queens," he explained. "I had done a little voice training, but I think the director hired me because I looked like a nice kid and he figured he could squeeze me in." Than had some difficulty in rehearsals because he couldn't read music, but this was his one opportunity to get an Equity card. Wyenn got his card not as an actor, but as a dancer and singer. "In other words, I was in an Equity show. That's the big problem," he explained. "To get into a Broadway show or an Equity company, you need to be a member of the union, and you can't be a member of the union unless someone invites you to be in a professional show."

"I'll tell you another little story," he said. "When I was nineteen years old I was making the rounds on Broadway and it was deep frustration. It was very hard for me to want and not get; not even to touch. They say 'Yes' in such a way you know it's a negative." He took his wife around one day so she could see what an actor goes through. At the end of the day she asked him, "How can you take it?" He went on to tell us of this frustration, "The dream is up here and the bubble is bursting every time you walk out." One time he saw an actor in his fifties at Walgreens or Schrafts Drug Store talking to some young people. This actor was a member of the Group Theatre that was currently performing *Awake and Sing*; an actor who had been doing small bit parts all his life. Wyenn looked at him and suddenly realized that his life was a tragedy. "There's no life. He wasn't married, had no family. It was like he was still proving himself in the eyes of these kids. And I said that from the way it looked that could happen to me; and I didn't even have the bit parts, outside of occasional things. So I realized that I must divide my life and have something else going on while I have acting."

So Than studied. He learned to solder silver wedding gifts and to work on jewelry. "I became very good at it," he remarked. "But every time I would see a good performance I would quit the current job and start looking." But Than realized that this thought of making a living, not by acting alone, was going to stay with him.

Eventually Than started directing little theatre groups, children groups and young adult groups around town, but not enough headway. Even landing a few narrating jobs didn't bring in the necessary money to be able to make a living. So Than and his wife decided to leave New York. He had learned of an opening in the Jewish Education Network in the Los Angeles area. "The Bureau of Jewish Education is like the Board of Education in New York, and they had ninety schools and twenty-five thousand children," Than explained. They told him that there was a job opening as a Dramatic Arts Consultant. He went through the required interviews and was hired. He held this position until his retirement in 1985. He had first come to Los Angeles in 1947. His full-time position at the Bureau became a half-time position because of budget problems. With half an income lacking he decided to try acting again. He went back to study with Benjamin Zemach, an outstanding coach, who later became one of the teachers of Alan Arkin. His acting skills came back rapidly. Around that period, the play *Once Upon a Tailor* by Baruch Lumet was being cast and Than went to read for it. When he first walked in, he was informed "You're too young." So he left, and got mad outside the theatre. They hadn't even give him a chance to read for the part. So he returned and said, 'At least give me a chance to read.' Ten minutes later they selected him for the starring role in the play. By the way, this play featured Alan Arkin in his first professional acting role.

"I invited agents to represent me, but none came," Than told us. "The play opened with great reviews in every Los Angeles newspaper, calling it comic brilliance – it was a smash hit. I left after six months. The play started my career and I got an agent, Meyer Mishkin." He represented such performers as Lee Marvin and Chuck Connors. He came to see the show, but he didn't know how to interpret Than as a client. Mishkin consulted Mildred Gussie, who was one of the top casting directors for the old Republic Studios. She liked the show enough to see it several times. Mishkin was actually asking her, "What do I do with Than? How do I sell him to casting agents? How do I promote him?" "Eventually he signed me,"

Than stated. "He's responsible for getting my film career off the ground. Strangely enough, I did have an agent previously for a while, which came to nought. It seemed that casting people did not have confidence in her choice of clients. I won't mention her name because she may still be in the business," he commented.

"I'd like to interpolate a little story about someone else who was truly helpful to me before I met Mishkin. While working for the Los Angeles Bureau of Jewish Education, I was invited to direct a children's camp for the Wilshire Boulevard Temple during my summers. There, I fortunately met Lew Landers who loved children and, as a layman, helped support this camp called Camp Hess Kramer. Landers directed such television shows as *Whirleybirds*. In casual conversation he learned that I was an aspiring actor. He was the one who got me my first film role. It was an episode of *Whirleybirds*," Than said. He went on a number of interviews without landing any roles, and Landers told him, "Let's keep trying. I'll get you in, don't worry." Than told us that "I got the role of the lead heavy in this episode." Doing the fight scenes came easy to Than because of his dance training. "Landers discovered in that episode that I was new to acting in films," he explained. "When you do a tight close-up with lights practically on top of you, you enter the scene by so-called 'cheating.' You 'cheat' your foot into the scene first; then carefully move your body into the scene. Your movements must be very smooth and slow in entering. Before the scene got going, Landers asked me to cheat my movements into the waiting chair. Frankly, I didn't know what that word meant for the actor. He explained, but that showed my ignorance. Landers remembered. After the fighting sequence, Landers said to me, 'It's a big jump, isn't it?' A big smile on his face." It meant, "First time, right?" Than answered, "Yeah." "You're doing fine," Landers replied.

After finishing *Once Upon a Tailor,* Mishkin introduced him around and landed him a role in *Good Morning Miss Dove* with Jennifer Jones. In this film Than played a thirty-five year old and a sixty year old man. "It was a larger part," he stated, "but part of it was cut out by Darryl Zanuck because it had too much Jewish ritual. Then *Marjorie Morningstar* came out and that had a lot of Jewish ritual. But the point was, it was a good beginning and I was paid four hundred dollars a week at that time." He was offered a higher salary, but then they found out through the grapevine what he was paid on his last job and insisted on paying him four hundred. "But I was glad for the opportunity," Than added.

On television, Than began to work on such shows as *Rifleman, Naked City, The Untouchables, Route 66,* and four episodes of *Gunsmoke*. "Among the different shows I did you began to grow; they got to trust me and I was well respected. They first give you a few lines to begin with. They don't want you to freeze on the set, and eventually they open up, as they begin to recognize you."

Mishkin landed Than a role on *Dragnet,* and he told us of his experience working with Jack Webb, saying that Webb was kind of a tough master. "He makes demands and he was shooting his *Dragnet*'s in a day and-a-half by using teleprompters." Webb put up a prompter in front of Than and said, "Read these lines," and Wyenn replied, "I prefer not to use the teleprompter." Jack wasn't happy with that and came back with, "Okay, it's your ass." "Simple as that," Than told us, "because Webb was filming by time." When this scene was finished, the assistant director came over and said to Than, "I think Jack likes you." He was later called back to do another *Dragnet*. Once again he was told that Webb liked him, and Than replied, "I can't tell." The assistant director then said, "He'll use you."

Eventually Than received word from Jack Webb that they were doing the feature film, *Pete Kelly's Blues*, and was interested in using him as one of the featured players. The idea of doing a dramatic lead thrilled Wyenn. "I didn't know then that Webb was fighting Warner Brothers because they thought I was too young," he mentioned, "but he fought it through. It was a wonderful cast and it was a big moment for me."

Sometime after the film was completed, Jack Webb asked Than to work with him in the television series, *Pete Kelly's Blues*, playing the same character he did in the feature film. He told us they had some of the most marvelous jazz musicians in America on that show. "So I had the pleasure of a series," Than smiled. "Jack Webb was a very loyal guy. His assistant director had a heart attack and he kept him on salary for two years."

Wyenn appeared in a number of *Wanted: Dead or Alive* episodes with Steve McQueen, whom he said "was an enjoyable guy to work with." Then word came from his agent that they wanted him for seven segments of *Zorro* over at Disney's. When he met with the director and producer, he was told that if they saw him two weeks earlier he would have had the part of the mute. He was cast as Pina Liciencade, a lawyer and adviser to Britt Lomond's Commandante. "Britt Lomond and Guy Williams were excellent fencers. It was a marvelous series," Than told us. Wyenn had learned fencing earlier for his part in a film being taught by the actual teacher of Douglas Fairbanks Senior.

In the film, *Beginning of the End*, Than played a mute who had lost the use of his voice through radiation. His character did have dialogue, using sign language. Later, Than would use sign language working with a chimp in an episode of *Simon And Simon*. "I learned sign language for the role. Once, while rehearsing by myself, one of the producers comes by and says, 'Oh, are you really signing the dialogue?' I said, 'Yes, of course.' He called the other producer over and said, 'He knows what he's doing!' Whenever I play a person from a minority group, I never want to insult them." In other words, Than does his homework in making his roles as true and believable as possible.

He appeared in a classic *Twilight Zone* episode in which Albert Salmi played a cowboy who's about to be hung in the last century and is brought into the present time by a time capsule. Salmi kills the scientist, and Than played the two-bit hoodlum who comes in to rob the place. Wyenn ends up choking Salmi with a window blind cord. "So I look around and wind up in this capsule," he mentioned, "and I wind up back in time, hanging in the place of Salmi. It was a very clever thing. That became a classic, which I was very proud of."

Than auditioned for a role in the play, *Me Candido*, which was being produced by the Players Ring. "They would do original things mostly," he stated. "*Me Candido* was mostly a

Puerto Rican cast which also featured Dabbs Greer and Henry Corden. I had the lead role of a father who adopts five kids. He doesn't have the money, but wants to adopt a sixth kid who was played by Rafael Campos." He was working with a Puerto Rican cast, so he went to work on his Puerto Rican dialect. A wife of a friend of Than's was writing a book on Puerto Rico, so he went to work with her. "There was more than dialect," Than continued. "I would ask her how does a Puerto Rican man who lives in Puerto Rico and works in the field, get angry? It's a slow build up. I asked her what does he do when he comes home from work? How does he greet his kids? The first thing he does, she said, is sit down and remove the fungus off his feet because he farms with an ox on a hill. I asked what is he most proud of? She said, 'Making babies.' She then said she has a favor to ask of me: to give him dignity. When it was over, she gave me a hug. It's the inner attitude you play. I felt very good about that."

He went on to play the Italian lawyer in Arthur Miller's play, *A View from the Bridge*, directed by Paul Stewart. The play opened at the Players Ring and moved over to the Ivar Theatre, and ran for about a year and-a-half. The original cast left after six months, but were called back to open it at the Ivar Theatre. "It was a thrilling experience," Than remarked. "In doing a play, when you finish rehearsal it doesn't mean you finished research on the piece. And once you find a new element it can change many elements along the way."

Than performs a one man show, both locally and nationally, titled *Turning the Pages of Jewish Humor and Drama*. It's a program of dramatizations in English, based on the characters in Jewish literature. "I perform for interested organizations," he informed us. Recent performances were done in Denver, Colorado and Dallas, Texas for the Jewish communities of these cities. "Frequently, while rehearsing for a performance, I discover something new in the material. It could be a certain attitude, a gesture, a tone of voice. My performance changes and it's for the better and as a result I take on a new energy and my performance takes on new colors." As for his theatre training, Than mentioned that he had studied acting with Lee Strasberg; modern dance with Katherine Dunham, and voice with Eugene Morgan of the Salmaggi Opera Company in Brooklyn, New York. Than said that he had also studied with Michael Chekhov, the nephew of writer Anton Chekhov. Michael was one of the colleagues of Constantin Stanislavsky in the Soviet Union, but they had split because of certain theoretical differences. "I studied with him in his later years," Than commented. "He helped actors trust more of what comes unconsciously. He was also one of the great actors. I have seen him on the stage with the Moscow Art Theatre and he blows your mind away because of his simplicity."

When asked if he has any favorites amongst the roles he played, Than stated, "I'm trying to think because I happen to be one who doesn't localize my favoritism. In other words, I find each role challenging." On stage, he mentioned that he felt a deep satisfaction from his roles in *View from The Bridge* and *Me Candido*. In motion pictures, he stated, "Of course the big scene was cut, but I enjoyed *Good Morning Miss Dove*." There was a role in a TV movie titled *Two Lives of Carol Letner* in which Than played a Jewish fellow. "I rarely played Jewish characters actually," he said. His character in this film was once beaten up by gangsters, and he sees the same gangsters coming to make a deal with a man he's now working for. "He lost his business because they broke his leg," Than said of the part. "The dialogue was written in such a way that was just very moving to me, and I remember the crew and people applauding after the scene." He told us that he very much enjoyed the featured roles he played in the film and television series, *Pete Kelly's Blues*, and the television series of Walt Disney's *Zorro* with Guy Williams. "I must say there were a number of good roles. There was a *Lou Grant* episode, where I played a rabbi whose former student was a young Jewish boy who joined the Nazi party and later committed suicide. It was based on a true story. The story touched me deeply."

Than's talents and mastery of various dialects have made him a very versatile actor. The characters he played have included such nationalities as Arabs, Mexicans, Cubans, Russian, Hungarian, Spanish, Israeli, Indian and French.

Apart from acting, Than and his wife have traveled extensively, visiting over forty countries and making friends throughout the world. "I also began leading tours," he said, "and two years ago I took a group of tourists to India. It was a great adventure. India is a fascinating country. I photograph like mad and some of my photographs have won prizes." The first year that the Museum of the Diaspora in Israel sponsored a worldwide photographic contest, Than won third prize. "Diaspora, of course, means the Jewish people that are scattered throughout the world, not residing in Israel," he explained. "We were in Israel about a year ago, and the museum will eventually receive my entire slide collection, depicting Jewish sites and people from the countries I have visited. There is no money involved, but I will know that my slide collection will have a home, where it can be made available to schools."

In Los Angeles, Than has been very much involved with the Jewish Community on several levels. He did taped interviews with holocaust survivors for the local Museum of the Holocaust. "I also produced a television show for the Jewish Federation Council, in which I would present a narrative on camera together with my slides each week, of a particular country." In his home, he has a wonderful collection of Jewish and other artifacts from around the world, some dating back hundreds of years. After viewing some of his photographs, it was obvious to see that Than has a very artistic sense with the camera. At one time, Than also organized a Yiddish speaking Jewish Children's Theatre, training the young people for a year before putting them on the stage.

In summing up his feelings about his career, he told us, "I do feel quite successful. I've had the opportunity to become the kind of actor I dreamed about as a young man, a character actor. My ideal in my younger years was Burgess Meredith. I sometimes do roles that are not particularly significant, but in many instances there are good scripts and meaningful roles which are very rewarding. Being creative has made my life meaningful."

"Of course, there were some difficult periods along the way, periods of unemployment between acting assignments. I feel fortunate to have made my decision in my younger years, not to put all my eggs into one basket – acting. It helped pay the bills to have been on the staff of the Los Angeles Bureau of Jewish Education as the Dramatic Arts Consultant. It was also convenient, as I could arrange my time in such a way that I could accept acting assignments. It was an ideal arrangement.

"I feel fortunate also that my wife Guy loved this industry and gave me the support I needed along the way. It isn't all fun and games, there are also pressures from time to time. When you're shooting a scene on the set, although you are with other actors, you are essentially alone in a way. No hand can reach out to you, no one is giving you your cue, the responsibility is in your hands. When you walk onto the set and the assistant director hands you a page with two paragraphs of new dialogue and says, 'These are your new lines; we're shooting in forty minutes.' You've got to be able to handle that. Shaking a bit, you manage to get through it.

"In any case the industry has been wonderful to me. I've been able to raise two sons who are now well married and I have five grandchildren, whom I adore. To think of this industry that frequently sparsely supports actors; that it made possible a nice home which came about from both my theatre and non-theatre work, what is to complain about? You know what I mean! So the only important thing left is one's health, and my wife has been a great partner there. She knows her vitamins backwards and forwards and our diet, we eat very little meat, and we like the idea. But in looking back to the theatre, it was very very gratifying. My heart goes out for the thousands who stream into the film and stage world where there is no room for them. I've always dreamt when I was with the International Ladies Garment Workers Union that unions would pick up and do plays about their causes, but that disappeared. Only the one union had that. I felt little towns would have their professional theatres, and some of them do have, but not enough to use the incredible talent that sometimes has no chance even to emerge. And I'm aware of that too, so occasionally when I have taught actors I would let them know what I know. That fills your life not only with theatre but with other things that can bring you support for a family, so you can have the pleasure of having children, and music, books, etc. So when I look back it's a very good feeling because of the friends along the way, the fact that I was trained by excellent people, and that's important if you go after any field. To be the best in it, not to be the best just to be competitive, but you for yourself, to be getting the brass ring in terms of your feeling about the quality of your work. And that's what keeps you working, so at least you would have that satisfaction. I'm very happy with my family, thank God, and I've had the best of both worlds. My wife had a thyroid operation, and in the hospital someone came over and said, 'Than Wyenn?' 'Yes.' 'I want to thank you. You were my teacher in the Yavneh Hebrew Academy years back. You got me interested in theatre, and I'm a lawyer now, but I have the theatre sense when I'm in the courtroom.' People saying that you have touched their life in some important way. In the street someone would walk up and say, 'You're an actor aren't you?' 'Yes.' 'You're good.' You know, just that comment. It's a nice feeling that you've somehow touched the lives of people you don't know, because of this giant medium."

Film Credits: **1953:** Prisoners of the Casbah; A Slight Case of Larceny. **1954:** The Human Jungle; Black Tuesday; Tennessee Champ; The Adventures of Haji Baba. **1955:** ; Good Morning, Miss Dove; The Naked Street; Pete Kelly's Blues; Prince of Players. **1956:** The Ten Commandments. **1957:** Hot Rod Rumble; The Beginning of the End; The Invisible Boy. **1958:** I Want to Live!; The True Story of Lynn Stuart; The Brothers Karamazov. **1959:** Imitation of Life. **1960:** Sign of Zorro; The Boy and the Pirates. **1963:** The Greatest Story Ever Told. **1966:** Gambit; The Money Trap. **1967:** Rosie; Sullivan's Empire. **1968:** The Pink Jungle; Now You See It, Now You Don't (TV). **1973:** Thunderbolt; Runaway! (TV); Ellery Queen: Don't Look Behind You (TV). **1975:** Adventures of the Queen. **1976:** Victory at Entebee (TV). **1977:** Black Sunday; The Other Side of Midnight. **1979:** Being There; Billion Dollar Threat (TV). **1980:** Wholly Moses; Power (TV); Enola Gay (TV). **1981:** Madame X (TV); Two Lives of Carol Letner (TV). **1982:** Mae West (TV). **1984:** Splash.

H.M. WYNANT

H.M.'s parents and siblings came to America from the border region of Austria and Poland, and settled in Detroit, Michigan, where he was born Haim Winant on February 12, 1927. "I didn't even speak English until I was about five years old," Haim reflected. "And being a Detroit person I got fascinated with automobiles. I loved cars and still do. I drive an old Mercedes that I wouldn't trade for anything brand new."

Haim stated that he was dyslexic and at that time nobody understood what dyslexia was. "They figured a good career in the army was for me because I was not doing well, but for some reason in a pool hall in Detroit I discovered Shakespeare. Why, I don't know, but I was able to read it and became very interested in Shakespeare and that turned my life around."

Haim attended a vocational school because "they thought I was hopeless and tried to teach me a trade. They thought that was better than the pool hall, and I couldn't learn a trade in the army." While at the school, Haim was trained to be a draftsman. "But, as I said, I got interested in Shakespeare, and went to Wayne University and got very interested in dance."

When Haim turned twenty, he stated he was going to go to New York. "Nobody thought I would," he informed. "I had $110 in my pocket at the time. Nobody even bid me farewell, they thought I was kidding, but I packed up a suitcase and away I went. I lived in New York and got a straight job with a potash mining company as a draftsman. I was down to my last nickel when I went to an open call audition as a dancer in January 1949. Jerry Robbins, who was holding the auditions, picked you, you, and you to come back tomorrow. I said, 'I can't. I got a job.' He said, 'Quit,' and I've never had a straight job since. I'm very lucky. I've earned my living as an actor ever since."

Haim's first job on stage was with the National Theater as dancer and member of the chorus in *High Button Shoes* with Eddie Foy, Audrey Meadows and Jack Whiting. "I ended up understudying the two leads and for most of the tour I took over the part of Uncle Willie, which was a comic tango he danced, but it was also an acting role," Haim reflected. "I toured the whole country for eighty-five weeks. I love the road and it was a wonderful tour."

After *High Button Shoes*, Haim auditioned in 1951 as a dancer for *Guys and Dolls*. "I got into it and was in it for three days because I had also auditioned for Katherine Hepburn's company of *As You Like It* and they wanted me. So I quit *Guys and Dolls* and went into *As You Like It*. From that point on I never danced again and became only an actor." In *As You Like It*, Haim understudied the part of Sylvius, but ended up playing that role."

Haim's next interview was for the part of Nicky in *Bell, Book and Candle*. "John Van Druten was looking for someone to play that part and Irene Selznick was producing it. Irene and Katherine Hepburn were great friends, and she told Irene that there was a person in her play who could play this part. Irene told her secretary, Ethel Wald, to find me. She found me and I met Van Druten. I didn't get the part, but I married Ethel. She became Ethel Winant and was my first wife and mother of my three children." Ethel went on to become a top Hollywood casting director, an Emmy winning producer, and vice president of Metromedia and CBS. "She rose beautifully," Haim commented.

After the close of *As You Like It*, Haim obtained a role on Broadway in *Venus Observed*, directed by Laurence Olivier. "Olivier was brilliant," Haim stated. "I just loved that man. I'll never forget when I arrived early at the theater once during rehearsal. Nobody was there, and I walked across to the other side of the stage, and the door opened, and in came Olivier. He didn't notice me. He walked to the center of the stage, then to the footlights, and looked at this big empty theater and screamed at the top of his lungs, 'I'm not afraid of you,' and turned and walked out. He was a great guy and sent me a wonderful opening night telegram."

Haim next worked opposite Rex Harrison and Lili Palmer in *Love of Four Colonels*. "Rex Harrison was a wonderful man," he reflected. "Lili Palmer, Bob Coote -- Those were good times." After this closed Haim opened in another play with Ann Jackson and Hugh Reilly called *Never Say Never*. "It was a flop," he told us. "Nobody knew much about it, but I actually liked the play."

In addition to his stage performances, Haim also performed a small role in Paul Henreid's film, *So Young, So Bad*, and in a number of live television shows. "I did a lot of live TV in New York," he related. "In the early days it was not regulated under any union and they paid you anything they wanted. I did *Ken Murray's Blackouts* for ten dollars a show," he laughed. "I did a *Studio One* with Charlton Heston around 1950. It was *Taming of the Shrew*, and we rehearsed for eighty hours or more. I think Chuck Heston got about one hundred and twenty dollars and I made forty or sixty. That was before the unions, and then we created a little union called TVA (Television Authority) which had no power, and that eventually merged about 1954 with AFRA (American Federation of Radio Artists) and became AFTRA."

Haim was working on stage with David Wayne and John Forsythe in *Teahouse of the August Moon* when Hollywood agent Henry Wilson sent him a message through David Wayne that he would like to meet him. "We met at the Plaza Hotel and he said he would like to represent me, and I said, 'Terrific.' He asked 'When are you coming to California?' and I said 'Never.' We left it where I would let him represent me and when something came up he would call. Toward the end of the run of *Teahouse of the August Moon* I got a call from Henry saying he got me a co-starring role in a picture that Sam Fuller was doing called *Run of the Arrow*. I quit *Teahouse* two weeks before it closed and went to California. I got there early enough to do a couple of things before that picture." Haim worked in television on *General Electric Theater* and an *Alfred Hitchcock Presents*, as well as the 1956 Easter show for *Matinee Theater* under the credit of Haim Winant. "I did *The Book of Ruth* with Sarah Churchill, Winston's daughter, and after that I did *Run of the Arrow*."

Reflecting on his being cast in *Run of the Arrow*, Haim said, "It's amazing that in those days he hired me for this wonderful role sight unseen, simply on my reputation, and from the recommendation of this rather unique agent. For two or three weeks before the picture started shooting in St. George, Utah, the limousine would come to my little apartment, pick me up, and I'd get archery lessons and horseback riding lessons on full salary. I learned to shoot a bow and arrow off a horse while riding bareback."

Run of the Arrow, in which Haim played Crazy Wolf, is considered to be one of Samuel Fuller's classics, and co-starred Rod Steiger, Brian Keith, Ralph Meeker and Charles Bronson. "I'm a Rod Steiger fan. I like Rod and think he was an extremely talented man," Haim told us. "That was my first big movie and from then on I did a lot of Indian roles. It typecast me for a while, and, as certain people in this town know, I'm credited with creating Indian gibberish," he said. "Sometimes you do certain roles where you talk only Indian. That came later, of course. But sometimes in order for the camera to come in for over the shoulder shots for a close-up it has to match. Therefore, you have to know your gibberish so you could constantly repeat it. But those days are gone, now they use real Indians. Only in one Indian picture did I actually speak true Indian language. I spoke Shoeshone in a picture I did with John Ericson called *Oregon Passage*."

When he worked in *Run of the Arrow* the studios changed his name. "They changed the spelling of my last name to Wynant, and dropped Haim, and gave me H.M." Asking for the reason that the studios changed the name, he replied, "It's ethnic. They didn't want ethnic in those days. Today it would be fine, but this was back in 1956 and they didn't think I should have an ethnic name."

Haim worked as a half-breed in a Western with Randolph Scott titled *Decision at Sundown*, directed by Budd Boetticher. "He was a wonderful director and it was a great experience," Haim told us, "but I remember before I did that part they wanted me to shave my head for a *Playhouse 90*. All of the *Playhouse 90*'s were live shows except for four that were done on film. I did two of them, one I did was called *Without Incident* with Errol Flynn and I had to be baldheaded for it.

It was a cavalry picture and I was a deserter and therefore they shaved his head. So I'm bald in the movie but I told them, 'No, I can't shave my head and do this part because I have this movie to do with Randolph Scott as soon as I finish this.' So they made me a bald wig for that movie. I did another movie earlier for *Playhouse 90* called *Massacre at Sand Creek*.

Haim enjoyed working in live television and performed opposite Jack Palance in *Death of Manolete* and opposite Mickey Rooney in *The Comedian*, both on *Playhouse 90*. "I loved doing live TV," he commented, "I'd rather do live TV." They would do an hour and a half show in five days. The first four days would be rehearsal and on the fifth day they would go on the air with the show. "I remember on the air-day at two I went to my dressing room, changed my clothes, and was ready to leave when they came to get me and said, 'Hey! You're not done yet.' You're under such pressure that I'd forgotten about Act III. I thought I'd done it already. So they pushed me on the set through a wall," he laughed. "I didn't enter through the door, I came through a wall. It was wild. We did the dress rehearsal but for some reason or other at one point I'd thought I had finished the show. I was ready to leave and this was live. You don't have much time to prepare so it's instant acting, and sometimes instant acting is the best acting. I loved it."

Haim worked in over 140 television shows during his career, including almost every genre there was. He appeared in such series as *Gunsmoke*, *Perry Mason*, *Cheyenne*, *One Step Beyond*, *Peter Gunn*, *Rawhide*, *M-Squad*, *Death Valley Days*, *The Deputy*, *77 Sunset Strip*, *Thriller*, *Wagon Train*, *Disneyland*, *The Restless Gun*, *Route 66*, *The Untouchables*, *Bat Masterson*, *Dr. Kildare*, *Branded*, *Combat*, *Profiles in Courage*, *Wild, Wild West*, *Batman*, *Get Smart*, *The Virginian*, *The Big Valley*, *Hogan's Heroes*, *Mission: Impossible*, *The Doris Day Show*, *Mannix*, *Cannon*, *The Rockford Files*, *Quincy*, *Airwolf*, and *The Young Riders*. One show that has become sort of a cult episode is *The Howling Man* for *The Twilight Zone*. "You know how I got that part?" he asked. "I was taking my children to the kiddy park and standing next to me with his children was Doug Heyes, and we said hi. He saw me and thought I'd be good for this role, and the next day I get a call for this wonderful part in *Twilight Zone* that Doug was directing. Another weird casting was when I was at the airport picking up my wife and I went into the john to go to the bathroom and at the next urinal was Paul Bogart. 'Hi H.' 'Hi Paul.' The next day I get a call and I'm in *Marlowe* playing the lead heavy. This is casting in the bathroom. You never really know. If I hadn't been at the airport in that bathroom at that time I wouldn't have had that role. I'm sure he interviewed a hundred people but for some reason this worked. It's really weird. You go on these auditions and wonder why you didn't get the part---Because that guy in the bathroom got it," Haim laughed.

Haim played the part of Inspector Hoskyns in *The Conquest of the Planet of the Apes*. "I liked the series," he said, "but unfortunately I'm not in it as much as I'd like to have been. I had more, but the script was edited just before we were shooting, so I lost a rather good scene. I liked the work. And then you had Don Murray, who's usually playing the nice guy, as the heavy in there. It's so funny because I go back to *High Button Shoes* and Don Murray's father was the stage manager. His name was Denny Murray. I loved him; he was a great man. He was the one who encouraged me to become an actor and get out of dancing."

When asked if he was ever in a dangerous position while performing in a movie, Haim replied, "In *Run of the Arrow* I was very macho, and that's why I have a very bad knee today. I had to run up about a sixty-degree angle hill and then shoot the arrow that begins the run of the arrow. Then I scream and run down for the chase, where I'm chasing Rod Steiger. But on the way down it was very steep and I didn't realize that the momentum got so great. I had to jump and landed on my heels, and my body folded like an accordion. Luckily that happened as I passed the camera so we didn't have to do it again, but I was young and able to recover rapidly. But those injuries are with me today. On that picture I did with Errol Flynn, *Without Incident*, there's one scene where I'm out on a balcony in a fight scene with Flynn and he hits me and I have to roll down the stairs. A stunt double is there but the director talked to me, saying, 'Listen, you should really do this because I'm going to follow you down with the camera and at the bottom of the stairs I pull up real tight on your face.' I say okay, and I roll all the way down the stairs and the camera comes in on me, but when the picture's cut together Flynn hits me and they cut away. I should never have done it. I'm not a stunt man. They know what they're doing, I don't. But you're young and you do all sorts of crazy things."

Haim mentioned that working with some of the stars he worked with that "I was in awe of these people. When I did *Without Incident* and we were put up in the hotel where we were shooting in Arizona, I thought, 'Wow. The next morning I get to work with Errol Flynn.' I had a big scene with him that we were going to shoot the next morning. So we get out on the desert and Flynn is sleeping in his chair with his boots off, and I'm sitting in my chair while the stand-in's are working in front of the camera getting lit. Then, 'Mr. Wynant. Mr. Flynn. We're ready for you.' I ran up to my spot and looked back at Flynn and he moved very slowly, putting on one boot and then the other. He then reached into his pocket and pulled out a big wad of toilet paper from which he took out his teeth and put them in. He looked a hundred and fifty years old. Then he started coming toward the spot and every step he took he got younger, and by the time he got to his mark there was Errol Flynn in all his glory. It was really a great experience working with him. He and Johnny Ireland were two wonderful guys. Working with Clark Gable in *Run Silent, Run Deep* was wonderful. A sweet, wonderful man, but he had palsy and did only a few films after that before he died. When it came five o'clock, every shooting day someone would come and pick him up, and they would leave. Five o'clock on the dot, he was gone, no matter what. He was not a well man, but a wonderful man. So I got to work with some of these guys. I came in just before they went out. I feel lucky. Errol Flynn, Randolph Scott -- that was good for me."

Haim went on a six-month national tour in 1977 with Shirley Jones in the stage production of *The Sound of Music*. "We played all the starlight theaters, four to six thousand seat theaters, and wound up that tour in Chicago." When asked what it was like playing to eight thousand people, Haim replied, "That's wild. The theater was so large they didn't have a curtain, so for the curtain there's a blackout. When you blackout, the lights in the audience go up and you look at that sea of people and it is unbelievable. Shirley Jones did draw them in. She really had draw power because there were a lot of shows touring that year like *The King and I* with Yul Brynner, and they weren't doing very well, but our show was sold out. You got to hand that to Shirley."

Haim and his wife Ethel were divorced in 1971, and later he married his second wife, Cynthia. During this time, in addition to his acting work, Haim took up sculpting. "Richard Basehart and I were great friends, and his wife Diana was a sculptress. She gave Cynthia a tiny piece of stone to work and gave her a tool to work with to calm her nerves. She fussed and fussed with it and finally I couldn't stand looking at it anymore so I took it out of her hand and made something out of it, and that started me. That was twenty-five years ago. The sculptures have become bigger and better. I work in marble and my sculptures are sort of realistic religious art. Why? I don't know because I'm not religious at all. My paintings are visceral and nightmarish, but my sculptures are thematic, usually more than one figure, and based on religion and in the Bible. I stopped after my second divorce, but I have to get back to it. It's not easy working in marble. It's hard work. Also you have to have the space to do it and I don't have a proper studio now so it's very difficult."

Haim and Cynthia also built a theater that he named the Richard Basehart Theater. "I named it after Richard before he died," Haim told us. "We basically designed it, built it, and ran it. It was probably one of the nicest small theaters in this town. The work that was done in the theater was rather good, but it was way out in Woodland Hills and that location didn't work. When I got divorced from Cynthia I left the theater to her and eventually it had to close."

In 1992 when the European version of Disneyland was opened in France, Haim was asked to perform as Buffalo Bill in their Wild West show. "They built a special arena for it and it was the biggest live show ever. I said okay and thought this was going to be my swan song. I'm going to go, do it, retire and that's it. So I went and did it. I loved the show but hated the French management. The thing that most made it miserable for me was their horse wrangler choreographer. I loathed him and I'm sure he loathed me. He had a tremendous ego and we didn't get along. He had the power to fire everybody except me because I was the star of the show. So I had a year of misery. Again, I enjoyed doing the show but when my contract was up I said good bye. They thought I would re-sign but I fooled them. I said 'Bye-bye,'" he laughed, "and I left."

Haim returned to California and in 1993 married for a third time to Paula Davis. "I realized I had to go back to work," he stated. "I had really cut all my ties, so I started calling my agents. I used to have the biggest and best, but they weren't very keen on taking me back so that's why I'm doing a play. I'm trying to re-establish myself in the minds of these people that I'm here and alive and well. I have to go back to work for many reasons because I'm extremely bored." Prior to our interview, Haim had performed locally on stage in *Karlaboy*, a ghost story, and was preparing to open in *The Sister's Rosensweig*.

When asked if he had any favorite roles, he replied "The first one. It is the one that stayed with me the most. I did about nineteen features and *Run of the Arrow* is the one I have the sharpest memories about." Does Haim have a preference between acting on stage or in front of the camera? "Both. It depends. I get most satisfaction out of a big role," he laughed.

Haim is the father of three sons through his first marriage: Bruce Winant, who is a stage and film actor; Scott Winant, an executive producer and director for television; and Bill Winant is a professor at Mills College and the University of California in Santa Cruz, as well as a musician who has performed concerts all over the world.

In summing up his feelings about his career thus far, Haim stated, "It was good, but it ended at a certain point and now I want to start it over again at an older age. I'm still in very good shape and I'd like to go out singing and dancing like I came in, rather than in a rocking chair watching TV. I can't handle that. I reached a point to where I've just got to get back."

Since our interview, Haim has performed on stage in *The Philadelphia Story* and has begun obtaining work on television in shows like *The West Wing* and *Huff*. He has become a father again, this time of a daughter he named for his mother, Pasha. "That's why I have to go back to work, so I am back in the saddle again," he told us. Haim has also just completed a lead part in a new film titled *Trail of the Screaming Forehead*, which is scheduled for release in the spring of 2007. It is a spoof on the 1950's horror films in a Boris Karloff type role.

Film Credits: **1950**: So Young, So Bad. **1956**: Massacre at Sand Creek (TV). **1957**: Run of the Arrow; The Comedian (TV); Decision at Sundown; Without Incident (TV). **1958**: Oregon Passage; Run Silent, Run Deep; Tonka. **1963**: It Happened at the World's Fair; The Wheeler Dealers. **1965**: The Slender Thread. **1967**: Track of Thunder; He Lives. **1968**: The Helicopter Spies (TV). **1969**: Marlowe. **1972**: Conquest of the Planet of the Apes. **1973**: Horror at 37,000 Feet (TV); The Stranger (TV). **1976**: Grand Jury; Gemini Man (TV); The Last Tycoon. **1979**: The Last Ride of the Dalton Gang (TV). **1980**: Hangar 18. **1981**: Earthbound. **1988**: The Diamond Trap (TV). **1990**: The Solar Crisis. **1998**: The Big Empty. **2005**: Whigmaleerie. **2007**: Trail of the Screaming Forehead. **2008**: Yesterday Was a Lie;. **2009**: The Lost Skeleton Returns Again Dark and Stormy Night; Footprints.

ABOUT THE AUTHORS

Tom and Jim Goldrup, sons of Eugene and Fernita (McKillop) Goldrup, were born in Palo Alto, California, and raised in the historic town of Sonoma in that state. They, with older brothers Bill and Ray, had a strong love of the movies, which was aided by their father building their first television set in 1949. After growing to adulthood, Ray made a living as a screenplay writer, and Tom and Jim pursued a less successful career as actors. They also turned to writing, having a book, *Growing Up on the Set*, a book based on former child performers in Hollywood, published in 2001. They have also interviewed over one hundred and fifty actors—these interviews serve as the basis for this book. They reside in Ben Lomond, California, where they are active in the local theater. In between their writing and acting they enjoy travel, having recently visited Nepal and India where they trekked in the Himalaya Mountains.

www.ingramcontent.com/pod-product-compliance
Lightning Source LLC
Chambersburg PA
CBHW071825230426
43672CB00013B/2761